**W9-CFB-292**

# This Is Who We Were In The 2000s

# This Is Who We Were In The 2000s

Based on material from Grey House Publishing's
*Working Americans* Series by Scott Derks

Grey House
Publishing

|                      |                  |
|----------------------|------------------|
| PUBLISHER:           | Leslie Mackenzie |
| EDITORIAL DIRECTOR:  | Laura Mars       |
| EDITORIAL ASSISTANT: | Alyssa Hurley    |
| PRODUCTION MANAGER:  | Kristen Hayes    |
| MARKETING DIRECTOR:  | Jessica Moody    |
| COMPOSITION:         | David Garoogian  |

Grey House Publishing, Inc.
4919 Route 22
Amenia, NY 12501
518.789.8700
FAX 845.373.6390
www.greyhouse.com
e-mail: books@greyhouse.com

Publisher's Cataloging-In-Publication Data
(Prepared by The Donohue Group, Inc.)

Names: Derks, Scott. Working Americans. | Grey House Publishing, Inc., compiler, publisher.
Title: This is who we were. In the 2000s / [compiled by] Grey House Publishing.
Other Titles: In the 2000s
Description: [First edition]. | Amenia, NY : Grey House Publishing, [2018] | "Based on material from Grey House Publishing's Working Americans Series by Scott Derks." | Includes bibliographical references and index.
Identifiers: ISBN 9781682177167 (hardcover)
Subjects: LCSH: United States—Economic conditions—2001-2009. | United States—Social conditions—21st century. | United States—Civilization—21st century. | United States—History—21st century. | Two thousands (Decade)
Classification: LCC HC106.83 T45 2018 | DDC 330.973090511—dc23

# Table of Contents

## Section One: Profiles

*This section contains 27 profiles of individuals and families living and working in the 2000s. It examines their lives at home, at work, and in their communities. Based upon historic materials, personal interviews, and diaries, the profiles give a sense of what it was like to live in the years 2000 to 2009.*

## Section Two: Historical Snapshots

*This section includes lists of important "firsts" in America, from technical advances and political events to new products, books, and movies. Combining American history with fun facts, these snapshots present an easy-to-read overview of the 2000s.*

# Essay On The 2000s

The first decade of the new millennium is most often called simply the "2000s," although other monikers include the "Aughts," "Twenty-ohs," "Zeros," and "Aughties." This decade was characterized by expanding globalization due to massive advances in technology. Companies like Apple, Google, Microsoft, and Facebook made the world increasingly smaller by putting the Internet in the world's back pocket, increasing the impact of ordinary citizens around the globe.

Transitioning to a more global outlook did not come without struggles for the U.S. The 2000s saw the increase of terrorist attacks, rising unemployment rates, a Great Recession, and several natural disasters that threatened to damage the American spirit. Change is what dominated this decade, culminating in the election of the country's first African American president, Barack Obama in 2008. Indeed, changes that began in the 2000s will resonate for decades to come.

### Current Events

No event had greater impact on the nation in this decade than the September 11, 2001 terrorist attack. Nineteen men hijacked four planes, and crashed them into the Twin Towers of the World Trade Center in New York City, and into the Pentagon in Washington D.C. Nearly 3,000 people lost their lives. The event sparked a national outcry against terrorism and especially against Islamic terrorist group al-Qaeda, leading to both the War in Afghanistan and the Iraq War.

Following the Introduction is the story of a survivor of that terrorist attack, Ron DiFrancesco. Other chapters in this work also give a sense of how far-reaching the impact of this horrendous event was. 9/11 touched every American old enough to remember, and the story lives on through them.

- Waitress and single mom Lana Evergood (p. 19) was terrified when she couldn't get through to her daughter's school after hearing the news; afterward, business in the Atlanta restaurant she worked in declined and her tips dropped dramatically, adding to her money trouble.

- PR specialist Chris Thatcher (p. 39) was in the tenth grade on that day, and remembers teachers whispering but no one ever explaining what had happened - puzzling to this day.

- Elementary school principal Ellen Boshe (p. 81) lived in Massachusetts, but had family in NYC. Her brother Tom—who worked in Tower Two—was not at work that day, but her nephew Peter, who worked with his father, was. His body was never recovered.

- Telemarketer Anna Reynolds (p. 87) found it more difficult to connect with potential customers from her Seattle office after the attack—people weren't interested in talking about diabetic supplies.

- National Guardsman Andros Thomson's (p. 115) decision to join the military became urgent as he watched the events of 9/11 unfold. He described his deployment in Iraq as a nightmare.

- CNN Producer Andrea Getz, (p. 137) who was in high school on that day, panicked when she heard the news. Her brother worked in Manhattan and her parents were in Washington D.C. Able to reach only her brother, they were both terrified until the family was slowly reunited, using the country's crippled transportation system.

The years after the 9/11 attacks were filled with color-coded threat levels, increased airport security, and a general sense of uncertainty. Both the national and global economies declined, and unemployment rates rose as manufacturers began outsourcing to China, India, and Mexico. Several natural disasters, most notably Hurricane Katrina in 2005 in New Orleans, wiped out local communities.

In 2008, Barack Obama was elected the first African American president of the United States. His campaign messages of hope and "Change we can believe in" resonated with the majority of Americans and his impact, which continues to be evident, began in the 2000s.

### Economy

The economy suffered greatly in the 2000s, first when the Dot-Com bubble burst and then with the mortgage crisis in 2007. Early in the decade, inspired by the growth of the Internet in the late 90s, many information technology companies (dot-coms), were created. About half of these companies failed between 2000-2002, but because 48% of those dot-coms survived, the nation avoided an economic crisis.

The mortgage crisis had a far worse outcome-a global financial crisis often referred to as the "Great Recession." Mortgage delinquencies soared in mid-2006 after a trend of lowered lending standards and higher-risk mortgage products. The ratio of household debt to disposable personal income rose from 77% in 1990 to 127% by the end of 2007. Unemployment also spiked, with roughly 9 million jobs lost in 2008 and 2009. The stock market fell by about 50% from 2007 to 2009, and U.S. housing prices fell nearly 30%. Much of the next decade was focused on rebuilding the national and global economy.

### Political and Social Change

If the 1990s were media-obsessed, the 2000s were even more so. Politics and current events could be debated at any hour of any day from any part of the world. A major political controversy opened the decade, when George W. Bush won the 2000 presidential election in an extremely close, highly contested election. Recounts in Florida started and stopped several times, delaying the official results until mid-December, when it was declared Bush had defeated Democratic opponent Al Gore. Bush was sworn in January 2001, and nine months later dealt with the most devastating terrorist attack on this country in history.

Bush's strong stance on terror and his willingness to engage the Middle East in conflict contributed to his second presidential victory in 2004, when he defeated Democratic candidate John Kerry. The Republican Party continued to control Congress until 2006, when the nation made a big sweep in the liberal direction, leasing to election of Barack Obama in 2008, the nation's first African American president. Obama defeated Republican candidate John McCain with his slogan of "Change we can believe in" and the chant "Yes We Can." His optimism was a balm for the American people in troubling times.

Many social movements began and/or continued in the 2000s. LGBTQ activists continued to fight for equal rights, most significantly for marriage equality. Women and minorities fought for equal pay and equal treatment. Climate change and global warming became household terms and new advances in technology better predicted weather and environmental patterns. Former U.S. Vice President Al Gore was at the forefront of eco-activism during this time, and there was a massive international push to move to "greener" technologies and industries. Still, the global temperature kept rising, and in December 2009, the World Meteorological Organization announced that the 2000s may have been the warmest decade since 1850.

### Technology and Culture

New technology in the 2000s meant that art, music, and entertainment were controlled, more than ever, by the consumer. The advent of steaming services like Napster, iTunes, YouTube and Netflix, and cheap, portable home software made it possible for the average American to not only create their own content, but to distribute it as well. This caused the entertainment industry to rethink strategies to stay competitive in an ever-expanding market.

Technology also meant more information. More individuals used the internet, and smaller, cheaper cell phones and computers allowed information to be taken with you anywhere. Social media sites like MySpace, Facebook, and Twitter allowed people to easily and quickly share details of their lives. Mainstream media developed the 24-hour news cycle, so the press could report on any issue at any time.

Obsession with technology paralleled an obsession with celebrity, and this decade saw the public frenzy with celebrity reach its height. Reality television exploded, as shows like *Real Housewives*, *Keeping Up with the Kardashians*, *The Simple Life*, *Survivor*, and *The Real World* followed the lives of ordinary people and celebrities up-close. Some stars, like Lindsey Lohan and Britney Spears, struggled with the constant media attention, often turning up in the headlines more for their drug use and erratic behaviors than their talents.

**Sports**

Athletes continued to push themselves like never before in the 2000s. One of the biggest events of the decade was the 2008 Summer Olympics in Beijing, when American swimmer Michael Phelps won eight gold medals, the most ever won by an individual athlete at a single Olympics. Serena Williams dominated tennis, and holding all five Grand Slam singles titles simultaneously was called a "Serena Slam." LeBron James and Tom Brady emerged as superstars of basketball and football, respectively. In 2004, the Boston Red Sox finally overturned the 86-year old "Curse of the Bambino" by winning the World Series against the St. Louis Cardinals.

The sports world was also full of controversy during the 2000s. Big name major league baseball players like Barry Bonds, Mark McGwire, Sammy Sosa, and Alex Rodriguez were accused of steroid use and "doping," allegations that also followed cyclist Lance Armstrong throughout the decade. Football's Atlanta Falcon's quarterback Michael Vick was charged and imprisoned for his involvement in an illegal dog fighting ring. Tiger Woods, once the most popular golfer in the world, faced controversy as an extramarital affair scandal in 2009 caused many of his biggest sponsors to drop him and threatened to end his professional career.

# Introduction

*This Is Who We Were In The 2000s* is an offspring of our 14-volume *Working Americans* series, which is devoted, volume by volume, to Americans by class, occupation, or social cause. This new edition is devoted to the 2000s. It represents various economic classes, dozens of occupations, and all regions of the country. This comprehensive look at this decade is through the eyes and ears of everyday Americans, not the words of historians or politicians.

*This Is Who We Were In The 2000s* presents 27 profiles of individuals and families-their lives at home, on the job, and in their neighborhood-with lots of photos and historical images. These stories portray struggling and successful Americans, and capture a wide range of thoughts and emotions. With government surveys, economic data, family diaries and letters, and newspaper and magazine features, this unique reference assembles a remarkable personal and realistic look at the lives of a wide range of Americans between the years 2000-2009.

The profiles, together with additional sections outlined below, present a complete picture of what it was like to live in America in the 2000s.

## The 2000s and 9/11

There can be no doubt that the one event that had the most impact on this decade is the 9/11 terrorist attack in New York City. Every single American old enough to remember knows exactly where they where when they heard the news. And those Americans too young to remember have been told the story. No matter where in the country you lived, you either missed work or school, or had your flight cancelled, or comforted family members, or lost a loved one. You saw American flags flying everywhere.

Following the Introduction is the story of Ron DiFrancesco, a survivor of the attack. Many of the profiles following Ron's story offer glimpses into how the events of that day affected Americans all over the country.

- Waitress and single mom Lana Evergood was terrified when she couldn't get through to her daughter's school after hearing the news; afterward, business in the Atlanta restaurant she worked in declined and her tips dropped dramatically, adding to her money trouble.
- PR specialist Chris Thatcher was in the tenth grade on that day, and remembers teachers whispering but no one ever explaining what had happened-puzzling to this day.
- Elementary school principal Ellen Boshe lived in Massachusetts, but had family in NYC. Her brother Tom-who worked in Tower Two-was not at work that day, but her nephew Peter, who worked with his father, was. His body was never recovered.
- Telemarketer Anna Reynolds found it more difficult to connect with potential customers from her Seattle office after the attack-people weren't interested in talking about diabetic supplies.
- National Guardsman Andros Thomson's decision to join the military became urgent as he watched the events of 9/11 unfold. He described his deployment in Iraq as a nightmare.
- CNN Producer Andrea Getz, who was in high school on that day, panicked when she heard the news. Her brother worked in Manhattan and her parents were in Washington DC. Able to reach only her brother, they were both terrified until the family was slowly reunited, using the country's crippled transportation system.

## Section One: Profiles

Each of the 27 profiles in Section One begins with a brief introduction. Each profile is arranged in three categories: Life at Home; Life at Work; Life in the Community. Photographs and original advertisements support each chapter, and many include industry or social timelines and contemporary articles.

## Section Two: Historical Snapshots

Section Two is made up of three long, bulleted lists of significant events and milestones. In chronological order-Early 2000s, Mid 2000s, and Late 2000s-these offer an amazing range of firsts and turning points in American history, including a few "can you believe it?" facts.

## Section Three: Economy of the Times

One of the most interesting things about researching an earlier time is learning how much things cost and what people earned. This section offers this information in three categories-Consumer Expenditures, Annual Income of Standard Jobs, and Selected Prices-with actual figures from three specific years for easy comparison and study.

At the end of Section Three is a *Value of a Dollar Index* that compares the buying power of $1.00 in 2016 to the buying power of $1.00 in every year prior, back to 1860, helping to put the economic data in This Is Who We Were In The 2000s into context.

## Section Four: All Around Us

There is no better way to put your finger on the pulse of a country than to read its magazines and newspapers. This section offers 50 original articles, book excerpts, speeches, and advertising copy that influenced American thought from 2000-2009.

## Section Five: Census Data

This section includes invaluable data to help define the 2000s such as State-by-State comparative tables, and reprints from the 2010 Census, including 11 Census Briefs. Here you will find detailed population, social and economic characteristics. This section also includes dozens of maps and charts for easy analysis.

*This Is Who We Were In The 2000s* ends with a Further Reading section and detailed Index.

The editors thank all those who agreed to be interviewed and share their personal photos for this book. We also gratefully acknowledge the Prints & Photographs Collections of the Library of Congress.

*The 2000s will aways be remembered in American history for the terrorist attacks in New York City and Washington D.C. on September 11, 2001. We begin this work with this story of Ron DiFrancesco, who survived the attack of the World Trade Center in New York City, written on its 15th anniversary. We dedicate this work to all who survived.*

## "The Last Known Survivor of the South Tower of the 9/11 World Trade Center Attack,"
### Andy J. Semotiuk, *Forbes*, September 12, 2016

Ron DiFrancesco was a Canadian working on a U.S. immigration work visa in the South Tower of the World Trade Center on 9/11. He was a manager at Euro Brokers' office on the 84th floor. As a Canadian he felt as if it was a unique honor for him to have been appointed to his position and to be working in the World Trade Center, regarded by many as the most prestigious building in Manhattan.

When the first plane hit the North Tower, the people in his office heard the crash and saw the flames and smoke emanating from that building. They did not know yet that a hijacked plane had been involved. As the phones started ringing and people started asking Ron and the other employees there what happened, they surmised that a small plane had lost its way and accidentally hit the building. They could see that the flames from the crash were forcing people in the North Tower to flee and in some cases to jump to escape the fire. As news reports started coming in giving more accurate accounts of what was happening, Ron got a telephone call from his good friend in Canada telling him to get out of his building. He heeded the warning and made his way over to the elevators. Just then the second plane hit his tower.

Ron says that the impact of the crash was so violent that the building swayed some seven or eight feet. He thought for the moment that the building would tip over but instead it simply swayed back the other way. After the building stopped swaying, Ron made his way to the staircase. Unlike in the North Tower where the plane came in level, in the case of the South Tower, the pilot of the plane came in on an angle evidently to cause maximum damage. In a sense that was fortuitous for Ron in that the right tip of the wing of the airplane plowed into the tower above the 84th floor although the body of the plane crashed into the building below it.

*Survivors at the scene, after the collapse of the towers.*

*The north face of Two World Trade Center (south tower) immediately after being struck by United Airlines Flight 175.*

Ron quickly made his way to the staircase. Smoke was coming up the stairs from the lower floor. He tried to make his way down but people from lower floors were coming up to escape the fire below. So he turned around and tried to go up.

Since the right tip of the wing of the plane hit the tower above his floor, that part of the tower was on fire. There was no way to proceed upward. For perhaps the first time, Ron DiFrancesco realized he was no longer in control of the events in his life. A sense of doom descended on him and the rest of the

*Urban Search and Rescue Task Force German Shepherd dog works to uncover survivors at the site of the collapsed World Trade Center after the September 11, 2001, attacks.*

people trapped between the floors. Unable to go up, once again he turned to go down facing the billowing smoke coming up the staircase like a smokestack. Now there was also fire down below and despite using a piece of drywall to shield himself from the heat, as he proceeded his body was being burned.

He thought it was all over. Overcome with smoke he was about to give up. Just then Ron says he heard a voice. He cannot really explain exactly whose voice it was, but he drew strength and faith from it to continue downward despite the burns. Then he heard a second voice, the voice of a firefighter. While he could not see in the smoke, the firefight said to come in the direction of his voice further down the stairs.

Ron reached the firefighter and told him he couldn't breathe. The firefighter examined him and told Ron to go down to the bottom where he would be cared for. That's what he did. Since he was now below the crash site the sprinklers had come on making the descent much easier. When he finally emerged on the ground floor he was blocked from exiting the building by firefighters who said it was too dangerous because of falling debris and the bodies of those who jumped. Instead he was directed into the basement of the building to exit there.

*The remains of three World Trade Center buildings on September 17, 2001.*

Ron descended below. He was especially impressed by a heavy set man who had also come down from his tower and was now descending with Ron into the bowels of the building. As they reached downstairs they suddenly heard the rumble of the building pancaking down on them. They turned to look back down the corridor where they saw a huge fire ball coming at them. They turned around and ran for their lives.

*The Tribute in Light on September 11, 2014, on the thirteenth anniversary of the attacks, seen from Bayonne, New Jersey. The tallest building in the picture is the new One World Trade Center.*

Ron woke up in the hospital. There were burns to the great majority of his body. His contact lenses had melted to his eyes. It took years to recover. But he had made it. He was the last known survivor of the South Tower of the World Trade Center bombing. Since then Ron and his family have moved back to Canada. Yesterday, however, he returned to New York to the site where exactly 15 years ago he was lucky enough to survive America's worst terrorist attack. His story is a testament to resilience in the face of adversity. It is one that reminds us of how precious life can be and of the fact that eternal vigilance is the price of liberty.

*Andy J. Semotiuk is a U.S. and Canadian immigration lawyer, published author and former UN Correspondent with offices in New York and Toronto. Article reprinted with permission of Forbes Media LLC.*

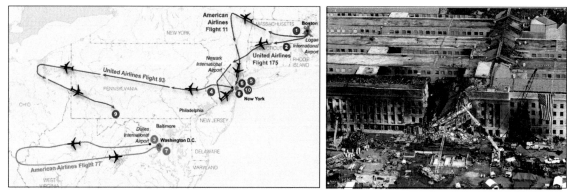

*Flight paths of the four planes used in the terrorist attacks on September 11, 2001. The Pentagon in Washington, D.C. (right) was hit by American Airlines Flight 77.*

*The following accounts are just a few the final words between victims of the attack at the World Trade Center and their loved ones. Many of the victims died with no idea of what had happened.*

**Robert McCarthy**, who worked at Cantor Fitzgerald, was on the 104th floor of the North Tower. His spoke to his wife, Annie. This is her account:

He called me right after the impact. He really didn't say anything to me. He sounded like he was kind of crying. I don't know. He said, "What are you doing?" I said, "I'm sleeping." He said, "You have to call my sister. I think Gerry's dead." (Mr. McCarthy's brother-in-law, Gerald O'Leary, worked as a sous-chef for the company in a kitchen several floors below.)

I called his sister right away. She turned on the TV. She saw. I believe Rob called her. Basically said the same thing he said to me.

Apparently, he had said to his mom, "There are no stairs."

It didn't sound like there was any panic going on in the background. I talked to him right after it happened. He didn't sound like he was running to get out at that point because it had just happened.

*Interview by James Glanz, The New York Times*

**Garth Feeney** was a vice president with Data Synapse. He was attending a business conference at Windows on the World on the 106th floor of the north tower when the plane hit. About five minutes after the crash, he called his mother, Judy Feeney, in Florida. This is her account:

I had just turned on "Good Morning America." They had something on about the plane and I had just mentioned it to my husband when the phone rang and it was my son. I simply said something like, "Hi. What's new?" He said, "Mom, I'm not calling to chat. I'm in the World Trade Center and it's been hit by a plane." I said, "Please tell me you are below it." He said, "No, I'm above it. I'm on the top floor. There are 70 of us in one room. They have closed the doors and they are trying to keep the smoke out."

*Interview by Kevin Flynn, The New York Times*

**Patricia Alonso**, worked at Marsh & McLennan. She managed one phone call to her husband, Robert. This is his account:

She worked in Tower 1, 95th floor. She was on the southeast side looking over the Brooklyn Bridge.

I talked to her while she was evacuating. She called me on her cell phone at 9:07. She said she was leaving. She was evacuating.

I said, "I'm coming down to get you." And I told her I loved her. And she told me she loved me.

She didn't know that a plane had hit the building. She just said there was smoke.

*Interview by Jim Glanz, The New York Times*

**Steven Jacobson** was a transmitter engineer for WPIX-TV and had an office on the 110th floor of the north tower, just below the station's rooftop antenna. When the first plane hit that tower, a friend and colleague at WPIX, Victor J. Arnone, called twice from the station to see how he was doing. This is his account:

I punched in his extension. I said, "Steve are you O.K.?" I was shocked the phone lines were still working. He said, "It's getting hot up here. What happened?" I told him to get one of the one air packs we had. After the 1993 bombing, we got these air packs. They're the same kind that the coal miners use when they need air while they wait to be rescued. They give you like five hours of air.

The second conversation was just after the second plane hit. I said "They're terrorists. They hit the other tower. Try to get to the roof." But he said, "It's too hot to leave the room. Get me out of here. Send help." And then the line went dead.

*Interview by Kevin Flynn, The New York Times*

**Jeff Shaw**, Forrest Electric I.B.E.W. Local 3 was working on the 105th floor.

His wife, Debra, talked to him after the first plane hit. This is her account:

I called him on his cell. I called him right after the first plane hit. He was up on the 105th floor at the time. He asked me first of all what happened. I said a plane hit. He said the room is full of heavy black smoke. They can't even see in front of them. And it was hard to breathe. He said they are trying to get the people out.

"But it doesn't look good babe," he said. I called him back a little while later. And of course the phone went dead. I called him at 10 to 9 and then 5 after 9. Actually, just as the second plane hit was the time I got back to him. That's when he was just screaming, "Bye."

He knew that building like the back of his hand. He slept in there. I'm sure he went down searching, doing everything he could.

*Interview by James Glanz, The New York Times*

*Reprinted with permission of The New York Times.*

*A fireman looks up at the remains of the South Tower.*

*"Defiant Prayers Surface on the South's Gridirons," by Erin McClam,*
*Atlanta Constitution, September 23, 2000:*

...AS, Ga.—The horns of the Paulding County High School marching band blew the last note of the national anthem, and there wa...
...e. Then one voice, then another, then thousands.
...on, the chorus dominated the modest stadium—asking this day for their daily bread, forgiving those who trespass against them
...g to be led not into temptation but delivered from evil.
...his recitation of "The Lord's Prayer" was simple but fundamentally defiant. Fans here compared themselves to Christian soldiers
...g to save religion's place in schools before the courts strip it away.
...e scene is being repeated on Friday nights, carrying forms but with an identical message, on the South's most hallowed battle...
...ds—its footba... ...ation from half a me...
...eople underst... ...arch-rival East Paulding. "It shouldn't be confined
...lis away to pas... ...ation from half a me...
...if we confine it? They'll do it like a smoking ban."

## 2000: Real Estate Lawyer

*Rita Willis found herself embroiled in a school prayer debate when a dozen teens gathered at her home after a football game at which a student had led the crowd in reciting the "Lord's Prayer." Rita's stand against prayer in school led to a five-year court battle.*

### Life at Home

- At 51 years old, Rita Willis was sure she was well past her rebel stage.
- Of course, when she went to law school in the early 1970s, she was considered a token female admission and a rebel of sorts.
- After all, the world seemed firmly convinced that only men were capable of coping with the rough-and-tumble world of "the law."
- "The law" appeared to rank above religion, presidential edicts, congressional mandates and the traditions of local practice.
- So, as she sat through the intoxicating world of constitutional law, she dreamed of fighting for the civil rights of the downtrodden and oppressed.
- Reality arrived quickly when she clerked for the first time at a major law firm where she was the lowest member of a very tall totem pole.
- Twelve-hour days of arcane research regarding commercial transactions hardly squared with her law school visions of glory.
- So after law school, marriage, and the birth of a child, Rita looked for an area of the law that balanced her love of legal precision and the tempo of her family.
- Real estate was booming in Macon, Georgia, as was the need for real estate lawyers.
- Real estate law paid reasonably well, was flexible enough to accommodate three very active children, and overall, it was an area of the law that was not festooned with conflict and controversy.
- Apparently, conflict was reserved for her personal life.
- Comfortable as a partner in one of Macon, Georgia's most respected law firms, Rita discovered that controversy could be thrust on anyone, at any age.
- And as a lifelong Episcopalian and choir member, she was shocked to discover that tackling the issue of school prayer would result in accusations that challenged her Christianity.

*Real estate lawyer Rita Willis took a stand against prayer in school.*

### Life at Work

- The issue of prayer at school officially arose more than five years earlier when a student chaplain delivered a prayer over the public address system before a home varsity football game.
- Rita was at the game with her husband to support her youngest daughter, a cheerleader on the varsity squad.
- She stood with the rest, listened passively to the prayer delivered by a student, held her hand over her heart for the playing of the national anthem and cheered the team as they roared onto the field.
- The rhythm and pattern had been unchanged for 30 years.
- Only later, when a dozen teens gathered at Rita's home after the game, did she come face to face with the inequity of public prayer.
- An argument broke out about that evening's prayer.

*Prayer at a football game ignited a five-year court battle.*

- A junior girl of the Muslim faith said she didn't think it right for everyone in the entire stadium to be asked to pray to "Jesus Christ our Lord" for protection and guidance.
- The boys quickly told her to "shut up or go back home," which made her cry, and made the other girls mad enough to berate the boys.
- Rita stepped in just as the disagreement reached a fevered pitch.
- Since 1962, she told them, the Supreme Court had consistently ruled that "Congress shall make no law respecting an establishment of religion."
- The Founding Fathers intended that no act of government—including laws governing public schools—should favor any one religion over others.
- That's hard to do, she said, because once someone mentioned God, Jesus, or anything even remotely "Biblical," he or she immediately pushed the constitutional envelope by "favoring" one practice of religion over all others.
- It may very well be that the only way not to favor one religion over others was not to favor any religion at all—a path now being chosen by many public schools already.
- The room was silent.
- "Shouldn't the majority rule?" her daughter asked to break the awkward silence.
- Rita knew that public opinion polls showed that a majority of people disagreed with the Supreme Court's religion-in-schools rulings and she told them so.
- Then she added, "While it's fine to disagree with them, it is not really fair to blame the Court for making them."
- The rulings were based on the way the Justices interpreted the First Amendment to the Constitution.
- The First Amendment spelled out America's guiding principles regarding religion, speech, press, assembly, and petition.
- Basically, it protected all Americans' right to worship as they wanted, to say what they wanted, to publish what they wanted, to gather in groups, and to make their concerns known to the government.

- It also prohibited the government from identifying with a particular religion, effectively separating church and state.
- Had the Supreme Court not been asked to interpret the Establishment Clause by private citizens, including some members of the clergy, they never would have done so.
- The Establishment Clause stated that Congress "shall make no law respecting an establishment of religion."
- "But," said Rita, "when you say, 'the majority rules,' does that include the majority that kept women out of law schools or medical schools or that said it was right for black people to ride in the back of the bus?"
- This time the room erupted into a flurry of questions and a few accusations of "Commie liberal talk."
- That's when Rita climbed out on the fragile limb that would support her life for the next five years.
- "Perhaps the most important job of the Supreme Court is to see to it that the will of the majority is never unfairly or hurtfully forced on the minority, and, that's a good thing because you never know when the minority might be you."
- All weekend she brooded over the conflict and what she had said.
- Her daughter seemed impressed with what had taken place.
- But Rita was unsure whether her daughter agreed with her comments or was simply pleased to see the boisterous boys shut down so effectively.
- When Monday arrived, Rita knew she had to act on her comments, so she made an appointment with the high school principal, a newcomer to Macon who might be sensitive to the needs of the students.
- In 1992, the Supreme Court had barred clergy-led prayers at graduation ceremonies, but there appeared to be unclear guidance about student-led prayer at football games.
- Her intent was to express her concerns and relate the weekend's events.
- But despite her best efforts, the first meeting went poorly.
- Early in the conversation, she casually mentioned the name of her law partner, and the principal immediately summoned his secretary to witness the remainder of the conversation.
- The second meeting involved the superintendent, the third a school district lawyer and the fourth was convened before the school board in open session.
- By the time she arrived home from the school board meeting, she was famous—or infamous.
- The 11 o'clock television news led with the word, "Prayer condemned as illegal by local attorney," beside an unflattering picture of Rita.
- The phone rang all night with calls that were mostly ugly and from people she didn't know.
- She attempted to take a low profile, but her timing was terrible.
- In Texas a case was brought by Mormon and Catholic students concerning the banning of prayer at football games.
- Nationally, school prayer became a hot topic once again.
- No matter what she said or how she framed her answers, every media outlet in the South portrayed her as a godless spokeswoman for the Devil who wanted to rip prayer from the mouths of America's youth.

*Rita felt "the will of the majority should never be forced on the minority" so she fought for the banning of prayer at football games.*

- During the lawsuit's five-year journey through the courts, Rita was vilified.
- After a time, the viciousness of the verbal assaults only served to remind her that the Constitution belonged to everyone, especially the Muslim girl who was verbally attacked by the boys that Friday night.
- In the intervening five years, her youngest daughter graduated from high school and college, her oldest daughter married and gave her a grandson, while her lawyer son took a job in Atlanta.
- Rita continually prayed for guidance and even joined a contemplative prayer group that gave her a measure of peace.
- And she began to explore the economic inequality of her community as a volunteer server at a local soup kitchen.
- By the time the courts ruled on the Texas prayer case, Rita was at peace with herself.
- But she could not keep from smiling at the results: the Supreme Court had ruled in favor of protecting the rights of America's minorities.

*Rita's daughter seemed impressed by her mother's stand.*

## Life in the Community: Macon, Georgia

- The city of Macon was called "The Heart of Georgia," as it lies nearly in the geographical center of the state.
- Before European settlers came to the area it was inhabited by indigenous peoples for over 13,000 years. These peoples built a powerful community, based on agriculture.
- President Thomas Jefferson ordered the Creek Indians of the area to leave their lands east of the Ocmulgee River so that a fort could be built at the most inland point of navigation on the river.
- Fort Benjamin Hawkins was built in 1809 and it was around this fort that modern Macon developed.
- Although the Fort burned down in the 1830s, Macon remained an important trade stop on the Ocmulgee River.
- Cotton was the most important crop in Macon's economy, and the community's reliance on this industry impacted its role in the American Civil War.
- During the Civil War, Macon was the official arsenal of the Confederacy.
- Macon was fortunately spared during General Sherman's march to the sea, in which he sacked many cities and villages in Georgia.
- After the war, Macon was able to transition relatively smoothly to an economy not based on slave labor.
- The city continued to serve as a transportation hub for the entire state.
- In 2000, there were 97,255 people, 38,444 households, and 24,219 families residing in the city.
- The racial makeup of the city was 67.94% African American, 28.56% White, 0.02% Native American, 0.65% Asian, 0.03% Pacific Islander, 0.46% from other races, and 0.77% from two or more races. Hispanic or Latino of any race were 2.48% of the population.

### *Santa Fe Independent School Dist. v. Doe* (2000)

- In 1995 two families filed a lawsuit against the Santa Fe, Texas school district over prayer in school.
- Unlike that of Rita, the identity of the two families who filed the lawsuit, one Catholic and one Mormon, was sealed by the courts.
- Their lawsuit alleged that the school district's policy of allowing students to lead prayers at home football games violated the First Amendment by creating a religious atmosphere, and a lower court agreed in principle.
- A federal appeals court ruled that student-led prayers that were not limited to one specific religion and did not attempt to create converts were allowed at graduations, but banned before football games which the court said were not serious enough to be "solemnized with prayer."
- The school district responded to the lower court ruling by implementing strict guidelines banning pre-game prayer, and warned senior Marian Ward, elected by fellow students to deliver religious messages before football games, that she would be disciplined if she prayed.
- Ward's family filed suit in September, arguing that the guidelines violated her free speech rights.
- A U.S. district court judge agreed that the guidelines the school had written were unconstitutional and ruled that the school could not censor Ward's speech.
- So it was up to the Supreme Court to sort out all of the lower court rulings and make a decision.
- In the summer of 2000, the U.S. Supreme Court ruled 6-3 that public schools could allow student-led prayer before high school football games.
- The central question was whether allowing prayer violated the First Amendment's Establishment Clause, which stated that Congress "shall make no law respecting an establishment of religion."
- "We recognize the important role that public worship plays in many communities, as well as the sincere desire to include public prayer as a part of various occasions so as to mark those occasions' significance," Justice John Paul Stevens wrote for the majority.
- "But such religious activity in public schools, as elsewhere, must comport with the First Amendment," he added.
- The 4,000-student southern Texas school district, until 1995, had a policy in which students elected student council chaplains to deliver prayers over the public address system before the start of high school football games.
- While the lower courts were considering the legal challenge, the school district adopted a new policy under which student-led prayer was permitted but not mandated.
- Students were asked to vote on whether to allow prayers and to vote again to select the person to deliver them.
- A lower court retooled that policy to allow only non-sectarian, non-proselytizing prayer.
- An appeals court found the modified policy constitutionally invalid and the nation's highest court agreed with the appeals court, rejecting the argument that the prefootball prayer was an example of "private speech" because the students, not school officials, decided the prayer matter.

## Timeline of Religion in Schools

1940   The Supreme Court ruled that a public school may require students to salute the flag and pledge allegiance even if doing so violated their religious beliefs.

1943   The Supreme Court overturned itself and ruled that no one can be forced to salute the flag or say the pledge of allegiance if it violates the individual conscience.

1948   The Supreme Court found religious instruction in public schools a violation of the Establishment Clause of the First Amendment and therefore unconstitutional.

1952   The Supreme Court ruled that release time from public school classes for religious instruction did not violate the Establishment Clause.

1962   The Supreme Court found school prayer unconstitutional.

1963   The Supreme Court ruled that Bible reading over the school intercom was unconstitutional.

The Supreme Court found forcing a child to participate in Bible reading and prayer unconstitutional.

1968   The Supreme Court ruled that states could not ban the teaching of evolution.

1980   The Supreme Court found the posting of the Ten Commandments in schools unconstitutional.

1985   The Supreme Court found that state laws enforcing a moment of silence in schools had a religious purpose and was therefore unconstitutional.

1987   The Supreme Court ruled that state law requiring equal treatment for creationism had a religious purpose and was therefore unconstitutional.

1990   The Supreme Court ruled that the Equal Access Act did not violate the First Amendment; public schools that received federal funds and maintained a "limited open forum" on school grounds after school hours could not deny equal access to student groups based upon religious, political, philosophical or other content.

1992   The Supreme Court found that prayer at public school graduation ceremonies violated the Establishment Clause and was therefore unconstitutional.

1993   The Supreme Court said that school districts could not deny churches access to school premises after hours if the district allowed the use of its building to other groups.

2000   The Supreme Court ruled that student-led prayer at a public high school athletic event violated the Establishment Clause and was unconstitutional.

❧❧❧❧❧❧❧❧

### Remarks of Principal Jody McLoud before a Roane County High School football game, Kingston, Tennessee, on September 1, 2000

It has always been the custom at Roane County High School football games to say a prayer and play the National Anthem to honor God and Country.

Due to a recent ruling by the Supreme Court, I am told that saying a prayer is a violation of Federal Case Law.

As I understand the law at this time, I can use this public facility to approve of sexual perversion and call it an alternate lifestyle, and if someone is offended, that's okay.

I can use it to condone sexual promiscuity by dispensing condoms and calling it safe sex. If someone is offended, that's okay.

I can even use this public facility to present the merits of killing an unborn baby as a viable means of birth control. If someone is offended, it's no problem.

I can designate a school day as Earth Day and involve students in activities to religiously worship and praise the goddess, Mother Earth, and call it ecology.

I can use literature, videos and presentations in the classroom that depict people with strong, traditional, Christian convictions as simple-minded and ignorant and call it enlightenment.

However, if anyone uses this facility to honor God and ask Him to bless this event with safety and good sportsmanship, Federal Case Law is violated. This appears to be inconsistent at best, and at worst, diabolical.

Apparently, we are to be tolerant of everything and anyone except God and His Commandments.

Nevertheless, as a school principal, I frequently ask staff and students to abide by rules that they do not necessarily agree with. For me to do otherwise would be inconsistent at best, and at worst, hypocritical.

I suffer from that affliction enough unintentionally. I certainly do not need to add an intentional transgression.

For this reason, I shall render unto Caesar that which is Caesar's and refrain from praying at this time. However, if you feel inspired to honor, praise and thank God, and ask Him in the name of Jesus to bless this event, please feel free to do so. As far as I know, that's not against the law yet.

❧❧❧❧❧❧❧❧

### "Defiant Prayers Surface on the South's Gridirons,"
### Erin McClam, *Atlanta Constitution*, September 23, 2000

DALLAS, Ga.—The horns of the Paulding County High School marching band blew the last note of the national anthem, and there was silence. Then one voice, then another, then thousands.

Soon, the chorus dominated the modest stadium—asking this day for their daily bread, forgiving those who trespass against them, seeking to be led not into temptation but delivered from evil.

This recitation of "The Lord's Prayer" was simple but fundamentally defiant. Fans here compared themselves to Christian soldiers, fighting to save religion's place in schools before the courts strip it away.

The scene is being repeated on Friday nights, in varying forms but with an identical message, on the South's most hallowed battlegrounds—its football fields.

"People understand we are a religious nation," said the Rev. Curtis Turner, who brought his Baptist congregation from half a metropolis away to pass out copies of the prayer before

Paulding County's game with arch-rival East Paulding. "It shouldn't be confined. What if we confine it? They'll do it like a smoking ban."

Turner's congregation, like others across the nation's Bible Belt, took offense with the Supreme Court's ruling this summer that amplified, student-led prayer approved by public school officials crosses the line in the separation of church and state.

Those leading the prayers are growing bolder every week, almost challenging the powers that be to stop them from praying.

Every Friday night this fall, Turner—who cuts an awkward figure in a dark suit and shiny necktie among football fans with pompoms and booster T-shirts—is leading his followers to a different game in metro Atlanta.

Each time, the church members pass out cards bearing "The Lord's Prayer" and encouraging fans to recite it after the national anthem. Each time, they claim they are fighting for God-fearing students who are losing their right to practice their religion in school.

"They've been intimidated," Turner said. "They're afraid to speak or pray. They think that prayer has been outlawed."

Church-state separatists argue that mass prayers in public, including school-sponsored events, infringe on the rights of religious minorities. Turner's caravanning prayers are "extremely inconsiderate," said Debbie Seagraves, executive director of Georgia's chapter of the American Civil Liberties Union.

"This is a group of people willing to stand up at a public school event, and very loudly over everyone else say, 'This is our prayer,' no matter what anybody else wants," she said.

But across the South, a region where devotion to football has been called religious itself, students and fans are bucking the high court's ruling, refusing to quiet their prayers.

In Alabama, most schools have replaced prayer with a moment of silence since the Supreme Court ruling. But Etowah County High School continues to broadcast students' prayers over the stadium public-address system.

"Number one, we think it's the right thing to do," principal David Bowman said. "And, number two, football is a contact sport where kids are apt to get hurt, and you need God on your side."

In rural South Carolina, a student body president took the press-box microphone at her school's football opener to lead fans in a pre-game prayer. In the face of a lawsuit threatened by the ACLU, other students at Batesburg-Leesville High School plan to sign up to lead prayers at future home games.

And in western Kentucky, high schools in two counties have no plans to stop holding public pre-game prayers. In another Kentucky town, a radio station broadcasting high school football is airing prayers before kickoff.

"The Christian people have rights, too," said Bob Kerrick, principal of Hancock County High School.

The ACLU contends it is not opposed to private prayer in school. But huge masses reciting prayers in football stadiums are both disruptive and offensive to fans of other religions, Seagraves said.

"Suppose a group decided to stand up during 'The Lord's Prayer' and sing a rap song," she said. "Wouldn't the school consider that a disturbance? It's important we be considerate of each other's differences in society."

The Supreme Court decision does not outlaw prayer in school, by students or otherwise. But schools violate the Constitution when they advocate a "particular religious practice" by sponsoring amplified, student-led prayer.

Turner insists he is not promoting Baptism, or even Christianity, by leading the prayers in metro Atlanta.

"The Lord's Prayer" is just what he knows best, he said, and members of other religions are free to pray to their gods at the same time.

Some of the pastor's followers believe the erosion of prayers in schools is responsible for the downfall of America's youth, including school shootings. They say schools bleached of religion are a sure sign of the country's moral destruction.

"Over 224 years, this has been part of our heritage. We can't rob the next generation of that," said Clint Andrews, 22, who passes out prayer cards with Turner's congregation. "They're trying to take away prayer altogether. So we're taking a stand. We're on the last straw. This is it, right here."

*Republished with permission of Atlanta Journal Constitution, from "Defiant Prayers Surface on the South's Gridirons," Erin McClam, September 23, 2000; permission conveyed through Copyright Clearance Center, Inc.*

*Mercer University, R. Kirby Godsey Administration Building in Macon, Georgia. The building is listed on the National Register of Historic Places.*

# 2000: Young Japanese Immigrant and Painter

*Stephen Teal left Japan in 1995 at the age of 15 to attend a private boarding school in Ohio and decided to stay in the United States because of the supportive community he found for pursuing his passion of painting.*

## Life at Home

- Stephen Teal was born in 1980 in Mito, Japan, to a Japanese mother and an American father.
- Stephen's father had come to Japan years before with his grandfather, who was a Catholic missionary.
- Stephen's father initially taught English to support himself but then returned to the United States and earned his Ph.D.
- When he returned to Japan, he got a job as a professor of English literature at a university, where he met Stephen's mother, who was working as a receptionist.
- The oldest of three children, Stephen was exposed to the English language and American culture at an early age by his father.
- At home his father would speak to him in English; Stephen would respond in Japanese.
- Life in Japan was sometimes difficult for Stephen; children of mixed-race marriages were often scorned.
- He tended to gravitate more toward American books, music and movies.
- As early as 10 years old, Stephen began thinking about attending high school in the United States.
- His parents encouraged him to enroll in a Japanese school first, but Stephen knew he wouldn't be there long.
- During his first year, he worked at a gas station to save up money for his trip to the United States.
- After one year, Stephen transferred to a private boarding school in Toldeo, Ohio; the plane fare to America cost $750.
- Fifteen-year-old Stephen had American Japanese dual citizenship through his father, so his entrance into America was smooth.
- His new school had many international students but only a few Japanese.
- Stephen became close friends with the other Japanese students and would continue to keep in touch with them.
- However, he didn't feel outcast by Americans or students of other nationalities.
- He was surprised by how many American students had divorced parents.
- Overall, he found American society much more open and accepting of diversity than that of Japan.

*Stephen Teal left Japan as a teenager.*

Stephen, left, with his brother and sister.

A young Stephen with his parents and grandmother.

His father exposed Stephen to American culture.

- Stephen did well in school and particularly enjoyed literature.
- He spent much of his time reading and writing, in both Japanese and English.
- He went back to Japan to see his family once a year around New Year's Eve.
- His high school graduation was very special because it was one of the few times that both his American and Japanese family celebrated together.
- After high school, Stephen enrolled in a small, private college on Long Island, New York, that specialized in foreign-relations studies.
- He was not particularly interested in the subject, but thought it was a good choice, given his background.
- Mostly he wanted to be close to New York City, and often skipped school to spend time in Manhattan.
- As a result, his grades suffered.
- He enjoyed the openness and freedom that New York offered.
- It was during this time that he began to paint and use his art to express his feelings as a young immigrant in the U.S.
- He painted mostly self-portraits.
- After one year, he dropped out of college and went back to Japan to decide where he wanted to settle down.
- After much contemplation, he decided to pursue his art more seriously and that the United States was a better place to do that.
- As a young artist who was not formally trained, he would be seen as an outcast in Japanese society.
- In America, he found people to be less judgmental.

**Life at Work**

- Stephen Teal moved to Housatonic, a small town in western Massachusetts, with a college friend in 1999.

- Despite longing for the city life, he felt that a quiet New England town, with fewer distractions, would better enable him to concentrate on his painting.
- Also, the cost of living was much lower than in the city.
- He rented a one-room apartment in an old farmhouse for $350 a month.
- Stephen initially found freelance work as a translator for a heavy-machinery company; he was paid $0.07 per word.
- He translated instruction manuals from Japanese into English but did not enjoy the work very much.
- Despite being a native speaker of both English and Japanese, Stephen found translation surprisingly difficult.
- The highly specialized nature of the work meant that he often didn't know the words either in Japanese or English, and he soon began looking for other work.
- When a friend offered to get him a job in a pizza restaurant, he agreed, just wanting a job to support himself so he could paint.
- Stephen had never worked in a restaurant before, but he was a quick learner.
- He began as a prep cook.
- He started in the early morning preparing all of the ingredients for the day and then worked the lunch shift.
- He liked this schedule because he was finished by 3:00 and would go home and paint.
- When he first started working, he was making $8 per hour.
- After six months he was promoted to line cook for the dinner shift and then to assistant manager.
- He got a raise to $15 per hour.
- He liked the benefits of the job, such as free food, a relaxed environment and a flexible schedule.
- He was able to schedule his hours to work double shifts four days a week, with three days off to paint.
- His boss also let him hang his paintings in the restaurant.
- He sold several paintings this way.
- The most he ever sold a painting for was $3,000.
- Stephen Teal didn't know any other Japanese people at work, but there were immigrants from other countries.
- Stephen worked with people from Mexico, Ecuador, Colombia, Venezuela and Brazil.
- Some of them spoke English fluently, while others spoke it very little or not at all.
- Although Stephen didn't speak Spanish or Portuguese, it was easier to communicate with non-English speakers because of his bilingualism.
- They often talked about Americans and how they were treated by them.
- Stephen found that he faced less discrimination than immigrants from Latin America because of American stereotypes about Japanese people.
- He was expected to be very smart, a math genius and good with computers.
- People were surprised to find out that he was an artist who worked in a pizza restaurant.
- Despite these misconceptions, Stephen had no trouble getting along with Americans or other immigrants.
- He befriended a bartender who let him use a converted barn behind her house as his studio.
- He repaid her by chopping firewood and doing yard work.

*Stephen painted mostly self-portraits.*

- He also became friends with the owner of a coffee shop.
- After a few months of persisting, Stephen convinced her to mount a show of his artwork in the coffee shop.
- Of the 12 paintings in the show, seven were sold—one for $2,000.
- Because of the personal nature of his paintings, Stephen felt that he could not relate to other artists, especially those with formal training.
- On his days off, Stephen would sometimes go to rock and alternative music concerts.
- He liked American bands that were similar in style to the Japanese bands he grew up hearing.
- He listened to Japanese music and followed his favorite Japanese bands through the Internet.
- His sister would also send him CDs from Japan.
- He would listen to Japanese rock during work at the restaurant, but didn't like explaining to the other employees what the lyrics meant.

*The flexibility of restaurant work made it possible for Stephen to work on his art.*

## Life in the Community: Housatonic, Massachusetts

- Housatonic was a tourist village and part of the town of Great Barrington, Massachusetts.
- Great Barrington was part of the Berkshire Mountains in Massachusetts, which included 15 towns in total.
- Berkshire County was a popular vacation spot for New Yorkers, with a variety of cultural events, including Tanglewood—the summer home of the Boston Symphony Orchestra—world class museums, art galleries and theaters.
- Great Barrington had the enviable combination of scenic beauty, sophistication and trendy fashion.
- The village of Housatonic was served by a diverse group of young people who worked in restaurants, hotels and other service-industry jobs.
- According to the 2000 census, 356 families resided in the village, which boasted a total population 1,335 people.
- Whites comprised 96.5 percent of the population, while 0.37 percent were Asian.
- The median income for a household in the village was $35,625.

*Stephen with his artwork.*

- In the 19th century, Housatonic's economic mainstays were textile and paper mills. Monument Mills, a textile manufacturer, and Rising Paper Mills employed hundreds of the towns employees, many of them immigrants.
- When Monument Mills closed in 1956, the town suffered a period of economic decline.
- However, in the 20th century the town experienced a revitalization, in part due to the presence of art galleries and related commercial activity.
- Although Housatonic had a thriving artist community, Stephen had little interest in connecting with it.

## Japanese Immigration Timeline

**1907** The United States and Japan formed a face-saving gentleman's agreement in which Japan ended the issuance of passports to laborers and the U.S. agreed not to prohibit Japanese immigration.

**1913** California's Alien Land Law stated that aliens "ineligible to citizenship" were ineligible to own agricultural property, further eroding Japanese immigrant rights.

**1915** The Supreme Court ruled that first-generation Japanese were ineligible for citizenship and could not apply for naturalization.

**1924** The Immigration Act of 1924 established fixed quotas based on national origin and virtually eliminated Japanese and Far East immigration.

**1929** Congress made the annual immigration quotas, passed in 1924, permanent.

**1941** Japan's surprise attack on Pearl Harbor, Hawaii, ignited a wave of anti-Japanese sentiment in America; more than 1,000 Japanese American community leaders were incarcerated for national security purposes.

**1942** President Franklin D. Roosevelt signed an executive order authorizing the building of relocation camps for Japanese Americans living along the Pacific Coast.

**1943** Congress repealed the Chinese Exclusion Act of 1882, and established quotas for Chinese immigrants, who also became eligible for US citizenship.

**1948** The U.S. Supreme Court ruled that California's alien land laws prohibiting the ownership of agricultural property violated the Constitution's Fourteenth Amendment.

A United States admitted persons fleeing persecution in their native lands, allowing 205,000 refugees to enter within two years.

**1952** The Immigration and Nationality Act allowed all individuals of all races to be eligible for naturalization.

**1965** The Immigration Act of 1965 established a new quota system that gave immigration preference to immediate families of immigrants and skilled workers.

**1980** The Refugee Act redefined the criteria and procedures for admitting refugees.

**1986** The Immigration Reform and Control Act legalized illegal aliens residing in the U.S. unlawfully since 1982.

**1988** The Civil Liberties Act provided compensation of $20,000 and a presidential apology to all Japanese American survivors of the World War II internment camps.

**"Arts In America; Japanese American Gloom on Canvas, Circa '42,"
by Bernard Weinraub, *The New York Times*, March 28, 2001**

Several months after the attack on Pearl Harbor, Henry Sugimoto, his wife and their six-year-old daughter were interned with other Japanese Americans in California and sent to an assembly center in Fresno. Mr. Sugimoto had been a rising artist, trained in France and known as a painter of the placid fields and lush landscapes of rural California. Almost as soon as he was interned he began sketching somber portraits of the Japanese American families devastated by government policy.

"The internment experience completely transformed him, and it continued for the rest of Sugimoto's life," said Kristine Kim, associate curator at the Japanese American National Museum in downtown Los Angeles, the only museum in the nation focusing on the Japanese American experience. "He no longer looked to nature for inspiration for his art but instead depicted on canvas his personal experiences, his beliefs."

*Tokyo, Japan*

The first retrospective survey of more than 100 paintings by Mr. Sugimoto, who spent his postwar years in Manhattan, opened on Saturday at the museum in the Little Tokyo section of Los Angeles. The show offers not only a glimpse into the internment which has rarely been explored in art and, for that matter, in movies and television, but also seeks to explore the life of a relatively unknown artist whose career was cut short by his incarceration and who never regained his footing.

Lawrence M. Small, secretary of the Smithsonian Institution, which has three paintings by Mr. Sugimoto in its permanent collection, said that the artist once wrote that he was most concerned about "leaving my mark on this world." Mr. Small said that he need not have worried, adding, "Initially in secret and then openly, Sugimoto created an extensive series of paintings that powerfully capture that painful time" and "he conveys the struggles, suffering and complexity of life in a detention camp." The show runs through Sept. 16. Mr. Sugimoto, who was born in Wakayama, Japan, and was the grandson of a samurai, moved to Hanford, Calif., when he was 19. He died at the age of 90 in 1990, living after the war in apartments on the Upper West

Side and in Hamilton Heights. His daughter, Madeleine Sumile Sugimoto, who lives in New York, said her father moved there after the family was released from an internment camp in Arkansas largely because he had always yearned to experience the artistic life in the city.

❧❧❧❧❧❧❧❧

### "No Place Like Home, Sometimes; Children's Author Illuminates Japanese American Identity," by James Sterngold, *The New York Times*, November 22, 2000

Allen Say never intended to become a children's book author, or any other kind of author for that matter. For years he worked as a commercial photographer in San Francisco, then did some freelance illustrations before deciding to write his own stories for children. These were truly his own stories, an immigrant's musings about a home he never quite seems to find.

In tales like "Grandfather's Journey," "Tea With Milk" and "Emma's Rug," he has produced characters who are restless misfits navigating their murky worlds like ships searching for a safe harbor, carried along by a gentle undercurrent of melancholy. Though different from traditionally upbeat children's fare, the books have won him many awards, including the prestigious Caldecott medal.

It is his vivid, slightly austere watercolors that bring his themes to life and underscore a deep connection with the Japanese American world, a fact powerfully on display at the first show of his works, at the Japanese American National Museum here, through Feb. 11.

It is a show with a poignant subtext, the confusion and complications of Japanese American identity. The museum itself is dedicated to unraveling and taking note of this complexity, and the show, "Allen Say's Journey: The Art and Words of a Children's Book Author," seems a metaphor for that experience.

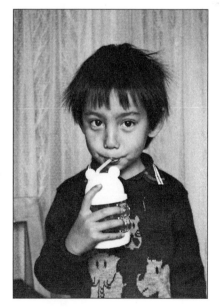

His realistically detailed illustrations for what are often autobiographical tales cleverly capture the spirit of being somehow linked to two worlds Japan, where Mr. Say, 63, whose name was originally James Allen Koichi Moriwaki Seii, and America, his adopted land, but completely at home in neither. The 55 paintings in the show are often dreamlike evocations of this rootlessness, characterized by broad, empty spaces with hints of loneliness and magisterial natural settings, much like the works of one of Mr. Say's prime influences, Edward Hopper.

That influence, and Mr. Say's clever use of it, is especially apparent in his most recent book, published this fall, The Sign Painter (Walter Lorraine Books/Houghton Mifflin Company), in which Mr. Say borrows readily recognizable scenes from this deeply American painter and populates them with bright Asian faces, sort of a Hopperesque perspective on the new America.

*The remains of one of the Twin Towers after the terrorist attack in New York City on September 11, 2001.*

## 2001: Waitress and Young Mother

*Before 9/11, Lana Evergood had eked out a living as a poorly paid waitress. When the United States was attacked by terrorists, her struggle to make ends meet got worse before it got better.*

### Life at Home

- At 42 years old, Lana Evergood thought she looked like an agitated, overweight, pink bumble bee in her waitress uniform that had been designed by the restaurant owner's wife.
- After dozens of restaurant jobs, Lana just chalked up the uniform to "getting by" and didn't worry about it unless an attractive single guy with money came in for a meal.
- Born Lana Louise Lovelace in 1960, Lana's early childhood education was mostly in geography: before she started the first grade, the family moved a dozen times—following work up and down the Eastern seaboard, especially where Wal-Marts were being constructed.
- "Any man who works for Wal-Mart will not want for work," her father liked to say.
- Her mother took in laundry and did daycare until she died when Lana was 13; the cause of death listed as "undetermined," but her father was convinced asbestos played a role.
- Lana's mother had grown up in houses built around Georgia's textile mills, many notorious for using discredited fiber once viewed as the low-cost answer to residential construction.
- Most of the houses' interiors also were painted with multiple coats of various lead-based paints.
- Lana liked school even when it was hard, but when she reached middle school, she realized that the teachers expected little from her except backtalk, so she grew dutifully uninvolved.
- By the time she was 16, Lana was pregnant; when she was 18, the father's parents sued for custody and won, allowing her only supervised visits every other weekend with her own child.
- A yearlong trip to Texas and a short stay in a Pennsylvania jail did little to enhance her position in the custody battle, or her relationship with her ex-boyfriend and his parents.
- Lana went back to school at 21 to get her GED; she waitressed nights and made at least two Alcoholic's Anonymous meetings each week.
- The meetings helped put her life back in perspective, kept her sober, and resulted in more than a few invitations to dinner and dessert.
- By the time she was 31, she had remarried, had another child, and regained her visitation rights.
- A decade later, Lana was married to a man who never came home, but she was enormously proud of her 11-year-old daughter, Laura, and delighted that she herself was about to be a grandmother—even though she hated thinking of herself in that way.

*Lana Evergood's struggle as a waitress seemed to get worse after 9/11.*

- Her first child graduated high school, attended two years of community college, and then married a man who had gotten an engineering degree from Georgia Tech.
- Their baby was due in September 2001.

## Life at Work

- Lana was working at another restaurant, Doug's Country Kitchen, when the September 11th attacks occurred.
- One of the reasons Lana had migrated to restaurants like Doug's Country Kitchen, where the tips were poor and the other waitresses mean, was alcohol.
- A few drinks with dinner not only enhanced the potential profitability of that customer, but also dramatically raised the amount of the tips Lana could receive.
- Restaurants like Doug's based their profitability on serving large numbers of people a fairly simple, nutritious menu that could largely be prepared ahead of time and easily stored for the next day.
- A typical menu offered customers a choice of four meats and twelve sides including cold slaw, green beans or sweet potatoes.
- Service was fast—very fast.
- Each table needed to turn over three times at lunch and five times at dinner to be profitable; dozens of customers sitting around savoring a glass of Chablis was not part of the formula.
- And for Lana, a Country Kitchen-type restaurant reduced the temptation to drink and the tendency of men to proposition her.
- When she worked nights at the Dutch Inn, the tips were excellent but the invitations to meet men after work became too frequent for her to feel comfortable; one night when her husband showed up at midnight, drunk and convinced she was cheating, she knew then she needed another job.
- Doug's Country Kitchen was the answer, even though her tips fell from $125 a day to $40.
- At Doug's, all the tips were shared; the hardest-working and the laziest waitresses were rewarded equally.
- Lana hated sharing her tips, and she hated the other women for talking about her behind her back.

*Lana hated her uniform, which was designed for perky young women.*

- She worked hard and deserved their respect, not their jealousy.
- Her boss operated a dozen restaurants throughout the Atlanta region, each based on the same formula—one that emphasized promptness; she was once laid off for three days for reporting to work five minutes late.
- She had planned to sleep late on Tuesday the 11th; she had worked the night shift, and once Laura was off to school, she planned to return to bed.
- On a whim, she turned on the TV and watched the television commentators ineptly attempt to make sense of an airplane hitting the World Trade Center in New York City.
- Transfixed, she watched, horrified, as a second plane appeared and also crashed into the famous Twin Towers, scattering debris for blocks.
- America was under attack and Lana was terrified; her first call was to Laura's school.
- When she realized that the phone lines were impossibly jammed, she drove to the school to rescue her child; Lana was convinced from past conversations that Atlanta would be a prime target when war broke out.

- She even realized that if Laura were to die, then she would consume the first bottle of alcohol she encountered—despite 20 years of sobriety.
- Her next call was to the cell phone of her pregnant older daughter; the stress of the morning's events had triggered labor pains—they were on the way to the hospital.
- By 2:30 in the afternoon, Laura was home and huddled around the television set with two friends watching videotaped replays of the Twin Towers collapsing over and over.
- Lana's older daughter was still in labor, and Lana had to go to work.
- People like to eat in good times and bad, she rationalized.
- But she was wrong.
- That day, the restaurant saw only a handful of customers.
- Her total tips for the night were $5.90—barely enough to cover her gas.
- The next night was just as still; even Atlanta's perennially clogged highways were quiet.
- America was hunkered down watching the TV version of Terror in America play out.

*After the Twin Towers were attacked on 9/11, Lana's money troubles got worse.*

- Meanwhile, young men lined up at military recruiting offices, thousands volunteered to give blood, and many more vowed vengeance on Osama bin Laden and his terrorist army.
- As the weeks passed, Americans became unglued from their television sets, home-centered projects like gardening gained momentum, and the country slowly returned to a disquieted mourning.
- Lana did not have her first $75-tip day until mid-December.
- By then, a car payment had been missed, she was behind in the rent, and gifts for her first grandbaby—a girl—were slim.
- But Lana figured she could always give love; three mornings a week she dropped Laura at school and picked baby Elizabeth up for a morning of grandmother time.
- The arrangement worked so well she also took in a neighbor's child—an October-born boy—and thought that she had found a way to make Christmas a celebration of birth and giving.
- Then she was notified that her Doug's Country Kitchen would be closing February 1.
- She was given a choice of working at a restaurant 40 miles away or finding another job.
- When she told baby Elizabeth about her troubles, the newborn simply wriggled.

### Life in the Community: Atlanta, Georgia

- Atlanta, which began as a settlement located at the intersection of two railroad lines, was incorporated in 1845 and quickly grew to become a major business city and transportation hub by 2001.
- Hartsfield–Jackson Atlanta International Airport had been the world's busiest airport since 1998; the city of Atlanta boasted the country's third-largest concentration of Fortune 500 companies.
- In addition, more than 75 percent of Fortune 1000 companies had business operations in the metropolitan area, including the world headquarters of The Coca-Cola Company, Turner Broadcasting, The Home Depot, AT&T Mobility, UPS, Arby's, Havertys Furniture, Cumulus Media, The Weather Channel, Chick-fil-A, Waffle House, and Delta Air Lines.
- Renowned for its robust cultural institutions, mild weather and dense tree coverage, Atlanta attracted an international community, with foreign-born people accounting for 13 percent of Atlanta's population.

*Downtown Atlanta, Georgia.*

- The city's population of 420,000 within its metropolitan area, comprising 5.3 million, made it the ninth-largest metropolitan area in the U.S.
- Atlanta got its start in 1836, when the Georgia General Assembly voted to build the Western and Atlantic Railroad to link the port of Savannah and the Midwest.
- The initial route was to run from Chattanooga to a spot called simply "Terminus," located east of the Chattahoochee River, which would eventually be linked to the Georgia Railroad from Augusta and the Macon and Western Railroad.
- The engineer chosen to recommend the location of the terminus drove a stake into the ground in what is now Five Points.
- A year later, the area around the railroad terminus had developed into a settlement, called Thrasherville, for John Thrasher, a local merchant who built homes and a general store in the settlement.
- The chief engineer of the Georgia Railroad, J. Edgar Thomson, suggested renaming the area "Atlantica-Pacifica" to highlight the rail connection westward, shortened to "Atlanta."
- The residents approved, and the town was incorporated as Atlanta on December 29, 1847.
- During the Civil War, the nexus of multiple railroads in Atlanta made the city a hub for the distribution of military supplies.
- On September 1, 1864, following a four-month-long siege of the city by the Union Army under the command of General William Tecumseh Sherman, Confederate General John Bell Hood made the decision to retreat from Atlanta.
- General Hood ordered that all public buildings and possible assets to the Union Army be destroyed; on November 11, 1864, Sherman ordered for Atlanta to be burned to the ground, sparing only the city's churches and hospitals.
- From 1867 until 1888, U.S. Army soldiers occupied the McPherson Barracks in southern Atlanta to ensure that the Reconstruction Era reforms were carried out.
- To train Georgians to develop new industries, the state established the Georgia School of Technology—today's Georgia Tech—in Atlanta in 1885.
- The Cotton States and International Exposition in 1895 successfully promoted the New South's development to the world, and was the site of Booker T. Washington's landmark speech encouraging racial cooperation.
- On May 21, 1917, the Great Atlanta Fire destroyed 1,938 buildings, mostly wooden, resulting in 10,000 people becoming homeless.
- On December 15, 1939, Atlanta hosted the film premiere of Gone with the Wind, the epic film based on the bestselling novel by Atlanta's Margaret Mitchell.
- Several stars of the film, including Clark Gable, Vivien Leigh, Olivia de Havilland, and its legendary producer, David O. Selznick, attended the gala event, which was held at Loew's Grand Theatre; African-American Hattie McDaniel, who had played Mammy in the film, was not invited.
- During World War II, Atlanta dramatically expanded, thanks to manufacturing industries such as the Bell Aircraft Company and the manufacture of railroad cars.

*Lana was enormously proud of her 11-year-old daughter, Laura.*

- Shortly after the war, the federal Centers for Disease Control and Prevention was founded in Atlanta.
- In the 1950s, the city's newly constructed freeway system enabled middle class Atlantans to relocate from the city to the suburbs.
- During the 1960s, Atlanta was a major organizing center of the Civil Rights Movement, with Dr. Martin Luther King, Jr., Ralph David Abernathy, and students from Atlanta's historically Black colleges and universities playing major roles in the movement's leadership.
- In 1961, Atlanta Mayor Ivan Allen Jr. became one of the few Southern white mayors to support desegregation of his city's public schools.
- African-Americans became a majority in the city by 1970, and exercised their new-found political influence by electing Atlanta's first black mayor, Maynard Jackson, in 1973.
- By 2001, Atlanta had transformed into a cosmopolitan city, becoming well known for its cultural offerings, driven by young, college-educated professionals who had moved into Atlanta by the thousands, seeking a lifestyle rich in cultural variety, diversity, and excitement.

# 2001: Collegiate Ultimate Frisbee Player

*The daughter of athletic parents in Greenville, South Carolina, Lola Martin excelled at many sports, but was most passionate about fast-growing ultimate frisbee, which showcased her athletic abilities.*

## Life at Home

- Lola Martin was raised in Greenville, South Carolina, the youngest of three children.
- Though her parents divorced when she was seven, she did not feel different from her classmates and enjoyed the opportunity to get to know both parents.
- Her father, as a basketball player, baseball player, and track runner in high school, encouraged all of his children to try different sports.
- Her mother, also athletically talented and a lover of the outdoors, encouraged her children to explore nature independently.
- As the youngest, Lola felt the need to keep up with her brother, three years older, and sister, seven years older.
- She started playing soccer at age eight on a coed team and soon joined a newly emerging all girls' team at age nine.
- An all girls' team was touted as progressive at the time, although other states had long ago created similar programs, making South Carolina a few steps behind even neighboring states like North Carolina and Georgia.
- She thought she would play soccer for the rest of her life, and did until her freshman year of college.
- In high school, she also played basketball, rock-climbed, and ran track and cross-country.
- In all, her teams won four state championships: one in soccer, one in basketball and two in track.
- She also found the time to play in one Ultimate Frisbee tournament, having been recruited for her ability to run and catch.
- Her previous experience with Ultimate Frisbee was at summer camp, where she enjoyed the constant movement but hated the tendency of the boys to rarely pass to the girls on the team.
- But at the tournament she was able to showcase all her athletic talents and had a ball.
- She also realized how much there was to learn about the rules, the throwing motion, when to cut and when to huck the disc (throw long).
- Ultimate, as it was more appropriately termed (Frisbee is a brand name), involved a field similar to that of a football field (40 yards wide by 70 yards long with 25-yard end zones on either end).

*Lola's love of sports stemmed from her parents.*

*Ultimate frisbee showcased all Lola's athletic abilities.*

- With seven players per team on the field at a time, the players' movements were a combination of soccer, basketball and football.
- The rules also mimic other sports: the need to establish a pivot foot was borrowed from basketball, the interference calls on receivers from football.
- In Ultimate, running with the disc was not allowed.
- Therefore, a team must move the disc down the field by throwing and catching with the eventual goal of catching the disc in the end zone to score.
- If the disc touched the ground during this progression, barring a foul, possession changed to the other team who then tried to score in the other end zone.
- Lola especially appreciated the multiple strategies that could be employed, including zone defenses, set plays on offense, various cutting strategies-all familiar because of her participation in basketball and soccer.
- The most unique aspect of the sport to Lola was the lack of official referees.
- Field conduct was regulated by "Spirit of the Game," a term used to describe each individual player's responsibility to uphold the rules and play with sportsmanship.
- Therefore, players must know all the rules of the game and call them when they felt there had been a violation.
- The opposing player had an opportunity to agree or disagree.
- There was a level of trust that each player would not cheat with rule calls to gain an unfair advantage.
- In higher-level games, official observers were used as passive referees; if there was a dispute on the field, the players asked the observer for his/her opinion, which was final.
- Since its conception, players have established the rules.

- Ultimate began with the invention of the disc, which World War II veteran Fred Morrison called the "Whirlo-Way" in 1948.
- By 1949 the disc was being marketed in the midst of the UFO craze as plastic flying saucers useful for tossing on America's beaches.
- Then, in 1955, Wham-O (best known for the hula hoop) provided national distribution and in 1957, the name Frisbee.
- By 1968 New Jersey high schools were experimenting with a variety of rules, and in 1972 Princeton and Rutgers Universities staged a collegian contest before 2,000 students.

*Lola loved to compete and was elected captain.*

- Also on hand were a local TV station, a reporter for The New York Times and a mention in Sports Illustrated.
- Twenty years later as many as 100,000 athletes were participating in organized games, mostly connected with colleges and universities.
- When Lola entered college, Ultimate was played in over 42 countries and was government sponsored in Sweden, Norway and Japan.

## Life at Work

- Lola Martin entered college with high expectations.
- Her plan was to study hard and play college soccer; after a summer of intense training and weightlifting she was in superb shape.
- But after discovering the pitfalls of no social life and a disagreeable coach at a Division I Soccer varsity program, Lola searched for another athletic outlet.
- She remembered her one Ultimate Frisbee tournament and thought that developing her skills in a new sport would be fun.
- Soon, she was hooked.
- She also found that her switch from soccer to Ultimate was not uncommon; many new college Ultimate players migrated from sports such as soccer, basketball and volleyball.
- Her college's women's team was formed only three short years earlier.
- So Lola believed she would have an opportunity to help the program build on itself.
- At the end of her freshman year, she was elected captain for the following year and soon began gaining regional recognition for her aggressive play.
- She also discovered the difficulties that came with balancing a leadership position and rigorous university classes.
- While varsity players enjoyed the support of professional tutors and some sympathy from professors, Ultimate players practiced four to five times a week without similar support or recognition.
- She even found that most people thought her sport involved a dog, was some variation of golf, or that marijuana-smoking hippies were the only people that played.
- Though she enjoyed the liberal attitudes that the sport attracted, Ultimate was much more intense than the majority of people thought.
- When deciding on a major, she was naturally drawn toward teaching.
- She initially knew that she loved teaching, but was also drawn to the flexibility of scheduling, allowing her to play Ultimate when she pleased.

- Many of her older Ultimate role models were teachers and advised her as to which avenues to pursue to maximize her ability to play and complete her studies.
- With her increasing recognition, she was scouted by club teams in the area to play Ultimate outside of school.
- The club season was primarily from the middle of the summer through the fall, and the college season was mostly during the spring semester, though there were tournaments for both divisions all year.
- The club division was composed of open (men's), women's, mixed (coed) and masters' (men over 30) categories.

*The game was much more demanding than most people thought.*

- Lola found herself recruited to play on mixed teams, but also one of the top women's teams in the country.
- With a lighter schedule her senior year, she switched from playing mixed to women's Ultimate, committing to coast-to-coast travel for tournaments and rigorous practice on the weekends.
- Because the women's team was not close by, she had to travel over two hours and would often stay at a teammate's house after practice on Saturday night before Sunday morning practice.
- She did not mind though; Ultimate was her life, and her best friends were her teammates.
- By the end of her senior year, her team had qualified for nationals for the first time in school history, and she was being mentioned on blogs by people from across the country.
- Though her team did not finish strongly at nationals, she was honored in an awards ceremony as being voted the fifth best college player (called the Callahan award) in the U.S. and Canada by other female college players.
- She was pleasantly surprised, since East Coast players and players from smaller schools tended not to rank very high in other female players' minds.
- Shortly after she graduated, tryouts for her club team began, along with track practices, agilities workouts, and weekend practices, a never-ending cycle.
- Sometimes she felt overwhelmed.
- But then she picked up a disc and hucked it downfield and smiled to herself.
- She loved this sport.

### Life in the Community: Maplewood, New Jersey

- Ultimate Frisbee was invented in 1968 by students attending Columbia High School in Maplewood, New Jersey.
- An early version of the game was taught to Columbia student Joel Silver by Jared Kass, an Amherst College dorm advisor.
- Joel and his friends further developed the game in Maplewood and the first sanctioned game was played at Columbia High School. The first opponents in this game were the student council and the student newspaper staff.
- The game took off quickly, and by the next year games were played in the student-designated parking lot, where students could play evening games under the lights.
- The first interscholastic games of Ultimate began in 1970 and were played by five New Jersey high school teams, including Maplewood.
- Ultimate spread throughout the country when alumni of that initial league brought the game to college.

- In 1975, Rutgers won the first collegiate Ultimate tournament.
- In that same year, Ultimate was introduced to the West Coast by way of the Second World Frisbee Championships at the Rose Bowl.
- The Ultimate Players Association, eventually renamed USA Ultimate, was formed in 1979 and has crowned a national champion every year since 1979.
- A plaque located at Columbia High School's student parking lot in Maplewood commemorated the advent of the sport.
- An annual CHS Ultimate Alumni game is played in the student parking lot on the night of Thanksgiving.
- Despite not being recognized as a sport and receiving no funding from the district, both the men's and women's Ultimate teams at CHS dominated regional and state championships.
- As of the 2000 census, Maplewood was home to 23,868 residents.
- The racial makeup of the township was 58.78% White, 32.63% African American, 0.13% Native American, 2.86% Asian, 0.03% Pacific Islander, 1.56% from other races, and 4.01% from two or more races. Hispanic or Latino of any race were 5.23% of the population.
- Its close proximity to Manhattan made Maplewood popular with Broadway and off-Broadway theater professionals.
- The downtown area of Maplewood was also a big draw for residents. Known as "the village" or "Maplewood Center," its structure has largely remained unchanged since the 1950s.

❧❧❧❧❧❧❧

### "'Ultimate Frisbee' Among Growing Outdoor Sports," by Jennifer Anderson, Associated Press, *Kerrville Times* (Texas), September 7, 2000

PORTLAND, Oregon—The plastic disc soars through the sky, tracing a long arc with a translucent glow before it floats for a frozen moment above the heads of two young men who leap to greet it.

Fwap! One claps the Frisbee between his hands while a player on defense lands on his feet and vows to knock it down the next time.

But there's no time for waffling.

"Stall one, stall two," he yells in Ultimate Frisbee lingo, counting the seconds his opponent has to fling the disc downfield in hopes of scoring the game point.

Before his defender can shout "stall three," he whips a hammer throw (Frisbee slang for a long vertical toss) into the end zone where a ponytailed teammate dives into the grass to catch it with her fingertips.

"Nice grab! Game!"

To these athletes, the familiar Frisbee that started as a toy more than 50 years ago has become a game enjoyed competitively by at least 100,000 people worldwide, about half in the United States.

Ultimate Frisbee—first played in 1968 by high school students in Maplewood, New Jersey—is a fastpaced non-contact sport that combines the speed of soccer, the objective of football and handling skills of basketball.

But what makes the sport unique is there is no referee, official scorekeeper or timekeeper.

Ultimate Frisbee relies on a "Spirit of the Game" rule, which, as defined in the game handbook, places responsibility for fair play on the player. It says that highly competitive play is encouraged, but never at the expense of the pure joy of the game.

"The people who play Ultimate really are virtuous people and play honestly," said Deana McMurrer, co-captain of Portland's only all-woman team, which last year took second place in the national tournament in San Diego and the world tournament in Scotland.

"It's a great quality that we can carry over to our lives." Perhaps because of the game's emphasis on fun and fair play, Ultimate is especially embraced in the laid-back Pacific Northwest.

"The spirit of the game is alive and well here," said Mark Aagenes, Missoula, Montana-based coordinator for the Northwest region's Big Sky section, which includes Utah, Idaho, Montana, part of Wyoming and Alberta, Canada.

"People play because they like each other and want to have fun with it". . . .

### "Frisbee Fans Get Fitness, Fun,"
### *Winnipeg Free Press,* June 4, 2001

It's just a round piece of plastic, but a Frisbee is the ultimate sport and fitness toy for growing fanatics like Jill Goddard.

Two nights a week, Goddard, a Toronto public health nurse, "hucks" and "backhands" a Frisbee at school and other fields, an oh-so-cool way to have fun, socialize and exercise.

Goddard is among Canadians who play Ultimate Frisbee, the trendy disc-throwing team sport that combines the nonstop running of soccer, the non-contact rules of basketball and the passing of football.

"You need to have good reflexes and you don't have to be a fitness freak, but you need a good cardiovascular base as there's lots of running around," the 28-year old said before joining her coed team, the Limp Diskits, for a Monday night game against an opposing team at a Toronto high school.

A huck, as Ultimate jargon goes, is a long throw, and sometimes Goddard is guilty of a "swill," a bad throw.

But she was on a high after scoring three points in her team's 14-4 win to open the spring-summer season at the beginning of May, her first year in the Ultimate Frisbee adult coed league run by the Toronto East Sport Social Club. There are about 30 teams in two divisions, for beginners and advanced players.

Ultimate, sometimes called Frisbee football, is said to have been invented by New Jersey high school students in 1968 (although some say that it has its roots in Eastern colleges in the '50s). The Frisbee was conceived in 1948 by a California army pilot who molded plastic in the shape of pie tins, which kids and soldiers had been playing catch with decades. . . .

Ultimate has since become an international phenomenon, and there are world championships and competitive bodies like the U.S.-based Ultimate Players Association. The sport makes its debut as a medal sport in the 2001 World Games in Japan this August as the only self-officiated sport of the Games. There's also talk of it in the Olympics.

The beauty of Ultimate Frisbee is that it's a cheap form of fitness: all you need is a disc, which costs a few bucks, the players and a field . . .

"Ultimate is for people who want exercise, fresh air, to run around and blow off some steam after a hard day at work," said Michael Lichti, a coordinator for the Toronto East Sport Social Club, which charges $400 for a team with 10 players to join the league. "There's also the social aspect, meeting people on your own and on other teams."

After games, for instance, Goddard and her teammates go out for drinks and bites and to conduct a friendly game of postmortem.

"What I like is that Ultimate isn't as competitive as some of the other sports I do," says Goddard, who iS also into running, hiking and paddling. "And most of the people in the league are of the same mindset, young professionals who are fit and into other sports, but who don't have the idea it's the be-all and end-all to win."

*Maplewood, New Jersey Municipal Building.*

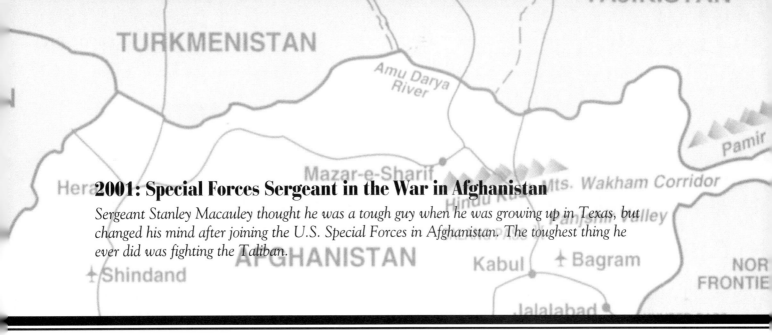

# 2001: Special Forces Sergeant in the War in Afghanistan

*Sergeant Stanley Macauley thought he was a tough guy when he was growing up in Texas, but changed his mind after joining the U.S. Special Forces in Afghanistan. The toughest thing he ever did was fighting the Taliban.*

### Life at Home

- Stanley "Mac" Macauley was broke, alone and desperate when he joined the army.
- The son of a truck driver, he grew up on the edge of suburban San Antonio, Texas.
- Because of emphysema, his father was often reduced to long stretches of TV watching, while his mother helped support the family by earning tips as a waitress.
- Mac considered himself a tough guy, capable of taking care of himself; he stayed in school primarily to play tight end on the football team.
- He boxed in the Golden Gloves program because he loved to see fear leap into the eyes of his opponent.
- After high school, he got married, agreed to attend community college, worked at the local garage and began to run with the nightclub crowd—with an impromptu brawl tossed in every once in a while for good measure.
- It was a plan that worked for 13 months, until he flunked out of school, showed up drunk for work and found out his wife was leaving him for another man.
- Suddenly, escape and the military looked good.
- Immediately, he discovered that he liked the structure of military life, and enjoyed learning practical things.
- In the army, he also discovered a goal: joining the Special Forces, reputed to be the toughest, smartest, trickiest soldiers around.
- He finally got his shot on the Special Forces Qualifying Course, but realized the competition was stiff, and felt no more than average.
- When it came time to swim the length of the pool and back wearing fatigues, boots and a 40-pound pack, he knew this was the way to set himself apart from the crowd.
- He dove in and breast-stroked the length of the pool underwater and back before resurfacing, though he was ready to pass out.
- The commanding officer was impressed.

us former *mujahedin* leader— nd briefly Prime Minister f Afghanistan—who lipped back into the ountry around February. Hekmatyar should be een as quite as much a worry as Omar," says a Western intelligence fficial in Kabul. "If he two are cooper- ting, then the anger of a rowth in terrorist ttacks and assassi- ations is very real."

What's more, al- Qaeda seems to be aving little trouble unding its continuing perations. According o a draft of a report by United Nations group harged with monitoring in- ernational controls on ter- orist groups, only about 10 million of identified ter- orist assets have been frozen ince the beginning of the ear, compared with $112 mil-

**MUDDLED VICTORY A special- orces soldier in Afghanistan**

Afghanistan itself, says Lieut. Colonel David Gray, director of operations for the 10th Mountain Di- vision, "we have certainly defeated if not destroyed the al-Qaeda net- work as it exist- ed before the war." Mili- tary and in- telligence an- alysts agree that the com- bined power of Taliban and al-Qaeda forces in Afghani- stan has been re- duced to not much more than several hundred men, none of them assembled in large groups. Another few hundred al-Qaeda fighters are thought to be across the border in Pakistan. One by one, two by two, they are being hunted down.

*Stanley Macauley joined the Special Forces in the Army.*

*Being behind enemy lines was more difficult than Mac had imagined.*

- Within the Special Forces environment, Mac began to grasp his full potential, taking college courses and becoming fluent in Arabic, Russian and Dari.
- He also became proficient in a variety of light weapon and hand-to-hand combat techniques.
- His particular specialty was his ability to work with horses, which quickly became an off-duty passion.
- Each 14-man Special Forces team included two specialists in intelligence, medicine, demolition, communications, weapons and, thanks to a recent change, two air force "targeteers" to help call in air strikes.
- Mac's area of expertise was intelligence.
- Two of each specialty were employed to allow the team to be divided into two equally qualified groups, if necessary.
- Since his team was part of the 5th Special Forces Group that specialized in the Middle East and Central Asia, he observed the tragedy of September 11 with special insight.
- The fight ahead was the one for which he had been trained.

## Life at Work

- Sgt. Macauley was on his way back from a visit with his sister, brother-in-law and two adoring nieces in Texas when his cell phone rang.
- "Stop shaving immediately and report to the base for deployment," he was told.
- Shortly thereafter, with his beard just beginning to look respectable, he and the rest of his team shipped out for Central Asia.
- Soon, they were helicoptered into a remote spot high in the mountains—far behind enemy lines.

- Their mission was twofold: to direct American air assaults from the ground, and assist and support the Northern Alliance, which would be conducting the ground war.
- The Northern Alliance was a loose confederation of tribal chiefs, often called warlords in the American press, who were opposed to the Taliban.
- The Bush administration did not feel that domestic policy would allow for the insertion of large numbers of ground troops, especially if U.S. casualties resulted, so small Special Forces teams and native forces—some of questionable reliability—were selected to carry the brunt of the combat burden.
- Mac and his team were assigned to a particularly unsavory warlord, known for shifting sides and for his creative ways of killing those who displeased him.
- The entire U.S. team, now sporting beards, wore clothing similar to that of the Northern Alliance, including the round wool hats, or "pakols," and long checked scarves.
- Each person also carried a pack with approximately 200 pounds of equipment and supplies.

- To help them move through the mountain trails to the warlord's camp, they arranged for a string of sturdy mountain horses.
- Since it was Mac's responsibility to supervise the loading of the animals, he also brought up the rear in case any of the team members, less accustomed to mountain horseback riding, ran into trouble.
- Ahead were 24 hours of difficult riding without rest.
- When they finally arrived exhausted and sore into camp, Mac, as the team's only Dari speaker, was pressed into service as a translator.
- One of the first orders of business was the treatment of Afghan wounded and injured; Mac's team included two medics.
- Unfortunately, one of the most seriously wounded required the amputation of his leg just below the hip.
- To bolster the fighting morale of the native fighting force, long deprived of supplies, the captain ordered food and medical supplies air-dropped to the site as soon as possible.
- The warlord claimed to have 2,000 men in his command, though Mac figured his strength to be no more than 1,200, many without much training.

- When they moved out toward a Taliban stronghold to the south, progress through the mountains was slow, taking two days.
- The enemy position was a seemingly impregnable fortress atop a crag, where Taliban soldiers were reported to be armed with machine guns, some light artillery, mortars and several Russian-made shoulder-mounted rocket launchers.
- While Afghan soldiers surrounded the crag, the Special Forces team divided into two groups.
- Mac and his team members carried the M-4, a shorter M-16 with collapsible stock, scope and laser designator.

- He helped pepper the enemy soldiers with automatic fire, while the second team used satellite radios to guide the first of the air strikes.
- The first to arrive were the F-14s with rockets and bombs to soften the enemy position.
- As they approached, Mac's team picked out targets and "painted" them with a laser beam capable of guiding the smart munitions to their targets.
- The Afghan allies watched in amazement as a cave entrance was first marked by a mysterious red beam followed by a pinpoint explosion on that exact spot, sending debris and bodies into the air.
- An AC-130 Spectre gunship followed the bombing run, making several passes designed to further pummel the Taliban position.
- The crag was quiet for only a few minutes before small-arms fire erupted again.
- Mac and his team were enthusiastically returning fire, when Warrant Officer Stephen Amato called out, "Here comes the big girl!"
- Overhead, the shape of a B-52 bomber emerged in the sky and released a dozen 500-pound bombs.
- The crag, nearly flattened by the explosions, took on an eerie silence, and the Northern Alliance headed up the rise.
- The few remaining Taliban surrendered immediately, and Mac wondered what plans the warlord had for these men.
- Mac and his team were surveying the beautiful brutality of modern weaponry when the captain took a radio call.
- Several hundred Taliban troops had been spotted to the southeast.
- All around him, the Afghan fighters were talking about the powerful explosions they had seen; surely the Taliban could not withstand this force for long, they remarked to him in a mixture of Russian and Dari.
- He had heard that about 100 Special Forces men were on the ground in Afghanistan—more than enough, he thought, to teach the Taliban not to mess with the U.S.A.

### Life in the Community: San Antonio, Texas

- San Antonio, Texas has Spanish roots: it was founded as a Spanish mission and colonial outpost and contained five 18th-century Spanish frontier missions, including The Alamo.
- The city was named for Saint Anthony of Padua by a Spanish expedition in 1691.
- One of the most famous battles in history, the Battle of the Alamo, took place in San Antonio in 1836.
- Although the Mexican army won the battle and killed all of the defenders of the Alamo, the Texan soldiers were so spurred on by revenge and cries of "Remember the Alamo!" that they eventually defeated the Mexicans and ended the Mexican Revolution only one month later.
- However, when Texas officially became a state by annexation in 1845, the Mexican-American War began anew.

*The Alamo, in San Antonio, Texas*

- Eventually the Americans won the war, but San Antonio was devastated.
- Only 800 residents lived in San Antonio by the end of the war in 1848.
- However, the city bounced back quickly, and by the start of the Civil War in 1860, San Antonio was a city of 15,000 people.
- San Antonio's population only continued to grow.
- It was the fastest-growing of the top ten largest cities in the United States from 2000 to 2010.
- According to the 2000 census, San Antonio had a population of over 1.1 million people.
- In 2000, the United States Census Bureau reported San Antonio's population as 58.7% Hispanic, 6.8% black, and 31.8% non-Hispanic white.

## Life in the Community: Afghanistan

- Afghanistan's geographic location between the Persian Gulf, Central Asia and the Indian subcontinent made it a significant world player, and created the potential for Afghan rulers to spread their authority east and west.
- It also made the country a target for international powers focused on global control.
- Of the 25 million people in Afghanistan, 20 percent live in urban areas, the rest in the vast rural stretches.
- The mountainous features of the country make it necessary for many villages to be self-sufficient.
- The population comprises eight major ethnic groups: Pashtuns (38 percent); Tajiks (25 percent); Hazaras (19 percent); Uzbeck (six percent); Turkmen, Aimaqs, Kirghiz, and Baluchis (12 percent).
- Eighty-five percent is Sunni Muslim, 15 percent Shiite Muslim.

*Eighty percent of Afghans lived in the country's vast rural areas.*

- The main national languages are Dari and Pushto; in addition, there are 20 languages and 40 dialects spoken.
- The modern state of Afghanistan emerged in 1747.
- The establishment of the first Republic of Afghanistan took place from 1973 to 1979.
- The People's Democratic Party of Afghanistan led a coup d'état in April 1978.
- The Soviet invasion began in December 1979, and lasted for almost 10 years.
- The Islamic State of Afghanistan existed from 1992 to 1996, followed by the rise of the Taliban movement and the establishment of the Islamic Emirate of Afghanistan.
- The rise of the Taliban was unanticipated, springing from the southern villages of Qandahar and the refugee camps in Pakistan.
- Many ex-military officers participated in the Taliban, whose supreme leader had a combined spiritual and political status in the high council and the affairs of the people.

## 2002: Public Relations Specialist

*Realizing he wasn't cut out for small town life, Christopher Thatcher enjoyed the fast-paced, high-energy lifestyle of New York City. As his confidence increased, so did his success as a division head at his public relations agency.*

### Life at Home

- Chris was born in Nyack, New York in 1986.
- He grew up in a small town in Dutchess County, New York: Stanfordville, 20 minutes from both the Massachusetts and Connecticut borders.
- His mother worked for 39 years as a project executive for IBM, managing multi-million dollar accounts, and his father worked for AT&T, took an early retirement and started his own telecommunications business.
- Chris had one older sister.
- As a child, his family celebrated the typical holidays—Thanksgiving, Easter, Christmas—always with lots of food and fun.
- He went to Stissing Mountain Jr./Sr. high school—his graduating class was the largest in the school's history at 110.
- He was involved in high school theater, and remembered this being part of the best times growing up.
- He also worked a lot during high school, and his first job was one of his best—working in a video store getting paid to watch movies.
- Other early jobs included ski instructor, wedding hall waiter, and cashier at Kohl's and Sam's Club in Kingston, New York.
- Chris always knew he wasn't cut out for small town life in a farming community.
- His most memorable childhood friend was Christina, with birthdays five days apart, and mothers with similar tastes, they became fast friends and had lots of adventures together.
- Chris was in the 10th grade during the 9/11 attacks.
- He was sitting in class and another teacher walked in, whispered something to his biology teacher, and walked out.

*Working in public relations thrust Chris into the high-energy, exciting lifestyle that Manhattan is known for.*

- Nothing was mentioned to the students and to this day he doesn't understand why they were so secretive about it.
- When he was young, his family took road trips to Canada, Hilton Head Island, Virginia Beach, Florida, and frequently to Lake George, renting cabins or camping.
- In high school he went on a school trip to France and Spain—a great experience, but one he would appreciate more when he returned as an adult—and a senior trip to the Bahamas, which was really great.
- His senior year, Chris would leave school at noon, drive to Norrie Point, a local fishing hole, and fish for hours.
- He spent his weekends at the drive-in with his friends.

*Chris with his younger sister.*

- A challenge that Chris faced growing up was being worried what people thought about him—his clothes, his first car, etc.
- Once he let go and cared less about what people thought, he became a more likeable person, with more friends and fun times.
- His most influential high school teacher was his theater coach, Sarah Combs, who taught him acting techniques and encouraged him to take chances to step out of his comfort zone.
- Chris went to SUNY Oswego, although he originally wanted to just go to the local community college.
- But he changed his mind after getting accepted to all his choices and visiting campuses, and decided on SUNY Oswego because it was on a lake.
- Sounds silly, but for whatever reason, it was the right choice—Oswego became his happy place.
- He remembered fondly his fraternity, and stayed in touch with members of Delta Sigma Phi even after graduation.

*Cocktails with a view were not uncommon for Chris and his co-workers.*

- After graduation, Chris quickly got a job in public relations—his major—moved in with his grandmother and commuted into New York City every day—2 hours door to door.
- The pay was awful, but he was grateful for work in his field, as he saw his friends struggling to find work.
- The Great Recession caused his agency many clients and he was forced to take a furlough.
- Fifteen months later, using Twitter to network, he was hired by another agency.

## Life at Work

- Chris became Associate Vice President at one of the top 15 Public Relations agencies in the country, managing the B2C (Business to Consumer) Technology division, with clients that dealt with online services, e-commerce platforms, mobile devices, adult web sites, apps, and anything with batteries.
- Prior to this position, he ran the agency's health division, responsible for products that included a herpes vaccine, erectile dysfunction pills, and the like.
- He had more than 90 different clients, and so became a generalist in PR, knowing enough to have a 10 minute conversation on just about any topic in the field.
- He credited his success in part to his background in high school theater—every new business presentation was a performance, and he knew how to adapt to or "own" any room.
- Chris chose a PR career because he was told that he could become a publicist for Jennifer Lopez.
- That didn't happen, but he worked with a number of celebrities over the years, learning that "celebrity publicist" is really a nice way to say "personal assistant."
- Other enticements for Chris included TV shows about working in public relations—*Power Girls* and *Sex and the City*—but he found few similarities.
- He also found that it's definitely a "who-you-know" world when he got his first job due to his connection to his college alumni association.

*Chris and his public relations team.*

*Chris at an event for reality star Jacqueline Laurita (second from right) of* The Real Housewives of New Jersey *fame.*

- That first job was basically administrative, which helped him get his next position, where he realized that he enjoyed working in public relations, which meant taking chances and being creative.
- Although his family was supportive of his career choice, he always felt that they—or anyone outside of the industry—really didn't understand what his job entailed.
- For the most part, Chris liked what he did and learned to deal with the stress of constantly needing to find creative ways to get his clients into the news.
- Nothing was more satisfying than seeing his work have a meaningful impact on his client's business.
- His absolute favorite thing that ever happened at work was launching an electronic cigarette brand, which nobody wanted to cover.
- It started out being the hardest client to get media coverage for, but momentum built slowly, article by article, until Chris was getting calls nonstop for the executives to appear on TV or be interviewed.
- The company went from a small brand with limited distribution to a billion dollar business in two years, largely due to smart messaging and being ahead of regulations.
- His share of "worst moments" included TV segments canceling due to breaking news and exclusive newspaper interviews being reduced to a one line mention.
- Routines were difficult to maintain for Chris.
- He went into work every day with a plan—read the morning news and take action on anything related to his clients, trying to leverage that news into coverage.
- Since he became the head of a division, he made sure that his team was successful in getting coverage and that they were sticking to the plan that had been developed for each client.
- Public relations was essentially sales—Chris and his team were selling clients to the media.

- The more media they got, the more likely their business would be impacted by the created perception, moving the needle for their business.
- One thing that would have made his job easier was more hours in the day.
- His commute was short—10-15 minutes, depending on the subways.
- Chris traveled for work from time to time, like when he spoke at a convention in Salt Lake City for Lice Clinics of America about how they can get media.
- The only time he attempted a career change was a four-month stint at a big pharmaceutical company whose product was constipation and diarrhea medications.
- It was boring, and he was happy to get the call from his former PR agency asking him to return to lead the B2C tech division.
- Sometimes Chris wished he had built a career on his interest in technology, but didn't have the energy to dive into a new career, let alone one that was constantly evolving.
- He had never lost a job, and had always gotten the job he interviewed for—an interview is just another performance!
- Chris felt confident about his future in this constantly changing industry, an industry he felt would always be needed as long as it evolved with the times.

## Life in the Community: Oswego, New York

- Chris attended the State University of New York at Oswego, which would become his "happy place."
- The college town was located on Lake Ontario in north-central New York.
- The Iroquois people migrated to the area beginning in the 13th century and "Oswego" is an Iroquois word meaning "a pouring out place."
- Oswego has been the site of a fort since the British first established a trading post in the area in 1722.
- The fort was held by French, British, and American forces, and was used after World War II to house Jewish refugees from the Holocaust.
- Oswego's location on Lake Ontario made it a strategic port and major railroad hub, which led to the town's growth.
- The city's lakeside location also put it in the center of the Snowbelt and Oswego was considered one of the snowiest towns in America.
- In 2007 the city saw a record 130" (almost 11') of snow fall within two weeks.
- Also in 2007, the SUNY Oswego Lakers won the men's NCAA Division III Ice Hockey Championship.
- Oswego was also the home of the Oswego Speedway, a nationally known auto- racing facility.
- As of the census of 2000, there were 17,954 people residing in the city.

*Light house and Fort Ontario, Oswego, New York, ca. 1900.*

## Life in the Community: Midtown, Manhattan

- Chris lived and worked in New York City.
- He didn't know the other people in his building, or his next door neighbors, but that was how it was in the city.
- He chose his neighborhood—Midtown—because it was close to work, and he could work late and be home quickly.
- In his spare time, he refereed intramural dodgeball for a NYC league.

*Times Square, in New York City, is one of the world's busiest pedestrian intersections.*

- The Midtown community was very different from where he grew up.
- In Manhattan, he was surrounded by neighbors, buildings and noise—with a strip club next to his building.
- His typical day off started with a breakfast sandwich at a local bagel shop, after which he met up with friends, usually for something relaxing to counter the crazy hard work week.
- The best thing about his neighborhood was the seven subway lines close to his building, making it easy to go wherever, whenever.
- The worst thing is how far the grocery store is—he has his groceries delivered instead.
- Chris didn't see much change in his immediate future—he thought for a while that he wanted out of NYC, but no longer.

# 2002: Shaman and Energy Healer

*Rebecca Singer experienced supernatural phenomenon in her early life that would eventually lead her to travel the world, working with people and animals, helping them achieve physical and spiritual well-being.*

## Life at Home

- Rebecca was born in Sioux City, Iowa in 1949.
- Her family moved to Colorado Springs, CO when she was three years old, and then to Ohio when she was 12.
- When Rebecca was 15, she was sent to a boarding school in Vienna, Austria.
- When she returned to the States, she lived in Atlanta, Georgia.
- Her mother taught elementary school and her father was a TV and radio newscaster, who also worked for the CIA, something Rebecca discovered after his death.
- Rebecca had an older sister and an older brother.
- She was raised in a reform Jewish household.
- When she was 10, she refused to celebrate her religion and stopped going to temple.
- During high school, Rebecca was active in the Drama Club, and had a job working in a theatre.
- She also played the French Horn in middle school, and remembered being so nervous when her solo came that she couldn't even lift the horn to her lips.
- As a sophomore, she also studied how to be popular.
- She became the Junior High School prom queen attendant, riding around the football field on the back of a big car waving and thinking, "Aha, I did it."
- Despite this, she detested the social aspect of school, and didn't like math or science (or homework!), but loved reading, writing, and theatre.
- Rebecca's favorite childhood friend, Margaret, was fun, funny, kind and, at nearly 6 feet tall, embraced the challenges of having a much shorter friend (Rebecca was 4 feet 11 inches).
- Rebecca initially attended Bard College, Annandale on Hudson, in New York because her high school counselor in Vienna recommended it.
- If she had more guidance in this regard, she would have chosen Columbia University in NYC.

*Rebecca Singer found her life's work as a natural healer.*

"I'm not mixed up--just nobody understands me!"
. . . "Oh, that's gross!!! . . . cool earrings . . .
colored stockings . . . is, but isn't a heim girl . . .
loves to laugh, anywhere and anytime . . . thrives
on coffee, gum and Warren . . . animal imitations?
. . . "Maybe when my hair's long I'll look sexy??" . . .
great actress . . . "Miss Paton, may I drop English?"
. . . goes up to the woods to read . . . "Aw, c'mon,
you guys!" . . . main interest-people (Grotchens)
. . . writes peotry, letters, and songs like "Love is for
the Anteaters" . . . to the States to study whatever
she decides to study.

*Rebecca's high school yearbook page.*

- While in college, Rebecca participated in lots of theatre, and rode her motorcycle with a small group of guys.
- As a young woman, she traveled to Yugoslavia to work as a script supervisor on a movie, worked with famous people who were very kind and funny, and learned a great deal about film making.
- Other trips included one to New Mexico where she fed her feelings for Native American culture, and one to Hawaii where she learned to scuba dive and encouraged her in her 20s to go back to school to become a marine biologist.
- The most challenging thing in her early life was her father's anger and the best thing was theatre.
- She remembered a creative dramatics teacher as her lifeline, who encouraged her to express herself without judgment.
- When she was 58, Rebecca met her future husband, who is kind, funny, light hearted, honest and adventurous, on EHarmony.com.
- She singly raised her son, who is 35 and creative, hilarious, hard working, intelligent, and independent.

## Life at Work

- Rebecca worked as a shaman, or healer, with people and animals to help with their life path, physical well being, spiritual path, relationship issues, and connection to the natural world.
- As a child, she would see and hear spirits, experiences that she tried to ignore or stop.
- She always thought she wanted to be an actress, until she wanted to be a healer.
- In her 30s, she prayed for a teacher, and she started on her path as a healer with a teacher who was part Native American—Lakota.
- Rebecca traveled to Costa Rica to learn from shaman there, and then lived in Mongolia with The Reindeer People to learn from their woman shaman.

*Rebecca performed smudging ceremonies that involved the burning of sacred herbs, often for spiritual cleansing.*

*Rebecca's studio and healing room at her home in Woodstock.*

- She started working as a shaman by offering healing sessions to people.
- Her parents were both encouraging and discouraging of her chosen path.
- Encouraging because they thought her first choice— acting—was a bad idea, and discouraging because they weren't too keen on her being a shaman either.
- Rebecca loved her work and it was constantly rewarding.
- Each day was different, working for herself in a beautiful healing room in her home.
- She worked with both people and animals, and also led healing ceremonies all over the country.
- Sometimes students stayed at her home for 5 days, 4 times a year for intensive classes.
- Rebecca's path took several turns, first as a professional actress, then a professional masseuse, then a professional theatre teacher, then a Violence Prevention Specialist and, finally, a Healer.
- The two things she would have done differently, was 1. applied to Columbia University, had she known it existed and 2. Defied her father when she was 17, to take an acting part offered by a famous director.
- She is not concerned for her future, but for the future of young people, and for the future of our planet.

*Rebecca often made food with healing properties using ancient recipes.*

### Life in the Community: Woodstock, New York

- Rebecca lived in upstate New York, near the town of Woodstock, in the lap of the Catskill Mountains with lots of forests and water.
- The community was very liberal with lots of healers, artists and small businesses.
- Woodstock was known for the legendary festival of the same name that was held in 1969, though the event was actually held on a dairy farm about 60 miles south of the town in Bethel, NY.
- The art community in Woodstock went back to 1903, when the Byrdcliffe art colony came to the area, attracting the town's first artists and craftspeople.
- Rebecca loved the feeling of community in the town, but wished there was more diversity, something that was offset by the onslaught of tourists of all cultures that visited the area all year long.
- Rebecca's immediate neighbors were all friendly and dependable, but generally kept to themselves—including a lesbian couple into rescue animals, another who came up to his second home about once a month, and another who plowed everyone's driveway in the winter.

*Woodstock, New York Town Hall.*

- Rebecca and her husband settled near Woodstock because it was within 2 hours of New York City, had lots of land, and was a liberal community.
- Rebecca participated in political marches, fed those in need around the holidays, and helped her community prevent a local lake from being purchased by Nestle's.
- A typical day off for Rebecca involved shopping at the local produce market, practicing movement in her studio, hiking, reading, gardening, and enjoying her animals.

*Stone circles celebrate power in balance and our interconnectiveness. Healers often use them to focus on natural rituals, like the four seasons.*

*In Mongolia, Rebecca connected with the healing powers of the natural environment.*

*Rebecca drumming.*

# 2003: Heavy Machinery Operator

*After years of struggle and hard work, Ben Barber had gained a reputation as a dependable, heavy-equipment operator who could handle complicated circumstances. When his business began to decline after more than 20 years of success, Ben was ready to slow down.*

## Life at Home

- When the twenty-first century arrived, Ben Barber was convinced this was his time; pay was good, his marriage was going well, and he loved fishing with his teenage son.
- Born on July 4, 1961, Ben grew up pleased that the city of Olive Hill, Kentucky, staged an annual celebration on his birthday and shot up so many fireworks.
- As a boy, Ben worked alongside his father in the cattle and tobacco business; his mother managed to build a successful florist business.
- Family stories included the tale of fighting off Indians.
- Ben often found arrowheads and spear points during spring plowing and planting, evidence of the Native American tribes who once hunted the lush land.
- He respected his mother's German heritage and his father's Scotch-Irish ancestry.
- The state that was known for bourbon and whiskey distilling, tobacco, horse racing, and college basketball was also influenced by the substantial migration of Germans.
- In all, the farm encompassed 300 head of cattle and two large patches of tobacco.
- Ben had dreams of farming his entire life: He loved the problems, the solutions and the work; as far as he could see, his future was in agriculture.
- Then, Ben's parents divorced when he was 14, just as the cattle market crashed; Ben was needed on the farm if the land was to stay in the family.
- He dropped out of school in the ninth grade to help his father on the farm; he was accustomed to hard work and long hours and never returned to school.
- He also spent some of his teenage years running wild; "After the divorce, I was like a herd of cattle that has been penned up too long; when the gate opened, I ran, bucked, jumped and enjoyed my freedom."
- The mid-1970s were hard times for the average farmer, and Ben's father had compounded the problem by going into debt to install a cattle feeding system just as the bottom fell out.

*Ben Barber transitioned from cattle farmer to successful heavy machinery operator.*

51

*When Ben's father turned his farmland into airplane runways, Ben moved to Kansas.*

- Then the gas crisis and price increases changed the economics of beef farming; the prices of feed and supplies were exaggerated by rampant inflation just as the government's campaign against tobacco smoking got underway.
- The family managed to keep the farm, thanks to Ben's willingness to drop out of school; his brothers and three sisters were grown and gone.
- It was left to the baby boy to help his dad; "I was the hind teat boy who had to work for his supper. Didn't have money for clothes, but I always had plenty of work to do."
- Ben loved farming: the seasonal rhythms, the sense of accomplishment that came so often on a farm, the smells and the way his muscles felt after a difficult day of harvesting or rebuilding tractor engines in the shop.
- All the while, there were those who predicted failure: "Just a bunch of vultures flying over you waiting for you to go belly up. They are always around."
- By the time he turned 19 in 1980, his father decided to push Ben out of the nest.
- After five years of working full time beside his father, Ben was told his services were no longer needed.
- His father was bored with farming, resentful of the continually rising cost of cattle feed and the stagnating market price of beef, and ready to convert his most level fields into grass runways for airplanes.
- He wanted to use his energy to operate a private airport, where pilots could come for fuel, maintenance and repainting of their planes.
- It was time for his father's avocation to become his occupation; he had no patience for any conversation that did not involve flying.
- Even the death of his brother in a dramatic crop dusting accident had not tempered his joy of flying small aircraft—including several he had built himself.
- Ben, who shared his father's enthusiasm for flying, felt betrayed and abandoned.
- His father sold 100 acres to finance the aircraft operation and his retirement.
- "He just shooed me off like an unwanted weed—took me a long time to get over that," Ben said.
- So Ben left Kentucky and traveled west to find himself—until he ran out of money in Wichita, Kansas, where he took a job as a pump jockey and auto mechanic.

- By day he pumped gasoline and washed windshields at one full-service gas station, then spent his evenings repairing cars at a second service station just down the street.
- When his earnings at the part-time night job began to exceed his full-time day job, he quit pumping gas to be a mechanic full time.
- There he discovered, outside the shadow of his father, that he had valuable skills, and was appreciated for his magical ability to bring cars back to life.
- At the same time, the Federal Reserve was beginning to wage war against the persistent inflation within the United States by clamping down hard on the money supply.

*Ben expanded a small house for his wife and baby.*

- By refusing to supply all the money an inflation-ravaged economy wanted, the Fed caused interest rates to rise even further.
- As a result, consumer spending and business borrowing slowed in the late 1970s and early 1980s, the economy fell into a deep recession, and unemployment began to rise just as Ben grew restless of being a grease monkey.
- He didn't like punching a clock or taking orders; he was highly suspicious of deals that appeared too good to be true.
- In 1982, business bankruptcies rose 50 percent over the previous year, and farmers suffered as agricultural exports declined, crop prices fell, and interest rates rose.
- But the aggressive, government-sponsored slowdown did break the destructive cycle in which the economy had been caught.
- By 1983, inflation had eased, the economy had rebounded, and the United States began a sustained period of economic growth.
- Ben returned to Kentucky and made a fragile peace with his dad.
- Soon after, Ben married a local girl and helped pay her way through cosmetology school.
- He and his young family moved into an 800-square-foot starter house that his stepfather had bought and fixed up.
- Originally, the house had been built as a worker's home for a clock-making factory nearby.
- Ben personally expanded the house over the next decade, until their home contained 2,400 square feet and a little baby.

## Life at Work

- With the confidence he had earned in Kansas, Ben Barber returned to Kentucky in the early 1980s and started working as a motor grader, developing major construction projects.
- He learned to prepare a sprawling woodland site for the largest shopping mall in the area; for a residential subdivision, he learned scraping, how to form the crown in the road, the slope of the ditch, and the most economical ways to move dirt from one place to another.
- Throughout Kentucky, West Virginia, and North Carolina, subdivisions were being built on abandoned farmland, where the land was cheaper and carried fewer zoning restrictions.
- Ben was often left to work on his own because of his ability to work independently, economically, and honestly.
- Developers knew he would deliver an honest day's pay and not fall prey to the emerging culture of drug use.
- His skills were in such demand that by the late 1980s, he was running crews with 10 men or more clearing huge tracts of land.

- In the beginning he was paid $12 an hour, but by the 1990s, his pay had more than doubled to $25 per hour.
- From walking through the woods putting ribbons on trees that needed to be plowed to grading the final project for the whole crew of men, he could do it all.
- Some weeks he would show up at 6 a.m. and work until 6 p.m., six days a week, and often drove more than an hour to get to the development site.
- Heavy construction jobs were plentiful.
- As an independent contractor, Ben received no insurance benefits, paid vacations or regular holiday pay.

*Ben developed major construction projects.*

- What he got instead was independence, including the freedom to move from job to job.
- Ben loved problem solving; he liked for each job to be different.
- In low-lying areas, a 96-inch pipe might be required to divert the water so the property could be developed; on other projects, the issue might be cost containment when scraping a storm drain or building a road.
- After all, potential buyers would judge the quality of the subdivision based on roadwork long before they viewed a house for sale; plus, the more efficiently Ben and his crew did their work, the lower the lot price.
- The costs of developing a subdivision's roads and ditches were directly reflected in the price of a house.
- But finding quality help for his work crews was becoming harder; many of the workers showing up claiming to possess the necessary skills to drive a motor grader, front-end loader, or excavator were on drugs.
- "Sometimes we were scraping the bottom of the barrel," Ben said. "If they weren't high on drugs when they arrived for work, then they needed time off to report to their probation officer."
- And when the equipment was not running on a job, the contractor was losing money; everything had its cost.
- By the late 1990s, meth and marijuana were becoming cheaper and more widespread; many of the potential employees appeared to consider dope smoking the "breakfast of champions."
- Ben also came to believe that President Ronald Reagan was right when he said, "Government is not the solution to our problem. Government is the problem," and supported slashing taxes for the rich, outlays on public services, and investments as a share of national income.

*Ben felt right at home in the cab of giant earth-moving machines.*

- At the same time, Ben witnessed the impact of the rise of global competition in the information age as dozens of local businesses and thousands of jobs decamped the region for Mexico, China or the Philippines.
- Factories closed, grocery stores disappeared, "For Sale" signs popped up like dandelion weeds, and neighbors declared bankruptcy.
- Then, 2003 arrived, and many building projects came to halt; Ben intentionally took a layoff and collected unemployment benefits while he cared for his father, who was sick with lung cancer.

- It was time to be close to home and family.
- Besides, his son was now playing high school football, and Ben never missed a game.
- His son looked like a football player and played like a demon; the newspapers referred to him as the "iron man" because he played on both the offensive and defensive lines.
- One opposing player confessed to his coach that he had faked an injury "so I wouldn't get hit by him anymore."
- Several colleges expressed interest in Ben's son, thanks to his ability to block and tackle, but more school was not a high priority.
- During breaks in the school year, the entire family headed east to North Carolina's beaches, where they surfed and fished for red drum, spots and sharks.
- Ben's wife continued to style women's hair—a business that remained steady; hair continued to grow in good times and bad.
- As the business began to dry up, Ben made calls to the region's biggest developers to see what dirt needed moving—just in case he needed to climb back into the cab of a giant earthmoving machine.

## Life in the Community: Olive Hill, Kentucky

- Early in its history, Kentucky gained recognition for its excellent farming conditions, and was the site of the first commercial winery in the United States in 1799.
- Because of the high calcium content of the soil, the Bluegrass region quickly became a major horse-breeding area.
- By 2003, Kentucky ranked fifth nationally in goat farming, eighth in beef cattle production, and fourteenth in corn production.
- The state's economy expanded to include auto manufacturing, energy fuel production, and medical expertise.
- Kentucky ranked fourth among U.S. states in the number of automobiles and trucks assembled, to include the Chevrolet Corvette, Cadillac XLR , Ford Explorer, Ford Super Duty trucks, Ford Excursion, Toyota Camry, Toyota Avalon, Toyota Solara, and Toyota Venza.
- Located in eastern Kentucky, the town of Olive Hill began as a rural trading post established by the Henderson brothers in the early nineteenth century.
- In 1881, the town was moved from a hillside location to its current one in the Tygarts Creek Valley, where the Elizabethtown, Lexington and Big Sandy Railroad had laid tracks.
- The hillside location become known as Old Olive Hill and served as the city's residential area.
- On March 24, 1884, Olive Hill was incorporated as a city and served as the county seat of the shortlived Beckham County from February 9 to April 29, 1904.
- In 1917, hundreds of white laborers went on strike at the brick-making General Refractories Company, demanding that all African American employees be dismissed. Company managers eventually ceded to the striker's demands and fired all black employees.
- According to the 2000 Census, Olive Hill had a population of 1,813, composed of 98.73 percent whites, 0.17 percent African-Americans, 0.50 percent Native Americans, and 0.6 percent other races.
- The median income for a household in the city was $22,958, compared to $28,513 in the state as a whole—forty-third in the nation.

*Kentucky is a significant horse-breeding area.*

Being a good corporate citizen starts with hiring lots of good citizens.

WHAT'S A GOOD CORPORATE CITIZEN? It's not about awards or mission statements or press releases. It's about people. People who care about what they do and how they do it. And at Toyota, we know these people pretty well, because we hire them every chance we get.

You see it in every vehicle we build here.** Our over 32,000 team members take pride in everything they do. Quality, teamwork and dependability, that's what they are all about.

Our team members care about doing what's right; at work as well as in their local communities. They really are good citizens. Which in turn makes Toyota a better corporate citizen. Isn't it nice when things work out?

TOYOTA

Manufacturing Facilities

| Toyota U.S. Operations | |
|---|---|
| Plants | 10 |
| Jobs | 386,000* |
| Investment | $13 B |

TOYOTA

*Toyota is a major employer in Kentucky.*

# 2003: Workshop and Retreat Leader

*Priscilla Bright fell in love with the ocean at an early age growing up in her family's boat marina. Her love of the natural environment led to her study of the natural world and the way humans shape, and are shaped by, their environments.*

## Life at Home

- Priscilla was born in Atlantic City, New Jersey in 1956.
- She grew up in Wildwood, NJ in a boat marina on a barrier island off southern New Jersey, which her grandparents had helped settle in the 1800s.
- On one side, her grandmother was a women's rights suffrage activist, and her grandfather was the town mayor and President of the New Jersey State Senate; and on the other side, both grandparents were from fishing families.
- Her father owned a boat marina, starting with one dock and building it into the largest on the New Jersey coast.
- The family loved the ocean, living in the marina with a ship's steering wheel for a table, and even spending vacations on boats.
- Priscilla was sure that she would grow up to be an oceanographer and live on a sailboat, and absolutely could not imagine ever living away from the ocean.
- She and her older sister were raised Catholic.
- They went to the public school on the island until her father died unexpectedly when she was 12.
- Then Priscilla spent two years at Springside School for Girls where she learned field hockey and lacrosse in an environment very different from what she was used to, but she adapted and enjoyed it, especially playing sports.
- At 14, when her mother became chronically ill, she went to a Quaker boarding school—a gentle and wonderful place in the open country of Pennsylvania.
- The teachers were wonderful and they lived on campus, creating a comforting community which was very healing after the loss of her father and her mother's long-term illness.
- Many of the students came from stressful home situations, so they supported each other and had fun as well.
- Priscilla always had some sort of job, from sweeping or another chore on the docks, to running a small hamburger

*Priscilla loved living in the natural environment of upstate New York.*

*Priscilla's workshops and retreats promote learning how to achieve personal well being from within.*

stand at a local sailing club, to sailing instructor (her favorite) to bus-girl to waitress.

- She met her best, and oldest to this day, childhood friend, Sally, in second grade and they loved to explore the bay in Priscilla's small motorboat.
- She went to college on an island in Maine, wanting to be back on the ocean after her time at boarding school.
- The school was known for its environmental studies and Priscilla wanted to help save the natural environment. She studied whales, solar energy, organic gardening and farming.
- At college, Priscilla discovered that her love of the ocean and boating did not necessarily translate into a serious interest in the science of oceanography.
- By working in the school's greenhouse and gardens, however, she became interested in how environment and nutrition affected plant health and disease resistance.
- From here, she became interested in how this related to human health, specifically in emotional and psychological health factors and the effects of stress, particularly based on her own childhood history of stress and loss.
- When Priscilla attended the College of the Atlantic (which was only three years old), from which she received a BA in Human Ecology, students lived in off-campus houses, sharing domestic chores.
- The college itself was housed in several donated mansions along the coast and lots of time was spent hiking and exploring the natural beauty of the island.
- As a young girl, Priscilla traveled with her family to the Caribbean, Mexico, and Europe and both her parents believed travel was valuable to broaden your worldview, and had a great respect for other cultures.
- In fact, during the Great Depression, her father, with a college degree but no job and no money, took a job shoveling coal in the boiler room of a steamship hauling cargo halfway around the world just so he could travel.

- He even had American Express card #99, for which he saw an ad in the New York Times to "fly now/pay later" (a new concept back then).
- Her most memorable travel was a six-week survival wilderness program in Wyoming when she was 16.
- Studying the health of the environment and the effects of humans on it, they canoed, carried heavy backpacks, and camped the entire time—often finding their own food from nature.
- After graduating college, Priscilla felt very directed, supporting herself and passionate about her holistic health work.
- She was offered a position as a counselor for a holistic physician in Boston, for whom she had interned during college, and designed and ran a program in holistic health for health care workers that became the root of her ongoing career.

## Life at Work

- Although in various forms, Priscilla has always worked on stress reduction and inner healing for both the general population and for caregivers, health care workers, advocates, etc.
- Learning to promote wellbeing from within was important for her own ongoing wellbeing, and also for the many individuals dealing with stress and burnout.
- A few years after college she earned a Masters in Public Health in Health Behavior and Health Promotion from Boston University School of Medicine.
- Priscilla's list of past jobs included consultant to national corporations, hospitals and health care organizations, speaker at national health conferences, HR for large corporations (Met Life, AT&T), and Dean of an international college of healing.
- All of her past jobs and businesses taught her valuable lessons and mistakes that she used for her career—it was an ongoing creative process.
- Her mother was always in her corner, and said as long as it was what she wanted to do it was good with her and Priscilla heard the family motto—you can choose any career you want as long as you give it your best—many times.
- The most rewarding parts of her job were running "wellbeing' workshops and retreats, and helping build a sense of respectful community where participants find a sense of peacefulness and renewal.
- She did a lot of work with professional caregivers and health care workers whose jobs came with a high risk of emotional burnout.
- One of the worst things that happened at work was when, at 23 and broke, Priscilla borrowed money to print 13,000 flyers for her business. The colors she used made it very hard to read, and ended up being a waste of money, teaching her to always approve print runs in person.
- Lesson learned—pay attention to the details right through to the end—never rely on others when something is important to you.
- One thing that would make her job easier would be a full-time secretary.

*Priscilla and her husband settled in New York's Catskill Mountains seeking privacy and wilderness.*

*The Hudson River was close to Priscilla's home, and allowed her to be near her life-long love—the water.*

- Priscilla often traveled to teach weekend workshops, nationwide and overseas.
- She soon realized that she needed to lessen the stress of traveling, which also made it difficult to build any real community at home.
- She began the gradual process of transitioning from work commitments that required long periods of travel to building business opportunities closer to home.
- This was the beginning of a big change for her and though it was very challenging, it gave her great joy and peace of mind to be an integral part of her local community, focusing on family, health, and friends, while still doing good work in the world.
- She also had time finally to travel from her mountain home to visit her beloved ocean.

## Life in the Community: Bar Harbor, Maine

- Priscilla attended school at the College of the Atlantic, which was located in Bar Harbor on Mount Desert Island, Maine.
- The Wabanaki Native Americans called Mount Desert Island "Pemetic," or "range of mountains" and revered it as an abundant clam-gathering place.
- The town became a popular tourist destination in the mid-1800s after several Hudson River School painters showcased its rugged maritime scenery.
- In mid-October 1947, a wildfire ignited that would intensify over ten days, and not be declared out until mid-November. Nearly half the eastern side of Mount Desert Island burned, including 67 palatial summer houses on Millionaires' Row. Five historic grand hotels and 170 permanent homes were destroyed.
- Hikers and bikers came from all over the world to use the trails in Acadia National Park, one of the oldest parks in the country.
- The park was also damaged in the fire of 1947, but the natural regrowth actually added to the diversity of its tree populations.

- The College of the Atlantic was founded on the island in 1968, and its first class of students numbered only 32.
- The school offered only one major: human ecology, and used the natural beauty and ecology of Bar Harbor and Mount Desert Island in its courses.
- The College of the Atlantic was the first school in the nation to become carbon-neutral.

## Life in the Community: Catskills, New York

- Priscilla lived and worked in the Catskill Mountains—around two hours north of New York City.
- Her town was very small and extremely close-knit, where she participated in weekly music-making and potluck dinners with friends.
- Her neighbors were all very helpful and friendly, loved nature and country living.
- They all helped each other dig out during snow storms, watched each other's animals, etc.
- Priscilla and her husband wound up in the Catskills looking for privacy and wilderness.
- The Catskills used New York City drinking water, so there was very little development and the environment was closely guarded, with park trails going up the mountains and clean streams and rivers.
- Much like during her childhood, she was closely aligned and nourished by nature and solitude.
- A typical day off for Priscilla usually included riding her bike in the woods, hiking, swimming in the river, listening and dancing to local live music, and playing with her dog.

*Slide Mountain and the peaks around it as seen from Twin Mountain in the northern Catskills.*

The Catskills, *a painting by Asher Brown Durand.*

## 2003: Lieutenant Colonel in the War in Iraq

*Lieutenant Colonel Joshua Cohen, who modeled himself on General George S. Patton, believed he was leading an assault in Iraq that would be an example of superb tactical warfare, taught in schools for years to come.*

### Life at Home

- When asked his profession by civilians, Lieutenant Colonel Joshua Cohen always replied, "Warrior."
- The term "soldier" might apply to people in the Quartermaster Corps, but not to the commander of a tank battalion spearheading the drive to root out Saddam Hussein and his regime.
- The Cohen family was deeply religious, patriotic and dedicated to doing well.
- Joshua's straight "A" report card was an expectation; he also pushed himself to excel at wrestling, debate and military history.
- He had seen the movie Patton too many times to count and, well aware of the origin of his name, knew all the great warriors of scripture.
- Graduating in 1986 from West Point near the top of his class, he was known for his keen intelligence, salty language and stentorian voice.
- In the evenings, he often circulated among the troops, blending bawdy stories with quotes from the Classics.
- A company commander in Desert Storm, he had been outraged at President George Bush when his troops were not allowed to proceed into Baghdad and take out Saddam.
- Now, with Gulf War II declared, that mistake was about to be rectified, ironically by a second President Bush.

### Life at Work

- Lieutenant Colonel Cohen was extremely proud of his unit and very protective of his men.
- He hated that the modern army included women and homosexuals, and thought that only men—real men—were suited for combat.
- One particular focus for his anger was Captain Rachael Greene, who joined the military for all the wrong reasons.
- Not only was she National Guard, but her motivation for going into the military was extra money for graduate school.
- Yet she commanded a five-person team of Arabic linguists in the Guard's 300th Military Intelligence Brigade.
- He was particularly irritated by the sign she and one of the other women had drawn and placed in front of her Humvee, reading "One weekend a month, my butt!" referring to the customary terms of her National Guard service.

*Lt. Colonel Joshua Cohen was dedicated to leading tactile attacks against the enemy in Iraq.*

- When word came down for Joshua's battalion to move out in the opening wave of the war, he was jubilant.
- His unit was to be at the tip of the spear on the army's drive to Baghdad.
- During the first Gulf War a decade earlier, all of the foreign allies had wimped out when it came time to eliminate Saddam, but nothing could stop America this time.
- Joshua could feel victory in his bones.
- When he addressed his troops in preparation for battle, he was clear: Confront the enemy and kill with extreme prejudice.
- When he finished his talk with a monologue from Shakespeare's Henry V, several rolled their eyes.
- As the battalion's M1A1 Abrams tanks moved through the scrubland of Iraq, they met only token resistance.

*Joshua always made sure his troops were ready for battle.*

- All enemy soldiers were quickly vanquished in the assault.
- As in the previous Gulf War, others quickly surrendered—so many that the column's progress was slowed.
- Those Iraqis with command seniority were sent back to division HQ for interrogation by Captain Greene and her team.
- As they proceeded, the U.S. tanks drew fire.
- At one point, Joshua's tank was hit, though he was not badly hurt.
- The tanks annihilated the Iraqis.
- Afterwards, Joshua stood among the smoldering remains of the Iraqi position and told his men, "God has been good to us this day," echoing the words of Confederate General Stonewall Jackson following the battle of Antietam.
- But the lightning pace of the attack left little room for reveling in victory.
- Soon, the column of tanks and Bradley fighting vehicles were thundering into the farmlands of Iraq near the Euphrates River.
- As they prepared to cross the river, an Iraqi military contingent offered stiff resistance.
- Rapidly, Joshua's men counterattacked, firing shell after shell into the Iraqi positions.
- When several Iraqi vehicles appeared disabled, Joshua ordered an all-out attack, destroying everyone.
- The remaining Iraqis fled.
- Quickly, Joshua collected the necessary data for the future awarding of bronze and silver stars for his men.
- Ahead was Saddam International Airport, only 10 miles from the center of Baghdad.
- There, Joshua knew, the real fighting would happen.
- His knew his men were exhausted from battle and lack of sleep, but he also knew they would fight ferociously when called upon.
- "Whatever emotions you're feeling, you've got to take the pain," he told his men; "Let your instincts take over. You've got to concentrate

*Joshua was extremely proud of his unit.*

*The rules of combat were clear: confront the enemy and kill with extreme prejudice.*

on the guys who are alive. The dead are just bodies; their spirits are gone."
- The threat of chemical warfare forced his men into special protective suits that were bulky and hot, especially in the 100-degree heat.
- The first obstacle they encountered at the perimeter of the airport was a high wall, which Cohen ordered his tanks to clear.
- After pounding the wall, the tanks finally broke through and flooded through the gap.
- Almost immediately, one of the tanks destroyed an airplane.
- The men cheered the explosion, but the officers were upset because they had wanted the planes left alone.
- To their surprise and Joshua's disappointment, the airport was largely deserted, littered only with empty vehicles and foxholes, shrapnel, and destroyed palm trees.
- Joshua and his vehicles surrounded the terminal and carefully searched for combatants, but found no one.
- Their mission to take the airport accomplished, he hoped his assault on Iraq would one day be taught in military schools around the world.

## Life in the Community: West Point, New York
- West Point was the oldest continuously occupied military post in the United States, located on the Hudson River in Orange County, New York.
- The location of West Point was chosen because of the unusual S-shaped curve of the Hudson River at this point.
- Although it was never tested in actual combat, a giant iron chain was laid across the Hudson at West Point in 1778 to prevent the British from sailing further up the river.
- West Point was the site for perhaps the most infamous act of treason in American history: General Benedict Arnold attempted to turn the fort over to the British in 1780.
- The United States Military Academy was established at West Point in 1802, making it the country's oldest service academy. The academy is popularly referred to simply as "West Point."
- In 1841, Charles Dickens visited the academy and said "It could not stand on more appropriate ground, and any ground more beautiful can hardly be."

- During the Civil War, graduates of West Point fought on both sides. 294 graduates served for the Union, while 151 served for the Confederacy.
- After the war, the academy struggled with reintegrating Union, Confederate, and the first black cadets into a cohesive student body.
- As a result, West Point dealt with issues of hazing by upperclassmen on entering freshmen. When Douglas A. MacArthur became superintendent in 1919, he began to institute policies that would discourage this practice.
- Both World Wars required so many soldiers that West Point academic years were accelerated and students graduated early so they could immediately deploy overseas.
- West Point began admitting female cadets in 1976, after Congress authorized the admission of women to the federal service academies in 1975.
- Notable graduates of West Point include Dwight D. Eisenhower, Ulysses S. Grant, and Buzz Aldrin.

---

### The 300th Military Brigade

- The 300th Military Intelligence Brigade (linguist) comprises trained and ready linguists and military intelligence soldiers.
- The organization is built from the bottom up with five-soldier teams possessing unique language skills.
- The brigade has 1,400 documented linguist team positions covering 19 languages.
- Arabic, Persian-Farsi and Korean are heavily represented; other languages include Russian, Chinese, Vietnamese, Thai, Spanish, French, Turkish, Serbo-Croatian and German.

---

## 2004: Salesperson and Training Director

*Michele Kyle was a rambunctious rule breaker as a young girl. Growing up with Catholic parents and strict nuns, she learned early how to talk her way into and out of any situation, skills that well prepared her for a successful career in sales.*

### Life at Home

- Michele was born in July 1962 in Nyack, New York.
- She grew up in a small paper mill town on the water called Piermont.
- She lived there for 28 years.
- Her parents owned an Italian restaurant and her father, in addition to the restaurant, was a packing manager in a paper company in Ridgefield, New Jersey.
- Michele and her older sister both worked at her parent's restaurant from a young age.
- Growing up, a favorite Easter tradition was making Easter pies with her mom (the youngest of ten children).
- Each pie used homemade pie dough, Italian meats, provolone, mozzarella, ricotta, parmesan, and 12 eggs.
- She went to St. Ann's Catholic Elementary School and Rosary Academy High School.
- Michele didn't like being in an all girl's Catholic high school, didn't like sports, and wanted nothing to do with school activities or clubs.
- She and her friends hung out together, laughed and caused trouble.
- In the 9th grade, her home room teacher "Sister Blinky" came looking for her in the bathroom, where she was caught smoking—detention again!
- In her senior year, the class trip to Bermuda was amazing, and involved a local guy named King.
- On the last night of the trip, she got back to the hotel an hour after curfew and found Mother Superior waiting for her, tapping her foot.
- Due to behavior not befitting of a "Rosary girl" she was told she would not graduate from Rosary Academy.
- After some serious acting, pleading and promising, she did graduate, but not before detention for the rest of her senior year.
- Her parents thought Catholic school would give Michele the discipline they thought she needed, but not so much!

*Michele Kyle was proud of the life she built.*

*Michele and her husband Rich in Las Vegas.*

- Working in the restaurant through her high school years and beyond, Michele did everything—cooked, washed dishes, bartended, waitressed and hostessed.
- She wouldn't admit it at the time, but working at the restaurant helped her achieve success in sales. It also helped her be comfortable around people.
- Michele's best childhood friend was Lisa Cornetta, whose parents also owned a restaurant.
- The girls were inseparable, often having sleepovers and getting in trouble together.
- Once, the girls snuck some boys into the house, and they eventually had to climb out the bedroom window onto the roof and slide down the drain pipe to avoid getting caught.
- At 19, Michele enrolled in Beauty School, trying to get away from the restaurant.
- She always dreamed about being a hairdresser, watching her aunt run a full service beauty salon from her house.
- Her parents paid the $995.00 for Beauty School—a lot of money at the time, and Michele became friends with the head of the school's son, Artie.
- She partied a lot, and did fine in school, but knew that it wasn't the life for her.
- With 300 hours left till graduation, Michele left school, but not without a fight from her parents.
- Her biggest challenge growing up was making sure she fit in—that she was popular and accepted.
- She remembered her father telling her the story of the Ugly Duckling and singing to her, "Micheline Ponavine my pretty swan you will be."
- "My daddy is the best thing I remember, he was right, he was always right."
- Michele was inspired by Og Mandino, author of *The Greatest Salesman in the World*.
- His quote set her career in motion: "I will persist until I succeed. I was not delivered unto this world in defeat, nor does failure course in my

*Many famous patrons frequented her parent's restaurant, the Hudson Terrace, including Bill Murray, who just wanted to "pose" for the camera with a bowling trophy.*

*Michele's father, sister, niece and nephew.*

veins. I am not a sheep waiting to be prodded by my shepherd. I am a lion and I refuse to talk, to walk, to sleep with the sheep. I will hear not those who weep and complain, for their disease is contagious. The slaughterhouse of failure is not in my destiny. I will persist until I succeed. I will win."

- After graduation, Michele worked at the family restaurant on weekends, plus at the local paper mill, which was BORING.
- After a medical procedure, she lived with her sister and brother in-law and beautiful baby niece—she loved living there, away from her mother.
- Michele met her husband at a party and they were married in 1993.
- He was handsome and a "good/bad boy," just her type.
- After unsuccessful attempts to have children, Michele focused on nieces, nephews, her cat Dusti, and dog Bella.

## Life at Work

- The first job Michele really loved was as a micrographics supervisor at Volvo, until she met someone on vacation in Florida, and opened up a bikini store in Daytona Beach—the start of her sales career.
- She traveled all over Florida, doing bikini fashion shows and meeting interesting people, like the owner/creator of Hawaiian Tropic suntan products, and a fashion designer in CoCo Beach who had a pet cheetah!
- For her bikini store, Michele would buy bathing suits in the Bahamas and California and had lots of fun.
- After sales started dropping—most of her clientele were strippers who only purchased bikini bottoms—she closed up shop and moved back to New York.
- Her computer experience at Volvo gave her confidence to apply for a job at a software company.

- With a newspaper article about her bikini store instead of a resume, she successfully sold herself and was hired on the spot.
- After she got married, Michele attended Saint Thomas Aquinas for a Real Estate course and loved it.
- For the first time, she was the perfect student and worked as a successful realtor for a number of years, but went back to the corporate world for the benefits.
- As Training Director for a large IT firm, Michele worked with Fortune 500 and 1000 clients, selling cloud solutions, managed services, Identity and Access Management, third party risk solutions and cyber security services and products.
- Although she did not have a college degree—her one regret—she took business courses at Fairleigh Dickinson University, computer related, and held several technical sales certifications.
- Looking back, Michele realized that because of her social nature, the natural way she talked to all kinds of people, and even working at her parent's restaurant, a successful sales career was inevitable.
- She especially enjoyed the technology aspect of her job—being a woman in this industry was empowering.
- The most rewarding thing that happened at work was being awarded President's Club five times—a very luxurious award trip was given to top performers.
- The challenges of her job involved unhappy clients.
- Satisfied customers are the key to success, so resolving issues to make things right was an important aspect of her job.
- Each day at work was different for Michele, contacting clients through phone calls, email, social media, conference calls and virtual meetings.
- She attended vendor partner webinars to hear and learn about the latest and greatest, worked on P&L spreadsheets for her department, created marketing email blasts, attended sales technical training, and wrote a quarterly technical training piece for the company newsletter.
- Every day she was in ABS mode—Always Be Selling.
- The only time her income was negatively affected was during the Great Recession, when she reinvented herself a bit with additional training and new techniques.
- Since she worked at home, having someone else walk her dog would have made her job easier!

Daytona Today     May 16-29, 1988

# Bikini Beach Bares All

By Dick Dugan

Some great things really do come in small packages — or in this case, in small stores.

Bikini Beach, 319 Seabreeze Blvd., purveyors of head-turning swimwear, is such a store. With only 350 square feet of floor space, Bikini Beach displays more than 50 lines of swimwear in hundreds of styles.

Owner/operators Michele Naglieri and Barry Wilson enjoy offering exotic originals such as those designed by Fay Francis of Cocoa Beach. To procure the rest of their unusual lines, Naglieri and Wilson attend exhibits in France, New York, California and Hawaii.

Then, according to Wilson, "We only buy three to six items from each line; then, no matter how well it sells, we will not order that particular style again. That way we continuously offer new and different swimwear to our customers."

It hardly seems possible in such small quarters, but in addition to the swimwear, Bikini Beach sells sunglasses, socks, jewelry, blouses and skirts, and has recently added a line of men's casual wear.

Says Wilson: "We're able to offer quality merchandise by keeping overhead low — we do all the buying and retailing ourselves."

Bikini Beach recently entertained patrons at Danny's Marker 32 restaurant with a show featuring a bevy of local ladies ensconced in the store's latest exotic beach and casual wear.

Future shows will be held alternate Wednesdays at 6 p.m., with the next showing scheduled for May 18.

**Bright Smile, Small Store**—Co-owner Michele Naglieri pulls a suit from packed rack in tiny swimwear shop.

**Bikini Clad Beauty**—shows what the right form can do for a little cloth. 21-year-old area resident Debbie Brickle was one of a bevy of local women who modeled Bikini Beach fashions at a recent show at Danny's Marker 32 restaurant.

*Michele's sales career started by selling bikinis in Daytona Beach, Florida.*

*Michele with the New York Knicks cheerleaders at a company event.*

- Michele was also VP of her husband's successful painting company—28 years and counting.
- The only things about her younger life she would change would be going to college and travelling in Europe for a year.

## Life in the Community: Suffern, New York

- Michele and Rich lived and worked in Suffern, New York, about an hour north of Manhattan.
- The area around Suffern was originally home to the Munsee Native Americans, a branch of the great Lenape nation.
- Suffern was also home to Avon Product's R&D facility, a large employer.
- The town was small and close knit, with several generations of families staying in the town for many years, including Michele's in-laws.
- Michele's neighbors were kind and friendly—available for cat sitting and exchanging holiday gifts (mostly food).
- Suffern was similar to where Michele grew up, except one was on the water and the other in the mountains.
- At one point her and her husband owned a comic book and collectible store in town, belonged to the Suffern Chamber of Commerce and participated in the town's annual street fairs.
- On her day off, Michele would typically run errands and take a Pure Barre class.
- The best things about her neighborhood were the many ethnically diverse restaurants, the proximity of the commuter train to NYC, and bordering Mahwah, New Jersey (which had no sales tax on clothing).
- Having the train so close was also a challenge—soot from the train station filled her house with dust, so she cleaned constantly to keep it spotless.

*Washington Avenue Soldier's Monument, at junction with Lafayette Avenue (NY 59), Suffern, NY*

## 2004: High School Girls' Basketball Coach

*John Walker Hall, a high school girls' basketball coach, became frustrated at the inferior practice facilities, meager transportation to away games, and even lack of uniforms suffered by his players.*

### Life at Home

- Hailing from Roanoke, Virginia, John Walker Hall graduated from Longwood College in Farmville, Virginia, in 1990.
- While still a student and a member of the basketball team there, he decided on a coaching career.
- In college, he met and wooed his future wife Dawn, a 6'3" center for the Longwood women's team.
- After graduation John taught and coached at several middle schools in the Roanoke, Virginia area, while Dawn worked as a pharmacist.
- John's plunge into controversy occurred after he was hired as a history teacher and girls' high school varsity basketball coach in Hemphill, West Virginia, in 2002.
- From the outset of his coaching stint, John was struck by the differences in the way the athletic programs were run in Hemphill in comparison to those in the Roanoke area.
- In particular, he was concerned that the girls' basketball program was consistently short-changed.
- Despite inconsistent support, he discovered that his team, the Lady Hawks, was a skilled bunch.
- The Lady Hawks had won multiple district and regional championships despite their being relegated to inferior practice space at a local elementary school.
- The only time the girls' team used the high school gym was for games, virtually eliminating their home team advantage.
- In addition, because of the distance between the high school and elementary school gymnasium, they had to carpool, often resulting in delayed practice times.
- And, the most obvious affront of all, the girls' basketball team had to share their uniforms with the girls' track team, despite occasional scheduling overlaps.
- Sounding out his rising senior players on the issue, he discovered the prevailing attitude was, "That's the way it's always been."
- So for the first two years, he said little.
- Besides, he had six solid players returning from the previous year's 16-4 season and had his eyes on a state championship in 2004.
- The Halls enjoyed a good life in a comfortable house with their two girls actively involved in the youth basketball league.
- But Coach Hall couldn't shake his frustration concerning the inequities between the boys' and girls' teams.
- So he began researching Title IX, which was signed into law in 1972, specifically aimed at creating parity in education and athletics.

*Coach John Hall fought for equality for his female basketball team.*

- Using the Web, he found detailed examples of other high schools in New Orleans and Michigan that relegated girls teams to inopportune conditions and times in order to accommodate the boys' teams.
- He became familiar with the opposing sides' arguments, including the argument that reducing male funding and increasing female funding could also be considered unequal.
- And he found the story of Coach Roderick Jackson, who lost his job for speaking up for the girls' team.
- But Coach Hall knew there was a middle path that would bring fairness to his high school; reasonable people could find reasonable solutions.

*Hemphill was in the Blue Ridge Mountains.*

## Life at Work

- John Hall could not have been happier with his team.
- The Lady Hawks were halfway through an undefeated season and the entire community was buzzing about the possibility of a state championship.
- His team's reputation for tough, smart play was drawing college recruiters from as far away as Washington State University.
- While he found the accolades rewarding, he grew increasingly angry.
- Underneath the praise, he knew about the adversity his young women had to overcome daily.
- No one seemed to care that the team practiced in an elementary school gymnasium, which had 1950s-style crescent-shaped, non-regulation metal backboards.
- Instead of a customary wooden floor, they practiced on a slick metal floor with a concrete sub-floor.
- Sure that the rock-hard surface would impact his girls' knees and joints, he prayed that it would not result in a season-ending injury.
- Knowing younger women were more susceptible to anterior cruciate ligament (ACL) injuries because of their wider hips, he sometimes shortened practice to prevent injuries that might be exacerbated by the outdated practice facilities.
- John was also frustrated that his girls had to arrange carpools to away games, while the boys' team traveled by bus.

*Coach Hall's team was a fierce competitor.*

- And even though the school owned two whirlpool tubs to ease muscle injury, access was limited.
- The boys used the whirlpools after practice; John could only schedule his girls for whirlpool therapy in the early morning hours before school.
- Funding was also an issue.
- Thanks to a tradition of winning, the Lady Hawks attracted standing-room-only crowds, nearly always out-drawing the boys.
- But he was continuously told that girls' teams were money losers and not to ask for too much.
- So, by the time Coach Hall was ready to take his grievances to his superiors, he had a full head of steam.
- Having already familiarized himself with the basics of Title IX, he proceeded to learn about contemporary developments in its history.

- He learned that requiring equal access was impacting the entire educational process, not just athletics.
- He discovered that half of all law and medical students were female, as were roughly three of every four veterinary students.
- In 1972, the year Title IX was enacted, women earned 7 percent of the nation's law degrees.
- That same year, 18 percent of female high school graduates were completing at least four years of college compared to 26 percent of their male peers.
- The studies showed that in 2004, 32 years after Title IX was enacted, women were earning 57 percent of bachelor's degrees, outpacing men.
- Nationwide, in 2002 girls and women accounted for four out of every 10 high school and varsity athletes.
- But not all had changed.
- Male coaches still led 50 percent of college women's teams; few women coached men's teams.

*The Lady Hawks were a winning team.*

- Coach Hall also learned that many high schools and middle schools continued to short-change girls' athletic programs.
- At the midpoint of the season, John met with the athletics director and the head football coach to lay out his concerns.
- They assured John that change was imminent and presented him with order forms for new uniforms for his team.
- Also, they agreed that the girls' team could use school transportation for away games.
- Then, after much discussion, they even ordered that the boys' and girls' teams alternate the use of the practice gymnasium and whirlpool facilities.
- That's when the trouble started.
- It was okay to give the girls equal treatment as long as it did not impact the boys.
- At first it was anonymous phone calls to his home after midnight with a single message: "Stop screwing with the boys' basketball team. Get out of our gym."
- Then came calls to his wife: "Don't think you are too big to be messed with."
- Finally, he learned that his starting five were being threatened by scrawled notes and angry outbursts in the hallways.
- Obviously, challenging the system was not going to be easy.
- The showdown came just days before the regional tournament.
- Both the boys' and the girls' teams were eligible for regional tournament play; both were favored to make the state tournament.
- Both had tough opponents.
- Coach Hall was anxious to practice his team against the high-pressure defense they would face next.
- Also, college scouts from five Division I schools were scheduled to be at the game to recruit his best players.
- But the boys' team was occupying the high school gym on a day they were scheduled to be at the tiny elementary school gym and refused to leave.
- Polite requests turned to harsh words, then frustration, then shouting.
- Both teams were at the peak of anxiety over the upcoming tournament play.
- Both refused to give ground.
- Controlling his temper, Coach Hall called the athletic director to mediate.

- The athletic director was calm and clear: the boys' tournament game was more important, and yes, he had given the boys permission to use the high school facilities at this important time of the season.
- Coach Hall was stunned.
- How could he tell the girls they were second-class citizens again?
- When he broke the news, his voice was clear, breaking only once with disappointment.
- The girls' reaction was immediate; first a chorus of "no fair," followed by fervent denunciation of the boys' team, and then, resignation.
- Half of the girls then said, "It's okay coach; the little gym will do just fine."
- The other half wanted revenge, and the opportunity came quickly.
- The next day an all-school pep rally was scheduled for the two basketball teams.
- The athletic director and principal traditionally enjoyed showing the teams that the student body was behind them all the way.
- As usual, the girls' team was introduced first, as a warm-up to announcing the boys' team.
- Coach Hall spoke to a packed auditorium about the dedication, skill and teamwork his team displayed, to rousing cheers.
- He then left the stage, but the girls' team stood still and refused to exit.
- Even after the boys' team was announced, the girls' basketball team stayed in place, refusing to give ground.
- The auditorium was filled with laughter, shouting, catcalls and cascading noise when Carrie, the smallest member of the team, walked to the microphone, and told the students about the battle for practice space, and said, "We will move when we are treated equally."
- The auditorium exploded with energy.
- Then the boys' team members attempted to physically push the girls' team members off the stage, at which point the principal took back the microphone and shouted at the girls' team, "Leave the stage or be suspended."
- The student body president shouted, "You can't suspend us all," and led the students out of the auditorium, including the entire girls' team.
- When the room fell silent, only one-third of the students, mostly freshmen, remained.
- In front of that timid gathering, the principal stormed up to Coach Hall and shouted, "You will pay for this!"
- Equally frustrated, they both went outside to meet with the students.

## Life in the Community: McDowell County, West Virginia

- Hemphill was located in McDowell County, West Virginia, in the Western Blue Ridge Mountains off I-77 in Appalachia coal mining country.
- Most of the employed citizens of Hemphill and nearby Welch were employed by either the Kingston Pocahontas Coal Company or Solvay Collieries Company at the time John Walker Hall began his high school coaching career.
- McDowell County started in Virginia, created in 1858 by the Virginia General Assembly.
- The county is named for James McDowell, a Virginia Governor and Congressman.
- It became a part of West Virginia when several counties seceded from Vrginia in the midst of the Civil War.
- A local newspaper editor called the county the "Free State of McDowell" to refer to the political atmosphere and demographics and the name stuck.
- The coal mining industry caused McDowell's population to boom, reaching nearly 100,000 residents in the 1950s.
- However, with that industry's decline, young people began to move out of the county in search of better work and the population declined rapidly, reaching half that number in only two decades.

- As of the 2000 census, McDowell County had a population of a little over 27,000 residents.
- With the population leaving McDowell County, poverty rates increased dramatically.
- The county even began garnering national attention. In a speech in May, 1963, President John F. Kennedy remarked "I don't think any American can be satisfied to find in McDowell County, in West Virginia, 20 or 25 percent of the people of that county out of work, not for 6 weeks or 12 weeks, but for a year, 2, 3, or 4 years."
- Several counties in Appalachia, including McDowell, were targets in the War on Poverty, an effort began by President Lyndon B. Johnson.

*McDowell County Courthouse in Welch, West Virginia.*

- The closing of all coal mines and facilities by the United States Steel Corporation in the mid-1980s not only caused a further mass exodus from McDowell County, but also increased the poverty levels dramatically.
- Personal income dropped by 66% after US Steel's departure from the county. Housing values plunged and many had no choice but to abandon their homes and mortgages.
- The economic turmoil in McDowell County also affected the school system; many school buildings were in disrepair, enrollment was low, and half of the children lived in poverty.
- In December 2001, the state intervened, and through emergency funding and reorganization, the West Virginia Department of Education assisted McDowell County in repairing or closing old buildings, and building new ones.
- Flooding in 2001 and 2002 demolished several towns in McDowell County. In some areas, over 10 inches of rain fell over a period of 12 hours. The mountains channeled the rainfall into violent flows of water that leveled whole towns.
- Several charitable groups, both religious and secular, have organized support for McDowell County's residents in need, assisting with home repair, providing clothing and supplies, and performing other mission work.

## The Origins of Title IX

- Congresswoman Edith Green of Oregon, who later was acknowledged as the mother of Title IX, began House Higher Education Style committee meetings on discrimination against women in June and July 1970.
- Over seven days, distinguished women, scholars and government officials outlined the ways in which women were left out of educational opportunities.
- State universities in John Hall's home state of Virginia had turned away thousands of qualified women since the early 1960s because of gender, not qualifications.
- The freshman class at the University of North Carolina consisted of 1,900 men and just 426 women.
- At the University of Michigan, more qualified women applied than men, so the school adjusted its requirements to keep women to less than half of the incoming class.
- Quotas at many medical and law schools limited females to just 10 students out of every 100.
- Even though most teachers from grade school through high school were women, most principals were men.
- Ms. Green's key supporters on the House Labor and Education Committee included Shirley Chisholm of New York, the first African American congresswomen, and Patsy Mink of Hawaii, the first woman of color elected to Congress, who helped write the section of Title IX that would apply to girls and women.

- Congressman Ed Koch of New York also spoke out in support of Title IX, accusing his fellow lawmakers of slow, incremental movement of rights to women.
- In the opening days of Title IX, the main thrust was directed at leveling the field in education itself.
- Only later was the emphasis shifted to athletics, thanks to the efforts of former Olympic swimming champion Diane Di Palma and tennis great Billie Jean King, who trounced Bobby Riggs in the Battle of the Sexes televised tennis match.
- Billie Jean King became pivotal in transforming American attitudes about women in sports.

*The struggle for women athletes was decades old.*

- Cartoonist Charles M. Shultz of Peanuts fame also helped through the creation of comic strip character Peppermint Patty, the epitome of the modern, competitive girl of the 1970s.
- Civil rights laws such as Title IX have historically been a powerful mechanism for effecting social change in the United States.
- Title IX of the Education Amendments of 1972 was modeled on Title VI of the Civil Rights Act of 1964 prohibiting discrimination on account of race, color and national origin.
- Title IX was followed by three other pieces of civil rights legislation: Section 504 of the Rehabilitation Act of 1973 prohibiting disability discrimination; the Age Discrimination Act of 1975; and Title II of the Americans with Disabilities Act of 1990 prohibiting disability discrimination by public entities.

### Title IX Timeline

**1972**  Title IX of The Educational Amendments of 1972 was signed into law by President Richard Nixon.

**1973**  The Association for Intercollegiate Athletics for Women (AIAW) adopted legislation to permit the first college scholarships for female athletes.

The U.S. Open was the first tennis tournament to offer equal prize money—$25,000—to men and women.

**1974**  The first women's professional football league began with seven teams; players earned $25.00 a game.

The Women's Sports Foundation was established by Billie Jean King.

**1976**  The first women's rowing and basketball competitions took place in the Olympics.

**1977**  Janet Guthrie became the first woman driver in the Indianapolis 500.

**1978**  The courts ruled that female sportswriters should have equal access to male athletes' locker rooms in the United States.

The Amateur Sports Act passed, which prohibited gender discrimination in open amateur sports in the United States.

**1982** The Supreme Court ruled that Title IX covered employees, such as coaches, as well as students.

The Association for Intercollegiate Athletics for Women, which previously governed many women's collegiate sports, closed its doors and filed an unsuccessful antitrust lawsuit challenging the NCAA's authority over women's sports.

**1984** Title IX was limited by the Supreme Court's ruling in *Grove City v. Bell*, which stated that only educational institutions receiving direct federal funds were affected by Title IX.

Joan Benoit Samuelson won the gold medal in the first official Olympic women's marathon.

**1986** The first woman to play on an all-male professional basketball team, Lynette Woodard, debuted with the Harlem Globetrotters.

**1988** The Civil Rights Restoration Act became law following a congressional override of a veto by President Ronald Reagan; the law mandated that all educational institutions that received federal money were bound by Title IX.

Judith Davidson became the first female athletic director at a Division I school—Central Connecticut State University.

**1990** Jodi Haller became the first woman to pitch in a college baseball game as a member of Pennsylvania's St. Vincent College team.

**1991** Judith Sweet became the first female president of the NCAA.

The U.S. women's soccer team won the first-ever Women's World Cup.

**1993** There occurred the first of nine straight sellouts for the NCAA Women's Final Four basketball championship.

**1995** Mighty Mary, the first almost all-women's yachting team, competed in the America's Cup Race and advanced to the final round.

**1996** A record number of women competed in the 1996 Olympic Games in Atlanta—close to 1,000 more than in any previous games—3,684 women as opposed to 7,059 men.

**1998** Women's ice hockey made its Olympic debut in Nagano, Japan; the U.S. team won the first gold medal.

**2000** The National Women's Football League (NWFL) was formed.

The women's United Soccer Association was formed, attracting investors such as Time Warner, Comcast Corporation, and Cox Communications.

No person in the United States shall, on the basis of sex, be excluded from participation in, be denied the benefits of, or be subject to discrimination under any educational programs or activity receiving federal financial assistance.
—*Preamble to Title IX of the Education Amendments of 1972*

### "Clarifying Title IX,"
### Editorial, *St. Petersburg Times* (Florida), July 19, 2003

The formal clarification the U.S. Department of Education has issued on Title IX ought to satisfy all who sought fair play for women and men in collegiate sports. But it hasn't. And those who now complain are revealing an agenda that has little to do with gender equity.

The DOE letter makes two abundantly clear points about the continued enforcement of Title IX:

1. Universities do not have to prove that their sports opportunities for women are "substantially proportionate" to their numbers on campus in order to comply. They can show they have a history of advancing women's sports or that they are "fully and effectively" serving women athletes. "Each of the three prongs of the test is an equally sufficient means of complying with Title IX, and no one prong is favored over the other," the letter advises.

2. Universities are not required and not encouraged to eliminate men's teams to bring equity between genders. Says the letter: "Nothing in Title IX requires the cutting or reduction of teams in order to demonstrate compliance with Title IX, and . . . the elimination of teams is a disfavored practice."

Those two points go directly to the allegations of unfairness that have been leveled by male wrestlers, gymnasts and swimmers who say their teams were eliminated to comply with Title IX. The National Wrestling Coaches Association even sued DOE in 2001, claiming that male wrestlers were losing their scholarships because of Title IX. But U.S. District Judge Emmet Sullivan, in ruling against the wrestlers last month, reached the same conclusion as Gerald Reynolds, the U.S. assistant secretary for civil rights who wrote the advisory letter. Both say that the sports teams were dropped because of financial pressures, not gender compliance. The record bears them out.

Title IX, an amendment to the Education Act passed by Congress 31 years ago, has been hugely successful in providing educational and athletic opportunities for women. In college, the number of women playing varsity sports has increased fivefold and, in high school, 10-fold. At the same time, there has been no credible evidence that those opportunities have come at the expense of men. In fact, the number of men playing intercollegiate sports has continued to grow, albeit at a smaller rate than for women, and 53 of the universities that eliminated wrestling teams did so during a four-year period in the mid-1980s when Title IX was not enforced.

The documented trends of sports participation haven't dissuaded some male athletes from pointing the finger at their female counterparts, however. And the groups that represent them are not satisfied with a DOE letter that specifically condemns the elimination of male sports teams. When asked for his reaction, Eric Pearson, chairman of the Washington-based College Sports Council, told reporters that "the Bush Administration has completely caved in to the gender-quota advocates."

While it is likely true that the Bush Administration calculated the politics of overturning a widely embraced gender-equity measure, it can hardly be argued that the president is a quota advocate. DOE appointed a special commission to examine Title IX in part because the president expressed precisely the same concern about quotas. The course he ultimately chose was a moderate one, but its effect is the same. Under Title IX, universities are being told they need not turn to quotas; they need only serve women equitably. Sometimes the guys don't always like that.

## 2004: Elementary School Principal

*Following in her mother's footsteps, Ellen Boshe dedicated her life to education. She started her career as a speech language pathologist, then moved to special education teacher, regular education teacher and finally, after 20 years of teaching, elementary school principal.*

### Life at Home

- Ellen was born on September 1, 1951 in the Bronx, New York.
- She moved to Long Island as a child and grew up in Amityville.
- Her mother was a middle school English teacher and her father was a New York City police officer.
- Ellen was the middle child in a family of seven children—5 brothers and 1 sister.
- She was raised Roman Catholic and celebrated the traditional holidays—Thanksgiving, Christmas, and Easter were always spent with extended family.
- Since both her parents were Irish, St. Patrick's day was always celebrated with food and corsages for female family members.
- She loved this as a child but was embarrassed as a teen—it wasn't cool wearing a green carnation to school.
- In high school, Ellen was an average student and played the violin, officiated intramural sports, played volleyball and field hockey, and was class secretary.
- She loved school more for the social outlet than the academic challenge, and her parents emphasized being respectful and happy more than getting top grades.
- Her summer jobs gave her spending money.
- Ellen met Peggy in 5th grade and they remained best friends through college, which they attended together.
- Ellen went to SUNY Plattsburgh for two reasons—money and family.
- The fact that two of her brothers were already attending Plattsburgh seemed like a good reason at the time, and she liked the security of being close to family.
- She joined a sorority for a short time, quitting after her first rush experience as a "sister."
- Once she saw the acceptance process, she wasn't interested in being a part of what seemed like a mean girls club, even though it did some good around campus.

*Ellen Boshe was a dedicated educator.*

- She graduated with a degree in speech and language pathology.
- In her early 20s, Ellen took a month long cross country trip with a boyfriend, camping from Plattsburgh to California, with the highlight of hiking and rock climbing in the Canadian Rockies.
- She also traveled to Ireland for 2 weeks—this time alone.
- In Ireland she mostly traveled by bicycle through much of the country, visiting relatives along the way, and gaining confidence in spending time alone—something she enjoys to this day.
- One of the more challenging decisions Ellen made as a young woman was deciding to move in with her boyfriend in the summer of 1974.
- Three of her brothers were already married when she decided to be the first one in her family to openly live with someone of the opposite sex.
- Because of the close relationship she had with her family, it was difficult to hide, and while they accepted her decision, their apparent disappointment created a small and short-lived, rift.
- Ellen was clearly inspired by her parents, remembering them as kind, loving, open, and non-judgmental.

*Ellen and part of her family in the 1960s.*

- While they carried many traditional values, they were ahead of their times in many ways, most evidenced by her mother going to college and teaching while her children were growing up.
- Her parents necessarily shared the household chores including cooking, shopping, cleaning and raising children.
- The respect and love they showed toward one another and others had a huge impact on Ellen's life—their optimism was contagious.
- Right after college, Ellen got a job as a speech/language pathologist, was involved in a serious relationship, and open to trying new things, including hiking, rock climbing, sky diving, and flying lessons.

*Ellen and part of her family today.*

- She soon realized that she wanted to learn how to educate the whole child with special needs—not just speech and language deficits.
- At the time, George Washington University had an excellent program, offered a generous financial package, and afforded Ellen the opportunity to live in a city—something she hadn't yet experienced.
- Ellen met her husband of 41 years in college, where they dated.
- After he graduated and left for Utah and Alaska, they tried a long distance relationship but soon became involved with other people.

- Four years later they reconnected and he visited Ellen in Washington, DC where she was a graduate student at George Washington University.
- After a few months together he asked her to join him in Utah which she did, but "Only if we are married"!
- He was still the love of her life 41 years later—adventurous, impulsive, kind, sensitive, giving and real
- Ellen and her husband had 4 children, two boys and two girls, and three grandchildren

## Life at Work

- Ellen's career path had always been in education, from speech and language pathologist to special education teacher to regular education teacher to program coordinator and lastly to elementary school principal.
- Her career decision was more a natural outgrowth of her environment and personality than a driven desire.
- Her mother was a teacher who loved what she did, shared many of her teaching experiences with her family, and often had colleagues at the house.

*A speech language pathologist worked one on one.*

- And the fact that most girls she knew either went into nursing or teaching and that Ellen loved being around children didn't hurt.
- On September 11, 2001, she had just returned to work after the death of her mother on August 30th.
- As she was sitting with her kindergarten students, beginning their morning circle routine, the assistant principal came into her room to tell her (away from the students) that a plane had flown into one of the towers of the World Trade Center and she could expect parents to come and take students home.
- Unbeknownst to him, Ellen had two relatives working in the towers—her brother Tom (a founder of Sandler/O'Neill—an investment banking firm in Tower Two) and her 21 year old nephew, Peter, who had recently started working at his uncle's firm.
- She immediately started making calls to family members who lived in New York; all lines were busy and she couldn't get through to anyone.
- Shortly after, she watched on TV as the second tower got hit and immediately began to fall, learning later that both Tom and Peter worked in that tower.
- She also learned that Tom was in the state of Washington during the attack, but that Peter was at work.
- The last his parents heard from him was shortly after the first tower was hit, when he told them that he was ok and was awaiting evacuation directions.
- Peter's remains were never found and the lives of Ellen and her family were changed forever.

*Ellen's nephew is part of the 9/11 memorial at ground zero. This photo shows a rubbing that she did of his name.*

*Ellen Boshe, principal, and Peter Pan in the school play!*

- Ellen was teaching for 20 years when she decided to become certified as a school principal.
- While still teaching full time, she enrolled in a local college for weekend and evening classes—a tough year.
- She loved being an elementary school principal, especially interacting with struggling students and making a difference in their day.
- The worst thing that happened at work was being accused by a parent of not addressing bullying.
- No two days were ever the same—but it was always very rewarding to work collaboratively with others to provide opportunities for children.
- The one thing that would have made her job easier was a longer day with more time for teachers to collect their thoughts and prepare for challenges.
- Her commute to work from home was 45 minutes.
- The one thing she might have done differently was to teach courses at the college level, which would have put her in a good position to teach a class or two a semester after retiring.
- Although Ellen never lost a job, she didn't get two principal positions after feeling confident after final round interviews.
- The fact that they were in the district where she had been teaching for almost 20 years made it that much more disappointing.
- In hindsight, however, getting a position in a new district where everything and everyone was new, allowed her to start fresh with new ideas.
- It was a challenge dealing with students whose lives were affected by parents losing their jobs, or by abuse.
- It was necessary to be more aware and seek out training on how to support children and families who were experiencing the resulting stress.

*Ellen loved teaching in a classroom of students with diverse capabilities and needs.*

## Life in the Community: Washington, DC

- Ellen was a graduate student at George Washington University in Washington, DC, the nation's capital.
- Washington became the capital in 1790, when George Washington selected the location on the Potomac River.
- The city was modeled to mimic European cities such as Paris and Milan and the architecture resembled Renaissance-style design.
- George Washington advocated for the establishment of a national university located in the capital from his first State of the Union address in 1790 until his death.
- He left his shares in the Potomac Company to go towards this university, though it was not until 1821 until the university was chartered.
- The first commencement was held in 1824 and was an important even for the city. President Monroe, John C. Calhoun, Henry Clay, and other dignitaries were in attendance.
- The college's buildings were used as a hospital and barracks during the Civil War, when most students left to join the Confederacy.
- Famous American poet Walt Whitman was one of the volunteers working on campus during the war.

*GWU's Corcoran School of the Arts and Design is located on The Ellipse, south of the White House. The building is a National Historic Landmark and one that Ellen often visited during her time in Washington.*

• George Washington University's campus is mainly located in the Foggy Bottom neighborhood of Washington, D.C., one of the oldest late 18th- and 19th-century neighborhoods.

## Life in the Community: Great Barrington, Massachusetts

• Ellen and her husband lived in Great Barrington, Massachusetts for most of their married life.
• He worked as a specialist in building solar rooms for most of those years and as a business owner of Four Seasons Greenhouses. His psychology degree came in handy on a daily basis dealing with customers.
• They chose Great Barrington for several reasons, including good schools, good for his business and lots of open space.
• Ellen had little time to participate in community activities, other than those that revolved around the school she worked in and a support group for families who had a loved one suffering from an opiod addiction.
• The best part about her neighborhood was the location—walking distance to both the main street and the neighborhood's community lake—close to the action and private at the same time.

*The Boshe's family home in Great Barrington.*

*Great Barrington was voted Best Small Town in America by Smithsonian Magazine. The flowering pear trees on its quaint Main Street (above) and eclectic shopping and restaurants along downtown's Railroad Street (below) are two reasons why.*

# 2005: Telemarketer

*Anna Reynolds quickly realized that telemarketing could be extremely lucrative, depending upon the products sold and the ways the fees were split. And she thrived in the industry's fast-paced, competitive environment.*

## Life at Home

- Growing up in Seattle, Washington, Anna had dreamed of being a nurse—even a doctor.
- But that was all before she met charming Alexander her junior year in high school.
- For the first time in her life, she cut school and declared homework to be unimportant.
- Her father, a postal service worker on disability, pleaded with her to keep her grades up; her mother tried to lock her in her bedroom.
- All she wanted was more time with Alexander, who dumped her and moved on.
- Anna's resulting depression made her rebellious and apathetic.
- As her senior year in high school came to an end, Anna left home on a bus bound for San Francisco on the day her parents expected her to graduate.
- She would not return to Seattle for two years.
- Anna's parents welcomed her home: her bedroom was exactly as she had left it.
- But she quickly chaffed under the glare of anxious parents.
- It was not their business where she was going or when she would be back.
- They didn't approve of her "more expressive" vocabulary, they hated her tattoo, and they wanted to hover.
- She just wanted a place to crash that didn't require sex in exchange.
- Quickly it became clear that having her own cash would reduce parental control; cash was king in Seattle—a city still influenced by the dot-com stock market meltdown of 2000.
- Anna didn't actually own any stock, but since she wanted to, it was only natural for her to feel connected to the roller coaster ride now being experienced by investors.
- Nearly everyone secretly dreamed of becoming an overnight dot-com millionaire.
- Almost a decade earlier, venture capitalists who were investing in dot-com companies experienced meteoric rises in their stock prices, driven by the potential of the emerging Internet, low interest rates in 1998-1999 for startup capital, and thousands of fascinating ideas.

*Anna Reynolds thrived in the fast paced, competitive field of telemarketing.*

- A typical dot-com company's business model relied on harnessing network effects by operating at a sustained net loss to build market share; the mantra "get big fast" reflected this strategy.
- Many dot-coms named themselves with onomatopoeic nonsense words that they hoped would be memorable, and 17 dot-com companies each paid more than $2 million for Super Bowl XXXIV ads in January 2000.
- By contrast, in January 2001, just three dot-coms bought advertising spots during Super Bowl XXXV.
- Dozens of American cities competed to become the "next Silicon Valley" by building network-enabled office space to attract Internet entrepreneurs.
- Communication providers, convinced that the future economy would require ubiquitous broadband access, went deeply into debt to improve their networks with high-speed equipment and fiber optic cables.

*As a young girl, Anna loved school and got perfect grades.*

- Then, in 2000, the U.S. Federal Reserve increased interest rates six times, and the economy began to lose speed.
- The dot-com bubble peaked on Friday, March 10, 2000, when the technology-heavy NASDAQ Composite index peaked at 5,048.62—more than double its value just a year before.
- The stock market crash of 2000-2002 caused the loss of $5 trillion in the market value of companies from March 2000 to October 2002; the 9/11 terrorist attacks on America in 2001 further disrupted the well-being of the U.S. and its financial markets.

## Life at Work

- The craigslist advertisement Anna Reynolds answered described the job as "sales," but failed to say the position required non-stop outbound telemarketing.

*When her boyfriend, Alexander, dumped her during high school, Anna rebelled.*

- The woman who interviewed Anna told her she had a lovely voice; the women at the phone station where she was assigned told her she was the third person that year to occupy that seat.
- When Anna took the new job, few would dispute that telemarketing and teleservices needed an image makeover.
- Telemarketers regularly ranked last in polls concerning business ethics.
- Millions of Americans had rushed to join the National Do Not Call Registry in hopes of eliminating the intrusive calls.
- And some financial advisors told their clients to hang up on anyone they didn't personally know.
- On Anna's first day on the job selling diabetic supplies which she barely understood, she was yelled at, cursed, and hung up on.
- She quickly developed "phone fear" and was caught by her supervisor pretending to make sales calls so she would not be told "no" again.
- It was especially painful to call the homes of individuals who had signed up to be on the Do Not Call Registry.

- Unfortunately for Anna, the Do Not Call Registry was less effective than advertised; exclusions to the program were not well understood.
- Companies like TTR Networking used pre-established relationship and partner programs, surveys, and political and charity exceptions to get around the legislation.
- Consumers still got calls they didn't want, only now they thought Anna was breaking the law when she called.
- Then it happened: Anna made a sale to an elderly lady who was extremely pleased that someone had called at all.

*Anna enjoyed working with her fellow telemarketers.*

- The customer was also ecstatic that "a real American" was calling, not "some foreigner."
- For many Americans, the evolving world of globalization was symbolized by the accented voice on a telemarketing call.
- The very legislation created to govern and police the industry's ethics and practices had only tarnished telemarketing even further.
- And Anna loved it; the verbal duels with unseen customers brought a particular joy.
- The interplay reminded her of dating and the musky intrigue that it engendered; the buyer had all the power but she had all the tools.
- They had the power to hang up and end the verbal arm wrestling; she had the motivation to keep them talking until they said yes to something.
- After all, Americans really did buy over the telephone, despite what they told their friends.
- A 2003 survey by the Direct Marketing Association showed that one-third of adult Americans (66 million) bought products or services by phone as a result of an outbound telemarketing campaign.
- These customers, equally comprising men and women, spent $9 billion on products averaging about $135.
- Nearly 60 percent said their purchase specifically suited their needs.
- Nearly 40 percent felt the savings and trial offers they received over the phone were a strong reason they made the purchase.
- Anna's training sessions included the psychology of selling over the phone to help her prevail over rejection and to uncover a physical stamina to handle a minimum of eight hours of quality phone calls a day.
- Burnout was discussed and closely monitored, along with phonetics and her mastery of a long checklist of skills necessary for success: the tone, rate, pitch, duration, pause, pregnant pause, delivery and timing of open- and close-ended questions.
- She also learned how body posture, facial expressions, hands as an illustrator and motion can dramatically improve a voice and projection—even if it goes unseen over the phone.
- Her new job also taught her about accepting criticism as well as self-monitoring and reflection.
- Within months, Anna was given a raise to $9.90 an hour, a spot bonus of $150, and the right to compete in the daily music rodeo.
- As a motivational tool, TTR Networking permitted each day's winning team to select the music that would be played in the background.
- Before Anna arrived, the Red team had dominated the sales each day, and they always selected urban rap.
- Anna and her Blue team were determined to alter that trend; they even decided they wanted an entire day featuring Garth Brooks.

- The pace was brutal but rewarding; the Red team was astonished that it had been defeated.
- For Anna, winning was sweet—she had put a lot of distance between her victories.
- She also discovered that she liked hanging out with her fellow telemarketers.
- Nationwide, African-American women made up half the total number of employees.
- Working mothers were more than 60 percent, and more than one-quarter were single working mothers.
- Only five percent had a college degree.
- And nearly one-third reported being "recently" on public assistance or welfare.
- The industry estimated that six million people worked in telemarketing, many of whom were unemployable.
- After a year, Anna changed jobs to handle in-bound calls for a bank whose center in a suburb of western Seattle was the area's second-largest employer.

## Life in the Community: Seattle, Washington

- The seaport city of Seattle, with 608,000 residents, was the largest city in the Northwestern United States; its metropolitan area of about 3.4 million inhabitants was the fifteenth-largest metropolitan area in the country.
- The Seattle area was inhabited by Native Americans for at least 4,000 years before the first permanent white settlers arrived.
- The settlement was named "Seattle" in 1853, after Chief Seattle of the local Duwamish and Squamish tribes.
- Logging was Seattle's first major industry, but by the late nineteenth century the city had become a commercial and shipbuilding center as a gateway to Alaska during the Klondike Gold Rush.
- By 1910, Seattle was one of the 25 largest cities in the country, but a combination of strikes and the Great Depression severely damaged the city's economy.
- Growth returned during and after World War II when the local Boeing Company established Seattle as a center for aircraft manufacturing.
- Seattle developed as a technology center in the 1980s.
- The stream of new software, biotechnology, and Internet companies led to an economic revival, which increased the city's population by 50,000 between 1990 and 2000.
- More recently, Seattle has become a hub for "green" industry and a model for sustainable development.
- The birthplace of rock legend Jimi Hendrix and the rock music style known as "grunge," Seattle birthed Nirvana, Soundgarden, Alice in Chains, and Pearl Jam.
- Beginning with Microsoft's 1979 move from Albuquerque, New Mexico, to nearby Bellevue, Washington, Seattle and its suburbs became home to a number of technology companies including Amazon.com, RealNetworks, McCaw Cellular and biomedical corporations such as HeartStream (later purchased by Philips), Heart Technologies (later purchased by Boston Scientific), Physio-Control (later purchased by Medtronic), ZymoGenetics, ICOS (later purchased by Eli Lilly and Company) and Immunex (later purchased by Amgen).
- This success brought an influx of new inhabitants and saw Seattle's real estate become some of the most expensive in the country.

*Microsoft is one of many technology companies who moved to Seattle and its suburbs.*

## 2005: Pool Player

*Alfredo Lenzi grew up in an Italian neighborhood, in a large family of first- and second-generation Italians. He learned how to hustle for what he wanted, and developed a competitive edge that served him well as a winning pool player.*

### Life at Home

- Alfredo—Al to his friends—Lenzi learned at an early age that it was who you knew that mattered.
- Al knew plenty of the right people.
- He never had to look far for a way to make a buck.
- Like any college student, Al came home during school breaks and summers.
- Unlike most college students, however, his jobs usually found him.
- One of Al's uncles—he had eight—belonged to the bartending union, so Al bartended.
- Similar connections got him jobs on a railroad crew and in the Highway Department.
- His father owned a waste removal company and worked long hours.
- His mother was the firm hand of this middle class Italian family, and Al's two older sisters often took her lead.
- But Al was the "baby," the only boy, and spoiled rotten.
- He was given two rules growing up—be home for dinner and stay out of trouble.
- He loved all sports in high school but football was his passion.
- Al was a starting quarterback at Notre Dame High School in West Haven, Connecticut, where he developed a competitive nature, believing that winning was everything.
- Coming close was like a boy kissing his sister—it didn't count.
- He became interested in pool at age 14 after watching the 1960 film *The Hustler*.
- He read *Willie Mosconi on Pocket Billiards*, and Mosconi became his hero.
- When he wasn't on the football field, Al hung around pool halls.
- He learned from watching the older men play.
- There wasn't much mentoring—pool players weren't about to give away their secrets.
- Al had his best lessons by challenging the old pros for a dollar or two a game.
- He was a quick study and perfected his game of straight pool—in which each player received one point for each ball pocketed.
- When he started college, Al began playing pool in earnest.

*Al had that competitive edge necessary for pool players.*

- In addition to straight pool, he became a pretty good 8-ball player—a game where you shot either the seven solid balls or the seven striped balls, and then the 8 ball.
- He learned which bars had the fastest tables and the drunkest crowds—Al rarely drank while playing and made money by betting on winning the game.
- On a good night, he could make $60, betting $3 or $4 a game.
- Al perfected two sure-fire strategies for winning— sharking and hustling.
- Sharking was startling your opponent to the point of making him miss a shot.
- This included coughing, dropping something, or walking into your opponent's line of vision when he was down on a shot.
- Hustling was tricking your opponent into thinking that you were not very good—and losing a few games to prove it.
- The key was getting him to bet the farm on you losing, after which, of course, your luck miraculously turned and you won it all.
- These schemes might sound easy, but they can be dangerous.

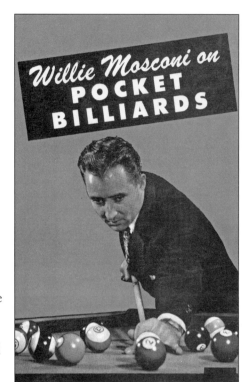

*Willie Mosconi was Al's hero.*

- If your opponent became wise to your strategy, you risked getting into a fight or being banned from the bar.
- All in all, Al found pool a profitable pastime.
- Always generous with his time, Al once accompanied a college buddy to New Orleans to find a car he had "lost" during Mardi Gras.
- They were determined to find the car and drive it back.
- They found the car, but ran out of money.
- Al's pool playing skills came in handy in a Bourbon Street bar, where he hustled an Oklahoma City man for $75, at $5.00 a game.

*Al joined the Navy after college.*

- The pair quickly got into the car and drove back to college.
- After graduating college, Al joined the Navy.
- He was stationed in Virginia Beach, where he found the best pool bars, but also found himself the victim of the "double hustle."
- This is when you think you are hustling an unassuming opponent, only your opponent is hustling you better.
- Not liking being suckered, Al sharpened his intuition skills after that.
- He continued to practice pool in Bremerton, Washington, where his submarine, the Patrick Henry, was stationed for a maintenance overhaul.
- Al became pool buddies with Slim, an old-time road pool player who lent Al a custom pool stick,

inlaid with mother of pearl, to use in the Northwest Regional Straight Pool Tournament at the Navy Base on Widbey Island.

- Generally, Al played with house sticks.
- Hustlers never carried their own stick; that was a dead giveaway that you were good.
- Not only did he win first place with Slim's borrowed stick, but he developed an appreciation for expensive pool sticks.

## Life at Work

- After the Navy, Al Lenzi married his high school sweetheart and they followed a job to Sheffield, Massachusetts, 125 miles north of Manhattan.
- There he taught physical education at the local high school and coached football and wrestling.
- His wife concentrated on her hair stylist career while they raised their two sons.

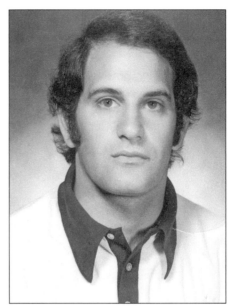

*In Sheffield, Al taught high school.*

- In 1995, Al retired early from teaching and worked as a stylist in their beauty salon—a surprisingly successful second career for him.
- His marriage wasn't as successful, however, and ended in divorce.
- His newfound freedom drew him back into the pool playing circuit.
- But finding places to play and decent competition wasn't easy in Sheffield.
- Al encouraged a bar owner in a neighboring town to start a pool league.
- As the league grew, area bars and restaurants installed pool tables.
- League officers would create detailed schedules, alternating weekly matches among a number of available places.
- Over the next 10 years, Al would play in several leagues at once—cutting hair by day and playing pool as many as four nights a week.
- As the captain of his teams, he coached his players to win season after season.
- His beauty salon doubled as his trophy room.
- Alone and with his teams, he traveled up and down the East Coast to compete in eight- and nine-ball tournaments.

*Al's team competed nationally.*

- Tournaments were often double elimination, two-day affairs.
- If a player lost one match, he was put in the loser's bracket and kept playing until he lost the second time.
- Al won his fair share of these tournaments, but he never stopped practicing.
- Unlike his younger days, winning now felt better when he played his best, not when his opponent made mistakes.
- There were often long waits in between matches, encouraging side games and individual betting.
- Official cash payouts for these tournaments could be as much as several thousand dollars.
- Al was a voracious collector of pool equipment, gadgets and supplies.

*Pool tournament trips combined playing pool and shopping.*

- He owned dozens of custom pool cues, including specialty break cues to break the balls at the beginning of a game, and jump cues to jump the cue ball over another ball.
- While at pool tournament trips, Al was on the prowl for the latest and greatest pool thing, including instructional videos and pool books.
- He had hundreds of instructive videos and books that he would often lend out to anyone who wanted to improve his or her game.
- Before an important match, Al would practice with members of his team at his home on his professional nine-foot table.
- They would review rules and practice certain shots over and over.
- Al's team often would win a trip to Las Vegas to compete in the national tournament.
- These tournaments included hundreds of teams from all over the country.
- Rules were strictly enforced—no jeans, sandals, flash photography or smoking.
- He and other team members would often play in single contests as well as the team event.
- Players would watch the bracket board to see where and when their friends were playing, so they could be on hand to support them during a match.
- In addition to playing in matches, Al would take advantage of the pool vendors at the tournament and get his sticks serviced.
- They did it all, from cleaning and smoothing to putting on new tips and new wraps.
- Al also looked forward to seeing his favorite professional players, like Johnny Archer and Corey Deuel, compete in Las Vegas.
- He loved watching them make great shots, and when they missed, he was reminded that even the pros make mistakes.

### Life in the Community: Sheffield, Massachusetts

- The Berkshire Mountains in Massachusetts are composed of 15 rural New England towns including Sheffield.
- Sheffield had the enviable combination of scenic beauty, sophistication and trendy fashion.
- It was also home to a wide variety of food, from organic farm markets to fine dining that rivaled the best Manhattan restaurants.
- Still, Al complained that he couldn't find "good, Italian food."
- Menus were too creative and portions too small for his taste.

*Sheffield is home to typical New England beauty.*

*Sheffield Town Hall and the Old Stone Store.*

- When he won the lottery, he would open an Italian restaurant and pool hall in town.
- The Berkshires also offered a variety of education choices, from progressive nursery schools and private prep schools to award-winning public schools.

## Life in the Community: Las Vegas, Nevada

- Las Vegas, Nevada could be considered a desert oasis.
- Its name in Spanish means "the meadows," and it was named after the abundant wild grasses and desert springs in the valley.
- The city was situated at the bottom of a basin in the Mojave Desert, which occupies a total of 47,877 sq mi.
- The city is also surrounded by mountain ranges, with peaks rising to above 10,000 feet.
- Las Vegas' repuation as "The Entertainment Capital of the World" and "Sin City" began in 1931, when the state of Nevada legalized casino gambling and reduced residency requirements for divorce to six weeks.
- That same year, construction on the Hoover Dam began, located just east of the city, drawing thousands of laborers to Las Vegas.
- These laborers would relax by spending time on Fremont Street, the cities only paved road, along which several casinos and showgirl venues opened.
- Over the next several decades, the city exploded with high-end resorts, casino-hotels, fine dining, and a variety of entertainment venues.
- However, technically the majority of casinos and resorts, including the famous Las Vegas Strip, were situated outside city limits, in nearby towns of Paradise and Winchester (both unincorporated).

- Gambling, prostitution, and the city's repuation for being lax with the law began to draw a certain unsavory crowd from some of America's other major cities.
- Mobsters and gangsters began funding the development of the Strip, creating new and fancier casino-hotels and resorts.
- Still, it was not until 1989 that the Mirage opened, the city's first mega-resort.
- The next two decades saw casino-hotels transform into massive complexes, many of which were designed to resemble other glamorous cities, such as Paris, Rome, Venice, and New York.
- Las Vegas was the home to the American Poolplayer's Association's World Pool Championships, the largest pool tournament in the world.
- With nearly 250,000 members throughout the United States, Canada and Japan, the APA awarded nearly $2 Million in guaranteed prize money every year during the APA Championships in Las Vegas.

*Downtown Las Vegas, Nevada.*

## 2006: Olympic Hockey Player

*Taught how to skate as soon as she could walk, Jamie Hagerman grew up to become a powerhouse hockey player—eventually landing on the U.S. Women's Olympic ice hockey team in 2006.*

### Life at Home

- Jamie Hagerman was born in 1981 in Deerfield, Massachusetts, the third child, with two older sisters, Casey and Kully; her younger sister Whitaker was born in 1987.
- Her parents both worked at the local preparatory high school, Deerfield Academy.
- Her father Dave was the head of athletics at the school, and her mother Parny was the director of admissions.
- Jamie's father was a hockey player at the University of New Hampshire and a hockey coach at Deerfield, so it was only natural that his children would play as well.
- Jamie hit the ice at age three.
- As she was learning to take her first strides on the ice, Jamie and her family relocated to another prep school, Hotchkiss School, in Lakeville, Connecticut.
- There, in the northwest corner of the state, she joined her first ice hockey team, becoming a "Cub" in Salisbury Youth Hockey.
- The Lakeville/Salisbury area had a small-town feel.
- The children with whom Jamie skated often attended the same school and church.
- Jamie attended the local public school, Salisbury Central School, up through eighth grade; just over 300 students attended the school.
- As she progressed through Salisbury Central, she also progressed through the different levels of youth hockey.
- After her three years as a Cub, she became a Mite, then a Squirt, Pewee, and finally a Bantam—spending about two years at each level.
- Jamie always made the "A" team—or the best team—at each level, going toe to toe with boys her age; she typically played right wing.
- She was usually the only girl on her youth hockey team; her parents were careful not to point out her unique position on the team.
- Some of her favorite memories on the youth hockey team were playing on frozen lakes in January with her Salisbury Youth Hockey teammates, who were also her best friends.

*Jamie learned to skate as a toddler.*

- In addition to playing in the youth hockey league, Jamie would practice with the Varsity girls' team at Hotchkiss School, which helped her become an even stronger player.
- The first time gender ever became an issue was when Jamie was 10.
- She was dressed in her hockey gear, eating at the dining hall at Salisbury School, where her dad was now working, when a boy walked up to her and said, "What are you doing?" She responded, "Going to hockey practice." The boy said, "Don't you know hockey is for boys and not for girls?"
- After graduating from Salisbury Central School, Jamie went to Deerfield Academy for high school from 1995 to 1999.
- While at Deerfield, she joined an all-girls' hockey team in Cromwell, Connecticut, called the Polar Bears, and also played on Deerfield's own girls' ice hockey, soccer and lacrosse teams.

*As a "cub," Jamie was the only girl on the Youth Hockey team.*

- At Deerfield, she switched from playing right wing to defense.
- Starting at 14, she went to the USA Hockey camps, which were designed for the best hockey players, broken down by age groups.
- Schoolwork at Deerfield did not come easy to Jamie.
- She had to work incredibly hard to master the subjects she was studying—if she didn't understand a topic or problem the first time, she'd try a second or third time until she eventually understood it.
- Her hard work endeared her to teachers at the time, and she became a top student at the school.
- By her senior year, she was captain of the hockey, lacrosse and soccer teams and was heading to Harvard to play hockey as well as lacrosse.
- Harvard was an essential step to her ultimate goal: to play hockey for the United States at the Winter Olympics.

*Jamie loved playing with her friends on her neighborhood's frozen lake.*

## Life at Work

- Jamie Hagerman thrived at Harvard.
- She loved her coaches and her teammates; in her freshman year, she was named to the conference All-Rookie team.
- Her second year at the school, she tore her anterior cruciate ligament, or ACL, during lacrosse practice.
- Her doctor told her she did not need surgery to play ice hockey since hockey is gentle on players' knees, but she could no longer play lacrosse.
- While she was at Harvard, she was once again selected to go to the USA camp for the best female players.
- At this level—the senior women's team—Jamie was being scouted for the Olympics.
- She also made it into the two critical tournaments a year—the Four Nations Cup in November, and the World Championships in April.
- She graduated from Harvard in 2003 and promptly moved to Canada to further her training for the Olympics.
- She was hoping to make one of the professional women's league teams in Canada.
- Only two Americans were allowed on each team, and there were eight teams in the country.
- In all, there were about 100 American girls fighting for those 16 spots.
- Jamie beat the odds and made a team in Toronto.
- She couldn't earn money in Canada for visa reasons, so she worked hard to save up money during the summer so she could financially survive the hockey season.
- When she headed up to Toronto, she was told by the team that she and the other American player needed to live with the Canadian Olympians until they got them their own house.
- The two women lived in an unfinished basement for four months—turning on the dryer at night to keep warm.
- Jamie moved back to the United States in April 2004 and made the World Championship Team, which brightened her hopes of making the 2006 Women's Olympic team.
- During this time, she moved back to Boston and worked as assistant coach on the women's hockey team at Harvard.
- She loved returning to her alma mater, her role as a coach, and the opportunity to stay in shape and practice for her possible Olympic bid.
- In the summer of 2005, she made the summer camp for the top 40 players in the country.
- Over the summer, the 40 Olympic competitor candidates were then cut to 25 hockey players.
- Those players then skated together from August to December, when the 25 were then cut to 20.
- Her family nervously awaited the announcement of the final roster outside the locker room of one of the exhibition games leading up to the Olympics.
- Jamie left the locker room in tears.
- Her parents thought the tears were because she did not make the team, but they were actually tears of joy—she was going to the Olympics.
- The 2006 Winter Olympic Games in Turin, Italy, were the third time women's ice hockey appeared in the Winter Games.
- Jamie and her team first played Switzerland and then Germany, beating both teams handily: 6-0 and 5-0, respectively.

*Jamie was a natural at playing hockey.*

- The third game against Finland was a bit tighter, but the United States came out on top, 7-3.
- After a three-day break, the women's hockey team headed into their semifinal game against Sweden.
- The United States had a 25-0 record against Sweden, so the odds were in their favor.
- The United States took the lead in the game, 2-0, with a goal in the first and second period each.
- But the Swedes caught up, scoring two goals little more than three minutes apart.
- Despite outshooting the Swedes 39-18, the United States could not get past the Swedish goalie Kim Martin, leaving the score tied through the third period and overtime.
- Now the teams were headed into a shootout.
- The United States failed to score during the shootout, and the Swedes scored their final two shots, leading them to victory and a spot in the finals against Canada.
- Brokenhearted at their loss, the United States gathered themselves for their bronze medal game against Finland.

*Jamie was excited to be a part of the Olympic team.*

- Beating Finland 4-0, the United States team showed they could bounce back—playing stronger, with sharper passes and deft puck handling.
- Jamie and her teammates were awarded a bronze medal for their victory against Finland.
- Although she did not win the gold, it was a thrilling experience for Jamie to be on the Olympic team.
- It was also a special moment for her father, Dave.
- After playing goalie at the University of New Hampshire, her father was good enough to attend the U.S. National Team training camp, in preparation for the Olympics.
- Before he even got to go to the camp, he was drafted to fight in Vietnam.
- Jamie not only fulfilled her dream of going to the Olympics, but also her father's.
- After the Olympics, she discovered she had torn her ACL again.
- She knew she had injured herself during the Olympics, but decided to keep quiet about the injury so she wouldn't jeopardize her chances to make the team.
- She had surgery on her knee.
- After the big win at the Olympics, she headed to Washington, DC, to teach advanced placement psychology in high school.
- But hockey was not left behind.
- During the summer, she taught at ice hockey camps, sharing her Olympic story with a new generation of female skaters.

## Life in the Community: Salisbury, Connecticut

- Salisbury, Connecticut, is located in the northwest corner of the state, on the borders of New York and Massachusetts.
- The town of Salisbury was incorporated in 1741, and it includes the villages of Salisbury and Lakeville, and the hamlets of Amesville, Lime Rock and Taconic.
- Salisbury is a rural area of rolling mountains, dotted with lakes and crisscrossed by the Housatonic River.
- During the Federal period, Salisbury was known for its iron production.

- Because the town was not near a river large enough to ship raw iron, the town instead handled much of the labor on their own—working the iron into wrought iron that was of such high quality it could be used for gun barrels.
- Salisbury iron became the choice iron for Connecticut's early nineteenth-century arms industry.
- Many of the arms were shipped South to be used by the Union army during the Civil War.
- Over the course of the twentieth century, Salisbury moved away from the iron industry and became a more upscale area, known as a weekend destination for New Yorkers.
- In 2000, Salisbury had a population of 3,977.

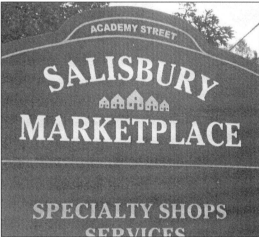

*Salisbury Town Hall, top left, and Salisbury Central School.*

## Trends in Women's Hockey

- The first organized all-women's hockey game took place in Barrie, Ontario, in 1892, two decades before the formation of the National Hockey League.

- In 1894, a female club team formed at Queen's University in Kingston, Ontario, known as the "Love-Me-Littles," incurred the wrath of the school's archbishop, who did not want women to play.

- Within two years, teams had formed at McGill University and in the Ottawa Valley.

- The first women's hockey championship for the province of Ontario was held in 1914.

- In 1916, the United States hosted an international hockey tournament in Cleveland, which featured both American and Canadian players.

- The Great Depression and World War II knocked the wind out of the gaining popularity of the sport; women did not start getting back into ice hockey until the 1960s.

- In 1967, the Dominion Ladies Hockey Tournament was held in Brampton, Ohio.

- The Dominion Ladies Hockey Tournament featured 22 teams, with players from ages nine to 50 competing.

- By the 1970s, several Canadian provinces moved to establish associations to govern female hockey teams.

- At the same time, American colleges and high schools started to form varsity and club teams for women.

- Canada held its first national championship for women's hockey in 1982.

- Eight years later, it hosted the first Women's World Ice Hockey Championships.

- Two years later, after the second world championships were held in Finland, the International Olympic Committee voted to include women's hockey in future Olympics.

- Women's ice hockey made its Olympic debut in 1998, at Nagano, Japan.

- With the World Ice Hockey Championships, and the introduction of the sport at the Olympics, women's ice hockey grew in popularity across the world.

- Canada and the United States still have the most female ice hockey players, and typically the most talented ones.

- In 1990-1991 season, there were 6,036 registered female hockey players in the United States; by 2001, there were 39,693—a 580 percent increase.

### "Women's Hockey Semifinal; Sweden 3, USA 2 (Shootout); Progress Stings," by Rachel Blount, *Star-Tribune* (Minneapolis, Minnesota), February 2006

They had seen the movie Miracle so many times that some of them could recite the lines. In the hours before Friday's Olympic semifinal against the United States, Swedish forward Maria Rooth and some of her teammates decided the time had come to give women's hockey its own version of that legend.

Sweden's 3-2 shootout victory will go down as a landmark in the women's game. While Rooth and her teammates hurled themselves into a blue-and-yellow pile on the Palasport Olimpico ice, the U.S. women bit their lips and felt the sting of a day they knew would come. As far back as September, coach Ben Smith warned that Finland and Sweden were at the doorstep of a historic upset. The Finns came close, and the Swedes made it happen, finally widening the women's hockey world beyond the U.S.-Canada axis.

The Americans had gone 73-0-2 against the six Olympic participants other than Canada. That included a 25-0 record against Sweden. In the past, Rooth said, her team never quite believed it could crack the icy wall that separated the North American powers from everyone else—until they arrived at the place where miracles are born.

"We said [Thursday] we were going to make a new miracle," said Rooth, a former Minnesota Duluth player who scored the shootout winner and both of Sweden's goals in regulation. "If we just believed we could beat them, we thought it could happen. Everyone was so committed. Everyone believed."

Except on the American side. The U.S. players felt only disbelief at losing their first Olympic semifinal. As Sweden's players got high-fives from NHL stars and countrymen Peter Forsberg and Mats Sundin, goalie Chanda Gunn fought a losing battle with tears, and Angela Ruggiero couldn't grasp the reality of playing for a bronze medal.

That will happen Monday against Finland, 6-0 losers Friday to Canada.

"I'm in shock right now," Ruggiero said. "It's a huge day for Sweden. It hurts, but we have to stay positive, because we can still win a medal.

"Everybody talks about the USA and Canada, but this may just open the world's eyes to the fact that there are other teams out there. We're back on our heels right now. But if you can take something positive away from this, maybe that's it."

Swedes' confidence grew.

Four years ago, Sweden's Olympic committee considered keeping its women's hockey team home for fear it would not be competitive in the Winter Games. The Swedes had finished fifth in the 1998 Olympics, the first to include women's hockey, and surprised with bronze in 2002.

Goalie Kim Martin was only 15 when she played in the Salt Lake City Games. Friday, her brilliance in the net provided the foundation for Sweden's greatest victory. Martin made 37 saves and thoroughly frustrated the Americans with her nimble, assured play.

The United States outshot Sweden 39-18, but the players' faces reflected the anxiety created by frequent miscues and breakdowns—and by Martin's impenetrability. Former UMD forward Erika Holst stripped the puck from Gophers' defenseman Lyndsay Wall behind the U.S. net and fired it to the charging Rooth for the tying shorthanded goal. The Swedes intercepted several passes deep in the American zone, and countless U.S. scoring chances sailed wide, struck the goal cage or banged off of sticks.

The United States also went 2-for-11 on power plays, including a two-player advantage that lasted more than three minutes in the second period.

"We had a lot of good opportunities on the power plays," forward Katie King said.

"We didn't put them home, and that's what hurts. We were maybe too pretty on plays and lost it a few times, and they capitalized."

A distinctly Swedish vibe began to take over the arena as Rooth's goals, little more than three minutes apart, negated a 2-0 U.S. lead. ABBA played on the sound system. Fans with horns and Tre Kroner jerseys outblared their American counterparts. The tension swelled through the scoreless third period, the overtime and the shootout.

The first five shooters missed or were stopped. Pernilla Winberg beat Gunn with a wrist shot to the stick side, and Rooth followed in similar fashion to cement one of the defining moments of these Olympics.

"When it was over, I had to ask people what happened," Holst said. "Tonight, we said, 'This is our night. We're going to win. No one can take this away from us.'"

"A breakthrough"

As Canada and the United States buried their opponents in pool play, their coaches were forced to answer questions about whether their sport belonged in the Olympics. A paucity of competitive teams recently got women's softball bounced from the Summer Olympics program.

The North American rivals had faced off in every world championship and Olympic final in history. It seemed a foregone conclusion that they would do so again, but even through their tears the U.S. players were able to acknowledge the impact their upset will have on the sport.

"It's a breakthrough for them and their program," said U.S. forward Natalie Darwitz of Eagan. "I wish it wasn't us, but it's great for women's hockey. It shows there's a lot more than the U.S. and Canada."

Sweden's coach, Peter Elander, said he took a cue from the late Herb Brooks in preparing his team. Like Brooks, who famously kept his players on the ice after a tie and made them skate to exhaustion, Elander drove his team relentlessly for the past three months.

Which goes to show that even American hockey movies have influenced the women's game abroad. Elander thanked the United States and Canada for playing the Swedes so often, allowing them to learn and develop. Many European players also are refining their games with U.S. college teams, including nine Olympians who have played for or been signed by Minnesota Duluth.

Sweden's victory resulted from its fearless and aggressive defense, a smart game plan, improved speed and conditioning, and a new attitude. Years of losses to the North Americans have affected the psyches of some opponents; the Finns, after seizing a 3-1 lead on the United States in pool play, tightened up and lost. By getting over that hurdle, the Swedes have opened a window of possibility for others.

Elander and his players speculated that Friday's upset will stimulate the growth of the game in Sweden. At the very least, it promises to give hope to hockey's have-nots.

"We said at the beginning that people were going to be surprised at how competitive this tournament was," said forward Jenny Potter of Edina. "This is disappointing, and it's hard. It's all you dream about. But they beat us. What else can you say?"

 спопросоросоро

### "Today's Players See Brighter Tomorrow; Growing Coaching Sorority Part of Long-term Hockey Plan," by Jill Lieber, *USA TODAY*, February 2006

TORINO—Sometimes, Jamie Hagerman, a defenseman on the U.S. women's ice hockey team, feels like a stranger in a strange land.

When she's not devoting energy to winning a gold medal, she's committed to her job as an assistant women's ice hockey coach at Harvard.

The Crimson are one of six NCAA Division I women's ice hockey programs with female head coaches—and the only Division I school with an all-female coaching staff.

"At Harvard, we talk about it a lot: 'We are the only allwomen staff. Why?'" Hagerman says.

The rest of the time, Hagerman feels like one of the crowd, playing one of the fastest-growing women's sports, with participation up 400 percent in the USA in the last decade, according to USA Hockey. She is one of seven women on the Olympic team who are, or have been, coaches of women's or girls' teams.

They include Katie King, an assistant at Boston College; Courtney Kennedy, head coach at Buckingham Browne and Nichols School in Cambridge, Mass.; and Jenny Potter, who coached at a Minnesota high school.

Also: Kathleen Kauth, a former volunteer assistant coach at Brown; Tricia Dunn-Luoma, a former assistant coach at New Hampshire; and Chanda Gunn, a former Massachusetts youth league coach.

"For a while, it was a male-dominated sport," Hagerman says. "It used to be women playing a men's sport. Now it's women playing hockey. A couple of years ago you couldn't make ends meet coaching. As a part-time first assistant at Harvard, I made $20,000 my first year. Now women can make a living."

Dave Ogrean, the executive director of USA Hockey, says increasing the pool of experienced female head coaches, especially at the national and international level, is a priority.

"We need to do a better job immediately," he says. In fact, Ogrean says his goal is to generate a list of women capable of coaching the 2010 or 2014 U.S. Olympic team. (The Canadian Olympic women's team is coached by Melody Davidson, on leave as head coach at Cornell.)

Ben Smith, in his third Olympics, became the first full-time head coach of the U.S. women's national and Olympic teams in 1996. He coached the USA to the Olympic gold medal in 1998 and silver in 2002. His contract is up after Torino.

Ogrean says he understands why none of the players from those first two U.S. Olympic teams are coaching at an elite level: "They're a collection of highly educated, high-achieving, exceptional women, not just women hockey players." But he hopes, over time, some team alumni will pursue coaching.

"When we sit down to talk about the next four years and the four years after that, I want there to be a lot of women whose names legitimately jump to mind as coaching candidates," Ogrean says.

# 2006: Music Copyright Lawyer

*William Bartlett Barrett IV was 58 and married with three children when he discovered the tangled web of music law, thanks to his oldest daughter's boyfriend, a bass guitarist in a cover band concerned about the upcoming release of their first CD.*

## Life at Home

- William Bartlett Barrett IV was an attorney just like his father, grandfather, great-grandfather and great-great-grandfather.
- Until he discovered the complexity of music copyright law, exposed by the rapid rise in technology, he hated being a lawyer.
- For Bill, the challenges of commercial law were financially rewarding, occasionally stimulating and perennially soul-sucking.
- For the past decade he had been attempting to negotiate the slow-moving field of copyright law vis à vis the lightning quick evolution of music technology.
- The Barrett dynasty, as Bill's father liked to say, was planted in Yuma, Arizona, more than 150 years earlier when settlers began wrestling fruits and vegetables from the parched ground.
- William Bartlett Barrett II had gone West from Oklahoma City to chase the sun, escape an arranged marriage, and hide from his father.
- As the eldest son of an ex-Confederate soldier who had moved West after the war, the expectations were high for William II.
- Since he was a baby, William II had repeatedly been told what his future was to be—as envisioned and constructed by his father.
- Working beside his father, he wrestled crops from the ground, fought over water rights and learned the law well enough to acquire an expansive track of farm land.
- By the turn of the twentieth century, the evolving legal issues of land ownership and future rights infringements dominated his time.
- By the turn of the twenty-first century, his great-grandson found himself knee-deep in ownership questions over music, questions about the future remuneration of artists, and deeply caught up in infringement cases that were robbing his clients of revenues.

*Attorney William Barrett discovered the complexity of music copyright law.*

- What was clear was that in the midst of technological change, the financial side of the music business was broken; digital technology had fundamentally changed the operating model as dramatically as electricity had altered American industry.
- The Internet had made many traditional corporate music jobs obsolete, while simultaneously broadening the reach of recorded music.
- Peer-to-peer file sharing had turned consumers into distributors; CD burners made everyone a potential manufacturer.

*Technology turned music listeners into music programmers.*

- The only job left exclusive to the music industry was as policeman—the enforcer of the copyright laws and stopper of progress.
- But to Bill's way of thinking, the financial train wreck had been inevitable; when only 5 percent of the musical artists were making 95 percent of the revenues, revolution was already in the air.
- The record industry was seen as greedy by consumers and artists alike so when technology stormed the gates of the giant companies' castle, there were few soldiers to defend them.
- Now, as Bill saw it, his job was to make sense of the mess.
- His daughter's boyfriend had come to him with a legitimate concern: how to protect his intellectual property from theft by other bands, powerful music companies or foreign distributors beyond the reach of U.S. law.
- The boyfriend and his band disappeared from his daughter's life only a few months later, leaving behind a reinvigorated commercial attorney with a curious mind.
- The music industry in the twenty-first century had become a brave new world; a virtual Wild West where the old rules no longer applied.
- After all, the entire power structure had been up-ended by technological change the courts were powerless to stop.
- In less than a decade, a new Internet-savvy music hierarchy had been created by artists themselves without asking permission from the reigning power structure: commercial radio, MTV, retail stores and record companies.

- At the same time, the once passive music-listening crowd had become music programmers fully capable of mixing together their own new musical ideas and communicating them via message boards, Web pages, e-zines and MP3s.
- Suddenly, the American music market had morphed into a gaggle of niche markets no longer focused on the mass market potential of a song or band; power had shifted from the highly paid corporate executives in suits to a 15-year-old girl relaxing in her bedroom with a brand-new laptop.
- It was a rude awakening for the record industry, which had spent decades consolidating its power; as the new millennium began, the industry had been reduced to only six multinational record labels and one corporation that dominated the concert and commercial radio business.
- They assumed the artists themselves would be up in arms over the piracy and the potential loss of revenues facilitated by technological innovations such as the file-sharing Napster.

- Instead, groups like the Beastie Boys and then Tom Petty and the Heartbreakers joined the insurrection; in March 1999, Tom Petty uploaded a free version of the garage-rock single "Free Girl Now."
- More than 150,000 fans downloaded the song in 56 hours before Warner Brothers shut down the giveaway.
- Where Warner Brothers saw no revenues from lost record sales, Tom Petty saw the acquisition of 150,000 e-mail addresses that could be used to promote his upcoming summer tour.
- Even with ticket prices at under $40 each, the concert—thanks to the e-mail promotion—grossed $27 million, legitimizing the concept; the rebellion was underway.

## Life at Work

- The first concept that Bill Barrett grasped was how unprepared the music industry was for change.
- They liked being in charge of what CDs were made, when they were distributed and how the revenues were divided.
- For decades artists had carped about the size of the industry's take from every record; by 2000 they had institutionalized the process with lawyers, accountants and contracts that resulted in company expenses and promotions absorbing virtually all the revenues from a hit record—fueling excellent industry profits.
- The Internet simply looked like a menace.
- It was a familiar pattern: phonograph machines were seen as a threat to live music in 1900; radio was attacked as a threat to the phonograph machine in the late 1920s; home taping was seen as the enemy of music makers in the 1980s, and Napster was decried as potentially a fatal blow.
- Bill knew through his children that the head-banger band Metallica had gained a wide following thanks to home taping of their first cassette, *Life 'til Leather*; obviously, the record companies were no longer in control of the music scene.
- Then Napster's simple-to-use file-sharing service ignited panic.
- The music industry moved quickly to shut down Napster, hardly recognizing that the tiny upstart was the beginning, not the end, of their problems.
- By the end of 2001, the number of homemade burned CDs topped 2.5 billion—the same number of CDs sold in retail stores; in 2002, industry revenues fell to $12.6 billion from their 1999 peak of $14.6 billion—a 13.7 percent decline.
- Even worse, the industry discovered that, unlike Napster, which required users to connect to its servers to download files, the emerging file-sharing companies only created software that had no control over user activity.
- Instead of neutralizing the problem, the industry opened the way for decentralized software that only made music file sharing far more efficient.
- The industry decided to fight back by suing file-sharing music lovers, who used to be their customers.
- They likened their action to a retailer prosecuting a shoplifter; most media stories portrayed the industry as giant bullies eager to intimidate 12-year-olds who had downloaded the music they loved.
- In September 2003, when the music industry filed its first major round of lawsuits, naming 261 consumers who

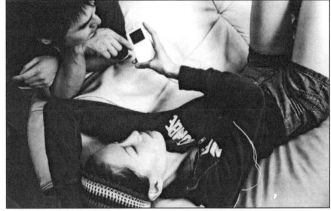

*Sharing music was easy between users and hard for the industry to control.*

had shared more than 1,000 songs each from music-swapping websites, Bill became much more visibly involved with the controversy.

- At the time, the average price of a compact disc was $18.98, of which 29 percent went to the label, 29 percent to retailers, 15 percent for marketing and promotion, 6 percent to the distributor, 5 percent for publishing royalties, 5 percent for packaging, 1 percent to the musicians' union, and 10 percent to the artist, minus recording expenses and other costs.
- Consumers thought CD prices were too high; the musicians thought they were being ripped off, colleges threatened their students with expulsion for file sharing, and a new concept known as iTunes attracted a million sales in a week by offering downloads at $0.99.
- The industry filed a slew of suits, Bill took the side of the consumer, and newly created file-sharing companies such as Grokster and BearShare were taken to court.
- Industry experts estimated that while iTunes stores produced $1 billion in sales, more than 20 billion songs were downloaded "illegally."
- Bill maintained that for distribution to take place, a physical copy had to change hands; peer-to-peer file sharing was no more a violation of the copyright than playing a CD for 20 people at a party at your home.
- In defense of college students sued by the industry, Bill argued that, even though the copyright laws were written in the days when mimeograph machines and vinyl records were king, it was the burden of the music industry to show that theft had occurred.
- He quoted Ken Waagner, a digital guru for Wilcox, who said, "the record industry suing the sharers is like the railroad industry trying to shoot down airplanes."
- And he refused to settle the suits, as many did, for $3,000.

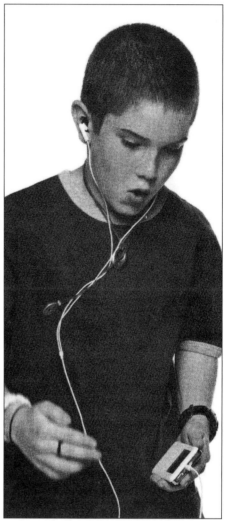

*Music lovers continued to download favorite songs despite the many lawsuits filed by the music industry.*

- Fundamental changes in the way music was made and sold were coming; the artists were gaining more control over their music and technology was their friend.
- By the end of 2006, the ratio of free downloads to paid downloads was 40 to one.
- The industry filed more lawsuits.

### Life in the Community: Yuma, Arizona

- Residents of Yuma like to say that its geography shaped the Southwest.
- Because Yuma was the safest spot to cross the Colorado River, all roads led to Yuma for travelers from Spanish explorers to Okies fleeing the Dust Bowl.
- During the California Gold Rush, Yuma became known for its ferry crossings and was considered the "Gateway to California."
- As a result, Yuma became a vibrant, multicultural community with a rich heritage, defined geographically by wide-open spaces and pristine desert scenery—all with a river running through it.
- Yuma featured a desert climate, with extremely hot summers and warm winters.

- According to The Guinness Book of World Records, Yuma was the sunniest place on earth; on average, Yuma received about three inches of rain annually.
- The year-round near-perfect flying weather attracted military interest in training its pilots, and in 1942, Major Gen. George S. Patton established the Desert Training Center, with Hyder, Horn, Laguna and Pilot Knob camps in the Yuma area.
- The Yuma Test Branch was opened in 1943; the flow of the river in the Yuma area could be controlled, so it was the perfect spot for testing bridging equipment. Italian prisoners of war were used to build the facilities, and were allowed to visit the town once a week.
- With the end of the war, Yuma's military activity also ceased and the Air Base emptied.
- In 1949, in a stunt designed to increase publicity for the area, the Yuma Jaycees set a record for nonstop flying: the plane (an Aeronca Sedan) took off on August 24, 1949 and did not touch down until October 10, 1949, for a total of 47 days in flight.
- A team of volunteers passed food and fuel to the pilots from a Buick which drove underneath the plane at 80 miles an hour.
- Possibly as a result of this publicity stunt, the Yuma air field was reactivated in 1951 and renamed Vincent Air Force Base in 1956.
- Yuma's estimated population was nearly 80,000 at the time of the 2000 census. However, as it is popular with seniors looking to escape the cold of the rest of the country, the population of Yuma nearly doubles during the winter months.
- The racial makeup of the city was 68.3% White, 3.2% Black or African American, 1.5% Native American, 1.5% Asian, 0.2% Pacific Islander, 21.4% from other races, and 3.9% from two or more races. 45.7% of the population were Hispanic or Latino of any race.

*The Sonoran Desert near Yuma, Arizona.*

Piracy? The biggest Pirates have been the record companies. The people running the record labels own lawyers and accountants, and they could be selling Brillo pads for all they care. It's not about the art at all. What has that got to do with music? So when people download a song, if it's a good song, people want the artist. People worship Eric Clapton or Ray Charles. What they do is bigger than any song. Downloading music gives people a chance to be exposed to an artist, not just a Brillo pad manufacturer.

*—Chuck D, Public Enemy*

❧❧❧❧❧❧❧

### "E-Commerce Report: Services for Downloading Music legally and With Making a Profit in Mind Are Gaining Momentum," by Bob Tedeschi, *The New York Times*, July 28, 2003

The dot-com frenzy has returned at least in one category.

The introduction last Tuesday of BuyMusic.com, an online music download store meant for consumers who eschew music piracy, was promoted by its owner as the first of many new single-song download services expected from online media sites and retailers.

The iTunes service from Apple Computer was there first, having demonstrated since April the demand for such services. But iTunes works with only Apple Macintosh computers, while BuyMusic.com is aimed at the far larger universe of PCs using the Microsoft Windows operating system.

BuyMusic.com's debut evoked memories of the Internet boom years for reasons that go beyond the company's news conference in Times Square and the coverage it generated. The founder is Scott Blum, one of a handful of dot-com entrepreneurs who got out of the market with his shirt still on his back. He earned $125 million or so from Buy.com stock before those shares, and the market that lifted them, lost nearly all their value.

Mr. Blum bought back the company for about $23 million in late 2001. He took it private and, he says, has nursed it to profitability through its sales of electronics, books and other items.

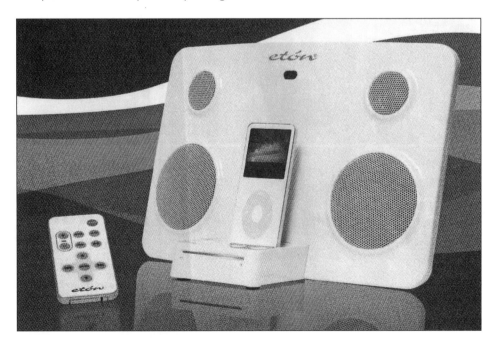

Other services, like AOL Time Warner's America Online and Listen.com's Rhapsody, have enabled Windows users to download single songs, but only as subscribers to a monthly service. BuyMusic.com is the first Windowsbased service to enable customers to buy songs à la carte à la Apple.

Mr. Blum, 39, says he sees a chance to gain an edge over Internet companies like Amazon.com that beat him to the market the first time around. Though it is true that many online merchants with the vaunted "first mover advantage" died after seeding the market for traditional retailers, eBay and Amazon are two first-mover notables that became market leaders in their own right.

"When I showed up on the Internet, I was a distant second to Amazon and I never made it up," Mr. Blum said. In his 20 years of being involved in entrepreneurial ventures, he said, "I haven't had this window ever in my life, so we're just going for it."

The BuyMusic.com service, which is not affiliated with Buy.com and is being financed entirely by Mr. Blum, is similar to iTunes, which has sold more than 6.5 million songs in about three months. BuyMusic.com shoppers can browse through more than 325,000 songs, which sell for $0.79 to $1.29. Full albums sell for $8 to $12.

BuyMusic.com customers retain different rights to the songs, depending on the artist's record label. Some titles, for example, can be downloaded and copied an unlimited number of times, though the technology is intended to prevent the sharing of them on music file-swapping services, while others can be copied just three times.

Mr. Blum said he expected his service to have a head start of perhaps three months before competitors appeared. He has begun a multimillion-dollar television advertising campaign in hopes of generating a loyal following before that happens.

When competition comes, it will take many forms, said Josh Bernoff, who covers online music for Forrester Research, a technology consulting firm. "There's a very long list of competitors," he said. "But that's good news, because it means someone will get it right."

Mr. Bernoff said that, besides BuyMusic.com, consumers could expect the rollout of online stores selling individual songs and subscriptions from online giants like Amazon, Microsoft and others. America Online, which began a music subscription service in February, plans to introduce an à la carte version later this year.

Other online companies are also lining up to sell digitized single songs without requiring subscriptions, Mr. Bernoff said, including RealNetworks, MusicMatch, and Roxio, which intends to revive the Napster brand it acquired for $5 million in November.

Roxio is set to unveil plans today for the new Napster service, which it will call Napster 2.0, Chris Gorog, Roxio's chief executive, said. The service will debut by Christmas and will include both subscriptions and à la carte downloads. Napster's technology will rely on the Pressplay music service it bought from Sony and Universal in May for close to $40 million in cash and stock.

# 2007: Avionics Mechanic in the National Guard

*After high school, Andros Thomson followed in his father's and grandfather's footsteps, and joined the National Guard. In the service, he found a way to combine his mechanical aptitude with helping his country fight terrorism.*

## Life at Home

- Andros was born in Bayshore, Long Island, New York in 1981.
- He grew up in Los Angeles, and his parents divorced when he was 7 years old.
- His father was in the United States Marine Corps active duty for almost 18 years, before working in manufacturing while being in the reserves.
- Andros remembered living off his father's reserve paycheck during a short unemployment stint.
- His mother went to college while Andros was in elementary school, and worked both as an interpreter for the deaf and in a school with mentally disabled children.
- When he was 11, Andros moved to Alabama with his father and step mother, where they moved around a lot.
- One year, during the First Gulf War, he went to two different schools in one year.
- At 13 years old, he moved to Connecticut, and graduated from high school in Falls Village.
- He lived too far from school to be involved in sports.
- He saw high school as a day care for teenagers where students were trained, not taught.
- Looking back, he wished that students were pushed towards their strengths instead being blanketed into a one-size-fits-all program.
- During high school, he worked—because his parents forced him—in a small deli/restaurant in West Cornwall called Hedgerows Market.
- One of his teachers—Mr. Looney—was his favorite because he saw potential in Andros and encouraged him.
- Despite Mr. Looney's encouragement, Andros did not graduate with the rest of his class.
- He was accused of hacking (having a .zip file of a video game on his personal drive), and forced to withdraw from his computer classes late in his senior year, despite doing A work in them.

*Andros Thomson joined the National Guard after high school.*

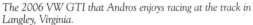

*The 2006 VW GTI that Andros enjoys racing at the track in Langley, Virginia.*

*Andros and his wife at a New Year's celebration.*

- He had one full sister, one half sister, one step sister, two half brothers, two step brothers and he was the oldest of the group.
- Andros was 20 years old when 9/11 happened.
- A friend woke him up with the news, but he didn't believe it until he turned on the TV to see the first tower on fire, and the second plane hit the building.
- What he saw made him more anxious than ever to start basic training in the Connecticut Army Reserve National Guard (ARNG), where he enlisted several months earlier.
- Andros went to the University of Connecticut, studying at regional campuses, with no time to participate in sports or other activities.
- He went to Egypt for about a month with the National Guard in 2005.
- The living conditions were horrible, like Kuwait during the war.
- It was interesting, though, flying around the Pyramids and touring some of the world's oldest structures—the Sphynx is really small in person!
- He also visited the Ancient city of Ur during his deployment in Iraq.
- He toured the ruins, climbing up the Ziggurat and walked through the house of Abraham, the father of Judaism, which was interesting to see.
- Andros and his wife had an 18-month old daughter with a second child on the way.
- His wife had a degree in business management and worked in publishing.

## Life at Work

- After high school and before college, Andros joined the Army National Guard, wanting to train as a power train mechanic.
- There were no power train openings, so he went through avionics training.
- Andros was an Avionics Mechanic on his first deployment.
- Always interested in aviation, he wanted to become a pilot, but medical issues prevented this path.
- Although his degree from University of Connecticut in American Studies was not related to his job, it still helped his career in some ways.

*With his unit in Iraq.*

- His full time job was Quality Assurance Manager of Turbine Technologies and Technical Inspector on helicopters in the CT-ARNG.
- His 18 years of experience doing almost every aspect of aviation within the Army, including being a Flight Engineer for 4 years—was solid preparation for his job.
- His parents were supportive of his chosen career path—especially since his father and grandfathers were also in the military.
- His mom was worried, but that's what moms do.
- Most of the time, he liked his job.
- Sometimes he thought that he would like to do something else, but it would have been difficult to start a new career with so much specific experience in one.
- The worst thing about work was his Iraq deployment—it was a nightmare.
- His job was somewhat routine, but every day was different and unpredictable—you never knew when something would break, or when issues would arise.
- The one thing that would have made his job easier was more employees, or winning the Powerball!
- His commute to work was 45 minutes with traffic.

*In 2003-2004, Andros' mission in Afghanistan involved door gunning.*

*At a mission launch in Iraq.*

## Life in the Community: Winsted, Connecticut

- Andros and his family lived in Winsted, Connecticut in a condominium complex.
- Winsted had a rich history; it was one of the first mill towns in Connecticut, and in 1871 The Gilbert Clock Company was founded in the town, becoming one of the largest clock manufacturers in the world by the start of the 20th century.
- Their neighbors were friendly, but quiet and kept to themselves.
- He wanted to buy a house with more space and privacy, but the value of their condo was not yet back to its pre-recession price.
- This part of Connecticut was considered rural, very different from the time he spent as a child in Los Angeles.
- Their living expenses were reasonable, especially compared to LA.
- One good thing about their condo was the two-car garage, with enough space for his 2006 MKV VW GTI, which he raced at the racetrack in Langley, Virginia.
- Andros also liked the fact that outdoor services were included in their association fee, as his job travels left him little time to take care of the property.
- One negative aspect of where he lived was that residents were not allowed to put solar panels on the roof.
- And the condo was too small for their second child—due in several months—so Andros and his family started looking for a bigger place.

*Winsted, Connecticut, where Andros lived, holds little similarity to this 1877 painting of Winsted by Sarah E. Harvey, save the mountains, churches and a few large factory buildings.*

# 2007: Jazz Saxophonist

*Jazz saxophonist and recording engineer Ryland Edwards moved from California to New York City, where he played in jazz and R&B bands to feed his passion, recorded and produced music to pay some of his bills, and worked in a restaurant to make it all work.*

## Life at Home

- Ryland Edwards was born in Berkeley, California, in 1982 and started playing alto saxophone in school when he was nine.
- His interest in machines and technology drew him to the saxophone because it had so many parts, and because his father had played saxophone as a young man.
- Ryland often could be found in his father's workshop adjusting the keys of his instrument with small screwdrivers to make his sax not only sound better, but play faster.
- Ryland found that the closer the keys were to the body of the instrument, the faster he could play.
- He wanted to play as fast as his hero, bebop saxophonist Charlie Parker, whose speed was legendary.
- Even as a teenager, Ryland was very disciplined, and practiced every day for three or four hours, which helped him strengthen the muscles in his lips and mouth.
- He also used a lot of reeds—which had to be soaked and properly filed down before they could be used.
- His parents were very supportive, and secretly happy he didn't play the drums.
- They gladly paid for the performing arts summer camp in the hills north of San Francisco.
- There he met musicians from many different walks of life who were all interested in different styles of music.
- The highlight of his time at camp was when the blues legend Taj Mahal came to see his daughter, who was a camper, play in the final concert.
- On the flight home from camp, Ryland nearly grounded the plane by insisting that he be allowed to carry on his instrument.
- In addition to playing music, Ryland discovered his talent for recording.
- Using a borrowed four-track tape recorder and a microphone, Ryland recorded himself playing four different parts on his saxophone and then layered them together into unique compositions.
- He even borrowed a baritone sax from his school to record bass parts in his harmonies.

*Ryland Edwards earned a living in New York City playing and recording the music that he loved—and waiting tables.*

- He and his friend Ben, who played the trumpet, practiced playing harmonies and backup parts in the style of Motown and soul records.
- Their favorite artists were Otis Redding, the Jackson 5, and Sam and Dave.
- In high school, the two friends joined a funk band together called The Confusion.
- The Confusion played cover songs by Stevie Wonder and Herbie Hancock, and got gigs at school dances, talent shows, and fundraisers.
- He loved the attention, but the money was terrible and they often played for free.
- Ryland recorded a five-song demo tape for the band, and enjoyed the challenge of figuring out the best way to record each instrument.
- Drums were hard to record because they required multiple microphones.

*Ryland was very dedicated to his music, from practice to performances.*

- The saxophone was also difficult because the sound came from different parts of the instrument.
- In addition to playing in the band, Ryland also played with the locally popular Berkeley High School Jazz Ensemble.
- When he joined the ensemble, there were no positions for alto saxophone players, so Ryland switched to tenor, and used his father's old tenor saxophone.
- Ryland was inspired by a fellow student, Scott, who played first chair saxophone in the ensemble, who encouraged him to pursue music in college—something he hadn't seriously considered before.
- When Scott left, he took his place as first chair in the jazz band and became a popular draw at school performances.

*Berkeley High School Jazz Ensemble helped Ryland develop his style.*

- His father was very proud of Ryland and recorded all his school performances, giving him a tape that spliced together all of his solos when he graduated.
- Ryland worked as much as he could to save money for college—as a sandwich maker at a bagel shop, a waiter at a Mexican restaurant, and a line cook at a gourmet pizza restaurant—making at most $10 an hour.
- It was at the pizza restaurant where he discovered that he liked to cook and experiment with different ingredients—not a bad Plan B if music didn't work out.
- Ryland took private saxophone lessons at $35 per hour and also gave lessons to elementary and middle school students, charging $20 per hour.
- One of his students went on to study saxophone in Chicago and, years later, Ryland took pride in seeing him perform.
- Ryland got his first professional performing experience while still in high school, playing

sax in a jazz trio at the wedding of the daughter of one of his teachers.
- They played jazz and bossa nova during dinner and got paid $150 for the gig—his share was $50.
- While Ryland was happy to be making money, he realized that he would need other ways to support himself—especially if he got into one of the New York City College music programs.
- Because he lived in a culturally rich area, there were many musicians at all stages of their careers.
- It wasn't unusual for Ryland to be watching a band at a restaurant in his hometown and be asked to play something with them; he learned to always carry his saxophone.
- To take advantage of the area and his passion for music, Ryland bought a digital multi-track recorder and began reading books on recording, mixing, and engineering.
- He was able to earn $25 per song by producing demo recordings for local bands before he left for college.

## Life at Work

- Many non-classical college music programs were focused strictly on jazz, but Ryland wanted a program that would allow him to study R&B, hip hop, and funk—as well as recording.
- He applied to several schools, but his first choice was the New School for Jazz and Contemporary Music in New York City, with a tuition of $21,000 per year.
- Since he had never been to New York, he was nervous.
- He lived in the school dorms during his first year, then found an apartment with friends in the basement of a Brooklyn brownstone.
- Being in the basement allowed Ryland to build a very small recording studio.
- Living in Brooklyn was less expensive than living in Manhattan where his school was located, and he saved even more by cooking many of his own meals.
- When he first moved to New York, he got a part-time job at a coffee shop, making $11.00 per hour plus tips.
- He then got hooked up with a local jazz club and played every Monday night, where he earned $25 plus dinner.
- This night job was a good fit with his school and music schedules because he had class in the afternoons and worked mornings at the coffee shop.
- At school, he met musicians who played a range of musical styles.
- The diversity of the people he met, and the energy of New York in general, provided him with a wide variety of freelance opportunities.
- He started playing dinner parties with a jazz trio; bars and nightclubs with a 10-piece funk band; church ceremonies with a saxophone quartet; and weddings with a 1980s cover band.
- Most gigs paid between $50 and $200 per person.
- He also played background on a variety of side projects, including for hip hop tracks and film scores, the most famous of these being a background track for Talib Kweli.
- Upon graduating, Ryland was intent on continuing his musician's lifestyle, and knew that he could make more money recording and engineering than by playing his sax.
- He was determined to meet as many musicians as possible—each one a potential recording and/or engineering job and easy to find in New York City.

*Ryland's first paying gig was at his teacher's daughter's wedding.*

- He charged $100 per song to record and mix a demo tape.
- The problem with this, however, was Ryland's friendly personality—because his friends and clients were the same, he often gave them a deal or worked for free.
- Living in the city was very expensive, and his share of the rent was $850 per month.
- The equipment that he needed to do professional recording and engineering work was also very expensive, with a microphone typically costing between $200 and $800.
- Also, to be able to compete with professional saxophone players, he needed a professional sax, which cost between $2,500 and $6,000.
- Needing to make more money, he got a job in a high-priced New York City restaurant where he could make up to $300 on a good night, and found it a good place to network.
- Actor Robert De Niro owned the restaurant and often ate there, along with actor Adrien Brody and singer John Mayer.
- Ryland loved to be able to get his friends hard-to-get reservations.
- While this cut into his time for performing, he hoped it wouldn't be long before he got his big break.
- It was during this time that he met up with his old roommate from camp, who was a blues guitar player.
- They played a few gigs together and introduced each other to their circles of friends and bandmates.
- Networking was very important for musicians in the city.
- It was not uncommon for musicians to play gigs for free if it helped them improve their reputations.

*John Mayer was co-owner of the restaurant where Ryland worked.*

- Ryland met a young soul singer named Arielle through a friend of a coworker, and began playing backup in her horn section, making $75 per show.
- As they got to know each other better, they began writing songs together.
- Arielle was very talented, but, having recently moved from Austin, Texas, didn't know many people.
- Ryland helped her record and mix a demo CD so she could get gigs at clubs and gain more exposure.
- He hoped that if she made it big, it just might be his big break.

### Life in the Community: New York City

- New York City was the most populous city in the United States, with a population of over 8,000,000 residents as of the 2000 census.
- The city drew in thousands of people a year from all over the world—seeking the opportunities that only a metropolis of New York's magnitude can offer.
- The population of New York was incredibly diverse as it was a major port of entry for immigrants.
- As a result, the music scene in New York was always diverse as well. Genres from Classical to Jazz to Hip Hop to Salsa have been able to find a foothold in New York's entertainment industry.
- Jazz blew up as the popular form of music nationwide in the 1920s.
- Though it had its origins in New Orleans and Africa, jazz was very quickly able to find a niche for itself in New York's music scene.
- Clubs like the Cotton Club, Cafe Society, and The Royal Roost were able to draw performers such as Cab Calloway, Ethel Waters, Dizzy Gillespie, and Billie Holiday.

- When Duke Ellington moved to New York City, he inaugurated a legion of jazz musicians that did the same and moved the center of jazz's development from Chicago to New York.
- Several offshoots of jazz, such as bebop, hard bop, and doo-wop originated in New York City before spreading to other parts of the country.
- Bebop was an incredibly fast-paced version of jazz, intended for the musician, rather than the dancer.
- Because it was not as danceable as other forms of jazz, like swing, bebop originally did not catch on.
- It was created in part as a response to white bandleaders who were profiting from black styles of music like swing.
- Pianist Thelonius Monk would describe the movement by saying "We wanted a music that they couldn't play" referring to those white bandleaders.
- Along with Monk, Gillespie, Charlie Christian and Kenny Clarke, famed bebop alto saxophonist Charlie Parker helped to popularize this style of music in New York's 52nd Street clubs.

### "What Music Is to Me,"
### J'Vontea Perminter, Age 16

What's music to me? It's more than an individual singing words. For me, it's an emotional stimulator. People like myself would listen to music all day. It helps to pass the time for a long day at work. Or it can even be something soothing to sleep to on restless nights.

For most people music is a form of entertainment. You can dance, sing along, it's even used to set the mood in movies. All songs have, as I like to think, a purpose. To understand that meaning, I just don't listen to the song; I try to interpret what the artist is saying. For example, classical music doesn't have very many words incorporated in it, but that's the gateway for your mind to explore and imagine anything you want.

Furthermore, hip hop music wasn't very popular among the majority. Hip hop to older audiences might just be artists cursing and being disrespectful. But to audiences of the ages between 13 and 30, it's the music of their era. Not saying that R&B or gospel doesn't have a place; just younger age groups can relate more to younger artists. It's not so much that we love to listen to them be disrespectful; its more when you experience or witness some of the things that they say, you become accustomed to hearing that artist.

In conclusion, hip hop, R&B, gospel, etc., all have their own style, but like fashion, style can become "outdated" as we say; so do music styles. If everyone listened to the same music with the same artist, what's going to happen when he or she becomes "outdated"?

### "JAZZ REVIEW;
### Saxophone, Bass and Drums, With an Equal Role for Everyone,"
### by Nate Chinen, *The New York Times*, May 13, 2006

The Village Vanguard has a history of spotlighting tenor saxophonists in trio settings, backed only by bass and drums. Sonny Rollins was the first prominent example, nearly 50 years ago; Joe Henderson memorably took up the challenge in the 1980s. (Both instances were documented on excellent live recordings.) What's attractive about the format, for such improvisers, is a precarious kind of freedom: few harmonic constrictions, but no safety net either. It's something like a Spartan endurance test for the thinking man.

This week the tenor saxophonist Mark Turner was playing at the Vanguard with a bassist, Larry Grenadier, and a drummer, Jeff Ballard, and some of the old challenges are still relevant. But the band, which calls itself Fly, doesn't heed the usual hierarchies of the saxophone trio, which cast the rhythm section in a supporting role. Instead, it proposes a collective model, in which all parts carry equal weight, and none necessarily takes the lead.

On Wednesday night that ideal was put to the test within the first few measures of "Fly Mr. Freakjar," a composition credited to all three musicians. (Fittingly, if awkwardly, the title is an anagram of their first names.) It began in quintuple meter, outfitted with complex rhythmic scaffolding by Mr. Ballard. Then Mr. Turner and Mr. Grenadier both entered, playing separate strands of a loosely braided melody. When, after several shifts in tempo, Mr. Turner ventured a solo, it was inextricable from his partners' commentary.

That's not to say that Mr. Turner's efforts were insufficiently heroic. Though disconcertingly egoless as a soloist—sometimes to the point of self-effacement—he left no doubt as to his command. Starting out with terse, scrappy phrases, he patiently developed a motif; gradually, he grew more emphatic, until he was unfurling eighth-note patterns in a billowing stream.

What apparently keeps Fly aloft is a modular sort of ensemble interaction, a flexible determination of roles. Mr. Turner's saxophone was often deployed as a rhythmic or harmonic tool, spelling out chords in shapely arpeggios. The most prominent feature of a funk number called "JJ" was Mr. Grenadier's strutting bass line; he also took the first solo on the tune. Another piece, the appropriately titled "Stark," suspended all three instrumental parts in a delicate equipoise, even during Mr. Ballard's feverish double time.

The sound of the band in the Vanguard was just as exquisitely balanced: Mr. Grenadier's resonant tone filled the space, and Mr. Ballard kept his polyrhythmic energies at a quiet roar. They both laid back considerably in one exceptional moment that seemed to acknowledge the lineage of the room: an austere arrangement of the standard "I Fall in Love Too Easily," complete with leading-man essay on tenor saxophone.

## 2008: Barack Obama Campaign Field Organizer

*David Moser began following Barack Obama's presidential run while he was a teacher living abroad. He knew that he wanted to work on Obama's campaign as soon as he returned to the States.*

### Life at Home

- David was born in Pittsfield, Massachusetts in 1984.
- He grew up in Great Barrington, a quintessential New England town, in a hilly residential neighborhood a short walk from downtown.
- His parents owned and operated the town bakery—Daily Bread—until he was 4, then pursued other careers—his dad got his Masters and became a therapist and his mom a librarian.
- He had one brother, younger by six and a half years.
- David was raised Jewish, had a Bar Mitzvah and was active in his synagogue, but also celebrated Christmas and Easter with his dad's family, only in a secular sense.
- Attending local schools, David played on the golf team throughout high school (he was captain his senior year), played basketball freshman and sophomore years, and ran cross country junior and senior year
- Cross country was a new pursuit, and he loved taking long practice runs in nearby Beartown State Forest and running on different courses for each race.
- He joined chorus his senior year, well out of his comfort zone, but because some of his best friends were there too, he had a good time with it.
- Also in senior year, David participated in an independent study program and made a video documentary about the Israeli/Palestinian conflict.
- It was a tremendous learning experience, and the first adult project he took on.
- His feeling about school got better over the years so that, by the time he graduated, he felt grateful for the community he grew up in and the school district and teachers, which had not always been the case.
- During his school years, David worked teaching at his synagogue, and as a summer camp counselor.

*David Moser loved working for the Obama campaign.*

- He didn't actually "need" the money, but it was always nice to have some financial independence over and above the allowance he got for doing household chores—and he never asked his parents for fun money, which always came out of his pocket.
- He met one of his lifelong friends, Sage, in pre-school and another, Mike, in elementary school, and in fourth grade the trio was in the same school for the first time.
- When Sage and Mike became friends independent from David, he was psyched that two of his best friends were now friends with each other—kismet!
- David attended Bard College, which he wasn't too keen on originally, but his parents made sure he looked at it closely, since his mother being an affiliated librarian meant free tuition.
- The more he looked, the more he liked and while a student at Bard, he enjoyed attending guest speakers/artists/film screenings/concerts on campus, many about US or Middle East politics.
- While in college David traveled to Nepal with a classmate who he invited to his parents' home for Hanukkah.

*Obama supporters welcomed David's efforts.*

- They had such a great time that the following year that he invited David to his parents' home—in Nepal.
- Nepal was in the midst of a Maoist insurgency and popular protests against a monarchy, making it scary at times to be there.
- They stayed with his friend's family in the city of Pokara, visited friends in the capital of Katmandu, and traveled to his father's ancestral village.
- Nepal could not have been more different from anywhere David had ever been, and it made the world beyond "the west" real to him in a new way.
- A favorite childhood memory for David was sleep away summer camp, giving him a kind of independence at a young age.
- His biggest challenge as a young person was finding a general sense of who he was or wanted to be and where that fit into the social world of school.
- David had many great professors, the best being those who taught systems for thinking and challenged students to consider ideas they hadn't before.
- He left many classes humbled by how little he knew, and how little he had thought through his opinions—always a good sign.
- Right after college, David taught for a year in Hong Kong at a Bard-affiliated university—Lingnan University.
- From there, David followed Barack Obama's primary victories and decided that he wanted to work for his 2008 presidential campaign.
- David's wife, Yael, was a Rabbi who he met in Jerusalem when he was working at a Bard program at a Palestinian university and she was studying as a first year rabbinical student.
- They were introduced through mutual friends and hit it off immediately.

## Life at Work

- David was a political field organizer for the Obama campaign.
- David's enthusiasm for Obama began by watching the presidential primaries from Hong Kong.
- He volunteered with a political party while in Hong Kong, which helped him get the job with the Obama campaign once he returned to the states.
- It was exactly what he wanted at that time.
- He was sent into a region—four counties in southeast Missouri—given an office, internet connection, and a few local leads with which to build a field campaign of Obama supporters to knock on doors, make phone calls, and generally ensure that his supporters came out to vote on Election Day.
- It was great to be dedicated to something nearly everyone he knew wanted to succeed, and his parents were very supportive.
- His work with the campaign was very hard—11 hour days, seven days a week.
- Despite the insane workload, David loved feeling like he was part of history, and part of a winning effort.
- His job, every day, was focused on cultivating local volunteers to be effective local advocates for the campaign.
- This meant working with known supporters and constantly trying to find new ones by making phone calls all day, working face to face with supporters, managing volunteer leaders, and sometimes traveling around the region to host or speak at local meetings.
- David wasn't sure that anything could have made his job easier.

*David was proud of his hard-working staff in Missouri.*

*David made sure that anyone who walked into his field office was put to work—and always with a smile.*

- If conditions became easier, they all just compensated by working harder—they left everything on the field.
- His housing, fifteen minutes from the office, was donated by a local family supportive of the campaign.
- There was a little travel involved, within his region or to statewide meetings, but most of the time he operated out of his office.
- The best part of the job was watching the election results with his team of volunteers, knowing that they had formed a new community within the region, and that they were part of a national movement that shook the world.
- The most challenging part of the work was the very conservative area he was organizing in, and the thick racial tension there.
- His volunteers were harassed for working on the campaign, and residents made threatening comments about Obama, so much so that the volunteers were provided with armed security at the office for the final ten days of the campaign.
- David felt good about the skills he acquired while working for the Obama campaign, and was confident about his future, even if he couldn't say exactly what that future was.

### Life in the Community: Poplar Bluff, Missouri

- David Moser worked on the Obama 2008 Presidential Campaign from Poplar Bluff, Missouri.
- This was a difficult place to campaign for a Democratic candidate, as the Republican Party controlled the government at all local levels in Butler County.
- However, in the 2008 Presidential primaries, a democrat won the most votes of any other candidate of either party.
- That was Hillary Rodham Clinton, who secured 2,490 votes to Barack Obama's 960.
- Poplar Bluff was first settled along the Natchitoches Trail, an old Native American Trail Ten Mile Creek and Cane Creek.
- The Ward Plantation was established as the largest and longest slave plantation in the State of Missouri, founded by Ephraim Ward in 1829 and continued until the end of the Civil War in 1865.

- A tornado leveled most of the city, especially the business district, in 1927.
- According to the 2000 U.S. Census, there were 16,651 people, 7,077 households, and 4,295 families residing in the city.
- The racial makeup of the city was 87.04% Caucasian, 9.71% African American, 0.55% Native American, 0.52% Asian, 0.48% from other races, and 1.71% from two or more races. Hispanic or Latino of any race were 1.35% of the population.

## Life in the Community: Chinatown, Manhattan

- After the campaign, David moved to Manhattan, and he and his wife lived in Chinatown, in Manhattan's lower east side.
- They enjoyed the excitement of the city, and the fact that things were always changing.
- The residents in their building were mostly first-generation Chinese families and older people who were friendly in the hallway, but they didn't know any of their neighbors well.
- Their neighborhood was an affordable pocket of Manhattan with vibrant and safe streets, an easy commute for both him and his wife, with many great restaurants and markets—and they sometimes checked out local neighborhood parades
- The lower east side of Manhattan was a world away from the mostly white, small, rural town he grew up in western Massachusetts
- David's typical day off involved shopping for groceries from street markets, eating great, cheap food, and walking the busy streets.
- Although they loved the energy of their neighborhood, David sometimes wished there was more green space and room to breathe, especially in the summer.
- After more than five years in Chinatown, the couple planned to move to a quieter neighborhood.

*David and his wife enjoyed living in Manhattan's Chinatown, home to the highest concentration of Chinese people in the Western Hemisphere. Mott Street, above, is central to the Chinatown neighborhood.*

*"Never waver," was David's motto!*

## 2008: Brigadier General

*Jim Schwitters was among the early recruits to the all-volunteer military. In a career that took him from private to brigadier general, he learned the value of initiative and critical thinking, and he applied those lessons to recruits training at Fort Jackson for combat in Iraq and Afghanistan.*

### Life at Home

- Jim Schwitters was in high school as the Vietnam War's death toll was accelerating.
- While just under 2,000 Americans were killed in 1965, when Jim was a sophomore, the death toll rose to 6,350 in 1966 and 11,363 in 1967.
- In 1968, the number of Americans killed, many of them the same age as Jim, rose to a peak of 16,899.
- Most young people of Jim's age were patriotic, but few wanted to go to Vietnam.
- Since 1940, young men had been forced into the military through the draft.
- Some sought exemptions, such as enrolling in a seminary to become a minister, while others had deferments, most commonly by being enrolled in college.
- Jim was among the latter.
- He enrolled at LeTourneau College in Longview, Texas, but in his junior and senior year, the U.S. government started the lottery.
- He had a high number (348, birthday November 3), "So I didn't have to worry about being drafted," he recalled.
- He worked summers and during the school year, graduating in 1972 with an engineering degree and working for the next three years for John Deere.
- In 1975, he enlisted in the Army for a four-year stint.
- "It sounds corny, but it was a sense of duty that every male needed to serve," he said.
- Jim joined the military at one of its lowest points.
- The long war in Vietnam ended swiftly in the spring of 1975.
- The South Vietnamese army, which had absorbed billions of dollars of U.S. aid, had been fighting without U.S. troops for the prior three years but retreated in the face of a North Vietnamese offensive, and then the retreat became a rout with some commanders abandoning their troops in the field.

*U.S. Army Brig. Gen. James Schwitters, above right.*

131

- The United States, whose president had resigned in disgrace less than a year earlier, looked weak.
- Then things got worse about two weeks after the fall of Saigon, South Vietnam's capital.
- Cambodian communists seized the U.S.-crewed cargo ship S.S. Mayaguez off the coast of Cambodia, to which the U.S. responded with a bungled rescue attempt.
- Even as the Cambodians were returning the crew unharmed, a force cobbled together of Marines and Air Force police were invading the Cambodian island where the hostages were no longer held.
- Ten U.S. soldiers were killed, and three Marines were abandoned on the island to be captured and killed by the Cambodians over the next few days.
- The American public knew little about the Mayaguez incident at the time, but it was one of the signals to military leaders that the United States needed a hostage rescue force.
- An example of what such a force might look like came in 1976 when the Israeli military carried out a stunning rescue mission.
- After a week of planning, 100 Israeli commandos flew 2,500 miles to the Entebbe Airport in Uganda

*Brig. Gen. Schwitters accepts flag during retirement ceremony.*

to rescue 94 hostages from a hijacked airplane; three hostages and one Israeli commando died in the mission, with the rest of the hostages freed.
- The mission was carried out in 90 minutes on the ground.
- U.S. military leaders decided they needed that kind of swift strike capability.
- The secretive Delta Force was started in November 1977 by Colonel Charles Beckwith, a Vietnam combat veteran who had been advocating for such a unit since working as an exchange officer with the British Special Air Service in 1962.
- When Jim Schwitters joined the Army, his first stop was Fort Jackson, South Carolina, where he was given his physical, issued a uniform, and sent to basic training at Fort Gordon near Augusta, Georgia.
- From there he went to advanced individual training, a three-week jump school, and was assigned to the 2nd Battalion Rangers at Fort Lewis, near Tacoma, Washington: "They were the Army's elite light infantry. They took pride in their training and standards," he explained.
- In winter of 1976-1977, he was sent to a communications course at Fort Bragg, North Carolina.
- "Some of my instructors at that course were later hired at Delta. They recalled me going through the course," he said.
- In the late summer of 1977, Jim was recruited for Delta Force; after discussing it with his wife, Rebecca, he decided to join as a radio operator and was assigned to the Fort Bragg-based unit in 1978.
- "I found the job at Delta was very rewarding. We were literally writing the book on our mission profile. We were developing the tactics," he noted.
- Jim was among the first cadre of Delta Force operational unit members.
- Like Beckwith, a great number of the members had combat experience in Vietnam and Special Forces training.
- Delta Force developed a selection system to ensure the unit kept the personnel with the right character, skills, and abilities to serve successfully.

- In the fall of 1979, Delta Force began a weeklong exercise to test the unit's abilities while senior officers, many of them highly skeptical, watched.
- "Those on the fence were gobsmacked on how well the organization performed," Jim said.
- Literally hours after that exercise, students in Iran who had supported the overthrow of the American-supported dictator stormed the U.S. embassy in Tehran on November 4, 1979, and took hostage 52 American diplomats and citizens.
- Delta Force began preparing for a rescue mission, which underwent numerous

*Basic Combat Training, above and lower left.*

revisions as they practiced worst-case scenarios, in which the prisoners were difficult to find and heavily guarded, and best-case scenarios, where they were found quickly and lightly guarded.
- After the U.S. planes and helicopters took off on April 24, 1981, they met in the desert for the final leg, but a series of mishaps led the mission's leaders to decide to abort.
- Before taking off to return, one of the C-130 planes was hit by a helicopter and caught fire.
- Jim was among the 60 soldiers and crew aboard the plane.
- The exit on one side was blocked by a wall of flames, but the other side was clear.
- Jim and most of those aboard made it out, but eight men died, and many more were burned.
- Jim realized more coordination was needed between the air and ground forces, and saw that the steps in training for the mission were insufficiently detailed.
- Lesson No. 1: "Pay attention to the details."
- Lesson No. 2: "You can't just assume it will all work."
- The failure of the mission was all the more painful when intelligence later showed the hostages had been right where they were expected to be and lightly guarded.
- "Their guards didn't even have ammunition in their weapons," Jim related.
- Later in 1981, Jim became an officer through direct appointment—an unusual method.
- "Colonel Beckwith kind of wanted to see if he could do it," Jim explained. "He thought I should be an officer. He told his adjutant to make it happen, and I was the victim."

- From 1982 to 1984, Jim served as a captain of an infantry battalion in Germany.
- He was back with Delta Force from 1984 to 1995, when he was promoted to lieutenant colonel.
- He commanded a training brigade at Fort Jackson from 1996 to 1998.
- "I became very familiar with how training was done. I saw how we trained in peacetime," he said.
- He was Delta Force commander in 2000-2002, and after the terrorist attacks of September 11, 2001, he oversaw units that were sent to Afghanistan.

- He was promoted to brigadier general in 2002 and sent to Iraq where, in the summer of 2004, he was assigned to help train a new Iraqi army, since its old military had been dismantled after the U.S. invasion in 2003.
- "At the institutional level, they were captives of their recent history. The institutions in their military were all limited by the regime in their scope of capability. Many were hobbled to support the regime instead of being a national asset," Jim remarked.
- The Iraqis developed a culture of self-serving officers and failed to develop a level of professional non-commissioned officers; they also treated their common soldiers like consumables.
- Under those conditions, the Americans were trying to help the Iraqis create a professional army that served the nation.
- "That was the hardest nut to crack, and frankly we didn't," Jim admitted.

## Life at Work

- Jim Schwitters returned in 2005 to Fort Jackson as the 42nd commander in the fort's history; he spent his last three years in the Army there before retiring.
- The year before he arrived, basic training at Fort Jackson and other posts was made tougher, especially for cooks, clerks, truck drivers, and others usually outside of combat.
- The irregular nature of the wars in Afghanistan and Iraq, where there were no "front lines," meant all personnel needed to be ready for combat.
- Also, the training needed to become more intense because many soldiers had little or no time for extra training before being deployed.
- Jim's assignment gave him the chance to apply the lessons of his career to new generations of soldiers, his goal was to change training to develop soldiers who were self-starters and self-disciplined.
- He wanted to cultivate "thinking soldiers" as opposed to soldiers who are robotic, simply obedient, and reliant upon leaders to do their thinking for them.

*President George Bush at the Army's training camp at Fort Jackson, Columbia, South Carolina.*

- "The opposite of that is you're taught a whole bunch of procedures," Jim explained. "We're not going to be able to train for every situation that occurs. There will be millions of situations, and we can't foresee each one."
- Jim had the honor of escorting President George W. Bush when he visited Fort Jackson on November 2, 2007; Bush was the first president to visit the installation in more than 50 years.
- While Bush was there, he met with family members of some of the soldiers killed in Afghanistan and Iraq.
- "Bush did a significant amount of that. He downplayed it in the press. He didn't want to make it a spectacle," Jim asserted.
- Bush delivered a 20-minute speech to 1,300 graduates of basic training, opening his remarks with a loud "Hooah!"
- The president gave a progress report on Iraq, saying the number of roadside bomb attacks had fallen in half in the last five months, and the number of American military deaths had fallen to its lowest level in 19 months.
- He said American troops and Iraqi allies had killed or captured an average of more than 1,500 "enemy fighters" per month since January.
- Moreover, he surmised that there were signs that internal divisions were healing as Shiite and Sunni leaders were beginning to cooperate with one another to fight against Al Qaeda.
- Bush told the graduates, "You have stepped forward and volunteered in this time of danger. You need to know you make Americans proud. Soldiers who have marched on this field have battled fascists, dictators, and terrorists. Our soldiers have brought freedom to millions of people they never knew. Because of their efforts, America is stronger; America is safer; and America is free."
- He ended the speech with Fort Jackson's motto, "Victory Starts Here!"

## Life in the Community: Fort Jackson, South Carolina

- Fort Jackson in Columbia, South Carolina, was the Army's largest training base, with more than 45,000 soldiers graduating each year from basic combat training or advanced schools.
- Camp Jackson first opened in 1917 as the United States entered World War I and was named for Andrew Jackson, president from 1829 to 1837.
- The camp was reactivated at the outbreak of World War II in Europe in 1939 and renamed Fort Jackson
- Active since then, it sprawled over 52,000 acres and was home to 3,600 active-duty soldiers and their 10,000 family members.
- The base directly supported nearly 8,000 full-time jobs, drawing $469 million in wages and benefits.
- The base had 1,150 buildings, including housing.
- In 2005, the Army began an eight-year, $1 billion plan to upgrade quarters.
- The Fort had one elementary school, one middle school, two bowling alleys, several park and picnic areas, a sport-shooting range, a miniature golf course, hunting and fishing grounds, a recreational water park, and a 36-hole golf course.
- A $4.5 million family water park opened in the summer of 2004.
- The base's mission was expanding; in 2007 the Army consolidated all of its training facilities for drill sergeants at Fort Jackson.
- In 2008, Fort Jackson became the site of the first of six national cemeteries to open under legislation signed by President Bush in 2003.

*Mazie Winter trained as an Army nurse at Camp Jackson, Columbia, South Carolina. Photo: Collection of Jim DuPlessis*

# 2008: Producer, CNN

*Andrea Getz was bitten by the news bug at an early age (CNN was her home page in high school). She interned on CNN's morning show while a junior in college and never looked back. Despite waking at 2 AM, she loved the fast pace and helping produce good content.*

## Life at Home

- Andrea was born in Salisbury, Connecticut in 1984.
- She grew up in a historical colonial house with two older brothers.
- Her parents both worked in book publishing.
- She attended public school through 8th grade and then an all-girls boarding high school.
- Growing up, Andrea remembered a Christmas tree and presents, although neither parent practiced any religion.
- She also remembered a particularly inspiring fifth grade teacher, Mr. Lunning, who assigned the 1994 Connecticut gubernatorial election; each student picked a candidate and followed their campaign in the Hartford Courant.
- Clipping articles and creating scrapbooks of the newspaper coverage was a great way to dive into politics.
- Sports were a big part of Andrea's high school life—as a tri-varsity athlete, she ran cross country, played ice hockey, and lacrosse
- Andrea was also the sports editor on the school's newspaper, and created a column called "Tales from the Field" written by the school's athletes about their experiences as a high school athlete.
- Overall, school was a positive experience for Andrea.
- The big learning curve from public school to the challenges of private school prepared her well for college.
- Summers during high school, Andrea worked at her parent's company and waitressed at the local country club.
- She had to have a summer job—parent's orders—but did not live off the money she earned.
- The morning of the 9/11 attacks, Andrea, who was in her senior year at boarding school, woke up late because of a free first period, and turned on the radio to her favorite music channel.

*Andrea Getz was production assistant at CNN.*

*Andrea's job was making sure that the show's graphics were in the right place at the right time.*

- Instead of music, however, she heard a report about a plane hitting the Twin Towers in NYC and alarmingly ran to her best friend's—Dinah's—room.
- Dinah was in a panic, on the phone with her sister, who lived in lower Manhattan.
- Normally not allowed to watch TV in the common area during the day, Andrea and a group of other seniors boldly broke that rule and watched the events unfold on CNN.
- She remembered one of the girls gasping as she saw the second plane hit.
- Another girl was panicking because her father worked in the Twin Towers—he was fine, out of the office at a dentist appointment that morning.
- When the Pentagon was hit by a third plane, the girls realized it was an attack on the country.
- Andrea became increasingly upset—her brother worked in midtown Manhattan, and her parents were in Washington, DC.
- She was the only person able to communicate with her brother through AOL Instant Messenger—all phone lines were down.
- She remembers him saying, "I'm so f*****g scared."
- When the towers collapsed, many of the students also collapsed in hysterics, fearing for friends and relatives—it was totally overwhelming.
- Later that day, the school held an assembly—Andrea remembered one of the other seniors sobbing in the back—her uncle had been killed in one of the towers.
- Upon graduating, she applied to the University of Wisconsin because her mother, who was an alumna, told her to!
- It was good advice—Andrea loved the campus, the school's strong spirit and strong academics.
- In university, she studied history and journalism, played intramural ice hockey and joined a sorority.
- Andrea studied abroad in Rome and was there when Pope John Paul II died and Pope Benedict was elected.
- To be able to witness the tradition and the media craziness surrounding it was incredible.
- Andrea also worked at a guest ranch in Montana, and was gobsmacked by the landscape and the adventurous lifestyle.

## Life at Work

- The summer after she graduated from college, Andrea got a job as production assistant at CNN.
- An internship on CNN's morning show during her junior year solidified her interest in broadcast news.
- She was bitten by the news bug at an early age, growing up with parents who always watched the evening news and were just naturally curious about the world around them.
- Always wanting to know the latest information, Andrea had CNN as her homepage in high school, mainly because they updated their website the most.

*Being able to monitor multiple screens at once was an important skill.*

- Andrea was also the subject of a story for ABC's 20/20 news show—they filmed her on an Outward Bound sea kayaking course while in high school.
- This experience taught her that she hated being on camera but loved seeing how things were done behind the scenes.
- This—and her internship at CNN—convinced her that working in broadcast news was what she wanted to do.
- Her family was very supportive of her chosen career path, offering good counsel when needed.
- One of the most rewarding things that ever happened at work involved the 2008 election.

*The newsroom was always bustling with on-air broadcasters.*

- As a graphics associate producer, Andrea learned CNN's complex system of election graphics—which were fed live data from across the country.
- On the morning after the election, she successfully pulled off complex playlists of graphics that were produced by much larger teams the night before.
- One of the worst things that ever happened at work was covering the Mumbai terrorist attack.
- It was terrifying to hear bombs and gunfire going off behind the CNN reporters, as they broadcast the news.
- A typical day at work had Andrea arriving at 2:00 am to prep graphics for air on the morning show at 6:00 am. Editorial staff (producers) requested polls, quotes or maps that she formatted and printed for the graphic artists, who would create the graphic.
- She constantly monitored workloads and deadlines to make sure the graphics made it on air.
- When a graphic was complete, she checked it for errors.
- If a graphic was not going to make air on time, she had to warn the producers about ten minutes before air time.
- She was also in charge of making sure the chyrons—the graphics on the lower third of the screen—were coded correctly and editorially sound.
- Two things that made her job easier were graphics being requested early, and fast, good artists.
- Because of Andrea's early start time, CNN paid for the 15-minute cab ride to work.

*It was exciting and a bit nerve-wracking to handle all the technology necessary for her job.*

- The only thing she might have done differently was starting at a local station—writing and producing a complete show—right out of college, instead of at a major national network.
- Her job was not affected by the Great Recession, but she distinctly remembered covering it—and starting to see weak numbers in the housing market starting in 2006.
- Her roommate, who worked at Lehman Brothers, got laid off.
- Andrea was positive about her future—despite the shifting landscape of media, there was always a desire for good content.

**Life in the Community: Upper West Side, Manhattan**

- Andrea lived in New York City, on the Upper West Side.
- Her walkup building had four apartments to a floor, with a mixed group of residents, including some who lived there for decades due to rent stabilized apartments.
- The neighborhood was a tight knit, urban one.
- There were amazing parks bordering the neighborhood—Central Park on one side, Riverside Park on the other—and it was very walkable and accessible to the rest of the city with two train lines close by.
- Andrea participated in an elderly visiting program called Dorot, and regularly visited an 83-year-old named Natalie.
- Her typical day off involved lots of sleep - recovering from the 2am schedule during the week.
- She joked that she lived in London during the week and came back to NYC on the weekends, feeling more or less jet lagged.
- She often went to movies in the neighborhood, and stopped at the local 24-hour French diner for food afterward.
- If Andrea had kids she might consider moving to the suburbs, but she loved her neighborhood and had no plans to move.

*Andrea loved living in Manhattan. This is a wide view of her neighborhood—the Upper West Side—from the Top of the Rock Observatory at Rockefeller Center.*

## 2008: Surfer and Surfboard Entrepreneur

*Surfer and materials scientist Rey Banatao and his brother, encouraged by their venture capitalist father, built surfboards using sugar beet oil instead of the industry's traditional, potentially carcinogenic materials.*

### Life at Home

- Thirty-four-year-old Rey Banatao and his brother Desi wanted to fundamentally change the way surfboards were built.
- The secret, they believed, was sugar beet oil.
- For decades the surfboard industry had been ripping through polyurethane foam cores, known as blanks, coated in petrochemical solvents and polyester resin—all wrapped in fiberglass.
- In most cases, modern surfboard blanks were so heavily packed with chemicals, including volatile organic compounds, they could be deemed carcinogenic by the EPA.
- This gave the impression that surfers, shapers, and glassers were willing participants in the destruction and soiling of the environment their lifestyle depended upon.
- Surfboard manufacturing, which had long been a garage-scale business, was dominated by shapers, who turned out a few hundred surfboards a year, priced at around $700 each, and netted maybe $40,000 a year.
- Rey and his brother, both surfers and materials scientists, were convinced that their semi-natural boards performed as well as those made from fiberglass.
- Now they had to prove it to the surfing community.
- When the two brothers began the project, they were definitely outsiders.
- Rey was finishing up postdoctoral research on nanomaterials at the University of California, Los Angeles.
- Desi had a master's degree in materials science from Berkeley, and had just lost his job at a Portland Oregon engineering company when his projection TV technology became obsolete.
- Their father, a venture capitalist and semiconductor engineer, proposed that they start a company to make use of their tech degrees.
- Growing up, the brothers fell in love with board sports: snowboarding, skateboarding and surfing.
- They started Entropy to make equipment for all these sports.
- They also wanted to understand and respect the traditions that had brought board sports like surfing to prominence.

*Rey Banatao resolved to make a better and greener surfboard.*

- The ancient Hawaiian people did not consider surfing a mere recreational activity, but something to be integrated into their culture.
- Prior to the surfer entering the ocean, a priest would bless the undertaking with a spiritual ceremony devoted to the construction of the surfboard.
- Hawaiians would carefully select one of three types of trees, including the koa, then dig the tree out and place a fish in the hole as an offering to the gods.
- Selected craftsmen of the community were then hired to shape, stain, and prepare the boards, employing three primary shapes: the 'olo, kiko'o, and alaia.

*With their father's advice, the Banatao brothers started their own company, Entropy.*

- The 'olo was thick in the middle and gradually got thinner towards the ends.
- The kiko'o ranged in length from 12-18 feet, while the alaia board was around nine feet long and required great skill to ride and master.
- Aside from the preparatory stages prior to entering the water, the most skilled surfers were often of the upper class, including chiefs and warriors who surfed the best waves on the island.
- These upper-class Hawaiians gained respect through their enduring ability to master the waves and this art the Hawaiians referred to as surfing.
- In 1907, George Freeth was brought to California from Hawaii to demonstrate surfboard riding as a publicity stunt to promote the opening of the Los Angeles-Redondo-Huntington Railroad owned by Henry Huntington.
- Surfing on the East Coast of the United States began in Virginia Beach, Virginia, in 1912, when James Matthias Jordan, Jr. captivated the locals astride a 110-pound (50 kg), nine-foot Hawaiian redwood.
- Around the same time, Hawaiians living close to Waikiki began to revive surfing, and soon reestablished surfing as a sport.
- Duke Kahanamoku, "Ambassador of Aloha," Olympic medalist, and avid waterman, helped expose surfing to the world.
- Author Jack London, already famous for his adventure books, wrote about the sport after having attempted it on his visit to the islands.
- As surfing progressed, innovations in board design exploded.
- In the 1960s, the release of the film *Gidget* boosted the sport's popularity immensely, moving surfing from an underground culture into a national fad and packing many surf breaks with previously unheard-of crowds.
- B-movies and surf music authored by the Beach Boys and Surfaris formed the world's first ideas of surfing and surfers, while the 1980s included portrayals of surfers represented by characters like Jeff Spicoli from Fast Times at Ridgemont High.
- The evolution of the short board in the late 1960s to the performance hotdogging of the 1980s and the epic professional surfing of the 1990s brought more and more exposure.

*Even Jack London had tried surfing on his visit to Hawaii.*

## Life at Work

- The Banatao brothers began working on bio-boards in 2006, opening a makeshift office in the basement of an office building owned by their father.
- They first focused on snowboards by combining epoxy resins with carbon nanotubes to create materials that would resist cracking.
- The nanotubes acted as barriers to a crack, preventing it from lengthening, but too many nanotubes make some materials unworkable.
- With the help of a Ph.D. student from Berkeley, they found the optimal concentration of tubes and proudly crafted a prototype for a custom snow ski company in Idaho.
- The technology was a success, but the company didn't like the design, so the brothers turned to surfboards created with nanotube technology and then shaped with simple hand tools.
- Again the bio-board was a success, but the grayish boards were a sleeper.
- That's when Rey went green.
- In December 2005, the surfboard blank manufacturing company Clark Foam shut its doors without warning, reportedly due to a mass of workers' compensation lawsuits and strict Environmental Protection Agency regulations.
- The vacuum left by Clark Foam's demise opened a giant door for new innovations in surfboard construction, including the manufacturing of "greener" surfboard materials.
- "It forced the industry to be open-minded," Rey said.
- Innovations included ways to effectively use bamboo in surfboard construction, as well as bio-plastic leash plugs and removable fin systems.
- For the committed, surfing was a spiritual enterprise—a connection with a divine energy unleashed by the interaction of wind, water and ocean-floor geography.
- The fact that the board used to tap into this energy was made from petroleum-based foam, polyester resins and chemically treated fiberglass had long been surfing's quiet contradiction.
- A broken board tossed in a landfill will take generations to biodegrade; the plastic fins probably never will.
- Even the thin strip of wood that runs down the middle to provide strength came at an environmental cost—a minuscule yield from the raw material from which it is milled.
- A wave of experimentation sought to detoxify surfboards by using materials that suggested the Whole Earth catalog rather than the periodic table of elements: hemp, bamboo, kelp and silk instead

*Movies and bands helped popularize surfing.*

of fiberglass; foam made from soy and sugar rather than polyurethane, which is composed of toluene diisocyanate, or TDI, a possible carcinogen that can be inhaled and absorbed through the skin; and adhesive resins made from linseed, pine and vegetable oils.

*Banatao searched for a way to make surf boards environmentally safer and "greener."*

- But changing the way surfboards were made had proved difficult.
- The few who sought to go greener struggled not only with finding just the right materials, but also with overcoming resistance from shapers and professional surfers reluctant to fix what they didn't consider broken.
- Making a performance surfboard—one that flexes and maneuvers correctly—was a black art.
- Shapers work quickly; their tools and techniques had been refined by years of working with Clark Foam.
- Rey had chosen to have their foam blanks made from sugar beet oil instead of polyurethane because chemically, the beet polymer was almost identical to polyurethane, but could be processed using much less toxic chemicals.
- Rey then wrapped the blanks in the layer of hemp cloth to fine-tune their flex and feel; the hemp rendered each board a yellowish color.

*Banatao's boards had to be strong, perform well, and look good.*

- Ray learned the craft from a do-it-yourself website and asked his friends to test his early efforts.
- "There have been a couple of boards breaking in bad situations, but everyone is still alive" said Desi.
- They finished developing the bio-board two years later, completing several dozen samples in their Santa Monica garage that doubled as the company headquarters.
- The challenge was then winning the respect of California surfers, who often maintained long-standing relationships with local shapers.
- The brothers had spent $150,000 on the bio-board, mostly borrowed from their wives; thus far, only two dozen boards had been sold.
- The company needed to move 300 boards to gross $200,000 and break even.
- Rey was hoping that several of the local superstars of the sport would embrace his enviro ethic and help launch the green board revolution.
- After all, Rey knew his philosophy was sound and the quality of his boards excellent; the only thing he didn't know was whether enough surfers would be willing to pay for them.
- Timing, Rey understood, was everything in surfing and in business.

## Life in the Community: Santa Monica, California

- Santa Monica, California, situated on Santa Monica Bay and surrounded on three sides by Los Angeles, had always been known as a resort town.
- Named for Saint Monica of Hippo, the area was first visited by Spaniards on her feast day.
- First incorporated in 1886, Santa Monica waged a battle with Los Angeles in the 1890s to be designated as the Southern Pacific Railroad's seaport and lost, thereby preserving the charm of the town.

- In 1895, Ocean Park was developed as an amusement park and residential project, followed by a race track and a golf course.
- By 1900, amusement piers were becoming enormously popular, stimulated by the Pacific Electric Railroad's ability to transport people from across the Greater Los Angeles area to the beaches of Santa Monica.
- After the Ocean Park Pier burned down in 1912, Fraser's Million Dollar amusement pier was built, which claimed to be the largest in the world at 1,250 feet long and 300 feet wide.
- The prosperity of the 1920s fueled a population boost from 15,000 to 32,000 and a downtown construction boom.
- Beach volleyball is believed to have been developed in Santa Monica during this time by surfing guru Duke Kahanamoku when he he took a job as athletic director at the Beach Club and brought a form of the game with him from Hawaii.
- Competitions began in 1924 with six-person teams, and by 1930 the first game with two-person teams took place.
- The Great Depression hit Santa Monica hard; numerous resort hotels went bankrupt.
- Muscle Beach, located just south of the Santa Monica Pier, started to attract gymnasts and body builders who put on free shows for the public.
- At the outbreak of World War II, the Douglas plant's business grew astronomically, employing as many as 44,000 people in 1943.
- To defend against air attacks, set designers from the Warner Brothers Studios prepared elaborate camouflage that disguised the factory and airfield.
- The Douglas plant closed in 1968, depriving Santa Monica of its largest employer.
- During the 1970s, a remarkable number of notable fitness- and health-related businesses started in the city, creating the Supergo bicycle shop chain, the Santa Monica Track Club, which trained Olympians such as Carl Lewis, and Gold's Gym.

*Amusement piers have been popular in California since the early 1900s.*

- The surf scene of Santa Monica also exploded in the 1970s. Rival surf gangs from different localities up the California coast fought for wave dominance.
- The "locals only" attitude and protectionism of the Santa Monica surf spots in the early 1970s was depicted in the 2005 movie *Lords of Dogtown*.
- The city's economy began to recover in the 1980s and with it, the resort feel of Santa Monica.
- After a hurricane badly damaged the pier, rundown stores and bars, the pier and shopping areas were extensively renovated.
- The increasingly upscale nature of the city was the cause of some tensions between newcomers and longtime residents nostalgic for the more bohemian, countercultural past.
- Nevertheless, with the recent corporate additions of Yahoo! and Google, gentrification continued.

*Arcadia Hotel and Bath House in Los Angeles County was home to the rich and famous.*

### "How to Shape a Surfboard,"
### by Jay DiMartino, *About.com Guide*, 2008

Watching your surfboard as it's shaped is a bit like watching your baby being born…just a little. If you haven't stood in the shaping room during this wondrous birth and felt foam dust waft up your nostrils as it blank to fully designed, you are missing out on a special moment. It takes the relationship between you and your surfboard to a deeper level, and may just lift your surfing to another level.

For those not familiar with the latest craze to invade the sun-drenched Pacific coast of Southern California, here is a definition of "surfing"—a water sport in which the participant stands on a floating slab of wood, resembling an ironing board in both size and shape, and attempts to remain perpendicular while being hurtled toward the shore at a rather frightening rate of speed on the crest of a huge wave (especially recommended for teen-agers and all others without the slightest regard for either life or limb).

—*Sleeve notes on The Beach Boys' 1962 album Surfin' Safari*

Our goal is to create high-performance resin systems that optimize the sustainability of endproducts by replacing petroleum-based chemicals with bio-based renewable resources. By employing bio-derived materials such as pine oil components sourced as a co-product from wood pulp processing and vegetable oil components sourced from the waste stream of bio-fuel processing, we are able to lower our resins' environmental impact from processing and improve the overall health and safety of our products.

—*Entropy website (www.Entropyresins.com)*

### "How Surfboards Became Danny Hess' Livelihood,"
### by Eric Gustafson, Special to *The San Francisco Chronicle*,
### November 11, 2009

Step into the workshops of most surfboard-makers and you'll find a fluffy, snowlike layer of polyurethane foam under your feet. The floor of Danny Hess' Outer Sunset garage is covered with sawdust. As with the ancient Polynesians who invented surfing, Hess builds his surfboards out of wood. However, unlike some shapers who are re-creating wooden boards from the past, mostly for the satisfaction of collectors who hang them on their walls, Hess chose wood to make a better surfboard.

Though they may help a rider peacefully commune with nature, most modern, high-performance surfboards have an environmental dark side. The polyurethane foam "blank" that is sculpted into a finished shape is made using a host of nasty chemicals, and the polyester resin used to cure a surfboard's fiberglass shell is toxic. The propensity of such boards to break in half only heightens their negative impact.

By synthesizing the woodworking techniques of cabinetmakers and boat builders with the standard foam-and-fiberglass approach, Hess creates surfboards that push the boundaries of environmental sustainability, aesthetic beauty and speed generation. They may cost twice as much as conventionally shaped surfboards, but they have the durability to last a lifetime.

The desire to build a better surfboard is not a new goal for Hess, 34. Ever since he started surfing regularly as a teenager in Ventura, he has been searching for superior equipment. As his skills progressed, so did his frustration with the boards available at the time. In the late '80s, surfboard design entered into a period of stagnation; the short, three-finned Thruster became the ubiquitous shape. Hess didn't like the way these boards surfed, and he was particularly unhappy with their short life spans.

By the time he turned 16, he was already making his own surfboards, inspired by older designs that were then seen as outmoded. His materials, however, were the usual fare. Hess' path to wood was a circuitous one. Oddly enough, it started with a straw-bale house. In the late '90s, having graduated from UC Santa Cruz with a double major in fine arts and marine biology, Hess found himself in Colorado, immersed in a sustainable-building project.

"It wasn't until I built that straw-bale house that I started seeing myself as a carpenter," says Hess. He learned another equally profound lesson during this landlocked period: "Living in Colorado made me realize how much I couldn't live away from the ocean."

Hess moved to San Francisco and quickly established himself in the Ocean Beach surfing lineup. It wasn't long before he had a contractor's license and a business doing sustainable remodels.

"Working with wood had become a fundamental part of my life at this point, and I wanted to incorporate it into as many parts of my life as possible," Hess says. The time had come for his two passions to merge. Problem was, there was no template for the wooden surfboard he had in mind.

Early hollow wooden surfboards, such as the "kook boxes" of the '30s, which were ostensibly lifeguard paddleboards, had some peripheral influence, but Hess' thinking was more directly shaped by his experience as a woodworker. Mastering techniques utilized for building radius cabinets—lamination, using molds and vacuum bagging, in which air pressure is used to bond glued pieces together—opened him up to the possibilities of wood. Taking courses at the San Francisco Institute of Architecture helped give structure to his thoughts.

"I spent something like a year constantly thinking about an approach, an idea," says Hess.

Then, in late 2000, he had an epiphany. He thought of constructing a surfboard using a molded perimeter frame, with the exterior decks supported by an interior skeleton and encased in a thin layer of fiberglass. Creating this design wasn't easy, however.

# Walking on Water

"It took me probably 140 hours to build that first board over a period of eight months," he says. During the next two years, he built about 10 experimental wood boards for himself and friends, making incremental improvements along the way.

But the boards didn't perform as well as he had hoped. They were too heavy and stiff. The solution was to ditch the wood skeleton and replace it with foam. This shed a significant amount of mass, taking the board down to the same weight as its conventional equivalent, and allowed it to flex more naturally because the decks were no longer rigidly linked. By using recycled expanded polystyrene foam instead of polyurethane, Hess was able to maintain both environmental and structural integrity. He says the resulting board was a "massive leap forward."

Until that point, he wasn't really thinking about making surfboards for a living—it was more of an artistic outlet. But the word got out, and demand for his boards quickly expanded beyond his circle of friends. In 2005, with 15 orders in hand, Hess finished his last remodel and "jumped into surfboard-making headfirst."

His timing couldn't have been better. Spurred in part by the closure of surf industry giant Clark Foam—which for decades had had a stranglehold on the foam blank business, stymieing innovation through standardization—and by a growing number of adventurous surfers looking for a more expansive range of designs, surfboard making was entering into a creative renaissance.

Hess admits that 10 years ago, there wouldn't have been a business case for selling $2,000 wooden surfboards. Today he has a seven-month backlog of orders.

Though he has nine basic surfboard models in varying sizes, several with Ocean Beach-related street names such as Noriega and Quintara, Hess custombuilds each one for a rider's weight and skill level.

Poplar is Hess's go-to material. It has the strength-to-weight ratio he demands, and the trees' fast growth makes the wood more sustainable than slower-growing redwood or cedar. Hess is particularly creative in what he does with his leftovers: He turns them into hand planes for bodysurfing. Designed to support the entire forearm, these boards function like a hydrofoil, elevating the rider's torso out of the water, allowing for higher speed and greater maneuverability.

Hess may not have chosen to use wood on purely aesthetic grounds, but his surfboards are nevertheless works of art. The clear epoxy fiberglass shell allows the viewer to revel in the uninterrupted flow of wood grains, with the intricately laminated rails framing each of these floating canvases. On his Singer model, Hess collaborates with Santa Cruz artist Thomas Campbell to add color and graphics. Still, this short, four-finned board is designed for high performance, not lofts with high ceilings.

In 2008, Hess shaped 170 surfboards; this year he hopes to surpass the 200-board mark. "Compared to a regular surfboard-maker, that's kind of laughable," says Hess. "For a wood surfboard-maker, I feel like it's a real accomplishment."

Given how labor-intensive his boards are to build, how is he able to make a profit?

"I've been able to refine the system down enough so that I can make a decent living," answers Hess, adding that each board takes 10 to 12 hours to build. "Nobody is getting rich building surfboards, and I never got into this to get rich. It's the love of doing it and making a living at the same time. I have time to surf—when I'm not too busy."

# 2009: Pastry Chef

*Sammy Barajas was adopted from South Korea and grew up in comfortable, suburban neighborhoods in Connecticut and Massachusetts. After several false starts, she finally found her groove when she enrolled in culinary school, where she loved being both creative and physically active.*

## Life at Home

- Sammy was born in South Korea in 1985, and adopted several months later by an American couple.
- She came to the United States with one porcelain doll to remember her heritage and country.
- Her childhood home town was New Britain, Connecticut—a charming, but typical, suburban neighborhood with a feeling of "sameness" to others in the community.
- Her parents divorced in 1992, when her mother moved the children—Sammy and two older brothers—to West Hartford, Connecticut and later to West Stockbridge, Massachusetts.
- Sammy's mother went to medical school and became an MD once her children were grown, an impressive example of "it's never too late."
- Her father was the president of U.S. Steel Company, following his father into the business after some overseas travel.
- As a child, she remembered celebrating Christmas and Easter.
- After the divorce, her mom observed the Winter Solstice, the Summer Solstice, and Eostre—a festival to welcome Spring.
- At Monument Mountain High School in Massachusetts, Sammy participated in track, soccer, and tennis, and was editor of the year book in her senior year.
- She was curious about trying new things and how they were structured, but discovered she was not passionate about any of them.
- Sammy went to high school in a relatively simple time—no cell phones, no social media, no PCs for note taking, and no high speed Internet for research assignments.
- She remembered eating lunch and then spending time outside to enjoy the foliage and mountain scenery—the school was in a beautiful New England setting.
- The nearby apple orchard and hiking trails provided ample opportunity for outdoor extra curricular activities.
- One summer during high school, Sammy worked at the only Japanese restaurant in town, a summer job that turned into a regular job during the school year.

*Pastry chef Sammy Barajas loved making cakes that celebrated her client's happy occasions.*

- She didn't have to work, but found that the extra money—$45-$80 a night—gave her more independence, not to mention gas money, new snowboarding gear, makeup, and whatever else she wanted at the time.
- Sammy met her best friend, Brighid, in kindergarten and they have stayed in touch ever since.
- The older she got, the easier it was to see people who were truly amazing.
- She went to the University of Vermont and studied Environmental Science, but became disillusioned in her second year.
- While in college, Sammy practiced yoga for the first time, and went snowboarding every weekend.

*Sammy and her husband at an event in Prospect Park in Brooklyn.*

- The most challenging part of her early life was being adopted and raised by divorced parents.
- Thinking about her background triggered questions and simultaneous feelings of sadness and gratitude—would her childhood have felt different if she was biologically connected to the people she grew up with?
- Sammy did not connect with teachers growing up, and was not very trusting of the adults in her life.
- After graduating from high school, Sammy felt extremely alone and undirected.
- She met her husband in middle school and they later connected as adults in their early 20s after he had been in New York for a few years.
- She found him very peculiar and methodical with a very simple yet sophisticated way of living, remembering that his room was free of clutter and personal belongings except a world history book!
- He was calm, controlled, and smart and taught her to trust and love.

## Life at Work

- Sammy worked as a pastry chef and specialized in cake design.
- She chose this path because it allowed her to be artistic while marketing a product to all types of people and occasions.
- After culinary school in Vermont, she worked for a few years as a pastry assistant and saved enough money to buy a motorcycle and put a small down payment on a condo.

*Creativity and the physical aspect of the work were both important to Sammy.*

- She cashed it all in to enroll in The French Pastry School of Chicago, taking L'Art du Gateau, which is a 6 month pastry intensive course.
- She wanted to strengthen the skills and techniques she would need to become a cake designer.
- As a college student studying the environment, she felt hopeless, anxious, and uncertain about the future.
- The turning point for her was watching chefs through the window of a culinary school in her college town, moving with vigor and so determined of their next physical move.

*Clients often dictated colors and themes, but she liked having the freedom to design her cakes.*

- She met with her advisor that very afternoon to arrange a year of absence, signed up for culinary school the next semester, and has worked in a kitchen ever since.
- Sammy always was creative and secretly wanted to go to art school, but worried that it would not lead to a satisfying career.
- Culinary school was a good choice because progress was based on what you physically and visually accomplish—recipes were structured, methods to complete the recipes were structured, and structure was exactly what she needed when she enrolled.
- She interned at Pebble Beach Resort in California, working her way up from line-cook to Pastry Chef of Club XIX, the fine dining restaurant of the club. Ressul Rassallat, the Head Chef there at the time, took her under his wing, teaching her to work hard and grow up.
- He encouraged Sammy to continue as a chef and demonstrated how to serve refined, composed cuisine using the finest ingredients.
- She stayed on at Pebble Beach for two more years, learning as much as she could—and the scenery and weather were easy to take!
- Her experience as a savory chef was a big help in her transition to a pastry chef.
- Her parents were supportive, but surprised that she wanted to pursue a life in the kitchen, especially her mother, since she never prepared a meal in her life.
- Her husband was a technical writer and project manager at Bloomberg Financial in Manhattan and enjoyed immersing himself in new projects.
- Sammy loved many elements of being a pastry chef and cake designer, especially working for herself, which allowed her to be creative and directly contribute to her business.
- She was in the business of celebration—a cake or special dessert order usually meant a happy occasion, and it was gratifying to get positive feedback from a client about how her product contributed to their celebration.

*Sports-themed cakes were popular.*

*Large, multi-tier cakes mean multi-bowls going at once.*

- The most challenging aspect of her job was the emotional and personal drama—kitchens are full of different personalities and working side by side with other people in stressful situations can be a challenge.
- Sammy's work day routine included spending mornings managing invoices and new orders, then making a list of the day's production (what needs to be baked/made), and then preparing the elements needed for any outgoing orders.
- The cake process could take from a few days to several months, depending on the design and the occasion.
- During the summer and fall, weddings were more popular, and the colder months meant baby showers and 1st birthday parties.
- Having a lump sum of money to invest in the business, like having her own dedicated van, would have helped a lot.
- Delivery times vary from 15 minutes to over an hour, and she depends on Uber and Lyft.
- If she had the opportunity to do things differently, Sammy would have started her business earlier, developed a viable business plan, and sought out a small business mentor.
- The Great Recession did not have much effect on her business—folks were looking for quick pick-me-ups that were not too pricey—desserts could quickly get your mind off those negative thoughts.
- Sammy's future had expansion written all over it!

## Life in the Community: Brooklyn, New York

- Sammy and her husband lived in Brooklyn, New York.
- When she first moved to Brooklyn, she felt distant from friends and what was familiar to her, but over the years she found smaller communities of wonderful people.
- The trick was to not ride the subway late at night and life got easier.
- Their apartment building was full of neighbors of all ages and walks of life, with lots of younger children.
- They chose Brooklyn because it is an easy commute to Manhattan and they enjoyed the endless amount of things to do and see in New York City.
- Sammy belonged to the Rising Tide Society, and started a Brooklyn Collective, companies that supported creative and small businesses by helping with networking.
- There was a big difference between Brooklyn and the Connecticut she grew up in—mostly the diversity of people and where they came from.
- The like-mindedness of the community she grew up in seemed unimaginative to her after Brooklyn, although she acknowledged that it could be comforting at times.
- A typical day off with her husband started with a big breakfast and usually included a walk around the neighborhood, especially

*Husband-to-be Michael and Sammy at their engagement party at her parent's Connecticut house.*

Prospect Park, or a subway ride to explore Manhattan—finding new dumpling spots was always fun.

- In the summer, a favorite Brooklyn place to visit was Coney Island, with its beach and frozen lemonade.
- They loved their neighborhood for the variety of food, markets, yoga studios and, of course, the people.
- They had no plans to move out of the city—maybe when they adopted kids of their own—something on the back burner.

*During a trip to South Korea, Sammy was impressed by the culture and tradition, like this Parade of Lights.*

*Seeing how food was packaged and displayed in South Korea was an interesting part of Sammy's trip. Take-out "deli" top, and fish market, bottom.*

# 2009: Irish Immigrant and Researcher

*After earning his PhD in biochemistry in the Republic of Ireland, David Cusack discovered far more ways to use his education in the United States than he would have if he had stayed in Dublin.*

### Life at Home

- David Cusack grew up in Beaumont, a suburb about four miles north of Dublin city center in the Republic of Ireland.
- He was the youngest child, with four older sisters.
- Their father was a building inspector for the city, and their mother was a homemaker.
- David went to O'Connell's Christian Brothers School in Dublin, although his Roman Catholicism lapsed when he was about 10 years old.
- Instead of going to mass every Sunday, he would go to the local convenience store.
- He later attended University College Dublin, part of the National University of Ireland, and obtained a B.Sc. (the equivalent of a US bachelor of science degree) in 1984 and a Ph.D. from the same university in 1989.
- When representatives from a Japanese pharmaceutical company came to the university to recruit researchers, David, who was 27 at the time, decided to work for them in Japan.
- After living and working in Osaka and Tokyo for four years, David went back to Ireland, where he stayed for about two months before deciding to do postdoctoral research in an academic setting.
- He applied for a couple of positions that he thought might be interesting—one at Columbia University in New York, and the other at Harvard University in Cambridge, Massachusetts.
- Consequently, he was offered both positions and chose the one at Harvard, whose international office took care of David's H1-B visa, which allows for employment at educational institutions.
- David left Dublin for Massachusetts in 1993.
- Having stayed with his cousins 10 years earlier in Dallas, Texas, as a college student for about four months, he was familiar with the US.
- David arrived in Cambridge on November 6, which was an unusually hot day for late fall.
- He discovered that Memorial Drive, which borders the north bank of the Charles River, was closed to traffic on

*David in 1993 at his first American football game and tailgate party.*

Sundays, and hundreds of people, most in shorts and t-shirts,were out roller blading, jogging, walking dogs, and playing Frisbee.

- He thought, "This place is really awesome!"
- He was to learn quickly that hot temperatures such as these were rare for November in Massachusetts.
- In fact, that year New England was heading into one of the worst winters for snowfall.
- The assistant for the Harvard lab where he would be working was away and kindly let David use her apartment, which was a two-minute walk from the lab, for about a week.

*The house in Dublin where David grew up.*

- This gave him time to find a more permanent place to live.
- During the hunt for an apartment, he was shocked by how expensive rentals were; for someone on a postdoc's salary, it seemed excessive.
- Also, after having lived in Japan, he found a lot of the apartments in the Cambridge area rundown and frankly crummy.
- However, he eventually found a lovely apartment in Union Square in Somerville, about a seven-minute drive from Harvard University.
- The building was owned by a wonderful Portuguese family, the Figureidos, who were originally from the Azores.
- The apartment was beautifully kept but expensive, so he advertised for a roommate.
- Sanjay, who was from India and was also a researcher, moved in and shared rent and expenses.
- Soon afterwards, while practicing karate at a local dojo, he met an intriguing woman named Rachel—an artist and graduate of Massachusetts College of Art.
- David had not intended to stay in the US, but after he and Rachel fell in love and were married, he decided to become a US citizen.
- This entailed a lot of paperwork, and multiple copies of forms had to be mailed; nothing was submitted electronically at the time.
- There were lengthy waits at the immigration office in Boston, along with a few extremely rude immigration officers, but eventually the paperwork was approved.
- He then studied for the citizenship test, which was not that difficult since he seemed to know more about American history than most Americans did.

*David and Rachel making their marriage vows at City Hall in Santorini, Greece.*

- The citizenship ceremony was held at Fenway Park, and was the largest in Boston to date.
- Thousands of people now formally called themselves Americans and the United States their new home.
- Rachel stood in the stands with the proud friends and families of the new citizens.
- Each country of the immigrants' provenance was called out in alphabetical order—from Afghanistan to Zimbabwe—and followed by cheers from the crowd; Rachel, whose grandparents had all come from Sicily, cheered loudly for both Ireland and Italy.
- David was profoundly moved by the ceremony: he was now a United States citizen.

## Life at Work

- Oddly enough, only the professor who headed the Harvard University lab and his assistant knew David Cusack was joining the lab, and they were both in Hawaii for a science meeting when he was due to start.
- When David arrived in the lab at 8 a.m. on a Monday, wanting to give a good impression, he found it locked.
- No one was around, and the lab, which was on the top floor of the four-story building in a back corner, was a bit creepy with its poor lighting, dull-colored walls, and strange vibe.
- It warmed up a bit once people began to arrive, but he was surprised to learn that none of the other researchers knew he was coming.

*David at work as a science writer and editor in his home office.*

- Eventually, he felt welcomed there.
- However, he noticed that the main difference between the US and Ireland is that Americans tended to keep more to themselves.
- After six years of performing bench research, David was ready for a change, and decided to become a freelance science writer for several publications and websites.
- Though the transition was not that difficult, making the decision to change careers was a bit agonizing.
- He knew that once he stepped away from research, he would never go back, and he worried that he might be making a mistake.
- Nevertheless, David ended up being very happy with his decision.
- David became the editor of a research news publication, assigning and editing articles written by a small staff of writers, and sometimes wrote news stories himself.
- Although he mostly worked from home, he attended about five scientific meetings a year in various parts of the world.
- Otherwise, most days were similar; covering the same beat for a few years was a bit dull, and he sometimes yearned for a change.

## Life in the Community: Stow, Massachusetts

- Stow, Massachusetts was a very small town about 25 miles west of Boston.
- It was known for its apple orchards, public golf courses, sheep farms, and original stone walls surrounding farms from colonial times.
- People kept to themselves and were unaware David Cusack was an immigrant, especially since he had only retained a nearly imperceptible trace of his Irish accent.
- In Ireland, David had lived in an urban setting with densely packed houses and lots of kids; in Stow, the minimum lot size was an acre, and children were rarely seen.
- In about 1660, the earliest colonial settlers in the area were Matthew Boon and John Kettell.

*David became enamored of the gardens in Japan, where he worked for several years, and created one in front of his house in Stow.*

*Winter at Delaney Pond in Stow, Massachusetts.*

- Their two families settled the land of the Tantamous (Jethro) Native Americans, called "Pompositticut," for which a school and a community center in Stow are named.
- Both families were involved in King Philip's War in 1676.
- Boon sent his family to the Sudbury Garrison House and proceeded to return home with one of his sons and a neighbor; all three were killed.
- John Kettell sent his family to the Lancaster Garrison, which was attacked and burned.
- The natives took 20 captives, including the famous Mary Rowlandson, who were all ransomed for £20 after several months of living a native life.
- Stow was officially incorporated as a town in 1683.
- The oldest existing house in Stow was built in 1690 and is now a historical museum.

*David enjoyed grilling and cooking, outside in summer and inside in winter.*

- In the 1920s, wealthy Bostonians made excursions to Stow—in summer to swim in and hike around the Assabet River, Elizabeth Brook, Lake Boon, and Delaney Pond, and in autumn to pick apples from the many orchards in the town.
- In the 1970s, a group of Harvard professors created an area within Stow called "Harvard Acres," with roads named after the streets around Harvard University in Cambridge.
- In the 2000s, Stow continued to capitalize from tourism. Apple orchards and several golf courses drew in thousands of wealthy weekenders and summer tourists from across New England.

## 2009: Roofing Crew Leader

*Jesus Mendez was a third-generation Mexican-American who had stayed in the construction trade his entire life simply because he enjoyed being a roofer.*

The Roof for All Reasons

### Life at Home

- Jesus Mendez spent almost his entire life in the construction industry, building a reputation as a dependable roofer in the St. Louis community.
- For three decades, Jesus had risen before dawn to tackle the steepest roofs in St. Louis; the jobs required skill, careful planning, and a certain level of tenacity.
- His current job was carrying a sign in front of a strip mall outside St. Louis, Missouri that read "We Buy Gold."
- Six days a week, six hours a day, Jesus carried a cardboard laminated sign along the narrow strip of grass in front of the mall, easy but monotonous work.
- Only three years earlier, he was on top of the world, financially, emotionally and physically.
- As the housing collapse progressed, however, housing construction came to a standstill and Jesus had to make other plans.
- Jesus was born April 21, 1961, in Belleville, Illinois.
- Both sets of Jesus' grandparents emigrated from Mexico after the Second World War, believing that their children would find greater opportunity in the United States.
- His maternal and paternal grandparents were married in the same ceremony; they even took the same train to Chicago for their honeymoon.
- Jesus' mother, Elizabeth, was the younger of two girls, and when Jesus came along, he was her and his father Pedro's second child, and the first boy.
- Ironically, the white flight from the city to the suburbs in the 1950s and 1960s provided Jesus' father with a steady stream of construction jobs and an opportunity for Jesus to learn his father's craft.
- Jesus could drive a 10-penny nail with three blows before he was six and was familiar with most common power tools before he was 10.
- At 12, he laid his first roof, and at 14 he ran his own crew—mostly Mexican immigrants older than Jesus.
- His father's one rule was school before work.
- He fully understood that a high school education was the ticket to success in America.

*Jesus Mendez enjoyed being a roofer.*

## Life at Work

- Jesus Mendez left St. Louis the day after he graduated from high school, because he wanted to see the world: starting with the ocean.
- When he arrived in Miami two days later, he was exhausted.
- After two weeks, he found the beaches too bright, the sun too hot, and the Spanish-speaking girls too cold.
- The attractive women of Miami—most with a Cuban background—had little time for an American-born construction worker suffering from a major sunburn.
- Jesus tried working on a shrimp boat, serving food, and cutting sugar cane.
- After six months he was ready to return to St. Louis.
- During the next two decades, he worked heavy construction, helped build several of the city's tallest buildings and handled renovations.
- By the time the twenty-first century dawned, Jesus had a wife, a small house, a boat and four children.
- Then cancer struck his youngest daughter, ending her life at 11 years old and putting the family $180,000 into debt.
- Jesus worked double shifts, got help from the Catholic Church and sold his boat, but could not make headway against the debt.
- His father suggested that Jesus run his own crew and specialize in roofing houses with complicated designs.
- The demand was great and the expertise rare.
- For three years, Jesus worked from 6 a.m. to 6 p.m. supervising three or four jobs at a time.
- At one point, he had 42 roofers employed—not counting office staff—and was building a reputation as the "go-to guy" for builders who had complex jobs.
- In 2006, Jesus reported an income to the IRS of $76,000—which did not include the jobs for which he was paid partially or fully in cash.
- His oldest son was attending an upstate Illinois community college, determined to use his hands for holding books, not sun-heated shingles.
- Jesus felt so good about the direction of his life, he purchased a house in the upscale neighborhood where his crews typically worked.
- The year 2007 was even more successful.
- American homeowners could not do renovations fast enough; Jesus was told by one homeowner, "if you move me to the head of your list, you can double your bid."
- Increasingly, Jesus and his crews took only the most difficult, high-end projects that promised the highest margin.
- Jesus even felt secure enough to become politically active and advocate for immigration policies that would allow Mexican workers with jobs to freely move back and forth between Mexico and the U.S.
- A guest worker program, he believed, would provide more stability to the worker's family by reassuring workers they could return home after a job.
- At the turn of the previous century, when more than a million immigrants a year were coming to America for economic opportunity, many Italians, Greeks and Irish periodically returned to their homeland, often to visit the family they had left behind.

*When cancer struck Jesus' 11-year old daughter, it depleted their savings and put the family in debt.*

- His political leanings cost him a few jobs and drew lots of unsigned hate mail.
- Despite having lived in St. Louis most of his life and having an ancestry with roots in the area going back 60 years, he was told "Go back to where you came from."
- The Census placed the Latino population of St. Louis at 3.5 percent.
- Business in 2008 was strong in the beginning, even though he was finding it harder to get final payment on some jobs.

- Then, overnight, the bottom fell out; the housing bubble had burst.
- Renovations were suddenly canceled, developers stopped calling, and customers quit paying.
- Two banks that had been courting Jesus for his business no longer had time to talk.
- A supplier sued Jesus for non-payment of specialized roofing materials, his new truck was repossessed, and he fell behind on the mortgage.
- By the end of 2009, Jesus' company was out of business, his house in foreclosure, his son was bitter that he was unable to afford college, and the hospitals were calling to collect the remaining debt on his daughter's medical bills.
- The only job the 50-year-old father of four could find at Christmas was carrying a placard up and down the street reading "We Buy Gold."

## Life in the Community: St Louis, Missouri

- Over its long history, St. Louis had seen itself as a city welcoming to newcomers.
- The French who had founded the city in 1764 mingled freely with the Irish, Scots and Anglo-Americans who came West in the early 1800s.
- Irish immigrants, scorned in many places, found St. Louis hospitable, so they established themselves in business, education, and state government.
- When the failure of Ireland's potato crop and repressive British policies in the late 1840s brought starvation to Ireland, thousands of Irish immigrants came to St. Louis.
- German immigrants came in large numbers between 1830 and 1850, spurred by the widely published letters of Gottfried Duden, who lived along the lower Mississippi River between 1824 and 1827.
- He extolled the glories of the region because it reminded him of the Rhine Valley.
- They were followed by the Bohemians, Slovaks and Croatians, who established native language churches and cultural centers.
- The Italians came to the city after the Civil War, Jews arrived around the turn of the century, Southern African-Americans arrived in large numbers during World War I, and Mexicans found St. Louis after World War II.
- Discrimination in housing and employment were common in St. Louis, and starting in the 1910s, many property deeds included racial or religious restrictive covenants.
- During World War II, the NAACP campaigned to integrate war factories, and restrictive covenants were prohibited in 1948 by the Shelley v. Kraemer Supreme Court decision, which had originated as a lawsuit in St. Louis.
- De jure educational segregation continued into the 1950s, and de facto segregation continued into the 1970s, leading to a court challenge and interdistrict desegregation agreement.
- St. Louis, like many Midwestern cities, expanded in the early twentieth century due to the formation of many industrial companies and wartime housing shortages.
- It reached its peak population of 856,796 at the 1950 Census.

- Suburbanization from the 1950s through the 1990s dramatically reduced the city's population, and although small increases in population were seen in the early 2000s, the city of St. Louis lost population from 2000 to 2010.
- By 2009, Greater St. Louis was ranked 18th-largest metropolitan area in the country and the fourth-largest in the Midwest.
- During most of the twentieth century, the economy of St. Louis was dependent on manufacturing, trade, transportation of goods, and tourism.
- The city was home to several major corporations, including Cassidy Turley, Express Scripts, Enterprise Rent-A-Car, Graybar Electric, Scottrade, Anheuser-Busch, Edward Jones Investments, Emerson Electric, Energizer, and Monsanto.
- St. Louis was also home to three professional sports teams, including the St. Louis Cardinals, one of the most successful Major League Baseball clubs.

*The Arch is a famous landmark in St. Louis, Missouri, symbolyzing the city as a gateway to the west.*

## 2009: Brewery Owner

*It had never occurred to William Thomas Davis that at age 72, he would spend his retirement years wrestling with a start-up business he called Thomas Creek Brewery in Greenville, South Carolina.*

### Life at Home

- William (Bill) Thomas Davis was familiar with many of life's challenges after 42 years as an architect.
- Often as a young boy, Bill helped his father work as a brick mason, laying brick in the hot South Carolina summers.
- It was during one afternoon that an architect visited the site with a set a blueprints.
- Meeting the architect and learning what he did helped Bill realize what he wanted to do for the rest of his adult life—design buildings as an architect.
- In the years after college and earning his degree, Bill Davis joined Craig Gaulden Architects, and within two years, he made partner in 1977.
- The firm changed its name to Craig Gaulden & Davis and went on to design a number of schools, libraries, and churches throughout the Southeast.
- Bill's hand was involved in a number of landmark buildings constructed in Greenville, including the Peace Center for the Performing Arts and the Greenville Art Museum.
- In addition to designing buildings, Bill traveled to committee meetings and conferences with the American Institute of Architects that met throughout the United States.
- It was during these travels that he discovered good brews in Oregon and Washington states.
- In the late 1970s, the craft beer renaissance was just beginning in the United States; start-up breweries were forming to create beers not made by the national distributors.
- "I've never brewed in my life, but I know what good beer tastes like," he told his son Tom.
- The stuff Bill was discovering was nothing like Pabst Blue Ribbon or the European imports found locally.
- Tom, who was then working as a bartender and manager of Henni's Restaurant in Greenville and had access to some of the better brands of beer, realized that his tastes were "slightly off kilter" because the choices his father suggested were limited in South Carolina.
- So 22-year-old Tom started to study home brewing books to learn how to create the craft beers his father was bragging about.

*William Thomas Davis started a microbrewery with his son at age 72.*

- After educating himself about home brewing, Tom skipped over 5-gallon extract brewing, which most beginners used, and started with 10-gallon all-grain batches.
- Discovering that he could make quality craft beer, Tom knew that he wanted to become a professional brewer and sell his own beer.
- Regretfully, he had an obstacle in front of him—the South Carolina law did not allow brewpubs until 1994.
- When the law passed, the owner of Henni's wanted to turn his restaurant in a brewpub and dreamed of creating a franchise of brewpubs throughout the state.
- Tom and Bill realized this was an opportunity and formed a leasing company.
- Bill financed the operation and agreed to lease the beer brewing systems to the restaurant for this possible franchise opportunity; Tom would be responsible for the restaurant's brewing.
- Bill purchased a tiny three and a half barrel system that could make over 150 gallons of beer for Henni's.
- Then, for the next couple of years, Tom crafted quality beer while Bill grew concerned about the lack of growth in the franchise.
- When Bill talked with Henni's owner, he learned the owner now wanted out of the franchise beer business and was only interested in operating a restaurant.
- Bill realized that his leasing approach was not going to work due to the limited number of brewpubs in South Carolina.
- Meanwhile, Tom wanted to take advantage of the economies of scale that a brewery could offer and reach a wider audience through a network of distributors.
- Setting up a chain of brewpubs to reach a larger population would be too costly.
- To sell beer in South Carolina, a businessperson had to either form a brewery that sold beer directly to distributors, who in turn sold it to retailers.
- The other option would be to have a brewpub, which required having a restaurant.

*Bill funded their new venture while son Tom honed his brewing skills.*

- It was one or the other—a company could not do both.
- Since Tom had improved his brewing prowess during the prior few years, both father and son were interested in creating a brewery while still providing product to Henni's.
- It would allow them to maintain revenues for their brewing operations.
- Much of the endeavor was really Tom's idea, and he encouraged his father to partner.
- The final decision required a number of weeks as father and son discussed their business ideas while enjoying Tom's homemade brew.

*The brewery started off as a three and a half-barrel system.*

- In 1997, Bill again provided the financing for the new brewing operation, but finding a lender proved difficult.
- Ultimately, Bill worked with a local bank that appeared to have little interest in the businesses, especially with the risk of lending money to a new company.
- Bill also questioned whether the loan officer had any interest in his product as well.
- To get a loan, Bill was required to mortgage his house to finance the operation and secure a $200,000 letter of credit, even though he was still active in his architecture career and carried no debt.
- Next, they began the search for a good commercial brewing system and an industrial building.
- This proved extremely difficult.
- To be successful, they needed to be in a warehouse facility with high ceilings, access to a lot of water, and have sloped drainage floors.

*Thomas Creek Brewery's new warehouse was a team effort.*

- The drainage floors are necessary for a brewery because workers constantly squeegee all the water and spilled beer off the floor.
- Unable to find a suitable location, Bill shared his woes with a neighbor during a Christmas party.
- The neighbor—and owner of Huskey Construction Company—was familiar with the Davis men's efforts.
- He agreed to build them a warehouse on the site of an old junkyard on Piedmont Highway on the south side of Greenville.
- The next step was a name for the brewery.
- "Thomas" was an obvious choice for both men, and they decided to focus on a water theme for their beer.
- Thus, Thomas Creek Brewery was created, which also provided a rustic image.

## Life at Work

- Starting a new business, Bill Davis knew preserving capital and limiting expenditures were a necessity in the first years of operations.
- When his son Tom discovered a discounted 60-barrel system from a defunct Kernersville, North Carolina brewery called Woodhouse Brewery, they made a purchase.
- In 1998, Thomas Creek Brewery fired up its brewhouse and began to make two brands of beer: Amber Ale and Multigrain.
- Six months later, the company started brewing its Red Ale, which became their flagship beer.
- Due to limited funds, Bill and Tom agreed to focus on a grassroots marketing effort.
- They did this by participating in festivals in the Southeast, such as the Brewgrass Festival in Asheville, North Carolina, and many others.
- They even offered private tastings for business clubs and community associations while sponsoring events in the Greenville community.
- A number of venues included the local chapter of the American Red Cross, Hands On Greenville, the March of Dimes, and the United Way.
- At all of the events, attendees enjoyed the beers produced by Thomas Creek Brewery and wanted to know where to buy more.
- But many had trouble finding Thomas Creek Brewery beer in their stores, even with the strong demand for its product.
- Bill grew frustrated with the limited distribution of the company's products.

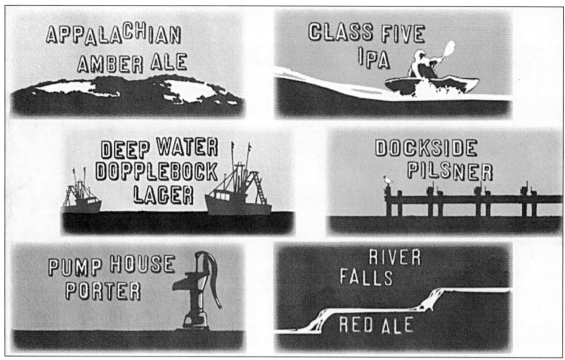

*Amber Ale was their first beer and Red Ale became their most popular.*

- By law in South Carolina, a brewery was classified as a manufacturing operation and could only sell its product to a distributor, who made sales directly to retailers.
- Bill was working with a local distributor, who feared that Thomas Creek Brewery's beer would only be in demand in the Greenville market.
- When Bill requested a statewide distribution, the distributor sold the distributing rights for Thomas Creek Brewery to another company that primarily handled wines.
- Finally, they could achieve statewide distribution.
- As sales improved, the men discovered that they needed to improve their product's image; distributors had noted that their bottle labels "looked homemade."
- So Bill Davis hired a Greenville marketing firm—Bounce—to do a complete makeover.
- Over several weeks, the ad people from Bounce created names for every beer while maintaining the theme of water referenced in the name Thomas Creek Brewery.
- Thomas Creek was brewing eight of their beers year-round; names included Up The Creek Extreme IPA, River Falls Red Ale, Deep Water Dopplebock, and Dockside Pilsner.
- The marketers also presented Bill with the overall theme of "Sink the Status Quo" for his product, and developed witty banners to appeal to a younger generation of drinkers.
- One read, "Yelling 'Play Free Bird' was funny about 23 years ago.... Come up with something original," referencing the Lynyrd Skynyrd song habitually requested at concerts, no matter the band.
- Bounce won local, regional and national Best in Show awards for the banner ads promoting Thomas Creek Brewery.
- Even with the new distributor and improved sales, however, Thomas Creek was struggling with its cash flow; Bill continued to finance the operations from his personal savings.
- It took five years for Thomas Creek Brewery to make a profit in one of its quarterly reports.
- It took an additional two years for the company to make its first annual profit.
- While many entrepreneurs would have quit, Bill and Tom were dedicated to make this family business a success.
- With sales growing by 2004, Bill realized they needed more equipment to support the new growth.

- At that time, Thomas Creek had a bottling system that took three days and 135 man-hours to empty a 60-barrel tank.
- Employees had to stack, package and label each bottle.
- At age 68, Bill found himself doing physical labor in bottling and stacking his product in this laborious manufacturing process.
- New equipment was needed to keep up with the business growth, and that required finding additional financing.
- Even though Thomas Creek was just becoming profitable, Bill knew that finding additional financing was going to be difficult with their current lender.

*Thomas Creek was gaining national recognition for quality and great taste.*

- After a number of conversations, Bill decided to change his banking relationship and collaborated with a few new investors.
- With the influx of fresh capital in business, Thomas Creek was able to buy the additional tanks, chillers and a bottling line.
- Finding good prices for the tanks and chillers was easy, but it was Tom's luck in discovering the company's new bottling system.
- Early one morning, Tom was on the Internet visiting a professional brewer's website when he discovered a brewery in Toronto selling its bottling line.
- Tom immediately posted an offer subject to inspection and approval.
- Several other offers followed later that day, but Tom's was first.
- Tom had a friend inspect the equipment a few days later, and he called Tom and told him to buy it.
- It was perfectly designed for a microbrewing operation.
- The bottling system would have traditionally cost as much as $400,000, but Thomas Creek secured it for only $80,000.
- Once installed, the new equipment was highly automated and improved efficiency.
- Thomas Creek could now bottle 60 barrels of beer within six to seven hours and package 50 bottles per minute.
- National brewers that produce established brands, such as Budweiser and Miller, typically bottle 500 to 600 bottles per minute.

*Thomas Creek beers won two awards in five years.*

- With the new equipment, Bill and Tom started producing more beer and expanding Thomas Creek's market into North Carolina, Georgia, Virginia, Florida and Alabama through a growing number of new distributorships.
- They also began doing contract brewing for a number of companies, including Charleston Brewing and Orange Blossom Brewing.
- Over the next several years, Thomas Creek became a more recognizable name by the various industry publications; they also continued to win regional and national awards.
- One of the most significant awards for Thomas Creek was the Silver Medal in both 2003 and 2008 at the World Beer Championships.

*Bill relied on local marketing to get the word out for their handcrafted brews.*

- The brewery won in the German-Style Strong Bock with its Deep Water Dopplebock beer, which was proclaimed to be outside the norm for the style with its prominent roasted malt character and chocolate notes.
- Even with all of the awards and national recognition, a phone call in 2009 caught Bill Davis by surprise.
- An agent representing a European distributorship was interested in Thomas Creek and seeking a regional microbrewery that could export product for the growing demand of quality American beers in Scandinavia.
- Without hesitation, Bill Davis shipped him a number of beers to sample and the agent loved them.
- The agent wanted to use Thomas Creek to introduce Scandinavians to "The microbrew from the United States' Southeast."
- Tom and Bill went to work providing a shipment to Sweden and delivered 50 barrels of Thomas Creek product by the fall of 2009.
- In addition to the quality of the product, many in Sweden liked the microbrews because they were less costly than European beers.
- European brewers must pay a value added tax throughout their manufacturing costs: a single beer may cost three times as much as a Thomas Creek beer exported to the country.
- Within the first week, the Scandinavian distributor had sold out of all the bottles shipped.

## Life in the Community: Greenville, South Carolina

- Greenville, South Carolina, was located in the northwestern corner of the state along Interstate 85, one of the busiest interstate highways in the nation.
- The area was centrally situated between two of the largest cities in the Southeast, Charlotte and Atlanta, and was one of the most rapidly growing areas of the country and the fastest in the state.
- Over the past decade, Greenville attracted more than $6 billion in new business investments and 43,000 new jobs.
- This growth allowed for more businesses to be created per capita than any other region in the Southeastern United States.

- National and international companies that can be found in Greenville include Michelin, Lockheed Martin, General Electric, Hubble Lighting, Samsung, 3M, and IBM.
- Much of the community's successes began in 1970s, when then Mayor Max Heller spearheaded a massive downtown revitalization project.
- The first and most important step in changing downtown's image was the streetscape plan, narrowing the street's four lanes to two, and installing angled parking, trees, and decorative light fixtures, as well as creating parks and plazas throughout downtown.
- By 2009, the city's Main Street possessed a lofty canopy of trees and shops that attracted a number of visitors annually.
- The pedestrian-friendly atmosphere has been compared to that of a European city.
- One of Greenville's biggest attractions was Falls Park on the Reedy, featuring two sets of waterfalls visible from the landmark Liberty Bridge.
- The pedestrian suspension bridge served as the community's icon.
- Connecting the various parks within the city were miles of walking and bicycle trails.
- One of the city's longest was the Swamp Rabbit Trail, a former railroad line that ran through the community during its textile days in the late nineteenth and early twentieth centuries.
- Greenville was rated one of Bike Magazine's "Top 5 Best Places to Live and Ride," which helped it attract the annual USA Pro Cycling Championships and many professional cyclists to live in the area.
- Greenville also boasted year-round arts and entertainment.
- The Greenville County Museum of Art, which specialized in American art, was noted for its collections by Andrew Wyeth and Jasper Johns, as well as a contemporary collection that featured such notables as Andy Warhol and Georgia O'Keeffe.

*Downtown Greenville, South Carolina was a great place for Thomas Creek Brewery.*

### "Opinion: South Carolina's Laws Too Hurtful on Breweries,"
### by Jaime Tenney of Coast Brewing Company,
### *The Digital Charleston*, May 14, 2009

So, we've been in the beer industry for over a decade now (and by we I mean David has been professional brewing for 12 years and we've have been operating COAST for over 2). We knew the laws when we started the brewery and ran Pop the Cap SC, which changed the law allowing beer over 6 percent to be made in SC. Fine and Dandy. Except, I am fed up with all the other laws that essentially annihilate small breweries to operate successfully.

We are not allowed to sell direct, self-distribute, or even give a tasting at our own brewery. Down right Ridiculous. With the passage of the Microdistillery Bill, distilleries now join wineries in the fact that they can have tours, do tastings and sell directly to consumers at their place of business. But STILL not beer. What gives?

The SC Beer Wholesalers oppose any legislation that "infringes on the 3-Tier system," that's what gives. Seems to me that this is downright unconstitutional to have these basic rights for wineries and distilleries but not beer. I have never seen such discrimination for a business sector in my entire life. Nor have I seen such absolute political power held by a special interest group (though I am sure it happens all the time).

❧❧❧❧❧❧❧❧

### "Thomas Creek's Appalachian Amber Ale,"
### by Jake Grove, *Independent Mail Newspaper*, August 20, 2009

For some strange reason, local breweries have been overlooked in this column of late.

Sure, a few regional brews have been reviewed, like those from the Highland family of beers in Asheville, N.C., or the Terrapin variations from Athens, Ga., but the very local breweries have been largely ignored.

That begins to change starting now.

A couple of weeks back, Greenville's Village Gallery on Pendleton Street threw its monthly First Friday art walk. During that time, the Upstate Visual Arts group was out there providing beer for those who donated to the cause and attended the event. And the beer they aptly put in their coolers was Greenville's own Thomas Creek.

They had four different brews available, but the one that caught this reviewer's eye was none other than the Appalachian Amber Ale.

For months I have been hung up on the amber ales. They typically have a roasted malt flavor with some nutty side tastes and a hint of hops on the back end. They are becoming more popular among brewers of late, much like the IPA of years past.

Since I only drank the Appalachian Amber out of a bottle at the event, I had to buy one on my way home to try from a pint glass to provide the full report. I was happy to do it.

The pour from the Appalachian Amber was just what you might expect. A deep red body followed up by an off-white head that lifted quickly, but vanished just as fast.

The aroma was light, mostly of malts and a slight citrus tone, with a nice grain tone to balance things out.

As for taste, there was more going on with this amber ale than one might expect. It starts off sweet with those roasted malts and nutty flavors coming out to start. As it goes along, things turn a bit bready, but with a light mouthfeel as the beer goes down. But the aftertaste is slightly of hops and a hint of orange.

The lacing is light if anything. The body of the beer doesn't promote anything thick or heavy, but it leaves a quality aftertaste that goes nicely with the crispness of the brew itself. Overall, this beer is a fine addition to a mix-and-six-pack or to try on tap in Greenville, but perhaps not something one would drink one after another with friends.

The nice thing is, Thomas Creek provides many different beers and a mixer of those would be ideal. Thomas Creek is available most everywhere, including specialty stores and grocery stores. They run around $7 per six-pack, and many varieties are available.

### Craft Beer—Associated Press Release

### Brewers Association Reports Mid-Year Craft Brewing Numbers: Number of U.S. Breweries the Highest in 100 Years

Boulder, CO. August 17, 2009—The Brewers Association, the trade association representing the majority of U.S. brewing companies, reports America's small and independent craft brewers are still growing despite many challenges, and are continuing to provide jobs to the U.S. economy. Dollar growth from craft brewers during the first half of 2009 increased 9 percent, down from 11 percent growth during the same period in 2008. Volume of craft brewed beer sold grew 5 percent for the first six months in 2009, compared to 6.5 percent growth in the first half of 2008. Barrels sold by craft brewers for the first half of the year is an estimated 4.2 million, compared to four million barrels sold in the first half of 2008.

"At a time when many of the giant beer brands are declining, small and independent craft brewers are organically growing their share and slowly gaining shelf and restaurant menu space one glass of craft beer at a time," said Paul Gatza, Director of the Brewers Association.

The U.S. now boasts 1,525 breweries, the highest number in 100 years when consolidation and the run-up to Prohibition reduced the number of breweries to 1,498 in 1910. "The U.S. has more breweries than any other nation and produces a greater diversity of beer styles than anywhere else, thanks to craft brewer innovation," Gatza added.

**"Beer Edges Out Wine, Liquor as Drink of Choice in U.S.,"**
*Gallup Online*, June 29, 2009

Among the nearly two-thirds of Americans who say they drink alcoholic beverages, 40 percent say they most often drink beer, 34 percent say wine, and 21 percent choose liquor.

కురాలికురాలికురాలికురాలికురా

**"Anheuser-Busch Introduces Wheat Beer Nationwide,"**
*St. Louis Business Journal*, October 5, 2009

Anheuser-Busch rolled out Bud Light Golden Wheat nationwide Monday in an effort to tap into the surge in popularity of sweeter beers and wheat beers from craft brewers.

Bud Light Golden Wheat marks the third brand extension under the Bud Light name following launches of Bud Light Chelada and Bud Light Lime in 2008.

The marketing budget for Bud Light Golden Wheat is about $30 million a year, similar to the marketing budget for Bud Light Lime.

St. Louis-based Anheuser-Busch is owned by Belgium-based Anheuser-Busch InBev, the world's largest brewer.

## Early 2000s

- A black monolith measuring approximately nine feet tall appeared in Seattle, Washington's Magnuson Park, placed by an anonymous artist in reference to the movie *2001: A Space Odyssey*

- A federal jury in Portland, Oregon, ordered abortion foes who had created "wanted" posters and a Web site listing the names and addresses of "baby butchers" to pay $107 million in damages

- After a letter containing anthrax was sent to Senator Tom Daschle's office, the Hart Senate Office Building was closed for three months

- Almost 3,000 were killed in the September 11, 2001, attacks at the World Trade Center in New York City; the Pentagon in Arlington, Virginia; and in rural Pennsylvania

- America Online was bought out by Time Warner for $162 billion in the largest-ever corporate merger

- An American businessman was admitted to the Vietnam France Hospital in Hanoi, Vietnam, with the first identified case of SARS; both the businessman and his doctor later died of the disease

- Barry Bonds of the San Francisco Giants broke the single season home run record with 72 home runs for the year

- Carlos Santana won eight Grammy awards, including Album of the Year for *Supernatural*

- CBS filmed the TV show *Survivor* on the Malaysian island of Pulau Tiga

- Charles Schulz, creator of the comic strip *Peanuts*, died at the age of 77

- China was formally granted permanent normal trade status, reversing a 20-year policy of requiring an annual review for the country to expand its human rights activities

- Despite the dot-com implosion, consumers purchased more than $2 billion worth of groceries online—three times the volume of 2000—leading to the sale of traditional grocery store chains such as Safeway and Albertson's

- During the last three months of the year, after nearly a million jobs had been lost, unemployment stood at nearly six percent, up from 3.9 percent a year earlier

- Education reform was approved, requiring annual standardized tests in grades three through eight by 2005-6

- Enron filed for Chapter 11 bankruptcy protection five days after Dynegy canceled an $8.4 billion buyout bid, triggering the largest bankruptcy in U.S. history

- Eric Rudolph, the suspect in the Centennial Olympic Park bombing in 1996, was captured in Murphy, North Carolina

- Facing an investigation surrounding allegations of illegal drug use, right-wing radio host Rush Limbaugh publicly admitted that he was addicted to prescription painkillers and would seek treatment
- FBI agent Robert Hanssen was arrested and charged with spying for Russia for 15 years
- FBI agents raided the corporate headquarters of HealthSouth Corporation in Birmingham, Alabama, on suspicion of massive corporate fraud led by the company's top executives
- Former President Jimmy Carter was honored with the Nobel Peace prize
- George Harrison, former lead guitarist of the Beatles, died of lung cancer at the age of 58
- George W. Bush was declared the winner of the presidential race in a highly controversial election against Al Gore becoming the 43rd president of the United States
- In California, President Bill Clinton created the Giant Sequoia National Monument to protect 328,000 acres of trees from timber harvesting
- In Terre Haute, Indiana, Timothy McVeigh was executed for the Oklahoma City bombing
- In the first such act since World War II, President George W. Bush signed an executive order allowing military tribunals against any foreigners suspected of having connections to terrorist acts or planned acts against the United States
- In The Netherlands, the Act on the Opening up of Marriage allowed same-sex couples to marry legally for the first time in the world since the reign of Nero
- Iraq's oil ministry, which produced 3.5 million barrels of oil a day only five years ago, produced only five percent of that number
- Judge Thomas Penfield Jackson ruled that Microsoft violated the Sherman Antitrust Act by tying its Internet browser to its operating system
- Leaders of developing nations called for a "New Global Human Order" to spread the world's wealth and power
- Martha Stewart and her broker were indicted for using privileged investment information and then obstructing a federal investigation; Stewart also resigned as chairperson and chief executive officer of Martha Stewart Living
- Millennium celebrations were held throughout the world despite fears of major computer failures from the "Y2K" bug
- More than 10 million people in over 600 cities worldwide protested the planned invasion of Iraq by the United States
- More than 600 people set out on a five-day, 120-mile protest march to Columbia, South Carolina, to urge state lawmakers to remove the Confederate flag from the state house dome
- NASCAR legend Dale Earnhardt died in a last-lap crash in the 43rd annual Daytona 500
- Nitrogen-based fertilizers were blamed for the rapid decline of the spotted frog in the Pacific Northwest
- Noah, a gaur, became the first individual of an endangered species to be cloned
- Officials announced that one of the Taliban prisoners captured after the prison uprising at Mazari Sharif, Afghanistan, was John Walker Lindh, an American citizen
- Pen Hadow became the first person to walk alone, without any outside help, from Canada to the North Pole
- Pope John Paul II begged for God's forgiveness for sins committed or condoned by Roman Catholics over the last 2,000 years, including wrongs inflicted on Jews, women and minorities
- President Bill Clinton awarded former President Theodore Roosevelt a posthumous Medal of Honor for his service during the Spanish-American War
- President Bill Clinton proposed a $2 billion program to bring Internet access to low income houses

- President George W. Bush limited federal funding for research on embryonic stem cells
- President George W. Bush said during his 2002 State of the Union address: "States like those (Iraq, Iran and North Korea) and their terrorist allies, constitute an axis of evil, aiming to threaten the peace of the world"
- School districts dominated by blacks and Hispanics spent $902 less per student on average than mostly white school districts
- Soyuz TM-32 lifted off from the Baikonur Cosmodrome, carrying the first space tourist, American Dennis Tito
- Surveys indicated that 80 percent of Americans were unwilling to sacrifice taste for more healthful, less flavorful foods
- Surveys indicated that 83 percent of children believed they would go to college, 68 percent thought they would get married, and 12 percent thought they would join the armed forces
- Surveys showed that 40 percent of all U.S. e-mail was spam
- Syracuse won the college basketball National Championship
- Thanks in part to file swapping, the sale of CDs was down 20 percent from the year 2000
- The 2001 anthrax attacks commenced as letters containing anthrax spores were mailed from Princeton, New Jersey, to ABC News, CBS News, NBC News, the New York Post, and the National Enquirer; 22 people in total were exposed and five of them died
- The 73rd Academy Awards selected *Gladiator* as the year's Best Picture
- The Baltimore Ravens defeated the New York Giants 34–7 to win their first Super Bowl title
- The book *Harry Potter and the Order of the Phoenix* sold more than five million copies in the first week
- The Colorado Avalanche won their second Stanley Cup
- The Concorde made its last scheduled commercial flight
- The Dow-Jones Industrial Average reached a high of 11,337 (May) for the year and low of 8,235 (September)
- The electorate of the Cherokee Nation of Oklahoma approved a new constitution re-designating the tribe "Cherokee Nation" without "of Oklahoma" and specifically disenfranchising the Cherokee Freedmen
- The female-oriented television cable channel Oxygen made its debut
- The Florida Marlins defeated the New York Yankees to win their second World Series title
- The Human Genome Project was completed, with 99 percent of the human genome sequenced to 99.99 percent accuracy
- The International Whaling Commission turned down requests from Japan and Norway to allow expanded whaling
- The Iraq War began with the invasion of Iraq by the U.S.; within days U.S. forces seized control of Baghdad, ending the regime of Saddam Hussein
- The journal *Nature* reported that 350,000-year-old upright-walking human footprints had been found in Italy
- The Millennium Summit among world leaders was held at the United Nations in New York
- The much-anticipated movie version of the book *Harry Potter and the Sorcerer's Stone* grossed $150 million in five days
- The National Labor Relations Board ruled that graduate students who work as teaching assistants may organize a union

- The *NEAR Shoemaker* spacecraft touched down in the "saddle" region of 433 Eros, becoming the first spacecraft to land on an asteroid
- The number of Internet users in China more than doubled in six months from four million to 8.9 million, most of them young, single men
- The number of U.S. golf courses had increased from 13,353 in 1986 to 17,701
- The number of unmarried couples heading U.S. households increased from 3.2 million in 1990 to 5.5 million in 2000
- The price paid for a typical set of childhood vaccinations was now $385, up from $10 in 1971
- The Russian space station *Mir* re-entered the atmosphere near Nadi, Fiji, and fell into the Pacific Ocean
- The Russian submarine *K-141 Kursk* sank in the Barents Sea, killing the 118 sailors on board
- The Space Shuttle *Columbia* disintegrated during re-entry over Texas, killing all seven astronauts on board
- The *Spirit of Butts Farm* completed the first flight across the Atlantic by a computer-controlled model aircraft; the flight set two world records for a model aircraft—for duration (38 hours, 53 minutes) and for non-stop distance (1,883 statute miles)
- The submarine USS *Greeneville* accidentally struck and sank the Japanese fishing vessel *Ehime-Maru* near Hawaii
- The Tribune Company bought the *LA Times* in a $6.5 billion merger with the Times Mirror Company
- The U.S. Government indicted Zacarias Moussaoui for involvement in the September 11 attacks
- The U.S. invaded Afghanistan, with participation from other nations in retaliation for the September 11 attacks
- The U.S. Justice Department announced that it no longer sought to break up software maker Microsoft, and would instead seek a lesser antitrust penalty
- The U.S. Supreme Court gave police broad authority to stop and question people who run from a police officer
- The U.S. Supreme Court upheld Affirmative Action in university admissions and declared sodomy laws unconstitutional
- The United States withdrew from the 1972 Antiballistic Missile Treaty, thereby allowing the military to test and deploy missile-defense systems without restraints
- The USA Patriot Act expanded the powers of the police to wiretap telephones, monitor Internet and e-mail use, and search the homes of suspected terrorists
- The War Against Terrorism legislation, authorizing the president to use force against those who perpetrated or assisted in the September 11 attacks, passed the House and Senate without objection
- The world's first self-contained artificial heart was implanted in Robert Tools
- Two Austrian banks agreed to a $40 million settlement with an estimated 1,000 Holocaust victims or their heirs for having confiscated their assets
- U.S. forces continued to search for terrorist mastermind Osama bin Laden; hundreds of al-Qaeda forces were believed to have escaped into Pakistan
- Using information leaked by George W. Bush's Administration, *Washington Post* columnist Robert Novak published the name of Valerie Plame, blowing her cover as a CIA operative
- Wikipedia, the online encyclopedia, was launched on the Internet

## Mid 2000s

- A computer worm, called MyDoom or Novarg, spread through Internet servers, infecting one in 12 e-mail messages
- A federal judge in San Francisco said the Partial Birth Abortion Ban Act was unconstitutional because it lacked a medical exception to save a woman's life, and it placed an unnecessary burden on women who sought abortions
- A Pew Research Center survey revealed that 81 percent of Americans believed it was "common behavior" for lobbyists to bribe members of Congress
- America was stunned by graphic photos of American soldiers grinning as they abused Iraqis in the Abu Ghraib prison
- Another second was added, 23:59:60, called a leap second, to end the year 2005; the last time this occurred was on June 30, 1998
- At the fourth annual Total Request Live Awards, Madonna won the Lifetime Achievement Award and Bono captured the Most Inspired Artist/Humanitarian Award
- Beyoncé Knowles released her second consecutive number one solo album *B'Day*, which sold 541,000 copies in its first week
- Bon Jovi's second single, "Who Says You Can't Go Home" from the album *Have a Nice Day* went to number one in the U.S. Hot Country Charts
- Cartoons that included depictions of Muhammad printed in the Danish newspaper *Jyllands-Posten* triggered Islamic protests and death threats
- Celebrations were held worldwide for the 250th anniversary of the birth of Wolfgang Amadeus Mozart
- Chicago rock band OK Go's video for their single "Here It Goes Again" became an Internet phenomenon on YouTube
- Deep Impact was launched from Cape Canaveral by a Delta 2 rocket
- Demonstrators marched through Baghdad denouncing the U.S. occupation of Iraq, two years after the fall of Saddam Hussein, and rallied in the square where his statue had been toppled in 2003
- Former Iraqi leader Saddam Hussein was sentenced to death by hanging after an Iraqi court found him guilty of crimes against humanity
- George W. Bush was inaugurated in Washington, DC, for his second term as the forty-third president of the United States
- Google bought YouTube for $1.65 billion
- In Super Bowl XL, the Pittsburgh Steelers defeated the Seattle Seahawks 21–10
- Justin Timberlake released his sophomore album FutureSex/LoveSounds
- Liquids and gels were banned from checked and carry-on baggage after London Metropolitan Police made 21 arrests in connection with an apparent terrorist plot to blow up planes traveling from the United Kingdom to the United States
- MahlerFest XIX, honoring Austrian composer Gustav Mahler, was held in Boulder, Colorado
- Mary J. Blige's single "Be Without You" was number one on the U.S. Billboard R&B chart for 15 weeks
- Massachusetts enacted Universal Health Coverage, requiring all residents to have either public or private insurance
- Massive antiwar demonstrations, including a march down Broadway in New York City, marked the third year of war in Iraq

- More than a million immigrants, primarily Hispanic, staged marches in over 100 cities, calling for immigration reform
- MTV celebrated its 25th anniversary
- NASA reported the discovery of a distant object in our solar system that closely resembled a planet
- NASA's Stardust mission successfully ended, the first to return dust from a comet
- *No. 5, 1948* by Jackson Pollock was sold privately for $140 million
- Pakistani scientists admitted to giving Libya, Iran and North Korea the technology to build nuclear weapons
- Paul O'Neill, former treasury secretary, told 60 Minutes that the Bush Administration had been planning an attack against Iraq since the first days of Bush's presidency
- *Pirates of the Caribbean: Dead Man's Chest* became the fastest film in Hollywood history to reach the billion-dollar mark worldwide in box office receipts
- PlayStation 3 and Wii were released in North America
- Pope Benedict XVI succeeded Pope John Paul II, becoming the 265th pope
- Pope John Paul II died, prompting over four million people to travel to the Vatican to mourn
- President Bush said in a national broadcast that to abandon Iraq would fuel anti-American sentiment around the world
- President George W. Bush proposed a plan the would allow illegal immigrants working in the United States to apply for temporary guest worker status and increase the number of green cards granted each year
- President George W. Bush used the fifth anniversary of the September 11, 2001, attacks to emphasize the link between Iraq and winning the broader war on terrorism, asserting that "if we give up the fight in the streets of Baghdad, we will face the terrorists in the streets of our own cities"
- Rapper Proof was shot and killed by a nightclub bouncer in Detroit, Michigan
- Rock group Panic! At the Disco won the MTV Video of the Year award for their hit single "I Write Sins Not Tragedies"
- Scientists announced that they had created mice with small amounts of human brain cells in an effort to make realistic models of neurological disorders
- Several hundred thousand demonstrators gathered in Washington, DC, to protest the Bush Administration's policy on reproductive rights
- Shakira's single "Hips Don't Lie" sold 266,500 downloads in its first week of availability, overtaking D4L's record of 175,000
- Smoking was banned in all Ohio bars, restaurants, workplaces and other public places
- Taylor Hicks won the U.S. television talent contest, American Idol, Season 5; Katharine McPhee was the runner-up
- Terrorists exploded at least 10 bombs on four commuter trains in Madrid, Spain, during rush hour, killing 202 people and wounding about 1,400
- The American military continued to engage in fierce fighting in Iraq
- The Blu-ray Disc format was released in the United States
- The Bonnaroo Music Festival in Manchester, Tennessee, featured Radiohead, Tom Petty, Phil Lesh and Friends, Beck, and Sasha
- The Bush Administration admitted that it failed to give the commission investigating the September 11, 2001 terrorist attacks thousands of pages of national security papers
- The California Supreme Court ordered San Francisco to stop issuing marriage licenses to same-sex couples

- The first thirteenth root calculation of a 200-digit number was computed mentally by Frenchman Alexis Lemaire
- The Human Genome Project published the last chromosome sequence in Nature
- The Huygens probe landed on Titan, the largest moon of Saturn
- The International Astronomical Union defined "planet" at its 26th General Assembly, demoting Pluto to the status of "dwarf planet" more than 70 years after its discovery
- The International Committee of the Red Cross found that military personnel used physical and psychological abuse at the Guantanamo prison in Cuba that was "tantamount to torture"
- The Kyoto Protocol went into effect, without the support of the U.S. and Australia
- The largest UN World Summit in history was held in New York City
- The Military Commissions Act of 2006 was passed, suspending habeas corpus for "enemy combatants"
- The one-billionth song was downloaded on iTunes; the song was "Speed of Sound" by Coldplay
- The People's Republic of China ratified an anti-secession law, aimed at preventing Taiwan from declaring independence
- The popular search engine Google went public
- The Provisional IRA issued a statement formally ordering an end to the armed campaign it had pursued since 1969, and ordering all its units to dump their arms
- The Rolling Stones gave a free concert to two million people in Rio de Janeiro, Brazil
- The Salvation Army reported that Joan Kroc, heir to the McDonald's fortune, had left the nonprofit entity $1.5 billion
- The second Chinese spacecraft, *Shenzhou 6*, was launched, carrying Fei Junlong and Nie Haisheng for five days in orbit
- The Superjumbo jet aircraft Airbus A380 made its first flight from Toulouse
- The U.S. required international travelers to be fingerprinted and photographed to enter the country
- Tickets for Madonna's Confessions Tour in North America, Europe, and Asia sold out in minutes; the tour grossed more than $260 million
- Two NASA Rovers landed on Mars and sent back spectacular images of the planet
- Two stolen Edvard Munch paintings, *The Scream* and *Madonna*, were recovered in a police raid in Oslo, Norway
- U2 won five awards at the 48th Annual Grammy Awards, Mariah Carey won three, and Kelly Clarkson became the first American Idol contestant ever to win a Grammy
- United Airlines emerged from bankruptcy after being in that position since December 9, 2002, the longest such filing in history
- United Nations Secretary General Kofi Annan said the war in Iraq was illegal and violated the U.N. charter
- Warren Buffett donated more than $30 billion to the Bill & Melinda Gates Foundation

## Late 2000s

- A 2,100-year-old melon was discovered by archaeologists in western Japan
- A five-year inquiry by the Intelligence Committee found that President George W. Bush and his staff repeatedly overstated evidence that Saddam Hussein possessed nuclear, chemical, and biological weapons and misled the public about ties between Iraq and al-Qaeda
- A Russian and an American satellite collided over Siberia, creating a large amount of space debris

- After an eight-month recount battle, Al Franken was sworn in as the junior senator of Minnesota, giving Democrats a majority of 60 seats
- AIG announced it would pay $450 million in bonuses to top executives, despite its central role in the global financial meltdown and receiving a $173 billion government bailout; a massive public outcry followed
- American swimmer Michael Phelps won eight gold medals at the Summer Olympics in China to beat a 36-year-old record set by countryman Mark Spitz
- Americans elected Barack Obama president, the first African American elected to that office
- An 8.3-magnitude earthquake triggered a tsunami near the Samoan Islands; many communities and harbors in Samoa and American Samoa were destroyed, and at least 189 were killed
- An economic recession began that rivaled the Great Depression of the 1930s and caused in large part by banks pushing securities backed by shaky, high-interest loans to homebuyers
- An outbreak of the H1N1 influenza strain, commonly referred to as "swine flu," was deemed a global pandemic, a designation that had not been used since 1967-68
- Analog television broadcasts ended in the United States as the Federal Communications Commission required all full-power stations to send their signals digitally
- Angela Hacker was voted the 2007 champion of the televised singing competition *Nashville Star*, earning her a record contract with Warner Bros. Records
- At a news conference in Baghdad, a reporter for a Cairo-based satellite television network hurled his shoes at President George W. Bush and called him a "dog"
- At the 51st Grammy Awards, Alison Krauss and Robert Plant won five Grammys for their duet album Raising Sand, which also won Album of the Year
- Australian actor and director Heath Ledger died from an accidental overdose at age 28, a few months after finishing filming for *The Dark Knight*. Ledger was posthumously awarded the Oscar for Best Supporting Actor for that role
- Barack Obama was inaugurated as the 44th president of the United States in front of a crowd of over one million
- Bernard Madoff was arrested and charged with securities fraud in a $50 billion Ponzi scheme
- Beyoncé launched The Beyoncé Experience in Tokyo, Japan
- Bill Gates ended his day-to-day management of Microsoft, the computer giant he founded
- Bolivia became the first South American country to declare the right of indigenous people to govern themselves
- California became the second state to legalize same-sex marriage after the state's own Supreme Court ruled a previous ban unconstitutional. The first state was Massachusetts in 2004
- Celine Dion made the final performance of her five-year engagement at Caesars Palace in Las Vegas
- Chris Cornell left Audioslave because of "musical differences"
- Christina Aguilera's Back to Basics Tour was the highest grossing tour for a female artist in 2007
- Colombian armed forces rescued politician and activist Ingrid Betancourt and 14 others after six years as hostages of the Revolutionary Armed Forces of Colombia (FARC)
- Danica Patrick won the Indy Japan 300, becoming the first woman to win an IndyCar race
- During a nearly 40-minute speech, presidential candidate Barack Obama explained the complexities of race in America
- Elton John played Madison Square Garden for the sixtieth time to celebrate his sixtieth birthday; he was joined by Whoopi Goldberg, Robin Williams, and former President Bill Clinton
- Fred Mascherino announced his departure from Taking Back Sunday to pursue his solo career called The Color Fred

- "Gimme More," Britney Spears' comeback single, sold one million copies shortly after its release
- Gold prices on the New York Mercantile Exchange hit $1,000 an ounce for the first time on March 13, 2008
- *Good Masters! Sweet Ladies! Voices from a Medieval Village* won the 2008 Newbery Medal for children's literature. The book, written by Laura Amy Schlitz and illustrated by Robert Byrd, tells the stories of 21 young inhabitants of a thirteenth-century England village and manor
- Governor John Lynch signed a bill allowing same-sex marriage in New Hampshire, the sixth state in the union to do so
- Grandmaster Flash and the Furious Five, R.E.M., The Ronettes, Patti Smith, and Van Halen were all inducted into Rock and Roll Hall of Fame
- Greg Maddux pitched his 5,000th career inning against the San Francisco Giants on September 19, 2008
- Gunman Robert Stewart entered a nursing home in Carthage, North Carolina, killing eight people and injuring two others before being shot by an off duty police officer
- Hilary Duff released *Dignity*, her first album in three years
- In Super Bowl XLIII, the Pittsburgh Steelers defeated the Arizona Cardinals 27-23
- Jordin Sparks of Arizona won Season 6 of American Idol
- Kelly Clarkson broke records for the biggest jump to number one on the Billboard Hot 100 when her single "My Life Would Suck Without You" soared from number 97 to number one, fueled by 280,000 digital downloads on the first week of release
- Lady Gaga's debut single "Just Dance" hit number one on the Billboard Hot 100 after 22 weeks—the second-longest climb to number one, since Creed "With Arms Wide Open" in November 2000
- Led Zeppelin reunited for their first show in 25 years
- Live Earth, a worldwide series of concerts to initiate action against global warming, took place
- Michael Jackson died in strange circumstances and brought a worldwide outpouring of grief
- Microsoft released Windows 7
- *Minutes to Midnight* by Linkin Park sold more than 600,000 copies in the U.S. and more than one million worldwide in the first week
- Mortgage giants Freddie Mac and Fannie Mae collapsed just days before investment bank Lehman Brothers declared bankruptcy
- NASA launched *Kepler Mission*, a space photometer which searches for planets in the Milky Way that could be similar to Earth and habitable by humans
- New York Governor Eliot Spitzer, known as a crusader against white-collar crime, was pressured to resign after he confessed to hiring prostitutes
- North Korean leader Kim Jong-il pardoned two American journalists, who had been arrested and imprisoned for illegal entry earlier in the year, after former President Bill Clinton met with Kim in North Korea
- Notable books for the year included *The Appeal* by John Grisham; *The Audacity of Hope* by Barack Obama; *Diary of a Wimpy Kid: Rodrick Rules* by Jeff Kinney; *Eat, Pray, Love* by Elizabeth Gilbert; *The Last Lecture* by Randy Pausch and Jeffrey Zaslow; and *Three Cups of Tea* by Greg Mortenson
- Paleontologists announced the discovery of an Ardipithecus ramidus fossil skeleton, deeming it the oldest remains of a human ancestor yet found
- Physician George Tiller, known for giving late-term abortions, was murdered during a Sunday service at his church in Wichita, Kansas
- Pope Benedict XVI visited the United States

- President George W. Bush signed a $700 billion bill on October 3, 2008 to bail out banks and stem a financial crisis
- President Obama announced vehicle emissions and mileage requirements; under the new federal rules, vehicles would use 30 percent less fuel and emit one-third less carbon dioxide by 2016
- President Obama ordered the deployment of 17,000 additional US troops to Afghanistan
- President Obama overturned a Bush-era policy that limited federal funding for embryonic stem cell research
- President Obama signed executive orders to close the Guantanamo Bay detention camp within one year and to prohibit torture in terrorism interrogations
- President Obama signed the Matthew Shepard and James Byrd Jr. Hate Crimes Prevention Act, extending federal hate crime law to include crimes motivated by a victim's gender, sexual orientation, gender identity, or disability
- President Obama won the Nobel Peace Prize
- RAINN Day, the Rape, Abuse and Incest National Network's annual campaign to stop sexual assault, was held on college campuses
- Researchers decoded the genome of a cancer patient and found mutations in the cancer cells that may have either caused the cancer or helped it to progress
- Russian President Vladimir Putin was announced as *Time* magazine's 2007 Person of the Year
- Seth MacFarlane signed a $100 million deal with the Fox television network to keep *Family Guy* and *American Dad* on the air until 2012, making MacFarlane the world's highest paid television writer
- *Slumdog Millionaire*, a movie about a young man from the slums of Mumbai, India, won the Academy Award for the best film of 2008. Altogether, the film won eight Oscars, the most of any 2008 film
- Sonia Sotomayor became the third woman and the first Latina to serve on the US Supreme Court
- Television shows winning an Emmy award included NBC's *30 Rock*, Comedy Central's *The Daily Show with Jon Stewart*, and the first season of AMC's drama, *Mad Men*
- The British alternative rock band Coldplay won the Grammy award for Song of the Year for "Viva la Vida," a Spanish phrase that can mean either "long live life" or "live the life"
- The Detroit Lions finished the football season 0-16, the first time in National Football League history that a team went winless in a 16-game season
- The final book of the Harry Potter series, *Harry Potter and the Deathly Hallows*, was released and sold over 11 million copies in the first 24 hours, becoming the fastest-selling book in history
- The Florida Gators defeated the Oklahoma Sooners 24-14 in front of a record crowd of 78,468 to win the 2009 BCS National Championship Game
- The Great Recession officially ended in 2009
- The Icelandic government and banking system collapsed as a result of the home mortgage crisis in America
- The International Criminal Court (ICC) issued an arrest warrant for Sudanese President Omar Hassan al-Bashir for war crimes and crimes against humanity in Darfur
- The International Red Cross and Red Crescent Movement adopted the Red Crystal as a non-religious emblem for use in its overseas operations
- The Iraqi government took command of 54,000 Sunni fighters who turned against al-Qaeda in Mesopotamia in 2007 and began siding with the United States
- The Justice Department announced the largest health care fraud settlement in history, $2.3 billion, involving Pfizer
- The longest total solar eclipse of the twenty-first century, lasting up to six minutes and 38.8 seconds, occured over parts of Asia and the Pacific Ocean

- The New York Yankees defeated the Philadelphia Phillies to win their 27th World Championship
- The New York Yankees played their final home game at Yankee Stadium against the Baltimore Orioles on September 21
- The Picasso painting *Portrait of Suzanne Bloch*, and Candido Portinari's *O Lavrador de Café* were stolen from the São Paulo Museum of Art
- The Police reunited for a tour after 23 years to mark the thirtieth anniversary of the release of "Roxanne" and subsequently announce The Police Reunion Tour
- The Senate passed a bill to impose new regulations on the credit card industry, curbing some fees and interest hikes and requiring more transparent disclosure of account terms
- The Spice Girls announced their reunion at the O2 in London in a press conference televised worldwide
- The Supreme Court ruled five to four that the Constitution protected an individual's right to possess a gun, but insisted that the ruling "is not a right to keep and carry any weapon whatsoever in any manner whatsoever and for whatever purpose."
- The Taliban released a video of Polish geologist Piotr Stanczak, whom they had abducted a few months earlier, being beheaded
- The U.S. Supreme Court ruled five to four that prisoners at Guantánamo Bay, Cuba, had a right to challenge their detention in federal court
- Three men wearing ski masks stole artwork from the Zurich Museum, including a Cezanne, a Degas, a van Gogh, and a Monet, with a combined worth of $163 million
- Toshiba recalled its HD DVD video formatting, ending the format war between it and Sony's Blu-Ray Disc
- Track and field star Marion Jones surrendered the five Olympic medals she won in the 2000 Sydney Games after admitting to doping
- US Airways Flight 1549 lost power in both engines shortly after takeoff from LaGuardia, forcing pilots Chesley Sullenberger and Jeffrey Skiles to land the aircraft in the Hudson River; all 155 passengers and crew were rescued with no casualties
- When insurance giant AIG reported nearly $62 billion in losses during the fourth quarter of 2008, the US government gave it $30 billion more in aid in a new bailout

# SECTION THREE: ECONOMY OF THE TIMES

The 2000s saw the bursting of two major economic bubbles: the Dot-Com Bubble burst in 2000 and the Housing Bubble burst in 2007, leading to the Great Recession. These bursts were characterized by rising costs and interest rates and led to persistently high unemployment rates nationwide. Economy of the Times illustrates three economic elements: Consumer Expenditures, Annual Income of Standard Jobs, and Selected Prices. We highlighted three years for each category-2002, 2005, and 2008. The Value of a Dollar chart at the end of the section shows the change in the value of $1.00 yearly, from 1860 to 2016.

## Consumer Expenditures

The numbers below are per capita expenditures in the years 2002, 2005, 2008 for all employees nationwide.

| Category | 2002 | 2005 | 2008 |
|---|---|---|---|
| Alcoholic Beverages | $376.00 | $426.00 | $444.00 |
| Auto Maintenance & Repairs | $697.00 | $671.00 | $731.00 |
| Auto Usage | $1,741.00 | $1,943.00 | $2,015.00 |
| Clothing | $1,749.00 | $1,886.00 | $1,801.00 |
| Drugs, Prescription & Non-Prescription | $487.00 | $521.00 | $482.00 |
| Education | $752.00 | $940.00 | $1,046.00 |
| Entertainment | $2,079.00 | $2,388.00 | $2,835.00 |
| Food | $5,375.00 | $5,931.00 | $6,443.00 |
| Footwear | $313.00 | $320.00 | $314.00 |
| Furniture | $401.00 | $467.00 | $388.00 |
| Gas and Oil | $1,235.00 | $2,013.00 | $2,715.00 |
| Health Care | $2,350.00 | $2,664.00 | $2,976.00 |
| Health Insurance | $1,168.00 | $1,361.00 | $1,653.00 |
| Housing | $13,283.00 | $15,167.00 | $17,109.00 |
| Mortgage Interest | $2,962.00 | $3,317.00 | $3,826.00 |
| New Auto Purchase | $1,753.00 | $1,931.00 | $1,305.00 |
| Per Capita Consumption | $11,390.00 | $12,110.00 | $12,905.00 |
| Personal Services | $331.00 | $322.00 | $383.00 |
| Personal Care | $526.00 | $541.00 | $616.00 |
| Public Transportation | $389.00 | $448.00 | $513.00 |
| Telephone | $957.00 | $1,048.00 | $1,127.00 |
| Tobacco | $320.00 | $319.00 | $317.00 |
| Utilities | $2,684.00 | $3,183.00 | $3,649.00 |

# Annual Income of Standard Jobs

The numbers below are annual income for selected jobs across America in the years 2002, 2005, and 2008.

| Category | 2002 | 2005 | 2008 |
|---|---|---|---|
| Architects | $62,530.00 | $68,560.00 | $76,750.00 |
| Athletes and Sports Competitors | $92,540.00 | $71,900.00 | $79,460.00 |
| Automotive Service Technicians and Mechanics | $32,830.00 | $35,140.00 | $37,540.00 |
| Chief Executives | $134,960.00 | $139,810.00 | $160,440.00 |
| Clergy | $36,080.00 | $41,700.00 | $45,440.00 |
| Coaches and Scouts | $34,170.00 | $32,050.00 | $35,580.00 |
| Computer Programmers | $63,690.00 | $67,400.00 | $73,470.00 |
| Dentists | $133,350.00 | $133,680.00 | $154,270.00 |
| Electrical Engineers | $70,480.00 | $76,060.00 | $85,350.00 |
| Farmworkers | $18,560.00 | $19,890.00 | $22,920.00 |
| Fashion Designers | $60,160.00 | $67,370.00 | $71,400.00 |
| Fine Artists | $43,750.00 | $46,670.00 | $48,300.00 |
| Fire Fighters | $37,530.00 | $40,420.00 | $45,700.00 |
| Hairdressers, Hairstylists, and Cosmetologists | $22,110.00 | $23,640.00 | $26,660.00 |
| Lawyers | $105,890.00 | $110,520.00 | $124,750.00 |
| Librarians | $44,430.00 | $49,110.00 | $54,700.00 |
| Massage Therapists | $33,720.00 | $40,210.00 | $39,850.00 |
| Models | $25,280.00 | $27,570.00 | $30,160.00 |
| Police and Sheriff's Patrol Officers | $43,390.00 | $47,270.00 | $52,810.00 |
| Postal Service Clerks | $38,930.00 | $46,820.00 | $50,150.00 |
| Registered Nurses | $49,840.00 | $56,880.00 | $65,130.00 |
| Roofers | $33,020.00 | $33,570.00 | $37,430.00 |
| Secondary School Teachers | $46,010.00 | $49,400.00 | $54,390.00 |
| Substance Abuse and Behavioral Disorder Counselors | $31,860.00 | $34,800.00 | $39,670.00 |
| Telemarketers | $22,330.00 | $23,500.00 | $24,770.00 |
| Ushers, Lobby Attendants, and Ticket Takers | $16,490.00 | $16,740.00 | $19,100.00 |
| Waiters and Waitresses | $15,770.00 | $16,310.00 | $19,580.00 |
| Writers and Authors | $50,300.00 | $53,850.00 | $64,560.00 |

## Selected Prices

### 2002

Advil, 50. . . . . . . . . . . . . . . . . . . . . . . . . . . . . . . . . . . . . . . . . . . . . . . . . . . . .$3.99
Airfare, New York to Miami, U.S Airways . . . . . . . . . . . . . . . . . . . . . . . . . . . . .$257.00
Airplane, Hawker 400XP . . . . . . . . . . . . . . . . . . . . . . . . . . . . . . . . . . . . . . .$387,500.00
Apartment, Studio, New York City . . . . . . . . . . . . . . . . . . . . . . . . . . . . . . . .$1,300.00
Automobile, Toyota Prius Hybrid. . . . . . . . . . . . . . . . . . . . . . . . . . . . . . . . . .$20,810.00
Bath Towel . . . . . . . . . . . . . . . . . . . . . . . . . . . . . . . . . . . . . . . . . . . . . . . . .$24.00
Binoculars . . . . . . . . . . . . . . . . . . . . . . . . . . . . . . . . . . . . . . . . . . . . . . . . .$29.99
Blender, Oster . . . . . . . . . . . . . . . . . . . . . . . . . . . . . . . . . . . . . . . . . . . . . . .$80.00
Breadmaker . . . . . . . . . . . . . . . . . . . . . . . . . . . . . . . . . . . . . . . . . . . . . . . .$129.99
Cell Phone . . . . . . . . . . . . . . . . . . . . . . . . . . . . . . . . . . . . . . . . . . . . . . . . .$49.99
Champagne . . . . . . . . . . . . . . . . . . . . . . . . . . . . . . . . . . . . . . . . . . . . . . . .$15.99
Compass. . . . . . . . . . . . . . . . . . . . . . . . . . . . . . . . . . . . . . . . . . . . . . . . . . . .$7.99
Computer Desk . . . . . . . . . . . . . . . . . . . . . . . . . . . . . . . . . . . . . . . . . . . . . .$999.00
Computer, Apple MAC Performa. . . . . . . . . . . . . . . . . . . . . . . . . . . . . . . .$2,699.00
Cordless Drill, DeWalt. . . . . . . . . . . . . . . . . . . . . . . . . . . . . . . . . . . . . . . . .$129.00
Cutlery Set, 22-Piece . . . . . . . . . . . . . . . . . . . . . . . . . . . . . . . . . . . . . . . . . .$19.99
Day Pack, Eddie Bauer. . . . . . . . . . . . . . . . . . . . . . . . . . . . . . . . . . . . . . . . .$34.99
Diapers, Pampers, 40 . . . . . . . . . . . . . . . . . . . . . . . . . . . . . . . . . . . . . . . . . .$14.99
Digital Camera. . . . . . . . . . . . . . . . . . . . . . . . . . . . . . . . . . . . . . . . . . . . . . .$800.00
Digital Video Camera, Fisher. . . . . . . . . . . . . . . . . . . . . . . . . . . . . . . . . . . . .$899.99
Dishwasher, Maytag. . . . . . . . . . . . . . . . . . . . . . . . . . . . . . . . . . . . . . . . . . .$429.00
French Bread, Each . . . . . . . . . . . . . . . . . . . . . . . . . . . . . . . . . . . . . . . . . . . .$0.99
Frisbee . . . . . . . . . . . . . . . . . . . . . . . . . . . . . . . . . . . . . . . . . . . . . . . . . . . .$12.00
iTunes Album. . . . . . . . . . . . . . . . . . . . . . . . . . . . . . . . . . . . . . . . . . . . . . . .$16.99
Laser Eye Surgery, Lasik, per Eye. . . . . . . . . . . . . . . . . . . . . . . . . . . . . . . . . .$599.00
Man's Belt, Italian Leather . . . . . . . . . . . . . . . . . . . . . . . . . . . . . . . . . . . . . .$42.00
Movie Ticket . . . . . . . . . . . . . . . . . . . . . . . . . . . . . . . . . . . . . . . . . . . . . . . . .$7.50
Palm Pilot. . . . . . . . . . . . . . . . . . . . . . . . . . . . . . . . . . . . . . . . . . . . . . . . . .$369.00

Pepper Grinder . . . . . . . . . . . . . . . . . . . . . . . . . . . . . . . . . . . . . . . . . . . . . . . . . . . . . . . .$12.99
Pizza, Little Caesar's. . . . . . . . . . . . . . . . . . . . . . . . . . . . . . . . . . . . . . . . . . . . . . . . . . . . . .$12.95
Reclining Sofa. . . . . . . . . . . . . . . . . . . . . . . . . . . . . . . . . . . . . . . . . . . . . . . . . . . . . . . . .$1,199.00
Shotgun, 12-Gauge . . . . . . . . . . . . . . . . . . . . . . . . . . . . . . . . . . . . . . . . . . . . . . . . . . . . . .$189.50
Sleeping Bag . . . . . . . . . . . . . . . . . . . . . . . . . . . . . . . . . . . . . . . . . . . . . . . . . . . . . . . . . . . . .$29.96
Steak, Ribeye, per Pound. . . . . . . . . . . . . . . . . . . . . . . . . . . . . . . . . . . . . . . . . . . . . . . . . . .$7.99
Tape Measure . . . . . . . . . . . . . . . . . . . . . . . . . . . . . . . . . . . . . . . . . . . . . . . . . . . . . . . . . . . .$19.99
Treadmill . . . . . . . . . . . . . . . . . . . . . . . . . . . . . . . . . . . . . . . . . . . . . . . . . . . . . . . . . . . . . . . .$399.88
Treadmill, ProForm . . . . . . . . . . . . . . . . . . . . . . . . . . . . . . . . . . . . . . . . . . . . . . . . . . . . . .$599.99
Weedwacker, Craftsman . . . . . . . . . . . . . . . . . . . . . . . . . . . . . . . . . . . . . . . . . . . . . . . . . . .$29.99
Wine Bottle Holder . . . . . . . . . . . . . . . . . . . . . . . . . . . . . . . . . . . . . . . . . . . . . . . . . . . . . . .$150.00
Woman's Purse, Kenneth Cole . . . . . . . . . . . . . . . . . . . . . . . . . . . . . . . . . . . . . . . . . . . . . .$148.50

## 2005

Apple, Red Delicious . . . . . . . . . . . . . . . . . . . . . . . . . . . . . . . . . . . . . . . . . . . . . . . . . . . . . . .$0.97
Automobile, Nissan Sentra. . . . . . . . . . . . . . . . . . . . . . . . . . . . . . . . . . . . . . . . . . . . . .$17,800.00
Baby Formula, Powdered, Case. . . . . . . . . . . . . . . . . . . . . . . . . . . . . . . . . . . . . . . . . . . . . .$75.00
Bathroom Scale, Digital . . . . . . . . . . . . . . . . . . . . . . . . . . . . . . . . . . . . . . . . . . . . . . . . . . . . .$49.99
Beach Towel . . . . . . . . . . . . . . . . . . . . . . . . . . . . . . . . . . . . . . . . . . . . . . . . . . . . . . . . . . . . . . .$20.00
BlackBerry Phone . . . . . . . . . . . . . . . . . . . . . . . . . . . . . . . . . . . . . . . . . . . . . . . . . . . . . . . . . .$649.99
Bluetooth Headset . . . . . . . . . . . . . . . . . . . . . . . . . . . . . . . . . . . . . . . . . . . . . . . . . . . . . . . . . .$99.99
Camera Flip Phone, Telos. . . . . . . . . . . . . . . . . . . . . . . . . . . . . . . . . . . . . . . . . . . . . . . . . . .$99.00
College Tuition, Annual, St. John's College . . . . . . . . . . . . . . . . . . . . . . . . . . . . . . . .$30,570.00
Computer, Toshiba Laptop . . . . . . . . . . . . . . . . . . . . . . . . . . . . . . . . . . . . . . . . . . . . . . . . . .$499.99
Digital Camera, Olympus. . . . . . . . . . . . . . . . . . . . . . . . . . . . . . . . . . . . . . . . . . . . . . . . . . . .$800.00
Disposable Camera, Kodak . . . . . . . . . . . . . . . . . . . . . . . . . . . . . . . . . . . . . . . . . . . . . . . . . . .$7.99
Four Loko, Alcoholic Energy Drink . . . . . . . . . . . . . . . . . . . . . . . . . . . . . . . . . . . . . . . . . . .$2.99
Gas Grill, Kenmore . . . . . . . . . . . . . . . . . . . . . . . . . . . . . . . . . . . . . . . . . . . . . . . . . . . . . . . . .$134.99

Gas, Gallon . . . . . . . . . . . . . . . . . . . . . . . . . . . . . . . . . . . . . . . . . . . . . . . . . . . . . . . . . . . . . . . . . . . . . . . . . . . . . . . . . . . . . . . . . . . . . . . . . .$3.18
GPS Navigator, Garmin . . . . . . . . . . . . . . . . . . . . . . . . . . . . . . . . . . . . . . . . . . . . . . . . . . . . . . . . . . . . . . . . . . . . . .$219.99
Handbag, Jill Stuart . . . . . . . . . . . . . . . . . . . . . . . . . . . . . . . . . . . . . . . . . . . . . . . . . . . . . . . . . . . . . . . . . . . . . . . . . . .$175.00
Handheld Computer, Palm One . . . . . . . . . . . . . . . . . . . . . . . . . . . . . . . . . . . . . . . . . . . . . . . . . . . . . . . . . . . . . . . . . . .$99.99
Hunting License, Texas, Seasonal . . . . . . . . . . . . . . . . . . . . . . . . . . . . . . . . . . . . . . . . . . . . . . . . . . . . . . . . . . . . . . . . . .$8.00
iPod Nano, 2GB . . . . . . . . . . . . . . . . . . . . . . . . . . . . . . . . . . . . . . . . . . . . . . . . . . . . . . . . . . . . . . . . . . . . . . . . . . . . . . . .$199.00
La-Z-Boy Recliner . . . . . . . . . . . . . . . . . . . . . . . . . . . . . . . . . . . . . . . . . . . . . . . . . . . . . . . . . . . . . . . . . . . . . . . . . . . . . .$499.99
Marriage License, New York City . . . . . . . . . . . . . . . . . . . . . . . . . . . . . . . . . . . . . . . . . . . . . . . . . . . . . . . . . . . . . . . . . . .$35.00
Motorcycle, Harley-Davidson Sportster(r) . . . . . . . . . . . . . . . . . . . . . . . . . . . . . . . . . . . . . . . . . . . . . . . . . . . $6,495.00
Nintendo DS . . . . . . . . . . . . . . . . . . . . . . . . . . . . . . . . . . . . . . . . . . . . . . . . . . . . . . . . . . . . . . . . . . . . . . . . . . . . . . . . . . .$129.99
Pampers, 176 Count . . . . . . . . . . . . . . . . . . . . . . . . . . . . . . . . . . . . . . . . . . . . . . . . . . . . . . . . . . . . . . . . . . . . . . . . . . . . . .$48.99
Plastic Surgery, Liposuction . . . . . . . . . . . . . . . . . . . . . . . . . . . . . . . . . . . . . . . . . . . . . . . . . . . . . . . . . . . . . . . . .$2,578.00
Printer, HP . . . . . . . . . . . . . . . . . . . . . . . . . . . . . . . . . . . . . . . . . . . . . . . . . . . . . . . . . . . . . . . . . . . . . . . . . . . . . . . . . . . .$178.22
Private School, Annual, Hotchkiss . . . . . . . . . . . . . . . . . . . . . . . . . . . . . . . . . . . . . . . . . . . . . . . . . . . . . . . . . . . . .$24,500.00
Radio/CD Player, Bose . . . . . . . . . . . . . . . . . . . . . . . . . . . . . . . . . . . . . . . . . . . . . . . . . . . . . . . . . . . . . . . . . . . . . . . . .$499.00
Refrigerator/Freezer, Whirlpool . . . . . . . . . . . . . . . . . . . . . . . . . . . . . . . . . . . . . . . . . . . . . . . . . . . . . . . . . . . . . . . . .$471.72
Scanner, Canon . . . . . . . . . . . . . . . . . . . . . . . . . . . . . . . . . . . . . . . . . . . . . . . . . . . . . . . . . . . . . . . . . . . . . . . . . . . . . . . .$49.00
Sirius Satellite Radio . . . . . . . . . . . . . . . . . . . . . . . . . . . . . . . . . . . . . . . . . . . . . . . . . . . . . . . . . . . . . . . . . . . . . . . . . . .$100.00
Software, Microsoft Office 2003 . . . . . . . . . . . . . . . . . . . . . . . . . . . . . . . . . . . . . . . . . . . . . . . . . . . . . . . . . . . . . . . . .$349.99
Sole F80 Treadmill . . . . . . . . . . . . . . . . . . . . . . . . . . . . . . . . . . . . . . . . . . . . . . . . . . . . . . . . . . . . . . . . . . . . . . . . . .$1,999.99
Telephone, Motorola . . . . . . . . . . . . . . . . . . . . . . . . . . . . . . . . . . . . . . . . . . . . . . . . . . . . . . . . . . . . . . . . . . . . . . . . . . . .$79.95
Tires and Wheels . . . . . . . . . . . . . . . . . . . . . . . . . . . . . . . . . . . . . . . . . . . . . . . . . . . . . . . . . . . . . . . . . . . . . . . . . . . . . .$449.00
Tractor, John Deere 790 . . . . . . . . . . . . . . . . . . . . . . . . . . . . . . . . . . . . . . . . . . . . . . . . . . . . . . . . . . . . . . . . . . . .$12,448.00
Vacuum, Hoover WindTunnel . . . . . . . . . . . . . . . . . . . . . . . . . . . . . . . . . . . . . . . . . . . . . . . . . . . . . . . . . . . . . . . . . . .$129.99
Walkman, Sony . . . . . . . . . . . . . . . . . . . . . . . . . . . . . . . . . . . . . . . . . . . . . . . . . . . . . . . . . . . . . . . . . . . . . . . . . . . . . . . .$200.00
Xbox 360 . . . . . . . . . . . . . . . . . . . . . . . . . . . . . . . . . . . . . . . . . . . . . . . . . . . . . . . . . . . . . . . . . . . . . . . . . . . . . . . . . . . . .$399.00

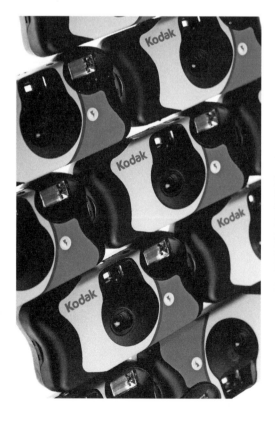

## 2008

| | |
|---|---|
| Backup Hard Drive | $44.71 |
| Book, The Picture of Dorian Gray | $13.50 |
| Bookcase | $119.00 |
| Bottled Water | $1.50 |
| Bubble Wrap Roll (Large Bubbles) 1/2" x 125' x 24" | $25.00 |
| Business Cards, 250 Count | $19.99 |
| CD, Billie Holiday, Lady in Autumn | $18.86 |
| Cell Phone, iPhone 8GB | $199.00 |
| Coffee Beans, Papua New Guinea, 5 Pounds | $48.88 |
| Coffee Grinder | $60.53 |
| Coffeemaker, Krups | $90.00 |
| Combination Router/Modem | $160.00 |
| Computer, MacBook Air | $1,799.00 |
| Concert Ticket, Allman Brothers | $159.00 |
| Converse Chuck Taylor All-Star Hi Tops | $44.99 |
| Digital Cordless Phone | $119.99 |
| Duraflame 00637 "Crackleflame" Fire Logs 5 Lb. | $49.99 |
| FLY on Time Lightweight Travel Alarm Clock | $7.99 |
| HP OfficeJet 7310 All-in-One Printer | $548.88 |
| Kindle 3G | $189.99 |
| Kindle Lighted Leather Cover | $59.99 |
| KitchenAid Blade Coffee Grinder | $27.99 |
| Leather Coin Purse | $7.95 |
| Lock Technology Tension Wrench | $11.99 |
| Logitech ClearChat Style Headset | $14.07 |
| Milk, Gallon | $3.06 |

Phone Service, Land Line, Monthly. . . . . . . . . . . . . . . . . . . . . . . . . . . . . . . . . . . . . . . . . . . . . . . . .$70.00
Phone, Camera Flip Phone . . . . . . . . . . . . . . . . . . . . . . . . . . . . . . . . . . . . . . . . . . . . . . . . . . . . . . . . .$99.00
Presto Hot Air Corn Popper  . . . . . . . . . . . . . . . . . . . . . . . . . . . . . . . . . . . . . . . . . . . . . . . . . . . . . . .$14.99
Printer Ink, Three-Pack . . . . . . . . . . . . . . . . . . . . . . . . . . . . . . . . . . . . . . . . . . . . . . . . . . . . . . . . . . . .$71.00
Rubbermaid Bucket. . . . . . . . . . . . . . . . . . . . . . . . . . . . . . . . . . . . . . . . . . . . . . . . . . . . . . . . . . . . . . . . .$5.09
Sofa . . . . . . . . . . . . . . . . . . . . . . . . . . . . . . . . . . . . . . . . . . . . . . . . . . . . . . . . . . . . . . . . . . . . . . . . . . .$899.00
Surfboard. . . . . . . . . . . . . . . . . . . . . . . . . . . . . . . . . . . . . . . . . . . . . . . . . . . . . . . . . . . . . . . . . . . . . . .$735.00
Tifosi Roubaix Sport Sunglasses, Iron Frame/Smoke. . . . . . . . . . . . . . . . . . . . . . . . . . . . . . . . .$49.09
Toaster, Krups . . . . . . . . . . . . . . . . . . . . . . . . . . . . . . . . . . . . . . . . . . . . . . . . . . . . . . . . . . . . . . . . . . .$90.96
Toolset, 137 Pieces . . . . . . . . . . . . . . . . . . . . . . . . . . . . . . . . . . . . . . . . . . . . . . . . . . . . . . . . . . . . . . .$99.99
Trimline Corded Telephone . . . . . . . . . . . . . . . . . . . . . . . . . . . . . . . . . . . . . . . . . . . . . . . . . . . . . . .$14.72
US Postage Stamp. . . . . . . . . . . . . . . . . . . . . . . . . . . . . . . . . . . . . . . . . . . . . . . . . . . . . . . . . . . . . . . . . .$0.44

# The Value of a Dollar, 1860-2016

### Composite Consumer Price Index; 1860=1

| Year | Amount | Year | Amount | Year | Amount | Year | Amount |
|------|--------|------|--------|------|--------|------|--------|
| 1860 | $1.00 | 1900 | $1.01 | 1940 | $1.69 | 1980 | $9.97 |
| 1861 | $1.06 | 1901 | $1.02 | 1941 | $1.77 | 1981 | $10.94 |
| 1862 | $1.22 | 1902 | $1.04 | 1942 | $1.96 | 1982 | $11.62 |
| 1863 | $1.52 | 1903 | $1.06 | 1943 | $2.08 | 1983 | $11.99 |
| 1864 | $1.89 | 1904 | $1.07 | 1944 | $2.12 | 1984 | $12.50 |
| 1865 | $1.96 | 1905 | $1.06 | 1945 | $2.17 | 1985 | $12.95 |
| 1866 | $1.92 | 1906 | $1.08 | 1946 | $2.35 | 1986 | $13.20 |
| 1867 | $1.78 | 1907 | $1.13 | 1947 | $2.68 | 1987 | $13.67 |
| 1868 | $1.71 | 1908 | $1.11 | 1948 | $2.90 | 1988 | $14.24 |
| 1869 | $1.64 | 1909 | $1.10 | 1949 | $2.87 | 1989 | $14.92 |
| 1870 | $1.58 | 1910 | $1.14 | 1950 | $2.90 | 1990 | $15.72 |
| 1871 | $1.47 | 1911 | $1.14 | 1951 | $3.13 | 1991 | $16.38 |
| 1872 | $1.47 | 1912 | $1.17 | 1952 | $3.19 | 1992 | $16.88 |
| 1873 | $1.45 | 1913 | $1.19 | 1953 | $3.22 | 1993 | $17.38 |
| 1874 | $1.37 | 1914 | $1.20 | 1954 | $3.24 | 1994 | $17.83 |
| 1875 | $1.32 | 1915 | $1.22 | 1955 | $3.23 | 1995 | $18.33 |
| 1876 | $1.29 | 1916 | $1.31 | 1956 | $3.28 | 1996 | $18.88 |
| 1877 | $1.26 | 1917 | $1.54 | 1957 | $3.39 | 1997 | $19.32 |
| 1878 | $1.20 | 1918 | $1.82 | 1958 | $3.48 | 1998 | $19.63 |
| 1879 | $1.20 | 1919 | $2.08 | 1959 | $3.50 | 1999 | $20.06 |
| 1880 | $1.23 | 1920 | $2.41 | 1960 | $3.56 | 2000 | $20.74 |
| 1881 | $1.23 | 1921 | $2.16 | 1961 | $3.60 | 2001 | $21.32 |
| 1882 | $1.23 | 1922 | $2.02 | 1962 | $3.64 | 2002 | $21.66 |
| 1883 | $1.22 | 1923 | $2.06 | 1963 | $3.68 | 2003 | $22.16 |
| 1884 | $1.18 | 1924 | $2.06 | 1964 | $3.73 | 2004 | $22.76 |
| 1885 | $1.17 | 1925 | $2.11 | 1965 | $3.79 | 2005 | $23.53 |
| 1886 | $1.13 | 1926 | $2.13 | 1966 | $3.90 | 2006 | $24.29 |
| 1887 | $1.14 | 1927 | $2.09 | 1967 | $4.02 | 2007 | $24.97 |
| 1888 | $1.14 | 1928 | $2.06 | 1968 | $4.19 | 2008 | $25.91 |
| 1889 | $1.11 | 1929 | $2.06 | 1969 | $4.42 | 2009 | $25.81 |
| 1890 | $1.09 | 1930 | $2.01 | 1970 | $4.67 | 2010 | $26.22 |
| 1891 | $1.09 | 1931 | $1.83 | 1971 | $4.88 | 2011 | $27.06 |
| 1892 | $1.09 | 1932 | $1.65 | 1972 | $5.03 | 2012 | $27.63 |
| 1893 | $1.08 | 1933 | $1.57 | 1973 | $5.35 | 2013 | $28.05 |
| 1894 | $1.04 | 1934 | $1.61 | 1974 | $5.93 | 2014 | $28.49 |
| 1895 | $1.01 | 1935 | $1.65 | 1975 | $6.47 | 2015 | $28.54 |
| 1896 | $1.01 | 1936 | $1.67 | 1976 | $6.85 | 2016 | $28.90 |
| 1897 | $1.00 | 1937 | $1.73 | 1977 | $7.30 | | |
| 1898 | $1.00 | 1938 | $1.70 | 1978 | $7.85 | | |
| 1899 | $1.00 | 1939 | $1.67 | 1979 | $8.74 | | |

# SECTION FOUR: ALL AROUND US

*This section offers a ringside seat to the issues and attitudes that were 2000s America. These 50 documents, listed in chronological order below, come from newspapers and magazines of the time. They show how America's changing ideas on education, politics, music, sports, immigration, and health were shaped.*

ॐॐॐॐॐॐ

**"How and Why America Voted,"**
**The Associated Press, *The Joplin Globe* (Joplin, Missouri),**
**November 8, 2000**

Voters were interviewed as they left the polls by Voter News Service, a consortium of the AP and the television networks. Early results were based on interviews with 8,364 voters as they left their polling places. The results have a margin of error of plus or minus 1.3 percentage points, higher for subgroups.

Here's a look at voter thinking in Tuesday's presidential election:

Who voted how:

- OVERALL: George W. Bush won solid majorities of men, whites and the wealthy. Al Gore was winning among women, blacks, Hispanics and those earning below $30,000.

- FAMILIES: Bush was leading among voters who were married, particularly those with children; Gore was doing better among those who were not married.

- RELIGION: Bush was leading among Protestants, and Gore was leading among Jews and those who did not identify with any religion. Bush and Gore were splitting the Catholic vote. The more likely a voter was to attend religious services, the more likely he or she was to vote for Bush.

- PARTY: Bush and Gore each had overwhelming leads among Republicans and Democrats, respectively. They were running even among independents, with a small chunk of independent voters favoring Ralph Nader.

Notable groups:

- LATE DECIDERS: Nearly one in five voters said they made up their minds in the last week, and Gore had a solid lead with this group. Bush and Gore were very close among voters who decided earlier.

- MODERATES: About half of voters considered themselves politically moderate, and they favored Gore. More voters called themselves conservative than liberal; conservatives heavily favored Bush and liberals heavily favored Gore.

- UNIONS: About one in four voters came from a union household, and a solid majority of them were supporting Gore.

Issues and qualities:

- MOST IMPORTANT ISSUES: Bush was winning among voters who cared most about world affairs and taxes. Gore was winning among voters who cared most about Medicare/prescription drugs. Social Security, health care, economy/jobs and education.

- MOST IMPORTANT QUALITIES: Bush was winning among voters who cared most about a candidate being honest, a strong leader and having good judgment in a crisis. Gore was winning those who cared most about someone who "cares about people like me," who has the right experience and who understands complex issues.

- BUSH-DRUNKEN ORIVING: About one in four voters said the revelation last week of Bush's 1976 arrest for drunken driving was very or somewhat important to their vote. Those voters went overwhelmingly for Gore.

- SMART ENOUGH?: Voters were more likely to believe that Gore had the knowledge needed to serve effectively as president than they were to think the same of Bush.

- HONEST ENOUGH?: More voters thought Bush was honest and trustworthy enough to be president than felt that way about Gore.

- RESERVATIONS: Four in 10 voters had reservations about their choice for president. Gore's supporters were more likely to have reservations about their vote than were Bush voters.

- INTERNATIONAL CRISIS: Voters were slightly more likely to believe that Gore would do a good job handling an international crisis.

- PRESCRIPTION DRUGS: Asked how the pvernment should help senior citizens pay or their prescriptions, a majority preferrea increased financing for Medicare, which Gore has proposed. Gore voters favored that plan overwhelmingly, while Bush voters more narrowly supported providing money for seniors to buy pnvate insurance coverage—Bush's proposal.

- MILITARY: Almost half of voters thought the U.S. military has become weaker since Clinton took office; more than one-third believed it stayed about the same. Bush's voters overwhelmingly said it was worse, while Gore supporters were divided on the question.

## Timeline of Dot-Com Bubble

1989    The World Wide Web began as a European Organization for Nuclear Research (CERN) project called "ENQUIRE." The purpose of ENQUIRE was to develop a system of interlocking/hyperlinked projects, which were similar to today's web sites, so that scientists could more easily find documents related to their research. While the ENQUIRE design was too rigid, it paved the way for the World Wide Web.

1990    The world's first web site and server went live.

1992    AOL, Inc. went public on the New York Stock Exchange (NYSE).

1994    The first online order was placed: a large pepperoni pizza, mushroom, and extra cheese from Pizza Hut.

1995    Craigslist, Inc., eBay Inc (NASDAQ:EBAY), Match.com, L.L.C., and MSN (owned by Microsoft Corporation (NASDAQ:MSFT)) were founded.

       Microsoft released "Windows 95," which included the first version of the Internet browser "Internet Explorer."

1997    The Taxpayer Relief Act of 1997 reduced several federal taxes in the United States.

1998    eBay went public on September 24 at $18.00 per share, but quickly climbed to $53.50 before closing at $47.35. That's a one-day gain of 163%.

2000    Super Bowl XXXIV Features Seventeen Dot-Com Companies

       On March 10, the NASDAQ hit a peak of 5132.52, a two-year increase of 226% and a four-year gain of approximately 390%.

On March 13, the NASDAQ opened 4.5% lower. Analysts saw it as a simple market correction.

On March 24, the S&P 500 topped out at 1553.51.

In December, eBay shares hit a low of $2.81. But, because of its unique platform and huge footprint, eBay continued to grow in popularity.

NASDAQ ended 2000 at 2470.52, a 52% drop from the March 2000 high of 5132.52.

Pets.com became the first listed US dot.com to collapse. Other notable failures that year included Garden.com and Furniture.com.

**2001**  In the fourth quarter of 2000, eToys reported a loss of $74.5 million and announced that it only has enough capital to last until March 31, 2001. By February 2001, the eToys stock price plunged to $0.09 per share. Just one month later, the company's shares were worthless. In less than three years, eToys exhausted $800.0 million in cash, went public, filed for bankruptcy, and shut its doors.

Monthly statistics for US dot.com lay-offs peak at 17,554 in April.

**2002**  On October 9, the NASDAQ closed at 1114.14, having lost 78% of its value over its March 2000 peak.

Also on October 9, Priceline's share price hit an all-time low of $6.60. Its share price was feeling pressure from both the bursting dotcom bubble and the September 11, 2001 terrorist attacks, which decimated the entire travel industry.

**2003**  A refocused Amazon reported its first annual profit of $35.3 million, compared to a 2002 loss of $149.1 million.

The Jobs and Growth Tax Relief Reconciliation Act of 2003 was signed into law by President George W. Bush on May 28, 2003. Among other provisions, the act accelerated certain tax changes passed in the Economic Growth and Tax Relief Reconciliation Act of 2001, increased the exemption amount for the individual Alternative Minimum Tax, and lowered taxes of income from dividends and capital gains.

&#8667;&#8667;&#8667;&#8667;&#8667;&#8667;&#8667;

### "Terrorists Hijack 4 Airliners; Destroy World Trade Center; Hit Pentagon; Hundreds Dead,"
### Michael Grunwald, *The Washington Post*, September 12, 2001

Rescuers fought through tons of debris in quest of victims at the Pentagon last night after terrorists seized an airliner outbound from Dulles International Airport and plunged it into the heart of American military power, killing an estimated several hundred people.

Hampered by fires that still raged as evening fell, emergency teams had carried out only six bodies, but they were preparing to remove many more, and rescuers were using dogs and listening devices to search for people they believed might be trapped alive.

Precise figures were hard to come by because portions of the building were under construction, and many of the military and civilian personnel had been temporarily relocated, according to Arlington Fire Chief Edward P. Plaugher.

Coming less than an hour after two hijacked passenger jets slammed into the twin towers of New York's World Trade Center, the assault on the Pentagon began an unprecedented day of office and school closings, panicked phone calls, wild rumors and extraordinary security in the Washington area.

Last night, downtown streets were largely deserted as D.C. National Guard units joined police in patrolling the city.

D.C. Mayor Anthony A. Williams (D), Maryland Gov. Parris N. Glendening (D) and Virginia Gov. James S. Gilmore III (R) declared states of emergency that broadened their power to govern without legislative authority.

Most of the region's school systems will be closed today, although President Bush announced that the federal government would reopen, after having shut down within an hour of yesterday's Pentagon attack.

At a late-evening news conference, D.C. Police Chief Charles H. Ramsey said that the attacks here and in New York would forever change security operations in Washington, and that there was no longer such a thing as "business as usual" here.

Originally headed for Los Angeles, the American Airlines Boeing 757—carrying 64 people and loaded with 30,000 pounds of fuel for the long flight to the West Coast—smashed into the five-story Pentagon's west facade about 9:40 a.m. after skimming above Arlington at breakneck speed.

Cmdr. Thomas P. Van Leunen, Jr., director of the navy's media operations, said the explosion was "similar to shooting a five-inch gun, only a little bit longer and louder."

The impact rocked the immense building, gouging a wedge deep into its interior, collapsing floors and touching off fires. Stunned, often disheveled employees stumbled from their offices and into the acrid smoke of what had been a perfect late-summer morning.

"People were yelling, 'Evacuate! Evacuate!' And we found ourselves on the lawn looking back on our building," Air Force Lt. Col. Marc Abshire said. "It was very much a surrealistic sort of experience. It was just definitely not right to see smoke coming out of the Pentagon."

At least 1,000 law enforcement officers, firefighters and Pentagon employees searched for victims and evidence, even as flames shot out of the building. Military helicopters and fighter aircraft prowled the skies, at times frightening those below, who believed another air assault might be under way.

Officials said most of the damage was in the E Ring, inflicted by an aircraft that disintegrated on impact. Parts of the wings were reportedly found outside the building.

The region's emergency medical system prepared for massive casualties, but by late afternoon, hospittals in Northern Virginia and the District had been able to cope easily with the approximately 70 brought to them. The busiest by far was Virginia Hospital Center-Arlington, where 36 patients were taken. Inova Alexandria Hospital treated 18, and 13 went to Washington Hospital Center, which has the region's only advanced burn-care center. Many patients were later released.

As rescue workers streamed toward the Pentagon, the federal government closed its offices in the area, telling its 260,000 local workers they were free to leave, and the D.C. government and many businesses followed suit. That unloosed an army of homebound drivers upon downtown's streets, causing temporary paralysis that, once cleared, was followed by the kind of emptiness and silence usually limited to snowstorms.

In the District, hundreds of members of the National Guard reported for duty in camouflage and took an oath to defend District streets. They patrolled in Humvees.

Cell phone networks stopped working as their patrons all tried to check on loved ones at once. Some school systems decided to send children home early, but even before they could be dismissed, parents showed up in droves to pick up their youngsters.

Historian David McCullough, author of the bestselling book on President John Adams, was staying at the Hay-Adams Hotel downtown, where he climbed to a high point in the building to view the smoke rising across the Potomac River at the Pentagon.

"This is going to be a dividing point in history," said McCullough, who was turned away when he went to George Washington University Hospital to try to give blood. "If they still teach history 100 years from now, children will still be reading about this day," he said, adding, "We haven't seen such destruction on our own soil since the Civil War."

### "Angry Americans Flock to Enlistment Centers,"
### *Doylestown Intelligencer* (Pennsylvania), September 13, 2001

Josh Gipe had been considering joining the Army to pay for college. The two recent attacks against the very symbols of American power steeled his resolve.

He went straight to an Army office Wednesday morning, filling out paperwork and answering recruiters' questions. The 24-year-old hopes to be in basic training in two weeks.

"As an American, I feel like I owe something to my country," Gipe said. "Our freedom has been put in jeopardy, and I want to be someone who helps defend that."

Across the country, military recruitment offices reported a jump in visitors and phone calls in the hours of the New York and Washington attacks. Recruiters heard from angry teenagers as well as sober veterans just calling to know how they could help.

An Army major in Florida called it a "patriotic swell" among Americans whose first reaction, after the horror wore off, was an urge to enlist to defend their country.

In Bakersfield, California, the Army recruitment office took dozens of calls and walk-ins Tuesday and Wednesday three to four times the normal activity, station commander William K. Hurley said.

### "Some Skimp on Tinsel as Others Splurge,"
### Melinda Ligos, *The New York Times*, December 5, 2001

This year, many managers are cutting back or canceling office parties, but Alfred Portale is not one of them.

Mr. Portale, chef and co-owner of Gotham Bar and Grill in New York, plans to close his Greenwich Village restaurant on Super Bowl Sunday for a post-holiday gathering that will include more than 400 employees and their family members.

Santa will be there. As will Winnie-the-Pooh, some characters from *Toy Story*, a host of Pac-Man and airhockey machines, five large-screen televisions, gift bags for the children, and an open bar and lavish spread for the adults. The annual event is the only time that many employees, from dishwashers to food servers, feel comfortable coming into the restaurant as patrons, Mr. Portale says.

"The show must go on," he said, adding that he "wouldn't dream in a million years" of abandoning a tradition he began 16 years ago.

Around half of all companies are pooh-poohing the idea of skimping on holiday gatherings this year. A survey last month by Battalia Winston International, an executive search firm, found companies split on the issue. Of those changing their plans, 82 percent said their holiday parties would be smaller or less expensive than in years past, and the remaining 18 percent will have no parties. Many gave the weak economy and the war on terrorism as rationales.

But for Mr. Portale and others like him, it is more important than ever to hold holiday parties, both to bolster employees' spirits and to defy the terrorists.

"We have all been through a lot of bad stuff this year," he said. "We need this party more now than we ever have before." The event will set him back more than $8,000, not counting the thousands in lost revenue from closing the restaurant for the day.

Michael Silver, president of Equis, a commercial real estate firm in Chicago, shares that sentiment. Not only is the Equis Chicago branch holding its regular holiday dinner at one of the city's most expensive restaurants, Naha, but for the first time it is inviting its 150 employees to bring along spouses. The five-hour party will include live entertainment and top-shelf liquor, even though profits are down 8 percent.

"I don't care if the economy's bad," Mr. Silver said. "I want our employees to feel a sense of community right about now." He derided managers who have canceled holiday parties this year as Scrooges.

Companies going ahead with elaborate celebrations are often tapping into nationalism awakened by Sept. 11.

"We're seeing a huge pro-America sentiment in the corporate parties we're planning," said Carey Smolensky, chief executive of Carey Smolensky Productions, an event-planning and promotions company in Wheeling, Ill. Mr. Smolensky said he had had an "unusually high number of requests" for items like flag pins and Christmas trees painted red, white and blue. At a party for a jewelry company, he had a large group of vocalists light candles and sing "God Bless America," he said.

"Everyone's looking not just to party, but to send employees a message that's more poignant and heartfelt," he said.

The HomeBanc Mortgage Corporation in Atlanta briefly considered canceling its festivities but decided to go ahead to bolster employee morale. The party in Atlanta, held on Monday, had 1,800 guests. HomeBanc also scheduled parties in late November and early December in Tampa, Orlando, Palm Beach, and Davie, Fla., in some cases expanding the guest lists by more than 40 percent from last year, according to Andrea Back, vice president for marketing.

"We have an awful lot to celebrate this year," Ms. Back said, noting that the company surpassed $4 billion in sales for the first time. "And many of our competitors are canceling their events, so this is our time to really shine." The theme was "home for the holidays," she said, and 18-wheeler trucks were commissioned to ship components of a life-size house to each event to serve as décor. Live bands played underneath a fake fireplace, and enormous windows and columns lined each ballroom.

In between feasting on chocolate fondue and made-to-order pasta, guests in floor-length gowns and tuxedos were asked to contribute to Habitat for Humanity, one charity the company supports. "Even though the events are huge, they're very touchy-feely this year," Ms. Back said.

## "The Manhunt,"
### Josh Tyrangiel, *Time Magazine*, December 24, 2001

The 12 bearded soldiers making their way up a pass in the White Mountains of Tora Bora were decked in flattopped Afghan caps and flowing *shalwar kameezes*. From a distance, only one detail gave them away as Americans. Afghan alliance fighters—dedicated but largely untrained—walk upright, making themselves easy targets for enemy fire. The Americans were shimmying up the hill on their bellies.

Late last week, American special operations forces quietly made their way to Tora Bora, to the very front of the front lines. The dozen U.S. soldiers used a translator to coordinate with an Afghan commander. To the Afghan fighters at their side, the Americans made it clear they were on a search-and-destroy mission. "We and the Americans had the same goal," said Khawri, an Afghan who was shoulder-to-shoulder with U.S. troops. "To kill all the al-Qaeda people." By Sunday, the Afghans were claiming victory, though the U.S. remained guarded.

The war in Afghanistan began nine weeks ago on a battlefield the size of Texas, and it may end in a high, narrow valley smaller than the city of Austin. After weeks of playing Where's Osama?, military officials believe they have overheard bin

Laden on handheld radios in the White Mountains, giving orders to his dwindling al-Qaeda forces. Afghan fighters said they had killed 200 and routed al-Qaeda, but the U.S. said too many nooks had yet to be searched. If bin Laden is in Tora Bora, he and his soldiers are trapped in a box: Snow-covered peaks loom on two sides, Afghan and American soldiers await on a third, and Pakistani border patrols stand guard on the fourth.

The cornered fighters have little room to maneuver. With no enemy antiaircraft fire, U.S. spy planes circle the sky, daring al-Qaeda fighters to step out of their caves and become glowing infrared targets. Few have done so. Bin Laden has resorted to giving orders on shortwave radio, U.S. authorities suggest, because there's no one else left to do so.

But inevitability almost slipped away last week. The three Afghan warlords in control of alliance forces began the week with a successful assault on the Milawa Valley, the lone entrance to Tora Bora from the north. Al-Qaeda soldiers fled quickly, though they did manage to kill a few alliance troops. Having taken the territory, the warlords committed a major tactical error: They withdrew from the valley. When alliance forces returned the next day, they were greeted by three al-Qaeda fighters armed with machine guns who opened fire from 200 meters. No alliance soldiers were killed, but the morning was spent fighting a battle for territory that had already been won.

The follies had only just begun. As al-Qaeda fighters scampered up the mountains in search of a safe haven, one of the warlords, Haji Zaman, agreed to a ceasefire without bothering to consult the other two Afghan commanders or the U.S. Zaman claims the Arab-speaking fighters reached him via wireless and offered to surrender on the condition that they be turned over to the United Nations. "They said they had to get in contact with each other and would surrender group by group," Zaman says. He then announced the ceasefire, halted his troops' advance and gave the opposition until 8 a.m. to give themselves up.

Zaman's fellow Afghan commanders were outraged, while U.S. officials appeared shocked. The Americans did not object to an al-Qaeda surrender, but any surrender had to be unconditional. As for the ceasefire, Air Force General Richard Myers,

the Chairman of the Joint Chiefs of Staff, simply ignored it. "Just for the record," said Myers, "our military mission remains to destroy the al-Qaeda and the Taliban networks. So our operation from the air and the ground will continue until our mission is accomplished."

The U.S. ignored the ceasefire and bombed relentlessly. Sure enough, the next day, the surrendering al-Qaeda troops had vanished. Zaman's aides insist that they were probably "confused" when the U.S. broke the ceasefire and scampered back into their holes. But other Afghan leaders thought Zaman had been duped. "It was a trick," said Haji Zahir, one of the warlords commanding Afghan troops in Tora Bora. "They were buying time."

The arrival of Western troops at the front lines had the added advantage of giving the Afghan fighters new resolve. During previous weeks, the Afghans withdrew from their positions during the day in time to break their Ramadan fasts at dusk. With the end—and the Americans—in sight, they held their positions.

From the start of the war, the U.S. has relied heavily on Afghan ground forces rather than deploy a sizable contingent of American troops. But the ceasefire screw-up was a reminder that the Afghans might be useful proxies for some jobs, but were perhaps not quite professional enough to finish this one. On Sunday, Zaman managed to get back into the U.S.'s good graces—and back into the race for the $25 million bounty on bin Laden's head—as he ferried Western commandos to the front. By then, U.S. warplanes were pounding al-Qaeda positions with hundreds of bombs and missiles, and more than 100 U.S. and British specialops soldiers had moved in, signaling to the Afghans and al-Qaeda that the time for mistakes was over.

"Al-Qaeda is finished," crowed Afghan commander Hazrat Ali from his battlefield perch below the caves on Friday afternoon. "They are surrounded." American military leaders were more cautious. "'Surrounded' probably is not a terribly good word," said General Tommy R. Franks, the regional commander of American forces. "But the view of the opposition leaders on the ground is that this al-Qaeda force is contained in that area."

### "Green Berets up Close,"
### Donatella Lorch, *Newsweek*, January 14, 2002

They landed in darkness on an early November night, deep in the mountains of northern Afghanistan. For six hours, they'd hunkered down in the freezing hold of the transport helicopter, tossed by heavy winds, before setting down 6,000 feet above sea level. Shouldering 200-pound packs stuffed with weapons, ammunition and communications gear, the U.S. Army's 1st Battalion 5th Special Forces A-Team piled out of the chopper and onto the snowy turf. The helicopter retreated, a roar of roto wash kicking dirt and ice into the men's faces. Then, silence. For weeks, the 13-man Green Beret team had trained and studied and obsessed about their mission. They were a tight-knit group, each man trusting the others with his life. Yet it wasn't until the chopper faded from view and the vastness of the landscape came into focus that they realized how far from home they were, and how alone: 90 miles behind enemy lines, in the heart of Taliban territory.

To the men, standing in the blackness that night, the mission ahead seemed almost impossible. The team was to find and win the trust of an elusive Northern Alliance commander they knew virtually nothing about and whose language they did not speak, supply his ragtag team of fighters and then, with his help, storm a key Taliban stronghold, the northern city of Mazar-e Sharif. After wrestling control from the enemy, they were to restore order and help local leaders begin rebuilding the ravaged city. Along the way, they were to sneak up on armed Taliban camps and caves, helping to laser-guide U.S. bombers to their targets.

In the harrowing, heroic days that followed, they did just that. The fall of Mazar-e Sharif turned out to be a critical moment in the Afghan war, setting off a domino effect that quickly led to the fall of the major cities of Kabul and Qandahar, and the collapse of Taliban rule. It also provided a dramatic victory for the élite Special Forces, whose daring missions in the past had sometimes gone disastrously wrong.

༙ঌ঺ঌ঺ঌ঺ঌ঺

### "Inside the Battle of Shah-i-Kot, Where the Enemy Has Nothing to Lose and U.S. Soldiers Had to Fight for Their Lives," Michael Elliott, *Time Magazine*, March 18, 2002

In the TV commercials, they call it "An army of One," and the phrase is intended to send a message: In the U.S. armed forces, every person counts. If you take a round, your buddies will come and get you. "The Ranger creed is that you do not leave a fallen comrade on the field of battle," says David Anderson, of Jacksonville, Fla., a former Ranger whose son, Marc Anthony Anderson, followed him into the army. "I really believed in what the creed says, and Marc did. He said, 'If something happens to me, don't worry, because you'll have a body.'"

Last week Marc's body, along with those of seven other American soldiers, was flown from Afghanistan to Ramstein Air Force Base in Germany before coming home for those proud, sad ceremonies that mark the death of young men in battle. The army had once more been asked to live up to the promise it makes to those who serve. "We don't leave Americans behind," says Brigadier General Jon Rosa, Jr., deputy director of operations for the Joint Chiefs of Staff. Last week, that word was kept. But the price for doing so was high.

For weeks, U.S. forces had been watching as Taliban and al-Qaeda fighters gathered south of Kabul. Code-named Operation Anaconda, the battle plan aimed at this force was a hammer-and-anvil strategy. Friendly Afghans, assisted by U.S. special forces, would flush the enemy from the north and northwest toward three exits of the Shah-i-Kot valley, where American troops waited. To the south, battle positions Heather and Ginger were divided by a hill christened the Whale, while to the east, battle position Eve guarded escape routes over the high mountains to Pakistan. But after two days of fierce combat, the al-Qaeda and Taliban fighters were still in place; one American had already been killed.

Before dawn on Monday, two huge MH-47 Chinooks, double-headed flying beasts like something out of Tolkein, chugged through the frigid air. They were on their way from Bagram Air Base, north of Kabul, to Shah-i-Kot and the most intense battle so far of the Afghan war. A force that would eventually grow to more than 1,000 Americans, drawn mainly from the 10th Mountain and 101st Airborne divisions, together with Afghan militias and about 200 special forces from allied nations, was engaged with perhaps 1,000 al-Qaeda and Taliban fighters—four times as many enemy men as the U.S. had expected. The battlefield spread over 70 square miles, at altitudes that ranged from 8,000 to 12,000 feet and temperatures that dipped at night to 15 degrees. The Chinooks headed for Ginger, at the southeast corner of the valley, where American forces had met intense opposition two days before. As the choppers prepared to set down, they came under heavy fire from small-arms and rocketpropelled grenades, one of which bounced, without exploding, off the armor of a Chinook. In the same bird, a hydraulic line was cut, and the pilots radioed back to Bagram that continuing with the mission would be suicide. Major General Frank (Buster) Hagenbeck, the force commander, agreed, and the choppers veered away to the north, climbing steeply. They found a place to set down and did a head count. On the damaged Chinook, one man was missing. They counted again. Navy SEAL Neil Roberts, the rear gunner who had been returning fire from the open back hatch, was no longer with his team. Roberts had apparently been jolted out when the chopper banked hard to the north.

The Rangers radioed Bagram for permission to go after their man. Hagenbeck agreed, and the undamaged Chinook dropped off six commandos to search for Roberts; then both helicopters returned to base. Unmanned surveillance aircraft searched for the missing man and found him moving across the valley. Images beamed from the drones to video monitors at Bagram showed three men approaching Roberts. They were at first thought to be friendly. Then Roberts was seen trying to flee. About three hours after the first incident, two more

Chinooks set off from Bagram on a dual mission: to rescue Roberts and to insert more troops at Ginger. One of the choppers took heavy machine-gun fire. It shuddered and spiraled toward the ground but managed to crash-land less than a mile from the place the first pair had come under attack. As the troops clambered out of the wrecked MH-47, they were ambushed. Hagenbeck ordered AC-130 gunships to the battle to provide close air support, but the al-Qaeda barrage was so intense that U.S. troops couldn't be lifted out during daylight. Fighting continued throughout the day, as the first team searching for Roberts fought its way to the downed Chinook. It was not until midnight that the last U.S. soldier was evacuated. The choppers also carried 11 wounded and the bodies of seven Americans—Roberts and six of his would-be rescuers. Roberts had died at the hands of his three pursuers.

Soldiers know the nature of their business. But death in war is no less painful to those left behind just because it goes with the mission. Roberts, 32, from a suburb of Sacramento, Calif., left a wife and two-year-old daughter. "He was a great guy," said his sister-in-law Denise Roberts. "His mother said at least she knew he died doing what he loved to do." Valerie Chapman, widow of Air Force Technical Sergeant John Chapman, 36, who lived in Fayetteville, N.C., had the same thought. "You have to love it to do what they do," she said of her husband, who died with Anderson and four others in the firefight after the Chinook crash-landed. "And he loved his job."

## Cost of Past Wars in 2002 Dollars

Revolutionary War, 1775-83 . . . . . . . . . . . . . 1.7 million
War of 1812, 1812-15 . . . . . . . . . . . . . . . . 975 million
Mexican War, 1846-48 . . . . . . . . . . . . . . . . 1.5 billion
Civil War, 1861-65 . . . . . . . . . . . . . . (Union) 38 billion
. . . . . . . . . . . . . . . . . . . . (Confederacy) 23.8 billion
Spanish-American War, 1898 . . . . . . . . . . . . 8.8 billion
World War I, 1917-18 . . . . . . . . . . . . . . . 564.5 billion
World War II, 1941-45 . . . . . . . . . . . . . . . . 4.6 trillion
Korean War, 1950-53 . . . . . . . . . . . . . . . 391.8 billion
Vietnam War, 1964-73 . . . . . . . . . . . . . . . . 840 billion
Gulf War, 1990-91 . . . . . . . . . . . . . . . . . . . 8.6 billion

## "End of Noise Is Music to Students' Ears,"
### *Chicago Daily Herald*, **April 8, 2002**

After months of living in a construction zone, you learn to adjust to your surroundings. And if you're like Leslie High School band conductor Steve Green, you incorporate the distractions into your daily routine. "That bulldozer outside is a little flat," Green told the class of freshmen on Friday.

Despite that bulldozer, members of the Music Department last week experienced the first physical proof that all the disruption of the school's $15.1 million renovation project wasn't in vain. The students finally got to rehearse in their recently completed band room.

The space has well-proportioned, lofty and has windows—a significant difference from the cramped room students and teachers were accustomed to. "When we did our sectionals for grading, we had to use a stage of the lunchroom," Green said. "We were teaching in the storeroom." Now the horn section no longer bumps into the woodwinds, and percussionists have room to swing a cymbal. Green and teacher Scott Gumina have separate offices instead of trying to squeeze into one closet-sized room.

"Overall, the increase in square footage and number of music rooms lets us have flexibility with our scheduling," Green said. Teachers hope the increased space will eventually clear the way for some new courses and start another band or chorus.

The band room is the first section to be completed as part of a 15-month renovation project to bring the school, which was built in 1974, into the new century.

৵৵৵৵৵৵৵৵

### "New Housing Development Could Tighten,"
### C. R. Ely Bond, *Cedar Rapids Gazette*, October 24, 2002

In something for pioneering venture, housing development in far southern Cedar Rapids is coming to a spot where city housing has never been—C Street, southwest of Hwy. 30 on Ely Road....

Local realtor Scott Olsen says the Wheatland Park addition, being planned by High Development Corp. of Cedar Rapids, is the start of the landscape change.

In 20 years, houses will stretch from this new development all the way to Ely, Olson predicted....

Housing development plans are slated for 50 acres recently annexed into the city.

The "mixed-use" development calls for a neighborhood of 67 single-family homes in the $150,000-$200,000 price range.

Closer to C Street will be a dozen 12-unit luxury apartment buildings and 80 townhouses, to be priced from the low 90,000s to about $110,000.

Darryl High, president of the development company told the City Planning Commission this week that he intends to create a place with "a real neighborhood feel."

High said the development would be a mix of "high class and affordability."

৵৵৵৵৵৵৵৵

### "Searching for New Thrills in Old Wheels, Investors Wary of
### Stocks are Taking the Collectible Car Market Out for a Spin,"
### Carol Buia, *Time Magazine*, March December 9, 2002

Americans who are fed up with the stock market's volatility are turning to an investment seeming to promise a smoother ride: collectible cars. According to a study by the automobile auction company Barrett-Jackson, the billion-dollar collectible car industry is growing at a 10 percent clip annually. "The baby boomers are fueling this long-term trend," explains Greg Jackson, president of Barrett-Jackson. "They want to own the cars of their youth." Coveted wheels include '50s sports cars like the Corvette and muscle cars in the late '60s and early '70s like the Pontiac Ram Air GTO.

As with most investments, there is no guarantee that your vintage find will appreciate five years from now. That's why experts recommend buying the car you've always wanted to drive. Hey, better to cruise in that '59 Cadillac Eldorado today than to sit on yesterday's Enron shares.

ᘒᘓᘒᘓᘒᘓᘒᘓ

### "Economic Hope Fades,"
### *Madison Capital Times*, February 26, 2003

Wisconsin residents are slightly less optimistic about state and local economies in the year ahead than they were five months ago, according to the latest Badger Poll. Their views on the direction of the national economy remain stable from last month but are still less optimistic than they were in September, the Poll also found.

The survey of 500 state residents, conducted February 11-19, found that 42 percent believe the national economy will stay "about the same" over the next nine months. A third of those polled said they expect the national economy to get better, while 23 percent said it would get worse.

These figures represent a substantial change from the first Badger Poll in March 2000, when 56 percent of those polled said the economy would get better and 12 percent said it would get worse.

At the state level, 47 percent said Wisconsin's economy will stay about the same in the coming year, roughly equivalent to 49 percent who gave the same answer last September. There was no change in the percentage who said the economy would get better, but 28 percent of those who said it will get worse rose from 18 percent to 23 percent.

This was a similar decline in optimism at the local level, said Poll director G. Donald Ferree, Jr. The percentage of those who expected the economy to get worse rose from 18 percent in September to 21 percent this month.

Ferree has noted a sharp difference in optimism between men and women. Men were more likely to be optimistic about the national economy and women less so. Republicans were also more likely to be optimistic about the economy than Democrats and Independents.

ᘒᘓᘒᘓᘒᘓᘒᘓ

### "Commercial Property Fallout From War; Hotel Use Declines;
### Office Sector Faces Uncertainty,"
### John Holuha, *The New York Times*, March 30, 2003

The war in Iraq is hurting the hotel industry in the New York metropolitan region, as airlines scale back their flight schedules and the threat of terrorist attacks makes people reluctant to visit the region, real estate executives say.

The effect on the office leasing and investment sales markets is not as easy to measure. Some executives say uncertainty about the conflict's duration and economic effects is causing companies to put off making decisions to buy or lease. Others, though, say it is a good time for bargain shopping, particularly for tenants who want to lock in a good deal.

Bookings at hotels started to drop even before the war broke out, said Thomas P. McConnell, senior managing director of the hotel group at Insignia/ESG, the brokerage and services company.

"The impact on travel took hold at the beginning of the year," he said, with hotel revenues down 5 to 10 percent from last year's level. "A lot of people blamed it on the weather, but a lot of travel was curtailed in anticipation of the war."

Hotels, he noted, are the most vulnerable of real estate sectors to shifts in public moods, because rooms are rented on a night-to-night basis. "Lodging is the most likely to be affected," Mr. McConnell said. "It is the first to go up and the first to go down."

Nicholas Buss, vice president of research for PNC Real Estate Finance Group, said: "The hotel sector is most at risk. It has been reeling since 9/11, and if travel continues to decline, we could see some distressed hotel owners."

The war is likely to delay, but probably not prevent, an expected upturn in occupancy rates and revenues, said Daniel H. Lesser, managing director of the hospitality industry group at Cushman & Wakefield, another major brokerage and services company. He said hotels have adjusted their marketing strategies to appeal to domestic travelers rather than the international tourists that previously sustained the local industry.

"The fly-to markets are softer than the drive-to markets, so hotels are reorienting toward the drive-to markets," he said. "In New York, hotels are marketing to people who live within 500 miles of the city, rather than the international travelers, who are not coming anyway."

He said the industry has been depressed for so long that a cyclical recovery can be expected. "It is not a matter of if, but when," he said. But, he conceded, the war could push back the time of the recovery.

"If we have a quick war and do not experience a terrorist attack, there will not be much impact on the industry in New York," he said, noting that outside investors are still interested in buying hotels in the city.

Nationally, Pricewaterhouse Coopers, the accounting and consulting company, said a brief war—defined as one lasting 30 to 45 days—would depress hotel revenues during the first half of this year, with normal growth resuming in the second half. Under this chain of events, the revenue per available room, a standard industry measurement, would increase only 0.5 percent in the first half of the year, compared with what had been anticipated as a growth of 2.1 percent. A war lasting more than a month and a half, however, would reduce first-half revenues to 0.1 percent and shrink them 3.6 percent in the second half, according to the study.

In other sectors of the market, the economic uncertainties produced by the war are seen as an opportunity for the determined to lock in deals when landlords are willing to make concessions to fill office space.

Quoting a saying that she attributed to an early Rothschild, "Buy when there is blood in the streets," Ruth Colp-Haber, a partner in Wharton Property Advisors, a tenants' broker, said, "There are good deals out there, and now is the time to lock in good long-term leases."

She said some of the best deals are to be found in sublease space that was expensively bought out for dot-com and telecommunications companies and then returned to the market. "They can be complicated deals, but they are among the best available," she said. "The space is built and the phones are installed, so a tenant can move in two weeks rather than waiting nine months if you are starting with raw space."

## "Counting Heads,"
## Peter Beinart, *The New Republic*, April 7, 2003

The 1.4 million American military personnel serving on active duty around the world represent a racial and ethnic cross-section of the United States. An overview of the troops:

### Race and Ethnicity, All Active Duty

Caucasian . . . . . . . . . . . . . . . . . . . . . . . . . . . . . . . . . . . . 64%
African-American . . . . . . . . . . . . . . . . . . . . . . . . . . . . . . . 20%
Hispanic . . . . . . . . . . . . . . . . . . . . . . . . . . . . . . . . . . . . . 9%
Asian . . . . . . . . . . . . . . . . . . . . . . . . . . . . . . . . . . . . . . . . 4%
Native American . . . . . . . . . . . . . . . . . . . . . . . . . . . . . . . 1%
Other . . . . . . . . . . . . . . . . . . . . . . . . . . . . . . . . . . . . . . . . 2%

### Military Compensation

Base pay for army private with one-year contract . . . . . . $15,480
Starting salary for second lieutenant . . . . . . . . . . . . . . . . $26,200
Average combat pay. . . . . . . . . . . . . . . . . . . . . . . . . $150/month
Death gratuity . . . . . . . . . . . . . . . . . . . . . . . . . . . . . . . $60,000
Life insurance. . . . . . . . . . . . . . . . . . . . . . . . . . . . . . . . $250,000
Dependency compensation . . . . . . . . . . . . . . Child: $247/month
Spouse: $948/month

### Education

| Education | Officers | Enlisted |
|---|---|---|
| College graduate | 94.7% | 3.5% |
| Two or more years college | 96.9% | 9.4% |
| Some college | 97.4% | 10.1% |
| High school graduate | 100.0% | 99.1% |

ও৶ও৶ও৶ও৶ও৶

## "The Sand and the Fury,"
## Arian Campo-Flores, *Newsweek*, April 7, 2003

Last Wednesday at around 3 p.m., in a patch of Iraqi desert where the 3/7th Infantry Battalion is camped, the wind whipped into a frenzy and the air began to glow a seemingly radioactive red. Tents strained against their poles, and any loose object fired away like a projectile. Minutes later, the sky turned dark and we were fully enveloped in dust. Then, thunder cracked the sky and it began to rain mud as moisture in the air gathered particles on its way to earth. It was the worst sandstorm I've yet experienced here—a three-day tour de force that battered the soldiers' morale as much as their equipment.

Despite the conditions, our unit had to embark on a mission to clear a militia compound that night. Before leaving, soldiers lined up for a hot meal—their first since the war started—and ended up eating ham and rice suffused with sand. Others scrambled to tie down equipment and shroud electronics tightly in plastic. For some, simply walking 100 feet to an adjacent squad required using a Global Positioning System. Those attempting to defecate in the field had to contend with dust surging at their backsides—and toilet paper being yanked from their hands by the howling wind.

When our Bradley fighting vehicle set off, visibility was practically zero. Through his night sight, Pfc. Giovanni Garcia, the driver, could only see a fuzzy, swirling mass and two lonely dots: the taillights of the vehicle in front of him, his only navigational reference along precarious terrain. A Bradley he trailed behind at one point threw him into a panic; only one of its taillights was working and Garcia couldn't tell if it was the right or left one. The difference mattered; drivers ride in each other's tracks to avoid potential mines and other hazards (one Bradley last week plunged into a deep crevice, killing one soldier and injuring another). Further along, we nearly crashed head-on with a Humvee that emerged suddenly from the murk. We arrived at our destination five hours later—after traveling just five miles. Once there, Staff Sgt. José Espada, the master gunner, exited his hatch to relieve himself from the Bradley's roof and was nearly knocked off by 60-mile-an-hour winds.

The sand—much of it as fine as flour—is inescapable. It infiltrates every sealed container and every orifice. It costs crucial pieces of equipment—guns, ammunition, engines, radios—rendering them useless if they aren't quickly and thoroughly cleaned. Worse yet, the lubricant necessary to keep guns functioning smoothly traps dust like flypaper, clogging machinery with gritty goo. Sandstorms exact a physical and psychological toll. Your breathing becomes labored (imagine enclosing your head in a discarded vacuum cleaner bag). Goggles and bandannas are *de rigueur*. Bombarded with fine particles, your body responds by emitting copious amounts of fluids. Your nose seeps brown snot. Your throat discharges dark phlegm. Your eyes—which quickly turn scarlet from irritation—shed tears continuously, releasing muddy rivulets down your face. Sgt. Brian Torres, the gunner, woke up the following morning with his eyelids welded shut from crust. Maj. Frank

McClary, the 3/7th's operations officer, who often travels with his head poking out of the Bradley's turret, had the skin on his eyelids and cheeks seared by the sand and wind. He now carries two sticks of lip balm—one for his lips and one for his face. Our only refuge that night was our sealed-up Bradley. All we could do was wait for the storm to pass. And wonder aloud, like many a soldier did: "Why would anyone want to fight over this place?"

### "Bolts in Rocks Have Climbers Screaming from Mountaintops," Dean Starkman, *Newsweek*, June 11, 2003

Patrick Seurynck was scaling a dangerous 400-foot granite cliff near Aspen, Colorado, last June when his partner above yelled down some disturbing news: "The anchors are gone!"

The 48-year-old Mr. Seurynck, who has been climbing rocks for 10 years, had just spent weeks drilling in place numerous stainless-steel bolts for securing ropes. He knew immediately what had happened: A bolt cutter had struck. He climbed down safely, fuming.

"It was just arrogant audacity," says Mr. Seurynck, still riled. Whether to bolt or not is a smoldering question in rock climbing these days as the sport comes to grips with growing popularity. Once the domain of a scruffy few that embraced an ethic of self-reliance, conservationism and risk, rock climbing is being overrun by a new generation less connected to its daring past. The result: a culture clash on the rocks.

Traditional, or "trad," climbers favor passive protection gear: metal nuts and spring-loaded retractable metal wedges called cams. These are slipped into cracks and then removed by the last climber to make an ascent. Climbers say newcomers put up permanent bolts merely to make hard climbs easier.

"They are entirely and utterly for the convenience of climbers, who, in my view, have just gotten incredibly lazy," says Richard Goldstone, a Poughkeepsie, New York, math professor, who has argued for fewer bolts in the Mohonk Preserve, a traditional climbing Mecca 80 miles north of New York.

The less-fastidious new-schoolers, sometimes called "sport climbers," dismiss the critique as elitist. They say bolted routes allow relatively safe climbs on even advanced routes and along the lines that otherwise could not be climbed at all. Besides, they say, bolts are becoming the norm....

With at least 450,000 regulars now on the rocks in the U.S., up from 200,000 a decade ago, land managers fear that bolting is getting out of hand. "All of them are looking to prevent the proliferation," says Randy Kaufman, a National Park Service official....

The nation's main rock-climbing group, the Access Fund, in Boulder, Colorado, is pro-bolt and favors leaving it up to climbers to decide when to place them. The group fears bureaucracy, so it is hoping the agencies provide "timely authorizations" for anchors, the spokesman says.

But a minority of climbers, including some big names in the sport, believe restrictions are needed. The anti-bolters echo the position of environmental groups that say permanent bolts degrade rock, look bad and allow climbers to disturb raptors' nests.

తొగోతొగోతొగోతొగోతొగ

### "2 Soldiers, 6 Kids, 1 Exhausted Grandmother,"
### Richard Jerome, Jason Bane, Cathy Free and Jane Sims Podesta,
### *People Magazine*, September 8, 2003

Major conflict in Iraq may have ended, but for families like the Holcombs, with both parents overseas, the battle continues at home and abroad.

Fort Carson, Colo., 6:25 a.m.: Inside a condominium on this dusty army base, Sue Bearer savors her last few moments of peace, sipping coffee and taking a drag from her cigarette.

6:35 a.m.: All hell breaks loose. It starts benignly enough, as nine-year-old Dustin trots downstairs and with a "Hi, Grandma!" and plants a kiss on Bearer's cheek. Then, the ceiling rumbles as if a *Riverdance* road company were rehearsing upstairs, and five other children tumble down to the kitchen. The boys—Tristan, 6, Skylor, 7, Forest, 11, and 12-year-old Jon—chatter and tease as they fix cereal and make bologna sandwiches for school; Taylor, 7, the only girl, plops down for Bearer to brush her strawberry-blond hair. Meanwhile her brothers—amped up over the new *Freddy vs. Jason* flick—taunt their sister for her loyalty to *Barney*. "Leave Taylor alone!" orders Bearer, 59. At 7:25, the backpacked brood moves out for school, and Bearer calls, "Hey, kisses!"

Then, silence.

This is the unseen Iraqi war, the quiet, unheralded heroism of the home front. For seven months now, since early February, Sue Bearer has been mother and father to her six grandkids because both their parents are on active duty in Iraq. For many, the war may have entered its final stage on April 9, when U.S. Marines helped topple Saddam Hussein's statue in central Baghdad. But the coda has been long and brutal—for the 140,000 U.S. troops still deployed in sweltering temperatures (up to 120 degrees F in some places) and under constant threat, and for their families back home for whom it won't end until they meet safely again.

Bearer's son Vaughn Holcomb, 40, and his wife, Simone, 30, don't know when they will be home; perhaps next spring. Vaughn, who left in March, is an army sergeant in the 3rd Armored Cavalry Regiment in charge of a tank platoon located outside the northern town of Al Quaim. Simone, a nursing student in civilian life, left home in January to serve as a National Guard medic stationed in Baghdad. Though husband and wife talk to each other by phone once a week, calls home are much rarer, and the uncertainty is beginning to take a toll. "It's hard. I miss my children," Vaughn told People via e-mail from Iraq. "Oh, and it's hot, sandy—and did I say hot?" Adds Simone, over a scratchy phone line: "It's beyond frustrating. At least if we had a [homecoming] date to look forward to, it would be much easier."

Bearer had been preparing since last fall to assume legal guardianship of the children (two are Vaughn's and four are Simone's, all from previous unions) just in case. "I volunteered," she says, "but I never thought it would happen. My whole life has been put on hold." A successful real estate agent, she had been living comfortably in Akron with her husband, Joe, 76, a retired postal worker, eating out for breakfast and dinner every day and enjoying her rose garden. Now, she has quit her job, cooks for seven every night and endures a wrenching separation: Joe is staying in Akron to mind the couple's two rental properties. "Joe and I went everywhere together," she says, tearing up. Back home in Akron, her husband's feelings run just as deep. "In the evening is when it hits you," he says. "Man, oh man, is it lonely."

Most of Bearer's time, however, is spent dealing with a greater separation: two parents and six young children, 7,000 miles apart, living under the ever-present spectre of tragedy—brought home when one of Jon's classmates lost a parent in the conflict. The stress weighs heavily on the kids, manifested in occasional bed-wetting, mood swings and sleepless nights. "I've just had nightmares all the time, that my mom blew up; it's horrible," says Forest, softly. "It stinks," adds Jon, looking at the floor. "I don't think it's fair that they left us."

### "Rebuilding Iraq: An Assessment at Six Months," *The New York Times*, November 4, 2003

Attacks against soldiers and occupation targets continue.

Here are the numbers as of Sunday [November 2, 2003]:

- Average number of U.S. soldiers killed per week since major combat ended: 5

- Number of U.S. soldiers wounded since major combat ended: 1,285

- Number of U.S. soldiers killed since major combat ended: 135

- Estimated bounty, in U.S. dollars, paid to Iraqis who kill U.S. soldiers: $300-$1,000

- Tons of weapons and munitions found and destroyed, per day: 100

- Average price of an Iraqi-made hand grenade in early May: 10 cents

- Average price now: $2.50

- Average price of a fully automatic Kalashnikov assault rifle in May: $5

- Average price now: $80

### "Remember the Alamo—in Music," *Orlando Sentinel*, April 8, 2004

SAN ANTONIO—When he heard there was a new movie being made about the Battle of the Alamo, Asleep at the Wheel's Ray Benson figured there would be a CD featuring music from the film.

Then the Alamo co-star Billy Bob Thornton told him there wasn't any such album in the works. "I said, 'Shoot, now there's an opportunity I can't resist,'" says the lead singer of the Western swing group.

*Asleep at the Wheel Remembers the Alamo* features a wide range of songs—from the melancholy trumpet standard "El Degüello" played by the Mexican army while it surrounded the Alamo in 1836, to a humorous ditty about the 1982 night Ozzy Osbourne was arrested for relieving himself in front of the shrine.

Benson had a lot of songs to choose from that focused on the battle—or merely mentioned the Alamo—between the Texans in Santa Anna's troops. "We just wanted to show how it permeates our culture," he says.

There are 10 verses of "The Ballad of Davy Crockett," made famous in the 1950s Disney classic *Davy Crockett, King of the Wild Frontier* that set off a coonskin cap craze among American boys.

Benson said the Crockett song has 31 verses in all, and that he took out as many of them as he could without shortchanging the frontiersman, who was among those who died at the Alamo.

### "Financial Firms Hasten Their Move to Outsourcing," Saritha Rai, *The New York Times*, August 18, 2004

BANGALORE, India—Last February, when the online lending company E-Loan wanted to provide its customers faster and more affordable loans, it began a program in India. Since then, 87 percent of E-Loan's customers have chosen to have their loans financed two days faster by having their applications processed in India.

"Offshoring is not just a fad, but the reality of doing business today," said Chris Larsen, chairman and chief executive of E-Loan, "and this is really just the beginning."

Indeed, seemingly a myriad of financial institutions including banks, mutual funds, insurance companies, investment firms and credit-card companies are sending work to overseas locations, at a scorching speed.

From 2003 to 2004, Deloitte Research found in a survey of 43 financial institutions in seven countries, including 13 of the top 25 by market capitalization, financial institutions in North America and Europe increased jobs offshore to an average of 1,500 each from an average of 300. The Deloitte study said that about 80 percent of this went to India.

Deloitte said the unexpectedly rapid growth rate for offshore outsourcing showed no signs of abating, despite negative publicity about job losses. Although information technology remains the dominant service, financial firms are expanding into other areas like insurance claims processing, mortgage applications, equity research and accounting.

"Offshoring has created a truly global operating model for financial services, unleashing a new and potent competitive dynamic that is changing the rules of the game for the entire industry," the report said.

Michael Haney, a senior analyst at research firm Celent Communications, said: "With its vast English speaking, technically well-trained labor pool and its low-cost advantages, India is one of the few countries that can handle the level of offshoring that U.S. financial companies want to scale to."

In a recent report, "Offshoring, A Detour Along the Automation Highway," Mr. Haney estimated that potentially 2.3 million American jobs in the banking and securities industries could be lost to outsourcing abroad.

Girish S. Paranjpe, president for financial solutions at Wipro, a large outsourcing company in India, said, "Pent-up demand, recent regulatory changes and technology upgrade requirements are all making global financial institutions increase their outsourcing budgets." His company's customers include J.P. Morgan Chase, for which it is building systems for measuring operational risk, and Aviva and Prudential, the British insurers.

Several recent studies concur that there has been an unexpected and large shift of work since the outsourcing pioneer Citigroup set up a company in India two decades ago. They cite cost advantages as the primary reason. According to Celent, in 2003 the average M.B.A. working in the financial services industry in India, where the cost of living is about 30 percent less than in the United States, earned 14 percent of his American counterpart's wages. Information technology professionals earned 13 percent, while call center workers who provide customer support and telemarketing services earned seven percent of their American counterparts' salaries.

Experts say that with China, India, the former Soviet Union and other nations embracing free trade and capitalism, there is a population 10 times that of the United States with average wage advantages of 85 percent to 95 percent.

"There has never been an economic discontinuity of this magnitude in the history of the world," said Mark Gottfredson, co-head of the consulting firm Bain & Company's global capability sourcing practice. "These powerful forces are allowing companies to rethink their sourcing strategies across the entire value chain."

A study by India's software industry trade body, the National Association of Software and Services Companies, or Nasscom, estimated that United States banks, financial services and insurance companies have saved $6 billion in the last four years by offshoring to India.

But cheap labor is not the only reason for outsourcing. Global financial institutions are moving work overseas to spread risks and to offer their customers service 24 hours a day. "Financial institutions are achieving accelerated speed to market, and quality and productivity gains in outsourcing to India," said Anil Kumar, senior vice president for banking and financial services at Satyam Computer Services, a software and services firm. Satyam works with 10 of the top global capital markets firms on Wall Street.

Mastek, an outsourcing company based in Mumbai, is another example. Two years ago, Mastek turned from doing diverse types of offshore work to specializing in financial services. The results are already showing. In the year ended in June, 42 percent of Mastek's revenues, $89.28 million, came from offering software and back office services to financial services firms, up from 22 percent last June.

Fidelity Investments, the world's largest mutual fund manager, started outsourcing to Mastek 18 months ago and is now among the top five clients in its roster.

Sudhakar Ram, chief executive of Mastek, said, "It is rare that within a year a new customer turns a top customer; this illustrates the momentum in the market."

Another Mastek customer, the CUNA Mutual Group, which is based in Madison, Wis., and is part of the Credit Union National Association, started a project billed at less than $100,000 two years ago. Now the applications that Mastek is building for CUNA, to handle disability claims, amount to a multimillion-dollar deal.

In the transaction-intensive financial services industry, offshoring of high-labor back-office tasks is becoming the norm.

ICICI OneSource, based in Mumbai, has added 2,100 employees in six months and signed on four new financial services clients, including the London-based bank Lloyd's TSB, for which it provides customer service.

In one year, from March 2003 to March 2004, ICICI OneSource grew to $42 million in revenues from $17 million. Today, more than 70 percent of its revenues come from the financial services industry, up from 40 percent two years ago.

For India's outsourcing firms, growth has not been without hiccups. Earlier this year, Capital One canceled a telemarketing contract with India's biggest call center company, Spectramind, owned by Wipro, after some workers were charged with enticing the credit-card company's customers with unauthorized free gifts. Weeks earlier, the investment bank Lehman Brothers canceled a contract with Wipro, saying it was dissatisfied with its workers' training.

In response, outsourcing companies are improving their offerings. Leading companies are investing in privacy and security due diligence as they handle sensitive customer data, doing reference checks on employees, providing secure physical environments with cameras, and banning employees from using cell phones and other gadgetry on the work floor.

Deloitte forecasts that by the year 2010, the 100 largest global financial institutions will move $400 billion of their work offshore for $150 billion in annual savings. Its survey forecasts that more than 20 percent of the financial industry's global cost base will have gone offshore in that period.

With competence levels rising, Indian companies are tackling more complex tasks. DSL Software, a joint venture of Deutsche Bank and HCL Technologies, a software company, is handling intricate jobs for the securities processing industry. "Indian firms are taking offshoring to the next level; in the banking industry, for instance, they are getting into wholesale banking, trade finance and larger loan processing type tasks," said Mr. Haney, the analyst from Celent.

But the relentless demand for skilled workers is putting pressure on wage rates, narrowing the wage gap with the United States and other Western economies. Simultaneously, companies are plagued by higher attrition rates that may lead to quality and deadline pressures.

For the moment, however, there is no indication the industry cannot cope with the unflagging demand to send work offshore. "If India can continuously pull less paid, less educated people into the labor pool," Mr. Haney said, "a substantial wage gap will continue to exist."

### "Terri Schiavo Dies,"
### *Wikinews*, March 31, 2005

Terri Schiavo died this morning in St. Petersburg, Florida, moments after 9 a.m. EST. Thirteen days ago, her feeding tube was removed after courts repeatedly ruled Schiavo would not want to be kept alive in her current state. Schiavo suffered severe brain damage in 1990 after a mysterious cardiac arrest.

Many news sources allege the cardiac arrest was caused by an eating disorder, while her family maintains she had no eating disorder at all. During the attack, her brain was starved of oxygen for 14 minutes, leading to the death of many of the neurons in her brain and possibly leaving her in a persistent vegetative state (PVS).

Michael Schiavo argued before the courts that his wife would not want to live for a prolonged period on a feeding tube. In 2001, the tube was removed, but was reinserted two days later after an appeal by Terri's parents, Bob and Mary Schindler. After the Schindler family had all of their appeals rejected, the tube was removed once again in 2003, but reinserted six days later when Governor Jeb Bush and the Florida legislature collaborated on a bill, allowing Bush to order the tube reinserted. After the law was overturned in May of 2004, and the Schindler family's numerous appeals were again rejected, the tube was removed on March 18th.

President George W. Bush held a press conference, in part to offer his condolences to the friends and family of Schiavo. The president commended those on both sides of the issue.

An autopsy is planned to be performed in the coming days, which both the Schindler family and Michael Schiavo hope will shed some light on the cause of her brain damage.

Schiavo is survived by her husband, parents and her younger siblings Robert Jr. and Suzanne; she had no children. Schiavo was 41 years old.

### "At Least 55 Killed by Hurricane Katrina; Serious Flooding across Affected Region," Wikinews, August 30, 2005

Thirty people died in the Gulf of Mexico resort of Biloxi when Hurricane Katrina demolished a water-side apartment block, Harrison County emergency operations center spokesman Jim Pollard told AP. However, the Mississippi Emergency Management Agency has yet to confirm the news.

At least another twenty have died across the rest of Harrison County; this number is expected to rise. The Governor of the state of Mississippi has asked people to stay away from the area for several days. The towns of Biloxi and Gulfport took the brunt of the hurricane's 140mph+ winds after it veered away from New Orleans as it made landfall.

Three more people have been killed by falling trees and at least two died in traffic accidents resulting from the hurricane. Hundreds of people have been rescued by boat and helicopter from the roofs of houses cut off by flood water.

The hurricane has caused a storm-surge—the force of the winds has piled the waters of the Gulf of Mexico against the coastline, causing widespread flooding reaching at least a mile inland in places.

A levee on the Lake Pontchartrain canal has broken in two places, causing massive flooding. Some parts of New Orleans are now under 20 feet of water. Flooding seems to have reduced to increasing at a rate of one inch an hour and Army Corps of Engineers are on the scene of the breaks. At aproximately 10:00 PM Central city officials confirmed that a major floodpump has failed, which could result in an additional nine feet of floodwaters.

The western part of New Orleans has been flooded after a two-block long stretch of the 17th Street Levee gave way on Monday afternoon. Much of the city lies below sea level and depends on flood defences to keep it safe. One hospital—that has 1,000 patients inside—has been surrounded by the water. The vice-president of the center has described seeing whitecaps on the waves of the water in a street outside.

A water main pipe has failed, meaning that tap water has been contaminated with flood water, and is no longer safe to drink.

The mayor of the city has described seeing "bodies floating in the water."

Some 10,000 people remain in the Superdome stadium, despite the electricity supply failing leaving the indoor stadium in darkness. The coverings of the concrete roof of the structure have been stripped away by the wind.

Electricity supplies to 1.3 million people across the south eastern parts of the US have been damaged, and it could be months before power is restored to all affected.

Two oil rigs have broken free of their moorings in the Gulf of Mexico, and a third drifted into a bridge in Mobile Bay, Alabama.

Katrina has now been downgraded to tropical storm status as it moves northwards across the US, and wind speeds have dropped to 60 mph. The current death toll does not include the 11 killed in Florida when Katrina struck there last week.

### "Enron Executives Kenneth Lay and Jeffrey Skilling Found Guilty," Wikinews, May 25, 2006

A jury in Houston found Former Enron Corp. CEOs Kenneth L. Lay and Jeffrey K. Skilling guilty of 6 kinds of white-collar crime on May 25. Lay was convicted of all ten counts against him, while Skilling was convicted of only nineteen of the charged twenty-eight counts. The variety of charges on which both men were convicted was astonishing; conspiracy, wire fraud, false statements to banks and auditors, and others. Both men now face many years in prison.

Outside the courtroom, Skilling continued to proclaim his innocence. "Obviously, I'm disappointed, but that's the way the system works," Skilling said after the verdict. He is expected to appeal. Lay did not immediately speak to reporters outside the courtroom.

The verdict was reached on the sixth day of deliberations after a four-month-long trial and brings to a close the first of the wave of accounting scandals earlier in the decade. The verdict also represents another major victory for the government, which has successfully prosecuted a number of high-profile executives involved in accounting scandals, as well as obtained sixteen guilty pleas from former Enron executives.

Sentencing has been set for September 11, 2006. U.S. District Judge Sim Lake ordered Lay to post a $5 million bond and surrender his passport before leaving the courtroom.

### "Pluto Loses Planet Status," Wikinews, August 24, 2006

Today, astronomers have endorsed a proposal about the definition of the word "planet." As a consequence, our solar system now counts only 8 planets. They are Mercury, Venus, Earth, Mars, Jupiter, Saturn, Uranus, and Neptune. Pluto no longer meets the criteria and loses its planet status, but becomes the prototype of a distinct class of dwarf planets.

Ceres and 2003 UB313 also have been recognised as dwarf planets. Charon, which was previously in the run for promotion, did not meet the final criteria for a dwarf planet.

Some 2500 astronomers from over 75 countries gathered this week in Prague at the Congress of the International Astronomical Union (IAU) to decide on several issues like a formal definition of a planet. Previously, there was no definition and with the discovery of new objects beyond Pluto there was much need for a clear criterion. The scientists also discussed new research findings in their field.

Louis Friedman, the executive director of the Planetary Society in California said: "The classification doesn't matter. Pluto—and all Solar System objects—are mysterious and exciting new worlds that need to be explored and better understood."

The final draft states: "A planet is a celestial body that is in orbit around the Sun has sufficient mass for its self-gravity to overcome rigid body forces so that it assumes a hydrostatic equilibrium (nearly round) shape has cleared the neighbourhood around its orbit.

A dwarf planet is a celestial body that is in orbit around the Sun, has sufficient mass for its self-gravity to overcome rigid body forces so that it assumes a hydrostatic equilibrium (nearly round) shape, has not cleared the neighbourhood around its orbit, is not a satellite.

All other objects except satellites orbiting the Sun shall be referred to collectively as "Small Solar-System Bodies."

Pluto did not meet one of the criteria for planet: its orbit is highly eccentric, causing it to overlap with Neptune's. The IAU has a dozen other objects similar to Pluto on its "watchlist" and is expected to announce new dwarf planets in the coming months and years.

Ever since its discovery by American Clyde Tombaugh in 1930, Pluto has been considered a planet, though its status has been questioned many times after it was discovered to be far less massive than earlier calculations suggested, and because of its many other eccentricities. As a consequence of the vote, many textbooks, encyclopedias and other sources will need rewriting.

$\approx\ll\approx\ll\approx\ll\approx\ll$

### "New Orleans Business Rebuilds to Help Homeowners Rebuild," *NewsUSA*, September 13, 2007

(NewsUSA)—Natausha Gaudin launched her own business—Risk Control, LLC—four years ago, after working for a big corporation. "I wanted to break away from the corporate environment and use my own innovative ideas to run my company," she said.

Gaudin combined her love of real estate and desire to help others as she defined the role of her company, which has become a resource for those who are building or rebuilding their homes.

However, an unexpected act of nature—Hurricane Katrina—knocked her business off course. Gaudin and her daughter lived just three blocks from the London Street canal levee in New Orleans, which resulted in the destruction of her home. Left with only her flash drive and laptop computer, she was challenged to keep her business afloat.

With the expense of rebuilding her business, she needed a small business loan to keep up with payroll and day-to-day business costs. After being denied by several financial institutions, Gaudin learned about Hope Community Credit Union, whose employees referred her to ACCION USA, a nonprofit organization committed to helping small business owners in the United States by providing micro-loans and financial training. Within 24 hours, Gaudin had completed her loan application online.

"The biggest struggle for small business owners is obtaining financing from traditional institutions," Gaudin said. "With this program—and the online micro-lending—the process was so smooth."

ACCION USA does not have a physical office in Louisiana, but its online loan application allows small entrepreneurs, like Gaudin, to apply from anywhere in the country. Within a few weeks, Gaudin's loan of $25,000 was approved, and she was back in business, providing a greatly needed service in post-Katrina New Orleans.

Since receiving her financing, Gaudin and her 12 employees have been working to help Katrina victims rebuild their homes. The company manages projects and helps homeowners locate contractors who are not performing and take legal action, rebuild within their budgets, screen contractors and subcontractors and receive services such as mold remediation.

"There are so many pieces needed for a well-oiled engine to run," said Gaudin. "ACCION USA's loan allowed us to continue moving in the right direction. You can get stalled if you don't have the oil to keep things moving."

And while the rebuilding is far from over, Gaudin and her team now have the financial security to continue to assist homeowners in the storm-torn Orleans and Jefferson Parishes.

෨ෟ෨ෟ෨ෟ෨ෟ෨ෟ

## "Congressional Democrats Prod President to do More to Head Off Foreclosures,"
### Jesse J. Holland, *The Daily Times* (Farmington, New Mexico), October 4, 2007

WASHINGTON—Congress's top Democrats demanded quick action on the subprime mortgage crisis, saying President Bush has been slow to address a situation that could cost millions of people their homes.

"This is a national crisis. Too bad it's taken so long to realize that we have a crisis," Senate Majority Leader Harry Reid of Nevada said at a joint news conference with House Speaker Nancy Pelosi of California.

Pelosi, Reid and other Democrats want the president to appoint a special adviser to coordinate the federal response to the subprime mortgage crisis.

"The subprime crisis demands action, and we're working to protect families who have lost their home or are in danger of foreclosure," Pelosi said.

For two years. President Bush has sought legislation revamping the Federal Housing Administration but has not gotten anything, said Housing and Urban Development Secretary Alphon-so Jackson. "To place even one family at risk is irresponsible, and Congress should stop playing politics with home-owners' financial security," Jackson said.

The Democrats are trying to pressure the White House and congressional Republicans into supporting their efforts to alleviate the mortgage mess.

Foreclosure filings in August more than doubled nationwide from the same period a year ago and jumped 36 percent from July, according to Irvine, Calif-based Realty Trac Inc. The filings include default notices, auction sale notices and bank repossessions.

Many of the foreclosures are caused by subprime mortgages—home loans made to people with weak credit histories. Many of those adjustable rate loans start out with low interest rates, but then reset to higher rates a few years down the road, bringing monthly mortgages up to prices many homeowners cannot afford.

More than 2 million adjustable rate mortgages are scheduled to reset by the end of 2008.

Bush last month acknowledged "some unsettling times" in the country's housing and credit markets. He has proposed expanding eligibility requirements for refinancing loans guaranteed by the Federal Housing Administration under a new program to be called FHA Secure.

Democrats say that is not enough. "If the administration does not act, then Congress should," said Sen. Charles Schumer, D-N.Y.

They repeated their demands for the White House to support more government spending to help homeowners avoid foreclosure, to increase the portfolio caps for home-loan finance companies Fannie Mae and Freddie Mac, and to agree to their plans to modernize the Federal Housing Administration.

The government last month slightly increased the investment portfolio caps for Fannie Mae and Freddie Mac, but the action did not go as fai- as Democrats had hoped.

"We predict at least 2.2 million people will lose their homes and the response from the Bush administration has been slow and small," said Rep. Carolyn Maloney, D-N.Y.

When asked what Congress was doing. Rep. Barney Frank, D-Mass., and head of the House Financial Services Committee, pointed out various bills that Democrats have been trying to move in the House and Senate this year.

The House in September passed legislation allowing the FHA to back refinanced loans for tens of thousands of borrowers who are delinquent on payments because their mortgages are resetting to sharply higher rates from low initial "teaser" levels. The Senate has passed a bill that would provide $200 million to help build up the network of nonprofit groups that help borrowers facing problems with subprime mortgages.

But Frank also accused the Republicans of blocking legislative efforts in 2005 to stop the subprime mortgage crisis from occurring.

"Republican House leadership sent word to (then-House Majority Leader Tom) DeLay: 'No action,'" Frank said. "We would have acted well over a year and a half ago at least, and a lot of these loans that are now going bad would have never been made."

ॐॐॐॐॐॐॐ

### "In Name Count, Garcias Are Catching Up to Joneses,"
### Sam Roberts, *The New York Times*, November 17, 2007

Step aside, Moore and Taylor. Welcome, Garcia and Rodriguez.

Smith remains the most common surname in the United States, according to a new analysis released yesterday by the Census Bureau. But for the first time, two Hispanic surnames—Garcia and Rodriguez—are among the top 10 most common in the nation, and Martinez nearly edged out Wilson for 10th place.

The number of Hispanics living in the United States grew by 58 percent in the 1990s to nearly 13 percent of the total population, and cracking the list of top 10 names suggests just how pervasively the Latino migration has permeated everyday American culture.

Garcia moved to No. 8 in 2000, up from No. 18, and Rodriguez jumped to No. 9 from 22nd place. The number of Hispanic surnames among the top 25 doubled, to six.

Compiling the rankings is a cumbersome task, in part because of confidentiality and accuracy issues, according to the Census Bureau, and it is only the second time it has prepared such a list. While the historical record is sketchy, several demographers said it was probably the first time that any non-Anglo name was among the 10 most common in the nation. "It's difficult to say, but it's probably likely," said Robert A. Kominski, Assistant Chief of Social Characteristics for the Census.

Luis Padilla, 48, a banker who has lived in Miami since he arrived from Colombia 14 years ago, greeted the ascendance of Hispanic surnames enthusiastically. "It shows we're getting stronger," Mr. Padilla said. "If there's that many of us to outnumber the Anglo names, it's a great thing."

Reinaldo M. Valdes, a board member of the Miami-based Spanish American League Against Discrimination, said the milestone "gives the Hispanic community a standing within the social structure of the country."

"People of Hispanic descent who hardly speak Spanish are more eager to take their Hispanic last names," he said. "Today, kids identify more with their roots than they did before."

Demographers pointed to more than one factor in explaining the increase in Hispanic surnames. Generations ago, immigration officials sometimes arbitrarily Anglicized or simplified names when foreigners arrived from Europe. "The movie studios used to demand that their employees have standard Waspy names," said Justin Kaplan, a historian and coauthor of *The Language of Names*. "Now, look at Renee Zellweger," Mr. Kaplan said.

And because recent Hispanic and Asian immigrants might consider themselves more identifiable by their physical characteristics than Europeans do, they are less likely to change their surnames, though they often choose Anglicized first names for their children.

The latest surname count also signaled the growing number of Asians in America. The surname Lee ranked No. 22, with the number of Lees about equally divided between whites and Asians. Lee is a familiar name in China and Korea and in all its variations is described as the most common surname in the world.

Altogether, the census found six million surnames in the United States. Among those, 151,000 were shared by a hundred or more Americans. Four million were held by only one person.

"The names tell us that we're a richly diverse culture," Mr. Kominski said. But the fact that about one in every 25 Americans is named Smith, Johnson, Williams, Brown, Jones, Miller or Davis "suggests that there's a durability in the family of man," Mr. Kaplan, the author, said. A million Americans share each of those seven names. An additional 268 last names are common to 10,000 or more people. Together, those 275 names account for one in four Americans.

As the population of the United States ballooned by more than 30 million in the 1990s, more Murphys and Cohens were counted when the decade ended than when it began. Smith—which would be even more common if all its variations, like Schmidt and Schmitt, were tallied—is among the names derived from occupations (Miller, which ranks No. 7, is another). Among the most famous early bearers of the name was Capt. John Smith, who helped establish the first permanent English settlement in North America at Jamestown, Va., 400 years ago. As recently as 1950, more Americans were employed as blacksmiths than as psychotherapists.

In 1984, according to the Social Security Administration, nearly 3.4 million Smiths lived in the United States. In 1990, the census counted 2.5 million. By 2000, the Smith population had declined to fewer than 2.4 million. The durability of some of the most common names in American history may also have been perpetuated because slaves either adopted or retained the surnames of their owners. About one in five Smiths is black, as is about one in three Johnsons, Browns, and Joneses and nearly half the people named Williams. The Census Bureau's analysis found that some surnames were especially associated with race and ethnicity.

More than 96 percent of Yoders, Kruegers, Muellers, Kochs, Schwartzes, Schmitts and Novaks were white. Nearly 90 percent of the Washingtons were black, as were 75 percent of the Jeffersons, 66 percent of the Bookers, 54 percent of the Banks and 53 percent of the Mosleys.

🙠🙢🙠🙢🙠🙢🙠🙢

### "Freed From Debt, a Hair Stylist Looks to a Brighter Future," Kari Haskell, *The New York Times*, November 20, 2007

The Jolie Femme hair salon is carved out of a barbershop in Harlem. Past the black combs soaking in blue Barbicide and the buzzing clippers, Aurea Casellas, 33, tends to her clients. She twists women's hair into up-dos, or irons spiral locks pin-straight. Her specialty, however, is weaves.

And like the hair she so skillfully interlaces with new tresses, Ms. Casellas, a mother of two, is slowly piecing together a brighter future with the help of a nonprofit organization, the Children's Aid Society.

"Children's Aid helped me realize my potential," Ms. Casellas said on a recent Friday morning at her home in Upper Manhattan. The Children's Aid Society is one of seven agencies supported by The New York Times Neediest Cases Fund.

Before she took part in the Children's Aid Society's Families With a Future program this year, Ms. Casellas said, insecurity had kept her from leaving a dead-end job as an assistant at a hair salon downtown. "I wasn't challenging myself—it was limited, what I could do there," she said.

As an assistant, she washed hair and swept trimmings from the floor, earning $200 a week, without benefits. Though rent subsidies covered all but $70.40 a month on her one-bedroom apartment, it was difficult to pay for utilities every month and to keep her daughters, Brazil, 4, and Shauna, 18, clothed and fed. When tips were good, she managed. When they weren't, she prayed.

Then in March, the $270 a month the family received in food stamps was cut off. "They said it was because Shauna wasn't attending her G.E.D. classes," said Ms. Casellas. That was enough to break her tenuous budget. "That was not a good time," Ms. Casellas said over the rattling of a passing subway train outside. "I didn't think I was going to get kicked out here," she said, sliding a barred window shut, "but I didn't have $100 for food."

By June, she owed two months' rent, $227.14 on an outstanding beauty school loan and $1,016.90 for dental work the previous year, when two teeth had to be replaced with implants because of gum disease. Her sisters and her mother, who live nearby, donated food stamps when they could, Ms. Casellas said.

"Fortunately, I am not the type to take it out on my children, but I know I wear sadness on my sleeve," she said. Her voice trailed off. "I lost myself long ago," she continued. "I was smart. I wanted to be a lawyer, but growing up I had no restrictions." At 15, pregnant with Shauna, she dropped out of school. Shauna's father had his own wild streak, which led to trouble with the law, she said.

What followed were years of lost opportunities, struggle and hardship. "I am dealing with what I am dealing with now because of the mistakes I've made," she said, then added, "I was too young with Shauna, but now I really understand how hard it is."

Coming to terms with her misspent past was one of the things she worked on during weekly visits with Rebeka Penberg, a life coach at the Families With a Future program. She also took part in a monthly support group. "It's good to be around a group of people speaking in a positive direction—it's not just my problems, my problems; it's about moving forward," she said.

During a session with Ms. Penberg, she mentioned her stifling debt. Ms. Penberg encouraged her to apply for a grant through the Children's Aid Society from the Neediest Cases Fund and guided her through the steps to have her food stamps reinstated. The grant was approved in July. "That was a good day," said Ms. Casellas. "It was a relief. I was very grateful."

The boost gave her the confidence to pursue the stylist position at Jolie Femme. She started in July, and little by little, her clientele is growing.

"Certain things just take time and patience," she said. "It will happen. I just have to stay focused."

**Timeline of Housing Bubble**

**1934** The National Housing Act of 1934, part of the New Deal, makes more affordable housing and home mortgages. It creates the Federal Housing Administration (FHA) (later United States Department of Housing and Urban Development, HUD) and the Federal Savings and Loan Insurance Corporation.

**1938** Fannie Mae is founded by the government under the New Deal. It is a stockholder-owned corporation that purchases and securitizes mortgages in order to ensure that funds are consistently available to the institutions that lend money to home buyers.

**1968** As part of the Housing and Urban Development Act of 1968, the Government mortgage-related agency, Fannie Mae is converted from a federal government entity to a stand-alone government sponsored enterprise (GSE) which purchases and securitizes mortgages to facilitate liquidity in the primary mortgage market. The move takes the debt of Fannie Mae off of the books of the government.

**1970** Federal Home Loan Mortgage Corporation (Freddie Mac) is chartered by an act of Congress, as a GSE, to buy mortgages on the secondary market, pool them, and sell them as mortgage-backed securities to investors on the open market.

**1980** The Depository Institutions Deregulation and Monetary Control Act of 1980 granted all thrifts, including savings and loan associations, the power to make consumer and commercial loans and to issue transaction accounts, but with little regulatory oversight of competing banks.

**1986** The Tax Reform Act of 1986 eliminated the tax deduction for interest paid on credit cards, encouraging the use of home equity through refinancing, second mortgages and home equity lines of credit (HELOC) by consumers.

New homes constructed dropped from 1.8 to 1 million, the lowest rated since World War II.

**1991** US recession, new construction prices fall, but above inflationary growth allows them to return by 1997 in real terms.

**1992** Federal Housing Enterprises Financial Safety and Soundness Act of 1992 required Fannie Mae and Freddie Mac to devote a percentage of their lending to support affordable housing increasing their pooling and selling of such loans as securities; Office of Federal Housing Enterprise Oversight (OFHEO) created to oversee them.

1997    Mortgage denial rate of 29 percent for conventional home purchase loans.

The Taxpayer Relief Act of 1997 repealed the Section 121 exclusion and section 1034 rollover rules, and replaced them with a $500,000 married/$250,000 single exclusion of capital gains on the sale of a home, available once every two years. This encouraged people to buy more expensive first homes, as well as invest in second homes and investment properties.

1997-2005    Mortgage fraud increased by 1,411 percent.

1999    Countrywide Financial and FannieMae ink a Strategic agreement which will lead Countrywide to become the country's leading mortgage provider to poor minorities by the end of 2000.

Fannie Mae eases the credit requirements to encourage banks to extend home mortgages to individuals whose credit is not good enough to qualify for conventional loans.

2001    US Federal Reserve lowers Federal funds rate eleven times, from 6.5% to 1.75%.

2002    Annual home price appreciation of 10% or more in California, Florida, and most Northeastern states.

2003    President Bush signs the American Dream Downpayment Act to be implemented under the Department of Housing and Urban Development. The goal was to provide a maximum downpayment assistance grant of either $10,000 or six percent of the purchase price of the home, whichever was greater.

2003-2007    The Federal Reserve failed to use its supervisory and regulatory authority over banks, mortgage underwriters and other lenders, who abandoned loan standards (employment history, income, down payments, credit rating, assets, property loan-to-value ratio and debt-servicing ability), emphasizing instead lender's ability to securitize and repackage subprime loans.

2005    Booming housing market halts abruptly; from the fourth quarter of 2005 to the first quarter of 2006, median prices nationwide dropped off 3.3 percent.

A total of 846,982 properties were in some stage of foreclosure in 2005.

2006    Continued market slowdown. Prices are flat, home sales fall, resulting in inventory buildup. U.S. Home Construction Index is down over 40% as of mid-August 2006 compared to a year earlier. A total of 1,259,118 foreclosures were filed during the year, up 42 percent from 2005.

2007    More than 25 subprime lenders declare bankruptcy, announce significant losses, or put themselves up for sale.

Many lenders stop offering home equity loans and "stated income" loans. Federal Reserve injects about $100B into the money supply for banks to borrow at a low rate.

Countrywide Financial Corporation, the biggest U.S. mortgage lender, narrowly avoids bankruptcy by taking out an emergency loan of $11 billion from a group of banks.

The Fed lowers interest rates by half a percent (50 basis points) to 4.75% in an attempt to limit damage to the economy from the housing and credit crises.

Federal Reserve injects $41B into the money supply for banks to borrow at a low rate. The largest single expansion by the Fed since $50.35B on September 19, 2001.

A consortium of banks officially abandons the U.S. government-supported "super-SIV" mortgage crisis bail-out plan announced in mid-October, citing a lack of demand for the risky mortgage products on which the plan was based, and widespread criticism that the fund was a flawed idea that would have been difficult to execute.

A total of 2,203,295 foreclosures were filed on 1,285,873 properties during the year, up 75 percent from 2006.

**2008** The National Association of Realtors (NAR) announced that 2007 had the largest drop in existing home sales in 25 years, and "the first price decline in many, many years and possibly going back to the Great Depression."

Dow Jones Industrial Average at the lowest level since October 2006, falling more than 20% from its peak just five months prior.

406 people were arrested for mortgage fraud in an FBI sting across the U.S., including buyers, sellers and others across the wide-ranging mortgage industry.

A total of 3,157,806 foreclosures were filed on 2,330,483 properties during the year, up 81 percent from 2007.

**2009** A total of 3,957,643 foreclosures were filed on 2,824,674 properties during the year, up 21 percent from 2008.

⤙⤚⤙⤚⤙⤚⤙⤚

**"Rights Groups: Forcing Wikileaks.org Offline Raises
'Serious First Amendment Concerns,'"
Wikinews, February 28, 2008**

The American Civil Liberties Union (ACLU) and the Electronic Frontier Foundation (EFF) have sided with Wikileaks.org and will defend them against a lawsuit which took the site off line in the United States. Wikileaks is a website dedicated to hosting leaked documents that are "anonymous, untraceable, uncensorable."

On February 18, 2008, a permanent court injunction issued in the California Northern District Court in San Francisco by judge Jeffrey White, California to Bank Julius Baer (BJB), a Swiss Bank, took the domain name offline. However the site remained online via its IP address and alternative domain names. Wikileaks previously published hundreds of documents obtained from a whistleblower of the Swiss Bank, "purportedly showing offshore tax evasion and money laundering by extremely wealthy and in some cases, politically sensitive, clients from the US, Europe, China and Peru."

"Blocking access to the entire site in response to a few documents posted there completely disregards the public's right to know," said Ann Brick a lawyer for the ACLU. At least 18 other organizations have signed documents in defense of Wikileaks. Those documents have been forged into a 'joint Amici Curiae ("friends of the Court") brief; which will be submitted to the court and used as defense evidence in a hearing scheduled for Friday February 29.

Despite the attempts by the ACLU and others, Bank Julius Baer says that their lawsuit has nothing to do with the rights of free speech. "This action has been brought solely to prevent the unlawful dissemination of stolen bank records and personal account information of its customers. Many of those documents have also been altered and forged," said the Bank.

Recently the Bank has made allegations that they have been "unable to negotiate with Wikileaks" at all before or during legal proceedings. Wikileaks, in a press release denies the allegations.

"Wikileaks at all times responded with grace and dignity to BJBs highly irregular demands and left communication open," said Wikileaks which also adds that the correspondence with the Bank is available on its website on servers in Denmark. "BJB did not submit the correspondence to the court, although it must be absolutely central to the issues held there. We wonder why?"

### "Who Should Heal Our Health Care System?," *NewsUSA*, March 13, 2008

(NewsUSA)—The growing number of Americans without access to medical care has sparked a national outcry and made health care reform a top issue in the 2008 presidential election. Candidates on both sides of the political spectrum are addressing the needs of American families by proposing ideas to reform the current health system.

Sen. John McCain, the Republican candidate, is a proponent of taking steps to deregulate the insurance market, which he believes would provide more insurance options. According to McCain, the resulting competition would drive costs down. He has also proposed a plan that would allow individuals to buy insurance through organizations and associations, making it more affordable for those not covered by an employer.

Democratic candidates Sen. Hillary Clinton and Sen. Barack Obama would provide a series of affordable insurance options, both public and private. Clinton has proposed insurance mandates that would require everyone to buy health insurance. Both she and Obama would require employers to provide health insurance or pay into a common fund to defray costs.

All three candidates are in favor of tax breaks for low-income Americans and support overturning laws that ban the importation of lower-cost drugs from other countries.

Meanwhile, some medical and health associations are offering further solutions that focus on physician involvement. The American College of Cardiology (ACC) has found-through proven quality outcomes—that health care providers are in a unique position to take responsibility for medical care and value. Since 40 percent of Medicare spending is used to treat heart disease alone, cardiologists have emerged as leaders in innovative health system reform.

In addition to the ACC's data collection and grassroots quality-improvement programs, the College has been active in developing and promoting the national standardization of performance measures and electronic medical data. Comprehensive electronic records and standards ensure coordination across sources and sites of care, further improving patient value. To ensure that practicing cardiologists are educated in the latest scientific advances and have the necessary tools to apply this information to patients in daily practice, the ACC helped create-and continues to update-clinical practice guidelines that focus on quality care.

The bottom line, the ACC says, is that national efforts to overhaul the health care system need to be based on quality improvement, health care provider involvement and partnership with patients. The ACC works to support its members in their efforts to deliver quality care and is expanding upon efforts to influence policymakers to align the health care system in ways that better support the delivery of patient-focused, evidence-based care.

**From the Blog of Major P. Alston Middleton, Jr., USMC**

**Thursday, July 3, 2008—Current Challenges in Iraq**

Dear Friends, Family and Fellow Marines,

I hope this email finds you all well. I guess we, those of us in my command, are victims of the Iraqi's success. The Ministry of Defense and the Iraqi Army are swelling with confidence and challenging us as a staff to stay up with them. The Iraqis are making major changes in their army on a weekly basis that would take us years to enact within our own force, yet they are having trouble getting approval to spend small sums of money. Much of the Iraqi leadership still tries to do things the old way while the lower ranking officers and younger staff seem to understand the need to modernize and improve their procedures.

It is both fascinating and frustrating. I must say that the future of Iraq is very bright. As long as the Iraqi Army/Police can maintain the security gains within Iraq, the potential is huge. This country has vast amounts of oil, is centrally located in the middle east, and has a very rich cultural heritage. In short, the only question remaining is how do we inform the citizens of the US of our success.

It has now been about 100 days sincewe lost the 4000th member of the US military in Iraq on March 24th. It was the day after Easter and Easter was the start of over 2 months of rocket attacks on the International Zone (IZ). Fortunately, we have not had any attacks in the past 3 to 4weeks and life seems to be returning to some sort of normalcy. The current count of US military deaths is 4113, which has been slowing over the past 2 months. Each loss is very painful including COL Scott, MAJ Wolfer and SSgt Frost, but the sacrifice being made over here must not be in vain. Afghanistan is now starting to surpass Iraq in the number of coalition losses. The fight and focus of the enemy seems to be shifting from Iraq to Afghanistan which is good news for this country.

The news over here is very encouraging, but will it sell in an American election year? I would expect the criminal elements of Al Qaeda and the Shi'ia "Special Groups" to possibly ramp up their attacks sometime in August through October in an attempt to sway public opinion of this war in the US press. Time will tell. Honestly, the biggest challenge is how do we back down and let the Iraqi government take the lead. The biggest trap over here is the temptation of performing tasks the American way. This temptation often creeps into play, and the Iraqis do the natural thing of stepping back and watching the US forces do the heavy lifting. Basically, it is a cultural difference that requires us to make a conscious effort to adjust.

I am very grateful for your continued support and I am looking forward to returning home in about 100 days, early to mid October.

Sincerely,

Alston

P. Alston Middleton, Jr., Major, USMC

**Monday, July 21, 2008—A Poolside Baptism**

Dear Friends, Family and Fellow Marines,

I hope this email finds you well. Life in Iraq has been churning on at a very intense pace with the weeks flying by but the days sometimes are painfully slow. It is becoming more and more apparent to those of us over here that the Iraqi leadership and the Ministry of Defense have their own ideas about Iraq and its future. Honestly, it is good to see them approaching these problems with their determination and grit. However, we are two different cultures with different ideas about communications, logistics, maintenance and supply. So, it appears that the coalition is now having less and less influence over Iraqi problems which may be a natural progression—but a difficult one.

On another note, last Saturday, I went to the liberty pool for a baptism. This pool was the hangout for Sadam's sons, Uday and Quesay.

It is now a nice facility run by the State Department. Seven of the Ugandan security guards in the IZ were baptized in a spirit filled ceremony. It was an amazing site which was made possible through one of the bible studies that occur locally. The singing and dancing during and after the baptism was incredible. I was truly impressed by their commitment and the musical talent of the other Ugandans attending.

I am now close to 80 days from heading home and I can't wait. A year-long tour over here gives you a new outlook on life. I really do appreciate the small things like a hug from my wife and children, the chance to go for a run down the beach or to watch a sunset over the Pacific Ocean.

Please join me in praying for the Coleman family which has experienced an unexpected loss last week. I will truly miss Walker, he was a Saint.

Sincerely,

Alston

P. Alston Middleton, Jr., Major, USMC


## Monday, August 11, 2008—A Chance Encounter

Dear Friends, Family and Fellow Marines,

The latest news from Iraq is truly amazing. In the month of July, there were a total of 11 US military fatalities in all of Iraq.

The number of combat related deaths was only five. While these low numbers are very encouraging, each of these fatalities have given the last full measure in order to bring peace to this nation and the region.

The Iraqi Army is still taking the fight to the enemy and going on the offense with strong support from the coalition.

One of the six noncombat related fatalities was a soldier named Specialist Andre D. Mitchell, 25, Elmont, NY assigned to the 2nd BN, 3rd Armored Cavalry Regiment, Fort Hood, TX. I was honored to be on the C-130 flight that carried Andre from Mosul to Kuwait International Airport. This redirected flight was originally scheduled to go from Baghdad International Airport (BIAP) to Al Udeid Air Base in Qatar; I was going on a 4 day pass at Camp As Sayliyah in Qatar. I have to credit the Air Force with making sure that this soldier was given what I perceived to be a very dignified entrance and exit on the C-130. Again, I was honored to be a Marine in the formation at 0300 in the morning on 1 August as he was carried off of the plane in Kuwait International Airport. I will never forget that moment.

I had a chance encounter on my trip to Qatar with a fellow Charlestonian at BIAP and at Camp As Sayliyah. Mr. Gibson, the incoming CEO for the USO, came over to the middle east to see how his organization can best support the troops in the field with tailored, deployable USO care packages. If you are looking for an organization to support that directly impacts deployed US military forces, give to the USO. It is hard to believe that our encounters were pure chance. I believe that my delayed departure from BIAP was directed by the good Lord in order to help him and one of his colleagues get to the MNC-I Headquarters at the Al Faw Palace on 31 July. We were able to link up with their POC by 0800 that morning. I also saw Mr. Gibson on 7 August at Camp As Sayliyah in Qatar as I was trying to get back to Iraq. My original flight from Al Udeid to BIAP on 6 August was canceled late that evening which gave me two extra days in Qatar. We had a nice meeting and I enjoyed the beer and spending time with 2 Navy LCDRs and an Air Force Major.

I am recharged and back at work pulling my MNSTC-I oar for the next 50 to 60 days as hard as I can. I need to stay focused on the mission and not redeploying, but I must say planning my redeployment is great.

Sincerely,

Alston

P. Alston Middleton, Jr., Major, USMC

### "Beijing 2008: Michael Phelps Wins Eighth Gold,"
### *Wikinews*, August 17, 2008

American swimmer Michael Phelps, 23, has set a new record for the most gold medals won in one Olympic games by winning his eighth gold medal of the 2008 Olympic games, beating the previous world record of seven that was set by Mark Spitz in the 1972 Olympic Games, which took place in Munich, Germany.

Phelps' eighth medal was won in the final of the men's 4 x 100m medley relay. In addition to Phelps, Aaron Piersol, Brendan Hansen, and Jason Lezak were in the winning Olympic team, which had a time of 3:29.34, which was a new world record. In seven of his eight races, Phelps set or contributed to a new world record time. He set an Olympic record time in the remaining race.

"With so many people saying it couldn't be done, all it takes is an imagination," said Phelps after realizing he had set the new medals record. "There are so many emotions going through my head and so much excitement. I kind of just want to see my mom."

"Without the help of my team-mates this isn't possible," he continued. "I was able to be a part of three relays and we were able to put up a solid team effort and we came together as one unit. For the three Olympics I've been a part of, this is by far the closest men's team that we've ever had. I didn't know everybody coming into this Olympics, but I feel going out I know every single person very well. The team that we had is the difference."

Grant Hackett, an Australian swimmer, praised Phelps for achieving his goal. "Michael Phelps - you can't put it in words what he has done here, his level of achievement is phenomenal and I don't think it will ever be seen again."

### "Foreclosures Open Up New Market,"
### *NewsUSA*, November 18, 2008

(NewsUSA)—To some, the current real estate market looks dismal. A weak labor market, rising mortgage rates and high energy prices have caused many American homeowners to lose their properties. To others, the real estate markets looks ripe for investment.

Deer Park Development Corporation, a company with over 30 years of experience in the real estate market, has developed a new approach for investors hoping to purchase and resell foreclosed properties for profit. Foreclosed houses sell at lower prices, helping investors buy properties with less money upfront. In the past, housing prices reflected overinflation; as the market evens out, the mortgage crisis might actually help stabilize home prices.

Marty O'Malley, CEO of Deer Park Development Corporation, noted that the current real estate market represents a once-in-a-lifetime opportunity for the astute buyer. "With one in every 360 homes in foreclosure nationwide, the opportunity to buy distressed property at significant discounts to their original appraisals is extensive," said O'Malley. "In Clark County, Nev., one in every eighty homes is in foreclosure, and on top of those statistics, one in every two homes is underwater, meaning that it's not worth the amount of money owed on it."

With this amount of inventory on the market, there are situations out there that present themselves as profitable ventures. Not all of the oreclosures are money-making deals, but with experience, professional investors know when and what to buy, so they can make successful ventures.

Being an individual investor in the real estate market can be a dangerous proposition for the inexperienced. But investors, in tying themselves to a group of experienced real estate players, can use experts' hard-earned knowledge to turn a profit in the down real estate market.

"Allowing individual investors to participate in ownership through direct partnership creates a risk-free vehicle for foreclosure players to work with," said O'Malley.

### "U.S. Celebrates as President Obama Vows New Era," CNN.com, January 20, 2009

WASHINGTON (CNN)—Barack Obama launched his presidency before an estimated 1.5 million people on the National Mall on Tuesday with somber yet confident tones, saying the country will overcome its serious economic and international challenges. "Today I say to you that the challenges we face are real," Obama said in his inaugural address. "They are serious, and they are many. They will not be met easily or in a short span of time. But know this, America: They will be met."

Obama's tempered optimism, however, was bookended by celebration in the Mall and across the country for the inauguration of the country's first African-American president. "This is America happening," said Evadey Minott, a Brooklyn, New York, resident who witnessed the inauguration. "It was prophesized by King that we would have a day when everyone would come together. This is that day. I am excited. I am joyful. It brings tears to my eyes."

Obama's address came before a crowd that had been building since 4 a.m. Tuesday down the National Mall. People sang, danced and waved flags as his swearing-in approached. Many in the crowd seemed moved as Aretha Franklin belted out a rousing version of "My Country 'Tis of Thee" before Joe Biden was sworn in as vice president. Wearing a navy suit and red tie, Obama repeated the oath of office, his hand on the same Bible used in President Abraham Lincoln's first inauguration.

When Obama took the podium, however, the jubilant crowd grew somber and quiet, hanging on his every word. There was only scattered applause—punctuated by an occasional "That's right" or "Amen."

Obama thanked those who sacrificed so much so "a man whose father, less than 60 years ago, might not have been served at a local restaurant can now stand before you to take a most sacred oath." He promised to end petty squabbles on Capitol Hill, bring "old friends and former enemies" into the fold, and invoked the Bible, saying, "The time has come to set aside childish things." He also vowed to leave Iraq to its people, responsibly, and to finish forging "a hard-earned peace" in Afghanistan. To Muslims, he promised "a new way forward, based on mutual interest," and to terrorists, he leveled a threat: "You cannot outlast us, and we will defeat you." The challenges are daunting, he said, but anyone who underestimates this nation has forgotten about its past perseverance. "Greatness is never a given. It must be earned," he said.

His words resounded with spectators and revelers who let out deafening cheers after his address. Spectator L.J. Caldwell likened Obama to some of the most heroic figures of the civil rights movement. "When you think back, Malcolm [X] fought, then we come a little further. Rosa Parks sat, then come up a little further, and [the Rev. Martin Luther King Jr.] spoke. Then today, President Obama ran and we won," said Caldwell, of Somerset, New Jersey.

Celebrations weren't limited to Washington. Across the country, friends and strangers gathered on the streets and in schools, bars and auditoriums to witness Obama's inauguration, united in their hope that he will deliver on his promise of change. In New York's Bronx borough, students huddled in the halls of a school to watch the ceremony on a projection screen. "They were cheering; they were clapping; they were in awe because everything we had talked about, they were able to see," teacher Marta Rendon said. Leaders around the world offered their congratulations. French President Nicolas Sarkozy said the United States expressed "its resolve to have an open, new, strong and caring America." Australian Prime Minister Kevin Rudd said Obama is "the hope of our time."

After Obama's address, hundreds of thousands remained on Washington's National Mall as Obama entered the Capitol and signed his first documents as the 44th president of the United States. Among those were his Cabinet nominations. The Senate approved most of those nominations later in the day. Obama then lunched with lawmakers at the Capitol's Statuary Hall, telling them, "What's happening today is not about me. It is about the American people."

Later, Obama's motorcade carried him past barricaded crowds along Pennsylvania Avenue toward the White House. He and his family watched the rest of the parade in a reviewing stand outside the White House. The president and first lady then began the rounds of 10 official inaugural balls scheduled over the course of the evening.

Many said before the festivities that they did not have tickets and would be happy to catch a mere glimpse of the nation's first African-American president. Some spectators were more than a mile from the swearing-in ceremony, watching on giant TV screens erected along the National Mall.

At St. John's Episcopal Church, where the Obamas kicked off a packed day, 9-year-old Laura Brueggeman waited with her mother, Wendy, and father, Jeff, of Bethesda, Maryland. The affable crowd tried to let shorter onlookers and children to the front for better views. "I want to see Obama. I think that would be really cool. I could tell all of my friends that I got to see him," the youngster said. Security was tight in Washington. However, no arrests related to the inauguration were reported as of Tuesday evening, an FBI spokesman said.

The ceremony also drew celebrities like Dustin Hoffman, Denzel Washington and Steven Spielberg. "It's beyond the dream. We're just here feeling it with the throngs of people. It's amazing grace personified," Oprah Winfrey said, sitting next to actor Samuel L. Jackson.

Obama and congressional leaders formally bade farewell to Bush, and the now-former president took a presidential jet to Midland, Texas, shortly afterward. As Obama and his wife, Michelle, made their way to the White House, they stepped out of their limousine amid another round of boisterous hoorahs.

The first couple beamed as they walked down Pennsylvania Avenue, waving to the throngs kept back by police barriers. They walked a few blocks before returning to their vehicle to finish the two-mile parade that took them to the White House. "I have a sneaky suspicion that Barack and Michelle will be out and about on the streets of Washington [during his term]. ...You'll see them again," said Tracy Miller, who was watching the Obamas. After arriving at the White House, Obama and his family watched the rest of the inauguration parade from a reviewing stand.

༺ৡৰ৾ৡৰ৾ৡৰ৾ৡৰ৾༻

### "Madoff Jailed after Pleading Guilty to $50 Billion Fraud Scheme," *Wikinews*, March 12, 2009

US financier Bernard Madoff, the former chairman of the Nasdaq stock index, has been jailed after pleading guilty to all 11 charges of fraud, money laundering, and perjury surrounding a US$50 billion Ponzi scheme.

"I'm deeply sorry and ashamed," the financier stated during a speech in the New York court. "I believed it would end quickly and I would extricate myself and my clients. This proved difficult and, in the end, impossible."

Some of Madoff's victims applauded when the former was handcuffed by officers and taken out of the courtroom to a holding cell where he will await sentencing. Madoff is facing 150 years behind bars, with no chance of parole. Sentencing is set for June 16.

Among the charges that Madoff plead guilty to were four counts of fraud, three counts of money laundering, perjury, and making false statements, among others.

Judge Denny Chin of Federal District Court ordered that Madoff be remanded as he was awaiting a sentence, rather than letting him out on bail and allowing him to return to his apartment in Manhattan. "He has incentive to flee, he has the means to flee, and thus he presents the risk of flight," the judge said. "Bail is revoked."

༺ৡৰ৾ৡৰ৾ৡৰ৾ৡৰ৾༻

### "In Down Economy, Cities Reach Out to Gay Tourists," *NewsUSA*, May 14, 2009

(NewsUSA)—As a stagnant economy has many Americans rethinking travel plans, cities are marketing to new travel demographics—including gay and lesbian tourists.

Unlike other travel brackets, gay travel has remained steady despite the economic recession. Gay and lesbian couples travel more often and spend more money while on vacation than straight couples. According to a 2006 study conduced by the U.S. Travel Association, gay men spend about $800 per trip. Straight men spend $540.

Cities are heeding the trend. In 2003, Philadelphia launched its $300,000 a year "Get Your History Straight and Your Nightlife Gay" marketing campaign. Now, the city ranks as America's 13th largest gay and lesbian travel destination. Southwest Airlines is currently working with the city to attract even more gay and lesbian visitors.

In addition to Philadelphia, Miami, with its historic art deco hotels, beaches and happening nightlife, continues to draw gay and lesbian vacationers. But as the gay tourism market becomes more competitive, the city is working to draw new visitors. In April 2009, the city held a Gay Pride Festival to celebrate gender rights and sexual equality. Twenty thousand visitors showed up to enjoy a parade and the Miami Gay Men's Chorus and to wave rainbow-colored flags.

"In the past few years, other cities like Key West have cut into Miami's gay tourism," says Frederic S. Richardson, CEO of MOD Hospitality (www.eastcoastventures.com), which owns the Astor and Clinton hotels—two of the top-ranked hotels in South Beach. "It's time that Miami reasserts itself as one of the gay cultural centers of the world."

Chicago, which hosted the 2006 Gay Games—a quadrennial athletic and cultural event—continues to pursue gay and lesbian tourists. The Chicago Convention and Tourism Bureau writes a quarterly newsletter directed toward gay, lesbian, bisexual and transgender travelers, and plans to host an International Gay and Lesbian Travel Association board meeting.

"Chicago, frankly, is just now catching up to other cities who have been aggressively wooing the pink dollar," said Mark Theis, executive vice president of the Chicago Convention and Tourism Bureau, in an interview with the the Chicago Tribune. "We want people to know how gay-friendly we are and the wealth of attractive assets we have."

სავ-ავ-ავ-ავ-ავ-ავ-ავ

### "The Earlier, the Better: Building Immune Defenses Against H1N1," *NewsUSA*, June 12, 2009

(NewsUSA)—Recently, scientists discovered that the 2009 H1N1 Swine Flu virus is more like the H5N1 avian flu than the historic 1918 pandemic H1N1 Spanish flu strain, and that current mutations of the virus have rendered previous flu vaccines less effective.

In a teleconference with colleagues, Dr. Roger Mazlen, an internist in Rosyln Heights, NY, discussed the current Swine Flu outbreaks. Aside from traditional medical school, Dr. Mazlen received specialized training at the National Institute for Health (NIH) and is the former Clinical Research Director for Immunotec, Ltd. in Canada. He has practiced internal medicine and nutrition for more than 30 years.

Swine flu, or H1N1, was first isolated in a pig in 1930, according to the Centers for Disease Control and Prevention. The virus has demonstrated an ability to migrate from domestic pigs to humans. Dr. Mazlen said there are several factors contributing to the current swine flu outbreak, including environmental, cultural and economic issues. "The current recession, loss of retirement funds, compromised nutrition, reduced exercise, obesity and other factors produce immune depression. A depressed immune system cannot fight off the invasion of viral and other pathogens that attempt to find a home to set up infections in our bodies," he says.

Dr. Mazlen suggests protection strategies for a potentially larger H1N1 outbreak during the 2009 through 2010 flu season. "Frequent hand washing is a start. Also, lots of daily water helps to hydrate the body and assist the immune system," he said. Vitamin and mineral supplements add fortification, but Dr. Mazlen suggested also adding fish oil because of its clinically-proven immune function support. Fish oil blends are available as gel capsules or in liquid form at health food stores, and several different brands are also available at www.puritan.com.

Dr. Mazlen said that Tamiflu, the currently recommended prescription medication used in flu and Swine flu, is most effective when used within a few hours of the first viral symptoms. But Swine Flu, as reported by the CDC, has an ability to mutate within hours. Tamiflu may be effective for Swine Flu in the morning, and may be ineffective by the end of the day because of viral mutation.

When asked whether the popular herbal remedy Echinacea could be effective, Dr. Mazlen explained that studies have proven the product has minimal effectiveness in stimulating the immune response. He said he prefers a natural immune-stimulating product that he has used with over 500 patients, including his family members. The product was originally developed in Russia but is now made in the U.S. Dr. Mazlen said he has had good results during the past years with patients fighting flu and other infections. The product, Del-Immune V, is available at www.delimmune.com.

Early measures to protect health might be the key to minimizing potentially serious infections this flu season. Dr. Mazlen closed the discussion by expressing his concern over whether it is Swine Flu H1N1 or a mutated form of the Swine Flu. "It is important to have an immune defense strategy this year—the earlier the better," he said.

 former

### "Michael Jackson Dead at 50 after Cardiac Arrest," CNN.com, June 26, 2009

(CNN)—Entertainer Michael Jackson died after being taken to a hospital on Thursday having suffered cardiac arrest, according to the Los Angeles County Coroner's office.

Paramedics took Jackson, 50, from his west Los Angeles home Thursday afternoon to UCLA Medical Center, where a team of physicians attempted to resuscitate him for more than an hour, said brother Jermaine Jackson. He said the famed singer was pronounced dead at 2:26 p.m. PT.

An autopsy is scheduled Friday, he said. Results are expected Friday afternoon, according to Lt. Fred Corral of the Los Angeles coroner's office, who also said Jackson was unresponsive when he arrived at the hospital.

Fire Capt. Steve Ruda told CNN paramedics were sent to a west Los Angeles, California, residence after a 911 call came in at 12:21 p.m.

Law enforcement officials said the Los Angeles Police Department Robbery-Homicide Division opened an investigation into Jackson's death. They stressed there is no evidence of criminal wrongdoing but that they would conduct interviews with family members and friends.

CNN Analyst Roland S. Martin spoke on Thursday with Marlon Jackson, brother of Michael Jackson.

"He talked to Frank Dileo, Michael's manager. Frank told me that Michael last night was complaining about not feeling well. He called to tell him he wasn't feeling well. Michael's doctor went over to see him, and Frank said, 'Marlon, from last night to this morning, he don't know what happened.' When they got to him this morning, he wasn't breathing. They rushed him to the hospital and couldn't bring him around."

"Janet Jackson is grief-stricken and devastated at the sudden loss of her brother," Kenneth Crear, her manager said. "She is…flying immediately to California to be with her family."

Michael Jackson, the music icon from Gary, Indiana, was known as the "King of Pop." Jackson had many No. 1 hits, and his "Thriller" is the best-selling album of all time. Jackson was the seventh of nine children from a well-knownmusical family. He is survived by three children, Prince Michael I, Paris and Prince Michael II. Jackson's former wife, Lisa Marie Presley, said she was "shocked and saddened" by Jackson's death. "My heart goes out to his children and his family," she said.

At the medical center, every entrance to the emergency room was blocked by security guards. Even hospital staffers were not permitted to enter. A fewpeople stood inside thewaiting area, some of them crying. Video footage shows a large crowd gathering outside the hospital. Some of Jackson's music was being played outside. The sounds of "Thriller" and "Beat It" bounced off the walls. Outside Jackson's Bel Air home, police arrived on motorcycles. The road in front of the home was closed in an attempt to hold traffic back, but several people were gathered outside the home.

Along with his success Jackson had some legal troubles later in his career. He was acquitted of child molestation charges after a well-publicized trial in Santa Maria, California, in March 2006. Prosecutors charged the singer with four counts of lewd conduct with a child younger than 14; one count of attempted lewd conduct; four counts of administering alcohol to facilitate child molestation; and one count of conspiracy to commit child abduction, false imprisonment or extortion.

கூக்கூக்கூக்கூ

### "During Visit by Bill Clinton, North Korea Releases American Journalists," Glenn Kessler, *Washington Post*, August 5, 2009

North Korea pardoned and released two detained American journalists after former president Bill Clinton met in Pyongyang on Tuesday with the country's ailing dictator, a transaction that gives Kim Jong II a thin slice of the international legitimacy that has long eluded him.

Although the White House and the State Department steadfastly insisted that the former president—the husband of Secretary of State Hillary Rodham Clinton—was on a "private humanitarian mission," the trip came about only after weeks of back-channel conversations involving academics, congressional figures, and senior White House and State Department officials, said sources involved in the planning.

North Korea rejected the administration's first choice for the trip—former vice president Al Gore, who co-founded the television channel that employs the journalists—and Bill Clinton left the United States only after North Korea provided assurances that the reporters would be released, the sources said.

U.S. officials said they hoped Clinton's trip would give Kim a face-saving way to end North Korea's provocative actions, such as recent missile launches and a second nuclear test, and begin the process of returning to the negotiating table on its nuclear programs. The American effort also appears to have been aided by South Korea's government, which in recent weeks has sought to ease tensions with its neighbor.

In Pyongyang, the official Korean Central News Agency (KCNA) reported that the release of Laura Ling, 32, and Euna Lee, 36, was ordered after Kim issued a "special pardon." The two had been sentenced to 12 years of hard labor after they were captured in March near the Chinese border while making a documentary about the trafficking of North Korean women to China.

The journalists and Clinton left North Korea on a plane en route to Los Angeles, where the women were to be reunited with their families.

"Clinton expressed words of sincere apology to Kim Jong II for the hostile acts committed by the two American journalists," KCNA reported. "Clinton courteously conveyed to Kim Jong II an earnest request of the U.S. government to leniently pardon them."

U.S. officials denied late Tuesday night that any apology was offered. During the visit, Kim hosted a banquet in Clinton's honor, and U.S. officials said the men held talks that lasted more than three hours. State media broadcast images showing a dour-looking Clinton and a smiling Kim. And the KCNA report summarizing the trip was remarkably positive, speaking of "building the bilateral confidence" and "improving the relations between the two countries."

Ling and Lee were in many ways pawns in a test of wills between North Korea and the United States. After their sentencing in June, North Korea reportedly kept them in a guesthouse near Pyongyang, allowing them to make occasional phone calls to relatives in the United States. The sentence to hard labor was not carried out.

North Korea had long made it clear that it expected a high-profile visit on behalf of the journalists, but Gore may not have been acceptable because he was viewed as their boss and thus not an appropriate symbol of the United States. Other potential envoys considered by the administration included Senate Foreign Relations Committee Chairman John F. Kerry (D-Mass.), New Mexico Gov. Bill Richardson (D) and a former ambassador to South Korea, Donald Gregg.

The discreet discussions to secure the women's release continued even as Hillary Clinton slammed North Korea last month, saying it had "no friends" and was acting like an unruly child. But in critical ways, she also moderated her tone with regard to the case, moving from declaring in June that the charges were "absolutely without merit or foundation" to saying last month that the journalists "are deeply regretful, and we are very sorry it's happened."

Some officials said the success of former president Clinton's trip could result in the first U.S.-North Korea bilateral meeting of the Obama administration. They also think the United States will have a somewhat stronger hand because China for the first time has backed tougher sanctions in the wake of North Korea's May nuclear test.

No government officials appeared to be aboard Clinton's plane, but the nature of the delegation gave the mission a quasi-official status. It included John Podesta, Clinton's White House chief of staff, who served as chief of Obama's transition team and is president of the Center for American Progress. Also seen in photos released by the Korean media were David Straub, a former head of the Korea desk at the State Department who is now at Stanford University; longtime Clinton aide Douglas J. Band; and Justin Cooper, who has worked with the William J. Clinton Foundation.

It is not clear who funded the trip. News of Podesta's role came as a surprise to staffers at the Center for American Progress; he was thought to be on vacation in Truckee, Calif. Colleagues of Straub's at Stanford were also surprised.

Clinton and his party were greeted early Tuesday at an airport in Pyongyang, the capital, by Yang Hyong Sop, vice president of the presidium of the Supreme People's Assembly, and by Vice Foreign Minister Kim Kye Gwan, according to KCNA. Kim is the chief nuclear negotiator for North Korea, suggesting that Pyongyang hoped to use the visit to make progress on the impasse over its nuclear weapons program.

The visit offered the United States its first direct look at the increasingly frail-looking Kim Jong Il, 67, who is thought to have suffered a stroke a year ago and whose health has triggered speculation that he has picked his third son to take over Asia's only communist dynasty.

"One of the most beneficial things that could come of this is that smart American observers can describe how sharp he is, how lucid he sounds," said Robert Carlin, a former U.S. intelligence analyst who has made nearly 30 visits to North Korea and is dubious about reports of a succession crisis. "It might put to rest a lot of garbage rumors."

The most senior U.S. official previously to have met Kim was then-Secretary of State Madeleine K. Albright in 2000, who traveled to Pyongyang aiming to arrange a presidential visit by Clinton. That visit did not take place as he turned his concentration to faltering

Israeli-Palestinian peace talks in the waning days of his presidency. "The visit that never happened has now happened," said a source involved in the talks with North Korea, noting that the meeting could help fill a gap in Kim's perceived legacy.

Special correspondent Stella Kim in Seoul, correspondent Blaine Harden in Seattle and staff writer Garance Franke-Ruta in Washington contributed to this report.

### "Unemployment by the Numbers,"
### Christopher Leonard, *The Hawk Eye* (Iowa), October 3, 2009

If the recession is really ending, someone forgot to tell the nation's employers. A net total of 263,000 jobs vanished from the economy last month, much worse than economists' expectations of 180,000 job losses.

The Labor Department figures set the stage for a scenario that labor analysts expect: joblessness will continue to rise after the economy starts to rebound.

The unemployment rate stands at 9.8 percent, a 26-year high. The rate would have been higher if 571,000 people had dropped out of the labor force, which many did in frustration over failing to find jobs.

That leaves 15.1 million Americans out of work, a huge pool of people. That's why the overall unemployment rate measuring people searching for work and who can't find it can continue to rise even after employers start creating thousands of jobs each month.

Even though economists think the economy has begun to grow, it could be well into 2010 before job creation ramps up. Here are some details by the numbers.

### Slack in the workforce

33: the number of hours in the workweek. This figure fell back to the record low earlier this year. It indicates many companies are not operating near full capacity, and they may boost the hours of their part-time workers before hiring more full-time staff.

103,000: the increase in people who hold a parttime job because they can't find full-time work. That number has climbed steadily this year, reaching 9.1 million in September.

$616.11: the average weekly earnings of prior private sector workers. This figure has fallen 1.3 percent since January, in part because employers are cutting hours.

$18.67: the average hourly wage. Up a penny from August.

### Dismal prospects

26.2 weeks: the average duration that unemployed workers are out of a job, a record high since the Labor Department started tracking the figure in 1948. The figure is up from 19.8 weeks in January.

5.4 million: The number of people unemployed longer than 27 weeks, also a post-World War II peak, though today's larger labor market is a contributing factor.

17 percent: the unemployment rate that includes frustrated workers who have dropped out of the labor market, people forced into part-time work, or those who want a job but haven't looked recently.

263,000: the number of jobs lost in September.

### Leading in job losses

64,000: the number of construction jobs lost in September, mostly in nonresidential and heavy construction. This sector has lost 1.5 million jobs since the recession began.

51,000: the number of manufacturing jobs lost in September. This sector has lost 2.1 million jobs since the recession began.

### One healthy sector

19,000: the number of healthcare jobs added in September.

559,000: the number of healthcare jobs added since the recession began.

22,000: the average monthly job gains in the healthcare sector this year.

30,000: the average monthly job gains in the healthcare sector last year.

### "Administration Eyes Ways to Help Jobless,"
### *The Bakersfield Californian*, October 4, 2009

The Obama administration is considering steps to ease the burdens of laid-off workers, including possible extensions of unemployment and health benefits, officials said Saturday.

The administration has stopped short of calling for a second economic stimulus package to augment the $787 billion measure approved this year. But with the jobless rate continuing to climb, President Barack Obama said Saturday he is exploring the "additional options to promote job creation."

Administration aides said possibilities include:

- Extending the enhanced employment insurance benefits beyond December 31, when they are set to expire.

- Extending the tax credit for laid-off workers who buy health insurance through the COBRA program. That program allows workers to keep their company's health insurance plan for 18 months after they leave their job, if they pay the premiums.

- Extending a tax credit for first-time home buyers. This credit also is set to expire soon.

The administration has discussed these possibilities with congressional leaders, officials said, but no decisions have been made.

White House economic advisor Lawrence Summers expressed interest in these ideas in an online interview with the Atlantic magazine. "I don't know what the term 'second stimulus package' exactly means," Summers said. "We certainly need to continue to support people who are in need, whether it's unemployment insurance, or a COBRA program that for the first time provides the people who are laid off get supported in being able to maintain their health insurance."

In his weekly radio and Internet video address Saturday, Obama said his proposed healthcare overhaul would create jobs by making small business startups more affordable. If aspiring entrepreneurs believe that they can stay insured while switching jobs, he said, they will start new businesses that hire workers.

Dismissive Republicans blamed the continuing job losses on Democratic policies and said the president's health proposals won't help.

The unemployment rate rose to 9.8 percent in September, the highest since June 1983, as employers cut far more jobs than expected.

### "Should Unemployed People Work for Free,"
### *Parade, Komono Tribune* (Indiana), October 11, 2009

More than half a million Americans file new unemployment claims each week, relying on state benefits to keep them afloat as they spend their days looking for jobs. But in Georgia, thousands of unemployed people are working without a salary in "auditions" for paying gigs.

Under the Georgia Works Program, jobless citizens work part-time for up to six weeks at businesses with job openings. They earn no salary, but the state pays unemployment benefits along with a weekly stipend for transportation, childcare, and other expenses. And while the businesses don't issue paychecks, they do provide valuable on-the-job training, according to Michael Thurmond, the state's labor Commissioner. So far, some 3,000 Georgians (58 percent of participants) have been hired at the places where they started working for free. Thurmond calls it a "win, win, win" program that has helped the unemployed find work; saved employers nearly $15 million in labor, hiring, and training costs; and saved the state $5.3 million in benefits that would have been paid to the people who remained unemployed. At least 17 other states have asked about starting similar programs.

Still, there are critics. Andrew Stettner of the National Employment Law Project says that unemployed workers should spend their time looking for the right job. He fears the Georgia program could lead to mandatory unpaid work for the unemployed if it were replicated in other states. "The purpose of unemployment had to be to enable people to search for suitable work, not give employers free labor," he says.

### "Thousands March in Washington for Gay Rights,"
### Katherine Skiba, *Los Angeles Times*, October 12, 2009

WASHINGTON—Tens of thousands of gays, lesbians and supporters marched through the nation's capital Sunday in a festive, forceful call for equality, culminating in a boisterous rally at the Capitol.

The National Equality March took place one day after President Obama made sweeping pledges to the gay community, including a vow to end the military policy of "don't ask, don't tell"—which bans gays and lesbians from serving openly in the armed forces. Obama gave no timetable for repealing the policy.

Marchers waving rainbow-colored flags were in no mood to wait. They came to a halt on Pennsylvania Avenue, in front of theWhite House, and chanted, "Hey, Obama, can't you see? We demand equality." Echoing the president's campaign slogan, they shouted, "Yes, we can" and "Si, se puede." Obama also said Saturday night, at a Human Rights Campaign gala, that he wanted Congress to repeal the federal Defense of Marriage Act. That legislation, passed in 1996 and signed by President Clinton, bars federal recognition of same-sex marriages. Obama has made these pledges before, and whether he can keep them could hinge on sentiments in Congress and the military.

In any event, to some in Sunday's crowd, his promises held little weight. "For this president to keep throwing us out of the military is unconscionable," Los Angeles City Councilman Bill Rosendahl, a gay man and Army veteran, said in an interview.

Later, at the Capitol rally, Rosendahl told the crowd that 36 states allow housing discrimination based on sexual orientation and 29 states permit firings on those grounds. Same-sex marriages are legal in only a handful of states—including Massachusetts, Vermont, Iowa and Connecticut. Depriving gays of the right to wed, Rosendahl said, deprives them of 1,100 rights. Organizers of Sunday's march said the LGBT community (lesbian, gay, bisexual and transgender people) is not satisfied with a piecemeal approach to civil rights. Forty years after the Stonewall riots in New York launched the gay rights movement, they are demanding "full federal equality" and singling out marriage, adoption, military service and workplace issues.

Some marchers wore purple T-shirts exhorting: "Legalize gay." Alex Miller, 23, of Ashburn, Va., waved a sign supporting her sister, Sam, 20, a lesbian. "Same womb. Same rights," it said. Another demonstrator held a sign that bore a swastika and the words: "You are not the first to hate us."

The U.S. Park Police does not provide crowd counts. Phil Siegel, a march spokesman, put the head count at "more than 150,000." A few counter-protesters also joined the crowd.

The rally drew impassioned speakers, including NAACP Chairman Julian Bond; Army 1st Lt. Daniel Choi, an Iraq combat veteran facing discharge for disclosing his sexual orientation; Babs Siperstein, a transsexual member of the Democratic National Committee; glam rocker Lady Gaga; and Michael Huffington, a Republican and former congressman from California. Bond linked gay rights to civil rights. "Black people of all people should not oppose equality, and that is what marriage is all about," he said. "We have a lot of real and serious problems in this country, and same-sex marriage is not one of them."

In California, black voters tended to support Proposition 8, the measure that passed last November and reversed a state Supreme Court decision permitting same-sex marriage. Choi appeared at the rally in his Army uniform. "Many of us have been discharged from the service because we told the truth," he said. "But I know that love is worth it."

One of the gay rights activists who took the stage said she had suffered personal and public heartbreak because of anti-gay violence. "I'm here today because I lost my son to hate," Judy Shepard said. Matthew Shepard, 21, a gay college student from Wyoming, was tortured, tied to a fence post and left to die 11 years ago. "We're all Americans," Judy Shepard said. "We're all equal Americans—gay, straight or whatever." Matthew Shepard is to be memorialized by legislation that would expand the definition of federal hate crimes to include sexual orientation. The House attached the provision to a defense bill that passed last week. The Senate is expected to pass it soon, and Obama has pledged to sign it.

At the rally, Lady Gaga raised her right fist and shouted, "Bless God and bless the gays." She also took a shot at House Democrat Barney Frank of Massachusetts, an openly gay lawmaker who shunned the march, saying on Friday: "The only thing they're going to be putting pressure on is the grass." Addressing Frank by name, Lady Gaga said: "Today this grass is ours. We will come away today and continue to do the work in our own backyards."

### "Authorities: 'Balloon Boy' Incident was a Hoax,"
### Greg Morrison and Janet DiGiacomo, *Los Angeles Times*,
### October 19, 2009

(CNN)—Three days after the world watched a giant balloon fly through the air as a tearful family expressed fears that their 6-year-old boy could be inside, authorities announced what millions suspected: The whole thing was staged.

The "Aha!" moment that led authorities to realize what had happened was an interview with the family Thursday night on CNN's "Larry King Live," Sheriff Jim Alderden of Larimer County said Sunday. In the interview with Wolf Blitzer, filling in for King, the Heenes asked their son why he had not come out from hiding when they called his name.

"You guys said we did this for the show," the boy responded.

On Sunday, Alderden called the incident a "hoax," adding that investigators believe the evidence indicates that "it was a publicity stunt" by the family in hopes of "better marketing themselves for a reality television show at some point in the future."

The parents, Richard and Mayumi Heene, met in a Hollywood acting school and "put on a very good show for us," Alderden said. Authorities know there was "a conspiracy" between them, he added.

He said charges are expected to be filed in the case.

The couple's attorney told CNN affiliate KMGH that he hasn't seen any evidence beyond "speculation," but the Heenes would turn themselves in if charges are filed.

"All I'm saying if you've got some reason to arrest him, let me know, he'll turn himself in," said Denver attorney David Lane referring to Richard Heene. "If you got the goods, just tell me."

The sheriff said investigators also want to interview 25-year-old researcher Robert Thomas who worked with Richard Heene for about two months last spring. Thomas was paid by Gawker.com—a popular gossip site—to write about his experience with Heene for a story published on Saturday.

In an interview arranged with the help of Gawker, Thomas told CNN Sunday that as a student at Colorado State University with an interest in electromagnetic studies, he sought out Heene for a job as a possible research assistant. He said he ended up as his "stenographer," taking down Heene's ideas and proposals for reality-show pitches.

Thomas said that at one point they were talking about the Roswell UFO incident of the late 1940s, when Heene said it would be easy to cook up "a media stunt that would be equally profound as Roswell, and we could do so with nothing more than a weather balloon and some controversy."

Thomas said he wrote up the balloon idea, which he says did not involve any kids going missing, as a potential reality show episode. "I didn't know that he was going to do something like this," Thomas told CNN Sunday.

Thomas said he eventually quit working with Heene in May.

The sheriff's announcement included an admission that authorities misled the media on Friday when they said they still believed it was not a hoax. After Falcon's remark on CNN Thursday night, "it became very clear to us at that point that they were lying," Alderden said.

The "nonverbal responses" and "verbal cues" from the children at that moment made it clear, Alderden said.

But to get to the truth, "it was very important during this time that they maintained their trust with us." So investigators misled the media while they carried out their "game plan" of gathering the truth.

That plan included pursuing separate interviews with the Heene parents and polygraph tests, partly by arguing that it could help end the media frenzy surrounding them, Alderden said. He added that by law he could not say whether those tests were taken.

The Heenes have repeatedly denied any hoax. In an interview Friday with CNN's "American Morning," Richard Heene said Falcon's remark was a reference to the media that had assembled in front of the family's home.

Charges have not been filed, but authorities expect to recommend felony charges including conspiracy, contributing to the delinquency of a minor and attempting to influence a public servant, Alderden said. They also plan to recommend a charge of filing a false police report, which is a misdemeanor.

He also said it is unlikely that someone convicted of these charges would face jail time.

One of the key questions that remain unanswered, Alderden said, is: Where was Falcon as police searched for him? On Friday, Alderden said it had been determined that the boy was hiding in an attic in the garage, and had fallen asleep. Now, authorities are unsure. Alderden said the boy may not have even been in the home.

"The biggest error we made is when we searched the house very clearly we didn't search the house as thoroughly as we should," he said. Authorities had assumed a 6-year-old boy could not have reached that attic, he said, so they took the Heenes at their word that he had hidden there the whole time.

The Heenes have previously appeared on the ABC program "Wife Swap." Richard Heene chases storms and brings the family along.

After the Hollywood gossip Web site TMZ.com reported that the Heenes had been "pitching a reality show about the wacky family," one of the networks mentioned—TLC, which produces the show "Jon and Kate plus 8"—told CNN that "they approached us months ago, and we passed."

Heene has been described as a meteorologist, but his education ended at the high school level, Alderden said.

Alderden also said authorities are concerned about the safety of the three children, ages 6, 8, and 10. In fact, authorities spoke with Mayumi Heene "at length about domestic violence" and the children's safety, Alderden said. "But we didn't have enough that would allow us or Child Protection Services to physically take the kids from that environment."

A 911 call was made from the home earlier this year that led authorities to a "suspicious circumstance" that Alderden said may have involved "domestic violence, perhaps against the wife."

Lane, the Heenes' attorney, told KMGH that he has "no reason to believe they're anything but loving parents."

In an interview Friday with CNN's "American Morning," the Heene parents—looking exhausted—expressed relief that their son was alive. "I'm feeling very, very grateful that Falcon is among us," Richard Heene said.

Mayumi Heene said that the family was sitting in their living room, distraught and terrified for missing Falcon, when he walked into the room.

"[It] felt like from nowhere. When he first saw him, I couldn't even believe it. I couldn't comprehend right away," she said, adding that the next moment she was "just jumping, calling his name." She began to "scream and cry, and I just enjoyed that moment."

### "Recliner No Decliner, Easy Chair Sales a Bright Spot for Furniture Industry," Emory Dalesio, *Arlington Heights Daily Herald* (Illinois), October 21, 2009

Ah, the recliner. The American invention that linked lazing in the living room to television and frozen dinners is one of the few bright spots in a well-worn U.S. household furniture industry.

Sales from planning shares are getting a lift from the growing popularity of high-tech TVs, home theater equipment, and video games, as well as an aging population that is less active. Even the recession, which forced many Americans to cancel vacation plans, seems to have helped sales of the comfy lounge chairs.

"People think 'I'm not going to travel. Doggone it, when I go home I'm going to be comfortable,' said Don Hunter, who heads Catnapper, a recliner focused division of Jackson Furniture Industries in Cleveland, Tennessee.

Sales for reclining chairs and sofas totaled $3.5 billion last year and are expected to climb to $4 billion within five years, according to trade magazine Furniture/Today and New York-based Easy Analytic Software Inc. Nevada and Arizona, both popular states for retirees, will see sales jump 25 percent.

That's a stark contrast to the nearly 13 percent drop in sales that furniture stores saw through September this year, compared with the same nine-month period last year, according to Census data. That bad news included a slight 1.4 percent rise in retail sales from August to September, the government reported this week.

On Saturday, as the household furniture industry assembles in High Point, North Carolina, for the start of its twice-a-year international tradeshow, several manufacturers will be showcasing recliners with more gizmos.

Berkline has introduced a recliner line starting at $699 with installed stereo speakers, a subwoofer, and a plug for an iPod. The company has an existing model that can be hooked up to a special amplifier that delivers the shakes and vibrations of the action in your home theater system.

Also new this year is a top end to the line of massage chair retailing for about $1,200-$2,400. The deluxe version offered this year cost $2,599, conforms to the shape of the user's body, and includes a system of pressurized air bags for a massage that mimics human hands.

### "Unemployment Hits 10.2 Percent," Chris Isidore, *CNNMoney.com*, November 6, 2009

NEW YORK (CNNMoney.com)—The nation's unemployment rate rose above 10 percent for the first time since 1983 in October, a much worse jump than expected as employers continued to trim jobs from payrolls.

The reading, reported by the government Friday, is a sign of the continued weakness in the labor market even though the economy grew in the third quarter following the longest and deepest downturn since the Great Depression.

The government reported that the unemployment rate spiked to 10.2 percent, up from 9.8 percent in September. It is the highest that this rate has been since April 1983. Economists had forecast an increase to 9.9 percent.

There was also a net loss of 190,000 jobs in October, according to the Labor Department, an improvement from a revised estimate of 219,000 job losses in September. However, economists surveyed by Briefing.com had forecast a loss of only 175,000 jobs in October. This was the 22nd straight month of job losses.

"The only good news is the number of layoffs are dropping off, but those who are laid off still aren't finding jobs," said David Wyss, chief economist with Standard & Poor's.

The jump in the unemployment rate was driven up by a large drop in the number of people who describe themselves as self-employed, as well as the number of teenagers who have jobs. The unemployment rate for teenagers in the labor force soared to 27.6 percent, up 1.8 percentage points and hitting a third straight record high.

Both teen workers and the self-employed are not captured very well in the government's separate survey of employers that is used to calculate the number of people on U.S. payrolls. That explains much of the disconnect between fewer job losses overall and the much worse unemployment rate.

The rise in unemployment was not spread evenly across the population. For those with college degrees, the unemployment rate fell to 4.7 percent from 4.9 percent in September, as the unemployment rate for those in management, professional, and related occupations slipped to 4.7 percent from 5.2 percent.

But the unemployment rate for production jobs, such as factory workers, jumped to 14.5 percent from 14.1 percent. The jobless rate for workers in construction, maintenance or natural resources industries such as mining rose to 15.5 percent from 14.3 percent.

"There's a real mismatch between the unemployed people out there compared to what job openings are available," said John Silvia, chief economist with Wells Fargo Securities. He said construction workers who lost a job when the housing bubble burst don't have the skills to compete for jobs in sectors that are hiring, such as health care and technology.

Government efforts to end job losses have had limited effects, although the Obama administration estimated last month that 640,000 jobs were created or saved by the federal stimulus package passed earlier this year. But that's modest compared to the 7.3 million jobs that have been lost since the start of 2008.

Christina Romer, chair of the President's Council of Economic Advisors, said the steady decline in monthly job losses since earlier this year is a hopeful sign for the economy.

But she acknowledged there's still significant pain for those looking for work. "Having the unemployment rate reach double-digits is a stark reminder of how much work remains to be done before American families see the job gains and reduced unemployment that they need and deserve," she said.

Friday's report comes one day after Congress voted overwhelmingly to extend unemployment benefits by up to 20 weeks. There are now a record 5.6 million people who have been unemployed for six months or longer, as the average time an unemployed person has been out of a job hit 26.9 weeks.

Prior to this report, most economists had believed that the unemployment rate would keep rising and that job losses would continue into next year. But the jump in unemployment in October took it to levels worse than what many previously had expected to be the peak.

According to a survey of top forecasters by the National Association of Business Economics last month, the consensus estimate among economists was that unemployment would hit a high of 10 percent in the final three months of this year and the first quarter of 2010.

The five economists with the most bearish forecasts had expected unemployment to rise to 10.2 percent in the fourth quarter of this year before hitting 10.5 percent in the first half of next year.

Wyss is one of those economists who had projected an unemployment rate of 10.5 percent in the middle of next year. He said Friday's report may force him to raise his worst case estimate.

"Some things aren't playing out the way I expected them to," he said. "There's just no good news in this report."

But others said they see some early signs of life for the labor market. Sung Won Sohn, economics professor at California State University Channel Islands, noted that the biggest increase in temporary employees in two years took place in October.

Employers typically bring in workers on a temporary basis before deciding to make more permanent hires. As such, he expects gains in payrolls by next spring.

"Despite the gloomy job picture, there are some encouraging signs," he said.

### "Officials: Fort Hood Shootings Suspect Alive; 12 Dead," CNN.com, November 7, 2009

(CNN)—A soldier suspected of fatally shooting 12 and wounding 31 at Fort Hood in Texas on Thursday is not dead as previously reported by the military, the base's commander said Thursday evening. A civilian officer who was wounded in the incident shot the suspect, who is "in custody and in stable condition," Army Lt. Gen. Robert Cone told reporters. "Preliminary reports indicate there was a single shooter that was shot multiple times at the scene," Cone said at a news conference. "However, he was not killed as previously reported."

The suspect, identified as Maj. Nidal Malik Hasan, opened fire at a military processing center at Fort Hood around 1:30 p.m., Cone said. Three others initially taken into custody for interviews have been released, Cone said. Hasan, 39, is a graduate of Virginia Tech and a psychiatrist licensed in Virginia who was practicing at Darnall Army Medical Center at Fort Hood, according to military and professional records. Previously, he worked at Walter Reed Army Medical Center. A federal official said Hasan is a U.S. citizen of Jordanian descent. Military documents show that Hasan was born in Virginia and was never deployed outside the United States.

In a statement released Thursday, Hasan's cousin, Nader Hasan, said his family is "filled with grief for the families of today's victims." "Our family loves America. We are proud of our country, and saddened by today's tragedy," the statement said. "Because this situation is still unfolding, we have nothing else that we are able to share with you at this time."

Hasan was scheduled to be deployed to Iraq "and appeared to be upset about that," Sen. Kay Bailey Hutchison, R-Texas, said. "I think that there is a lot of investigation going on now into his background and what he was doing that was not known before," Hutchison said. Hutchison said she was told that the soldiers at the readiness facility "were filling out paper processing to go to Iraq or Afghanistan," according to CNN affiliate KXAN in Austin, Texas. The readiness center is one of the last stops before soldiers deploy. It is also one of the first places a soldier goes upon returning to the United States. The base reopened Thursday night after being under lockdown for more than five hours.

At a news conference earlier in the day, Cone said at least 10 of the dead were soldiers. The shooter had two weapons, both handguns, Cone said. A witness in a building adjacent to where the shooting happened said soldiers were cutting up their uniforms into homemade bandages as the wounded were brought into the building. "It was total chaos," the witness said. Cone said a graduation ceremony was being held in an auditorium just 50 meters from where the shooting took place. "Thanks to the quick reaction of several soldiers, they were able to close off the doors to that auditorium where there were some 600 people inside," he said.

Peggy McCarty of Missouri told CNN affiliate KSHB that her daughter, Keara Bono, was among Thursday's wounded. She said she briefly spoke to Bono, who told her she had been shot in her left shoulder but was doing well. "She's being deployed to Iraq on December 7," McCarty said. "I thought I was more worried about her going over to Iraq than here, just doing training in Texas. She just got there yesterday."

A woman who lives on base, about eight blocks from the shooting, said she and her daughter were at home when her husband called and told them to stay inside. "And I asked him why, what was going on. He said that there was a shooting," said the woman, Nicole, who asked that her last name not be used. She said her husband called her back about 20 minutes later and told her to go upstairs, stay away from doors and windows and keep the doors locked. "It's just been crazy," she said. "Sirens everywhere." A soldier who asked not to be identified told CNN that an e-mail went out to all base personnel instructing them not to speak to the media.

President Obama called the shootings "tragic" and "a horrific outburst of violence." He expressed his condolences for the shooting victims. "These are men and women who have made the selfless and courageous decision to risk, and at times give, their lives to protect the rest of us on a daily basis," Obama said. "It's difficult enough when we lose these brave Americans in battles overseas. It is horrifying that they should come under fire at an Army base on American soil."

Scott & White Memorial Hospital in Temple, Texas, posted an online appeal for blood as it began receiving victims. "Due to the recent events on Fort Hood, we are in URGENT need of ALL blood types," it said.

Fort Hood, with about 40,000 troops, is home to the Army's 1st Cavalry Division and elements of the 4th Infantry Division, as well as the 3rd Armored Cavalry Regiment and the 13th Corps Support Command. It is located near Killeen, Texas. The headquarters unit and three brigades of the 1st Cavalry are currently deployed in Iraq. At least 25,000 people are at Fort Hood on any given day, an Army spokesman at the Pentagon said. Fort Hood is home to the Warrior Combat Stress Reset Program, which is designed to help soldiers overcome combat stress issues.

In June, Fort Hood's commander, Lt. Gen. Rick Lynch, told CNN that he was trying to ease the kind of stresses soldiers face. He has pushed for soldiers working a day schedule to return home for dinner by 6 p.m., and required his personal authorization for anyone working weekends. At the time, two soldiers stationed there had committed suicide in 2009—a rate well below those of other posts.

Nearby Killeen was the scene of one of the most deadly shootings in American history 18 years ago when George Hennard crashed his truck into a Luby's Cafeteria and began shooting, killing 23 people and wounding 20. Hennard's spree lasted 14 minutes. He eventually took his own life.

ॐॐॐॐॐॐॐॐॐ

**"Retaining Women in the IT Industry,"**
***NewsUSA*, November 24, 2009**

(NewsUSA)—Despite improving economic data pointing to a global recovery, unemployment remains at the highest levels since 1983. For those looking for work today, risk has become an important criteria in their decision-making.

One industry that is considered to be relatively recession-proof and actually growing is information technology (IT). For example, according to the U.S. Department of Labor, technology job opportunities are projected to grow at a faster rate than jobs in all other professional sectors, or up to 25 percent over the next decade.

However, IT still has a long way to go when it comes to its hiring practices, especially with regard to women. According to the National Center for Women and IT, the number of women in IT is the lowest since the 1980s. Meanwhile, the percentage of jobs held by women in almost all other sciences has increased significantly. Furthermore, women already employed in IT are leaving at an alarming rate: 56 percent of women leave at the mid-level point.

"Technical women value professional development above all else, yet many IT companies don't foster career advancement programs, says Telle Whitney, president and CEO, Anita Borg Institute for Women and Technology (ABI)." Companies should invest in career development practices as well as provide mentoring and networking opportunities for women, which could also help achieve greater gender balance in the workplace and encourage women to stay in more senior roles.

Some companies, such as CA, Inc., recognize the need to support and retain women in IT. Today, approximately one-third of CA's total workforce is female, which compares favorably with the technology industry average. CA sponsors various programs designed to mentor women and help them to network with each other. CA also partners with ABI and participates in the annual Women Leadership Conference in New York.

# SECTION FIVE: CENSUS DATA

This section begins with eighteen state-by-state ranking tables from the 2000 and 2010 Census and the 2016 American Community Survey, designed to help define the times during which the families profiled in Section One lived. Table topics are listed below. Following the state-by-state ranking tables are reprints from Census 2010. These maps, tables, graphs, charts and narrative help the reader visualize the environment at that time.

## State-by-State Comparative Tables: 2000, 2010 and 2016

Note: When reviewing the ranking columns, be aware that the District of Columbia is included in the list of states.

## Twenty-third Decennial Census of the United States

### 2010 Census

### 2010 Census Briefs

# Total Population

| Area | Population | | | 2000 | | 2010 | | 2016 | |
|---|---|---|---|---|---|---|---|---|---|
| | 2000 | 2010 | 2016 | Area | Rank | Area | Rank | Area | Rank |
| Alabama | 4,447,100 | 4,779,736 | 4,863,300 | California | 1 | California | 1 | California | 1 |
| Alaska | 626,932 | 710,231 | 741,894 | Texas | 2 | Texas | 2 | Texas | 2 |
| Arizona | 5,130,632 | 6,392,017 | 6,931,071 | New York | 3 | New York | 3 | Florida | 3 |
| Arkansas | 2,673,400 | 2,915,918 | 2,988,248 | Florida | 4 | Florida | 4 | New York | 4 |
| California | 33,871,648 | 37,253,956 | 39,250,017 | Illinois | 5 | Illinois | 5 | Illinois | 5 |
| Colorado | 4,301,261 | 5,029,196 | 5,540,545 | Pennsylvania | 6 | Pennsylvania | 6 | Pennsylvania | 6 |
| Connecticut | 3,405,565 | 3,574,097 | 3,576,452 | Ohio | 7 | Ohio | 7 | Ohio | 7 |
| Delaware | 783,600 | 897,934 | 952,065 | Michigan | 8 | Michigan | 8 | Georgia | 8 |
| D.C. | 572,059 | 601,723 | 681,170 | New Jersey | 9 | Georgia | 9 | North Carolina | 9 |
| Florida | 15,982,378 | 18,801,310 | 20,612,439 | Georgia | 10 | North Carolina | 10 | Michigan | 10 |
| Georgia | 8,186,453 | 9,687,653 | 10,310,371 | North Carolina | 11 | New Jersey | 11 | New Jersey | 11 |
| Hawaii | 1,211,537 | 1,360,301 | 1,428,557 | Virginia | 12 | Virginia | 12 | Virginia | 12 |
| Idaho | 1,293,953 | 1,567,582 | 1,683,140 | Massachusetts | 13 | Washington | 13 | Washington | 13 |
| Illinois | 12,419,293 | 12,830,632 | 12,801,539 | Indiana | 14 | Massachusetts | 14 | Arizona | 14 |
| Indiana | 6,080,485 | 6,483,802 | 6,633,053 | Washington | 15 | Indiana | 15 | Massachusetts | 15 |
| Iowa | 2,926,324 | 3,046,355 | 3,134,693 | Tennessee | 16 | Arizona | 16 | Tennessee | 16 |
| Kansas | 2,688,418 | 2,853,118 | 2,907,289 | Missouri | 17 | Tennessee | 17 | Indiana | 17 |
| Kentucky | 4,041,769 | 4,339,367 | 4,436,974 | Wisconsin | 18 | Missouri | 18 | Missouri | 18 |
| Louisiana | 4,468,976 | 4,533,372 | 4,681,666 | Maryland | 19 | Maryland | 19 | Maryland | 19 |
| Maine | 1,274,923 | 1,328,361 | 1,331,479 | Arizona | 20 | Wisconsin | 20 | Wisconsin | 20 |
| Maryland | 5,296,486 | 5,773,552 | 6,016,447 | Minnesota | 21 | Minnesota | 21 | Colorado | 21 |
| Massachusetts | 6,349,097 | 6,547,629 | 6,811,779 | Louisiana | 22 | Colorado | 22 | Minnesota | 22 |
| Michigan | 9,938,444 | 9,883,640 | 9,928,300 | Alabama | 23 | Alabama | 23 | South Carolina | 23 |
| Minnesota | 4,919,479 | 5,303,925 | 5,519,952 | Colorado | 24 | South Carolina | 24 | Alabama | 24 |
| Mississippi | 2,844,658 | 2,967,297 | 2,988,726 | Kentucky | 25 | Louisiana | 25 | Louisiana | 25 |
| Missouri | 5,595,211 | 5,988,927 | 6,093,000 | South Carolina | 26 | Kentucky | 26 | Kentucky | 26 |
| Montana | 902,195 | 989,415 | 1,042,520 | Oklahoma | 27 | Oregon | 27 | Oregon | 27 |
| Nebraska | 1,711,263 | 1,826,341 | 1,907,116 | Oregon | 28 | Oklahoma | 28 | Oklahoma | 28 |
| Nevada | 1,998,257 | 2,700,551 | 2,940,058 | Connecticut | 29 | Connecticut | 29 | Connecticut | 29 |
| New Hampshire | 1,235,786 | 1,316,470 | 1,334,795 | Iowa | 30 | Iowa | 30 | Iowa | 30 |
| New Jersey | 8,414,350 | 8,791,894 | 8,944,469 | Mississippi | 31 | Mississippi | 31 | Utah | 31 |
| New Mexico | 1,819,046 | 2,059,179 | 2,081,015 | Kansas | 32 | Arkansas | 32 | Mississippi | 32 |
| New York | 18,976,457 | 19,378,102 | 19,745,289 | Arkansas | 33 | Kansas | 33 | Arkansas | 33 |
| North Carolina | 8,049,313 | 9,535,483 | 10,146,788 | Utah | 34 | Utah | 34 | Nevada | 34 |
| North Dakota | 642,200 | 672,591 | 757,953 | Nevada | 35 | Nevada | 35 | Kansas | 35 |
| Ohio | 11,353,140 | 11,536,504 | 11,614,373 | New Mexico | 36 | New Mexico | 36 | New Mexico | 36 |
| Oklahoma | 3,450,654 | 3,751,351 | 3,923,561 | West Virginia | 37 | West Virginia | 37 | Nebraska | 37 |
| Oregon | 3,421,399 | 3,831,074 | 4,093,465 | Nebraska | 38 | Nebraska | 38 | West Virginia | 38 |
| Pennsylvania | 12,281,054 | 12,702,379 | 12,784,227 | Idaho | 39 | Idaho | 39 | Idaho | 39 |
| Rhode Island | 1,048,319 | 1,052,567 | 1,056,426 | Maine | 40 | Hawaii | 40 | Hawaii | 40 |
| South Carolina | 4,012,012 | 4,625,364 | 4,961,119 | New Hampshire | 41 | Maine | 41 | New Hampshire | 41 |
| South Dakota | 754,844 | 814,180 | 865,454 | Hawaii | 42 | New Hampshire | 42 | Maine | 42 |
| Tennessee | 5,689,283 | 6,346,105 | 6,651,194 | Rhode Island | 43 | Rhode Island | 43 | Rhode Island | 43 |
| Texas | 20,851,820 | 25,145,561 | 27,862,596 | Montana | 44 | Montana | 44 | Montana | 44 |
| Utah | 2,233,169 | 2,763,885 | 3,051,217 | Delaware | 45 | Delaware | 45 | Delaware | 45 |
| Vermont | 608,827 | 625,741 | 624,594 | South Dakota | 46 | South Dakota | 46 | South Dakota | 46 |
| Virginia | 7,078,515 | 8,001,024 | 8,411,808 | North Dakota | 47 | Alaska | 47 | North Dakota | 47 |
| Washington | 5,894,121 | 6,724,540 | 7,288,000 | Alaska | 48 | North Dakota | 48 | Alaska | 48 |
| West Virginia | 1,808,344 | 1,852,994 | 1,831,102 | Vermont | 49 | Vermont | 49 | D.C. | 49 |
| Wisconsin | 5,363,675 | 5,686,986 | 5,778,709 | D.C. | 50 | D.C. | 50 | Vermont | 50 |
| Wyoming | 493,782 | 563,626 | 585,501 | Wyoming | 51 | Wyoming | 51 | Wyoming | 51 |
| United States | 281,421,906 | 308,745,538 | 323,127,515 | United States | – | United States | – | United States | – |

Source: U.S. Census Bureau, Census 2000, Census 2010, American Community Survey, 2016 1-Year Estimate

# White Population

| Area | Percent of Population | | | 2000 | | 2010 | | 2016 | |
|---|---|---|---|---|---|---|---|---|---|
| | 2000 | 2010 | 2016 | Area | Rank | Area | Rank | Area | Rank |
| Alabama | 71.1 | 68.5 | 68.1 | Maine | 1 | Vermont | 1 | Maine | 1 |
| Alaska | 69.3 | 66.6 | 64.4 | Vermont | 2 | Maine | 2 | Vermont | 2 |
| Arizona | 75.5 | 73.0 | 75.8 | New Hampshire | 3 | West Virginia | 3 | New Hampshire | 3 |
| Arkansas | 80.0 | 77.0 | 76.6 | West Virginia | 4 | New Hampshire | 4 | West Virginia | 4 |
| California | 59.5 | 57.5 | 59.6 | Iowa | 5 | Iowa | 5 | Wyoming | 5 |
| Colorado | 82.7 | 81.3 | 84.0 | North Dakota | 6 | Wyoming | 6 | Iowa | 6 |
| Connecticut | 81.6 | 77.5 | 76.6 | Wyoming | 7 | North Dakota | 7 | Idaho | 7 |
| Delaware | 74.6 | 68.8 | 69.2 | Idaho | 8 | Montana | 8 | Montana | 8 |
| D.C. | 30.7 | 38.4 | 40.7 | Montana | 9 | Idaho | 9 | Nebraska | 9 |
| Florida | 77.9 | 75.0 | 75.5 | Kentucky | 10 | Kentucky | 10 | North Dakota | 10 |
| Georgia | 65.0 | 59.7 | 58.7 | Nebraska | 11 | Wisconsin | 11 | Kentucky | 11 |
| Hawaii | 24.2 | 24.7 | 25.0 | Minnesota | 12 | Nebraska | 12 | Utah | 12 |
| Idaho | 90.9 | 89.0 | 89.7 | Utah | 13 | Utah | 13 | Wisconsin | 13 |
| Illinois | 73.4 | 71.5 | 71.2 | Wisconsin | 14 | South Dakota | 14 | South Dakota | 14 |
| Indiana | 87.4 | 84.3 | 83.4 | South Dakota | 15 | Minnesota | 15 | Kansas | 15 |
| Iowa | 93.9 | 91.3 | 90.4 | Indiana | 16 | Indiana | 16 | Oregon | 16 |
| Kansas | 86.0 | 83.8 | 84.5 | Oregon | 17 | Kansas | 17 | Colorado | 17 |
| Kentucky | 90.0 | 87.7 | 87.1 | Kansas | 18 | Oregon | 18 | Indiana | 18 |
| Louisiana | 63.9 | 62.5 | 61.9 | Pennsylvania | 19 | Missouri | 19 | Minnesota | 19 |
| Maine | 96.9 | 95.2 | 94.4 | Rhode Island | 20 | Ohio | 20 | Missouri | 20 |
| Maryland | 64.0 | 58.1 | 56.4 | Ohio | 21 | Pennsylvania | 21 | Ohio | 21 |
| Massachusetts | 84.5 | 80.4 | 78.5 | Missouri | 22 | Rhode Island | 22 | Pennsylvania | 22 |
| Michigan | 80.1 | 78.9 | 78.5 | Massachusetts | 23 | Colorado | 23 | Rhode Island | 23 |
| Minnesota | 89.4 | 85.3 | 83.2 | Colorado | 24 | Massachusetts | 24 | Massachusetts | 24 |
| Mississippi | 61.3 | 59.1 | 58.5 | Washington | 25 | Michigan | 25 | Michigan | 25 |
| Missouri | 84.8 | 82.8 | 82.2 | Connecticut | 26 | Connecticut | 26 | Tennessee | 26 |
| Montana | 90.5 | 89.4 | 88.9 | Tennessee | 27 | Tennessee | 27 | Connecticut | 27 |
| Nebraska | 89.6 | 86.1 | 87.8 | Michigan | 28 | Washington | 28 | Arkansas | 28 |
| Nevada | 75.1 | 66.1 | 66.8 | Arkansas | 29 | Arkansas | 29 | Arizona | 29 |
| New Hampshire | 96.0 | 93.8 | 93.4 | Florida | 30 | Florida | 30 | Washington | 30 |
| New Jersey | 72.5 | 68.5 | 68.1 | Oklahoma | 31 | Arizona | 31 | Florida | 31 |
| New Mexico | 66.7 | 68.3 | 73.9 | Arizona | 32 | Oklahoma | 32 | Texas | 32 |
| New York | 67.9 | 65.7 | 63.4 | Nevada | 33 | Illinois | 33 | New Mexico | 33 |
| North Carolina | 72.1 | 68.4 | 68.8 | Delaware | 34 | Texas | 34 | Oklahoma | 34 |
| North Dakota | 92.3 | 90.0 | 87.2 | Illinois | 35 | Delaware | 35 | Illinois | 35 |
| Ohio | 84.9 | 82.6 | 81.5 | New Jersey | 36 | New Jersey | 36 | Delaware | 36 |
| Oklahoma | 76.1 | 72.1 | 72.4 | Virginia | 37 | Virginia | 36 | North Carolina | 37 |
| Oregon | 86.5 | 83.6 | 84.4 | North Carolina | 38 | Alabama | 38 | Alabama | 38 |
| Pennsylvania | 85.3 | 81.9 | 80.8 | Alabama | 39 | North Carolina | 39 | New Jersey | 39 |
| Rhode Island | 85.0 | 81.4 | 80.4 | Texas | 40 | New Mexico | 40 | Virginia | 40 |
| South Carolina | 67.1 | 66.1 | 67.3 | Alaska | 41 | Alaska | 41 | South Carolina | 41 |
| South Dakota | 88.6 | 85.9 | 84.6 | New York | 42 | Nevada | 42 | Nevada | 42 |
| Tennessee | 80.2 | 77.5 | 77.8 | South Carolina | 43 | South Carolina | 42 | Alaska | 43 |
| Texas | 70.9 | 70.4 | 74.3 | New Mexico | 44 | New York | 44 | New York | 44 |
| Utah | 89.2 | 86.0 | 86.3 | Georgia | 45 | Louisiana | 45 | Louisiana | 45 |
| Vermont | 96.7 | 95.2 | 94.3 | Maryland | 46 | Georgia | 46 | California | 46 |
| Virginia | 72.3 | 68.5 | 67.8 | Louisiana | 47 | Mississippi | 47 | Georgia | 47 |
| Washington | 81.8 | 77.2 | 75.6 | Mississippi | 48 | Maryland | 48 | Mississippi | 48 |
| West Virginia | 95.0 | 93.9 | 93.0 | California | 49 | California | 49 | Maryland | 49 |
| Wisconsin | 88.9 | 86.2 | 85.5 | D.C. | 50 | D.C. | 50 | D.C. | 50 |
| Wyoming | 92.0 | 90.7 | 92.0 | Hawaii | 51 | Hawaii | 51 | Hawaii | 51 |
| United States | 75.1 | 72.4 | 72.6 | United States | – | United States | – | United States | – |

Source: U.S. Census Bureau, Census 2000, Census 2010, American Community Survey, 2016 1-Year Estimate

# Black Population

| Area | Percent of Population | | | 2000 | | 2010 | | 2016 | |
|------|------|------|------|------|------|------|------|------|------|
| | 2000 | 2010 | 2016 | Area | Rank | Area | Rank | Area | Rank |
| Alabama | 25.9 | 26.1 | 26.7 | D.C. | 1 | D.C. | 1 | D.C. | 1 |
| Alaska | 3.4 | 3.2 | 3.2 | Mississippi | 2 | Mississippi | 2 | Mississippi | 2 |
| Arizona | 3.1 | 4.0 | 4.3 | Louisiana | 3 | Louisiana | 3 | Louisiana | 3 |
| Arkansas | 15.6 | 15.4 | 15.5 | South Carolina | 4 | Georgia | 4 | Georgia | 4 |
| California | 6.6 | 6.1 | 5.7 | Georgia | 5 | Maryland | 5 | Maryland | 5 |
| Colorado | 3.8 | 4.0 | 4.2 | Maryland | 6 | South Carolina | 6 | South Carolina | 6 |
| Connecticut | 9.1 | 10.1 | 10.6 | Alabama | 7 | Alabama | 7 | Alabama | 7 |
| Delaware | 19.2 | 21.3 | 22.0 | North Carolina | 8 | North Carolina | 8 | Delaware | 8 |
| D.C. | 60.0 | 50.7 | 47.0 | Virginia | 9 | Delaware | 9 | North Carolina | 9 |
| Florida | 14.6 | 15.9 | 16.0 | Delaware | 10 | Virginia | 10 | Virginia | 10 |
| Georgia | 28.7 | 30.4 | 31.5 | Tennessee | 11 | Tennessee | 11 | Tennessee | 11 |
| Hawaii | 1.8 | 1.5 | 1.8 | New York | 12 | Florida | 12 | Florida | 12 |
| Idaho | 0.4 | 0.6 | 0.6 | Arkansas | 13 | New York | 13 | New York | 13 |
| Illinois | 15.1 | 14.5 | 14.1 | Illinois | 14 | Arkansas | 14 | Arkansas | 14 |
| Indiana | 8.3 | 9.1 | 9.3 | Florida | 15 | Illinois | 15 | Illinois | 15 |
| Iowa | 2.1 | 2.9 | 3.5 | Michigan | 16 | Michigan | 16 | Michigan | 16 |
| Kansas | 5.7 | 5.8 | 5.7 | New Jersey | 17 | New Jersey | 17 | New Jersey | 17 |
| Kentucky | 7.3 | 7.7 | 8.2 | Texas | 18 | Ohio | 18 | Ohio | 18 |
| Louisiana | 32.4 | 32.0 | 32.3 | Ohio | 19 | Texas | 19 | Texas | 19 |
| Maine | 0.5 | 1.1 | 1.5 | Missouri | 20 | Missouri | 20 | Missouri | 20 |
| Maryland | 27.8 | 29.4 | 29.8 | Pennsylvania | 21 | Pennsylvania | 21 | Pennsylvania | 21 |
| Massachusetts | 5.4 | 6.6 | 7.4 | Connecticut | 22 | Connecticut | 22 | Connecticut | 22 |
| Michigan | 14.2 | 14.1 | 13.7 | Indiana | 23 | Indiana | 23 | Indiana | 23 |
| Minnesota | 3.4 | 5.1 | 6.0 | Oklahoma | 24 | Nevada | 24 | Nevada | 24 |
| Mississippi | 36.3 | 37.0 | 37.9 | Kentucky | 25 | Kentucky | 25 | Kentucky | 25 |
| Missouri | 11.2 | 11.5 | 11.5 | Nevada | 26 | Oklahoma | 26 | Massachusetts | 26 |
| Montana | 0.3 | 0.4 | 0.3 | California | 27 | Massachusetts | 27 | Oklahoma | 27 |
| Nebraska | 4.0 | 4.5 | 4.7 | Kansas | 28 | Wisconsin | 28 | Rhode Island | 28 |
| Nevada | 6.7 | 8.1 | 8.8 | Wisconsin | 29 | California | 29 | Wisconsin | 29 |
| New Hampshire | 0.7 | 1.1 | 1.2 | Massachusetts | 30 | Kansas | 30 | Minnesota | 30 |
| New Jersey | 13.5 | 13.7 | 13.3 | Rhode Island | 31 | Rhode Island | 31 | California | 31 |
| New Mexico | 1.8 | 2.0 | 1.9 | Nebraska | 32 | Minnesota | 32 | Kansas | 32 |
| New York | 15.8 | 15.8 | 15.6 | Colorado | 33 | Nebraska | 33 | Nebraska | 33 |
| North Carolina | 21.5 | 21.4 | 21.5 | Minnesota | 34 | Arizona | 34 | Arizona | 34 |
| North Dakota | 0.6 | 1.1 | 2.5 | Alaska | 35 | Colorado | 35 | Colorado | 35 |
| Ohio | 11.4 | 12.2 | 12.4 | Washington | 36 | Washington | 36 | West Virginia | 36 |
| Oklahoma | 7.5 | 7.4 | 7.3 | West Virginia | 37 | West Virginia | 37 | Washington | 37 |
| Oregon | 1.6 | 1.8 | 1.9 | Arizona | 38 | Alaska | 38 | Iowa | 38 |
| Pennsylvania | 9.9 | 10.8 | 11.0 | Iowa | 39 | Iowa | 39 | Alaska | 39 |
| Rhode Island | 4.4 | 5.7 | 6.3 | New Mexico | 40 | New Mexico | 40 | North Dakota | 40 |
| South Carolina | 29.5 | 27.9 | 26.9 | Hawaii | 41 | Oregon | 41 | New Mexico | 41 |
| South Dakota | 0.6 | 1.2 | 1.6 | Oregon | 42 | Hawaii | 42 | Oregon | 42 |
| Tennessee | 16.4 | 16.6 | 16.7 | Utah | 43 | South Dakota | 43 | Hawaii | 43 |
| Texas | 11.5 | 11.8 | 12.0 | Wyoming | 44 | North Dakota | 44 | South Dakota | 44 |
| Utah | 0.7 | 1.0 | 1.0 | New Hampshire | 45 | Maine | 44 | Maine | 45 |
| Vermont | 0.5 | 1.0 | 1.2 | South Dakota | 46 | New Hampshire | 46 | Vermont | 46 |
| Virginia | 19.6 | 19.3 | 19.0 | North Dakota | 47 | Utah | 47 | New Hampshire | 47 |
| Washington | 3.2 | 3.5 | 3.6 | Maine | 48 | Vermont | 48 | Utah | 48 |
| West Virginia | 3.1 | 3.4 | 3.8 | Vermont | 49 | Wyoming | 49 | Wyoming | 49 |
| Wisconsin | 5.6 | 6.3 | 6.2 | Idaho | 50 | Idaho | 50 | Idaho | 50 |
| Wyoming | 0.7 | 0.8 | 1.0 | Montana | 51 | Montana | 51 | Montana | 51 |
| United States | 12.3 | 12.6 | 12.6 | United States | – | United States | – | United States | – |

Source: U.S. Census Bureau, Census 2000, Census 2010, American Community Survey, 2016 1-Year Estimate

## American Indian/Alaska Native Population

| Area | Percent of Population | | | 2000 Area | Rank | 2010 Area | Rank | 2016 Area | Rank |
|------|------|------|------|------|------|------|------|------|------|
| | 2000 | 2010 | 2016 | | | | | | |
| Alabama | 0.5 | 0.5 | 0.5 | Alaska | 1 | Alaska | 1 | Alaska | 1 |
| Alaska | 15.6 | 14.7 | 14.5 | New Mexico | 2 | New Mexico | 2 | New Mexico | 2 |
| Arizona | 4.9 | 4.6 | 4.4 | South Dakota | 3 | South Dakota | 3 | South Dakota | 3 |
| Arkansas | 0.6 | 0.7 | 0.6 | Oklahoma | 4 | Oklahoma | 4 | Oklahoma | 4 |
| California | 0.9 | 0.9 | 0.7 | Montana | 5 | Montana | 5 | Montana | 5 |
| Colorado | 1.0 | 1.1 | 0.9 | Arizona | 6 | North Dakota | 6 | North Dakota | 6 |
| Connecticut | 0.2 | 0.3 | 0.2 | North Dakota | 7 | Arizona | 7 | Arizona | 7 |
| Delaware | 0.3 | 0.4 | 0.4 | Wyoming | 8 | Wyoming | 8 | Wyoming | 8 |
| D.C. | 0.3 | 0.3 | 0.2 | Washington | 9 | Washington | 9 | Idaho | 9 |
| Florida | 0.3 | 0.3 | 0.2 | Idaho | 10 | Oregon | 10 | Washington | 10 |
| Georgia | 0.2 | 0.3 | 0.3 | Utah | 11 | Idaho | 11 | North Carolina | 11 |
| Hawaii | 0.2 | 0.3 | 0.1 | Nevada | 12 | North Carolina | 12 | Nevada | 12 |
| Idaho | 1.3 | 1.3 | 1.5 | Oregon | 12 | Nevada | 13 | Minnesota | 13 |
| Illinois | 0.2 | 0.3 | 0.2 | North Carolina | 14 | Utah | 13 | Oregon | 14 |
| Indiana | 0.2 | 0.2 | 0.2 | Minnesota | 15 | Minnesota | 15 | Utah | 15 |
| Iowa | 0.3 | 0.3 | 0.3 | Colorado | 16 | Colorado | 16 | Colorado | 16 |
| Kansas | 0.9 | 0.9 | 0.7 | California | 17 | Nebraska | 17 | Wisconsin | 17 |
| Kentucky | 0.2 | 0.2 | 0.2 | Kansas | 18 | Kansas | 18 | Nebraska | 18 |
| Louisiana | 0.5 | 0.6 | 0.5 | Wisconsin | 19 | California | 19 | California | 19 |
| Maine | 0.5 | 0.6 | 0.5 | Nebraska | 20 | Wisconsin | 20 | Kansas | 19 |
| Maryland | 0.2 | 0.3 | 0.2 | Arkansas | 21 | Arkansas | 21 | Arkansas | 21 |
| Massachusetts | 0.2 | 0.2 | 0.1 | Michigan | 22 | Texas | 22 | Maine | 22 |
| Michigan | 0.5 | 0.6 | 0.5 | Texas | 23 | Louisiana | 23 | Louisiana | 23 |
| Minnesota | 1.1 | 1.1 | 1.1 | Louisiana | 23 | Maine | 24 | Michigan | 24 |
| Mississippi | 0.4 | 0.5 | 0.4 | Maine | 25 | Michigan | 25 | Missouri | 25 |
| Missouri | 0.4 | 0.4 | 0.5 | Alabama | 26 | Alabama | 26 | Rhode Island | 26 |
| Montana | 6.2 | 6.3 | 6.3 | Rhode Island | 27 | Rhode Island | 27 | Alabama | 26 |
| Nebraska | 0.8 | 1.0 | 0.8 | Missouri | 28 | New York | 28 | Texas | 28 |
| Nevada | 1.3 | 1.1 | 1.1 | New York | 29 | Mississippi | 29 | Mississippi | 29 |
| New Hampshire | 0.2 | 0.2 | 0.1 | Mississippi | 30 | Delaware | 30 | Delaware | 30 |
| New Jersey | 0.2 | 0.3 | 0.2 | Vermont | 31 | Missouri | 31 | New York | 31 |
| New Mexico | 9.5 | 9.3 | 9.3 | Delaware | 32 | South Carolina | 32 | Georgia | 31 |
| New York | 0.4 | 0.5 | 0.3 | Florida | 33 | Florida | 33 | Vermont | 33 |
| North Carolina | 1.2 | 1.2 | 1.1 | South Carolina | 33 | Virginia | 34 | Iowa | 34 |
| North Dakota | 4.8 | 5.4 | 5.4 | Iowa | 35 | Iowa | 35 | South Carolina | 35 |
| Ohio | 0.2 | 0.2 | 0.1 | D.C. | 36 | D.C. | 36 | D.C. | 36 |
| Oklahoma | 7.9 | 8.5 | 7.5 | Virginia | 36 | Maryland | 36 | Tennessee | 36 |
| Oregon | 1.3 | 1.3 | 1.1 | Hawaii | 38 | Vermont | 36 | Connecticut | 38 |
| Pennsylvania | 0.1 | 0.2 | 0.1 | Maryland | 38 | Illinois | 39 | Virginia | 38 |
| Rhode Island | 0.4 | 0.5 | 0.5 | Connecticut | 40 | New Jersey | 40 | Florida | 40 |
| South Carolina | 0.3 | 0.4 | 0.3 | Georgia | 41 | Georgia | 40 | Indiana | 40 |
| South Dakota | 8.2 | 8.8 | 8.9 | Tennessee | 41 | Tennessee | 42 | Maryland | 42 |
| Tennessee | 0.2 | 0.3 | 0.2 | Indiana | 43 | Connecticut | 43 | Kentucky | 42 |
| Texas | 0.5 | 0.6 | 0.4 | Illinois | 44 | Hawaii | 43 | Illinois | 44 |
| Utah | 1.3 | 1.1 | 1.0 | Massachusetts | 45 | Massachusetts | 45 | New Jersey | 45 |
| Vermont | 0.4 | 0.3 | 0.3 | New Hampshire | 45 | Indiana | 46 | West Virginia | 46 |
| Virginia | 0.3 | 0.3 | 0.2 | New Jersey | 47 | New Hampshire | 47 | Hawaii | 47 |
| Washington | 1.5 | 1.5 | 1.3 | Ohio | 48 | Kentucky | 48 | Massachusetts | 48 |
| West Virginia | 0.2 | 0.2 | 0.2 | Kentucky | 49 | Ohio | 49 | Pennsylvania | 48 |
| Wisconsin | 0.8 | 0.9 | 0.9 | West Virginia | 50 | Pennsylvania | 50 | Ohio | 50 |
| Wyoming | 2.2 | 2.3 | 2.2 | Pennsylvania | 51 | West Virginia | 51 | New Hampshire | 51 |
| United States | 0.9 | 0.9 | 0.8 | United States | – | United States | – | United States | – |

Source: U.S. Census Bureau, Census 2000, Census 2010, American Community Survey, 2016 1-Year Estimate

# Asian Population

| Area | Percent of Population | | | 2000 | | 2010 | | 2016 | |
|------|------|------|------|------|------|------|------|------|------|
| | 2000 | 2010 | 2016 | Area | Rank | Area | Rank | Area | Rank |
| Alabama | 0.7 | 1.1 | 1.3 | Hawaii | 1 | Hawaii | 1 | Hawaii | 1 |
| Alaska | 4.0 | 5.3 | 6.1 | California | 2 | California | 2 | California | 2 |
| Arizona | 1.8 | 2.7 | 3.1 | New Jersey | 3 | New Jersey | 3 | New Jersey | 3 |
| Arkansas | 0.7 | 1.2 | 1.4 | New York | 4 | New York | 4 | New York | 4 |
| California | 10.9 | 13.0 | 14.2 | Washington | 5 | Nevada | 5 | Nevada | 5 |
| Colorado | 2.2 | 2.7 | 3.1 | Nevada | 6 | Washington | 6 | Washington | 6 |
| Connecticut | 2.4 | 3.7 | 4.5 | Alaska | 7 | Maryland | 7 | Massachusetts | 7 |
| Delaware | 2.0 | 3.1 | 3.7 | Maryland | 8 | Virginia | 8 | Virginia | 8 |
| D.C. | 2.6 | 3.5 | 3.8 | Massachusetts | 9 | Alaska | 9 | Maryland | 9 |
| Florida | 1.6 | 2.4 | 2.7 | Virginia | 10 | Massachusetts | 10 | Alaska | 10 |
| Georgia | 2.1 | 3.2 | 3.8 | Illinois | 11 | Illinois | 11 | Illinois | 11 |
| Hawaii | 41.5 | 38.6 | 38.0 | Oregon | 12 | Minnesota | 12 | Minnesota | 12 |
| Idaho | 0.9 | 1.2 | 1.4 | Minnesota | 13 | Texas | 13 | Texas | 13 |
| Illinois | 3.4 | 4.5 | 5.3 | Texas | 14 | Connecticut | 14 | Connecticut | 14 |
| Indiana | 0.9 | 1.5 | 2.1 | D.C. | 15 | Oregon | 15 | Oregon | 15 |
| Iowa | 1.2 | 1.7 | 2.3 | Connecticut | 16 | D.C. | 16 | D.C. | 16 |
| Kansas | 1.7 | 2.3 | 2.7 | Rhode Island | 17 | Georgia | 17 | Georgia | 17 |
| Kentucky | 0.7 | 1.1 | 1.3 | Colorado | 18 | Delaware | 18 | Delaware | 18 |
| Louisiana | 1.2 | 1.5 | 1.6 | Georgia | 19 | Rhode Island | 19 | Rhode Island | 19 |
| Maine | 0.7 | 1.0 | 1.3 | Delaware | 20 | Arizona | 20 | Pennsylvania | 20 |
| Maryland | 3.9 | 5.5 | 6.2 | Arizona | 21 | Colorado | 20 | Arizona | 21 |
| Massachusetts | 3.7 | 5.3 | 6.4 | Pennsylvania | 22 | Pennsylvania | 22 | Colorado | 21 |
| Michigan | 1.7 | 2.4 | 2.9 | Michigan | 23 | Florida | 23 | Michigan | 23 |
| Minnesota | 2.8 | 4.0 | 4.6 | Kansas | 24 | Michigan | 24 | Kansas | 24 |
| Mississippi | 0.6 | 0.8 | 0.8 | Florida | 25 | Kansas | 25 | Florida | 25 |
| Missouri | 1.1 | 1.6 | 1.9 | Utah | 26 | Wisconsin | 26 | North Carolina | 25 |
| Montana | 0.5 | 0.6 | 0.8 | Wisconsin | 27 | North Carolina | 27 | Wisconsin | 27 |
| Nebraska | 1.2 | 1.7 | 2.1 | North Carolina | 28 | New Hampshire | 28 | New Hampshire | 28 |
| Nevada | 4.5 | 7.2 | 8.3 | Oklahoma | 29 | Utah | 29 | Iowa | 29 |
| New Hampshire | 1.2 | 2.1 | 2.4 | New Hampshire | 30 | Nebraska | 30 | Utah | 30 |
| New Jersey | 5.7 | 8.2 | 9.5 | Nebraska | 31 | Iowa | 31 | Nebraska | 31 |
| New Mexico | 1.0 | 1.3 | 1.5 | Iowa | 32 | Oklahoma | 32 | Indiana | 32 |
| New York | 5.5 | 7.3 | 8.4 | Louisiana | 33 | Ohio | 33 | Ohio | 33 |
| North Carolina | 1.4 | 2.1 | 2.7 | Ohio | 34 | Missouri | 34 | Oklahoma | 34 |
| North Dakota | 0.5 | 1.0 | 1.2 | Missouri | 35 | Indiana | 35 | Missouri | 35 |
| Ohio | 1.1 | 1.6 | 2.0 | New Mexico | 36 | Louisiana | 36 | Tennessee | 36 |
| Oklahoma | 1.3 | 1.7 | 2.0 | Tennessee | 37 | Tennessee | 37 | Louisiana | 37 |
| Oregon | 2.9 | 3.6 | 4.1 | Indiana | 38 | New Mexico | 38 | New Mexico | 38 |
| Pennsylvania | 1.7 | 2.7 | 3.3 | Idaho | 39 | South Carolina | 39 | South Carolina | 38 |
| Rhode Island | 2.2 | 2.8 | 3.4 | South Carolina | 40 | Vermont | 40 | Vermont | 40 |
| South Carolina | 0.9 | 1.2 | 1.5 | Vermont | 41 | Arkansas | 41 | South Dakota | 41 |
| South Dakota | 0.5 | 0.9 | 1.5 | Arkansas | 42 | Idaho | 42 | Idaho | 42 |
| Tennessee | 1.0 | 1.4 | 1.7 | Kentucky | 43 | Kentucky | 43 | Arkansas | 43 |
| Texas | 2.7 | 3.8 | 4.6 | Maine | 44 | Alabama | 44 | Kentucky | 44 |
| Utah | 1.6 | 2.0 | 2.3 | Alabama | 45 | North Dakota | 45 | Alabama | 45 |
| Vermont | 0.8 | 1.2 | 1.5 | Mississippi | 46 | Maine | 46 | Maine | 46 |
| Virginia | 3.6 | 5.5 | 6.3 | South Dakota | 47 | South Dakota | 47 | North Dakota | 47 |
| Washington | 5.4 | 7.1 | 8.1 | Wyoming | 48 | Mississippi | 48 | Wyoming | 48 |
| West Virginia | 0.5 | 0.6 | 0.7 | North Dakota | 48 | Wyoming | 49 | Mississippi | 49 |
| Wisconsin | 1.6 | 2.2 | 2.6 | Montana | 50 | West Virginia | 50 | Montana | 50 |
| Wyoming | 0.5 | 0.7 | 1.0 | West Virginia | 50 | Montana | 51 | West Virginia | 51 |
| United States | 3.6 | 4.7 | 5.4 | United States | – | United States | – | United States | – |

Source: U.S. Census Bureau, Census 2000, Census 2010, American Community Survey, 2016 1-Year Estimate

# Hispanic Population

| Area | Percent of Population | | | 2000 | | 2010 | | 2016 | |
|------|------|------|------|------|------|------|------|------|------|
| | 2000 | 2010 | 2016 | Area | Rank | Area | Rank | Area | Rank |
| Alabama | 1.7 | 3.8 | 4.1 | New Mexico | 1 | New Mexico | 1 | New Mexico | 1 |
| Alaska | 4.1 | 5.5 | 6.9 | California | 2 | California | 2 | Texas | 2 |
| Arizona | 25.2 | 29.6 | 30.9 | Texas | 3 | Texas | 2 | California | 3 |
| Arkansas | 3.2 | 6.3 | 7.1 | Arizona | 4 | Arizona | 4 | Arizona | 4 |
| California | 32.3 | 37.6 | 38.9 | Nevada | 5 | Nevada | 5 | Nevada | 5 |
| Colorado | 17.1 | 20.6 | 21.3 | Colorado | 6 | Florida | 6 | Florida | 6 |
| Connecticut | 9.4 | 13.4 | 15.7 | Florida | 7 | Colorado | 7 | Colorado | 7 |
| Delaware | 4.7 | 8.1 | 9.1 | New York | 8 | New Jersey | 8 | New Jersey | 8 |
| D.C. | 7.8 | 9.1 | 10.9 | New Jersey | 9 | New York | 9 | New York | 9 |
| Florida | 16.7 | 22.4 | 24.8 | Illinois | 10 | Illinois | 10 | Illinois | 10 |
| Georgia | 5.3 | 8.8 | 9.3 | Connecticut | 11 | Connecticut | 11 | Connecticut | 11 |
| Hawaii | 7.2 | 8.8 | 10.3 | Utah | 12 | Utah | 12 | Rhode Island | 12 |
| Idaho | 7.8 | 11.2 | 12.3 | Rhode Island | 13 | Rhode Island | 13 | Utah | 13 |
| Illinois | 12.3 | 15.8 | 17.0 | Oregon | 14 | Oregon | 14 | Oregon | 14 |
| Indiana | 3.5 | 6.0 | 6.7 | D.C. | 15 | Washington | 15 | Washington | 15 |
| Iowa | 2.8 | 4.9 | 5.7 | Idaho | 15 | Idaho | 16 | Idaho | 16 |
| Kansas | 7.0 | 10.5 | 11.5 | Washington | 17 | Kansas | 17 | Kansas | 17 |
| Kentucky | 1.4 | 3.0 | 3.4 | Hawaii | 18 | Massachusetts | 18 | Massachusetts | 18 |
| Louisiana | 2.4 | 4.2 | 4.9 | Kansas | 19 | Nebraska | 19 | D.C. | 19 |
| Maine | 0.7 | 1.2 | 1.5 | Massachusetts | 20 | D.C. | 20 | Nebraska | 20 |
| Maryland | 4.3 | 8.1 | 9.7 | Wyoming | 21 | Wyoming | 21 | Hawaii | 21 |
| Massachusetts | 6.7 | 9.5 | 11.4 | Nebraska | 22 | Hawaii | 22 | Oklahoma | 22 |
| Michigan | 3.2 | 4.4 | 4.9 | Georgia | 23 | Oklahoma | 23 | Maryland | 23 |
| Minnesota | 2.9 | 4.7 | 5.2 | Oklahoma | 24 | Georgia | 24 | Wyoming | 24 |
| Mississippi | 1.3 | 2.7 | 2.9 | Delaware | 25 | North Carolina | 25 | Georgia | 25 |
| Missouri | 2.1 | 3.5 | 4.0 | North Carolina | 26 | Delaware | 26 | North Carolina | 26 |
| Montana | 2.0 | 2.8 | 3.5 | Virginia | 27 | Maryland | 26 | Delaware | 27 |
| Nebraska | 5.5 | 9.1 | 10.6 | Maryland | 28 | Virginia | 28 | Virginia | 28 |
| Nevada | 19.7 | 26.5 | 28.4 | Alaska | 29 | Arkansas | 29 | Arkansas | 29 |
| New Hampshire | 1.6 | 2.7 | 3.5 | Wisconsin | 30 | Indiana | 30 | Pennsylvania | 30 |
| New Jersey | 13.2 | 17.6 | 19.9 | Indiana | 31 | Wisconsin | 31 | Alaska | 31 |
| New Mexico | 42.0 | 46.3 | 48.5 | Michigan | 32 | Pennsylvania | 32 | Indiana | 32 |
| New York | 15.1 | 17.6 | 18.9 | Arkansas | 33 | Alaska | 33 | Wisconsin | 33 |
| North Carolina | 4.7 | 8.3 | 9.1 | Pennsylvania | 34 | South Carolina | 34 | Iowa | 34 |
| North Dakota | 1.2 | 2.0 | 3.4 | Minnesota | 35 | Iowa | 35 | South Carolina | 35 |
| Ohio | 1.9 | 3.0 | 3.6 | Iowa | 36 | Minnesota | 36 | Minnesota | 36 |
| Oklahoma | 5.2 | 8.8 | 10.3 | Louisiana | 37 | Tennessee | 37 | Tennessee | 37 |
| Oregon | 8.0 | 11.7 | 12.7 | South Carolina | 38 | Michigan | 38 | Michigan | 38 |
| Pennsylvania | 3.2 | 5.6 | 7.0 | Tennessee | 39 | Louisiana | 39 | Louisiana | 39 |
| Rhode Island | 8.6 | 12.4 | 14.8 | Missouri | 40 | Alabama | 40 | Alabama | 40 |
| South Carolina | 2.3 | 5.1 | 5.5 | Montana | 41 | Missouri | 41 | Missouri | 41 |
| South Dakota | 1.4 | 2.7 | 3.7 | Ohio | 42 | Ohio | 42 | South Dakota | 42 |
| Tennessee | 2.1 | 4.5 | 5.2 | Alabama | 43 | Kentucky | 43 | Ohio | 43 |
| Texas | 31.9 | 37.6 | 39.0 | New Hampshire | 44 | Montana | 44 | Montana | 44 |
| Utah | 9.0 | 12.9 | 13.7 | Kentucky | 45 | New Hampshire | 45 | New Hampshire | 45 |
| Vermont | 0.9 | 1.4 | 2.0 | South Dakota | 46 | Mississippi | 46 | North Dakota | 46 |
| Virginia | 4.6 | 7.9 | 9.0 | Mississippi | 47 | South Dakota | 47 | Kentucky | 47 |
| Washington | 7.4 | 11.2 | 12.4 | North Dakota | 48 | North Dakota | 48 | Mississippi | 48 |
| West Virginia | 0.6 | 1.2 | 1.4 | Vermont | 49 | Vermont | 49 | Vermont | 49 |
| Wisconsin | 3.6 | 5.9 | 6.7 | Maine | 50 | Maine | 50 | Maine | 50 |
| Wyoming | 6.4 | 8.9 | 9.6 | West Virginia | 51 | West Virginia | 51 | West Virginia | 51 |
| United States | 12.5 | 16.3 | 17.7 | United States | – | United States | – | United States | – |

Source: U.S. Census Bureau, Census 2000, Census 2010, American Community Survey, 2016 1-Year Estimate

# Foreign-Born Population

| Area | Percent of Population | | | 2000 | | 2010 | | 2016 | |
|------|------|------|------|------|------|------|------|------|------|
| | 2000 | 2010 | 2016 | Area | Rank | Area | Rank | Area | Rank |
| Alabama | 2.0 | 3.4 | 3.4 | California | 1 | California | 1 | California | 1 |
| Alaska | 5.9 | 7.2 | 7.7 | New York | 2 | New York | 2 | New York | 2 |
| Arizona | 12.8 | 14.2 | 13.5 | New Jersey | 3 | New Jersey | 3 | New Jersey | 3 |
| Arkansas | 2.8 | 4.3 | 4.6 | Hawaii | 3 | Nevada | 4 | Florida | 4 |
| California | 26.2 | 27.2 | 27.2 | Florida | 5 | Florida | 5 | Nevada | 5 |
| Colorado | 8.6 | 9.8 | 9.8 | Nevada | 6 | Hawaii | 6 | Hawaii | 6 |
| Connecticut | 10.9 | 13.2 | 14.4 | Texas | 7 | Texas | 7 | Texas | 7 |
| Delaware | 5.7 | 8.2 | 9.4 | D.C. | 8 | Massachusetts | 8 | Massachusetts | 8 |
| D.C. | 12.9 | 13.0 | 13.3 | Arizona | 9 | Arizona | 9 | Maryland | 9 |
| Florida | 16.7 | 19.2 | 20.6 | Illinois | 10 | Illinois | 10 | Connecticut | 10 |
| Georgia | 7.1 | 9.6 | 10.1 | Massachusetts | 11 | Connecticut | 11 | Rhode Island | 11 |
| Hawaii | 17.5 | 17.7 | 18.4 | Rhode Island | 12 | Maryland | 11 | Washington | 12 |
| Idaho | 5.0 | 5.9 | 5.8 | Connecticut | 13 | D.C. | 13 | Illinois | 13 |
| Illinois | 12.3 | 13.6 | 13.9 | Washington | 14 | Washington | 14 | Arizona | 14 |
| Indiana | 3.1 | 4.4 | 5.3 | Maryland | 15 | Rhode Island | 15 | D.C. | 15 |
| Iowa | 3.1 | 4.1 | 5.1 | Colorado | 16 | Virginia | 16 | Virginia | 16 |
| Kansas | 5.0 | 6.3 | 7.1 | Oregon | 17 | Colorado | 17 | Georgia | 17 |
| Kentucky | 2.0 | 3.1 | 3.5 | New Mexico | 18 | New Mexico | 18 | Colorado | 18 |
| Louisiana | 2.6 | 3.6 | 4.1 | Virginia | 19 | Oregon | 18 | Oregon | 19 |
| Maine | 2.9 | 3.3 | 3.8 | Utah | 20 | Georgia | 20 | New Mexico | 20 |
| Maryland | 9.8 | 13.2 | 15.3 | Georgia | 20 | Utah | 21 | Delaware | 21 |
| Massachusetts | 12.2 | 14.5 | 16.5 | Alaska | 22 | Delaware | 21 | Utah | 22 |
| Michigan | 5.3 | 5.9 | 6.7 | Delaware | 23 | North Carolina | 23 | Minnesota | 23 |
| Minnesota | 5.3 | 7.0 | 8.2 | North Carolina | 24 | Alaska | 24 | North Carolina | 24 |
| Mississippi | 1.4 | 2.2 | 2.0 | Michigan | 24 | Minnesota | 25 | Alaska | 25 |
| Missouri | 2.7 | 3.7 | 4.1 | Minnesota | 24 | Kansas | 26 | Kansas | 26 |
| Montana | 1.8 | 2.0 | 2.1 | Idaho | 27 | Idaho | 27 | Nebraska | 27 |
| Nebraska | 4.4 | 5.9 | 7.0 | Kansas | 27 | Nebraska | 27 | Pennsylvania | 28 |
| Nevada | 15.8 | 19.3 | 20.0 | Nebraska | 29 | Michigan | 27 | Michigan | 29 |
| New Hampshire | 4.4 | 5.3 | 5.7 | New Hampshire | 29 | Pennsylvania | 30 | Idaho | 30 |
| New Jersey | 17.5 | 20.3 | 22.5 | Pennsylvania | 31 | New Hampshire | 31 | Oklahoma | 30 |
| New Mexico | 8.2 | 9.7 | 9.5 | Oklahoma | 32 | Oklahoma | 32 | New Hampshire | 32 |
| New York | 20.4 | 21.7 | 23.0 | Vermont | 32 | South Carolina | 33 | Indiana | 33 |
| North Carolina | 5.3 | 7.4 | 7.8 | Wisconsin | 34 | Wisconsin | 34 | Iowa | 34 |
| North Dakota | 1.9 | 2.4 | 3.2 | Indiana | 35 | Indiana | 35 | Wisconsin | 35 |
| Ohio | 3.0 | 3.8 | 4.4 | Iowa | 35 | Tennessee | 35 | South Carolina | 36 |
| Oklahoma | 3.8 | 5.2 | 5.8 | Ohio | 37 | Arkansas | 37 | Tennessee | 36 |
| Oregon | 8.5 | 9.7 | 9.6 | South Carolina | 38 | Iowa | 38 | Arkansas | 38 |
| Pennsylvania | 4.1 | 5.6 | 6.8 | Maine | 38 | Vermont | 39 | Vermont | 39 |
| Rhode Island | 11.4 | 12.6 | 14.1 | Arkansas | 40 | Ohio | 40 | Ohio | 40 |
| South Carolina | 2.9 | 4.7 | 4.8 | Tennessee | 40 | Missouri | 41 | Louisiana | 41 |
| South Dakota | 1.8 | 2.3 | 3.6 | Missouri | 42 | Louisiana | 42 | Missouri | 41 |
| Tennessee | 2.8 | 4.4 | 4.8 | Louisiana | 43 | Alabama | 43 | Maine | 43 |
| Texas | 13.9 | 16.1 | 17.0 | Wyoming | 44 | Maine | 44 | South Dakota | 44 |
| Utah | 7.1 | 8.2 | 8.3 | Alabama | 45 | Wyoming | 45 | Kentucky | 45 |
| Vermont | 3.8 | 4.0 | 4.5 | Kentucky | 45 | Kentucky | 45 | Alabama | 46 |
| Virginia | 8.1 | 10.8 | 12.3 | North Dakota | 47 | North Dakota | 47 | Wyoming | 47 |
| Washington | 10.4 | 12.7 | 14.0 | Montana | 48 | South Dakota | 48 | North Dakota | 47 |
| West Virginia | 1.1 | 1.3 | 1.7 | South Dakota | 48 | Mississippi | 49 | Montana | 49 |
| Wisconsin | 3.6 | 4.6 | 5.0 | Mississippi | 50 | Montana | 50 | Mississippi | 50 |
| Wyoming | 2.3 | 3.1 | 3.2 | West Virginia | 51 | West Virginia | 51 | West Virginia | 51 |
| United States | 11.1 | 12.7 | 13.5 | United States | – | United States | – | United States | – |

Source: U.S. Census Bureau, Census 2000, Census 2010, American Community Survey, 2016 1-Year Estimate

# Urban Population

| Area | Percent of Population | | | 2000 | | 2010 | | 2016 | |
|---|---|---|---|---|---|---|---|---|---|
| | 2000 | 2010 | 2016 | Area | Rank | Area | Rank | Area | Rank |
| Alabama | 55.4 | 59.0 | n/a | D.C. | 1 | D.C. | 1 | Alabama | n/a |
| Alaska | 65.7 | 66.0 | n/a | California | 2 | California | 2 | Alaska | n/a |
| Arizona | 88.2 | 89.8 | n/a | New Jersey | 3 | New Jersey | 3 | Arizona | n/a |
| Arkansas | 52.4 | 56.2 | n/a | Nevada | 4 | Nevada | 4 | Arkansas | n/a |
| California | 94.5 | 95.0 | n/a | Hawaii | 4 | Massachusetts | 5 | California | n/a |
| Colorado | 84.5 | 86.2 | n/a | Massachusetts | 6 | Hawaii | 6 | Colorado | n/a |
| Connecticut | 87.7 | 88.0 | n/a | Rhode Island | 7 | Florida | 7 | Connecticut | n/a |
| Delaware | 80.0 | 83.3 | n/a | Florida | 8 | Rhode Island | 8 | D.C. | n/a |
| D.C. | 100.0 | 100.0 | n/a | Utah | 9 | Utah | 9 | Delaware | n/a |
| Florida | 89.3 | 91.2 | n/a | Arizona | 10 | Arizona | 10 | Florida | n/a |
| Georgia | 71.7 | 75.1 | n/a | Illinois | 11 | Illinois | 11 | Georgia | n/a |
| Hawaii | 91.6 | 91.9 | n/a | Connecticut | 12 | Connecticut | 12 | Hawaii | n/a |
| Idaho | 66.4 | 70.6 | n/a | New York | 13 | New York | 13 | Idaho | n/a |
| Illinois | 87.8 | 88.5 | n/a | Maryland | 14 | Maryland | 14 | Illinois | n/a |
| Indiana | 70.8 | 72.4 | n/a | Colorado | 15 | Colorado | 15 | Indiana | n/a |
| Iowa | 61.1 | 64.0 | n/a | Texas | 16 | Texas | 16 | Iowa | n/a |
| Kansas | 71.4 | 74.2 | n/a | Washington | 17 | Washington | 17 | Kansas | n/a |
| Kentucky | 55.7 | 58.4 | n/a | Delaware | 18 | Delaware | 18 | Kentucky | n/a |
| Louisiana | 72.7 | 73.2 | n/a | Oregon | 19 | Oregon | 19 | Louisiana | n/a |
| Maine | 40.2 | 38.7 | n/a | Ohio | 20 | Pennsylvania | 20 | Maine | n/a |
| Maryland | 86.1 | 87.2 | n/a | Pennsylvania | 21 | Ohio | 21 | Maryland | n/a |
| Massachusetts | 91.4 | 92.0 | n/a | New Mexico | 22 | New Mexico | 22 | Massachusetts | n/a |
| Michigan | 74.7 | 74.6 | n/a | Michigan | 23 | Virginia | 23 | Michigan | n/a |
| Minnesota | 70.9 | 73.3 | n/a | Virginia | 24 | Georgia | 24 | Minnesota | n/a |
| Mississippi | 48.8 | 49.3 | n/a | Louisiana | 25 | Michigan | 25 | Mississippi | n/a |
| Missouri | 69.4 | 70.4 | n/a | Georgia | 26 | Kansas | 26 | Missouri | n/a |
| Montana | 54.0 | 55.9 | n/a | Kansas | 27 | Minnesota | 27 | Montana | n/a |
| Nebraska | 69.7 | 73.1 | n/a | Minnesota | 28 | Louisiana | 28 | Nebraska | n/a |
| Nevada | 91.6 | 94.2 | n/a | Indiana | 29 | Nebraska | 29 | Nevada | n/a |
| New Hampshire | 59.2 | 60.3 | n/a | Nebraska | 30 | Indiana | 30 | New Hampshire | n/a |
| New Jersey | 94.3 | 94.7 | n/a | Missouri | 31 | Idaho | 31 | New Jersey | n/a |
| New Mexico | 75.0 | 77.4 | n/a | Wisconsin | 32 | Missouri | 32 | New Mexico | n/a |
| New York | 87.5 | 87.9 | n/a | Idaho | 33 | Wisconsin | 33 | New York | n/a |
| North Carolina | 60.2 | 66.1 | n/a | Alaska | 34 | Tennessee | 34 | North Carolina | n/a |
| North Dakota | 55.8 | 59.9 | n/a | Oklahoma | 35 | South Carolina | 35 | North Dakota | n/a |
| Ohio | 77.3 | 77.9 | n/a | Wyoming | 36 | Oklahoma | 36 | Ohio | n/a |
| Oklahoma | 65.3 | 66.2 | n/a | Tennessee | 37 | North Carolina | 37 | Oklahoma | n/a |
| Oregon | 78.7 | 81.0 | n/a | Iowa | 38 | Alaska | 38 | Oregon | n/a |
| Pennsylvania | 77.0 | 78.7 | n/a | South Carolina | 39 | Wyoming | 39 | Pennsylvania | n/a |
| Rhode Island | 90.9 | 90.7 | n/a | North Carolina | 40 | Iowa | 40 | Rhode Island | n/a |
| South Carolina | 60.5 | 66.3 | n/a | New Hampshire | 41 | New Hampshire | 41 | South Carolina | n/a |
| South Dakota | 51.9 | 56.7 | n/a | North Dakota | 42 | North Dakota | 42 | South Dakota | n/a |
| Tennessee | 63.6 | 66.4 | n/a | Kentucky | 43 | Alabama | 43 | Tennessee | n/a |
| Texas | 82.5 | 84.7 | n/a | Alabama | 44 | Kentucky | 44 | Texas | n/a |
| Utah | 88.3 | 90.6 | n/a | Montana | 45 | South Dakota | 45 | Utah | n/a |
| Vermont | 38.2 | 38.9 | n/a | Arkansas | 46 | Arkansas | 46 | Vermont | n/a |
| Virginia | 73.0 | 75.5 | n/a | South Dakota | 47 | Montana | 47 | Virginia | n/a |
| Washington | 82.0 | 84.0 | n/a | Mississippi | 48 | Mississippi | 48 | Washington | n/a |
| West Virginia | 46.1 | 48.7 | n/a | West Virginia | 49 | West Virginia | 49 | West Virginia | n/a |
| Wisconsin | 68.3 | 70.2 | n/a | Maine | 50 | Vermont | 50 | Wisconsin | n/a |
| Wyoming | 65.2 | 64.8 | n/a | Vermont | 51 | Maine | 51 | Wyoming | n/a |
| United States | 79.0 | 80.7 | n/a | United States | – | United States | – | United States | – |

Source: U.S. Census Bureau, Census 2000, Census 2010, American Community Survey, 2016 1-Year Estimate

# Rural Population

| Area | Percent of Population | | | 2000 | | 2010 | | 2016 | |
|------|------|------|------|------|------|------|------|------|------|
| | 2000 | 2010 | 2016 | Area | Rank | Area | Rank | Area | Rank |
| Alabama | 44.6 | 41.0 | n/a | Vermont | 1 | Maine | 1 | Alabama | n/a |
| Alaska | 34.3 | 34.0 | n/a | Maine | 2 | Vermont | 2 | Alaska | n/a |
| Arizona | 11.8 | 10.2 | n/a | West Virginia | 3 | West Virginia | 3 | Arizona | n/a |
| Arkansas | 47.6 | 43.8 | n/a | Mississippi | 4 | Mississippi | 4 | Arkansas | n/a |
| California | 5.5 | 5.0 | n/a | South Dakota | 5 | Montana | 5 | California | n/a |
| Colorado | 15.5 | 13.8 | n/a | Arkansas | 6 | Arkansas | 6 | Colorado | n/a |
| Connecticut | 12.3 | 12.0 | n/a | Montana | 7 | South Dakota | 7 | Connecticut | n/a |
| Delaware | 20.0 | 16.7 | n/a | Alabama | 8 | Kentucky | 8 | D.C. | n/a |
| D.C. | 0.0 | 0.0 | n/a | Kentucky | 9 | Alabama | 9 | Delaware | n/a |
| Florida | 10.7 | 8.8 | n/a | North Dakota | 10 | North Dakota | 10 | Florida | n/a |
| Georgia | 28.3 | 24.9 | n/a | New Hampshire | 11 | New Hampshire | 11 | Georgia | n/a |
| Hawaii | 8.4 | 8.1 | n/a | North Carolina | 12 | Iowa | 12 | Hawaii | n/a |
| Idaho | 33.6 | 29.4 | n/a | South Carolina | 13 | Wyoming | 13 | Idaho | n/a |
| Illinois | 12.2 | 11.5 | n/a | Iowa | 14 | Alaska | 14 | Illinois | n/a |
| Indiana | 29.2 | 27.6 | n/a | Tennessee | 15 | North Carolina | 15 | Indiana | n/a |
| Iowa | 38.9 | 36.0 | n/a | Wyoming | 16 | Oklahoma | 16 | Iowa | n/a |
| Kansas | 28.6 | 25.8 | n/a | Oklahoma | 17 | South Carolina | 17 | Kansas | n/a |
| Kentucky | 44.3 | 41.6 | n/a | Alaska | 18 | Tennessee | 18 | Kentucky | n/a |
| Louisiana | 27.3 | 26.8 | n/a | Idaho | 19 | Wisconsin | 19 | Louisiana | n/a |
| Maine | 59.8 | 61.3 | n/a | Wisconsin | 20 | Missouri | 20 | Maine | n/a |
| Maryland | 13.9 | 12.8 | n/a | Missouri | 21 | Idaho | 21 | Maryland | n/a |
| Massachusetts | 8.6 | 8.0 | n/a | Nebraska | 22 | Indiana | 22 | Massachusetts | n/a |
| Michigan | 25.3 | 25.4 | n/a | Indiana | 23 | Nebraska | 23 | Michigan | n/a |
| Minnesota | 29.1 | 26.7 | n/a | Minnesota | 24 | Louisiana | 24 | Minnesota | n/a |
| Mississippi | 51.2 | 50.7 | n/a | Kansas | 25 | Minnesota | 25 | Mississippi | n/a |
| Missouri | 30.6 | 29.6 | n/a | Georgia | 26 | Kansas | 26 | Missouri | n/a |
| Montana | 46.0 | 44.1 | n/a | Louisiana | 27 | Michigan | 27 | Montana | n/a |
| Nebraska | 30.3 | 26.9 | n/a | Virginia | 28 | Georgia | 28 | Nebraska | n/a |
| Nevada | 8.4 | 5.8 | n/a | Michigan | 29 | Virginia | 29 | Nevada | n/a |
| New Hampshire | 40.8 | 39.7 | n/a | New Mexico | 30 | New Mexico | 30 | New Hampshire | n/a |
| New Jersey | 5.7 | 5.3 | n/a | Pennsylvania | 31 | Ohio | 31 | New Jersey | n/a |
| New Mexico | 25.0 | 22.6 | n/a | Ohio | 32 | Pennsylvania | 32 | New Mexico | n/a |
| New York | 12.5 | 12.1 | n/a | Oregon | 33 | Oregon | 33 | New York | n/a |
| North Carolina | 39.8 | 33.9 | n/a | Delaware | 34 | Delaware | 34 | North Carolina | n/a |
| North Dakota | 44.2 | 40.1 | n/a | Washington | 35 | Washington | 35 | North Dakota | n/a |
| Ohio | 22.7 | 22.1 | n/a | Texas | 36 | Texas | 36 | Ohio | n/a |
| Oklahoma | 34.7 | 33.8 | n/a | Colorado | 37 | Colorado | 37 | Oklahoma | n/a |
| Oregon | 21.3 | 19.0 | n/a | Maryland | 38 | Maryland | 38 | Oregon | n/a |
| Pennsylvania | 23.0 | 21.3 | n/a | New York | 39 | New York | 39 | Pennsylvania | n/a |
| Rhode Island | 9.1 | 9.3 | n/a | Connecticut | 40 | Connecticut | 40 | Rhode Island | n/a |
| South Carolina | 39.5 | 33.7 | n/a | Illinois | 41 | Illinois | 41 | South Carolina | n/a |
| South Dakota | 48.1 | 43.3 | n/a | Arizona | 42 | Arizona | 42 | South Dakota | n/a |
| Tennessee | 36.4 | 33.6 | n/a | Utah | 43 | Utah | 43 | Tennessee | n/a |
| Texas | 17.5 | 15.3 | n/a | Florida | 44 | Rhode Island | 44 | Texas | n/a |
| Utah | 11.7 | 9.4 | n/a | Rhode Island | 45 | Florida | 45 | Utah | n/a |
| Vermont | 61.8 | 61.1 | n/a | Massachusetts | 46 | Hawaii | 46 | Vermont | n/a |
| Virginia | 27.0 | 24.5 | n/a | Nevada | 47 | Massachusetts | 47 | Virginia | n/a |
| Washington | 18.0 | 16.0 | n/a | Hawaii | 47 | Nevada | 48 | Washington | n/a |
| West Virginia | 53.9 | 51.3 | n/a | New Jersey | 49 | New Jersey | 49 | West Virginia | n/a |
| Wisconsin | 31.7 | 29.8 | n/a | California | 50 | California | 50 | Wisconsin | n/a |
| Wyoming | 34.8 | 35.2 | n/a | D.C. | 51 | D.C. | 51 | Wyoming | n/a |
| United States | 21.0 | 19.3 | n/a | United States | – | United States | – | United States | – |

Source: U.S. Census Bureau, Census 2000, Census 2010, American Community Survey, 2016 1-Year Estimate

## Males per 100 Females

| Area | Males per 100 Females | | | 2000 | | 2010 | | 2016 | |
|---|---|---|---|---|---|---|---|---|---|
| | 2000 | 2010 | 2016 | Area | Rank | Area | Rank | Area | Rank |
| Alabama | 93.3 | 94.3 | 94.0 | Alaska | 1 | Alaska | 1 | Alaska | 1 |
| Alaska | 107.0 | 108.5 | 111.2 | Nevada | 2 | Wyoming | 2 | North Dakota | 2 |
| Arizona | 99.7 | 98.7 | 98.8 | Colorado | 3 | North Dakota | 3 | Wyoming | 3 |
| Arkansas | 95.3 | 96.5 | 96.7 | Wyoming | 4 | Nevada | 4 | Montana | 4 |
| California | 99.3 | 98.8 | 98.6 | Hawaii | 5 | Utah | 5 | Utah | 5 |
| Colorado | 101.4 | 100.5 | 101.5 | Idaho | 6 | Montana | 6 | Colorado | 6 |
| Connecticut | 93.9 | 94.8 | 95.3 | Utah | 7 | Colorado | 7 | South Dakota | 7 |
| Delaware | 94.4 | 93.9 | 93.6 | Arizona | 8 | Idaho | 8 | Hawaii | 8 |
| D.C. | 89.0 | 89.5 | 90.5 | North Dakota | 9 | Hawaii | 9 | Nevada | 9 |
| Florida | 95.3 | 95.6 | 95.5 | California | 10 | South Dakota | 10 | Idaho | 10 |
| Georgia | 96.8 | 95.4 | 94.8 | Montana | 10 | Washington | 11 | Washington | 11 |
| Hawaii | 101.0 | 100.3 | 101.1 | Washington | 12 | California | 12 | Kansas | 12 |
| Idaho | 100.5 | 100.4 | 99.9 | Texas | 13 | Arizona | 13 | Nebraska | 12 |
| Illinois | 95.9 | 96.2 | 96.6 | South Dakota | 14 | Nebraska | 14 | New Hampshire | 14 |
| Indiana | 96.3 | 96.8 | 97.1 | Oregon | 15 | Wisconsin | 14 | Minnesota | 15 |
| Iowa | 96.3 | 98.1 | 98.6 | Minnesota | 16 | Minnesota | 14 | Wisconsin | 16 |
| Kansas | 97.7 | 98.4 | 99.3 | Kansas | 17 | Texas | 17 | Arizona | 17 |
| Kentucky | 95.6 | 96.8 | 96.6 | Wisconsin | 18 | Kansas | 17 | Texas | 18 |
| Louisiana | 93.8 | 95.9 | 95.9 | Nebraska | 19 | Iowa | 19 | California | 18 |
| Maine | 94.8 | 95.8 | 95.6 | Georgia | 20 | Oregon | 20 | Iowa | 18 |
| Maryland | 93.4 | 93.6 | 94.2 | New Hampshire | 20 | Oklahoma | 20 | Oklahoma | 21 |
| Massachusetts | 93.0 | 93.7 | 94.3 | New Mexico | 22 | New Mexico | 22 | New Mexico | 22 |
| Michigan | 96.2 | 96.3 | 96.8 | Oklahoma | 23 | New Hampshire | 23 | Oregon | 22 |
| Minnesota | 98.1 | 98.5 | 99.1 | Virginia | 24 | West Virginia | 23 | Vermont | 24 |
| Mississippi | 93.4 | 94.4 | 93.1 | Indiana | 24 | Vermont | 25 | Indiana | 25 |
| Missouri | 94.6 | 96.0 | 96.7 | Iowa | 24 | Indiana | 26 | West Virginia | 26 |
| Montana | 99.3 | 100.8 | 101.8 | Michigan | 27 | Kentucky | 26 | Michigan | 27 |
| Nebraska | 97.2 | 98.5 | 99.3 | Vermont | 28 | Arkansas | 28 | Virginia | 28 |
| Nevada | 103.9 | 102.0 | 100.4 | North Carolina | 29 | Virginia | 29 | Arkansas | 28 |
| New Hampshire | 96.8 | 97.3 | 99.2 | Illinois | 30 | Michigan | 29 | Missouri | 28 |
| New Jersey | 94.3 | 94.8 | 95.5 | Kentucky | 31 | Illinois | 31 | Illinois | 31 |
| New Mexico | 96.7 | 97.7 | 98.0 | Florida | 32 | Missouri | 32 | Kentucky | 31 |
| New York | 93.1 | 93.8 | 94.3 | Arkansas | 32 | Louisiana | 33 | Ohio | 33 |
| North Carolina | 96.0 | 95.0 | 94.6 | Tennessee | 34 | Maine | 34 | Pennsylvania | 34 |
| North Dakota | 99.6 | 102.1 | 106.1 | Maine | 35 | Florida | 35 | Louisiana | 35 |
| Ohio | 94.4 | 95.4 | 96.1 | Missouri | 36 | Georgia | 36 | Maine | 36 |
| Oklahoma | 96.6 | 98.0 | 98.1 | West Virginia | 36 | Ohio | 36 | Florida | 37 |
| Oregon | 98.4 | 98.0 | 98.0 | South Carolina | 38 | Pennsylvania | 38 | New Jersey | 37 |
| Pennsylvania | 93.4 | 95.1 | 96.0 | Delaware | 39 | Tennessee | 38 | Tennessee | 39 |
| Rhode Island | 92.5 | 93.4 | 93.8 | Ohio | 39 | North Carolina | 40 | Connecticut | 40 |
| South Carolina | 94.5 | 94.7 | 94.1 | New Jersey | 41 | New Jersey | 41 | Georgia | 41 |
| South Dakota | 98.5 | 100.1 | 101.4 | Connecticut | 42 | Connecticut | 41 | North Carolina | 42 |
| Tennessee | 94.9 | 95.1 | 95.4 | Louisiana | 43 | South Carolina | 43 | New York | 43 |
| Texas | 98.6 | 98.4 | 98.6 | Maryland | 44 | Mississippi | 44 | Massachusetts | 43 |
| Utah | 100.4 | 100.9 | 101.7 | Pennsylvania | 44 | Alabama | 45 | Maryland | 45 |
| Vermont | 96.1 | 97.1 | 97.2 | Mississippi | 44 | Delaware | 46 | South Carolina | 46 |
| Virginia | 96.3 | 96.3 | 96.7 | Alabama | 47 | New York | 47 | Alabama | 47 |
| Washington | 99.1 | 99.3 | 99.8 | New York | 48 | Massachusetts | 48 | Rhode Island | 48 |
| West Virginia | 94.6 | 97.3 | 96.9 | Massachusetts | 49 | Maryland | 49 | Delaware | 49 |
| Wisconsin | 97.6 | 98.5 | 98.9 | Rhode Island | 50 | Rhode Island | 50 | Mississippi | 50 |
| Wyoming | 101.2 | 104.1 | 103.8 | D.C. | 51 | D.C. | 51 | D.C. | 51 |
| United States | 96.3 | 96.7 | 96.9 | United States | – | United States | – | United States | – |

Source: U.S. Census Bureau, Census 2000, Census 2010, American Community Survey, 2016 1-Year Estimate

## Median Age

| Area | Years | | | 2000 | | 2010 | | 2016 | |
|---|---|---|---|---|---|---|---|---|---|
| | 2000 | 2010 | 2016 | Area | Rank | Area | Rank | Area | Rank |
| Alabama | 35.8 | 37.9 | 39.0 | West Virginia | 1 | Maine | 1 | Maine | 1 |
| Alaska | 32.4 | 33.8 | 33.5 | Florida | 2 | Vermont | 2 | Vermont | 2 |
| Arizona | 34.2 | 35.9 | 37.5 | Maine | 3 | West Virginia | 3 | New Hampshire | 3 |
| Arkansas | 36.0 | 37.4 | 38.0 | Pennsylvania | 4 | New Hampshire | 4 | West Virginia | 4 |
| California | 33.3 | 35.2 | 36.4 | Vermont | 5 | Florida | 5 | Florida | 5 |
| Colorado | 34.3 | 36.1 | 36.7 | Montana | 6 | Pennsylvania | 6 | Connecticut | 6 |
| Connecticut | 37.4 | 40.0 | 40.9 | Connecticut | 7 | Connecticut | 7 | Delaware | 7 |
| Delaware | 36.0 | 38.8 | 40.6 | New Hampshire | 8 | Montana | 8 | Pennsylvania | 7 |
| D.C. | 34.6 | 33.8 | 33.9 | New Jersey | 9 | Rhode Island | 9 | Rhode Island | 9 |
| Florida | 38.7 | 40.7 | 42.1 | Rhode Island | 9 | Massachusetts | 10 | Montana | 10 |
| Georgia | 33.4 | 35.3 | 36.5 | Iowa | 11 | New Jersey | 11 | Michigan | 11 |
| Hawaii | 36.2 | 38.6 | 38.9 | Massachusetts | 12 | Michigan | 12 | New Jersey | 12 |
| Idaho | 33.2 | 34.6 | 36.1 | Oregon | 13 | Delaware | 13 | Massachusetts | 12 |
| Illinois | 34.7 | 36.6 | 37.9 | Hawaii | 14 | Ohio | 13 | Wisconsin | 14 |
| Indiana | 35.2 | 37.0 | 37.6 | Wyoming | 14 | Hawaii | 15 | Ohio | 15 |
| Iowa | 36.6 | 38.1 | 38.0 | Ohio | 14 | Wisconsin | 16 | Oregon | 16 |
| Kansas | 35.2 | 36.0 | 36.5 | North Dakota | 14 | Oregon | 17 | South Carolina | 17 |
| Kentucky | 35.9 | 38.1 | 38.7 | Missouri | 18 | Iowa | 18 | Alabama | 18 |
| Louisiana | 34.0 | 35.8 | 36.5 | Delaware | 19 | Kentucky | 18 | Hawaii | 19 |
| Maine | 38.6 | 42.7 | 44.5 | Maryland | 19 | New York | 20 | North Carolina | 20 |
| Maryland | 36.0 | 38.0 | 38.5 | Wisconsin | 19 | Maryland | 20 | Kentucky | 20 |
| Massachusetts | 36.5 | 39.1 | 39.5 | Arkansas | 19 | Tennessee | 20 | Tennessee | 22 |
| Michigan | 35.5 | 38.9 | 39.7 | New York | 23 | South Carolina | 23 | Maryland | 23 |
| Minnesota | 35.4 | 37.4 | 37.9 | Tennessee | 23 | Alabama | 23 | New York | 24 |
| Mississippi | 33.8 | 36.0 | 37.2 | Kentucky | 23 | Missouri | 23 | Missouri | 24 |
| Missouri | 36.1 | 37.9 | 38.4 | Alabama | 26 | Virginia | 26 | Virginia | 26 |
| Montana | 37.5 | 39.8 | 40.1 | Virginia | 27 | North Carolina | 27 | Arkansas | 27 |
| Nebraska | 35.3 | 36.2 | 36.3 | South Dakota | 28 | Arkansas | 27 | Iowa | 27 |
| Nevada | 35.0 | 36.3 | 37.9 | Oklahoma | 29 | Minnesota | 27 | Nevada | 29 |
| New Hampshire | 37.1 | 41.1 | 42.7 | Michigan | 29 | Washington | 30 | Illinois | 29 |
| New Jersey | 36.7 | 39.0 | 39.5 | Minnesota | 31 | Indiana | 31 | Minnesota | 29 |
| New Mexico | 34.6 | 36.7 | 37.7 | South Carolina | 31 | North Dakota | 31 | New Mexico | 32 |
| New York | 35.9 | 38.0 | 38.4 | Washington | 33 | South Dakota | 33 | Washington | 32 |
| North Carolina | 35.3 | 37.4 | 38.7 | Nebraska | 33 | Wyoming | 34 | Indiana | 34 |
| North Dakota | 36.2 | 37.0 | 35.0 | North Carolina | 33 | New Mexico | 35 | Arizona | 35 |
| Ohio | 36.2 | 38.8 | 39.3 | Kansas | 36 | Illinois | 36 | Wyoming | 36 |
| Oklahoma | 35.5 | 36.2 | 36.4 | Indiana | 36 | Nevada | 37 | Mississippi | 36 |
| Oregon | 36.3 | 38.4 | 39.2 | Nevada | 38 | Nebraska | 38 | South Dakota | 38 |
| Pennsylvania | 38.0 | 40.1 | 40.6 | Illinois | 39 | Oklahoma | 38 | Colorado | 39 |
| Rhode Island | 36.7 | 39.4 | 40.2 | New Mexico | 40 | Colorado | 40 | Kansas | 40 |
| South Carolina | 35.4 | 37.9 | 39.1 | D.C. | 40 | Kansas | 41 | Georgia | 40 |
| South Dakota | 35.6 | 36.9 | 36.8 | Colorado | 42 | Mississippi | 41 | Louisiana | 40 |
| Tennessee | 35.9 | 38.0 | 38.6 | Arizona | 43 | Arizona | 43 | California | 43 |
| Texas | 32.3 | 33.6 | 34.5 | Louisiana | 44 | Louisiana | 44 | Oklahoma | 43 |
| Utah | 27.1 | 29.2 | 30.7 | Mississippi | 45 | Georgia | 45 | Nebraska | 45 |
| Vermont | 37.7 | 41.5 | 43.1 | Georgia | 46 | California | 46 | Idaho | 46 |
| Virginia | 35.7 | 37.5 | 38.2 | California | 47 | Idaho | 47 | North Dakota | 47 |
| Washington | 35.3 | 37.3 | 37.7 | Idaho | 48 | D.C. | 48 | Texas | 48 |
| West Virginia | 38.9 | 41.3 | 42.3 | Alaska | 49 | Alaska | 48 | D.C. | 49 |
| Wisconsin | 36.0 | 38.5 | 39.4 | Texas | 50 | Texas | 50 | Alaska | 50 |
| Wyoming | 36.2 | 36.8 | 37.2 | Utah | 51 | Utah | 51 | Utah | 51 |
| United States | 35.3 | 37.2 | 37.9 | United States | – | United States | – | United States | – |

*Source: U.S. Census Bureau, Census 2000, Census 2010, American Community Survey, 2016 1-Year Estimate*

# High School Graduates

| Area | Percent of Population | | | 2000 | | 2010 | | 2016 | |
| --- | --- | --- | --- | --- | --- | --- | --- | --- | --- |
| | 2000 | 2010 | 2016 | Area | Rank | Area | Rank | Area | Rank |
| Alabama | 75.3 | 82.1 | 85.1 | Alaska | 1 | Wyoming | 1 | Wyoming | 1 |
| Alaska | 88.3 | 91.0 | 93.1 | Minnesota | 2 | Minnesota | 2 | Alaska | 2 |
| Arizona | 81.0 | 85.6 | 86.7 | Wyoming | 3 | Montana | 3 | Minnesota | 3 |
| Arkansas | 75.3 | 82.9 | 86.0 | Utah | 4 | New Hampshire | 4 | Montana | 4 |
| California | 76.8 | 80.7 | 82.4 | New Hampshire | 5 | Alaska | 5 | New Hampshire | 4 |
| Colorado | 86.9 | 89.7 | 91.4 | Montana | 6 | Vermont | 5 | North Dakota | 6 |
| Connecticut | 84.0 | 88.6 | 90.5 | Washington | 7 | Utah | 7 | Maine | 7 |
| Delaware | 82.6 | 87.7 | 89.3 | Colorado | 8 | Iowa | 7 | Vermont | 8 |
| D.C. | 77.8 | 87.4 | 90.5 | Nebraska | 9 | Nebraska | 9 | Hawaii | 9 |
| Florida | 79.9 | 85.5 | 87.4 | Vermont | 10 | North Dakota | 10 | Wisconsin | 10 |
| Georgia | 78.6 | 84.3 | 86.4 | Iowa | 11 | Maine | 10 | Iowa | 11 |
| Hawaii | 84.6 | 89.9 | 92.0 | Kansas | 12 | Wisconsin | 12 | Utah | 12 |
| Idaho | 84.7 | 88.3 | 90.4 | Maine | 13 | Hawaii | 13 | Colorado | 13 |
| Illinois | 81.4 | 86.9 | 88.8 | Oregon | 14 | Washington | 14 | South Dakota | 14 |
| Indiana | 82.1 | 87.0 | 88.4 | Wisconsin | 14 | Colorado | 15 | Nebraska | 15 |
| Iowa | 86.1 | 90.6 | 91.8 | Massachusetts | 16 | South Dakota | 16 | Washington | 16 |
| Kansas | 86.0 | 89.2 | 90.5 | Idaho | 17 | Kansas | 17 | Connecticut | 17 |
| Kentucky | 74.1 | 81.9 | 85.7 | Hawaii | 18 | Massachusetts | 18 | Kansas | 17 |
| Louisiana | 74.8 | 81.9 | 84.4 | South Dakota | 18 | Oregon | 19 | D.C. | 17 |
| Maine | 85.4 | 90.3 | 92.3 | Connecticut | 20 | Michigan | 20 | Idaho | 20 |
| Maryland | 83.8 | 88.1 | 90.1 | North Dakota | 21 | Connecticut | 21 | Massachusetts | 20 |
| Massachusetts | 84.8 | 89.1 | 90.4 | Maryland | 22 | Pennsylvania | 22 | Michigan | 20 |
| Michigan | 83.4 | 88.7 | 90.4 | Michigan | 23 | Idaho | 23 | Oregon | 23 |
| Minnesota | 88.0 | 91.8 | 92.9 | Ohio | 24 | Maryland | 24 | Maryland | 24 |
| Mississippi | 72.9 | 81.0 | 84.1 | Delaware | 25 | Ohio | 24 | Pennsylvania | 24 |
| Missouri | 81.3 | 86.9 | 89.6 | New Jersey | 26 | New Jersey | 26 | Ohio | 26 |
| Montana | 87.2 | 91.7 | 92.8 | Indiana | 26 | Delaware | 27 | Missouri | 27 |
| Nebraska | 86.6 | 90.4 | 90.9 | Pennsylvania | 28 | D.C. | 28 | New Jersey | 28 |
| Nevada | 80.7 | 84.7 | 86.0 | Virginia | 29 | Indiana | 29 | Delaware | 28 |
| New Hampshire | 87.4 | 91.5 | 92.8 | Illinois | 30 | Illinois | 30 | Virginia | 28 |
| New Jersey | 82.1 | 88.0 | 89.3 | Missouri | 31 | Missouri | 30 | Illinois | 31 |
| New Mexico | 78.9 | 83.3 | 85.4 | Arizona | 32 | Virginia | 32 | Rhode Island | 32 |
| New York | 79.1 | 84.9 | 86.3 | Nevada | 33 | Oklahoma | 33 | Indiana | 33 |
| North Carolina | 78.1 | 84.7 | 87.3 | Oklahoma | 34 | Arizona | 34 | Oklahoma | 34 |
| North Dakota | 83.9 | 90.3 | 92.4 | Florida | 35 | Florida | 35 | Florida | 35 |
| Ohio | 83.0 | 88.1 | 90.0 | New York | 36 | New York | 36 | North Carolina | 36 |
| Oklahoma | 80.6 | 86.2 | 87.8 | New Mexico | 37 | Nevada | 37 | Tennessee | 37 |
| Oregon | 85.1 | 88.8 | 90.3 | Georgia | 38 | North Carolina | 37 | Arizona | 38 |
| Pennsylvania | 81.9 | 88.4 | 90.1 | North Carolina | 39 | Georgia | 39 | South Carolina | 39 |
| Rhode Island | 78.0 | 83.5 | 88.5 | Rhode Island | 40 | South Carolina | 40 | Georgia | 40 |
| South Carolina | 76.3 | 84.1 | 86.6 | D.C. | 41 | Tennessee | 41 | New York | 41 |
| South Dakota | 84.6 | 89.6 | 91.2 | California | 42 | Rhode Island | 42 | Nevada | 42 |
| Tennessee | 75.9 | 83.6 | 87.0 | South Carolina | 43 | New Mexico | 43 | Arkansas | 42 |
| Texas | 75.7 | 80.7 | 82.9 | Tennessee | 44 | West Virginia | 44 | West Virginia | 42 |
| Utah | 87.7 | 90.6 | 91.7 | Texas | 45 | Arkansas | 45 | Kentucky | 45 |
| Vermont | 86.4 | 91.0 | 92.1 | Arkansas | 46 | Alabama | 46 | New Mexico | 46 |
| Virginia | 81.5 | 86.5 | 89.3 | Alabama | 46 | Louisiana | 47 | Alabama | 47 |
| Washington | 87.1 | 89.8 | 90.8 | West Virginia | 48 | Kentucky | 47 | Louisiana | 48 |
| West Virginia | 75.2 | 83.2 | 86.0 | Louisiana | 49 | Mississippi | 49 | Mississippi | 49 |
| Wisconsin | 85.1 | 90.1 | 91.9 | Kentucky | 50 | California | 50 | Texas | 50 |
| Wyoming | 87.9 | 92.3 | 93.2 | Mississippi | 51 | Texas | 50 | California | 51 |
| United States | 80.4 | 85.6 | 87.5 | United States | – | United States | – | United States | – |

Source: U.S. Census Bureau, Census 2000, Census 2010, American Community Survey, 2016 1-Year Estimate

# College Graduates

| Area | Percent of Population | | | 2000 | | 2010 | | 2016 | |
|---|---|---|---|---|---|---|---|---|---|
| | 2000 | 2010 | 2016 | Area | Rank | Area | Rank | Area | Rank |
| Alabama | 19.0 | 21.9 | 24.7 | D.C. | 1 | D.C. | 1 | D.C. | 1 |
| Alaska | 24.7 | 27.9 | 29.6 | Massachusetts | 2 | Massachusetts | 2 | Massachusetts | 2 |
| Arizona | 23.5 | 25.9 | 28.9 | Colorado | 3 | Colorado | 3 | Colorado | 3 |
| Arkansas | 16.7 | 19.5 | 22.4 | Maryland | 4 | Maryland | 4 | Maryland | 4 |
| California | 26.6 | 30.1 | 32.9 | Connecticut | 5 | Connecticut | 5 | New Jersey | 5 |
| Colorado | 32.7 | 36.4 | 39.9 | New Jersey | 6 | New Jersey | 6 | Connecticut | 5 |
| Connecticut | 31.4 | 35.5 | 38.6 | Virginia | 7 | Virginia | 7 | Virginia | 7 |
| Delaware | 25.1 | 27.8 | 31.0 | Vermont | 7 | Vermont | 8 | New Hampshire | 8 |
| D.C. | 39.1 | 50.1 | 56.8 | New Hampshire | 9 | New Hampshire | 9 | Vermont | 9 |
| Florida | 22.3 | 25.8 | 28.6 | Washington | 10 | New York | 10 | New York | 10 |
| Georgia | 24.3 | 27.3 | 30.5 | New York | 11 | Minnesota | 11 | Washington | 11 |
| Hawaii | 26.2 | 29.5 | 31.9 | Minnesota | 11 | Washington | 12 | Minnesota | 12 |
| Idaho | 21.7 | 24.4 | 27.6 | California | 13 | Illinois | 13 | Rhode Island | 13 |
| Illinois | 26.1 | 30.8 | 34.0 | Hawaii | 14 | Rhode Island | 14 | Illinois | 14 |
| Indiana | 19.4 | 22.7 | 25.6 | Illinois | 15 | California | 15 | California | 15 |
| Iowa | 21.2 | 24.9 | 28.4 | Utah | 15 | Kansas | 16 | Kansas | 16 |
| Kansas | 25.8 | 29.8 | 32.8 | Kansas | 17 | Hawaii | 17 | Oregon | 17 |
| Kentucky | 17.1 | 20.5 | 23.4 | Rhode Island | 18 | Utah | 18 | Utah | 18 |
| Louisiana | 18.7 | 21.4 | 23.4 | Oregon | 19 | Oregon | 19 | Hawaii | 19 |
| Maine | 22.9 | 26.8 | 30.1 | Delaware | 19 | Montana | 19 | Nebraska | 20 |
| Maryland | 31.5 | 36.1 | 39.3 | Alaska | 21 | Nebraska | 21 | Delaware | 21 |
| Massachusetts | 33.2 | 39.0 | 42.7 | Montana | 22 | Alaska | 22 | Montana | 21 |
| Michigan | 21.8 | 25.2 | 28.3 | Georgia | 23 | Delaware | 23 | Pennsylvania | 23 |
| Minnesota | 27.4 | 31.8 | 34.8 | Nebraska | 24 | North Dakota | 24 | Georgia | 24 |
| Mississippi | 16.9 | 19.5 | 21.8 | New Mexico | 25 | Georgia | 25 | North Carolina | 25 |
| Missouri | 21.6 | 25.6 | 28.5 | Arizona | 25 | Pennsylvania | 26 | Maine | 26 |
| Montana | 24.4 | 28.8 | 31.0 | Texas | 27 | Maine | 27 | Alaska | 27 |
| Nebraska | 23.7 | 28.6 | 31.4 | Maine | 28 | North Carolina | 28 | North Dakota | 27 |
| Nevada | 18.2 | 21.7 | 23.5 | North Carolina | 29 | Wisconsin | 29 | Wisconsin | 29 |
| New Hampshire | 28.7 | 32.8 | 36.6 | Wisconsin | 30 | South Dakota | 29 | Texas | 30 |
| New Jersey | 29.8 | 35.4 | 38.6 | Pennsylvania | 30 | Texas | 31 | Arizona | 30 |
| New Mexico | 23.5 | 25.0 | 27.2 | Florida | 32 | Arizona | 31 | South Dakota | 30 |
| New York | 27.4 | 32.5 | 35.7 | North Dakota | 33 | Florida | 33 | Florida | 33 |
| North Carolina | 22.5 | 26.5 | 30.4 | Wyoming | 34 | Missouri | 34 | Missouri | 34 |
| North Dakota | 22.0 | 27.6 | 29.6 | Michigan | 35 | Michigan | 35 | Iowa | 35 |
| Ohio | 21.1 | 24.6 | 27.5 | Idaho | 36 | New Mexico | 36 | Michigan | 36 |
| Oklahoma | 20.3 | 22.9 | 25.2 | Missouri | 37 | Iowa | 37 | Idaho | 37 |
| Oregon | 25.1 | 28.8 | 32.7 | South Dakota | 38 | Ohio | 38 | Ohio | 38 |
| Pennsylvania | 22.4 | 27.1 | 30.8 | Iowa | 39 | South Carolina | 39 | New Mexico | 39 |
| Rhode Island | 25.6 | 30.2 | 34.1 | Ohio | 40 | Idaho | 40 | South Carolina | 39 |
| South Carolina | 20.4 | 24.5 | 27.2 | South Carolina | 41 | Wyoming | 41 | Wyoming | 41 |
| South Dakota | 21.5 | 26.3 | 28.9 | Oklahoma | 42 | Tennessee | 42 | Tennessee | 42 |
| Tennessee | 19.6 | 23.1 | 26.1 | Tennessee | 43 | Oklahoma | 43 | Indiana | 43 |
| Texas | 23.2 | 25.9 | 28.9 | Indiana | 44 | Indiana | 44 | Oklahoma | 44 |
| Utah | 26.1 | 29.3 | 32.6 | Alabama | 45 | Alabama | 45 | Alabama | 45 |
| Vermont | 29.5 | 33.6 | 36.4 | Louisiana | 46 | Nevada | 46 | Nevada | 46 |
| Virginia | 29.5 | 34.2 | 38.1 | Nevada | 47 | Louisiana | 47 | Louisiana | 47 |
| Washington | 27.7 | 31.1 | 35.1 | Kentucky | 48 | Kentucky | 48 | Kentucky | 47 |
| West Virginia | 14.8 | 17.5 | 20.8 | Mississippi | 49 | Arkansas | 49 | Arkansas | 49 |
| Wisconsin | 22.4 | 26.3 | 29.5 | Arkansas | 50 | Mississippi | 49 | Mississippi | 50 |
| Wyoming | 21.9 | 24.1 | 27.1 | West Virginia | 51 | West Virginia | 51 | West Virginia | 51 |
| United States | 24.4 | 28.2 | 31.3 | United States | – | United States | – | United States | – |

Source: U.S. Census Bureau, Census 2000, Census 2010, American Community Survey, 2016 1-Year Estimate

# One-Person Households

| Area | Percent of Population | | | 2000 | | 2010 | | 2016 | |
|------|------|------|------|------|------|------|------|------|------|
| | 2000 | 2010 | 2016 | Area | Rank | Area | Rank | Area | Rank |
| Alabama | 26.1 | 27.4 | 30.7 | D.C. | 1 | D.C. | 1 | D.C. | 1 |
| Alaska | 23.5 | 25.6 | 25.1 | North Dakota | 2 | North Dakota | 2 | Rhode Island | 2 |
| Arizona | 24.8 | 26.1 | 27.3 | Rhode Island | 3 | Montana | 3 | North Dakota | 2 |
| Arkansas | 25.6 | 27.1 | 29.3 | New York | 4 | Rhode Island | 4 | South Dakota | 4 |
| California | 23.5 | 23.3 | 23.9 | Massachusetts | 5 | South Dakota | 5 | Alabama | 5 |
| Colorado | 26.3 | 27.9 | 27.3 | Pennsylvania | 6 | New York | 6 | Montana | 5 |
| Connecticut | 26.4 | 27.3 | 28.7 | Nebraska | 7 | Ohio | 7 | New Mexico | 7 |
| Delaware | 25.0 | 25.6 | 27.6 | South Dakota | 7 | Massachusetts | 8 | Ohio | 8 |
| D.C. | 43.8 | 44.0 | 43.8 | Montana | 9 | Nebraska | 8 | Louisiana | 9 |
| Florida | 26.6 | 27.2 | 28.8 | Missouri | 10 | Pennsylvania | 10 | Vermont | 9 |
| Georgia | 23.6 | 25.4 | 27.2 | Ohio | 10 | Maine | 10 | Pennsylvania | 11 |
| Hawaii | 21.9 | 23.3 | 24.5 | Iowa | 12 | Iowa | 12 | Maine | 11 |
| Idaho | 22.4 | 23.8 | 26.6 | West Virginia | 13 | West Virginia | 12 | New York | 13 |
| Illinois | 26.8 | 27.8 | 29.6 | Kansas | 14 | Missouri | 14 | Nebraska | 13 |
| Indiana | 25.9 | 26.9 | 28.6 | Maine | 14 | Wisconsin | 15 | Wisconsin | 15 |
| Iowa | 27.2 | 28.4 | 29.4 | Minnesota | 16 | Vermont | 15 | Michigan | 16 |
| Kansas | 27.0 | 27.8 | 29.6 | Illinois | 17 | New Mexico | 17 | West Virginia | 16 |
| Kentucky | 26.0 | 27.5 | 28.8 | Wisconsin | 17 | Wyoming | 17 | Illinois | 18 |
| Louisiana | 25.3 | 26.9 | 30.2 | Oklahoma | 19 | Minnesota | 17 | Kansas | 18 |
| Maine | 27.0 | 28.6 | 30.0 | Florida | 20 | Colorado | 20 | Iowa | 20 |
| Maryland | 25.0 | 26.1 | 27.3 | Connecticut | 21 | Michigan | 20 | Arkansas | 21 |
| Massachusetts | 28.0 | 28.7 | 28.9 | Colorado | 22 | Illinois | 22 | South Carolina | 21 |
| Michigan | 26.2 | 27.9 | 29.7 | Wyoming | 22 | Kansas | 22 | Minnesota | 23 |
| Minnesota | 26.9 | 28.0 | 29.2 | Washington | 24 | Oklahoma | 24 | Missouri | 23 |
| Mississippi | 24.6 | 26.3 | 28.8 | Michigan | 24 | Kentucky | 24 | Massachusetts | 25 |
| Missouri | 27.3 | 28.3 | 29.2 | Vermont | 24 | Oregon | 26 | Florida | 26 |
| Montana | 27.4 | 29.7 | 30.7 | Oregon | 27 | Alabama | 26 | Kentucky | 26 |
| Nebraska | 27.6 | 28.7 | 29.9 | Alabama | 27 | Connecticut | 28 | Mississippi | 26 |
| Nevada | 24.9 | 25.7 | 28.6 | Kentucky | 29 | Florida | 29 | Connecticut | 29 |
| New Hampshire | 24.4 | 25.6 | 26.4 | Indiana | 30 | Washington | 29 | Oklahoma | 29 |
| New Jersey | 24.5 | 25.2 | 26.3 | Tennessee | 31 | Arkansas | 31 | Tennessee | 29 |
| New Mexico | 25.4 | 28.0 | 30.4 | Arkansas | 32 | North Carolina | 32 | Nevada | 32 |
| New York | 28.1 | 29.1 | 29.9 | New Mexico | 33 | Indiana | 33 | Indiana | 32 |
| North Carolina | 25.4 | 27.0 | 28.5 | North Carolina | 33 | Tennessee | 33 | North Carolina | 34 |
| North Dakota | 29.3 | 31.5 | 32.3 | Louisiana | 35 | Louisiana | 33 | Wyoming | 35 |
| Ohio | 27.3 | 28.9 | 30.3 | Virginia | 36 | South Carolina | 36 | Delaware | 36 |
| Oklahoma | 26.7 | 27.5 | 28.7 | Delaware | 37 | Mississippi | 37 | Oregon | 37 |
| Oregon | 26.1 | 27.4 | 27.4 | Maryland | 37 | Arizona | 38 | Virginia | 37 |
| Pennsylvania | 27.7 | 28.6 | 30.0 | South Carolina | 37 | Maryland | 38 | Arizona | 39 |
| Rhode Island | 28.6 | 29.6 | 32.3 | Nevada | 40 | Virginia | 40 | Colorado | 39 |
| South Carolina | 25.0 | 26.5 | 29.3 | Arizona | 41 | Nevada | 41 | Maryland | 39 |
| South Dakota | 27.6 | 29.4 | 31.0 | Mississippi | 42 | Delaware | 42 | Georgia | 42 |
| Tennessee | 25.8 | 26.9 | 28.7 | New Jersey | 43 | Alaska | 42 | Washington | 43 |
| Texas | 23.7 | 24.2 | 25.2 | New Hampshire | 44 | New Hampshire | 42 | Idaho | 44 |
| Utah | 17.8 | 18.7 | 18.7 | Texas | 45 | Georgia | 45 | New Hampshire | 45 |
| Vermont | 26.2 | 28.2 | 30.2 | Georgia | 46 | New Jersey | 46 | New Jersey | 46 |
| Virginia | 25.1 | 26.0 | 27.4 | California | 47 | Texas | 47 | Texas | 47 |
| Washington | 26.2 | 27.2 | 27.0 | Alaska | 47 | Idaho | 48 | Alaska | 48 |
| West Virginia | 27.1 | 28.4 | 29.7 | Idaho | 49 | California | 49 | Hawaii | 49 |
| Wisconsin | 26.8 | 28.2 | 29.8 | Hawaii | 50 | Hawaii | 49 | California | 50 |
| Wyoming | 26.3 | 28.0 | 27.7 | Utah | 51 | Utah | 51 | Utah | 51 |
| United States | 25.8 | 26.7 | 28.0 | United States | – | United States | – | United States | – |

*Source: U.S. Census Bureau, Census 2000, Census 2010, American Community Survey, 2016 1-Year Estimate*

# Homeownership

| Area | Percent of Population | | | 2000 | | 2010 | | 2016 | |
|------|------|------|------|------|------|------|------|------|------|
| | 2000 | 2010 | 2016 | Area | Rank | Area | Rank | Area | Rank |
| Alabama | 72.5 | 69.7 | 68.5 | West Virginia | 1 | West Virginia | 1 | West Virginia | 1 |
| Alaska | 62.5 | 63.1 | 64.5 | Minnesota | 2 | Minnesota | 2 | Maine | 2 |
| Arizona | 68.0 | 66.0 | 63.2 | Michigan | 3 | Iowa | 3 | Minnesota | 3 |
| Arkansas | 69.4 | 66.9 | 64.6 | Alabama | 4 | Michigan | 3 | Iowa | 4 |
| California | 56.9 | 56.0 | 53.6 | Idaho | 5 | Delaware | 5 | Michigan | 5 |
| Colorado | 67.3 | 65.5 | 64.8 | Delaware | 6 | Maine | 6 | New Hampshire | 6 |
| Connecticut | 66.8 | 67.5 | 64.8 | Iowa | 6 | New Hampshire | 7 | Utah | 7 |
| Delaware | 72.3 | 72.0 | 69.8 | Mississippi | 6 | Vermont | 8 | Delaware | 8 |
| D.C. | 40.8 | 42.0 | 39.2 | South Carolina | 9 | Utah | 9 | Vermont | 8 |
| Florida | 70.1 | 67.3 | 64.1 | Maine | 10 | Idaho | 10 | Wyoming | 10 |
| Georgia | 67.5 | 65.7 | 61.5 | Utah | 11 | Indiana | 11 | South Carolina | 11 |
| Hawaii | 56.5 | 57.7 | 57.2 | Indiana | 12 | Alabama | 12 | Idaho | 12 |
| Idaho | 72.4 | 69.9 | 68.5 | Pennsylvania | 13 | Pennsylvania | 13 | Pennsylvania | 12 |
| Illinois | 67.3 | 67.4 | 65.3 | Kentucky | 14 | Mississippi | 13 | Alabama | 12 |
| Indiana | 71.4 | 69.8 | 68.3 | Vermont | 15 | Wyoming | 15 | Indiana | 15 |
| Iowa | 72.3 | 72.1 | 70.6 | Missouri | 16 | South Carolina | 15 | Montana | 16 |
| Kansas | 69.2 | 67.7 | 65.7 | Florida | 17 | Missouri | 17 | New Mexico | 17 |
| Kentucky | 70.8 | 68.7 | 66.8 | New Mexico | 18 | Kentucky | 18 | Mississippi | 18 |
| Louisiana | 67.9 | 67.3 | 64.3 | Wyoming | 18 | New Mexico | 19 | South Dakota | 19 |
| Maine | 71.6 | 71.3 | 71.9 | Tennessee | 20 | Tennessee | 20 | Kentucky | 20 |
| Maryland | 67.7 | 67.5 | 65.9 | New Hampshire | 21 | Wisconsin | 21 | Wisconsin | 21 |
| Massachusetts | 61.7 | 62.3 | 62.0 | North Carolina | 22 | South Dakota | 21 | Missouri | 22 |
| Michigan | 73.8 | 72.1 | 70.3 | Arkansas | 22 | Montana | 23 | Maryland | 23 |
| Minnesota | 74.6 | 73.1 | 71.3 | Kansas | 24 | Kansas | 24 | Kansas | 24 |
| Mississippi | 72.3 | 69.6 | 67.3 | Montana | 25 | Ohio | 25 | Ohio | 25 |
| Missouri | 70.3 | 68.8 | 66.1 | Ohio | 25 | Connecticut | 26 | Illinois | 26 |
| Montana | 69.1 | 68.0 | 68.0 | Oklahoma | 27 | Maryland | 26 | Nebraska | 26 |
| Nebraska | 67.4 | 67.2 | 65.3 | Wisconsin | 27 | Illinois | 28 | Virginia | 26 |
| Nevada | 60.9 | 58.8 | 54.9 | South Dakota | 29 | Florida | 29 | Tennessee | 29 |
| New Hampshire | 69.7 | 70.9 | 70.1 | Virginia | 30 | Oklahoma | 29 | Oklahoma | 30 |
| New Jersey | 65.6 | 65.4 | 63.2 | Arizona | 31 | Louisiana | 29 | Colorado | 31 |
| New Mexico | 70.0 | 68.5 | 67.4 | Louisiana | 32 | Nebraska | 32 | Connecticut | 31 |
| New York | 53.0 | 53.3 | 53.3 | Maryland | 33 | Virginia | 32 | Arkansas | 33 |
| North Carolina | 69.4 | 66.7 | 64.2 | Georgia | 34 | Arkansas | 34 | Alaska | 34 |
| North Dakota | 66.6 | 65.4 | 63.2 | Nebraska | 35 | North Carolina | 35 | Louisiana | 35 |
| Ohio | 69.1 | 67.6 | 65.4 | Colorado | 36 | Arizona | 36 | North Carolina | 36 |
| Oklahoma | 68.4 | 67.3 | 64.9 | Illinois | 36 | Georgia | 37 | Florida | 37 |
| Oregon | 64.3 | 62.1 | 61.7 | Connecticut | 38 | Colorado | 38 | Arizona | 38 |
| Pennsylvania | 71.3 | 69.6 | 68.5 | North Dakota | 39 | New Jersey | 39 | New Jersey | 38 |
| Rhode Island | 60.0 | 60.7 | 58.0 | New Jersey | 40 | North Dakota | 39 | North Dakota | 38 |
| South Carolina | 72.2 | 69.3 | 68.6 | Washington | 41 | Washington | 41 | Washington | 41 |
| South Dakota | 68.2 | 68.1 | 67.2 | Oregon | 42 | Texas | 42 | Massachusetts | 42 |
| Tennessee | 69.9 | 68.2 | 65.1 | Texas | 43 | Alaska | 43 | Oregon | 43 |
| Texas | 63.8 | 63.7 | 61.1 | Alaska | 44 | Massachusetts | 44 | Georgia | 44 |
| Utah | 71.5 | 70.5 | 69.9 | Massachusetts | 45 | Oregon | 45 | Texas | 45 |
| Vermont | 70.6 | 70.7 | 69.8 | Nevada | 46 | Rhode Island | 46 | Rhode Island | 46 |
| Virginia | 68.1 | 67.2 | 65.3 | Rhode Island | 47 | Nevada | 47 | Hawaii | 47 |
| Washington | 64.6 | 63.9 | 62.5 | California | 48 | Hawaii | 48 | Nevada | 48 |
| West Virginia | 75.2 | 73.4 | 72.4 | Hawaii | 49 | California | 49 | California | 49 |
| Wisconsin | 68.4 | 68.1 | 66.7 | New York | 50 | New York | 50 | New York | 50 |
| Wyoming | 70.0 | 69.3 | 68.8 | D.C. | 51 | D.C. | 51 | D.C. | 51 |
| United States | 66.2 | 65.1 | 63.1 | United States | – | United States | – | United States | – |

Source: U.S. Census Bureau, Census 2000, Census 2010, American Community Survey, 2016 1-Year Estimate

## Median Home Value

| Area | Median Home Value ($) | | | 2000 | | 2010 | | 2016 | |
|------|------|------|------|------|------|------|------|------|------|
| | 2000 | 2010 | 2016 | Area | Rank | Area | Rank | Area | Rank |
| Alabama | 85,100 | 123,900 | 136,200 | Hawaii | 1 | Hawaii | 1 | Hawaii | 1 |
| Alaska | 144,200 | 241,400 | 267,800 | California | 2 | D.C. | 2 | D.C. | 2 |
| Arizona | 121,300 | 168,800 | 205,900 | Massachusetts | 3 | California | 3 | California | 3 |
| Arkansas | 72,800 | 106,300 | 123,300 | New Jersey | 4 | New Jersey | 4 | Massachusetts | 4 |
| California | 211,500 | 370,900 | 477,500 | Washington | 5 | Massachusetts | 5 | New Jersey | 5 |
| Colorado | 166,600 | 236,600 | 314,200 | Connecticut | 6 | Maryland | 6 | Colorado | 6 |
| Connecticut | 166,900 | 288,800 | 274,600 | Colorado | 7 | New York | 7 | Maryland | 7 |
| Delaware | 130,400 | 243,600 | 243,400 | D.C. | 8 | Connecticut | 8 | Washington | 8 |
| D.C. | 157,200 | 426,900 | 576,100 | Oregon | 9 | Washington | 9 | New York | 9 |
| Florida | 105,500 | 164,200 | 197,700 | New York | 10 | Rhode Island | 10 | Oregon | 10 |
| Georgia | 111,200 | 156,200 | 166,800 | Utah | 11 | Virginia | 11 | Connecticut | 11 |
| Hawaii | 272,700 | 525,400 | 592,000 | Maryland | 12 | Oregon | 12 | Alaska | 12 |
| Idaho | 106,300 | 165,100 | 189,400 | Alaska | 13 | Delaware | 13 | Virginia | 13 |
| Illinois | 130,800 | 191,800 | 186,500 | Nevada | 14 | New Hampshire | 14 | New Hampshire | 14 |
| Indiana | 94,300 | 123,300 | 134,800 | New Hampshire | 15 | Alaska | 15 | Utah | 15 |
| Iowa | 82,500 | 123,400 | 142,300 | Rhode Island | 16 | Colorado | 16 | Rhode Island | 16 |
| Kansas | 83,500 | 127,300 | 144,900 | Illinois | 17 | Utah | 17 | Delaware | 17 |
| Kentucky | 86,700 | 121,600 | 135,600 | Delaware | 18 | Vermont | 18 | Nevada | 18 |
| Louisiana | 85,000 | 137,500 | 158,000 | Virginia | 19 | Minnesota | 19 | Vermont | 19 |
| Maine | 98,700 | 179,100 | 184,700 | Minnesota | 20 | Illinois | 20 | Montana | 20 |
| Maryland | 146,000 | 301,400 | 306,900 | Arizona | 21 | Montana | 21 | Minnesota | 21 |
| Massachusetts | 185,700 | 334,100 | 366,900 | Michigan | 22 | Wyoming | 22 | Wyoming | 22 |
| Michigan | 115,600 | 123,300 | 147,100 | Wisconsin | 23 | Maine | 23 | Arizona | 23 |
| Minnesota | 122,400 | 194,300 | 211,800 | Vermont | 24 | Nevada | 24 | Florida | 24 |
| Mississippi | 71,400 | 100,100 | 113,900 | Georgia | 25 | Wisconsin | 25 | Idaho | 25 |
| Missouri | 89,900 | 139,000 | 151,400 | North Carolina | 26 | Arizona | 26 | Illinois | 26 |
| Montana | 99,500 | 181,200 | 217,200 | New Mexico | 27 | Pennsylvania | 27 | Maine | 27 |
| Nebraska | 88,000 | 127,600 | 148,100 | Idaho | 28 | Idaho | 28 | North Dakota | 28 |
| Nevada | 142,000 | 174,800 | 239,500 | Florida | 29 | Florida | 29 | Pennsylvania | 29 |
| New Hampshire | 133,300 | 243,000 | 251,100 | Ohio | 30 | New Mexico | 30 | Wisconsin | 30 |
| New Jersey | 170,800 | 339,200 | 328,200 | Montana | 31 | Georgia | 31 | New Mexico | 31 |
| New Mexico | 108,100 | 161,200 | 167,500 | Maine | 32 | North Carolina | 32 | Georgia | 32 |
| New York | 148,700 | 296,500 | 302,400 | Pennsylvania | 33 | Tennessee | 33 | North Carolina | 33 |
| North Carolina | 108,300 | 154,200 | 165,400 | Wyoming | 34 | Missouri | 33 | Texas | 34 |
| North Dakota | 74,400 | 123,000 | 184,100 | South Carolina | 35 | South Carolina | 35 | South Dakota | 35 |
| Ohio | 103,700 | 134,400 | 140,100 | Indiana | 36 | Louisiana | 36 | Louisiana | 36 |
| Oklahoma | 70,700 | 111,400 | 132,200 | Tennessee | 37 | Ohio | 37 | Tennessee | 37 |
| Oregon | 152,100 | 244,500 | 287,100 | Missouri | 38 | South Dakota | 38 | South Carolina | 38 |
| Pennsylvania | 97,000 | 165,500 | 174,100 | Nebraska | 39 | Texas | 39 | Missouri | 39 |
| Rhode Island | 133,000 | 254,500 | 247,700 | Kentucky | 40 | Nebraska | 40 | Nebraska | 40 |
| South Carolina | 94,900 | 138,100 | 153,900 | Alabama | 41 | Kansas | 41 | Michigan | 41 |
| South Dakota | 79,600 | 129,700 | 160,700 | Louisiana | 42 | Alabama | 42 | Kansas | 42 |
| Tennessee | 93,000 | 139,000 | 157,700 | Kansas | 43 | Iowa | 43 | Iowa | 43 |
| Texas | 82,500 | 128,100 | 161,500 | Texas | 44 | Indiana | 44 | Ohio | 44 |
| Utah | 146,100 | 217,200 | 250,300 | Iowa | 44 | Michigan | 44 | Alabama | 45 |
| Vermont | 111,500 | 216,800 | 223,700 | South Dakota | 46 | North Dakota | 46 | Kentucky | 46 |
| Virginia | 125,400 | 249,100 | 264,000 | North Dakota | 47 | Kentucky | 47 | Indiana | 47 |
| Washington | 168,300 | 271,800 | 306,400 | Arkansas | 48 | Oklahoma | 48 | Oklahoma | 48 |
| West Virginia | 72,800 | 95,100 | 117,900 | West Virginia | 48 | Arkansas | 49 | Arkansas | 49 |
| Wisconsin | 112,200 | 169,400 | 173,200 | Mississippi | 50 | Mississippi | 50 | West Virginia | 50 |
| Wyoming | 96,600 | 180,100 | 209,500 | Oklahoma | 51 | West Virginia | 51 | Mississippi | 51 |
| United States | 119,600 | 179,900 | 205,000 | United States | – | United States | – | United States | – |

*Source: U.S. Census Bureau, Census 2000, Census 2010, American Community Survey, 2016 1-Year Estimate*

## Median Gross Rent

| Area | Median Gross Rent ($/month) | | | 2000 | | 2010 | | 2016 | |
|---|---|---|---|---|---|---|---|---|---|
| | 2000 | 2010 | 2016 | Area | Rank | Area | Rank | Area | Rank |
| Alabama | 447 | 667 | 743 | Hawaii | 1 | Hawaii | 1 | Hawaii | 1 |
| Alaska | 720 | 981 | 1,208 | New Jersey | 2 | D.C. | 2 | D.C. | 2 |
| Arizona | 619 | 844 | 976 | California | 3 | California | 3 | California | 3 |
| Arkansas | 453 | 638 | 701 | Alaska | 4 | Maryland | 4 | Maryland | 4 |
| California | 747 | 1,163 | 1,375 | Nevada | 5 | New Jersey | 5 | New Jersey | 5 |
| Colorado | 671 | 863 | 1,171 | Maryland | 6 | New York | 6 | Alaska | 6 |
| Connecticut | 681 | 992 | 1,115 | Massachusetts | 7 | Virginia | 7 | New York | 7 |
| Delaware | 639 | 952 | 1,048 | Connecticut | 8 | Massachusetts | 8 | Massachusetts | 8 |
| D.C. | 618 | 1,198 | 1,376 | New York | 9 | Connecticut | 9 | Colorado | 9 |
| Florida | 641 | 947 | 1,086 | Colorado | 10 | Alaska | 10 | Virginia | 10 |
| Georgia | 613 | 819 | 933 | Washington | 11 | Nevada | 11 | Washington | 11 |
| Hawaii | 779 | 1,291 | 1,483 | Virginia | 12 | Delaware | 11 | Connecticut | 12 |
| Idaho | 515 | 683 | 790 | New Hampshire | 13 | New Hampshire | 13 | Florida | 13 |
| Illinois | 605 | 848 | 950 | Florida | 14 | Florida | 14 | Delaware | 14 |
| Indiana | 521 | 683 | 768 | Delaware | 15 | Washington | 15 | New Hampshire | 15 |
| Iowa | 470 | 629 | 741 | Oregon | 16 | Rhode Island | 16 | Oregon | 16 |
| Kansas | 498 | 682 | 789 | Arizona | 17 | Colorado | 17 | Nevada | 17 |
| Kentucky | 445 | 613 | 707 | D.C. | 18 | Illinois | 18 | Arizona | 18 |
| Louisiana | 466 | 736 | 808 | Georgia | 19 | Arizona | 19 | Texas | 19 |
| Maine | 497 | 707 | 797 | Illinois | 20 | Vermont | 20 | Utah | 20 |
| Maryland | 689 | 1,131 | 1,314 | Utah | 21 | Georgia | 21 | Illinois | 21 |
| Massachusetts | 684 | 1,009 | 1,179 | Texas | 22 | Oregon | 22 | Rhode Island | 22 |
| Michigan | 546 | 730 | 818 | Minnesota | 23 | Texas | 23 | Georgia | 23 |
| Minnesota | 566 | 764 | 912 | Rhode Island | 24 | Utah | 24 | Vermont | 24 |
| Mississippi | 439 | 672 | 728 | Vermont | 24 | Minnesota | 25 | Minnesota | 25 |
| Missouri | 484 | 682 | 771 | North Carolina | 26 | Pennsylvania | 26 | Pennsylvania | 26 |
| Montana | 447 | 642 | 741 | Michigan | 27 | Louisiana | 27 | South Carolina | 27 |
| Nebraska | 491 | 669 | 769 | Wisconsin | 28 | North Carolina | 28 | Wyoming | 28 |
| Nevada | 699 | 952 | 1,003 | Pennsylvania | 29 | Michigan | 29 | North Carolina | 29 |
| New Hampshire | 646 | 951 | 1,026 | Indiana | 30 | South Carolina | 30 | Michigan | 30 |
| New Jersey | 751 | 1,114 | 1,244 | Idaho | 31 | Wisconsin | 31 | Louisiana | 31 |
| New Mexico | 503 | 699 | 804 | Ohio | 31 | Maine | 32 | Tennessee | 32 |
| New York | 672 | 1,020 | 1,194 | South Carolina | 33 | New Mexico | 33 | New Mexico | 33 |
| North Carolina | 548 | 731 | 839 | Tennessee | 34 | Tennessee | 34 | Wisconsin | 34 |
| North Dakota | 412 | 583 | 776 | New Mexico | 35 | Wyoming | 35 | Maine | 35 |
| Ohio | 515 | 685 | 759 | Kansas | 36 | Ohio | 36 | Idaho | 36 |
| Oklahoma | 456 | 659 | 744 | Maine | 37 | Idaho | 37 | Kansas | 37 |
| Oregon | 620 | 816 | 1,015 | Nebraska | 38 | Indiana | 37 | North Dakota | 38 |
| Pennsylvania | 531 | 763 | 881 | Missouri | 39 | Kansas | 39 | Missouri | 39 |
| Rhode Island | 553 | 868 | 948 | Iowa | 40 | Missouri | 39 | Nebraska | 40 |
| South Carolina | 510 | 728 | 841 | Louisiana | 41 | Mississippi | 41 | Indiana | 41 |
| South Dakota | 426 | 591 | 706 | Oklahoma | 42 | Nebraska | 42 | Ohio | 42 |
| Tennessee | 505 | 697 | 806 | Arkansas | 43 | Alabama | 43 | Oklahoma | 43 |
| Texas | 574 | 801 | 956 | Montana | 44 | Oklahoma | 44 | Alabama | 44 |
| Utah | 597 | 796 | 954 | Alabama | 44 | Montana | 45 | Iowa | 45 |
| Vermont | 553 | 823 | 925 | Kentucky | 46 | Arkansas | 46 | Montana | 45 |
| Virginia | 650 | 1,019 | 1,159 | Mississippi | 47 | Iowa | 47 | Mississippi | 47 |
| Washington | 663 | 908 | 1,135 | Wyoming | 48 | Kentucky | 48 | Kentucky | 48 |
| West Virginia | 401 | 571 | 682 | South Dakota | 49 | South Dakota | 49 | South Dakota | 49 |
| Wisconsin | 540 | 715 | 802 | North Dakota | 50 | North Dakota | 50 | Arkansas | 50 |
| Wyoming | 437 | 693 | 840 | West Virginia | 51 | West Virginia | 51 | West Virginia | 51 |
| United States | 602 | 855 | 981 | United States | – | United States | – | United States | – |

Source: U.S. Census Bureau, Census 2000, Census 2010, American Community Survey, 2016 1-Year Estimate

## Households Lacking Complete Plumbing Facilities

| Area | Percent of Households | | | 2000 | | 2010 | | 2016 | |
|---|---|---|---|---|---|---|---|---|---|
| | 2000 | 2010 | 2016 | Area | Rank | Area | Rank | Area | Rank |
| Alabama | 0.6 | 0.5 | 0.4 | Alaska | 1 | Alaska | 1 | Alaska | 1 |
| Alaska | 6.3 | 5.0 | 4.0 | New Mexico | 2 | New Mexico | 2 | New Mexico | 2 |
| Arizona | 1.1 | 0.8 | 0.7 | Arizona | 3 | Maine | 3 | Hawaii | 2 |
| Arkansas | 0.8 | 0.6 | 0.4 | Hawaii | 4 | Vermont | 4 | Arizona | 4 |
| California | 0.7 | 0.6 | 0.5 | West Virginia | 4 | Arizona | 5 | Maine | 4 |
| Colorado | 0.4 | 0.5 | 0.3 | D.C. | 6 | Nevada | 5 | California | 6 |
| Connecticut | 0.5 | 0.4 | 0.3 | Kentucky | 6 | Rhode Island | 5 | Oregon | 6 |
| Delaware | 0.4 | 0.8 | 0.2 | Mississippi | 6 | Delaware | 5 | Idaho | 6 |
| D.C. | 0.9 | 0.7 | 0.1 | Maine | 6 | Montana | 5 | Wisconsin | 6 |
| Florida | 0.5 | 0.4 | 0.3 | New York | 10 | Texas | 10 | South Dakota | 6 |
| Georgia | 0.6 | 0.5 | 0.3 | Arkansas | 10 | D.C. | 10 | Montana | 6 |
| Hawaii | 1.0 | 0.7 | 0.8 | Montana | 10 | Hawaii | 10 | New Hampshire | 6 |
| Idaho | 0.6 | 0.5 | 0.5 | California | 13 | Kentucky | 10 | Kentucky | 6 |
| Illinois | 0.5 | 0.5 | 0.3 | Texas | 13 | Mississippi | 10 | Mississippi | 6 |
| Indiana | 0.5 | 0.4 | 0.3 | Virginia | 13 | South Dakota | 10 | Vermont | 6 |
| Iowa | 0.4 | 0.4 | 0.2 | Idaho | 16 | West Virginia | 10 | West Virginia | 6 |
| Kansas | 0.4 | 0.3 | 0.4 | Massachusetts | 16 | California | 17 | Texas | 17 |
| Kentucky | 0.9 | 0.7 | 0.5 | Georgia | 16 | New York | 17 | New York | 17 |
| Louisiana | 0.6 | 0.5 | 0.3 | Oklahoma | 16 | Oregon | 17 | Washington | 17 |
| Maine | 0.9 | 1.1 | 0.7 | North Carolina | 16 | Washington | 17 | Kansas | 17 |
| Maryland | 0.5 | 0.5 | 0.2 | Louisiana | 16 | Oklahoma | 17 | Oklahoma | 17 |
| Massachusetts | 0.6 | 0.4 | 0.3 | South Carolina | 16 | Virginia | 17 | Arkansas | 17 |
| Michigan | 0.4 | 0.5 | 0.4 | Tennessee | 16 | Arkansas | 17 | Michigan | 17 |
| Minnesota | 0.5 | 0.5 | 0.3 | Alabama | 16 | Wisconsin | 17 | Alabama | 17 |
| Mississippi | 0.9 | 0.7 | 0.5 | South Dakota | 16 | New Hampshire | 17 | Missouri | 17 |
| Missouri | 0.5 | 0.5 | 0.4 | Vermont | 16 | Colorado | 26 | Nevada | 26 |
| Montana | 0.8 | 0.8 | 0.5 | Nevada | 27 | New Jersey | 26 | Florida | 26 |
| Nebraska | 0.4 | 0.2 | 0.3 | Florida | 27 | Illinois | 26 | Colorado | 26 |
| Nevada | 0.5 | 0.8 | 0.3 | New Jersey | 27 | Utah | 26 | Illinois | 26 |
| New Hampshire | 0.5 | 0.6 | 0.5 | Illinois | 27 | Idaho | 26 | Connecticut | 26 |
| New Jersey | 0.5 | 0.5 | 0.2 | Connecticut | 27 | Georgia | 26 | Rhode Island | 26 |
| New Mexico | 1.8 | 1.3 | 0.8 | Rhode Island | 27 | North Carolina | 26 | Utah | 26 |
| New York | 0.8 | 0.6 | 0.4 | Oregon | 27 | Maryland | 26 | Massachusetts | 26 |
| North Carolina | 0.6 | 0.5 | 0.3 | Washington | 27 | Pennsylvania | 26 | Nebraska | 26 |
| North Dakota | 0.4 | 0.2 | 0.3 | Wyoming | 27 | South Carolina | 26 | Georgia | 26 |
| Ohio | 0.4 | 0.5 | 0.3 | Maryland | 27 | Minnesota | 26 | North Carolina | 26 |
| Oklahoma | 0.6 | 0.6 | 0.4 | Wisconsin | 27 | Tennessee | 26 | Virginia | 26 |
| Oregon | 0.5 | 0.6 | 0.5 | Indiana | 27 | Michigan | 26 | Pennsylvania | 26 |
| Pennsylvania | 0.5 | 0.5 | 0.3 | Pennsylvania | 27 | Louisiana | 26 | Indiana | 26 |
| Rhode Island | 0.5 | 0.8 | 0.3 | Minnesota | 27 | Alabama | 26 | South Carolina | 26 |
| South Carolina | 0.6 | 0.5 | 0.3 | Missouri | 27 | Missouri | 26 | Minnesota | 26 |
| South Dakota | 0.6 | 0.7 | 0.5 | New Hampshire | 27 | Ohio | 26 | Tennessee | 26 |
| Tennessee | 0.6 | 0.5 | 0.3 | Colorado | 43 | Florida | 43 | Louisiana | 26 |
| Texas | 0.7 | 0.7 | 0.4 | Utah | 43 | Connecticut | 43 | Ohio | 26 |
| Utah | 0.4 | 0.5 | 0.3 | Kansas | 43 | Massachusetts | 43 | North Dakota | 26 |
| Vermont | 0.6 | 0.9 | 0.5 | Nebraska | 43 | Wyoming | 43 | New Jersey | 46 |
| Virginia | 0.7 | 0.6 | 0.3 | Delaware | 43 | Indiana | 43 | Maryland | 46 |
| Washington | 0.5 | 0.6 | 0.4 | Michigan | 43 | Iowa | 43 | Wyoming | 46 |
| West Virginia | 1.0 | 0.7 | 0.5 | Iowa | 43 | Kansas | 49 | Delaware | 46 |
| Wisconsin | 0.5 | 0.6 | 0.5 | Ohio | 43 | Nebraska | 50 | Iowa | 46 |
| Wyoming | 0.5 | 0.4 | 0.2 | North Dakota | 43 | North Dakota | 50 | D.C. | 51 |
| United States | 0.6 | 0.6 | 0.4 | United States | – | United States | – | United States | – |

Note: The reader is cautioned against comparing values across decades as the definition of plumbing facilities has changed over time.
Source: U.S. Census Bureau, 2000 Census; U.S. Census Bureau, American Community Survey, 2010 and 2016 1-Year Estimate

# 2010 Census: United States Profile

## Population Density by County[†]

### U.S. Race* Breakdown

Black or African American (12.6%)
American Indian and Alaska Native (0.9%)
Asian (4.8%)
Native Hawaiian and Other Pacific Islander (0.2%)
Some other race (6.2%)
Two or more races (2.9%)

*One race

White (72.4%)

### Hispanic or Latino (of any race) makes up **16.3%** of the U.S. population.

### Population by Sex and Age

Total Population: 308,745,538

85+ Years
80
70
60
50
40
30
20
10

12,000,000   6,000,000   0   6,000,000   12,000,000

Male          Female

### Housing Tenure

Total Occupied Housing Units: 116,716,292

65.1% Owner Occupied    34.9% Renter Occupied

Average Household Size of Owner-Occupied Units: 2.65 people

Average Household Size of Renter-Occupied Units: 2.44 people

### People per Square Mile by County[†]

3,000.0 to 69,468.4
300.0 to 2,999.9
160.0 to 299.9
88.4 to 159.9
7.0 to 88.3
1.0 to 6.9
Less than 1.0

State Boundary
County† Boundary
United States Mean Center of Population

U.S. density is 88.4

†County and statistically equivalent entity

### United States Population 1970 to 2010

| Year | Population |
|------|------------|
| 2010 | 308,745,538 |
| 2000 | 281,421,906 |
| 1990 | 248,709,873 |
| 1980 | 226,545,805 |
| 1970 | 203,211,926 |

0   100   300   500 Kilometers
0   100   300   500 Miles

0   300 Kilometers
0   300 Miles

0   100 Kilometers
0   100 Miles

United States Census Bureau

U.S. Department of Commerce   Economics and Statistics Administration   U.S. CENSUS BUREAU

# 2010 Census: Alabama Profile

## Population Density by Census Tract

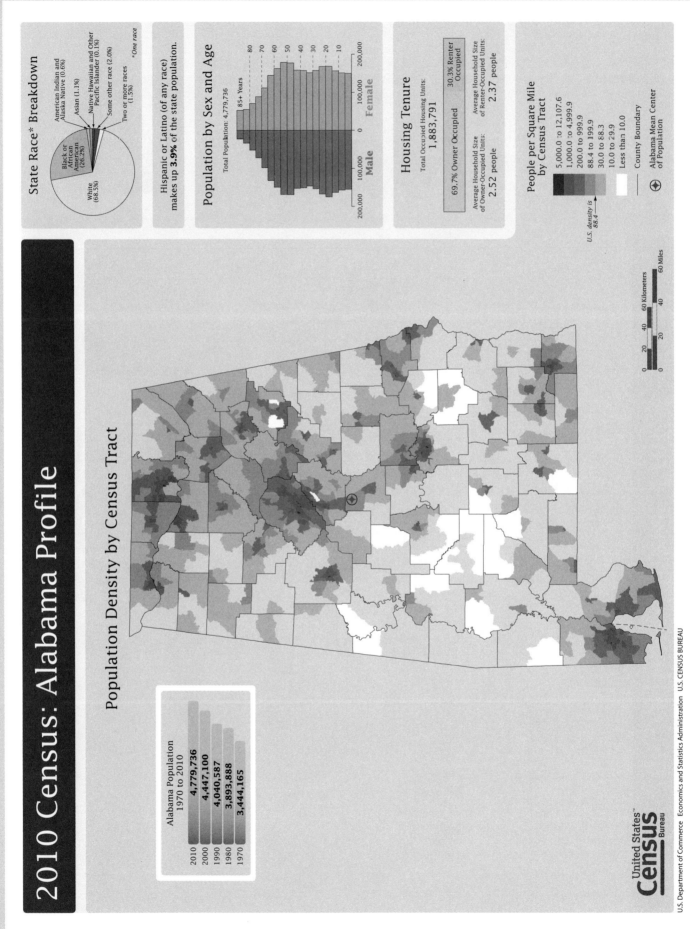

### State Race* Breakdown

American Indian and Alaska Native (0.6%)
Asian (1.1%)
Native Hawaiian and Other Pacific Islander (0.1%)
Some other race (2.0%)
Two or more races (1.5%)
*One race

Black or African American (26.2%)

White (68.5%)

### Hispanic or Latino (of any race) makes up **3.9%** of the state population.

### Population by Sex and Age

Total Population: 4,779,736

85+ Years
80
70
60
50
40
30
20
10

200,000   100,000   0   100,000   200,000

Male          Female

### Housing Tenure

Total Occupied Housing Units:
1,883,791

69.7% Owner Occupied     30.3% Renter Occupied

Average Household Size of Owner-Occupied Units:
2.52 people

Average Household Size of Renter-Occupied Units:
2.37 people

### People per Square Mile by Census Tract

5,000.0 to 12,107.6
1,000.0 to 4,999.9
200.0 to 999.9
88.4 to 199.9
30.0 to 88.3
10.0 to 29.9
Less than 10.0

*U.S. density is 88.4*

County Boundary
Alabama Mean Center of Population

### Alabama Population 1970 to 2010

2010   4,779,736
2000   4,447,100
1990   4,040,587
1980   3,893,888
1970   3,444,165

0   20   40   60 Kilometers
0   20   40   60 Miles

United States™
**Census**
Bureau

U.S. Department of Commerce   Economics and Statistics Administration   U.S. CENSUS BUREAU

# 2010 Census: Alaska Profile

## Population Density by Census Tract

### State Race* Breakdown

Black or African American (3.3%)
American Indian and Alaska Native (14.8%)
Asian (5.4%)
Native Hawaiian and Other Pacific Islander (1.0%)
Some other race (1.6%)
Two or more races (7.3%)
*One race
White (66.7%)

Hispanic or Latino (of any race) makes up **5.5%** of the state population.

### Population by Sex and Age

Total Population: 710,231

Male
Female
85+ Years
80
70
60
50
40
30
20
10

30,000  15,000  0  15,000  30,000

### Housing Tenure

Total Occupied Housing Units:
258,058

63.1% Owner Occupied
36.9% Renter Occupied

Average Household Size of Owner-Occupied Units:
2.76 people

Average Household Size of Renter-Occupied Units:
2.47 people

### People per Square Mile by Census Tract

2,000.0 to 8,336.8
500.0 to 1,999.9
88.4 to 499.9
20.0 to 88.3
5.0 to 19.9
1.0 to 4.9
Less than 1.0
Borough or Equivalent Boundary
Alaska Mean Center of Population

U.S. density is 88.4

### Alaska Population 1970 to 2010

2010  710,231
2000  626,932
1990  550,043
1980  401,851
1970  300,382

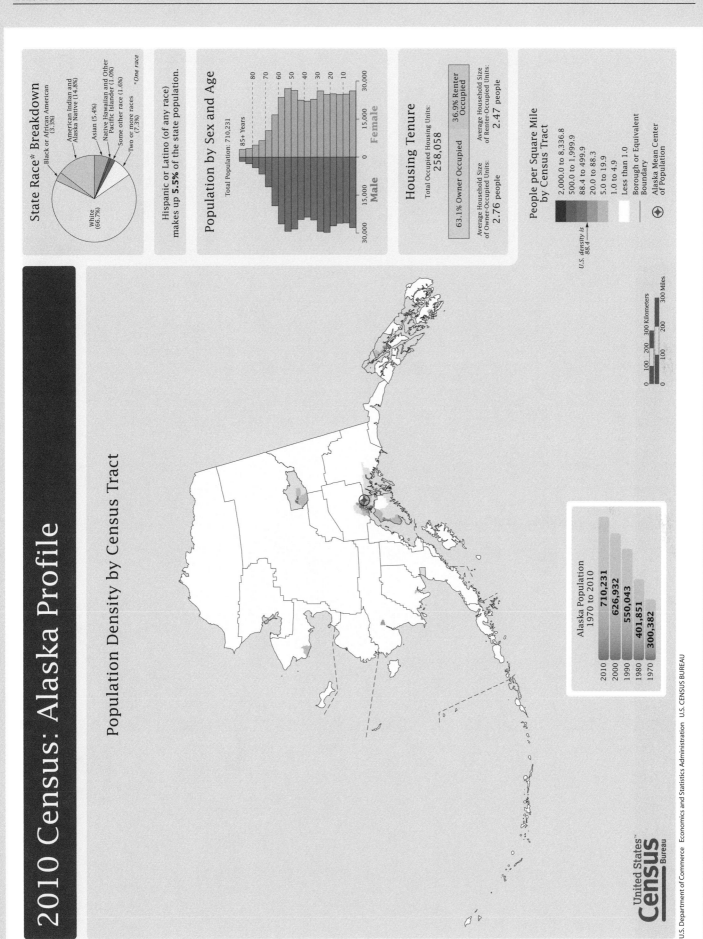

0  100  200  300 Kilometers
0  100  200  300 Miles

United States™
Census
Bureau

U.S. Department of Commerce  Economics and Statistics Administration  U.S. CENSUS BUREAU

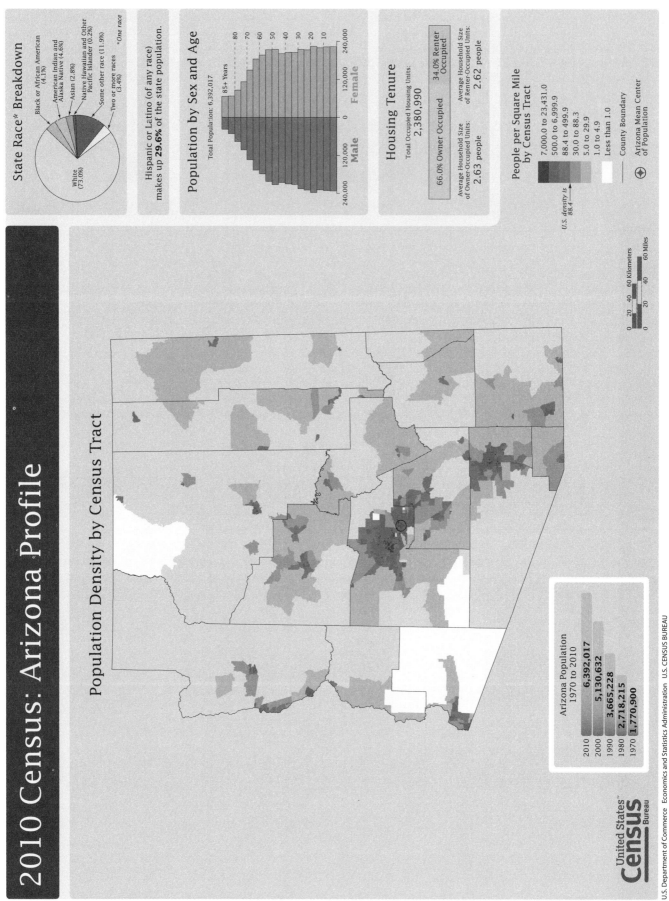

## 2010 Census: Arizona Profile

### State Race* Breakdown

White (73.0%)
Black or African American (4.1%)
American Indian and Alaska Native (4.6%)
Asian (2.8%)
Native Hawaiian and Other Pacific Islander (0.2%)
Some other race (11.9%)
Two or more races (3.4%)

*One race

Hispanic or Latino (of any race) makes up **29.6%** of the state population.

### Population by Sex and Age

Total Population: 6,392,017

85+ Years
80
70
60
50
40
30
20
10

Male
Female

240,000  120,000  0  120,000  240,000

### Housing Tenure

Total Occupied Housing Units: 2,380,990

66.0% Owner Occupied          34.0% Renter Occupied

Average Household Size of Owner-Occupied Units: 2.63 people

Average Household Size of Renter-Occupied Units: 2.62 people

### People per Square Mile by Census Tract

7,000.0 to 23,431.0
500.0 to 6,999.9
88.4 to 499.9
30.0 to 88.3
5.0 to 29.9
1.0 to 4.9
Less than 1.0

U.S. density is 88.4

County Boundary
Arizona Mean Center of Population

### Population Density by Census Tract

0  20  40  60 Kilometers
0  20  40  60 Miles

Arizona Population 1970 to 2010

2010  6,392,017
2000  5,130,632
1990  3,665,228
1980  2,718,215
1970  1,770,900

United States Census Bureau

U.S. Department of Commerce  Economics and Statistics Administration  U.S. CENSUS BUREAU

# 2010 Census: Arkansas Profile

## State Race* Breakdown

White (77.0%)
Black or African American (15.4%)
American Indian and Alaska Native (0.8%)
Asian (1.2%)
Native Hawaiian and Other Pacific Islander (0.2%)
Some other race (3.4%)
Two or more races (2.0%)

*One race

Hispanic or Latino (of any race) makes up **6.4%** of the state population.

## Population by Sex and Age

Total Population: 2,915,918

85+ Years
80
70
60
50
40
30
20
10

Male | Female

120,000 · 60,000 · 0 · 60,000 · 120,000

## Housing Tenure

Total Occupied Housing Units: 1,147,084

67.0% Owner Occupied
33.0% Renter Occupied

Average Household Size of Owner-Occupied Units: 2.51 people

Average Household Size of Renter-Occupied Units: 2.40 people

## People per Square Mile by Census Tract

5,000.0 to 7,426.8
1,000.0 to 4,999.9
200.0 to 999.9
88.4 to 199.9
30.0 to 88.3
10.0 to 29.9
Less than 10.0

U.S. density is 88.4

County Boundary

Arkansas Mean Center of Population

## Population Density by Census Tract

Arkansas Population 1970 to 2010

2010 — 2,915,918
2000 — 2,673,400
1990 — 2,350,725
1980 — 2,286,435
1970 — 1,923,295

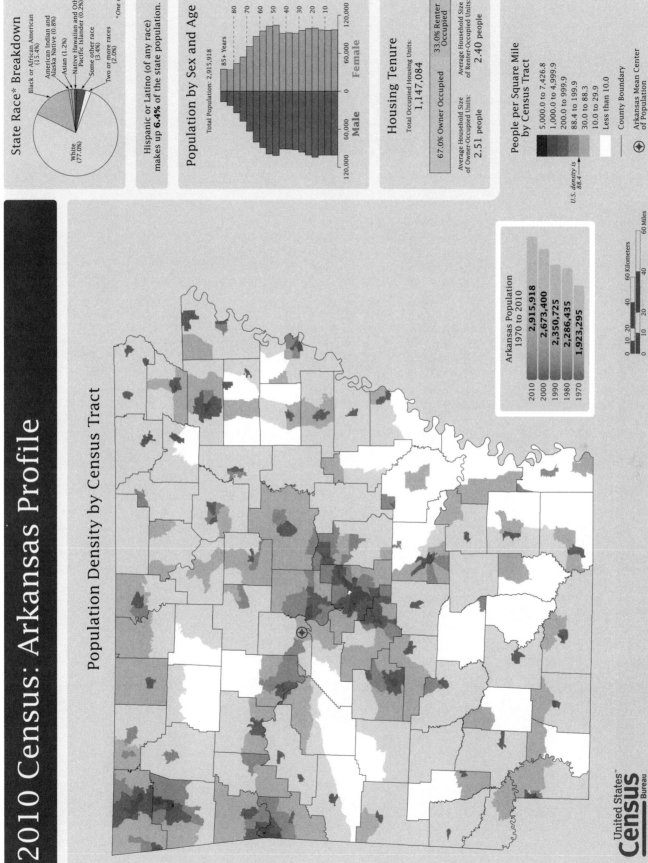

0 10 20 40 60 Kilometers
0 10 20 40 60 Miles

United States™ Census Bureau

U.S. Department of Commerce  Economics and Statistics Administration  U.S. CENSUS BUREAU

275

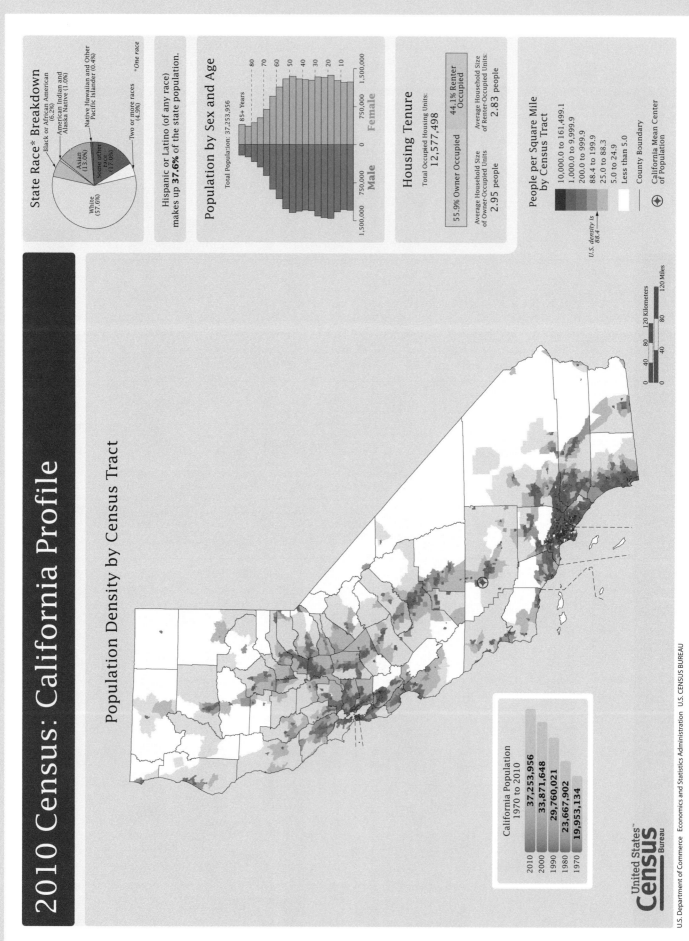

# 2010 Census: California Profile

## Population Density by Census Tract

### State Race* Breakdown

Black or African American (6.2%)
American Indian and Alaska Native (1.0%)
Native Hawaiian and Other Pacific Islander (0.4%)
Two or more races (4.9%)
*One race

White (57.6%)
Asian (13.0%)
Some other race (17.0%)

### Hispanic or Latino (of any race) makes up **37.6%** of the state population.

### Population by Sex and Age

Total Population: 37,253,956

85+ Years
80
70
60
50
40
30
20
10

1,500,000    750,000    0    750,000    1,500,000

Male    Female

### Housing Tenure

Total Occupied Housing Units:
12,577,498

55.9% Owner Occupied     44.1% Renter Occupied

Average Household Size of Owner-Occupied Units
2.95 people

Average Household Size of Renter-Occupied Units:
2.83 people

### People per Square Mile by Census Tract

10,000.0 to 161,499.1
1,000.0 to 9,999.9
200.0 to 999.9
88.4 to 199.9
25.0 to 88.3
5.0 to 24.9
Less than 5.0

U.S. density is 88.4

—— County Boundary

⊕ California Mean Center of Population

0   40   80   120 Kilometers
0   40   80   120 Miles

### California Population 1970 to 2010

2010    37,253,956
2000    33,871,648
1990    29,760,021
1980    23,667,902
1970    19,953,134

United States™ Census Bureau

U.S. Department of Commerce  Economics and Statistics Administration  U.S. CENSUS BUREAU

# 2010 Census: Colorado Profile

## Population Density by Census Tract

### State Race* Breakdown

Black or African American (4.0%)
American Indian and Alaska Native (1.1%)
Asian (2.8%)
Native Hawaiian and Other Pacific Islander (0.1%)
Some other race (7.2%)
Two or more races (3.4%)

White (81.3%)

*One race

### Hispanic or Latino (of any race) makes up **20.7%** of the state population.

### Population by Sex and Age

Total Population: 5,029,196

85+ Years
80
70
60
50
40
30
20
10

Male    Female

200,000    100,000    0    100,000    200,000

### Housing Tenure

Total Occupied Housing Units:
**1,972,868**

65.5% Owner Occupied    34.5% Renter Occupied

Average Household Size of Owner-Occupied Units: 2.57 people

Average Household Size of Renter-Occupied Units: 2.34 people

### People per Square Mile by Census Tract

7,000.0 to 31,336.2
500.0 to 6,999.9
88.4 to 499.9
30.0 to 88.3
5.0 to 29.9
1.0 to 4.9
Less than 1.0

U.S. density is 88.4

County Boundary

Colorado Mean Center of Population

0    20    40    60 Kilometers
0    20    40    60 Miles

Colorado Population 1970 to 2010

2010    5,029,196
2000    4,301,261
1990    3,294,394
1980    2,889,964
1970    2,207,259

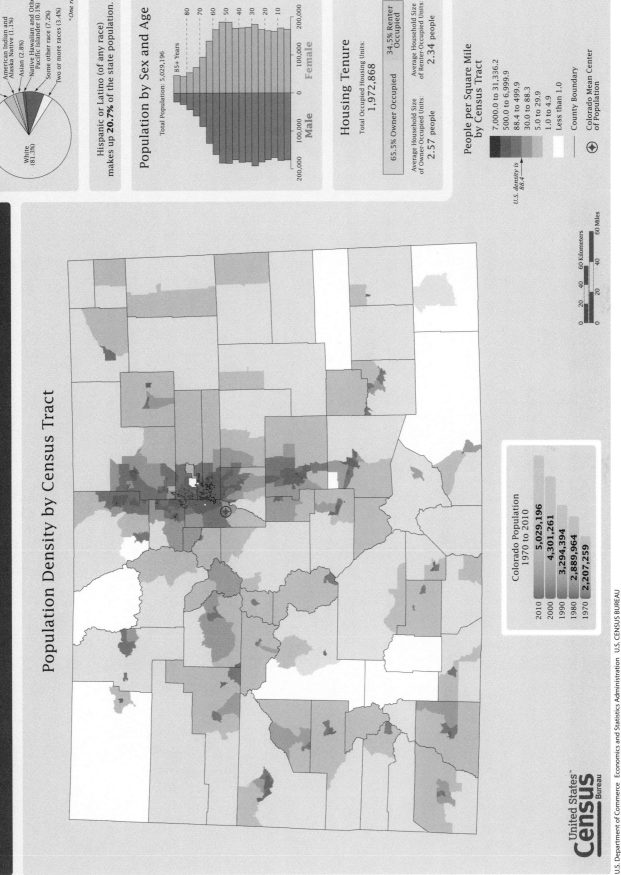

United States **census** Bureau

U.S. Department of Commerce   Economics and Statistics Administration   U.S. CENSUS BUREAU

# 2010 Census: Connecticut Profile

## Population Density by Census Tract

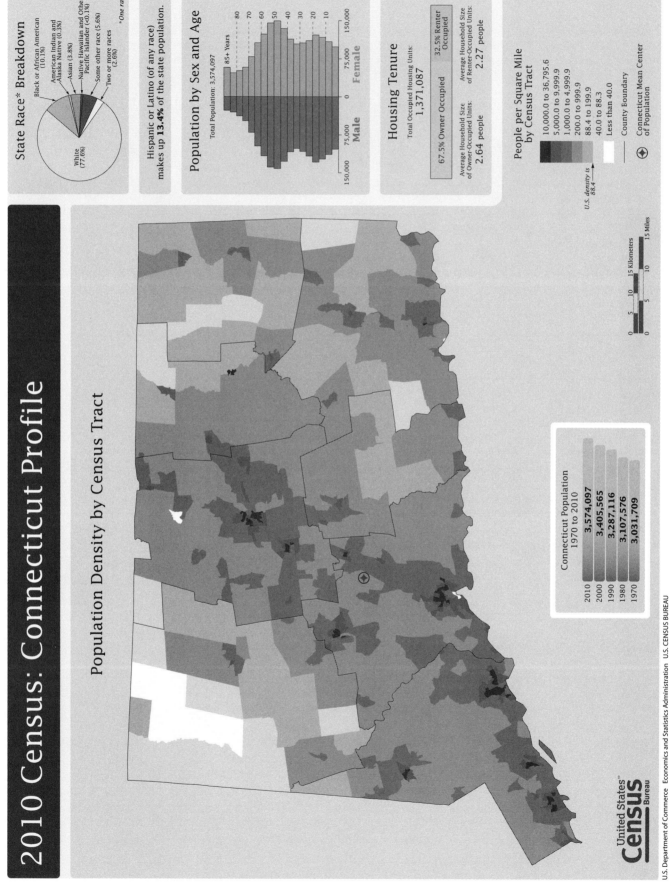

### State Race* Breakdown

- White (77.6%)
- Black or African American (10.1%)
- American Indian and Alaska Native (0.3%)
- Asian (3.8%)
- Native Hawaiian and Other Pacific Islander (<0.1%)
- Some other race (5.6%)
- Two or more races (2.6%)

*One race

### Hispanic or Latino (of any race) makes up **13.4%** of the state population.

### Population by Sex and Age

Total Population: 3,574,097

85+ Years
80
70
60
50
40
30
20
10

Male — Female

150,000   75,000   0   75,000   150,000

### Housing Tenure

Total Occupied Housing Units: 1,371,087

67.5% Owner Occupied    32.5% Renter Occupied

Average Household Size of Owner-Occupied Units: 2.64 people

Average Household Size of Renter-Occupied Units: 2.27 people

### People per Square Mile by Census Tract

- 10,000.0 to 36,795.6
- 5,000.0 to 9,999.9
- 1,000.0 to 4,999.9
- 200.0 to 999.9
- 88.4 to 199.9
- 40.0 to 88.3
- Less than 40.0

U.S. density is 88.4

— County Boundary

⊕ Connecticut Mean Center of Population

### Connecticut Population 1970 to 2010

| Year | Population |
|------|-----------|
| 2010 | 3,574,097 |
| 2000 | 3,405,565 |
| 1990 | 3,287,116 |
| 1980 | 3,107,576 |
| 1970 | 3,031,709 |

0   5   10   15 Miles

0   5   10   15 Kilometers

0   15 Miles

United States™
**census**
Bureau

U.S. Department of Commerce  Economics and Statistics Administration  U.S. CENSUS BUREAU

# 2010 Census: Delaware Profile

## Population Density by Census Tract

### State Race* Breakdown

White (68.9%)

Black or African American (21.4%)

American Indian and Alaska Native (0.5%)
Asian (3.2%)
Native Hawaiian and Other Pacific Islander (<0.1%)
Some other race (3.4%)
Two or more races (2.7%)

*One race

Hispanic or Latino (of any race) makes up **8.2%** of the state population.

### Population by Sex and Age

Total Population: 897,934

85+ Years
80
70
60
50
40
30
20
10

Male          Female

35,000   17,500   0   17,500   35,000

### Housing Tenure

Total Occupied Housing Units:
342,297

72.1% Owner Occupied     27.9% Renter Occupied

Average Household Size of Owner-Occupied Units:
2.58 people

Average Household Size of Renter-Occupied Units:
2.48 people

### People per Square Mile by Census Tract

10,000.0 to 32,786.7
5,000.0 to 9,999.9
1,000.0 to 4,999.9
200.0 to 999.9
88.4 to 199.9
40.0 to 88.3
Less than 40

*U.S. density is 88.4*

County Boundary
Delaware Mean Center of Population

Delaware Population 1970 to 2010

| Year | Population |
|------|-----------|
| 2010 | 897,934 |
| 2000 | 783,600 |
| 1990 | 666,168 |
| 1980 | 594,338 |
| 1970 | 548,104 |

0   5   10   15   20 Kilometers
0   5   10   15   20 Miles

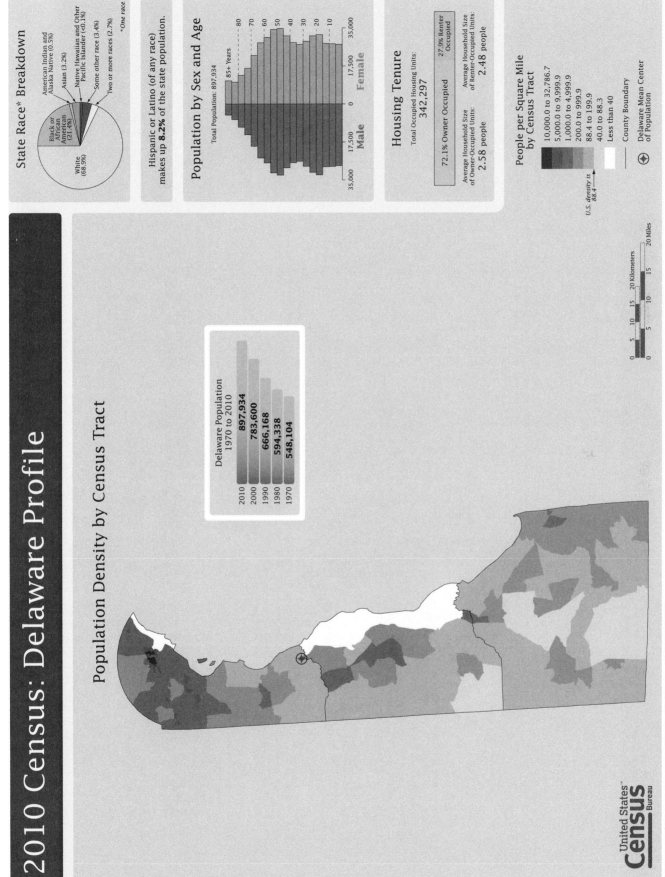

United States Census Bureau

U.S. Department of Commerce  Economics and Statistics Administration  U.S. CENSUS BUREAU

279

# 2010 Census: District of Columbia Profile

## State Race* Breakdown

American Indian and
Alaska Native (0.3%)
Asian (3.5%)
Native Hawaiian and Other
Pacific Islander (0.1%)
Some other race (4.1%)
Two or more races (2.9%)
*One race

Black or
African American
(50.7%)

White
(38.5%)

Hispanic or Latino (of any race)
makes up **9.1%** of the state population.

## Population by Sex and Age

Total Population: 601,723

85+ Years
80
70
60
50
40
30
20
10

40,000    20,000    0    20,000    40,000
Male                        Female

## Housing Tenure

Total Occupied Housing Units:
266,707

42.0% Owner
Occupied

58.0% Renter
Occupied

Average Household Size
of Owner-Occupied Units:
2.20 people

Average Household Size
of Renter-Occupied Units:
2.04 people

## People per Square Mile
by Census Tract

25,000.0 to 66,782.8
15,000.0 to 24,999.9
10,000.0 to 14,999.9
5,000.0 to 9,999.9
1,000.0 to 4,999.9
88.4 to 999.9
Less than 88.4

U.S. density is
88.4

District of Columbia Boundary

District of Columbia Mean
Center of Population

## Population Density by Census Tract

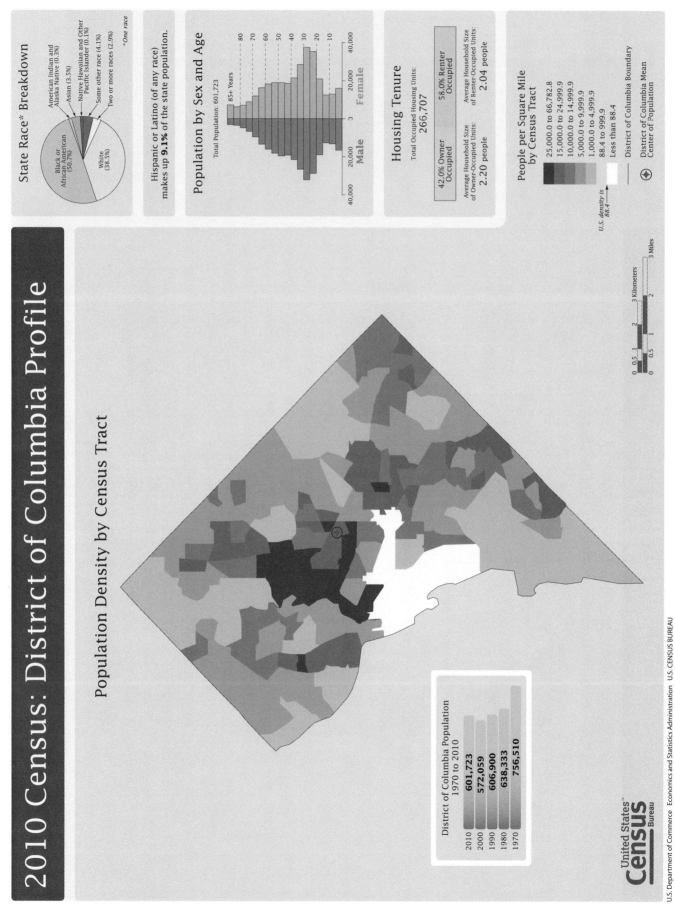

0   0.5   1        2        3 Miles
0   0.5   1   2   3 Kilometers

District of Columbia Population
1970 to 2010

2010  601,723
2000  572,059
1990  606,900
1980  638,333
1970  756,510

United States™
**Census**
Bureau

U.S. Department of Commerce   Economics and Statistics Administration   U.S. CENSUS BUREAU

# 2010 Census: Florida Profile

## Population Density by Census Tract

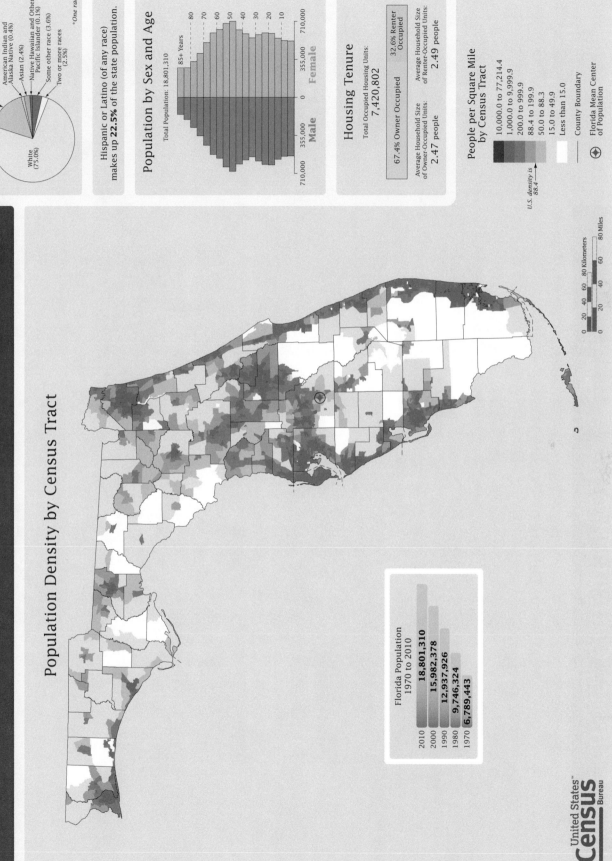

### State Race* Breakdown

- Black or African American (16.0%)
- American Indian and Alaska Native (0.4%)
- Asian (2.4%)
- Native Hawaiian and Other Pacific Islander (0.1%)
- Some other race (3.6%)
- Two or more races (2.5%)
- White (75.0%)

*One race

Hispanic or Latino (of any race) makes up **22.5%** of the state population.

### Population by Sex and Age

Total Population: 18,801,310

85+ Years
80
70
60
50
40
30
20
10

710,000   355,000   0   355,000   710,000

Male        Female

### Housing Tenure

Total Occupied Housing Units: 7,420,802

67.4% Owner Occupied

32.6% Renter Occupied

Average Household Size of Owner-Occupied Units: 2.47 people

Average Household Size of Renter-Occupied Units: 2.49 people

### People per Square Mile by Census Tract

- 10,000.0 to 77,214.4
- 1,000.0 to 9,999.9
- 200.0 to 999.9
- 88.4 to 199.9
- 50.0 to 88.3
- 15.0 to 49.9
- Less than 15.0

U.S. density is 88.4

County Boundary

Florida Mean Center of Population

### Florida Population 1970 to 2010

- 2010: 18,801,310
- 2000: 15,982,378
- 1990: 12,937,926
- 1980: 9,746,324
- 1970: 6,789,443

0   20   40   60   80 Kilometers
0   20   40   60   80 Miles

United States™ Census Bureau

U.S. Department of Commerce  Economics and Statistics Administration  U.S. CENSUS BUREAU

281

# 2010 Census: Georgia Profile

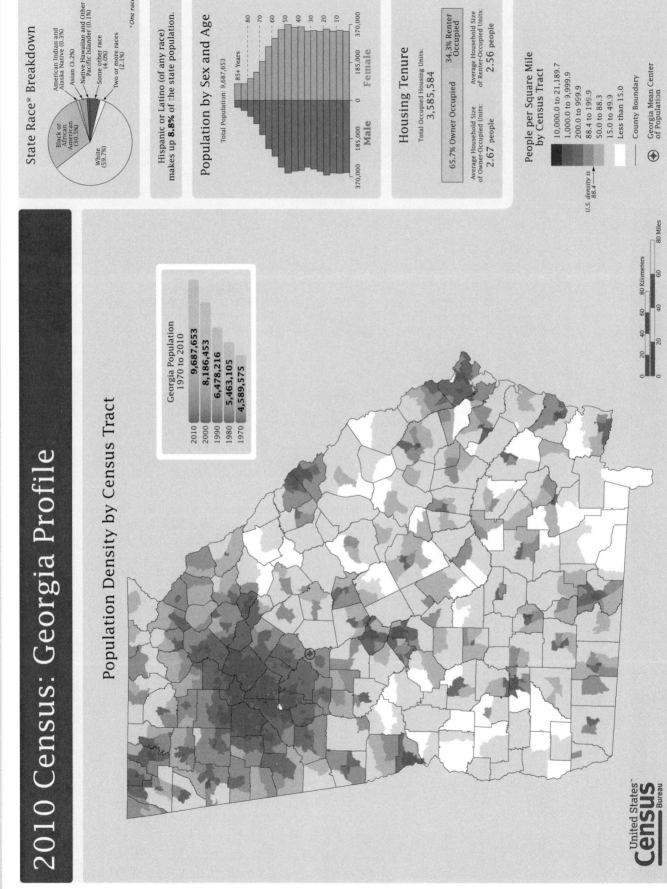

## State Race* Breakdown

- White (59.7%)
- Black or African American (30.5%)
- American Indian and Alaska Native (0.3%)
- Asian (3.2%)
- Native Hawaiian and Other Pacific Islander (0.1%)
- Some other race (4.0%)
- Two or more races (2.1%)

*One race

Hispanic or Latino (of any race) makes up **8.8%** of the state population.

## Population by Sex and Age

Total Population: 9,687,653

85+ Years
80
70
60
50
40
30
20
10

370,000   185,000   0   185,000   370,000
Male          Female

## Housing Tenure

Total Occupied Housing Units: 3,585,584

65.7% Owner Occupied     34.3% Renter Occupied

Average Household Size of Owner-Occupied Units: 2.67 people

Average Household Size of Renter-Occupied Units: 2.56 people

## People per Square Mile by Census Tract

- 10,000.0 to 21,189.7
- 1,000.0 to 9,999.9
- 200.0 to 999.9
- 88.4 to 195.9
- 50.0 to 88.3
- 15.0 to 49.9
- Less than 15.0

U.S. density is 88.4

— County Boundary

⊕ Georgia Mean Center of Population

## Population Density by Census Tract

### Georgia Population 1970 to 2010

| Year | Population |
|------|-----------|
| 2010 | 9,687,653 |
| 2000 | 8,186,453 |
| 1990 | 6,478,216 |
| 1980 | 5,463,105 |
| 1970 | 4,589,575 |

0   20   40   60   80 Miles
0   20   40   60   80 Kilometers

United States Census Bureau

U.S. Department of Commerce  Economics and Statistics Administration  U.S. CENSUS BUREAU

# 2010 Census: Hawaii Profile

## Population Density by Census Tract

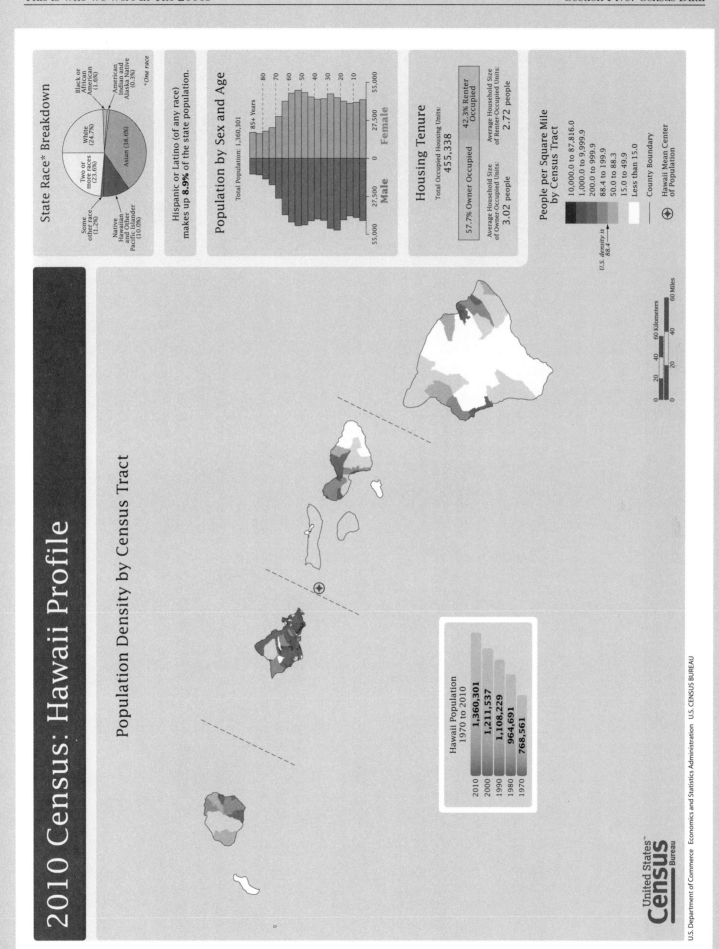

### State Race* Breakdown

White (24.7%)
Asian (38.6%)
Two or more races (23.6%)
Some other race (1.2%)
Native Hawaiian and Other Pacific Islander (10.0%)
American Indian and Alaska Native (0.3%)
Black or African American (1.6%)

*One race

Hispanic or Latino (of any race) makes up **8.9%** of the state population.

### Population by Sex and Age

Total Population: 1,360,301

85+ Years
80
70
60
50
40
30
20
10

Male
Female

55,000
27,500
0
27,500
55,000

### Housing Tenure

Total Occupied Housing Units:
**455,338**

57.7% Owner Occupied
42.3% Renter Occupied

Average Household Size of Owner-Occupied Units:
3.02 people

Average Household Size of Renter-Occupied Units:
2.72 people

### People per Square Mile by Census Tract

10,000.0 to 87,816.0
1,000.0 to 9,999.9
200.0 to 999.9
88.4 to 199.9
50.0 to 88.3
15.0 to 49.9
Less than 15.0

County Boundary
Hawaii Mean Center of Population

U.S. density is 88.4

0   20   40   60 Kilometers
0   20   40   60 Miles

### Hawaii Population
1970 to 2010

2010   1,360,301
2000   1,211,537
1990   1,108,229
1980   964,691
1970   768,561

United States™ Census Bureau

U.S. Department of Commerce   Economics and Statistics Administration   U.S. CENSUS BUREAU

# 2010 Census: Idaho Profile

## State Race* Breakdown

- Black or African American (0.6%)
- American Indian and Alaska Native (1.4%)
- Asian (1.2%)
- Native Hawaiian and Other Pacific Islander (0.1%)
- Some other race (5.1%)
- Two or more races (2.5%)
- White (89.1%)

*One race

Hispanic or Latino (of any race) makes up **11.2%** of the state population.

## Population by Sex and Age

Total Population: 1,567,582

85+ Years
80
70
60
50
40
30
20
10

65,000    32,500    0    32,500    65,000

Male            Female

## Housing Tenure

Total Occupied Housing Units: 579,408

69.9% Owner Occupied

30.1% Renter Occupied

Average Household Size of Owner-Occupied Units: 2.70 people

Average Household Size of Renter-Occupied Units: 2.56 people

## People per Square Mile by Census Tract

- 1,000.0 to 14,941.5
- 250.0 to 999.9
- 88.4 to 249.9
- 30.0 to 88.3
- 5.0 to 29.9
- 1.0 to 4.9
- Less than 1.0

U.S. density is 88.4

— County Boundary

⊕ Idaho Mean Center of Population

## Population Density by Census Tract

Idaho Population 1970 to 2010

| Year | Population |
|------|-----------|
| 2010 | 1,567,582 |
| 2000 | 1,293,953 |
| 1990 | 1,006,749 |
| 1980 | 943,935 |
| 1970 | 712,567 |

0    30    60    90 Kilometers

0    30    60    90 Miles

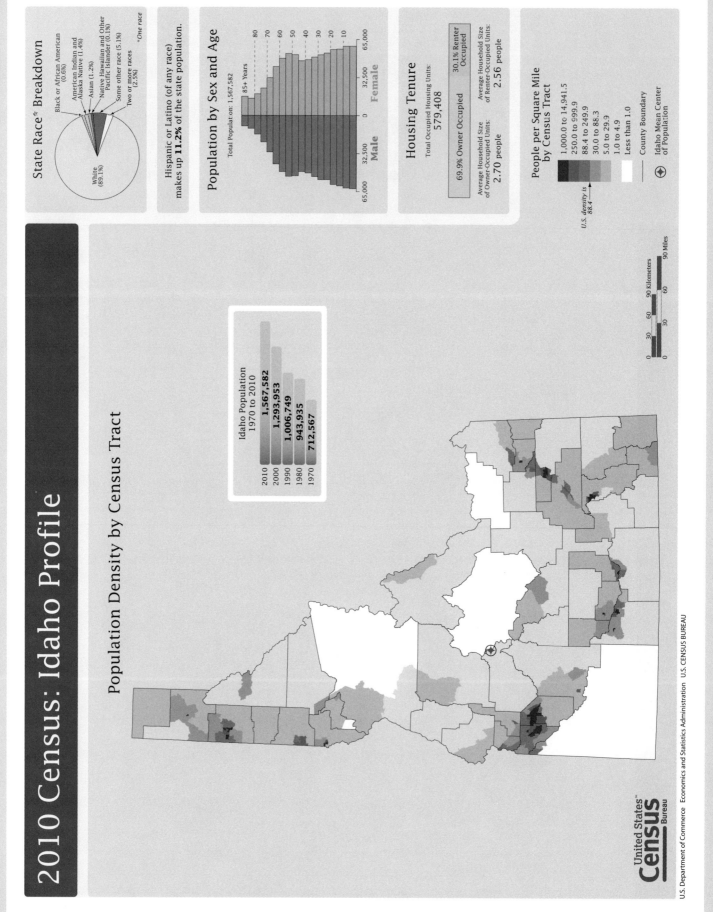

United States™ Census Bureau

U.S. Department of Commerce   Economics and Statistics Administration   U.S. CENSUS BUREAU

# 2010 Census: Illinois Profile

## State Race* Breakdown

Black or African American (14.5%)
American Indian and Alaska Native (0.3%)
Asian (4.6%)
Native Hawaiian and Other Pacific Islander (<0.1%)
Some other race (6.7%)
Two or more races (2.3%)
*One race

White (71.5%)

## Hispanic or Latino (of any race) makes up **15.8%** of the state population.

## Population by Sex and Age

Total Population: 12,830,632

85+ Years
80
70
60
50
40
30
20
10

510,000   255,000   0   255,000   510,000
Male                          Female

## Housing Tenure

Total Occupied Housing Units:
**4,836,972**

67.5% Owner Occupied      32.5% Renter Occupied

Average Household Size of Owner-Occupied Units:
**2.69** people

Average Household Size of Renter-Occupied Units:
**2.38** people

## People per Square Mile by Census Tract

10,000.0 to 508,697.5
1,000.0 to 9,999.9
200.0 to 999.9
88.4 to 199.9
50.0 to 88.3
15.0 to 49.9
Less than 15.0

U.S. density is 88.4

County Boundary
Illinois Mean Center of Population

## Population Density by Census Tract

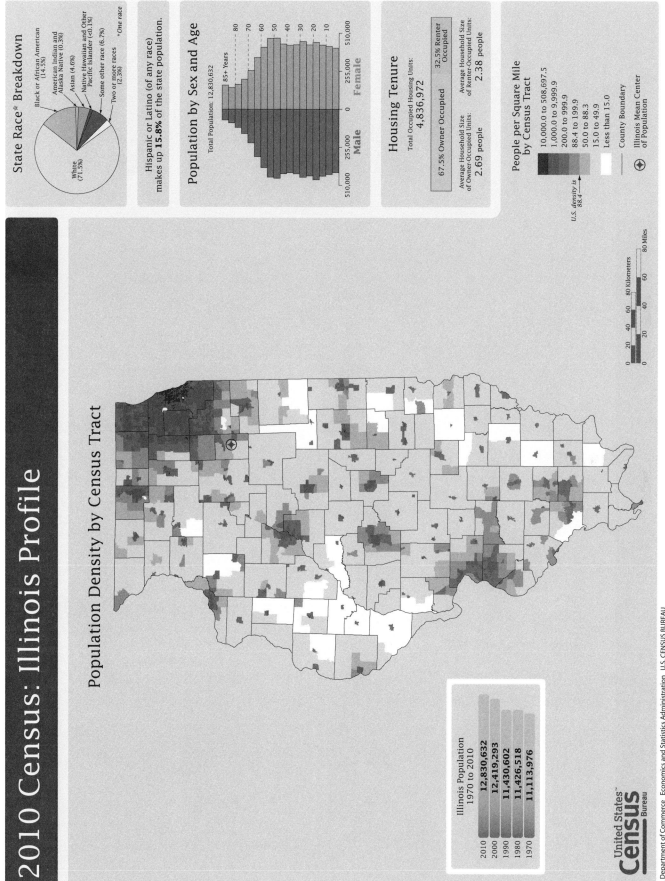

0   20   40   60   80 Miles
0   20   40   60   80 Kilometers

### Illinois Population 1970 to 2010

| Year | Population |
|------|------------|
| 2010 | 12,830,632 |
| 2000 | 12,419,293 |
| 1990 | 11,430,602 |
| 1980 | 11,426,518 |
| 1970 | 11,113,976 |

**United States Census** Bureau

U.S. Department of Commerce   Economics and Statistics Administration   U.S. CENSUS BUREAU

# 2010 Census: Indiana Profile

## Population Density by Census Tract

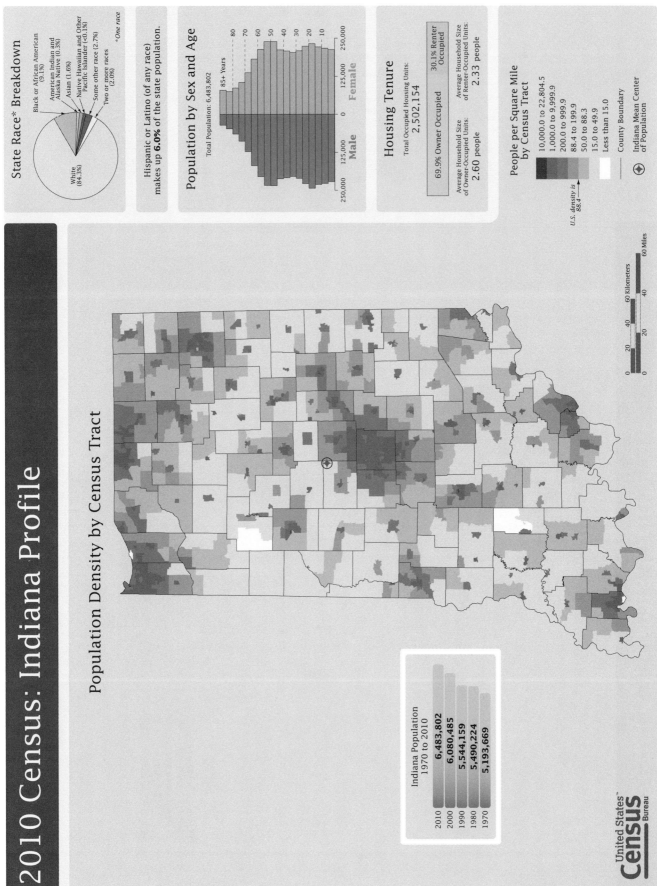

### State Race* Breakdown

White (84.3%)
Black or African American (9.1%)
American Indian and Alaska Native (0.3%)
Asian (1.6%)
Native Hawaiian and Other Pacific Islander (<0.1%)
Some other race (2.7%)
Two or more races (2.0%)

*One race

Hispanic or Latino (of any race) makes up **6.0%** of the state population.

### Population by Sex and Age

Total Population: 6,483,802

85+ Years
80
70
60
50
40
30
20
10

250,000   125,000   0   125,000   250,000

Male          Female

### Housing Tenure

Total Occupied Housing Units:
2,502,154

69.9% Owner Occupied     30.1% Renter Occupied

Average Household Size of Owner-Occupied Units:
2.60 people

Average Household Size of Renter-Occupied Units:
2.33 people

### People per Square Mile by Census Tract

10,000.0 to 22,804.5
1,000.0 to 9,999.9
200.0 to 999.9
88.4 to 199.9
50.0 to 88.3
15.0 to 49.9
Less than 15.0

U.S. density is 88.4

County Boundary

Indiana Mean Center of Population

### Indiana Population 1970 to 2010

| Year | Population |
|---|---|
| 2010 | 6,483,802 |
| 2000 | 6,080,485 |
| 1990 | 5,544,159 |
| 1980 | 5,490,224 |
| 1970 | 5,193,669 |

0   20   40   60 Kilometers
0   20   40   60 Miles

United States™ Census Bureau

U.S. Department of Commerce  Economics and Statistics Administration  U.S. CENSUS BUREAU

# 2010 Census: Iowa Profile

## Population Density by Census Tract

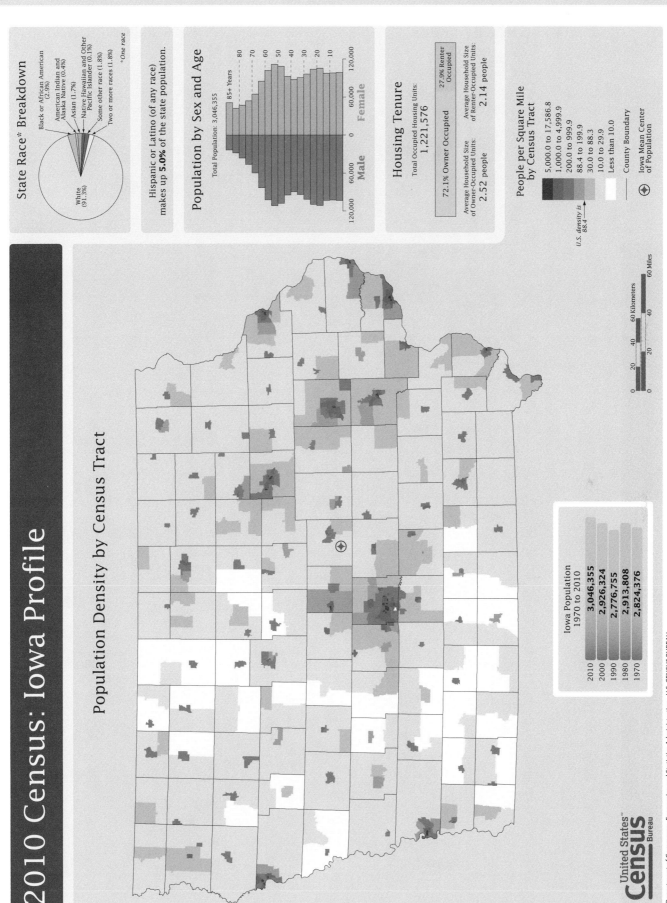

### State Race* Breakdown

White (91.3%)
Black or African American (2.9%)
American Indian and Alaska Native (0.4%)
Asian (1.7%)
Native Hawaiian and Other Pacific Islander (0.1%)
Some other race (1.8%)
Two or more races (1.8%)

*One race

Hispanic or Latino (of any race) makes up **5.0%** of the state population.

### Population by Sex and Age

Total Population: 3,046,355

85+ Years
80
70
60
50
40
30
20
10

120,000   60,000   0   60,000   120,000

Male          Female

### Housing Tenure

Total Occupied Housing Units: 1,221,576

72.1% Owner Occupied          27.9% Renter Occupied

Average Household Size of Owner-Occupied Units: 2.52 people

Average Household Size of Renter-Occupied Units: 2.14 people

### People per Square Mile by Census Tract

5,000.0 to 17,586.8
1,000.0 to 4,999.9
200.0 to 999.9
88.4 to 199.9
30.0 to 88.3
10.0 to 29.9
Less than 10.0
County Boundary
Iowa Mean Center of Population

U.S. density is 88.4

0   20   40   60 Kilometers
0   20   40   60 Miles

### Iowa Population 1970 to 2010

2010   3,046,355
2000   2,926,324
1990   2,776,755
1980   2,913,808
1970   2,824,376

United States™ Census Bureau

U.S. Department of Commerce   Economics and Statistics Administration   U.S. CENSUS BUREAU

# 2010 Census: Kansas Profile

## Population Density by Census Tract

### State Race* Breakdown

Black or African American (5.9%)

American Indian and Alaska Native (1.0%)

Asian (2.4%)

Native Hawaiian and Other Pacific Islander (0.1%)

Some other race (3.9%)

Two or more races (3.0%)

White (83.8%)

*One race

Hispanic or Latino (of any race) makes up **10.5%** of the state population.

### Population by Sex and Age

Total Population: 2,853,118

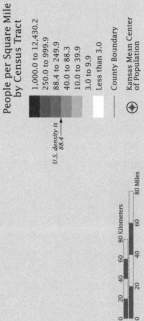

85+ Years
80
70
60
50
40
30
20
10

Male
Female

110,000  55,000  0  55,000  110,000

### Housing Tenure

Total Occupied Housing Units: 1,112,096

67.8% Owner Occupied | 32.2% Renter Occupied

Average Household Size of Owner-Occupied Units: 2.60 people

Average Household Size of Renter-Occupied Units: 2.27 people

### People per Square Mile by Census Tract

1,000.0 to 12,430.2
250.0 to 999.9
88.4 to 249.9
40.0 to 88.3
10.0 to 39.9
3.0 to 9.9
Less than 3.0

U.S. density is 88.4

County Boundary

Kansas Mean Center of Population

0  20  40  60  80 Kilometers
0  20  40  60  80 Miles

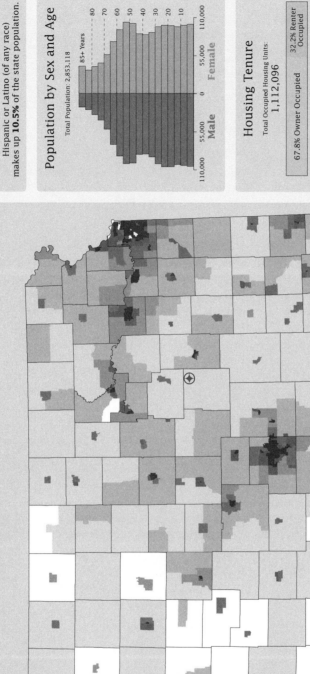

Kansas Population 1970 to 2010

2010  2,853,118
2000  2,688,418
1990  2,477,574
1980  2,363,679
1970  2,246,578

United States Census Bureau

U.S. Department of Commerce  Economics and Statistics Administration  U.S. CENSUS BUREAU

# 2010 Census: Kentucky Profile

## Population Density by Census Tract

### State Race* Breakdown

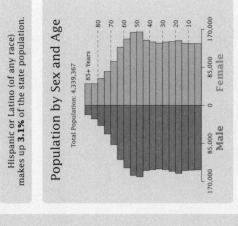

- White (87.8%)
- Black or African American (7.8%)
- American Indian and Alaska Native (0.2%)
- Asian (1.1%)
- Native Hawaiian and Other Pacific Islander (0.1%)
- Some other race (1.3%)
- Two or more races (1.7%)

*One race

Hispanic or Latino (of any race) makes up **3.1%** of the state population.

### Population by Sex and Age

Total Population: 4,339,367

Male | Female

85+ Years

80 · 70 · 60 · 50 · 40 · 30 · 20 · 10

170,000 · 85,000 · 0 · 85,000 · 170,000

### Housing Tenure

Total Occupied Housing Units: 1,719,965

68.7% Owner Occupied

31.3% Renter Occupied

Average Household Size of Owner-Occupied Units: 2.51 people

Average Household Size of Renter-Occupied Units: 2.31 people

### People per Square Mile by Census Tract

- 5,000.0 to 14,217.7
- 1,000.0 to 4,999.9
- 200.0 to 999.9
- 88.4 to 199.9
- 50.0 to 88.3
- 15.0 to 49.9
- Less than 15.0

— County Boundary

⊕ Kentucky Mean Center of Population

U.S. density is 88.4

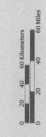

0 · 20 · 40 · 60 Kilometers
0 · 20 · 40 · 60 Miles

**Kentucky Population 1970 to 2010**

- 2010: 4,339,367
- 2000: 4,041,769
- 1990: 3,685,296
- 1980: 3,660,777
- 1970: 3,218,706

United States™ Census Bureau

U.S. Department of Commerce  Economics and Statistics Administration  U.S. CENSUS BUREAU

# 2010 Census: Louisiana Profile

## State Race* Breakdown

- White (62.6%)
- Black or African American (32.0%)
- American Indian and Alaska Native (0.7%)
- Asian (1.5%)
- Native Hawaiian and Other Pacific Islander (<0.1%)
- Some other race (1.5%)
- Two or more races (1.6%)

*One race

Hispanic or Latino (of any race) makes up **4.2%** of the state population.

## Population by Sex and Age

Total Population: 4,533,372

85+ Years
80
70
60
50
40
30
20
10

Male | Female

190,000   95,000   0   95,000   190,000

## Housing Tenure

Total Occupied Housing Units: 1,728,360

67.2% Owner Occupied    32.8% Renter Occupied

Average Household Size of Owner-Occupied Units: 2.61 people

Average Household Size of Renter-Occupied Units: 2.43 people

## People per Square Mile by Census Tract

- 10,000.0 to 38,351.7
- 1,000.0 to 9,999.9
- 200.0 to 999.9
- 88.4 to 199.9
- 50.0 to 88.3
- 15.0 to 49.9
- Less than 15.0

U.S. density is 88.4

— Parish Boundary

⊕ Louisiana Mean Center of Population

## Population Density by Census Tract

Louisiana Population 1970 to 2010

- 2010: 4,533,372
- 2000: 4,468,976
- 1990: 4,219,973
- 1980: 4,205,900
- 1970: 3,641,306

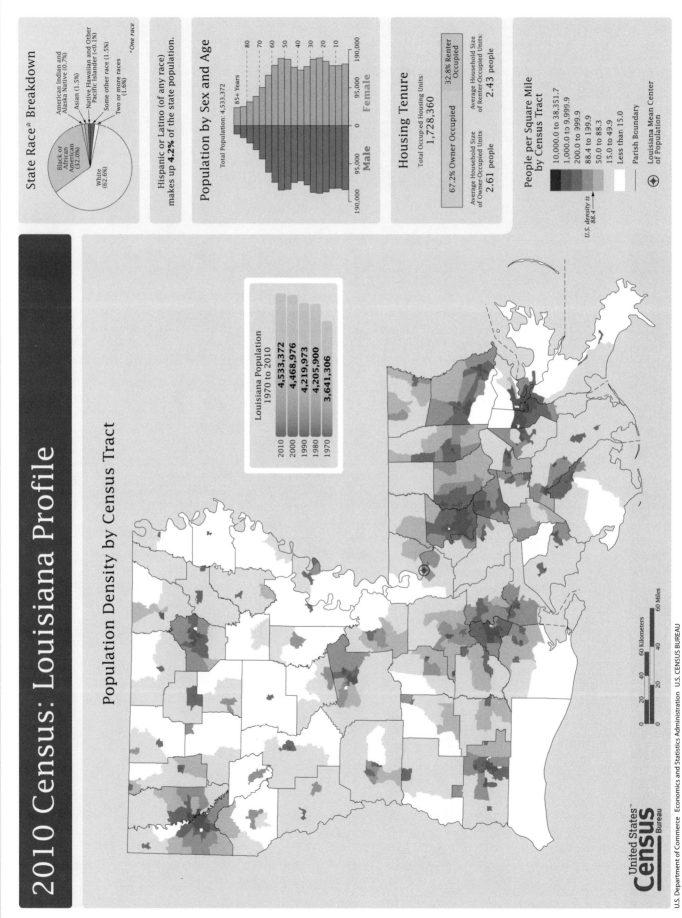

0   20   40   60 Kilometers
0   20   40   60 Miles

United States Census Bureau™

U.S. Department of Commerce  Economics and Statistics Administration  U.S. CENSUS BUREAU

290

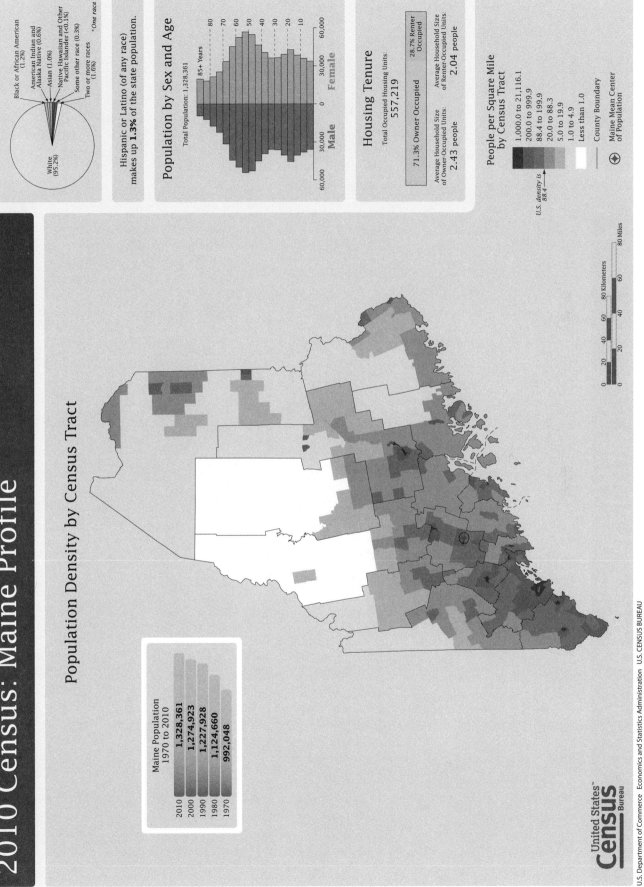

# 2010 Census: Maine Profile

## Population Density by Census Tract

### State Race* Breakdown

Black or African American (1.2%)

American Indian and Alaska Native (0.6%)

Asian (1.0%)

Native Hawaiian and Other Pacific Islander (<0.1%)

Some other race (0.3%)

Two or more races (1.6%)

*One race

White (95.2%)

Hispanic or Latino (of any race) makes up **1.3%** of the state population.

### Population by Sex and Age

Total Population: 1,328,361

85+ Years

80

70

60

50

40

30

20

10

60,000    30,000    0    30,000    60,000

Male    Female

### Housing Tenure

Total Occupied Housing Units: 557,219

71.3% Owner Occupied

28.7% Renter Occupied

Average Household Size of Owner-Occupied Units: 2.43 people

Average Household Size of Renter-Occupied Units: 2.04 people

### People per Square Mile by Census Tract

1,000.0 to 21,116.1

200.0 to 999.9

88.4 to 199.9

20.0 to 88.3

5.0 to 19.9

1.0 to 4.9

Less than 1.0

U.S. density is 88.4

County Boundary

Maine Mean Center of Population

0    20    40    60    80 Kilometers

0    20    40    60    80 Miles

### Maine Population 1970 to 2010

2010    1,328,361
2000    1,274,923
1990    1,227,928
1980    1,124,660
1970    992,048

United States™ Census Bureau

# 2010 Census: Maryland Profile

## Population Density by Census Tract

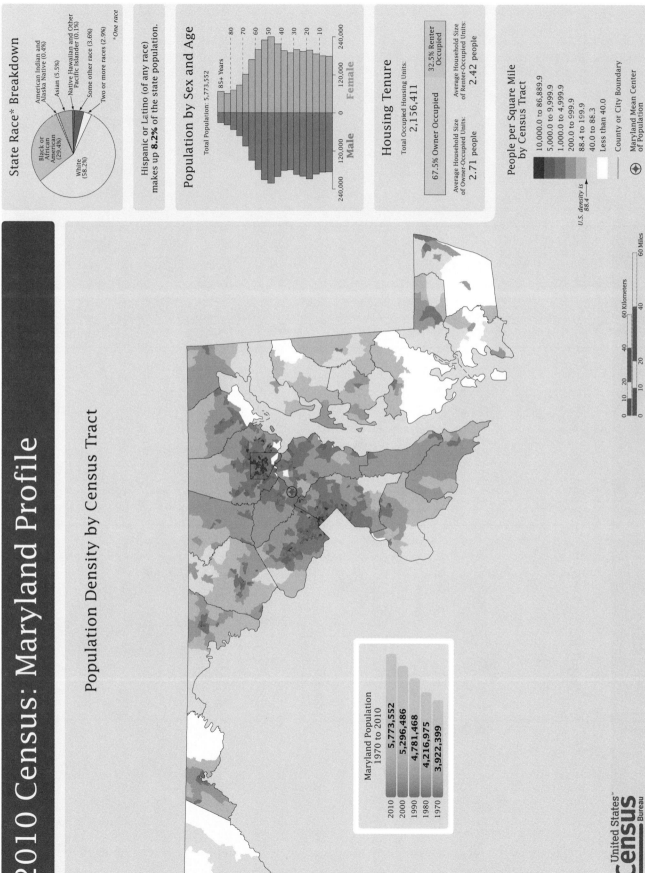

### State Race* Breakdown

- White (58.2%)
- Black or African American (29.4%)
- American Indian and Alaska Native (0.4%)
- Asian (5.5%)
- Native Hawaiian and Other Pacific Islander (0.1%)
- Some other race (3.6%)
- Two or more races (2.9%)

*One race

Hispanic or Latino (of any race) makes up **8.2%** of the state population.

### Population by Sex and Age

Total Population: 5,773,552

Male    Female

85+ Years
80
70
60
50
40
30
20
10

240,000   120,000   0   120,000   240,000

### Housing Tenure

Total Occupied Housing Units:
2,156,411

67.5% Owner Occupied     32.5% Renter Occupied

Average Household Size of Owner-Occupied Units:
2.71 people

Average Household Size of Renter-Occupied Units:
2.42 people

### People per Square Mile by Census Tract

- 10,000.0 to 86,889.9
- 5,000.0 to 9,999.9
- 1,000.0 to 4,999.9
- 200.0 to 999.9
- 88.4 to 199.9
- 40.0 to 88.3
- Less than 40.0

U.S. density is 88.4

— County or City Boundary

⊕ Maryland Mean Center of Population

### Maryland Population 1970 to 2010

| Year | Population |
|------|-----------|
| 2010 | 5,773,552 |
| 2000 | 5,296,486 |
| 1990 | 4,781,468 |
| 1980 | 4,216,975 |
| 1970 | 3,922,399 |

0   10   20   40   60 Kilometers

0   10   20   40   60 Miles

United States™ Census Bureau

U.S. Department of Commerce  Economics and Statistics Administration  U.S. CENSUS BUREAU

# 2010 Census: Massachusetts Profile

## Population Density by Census Tract

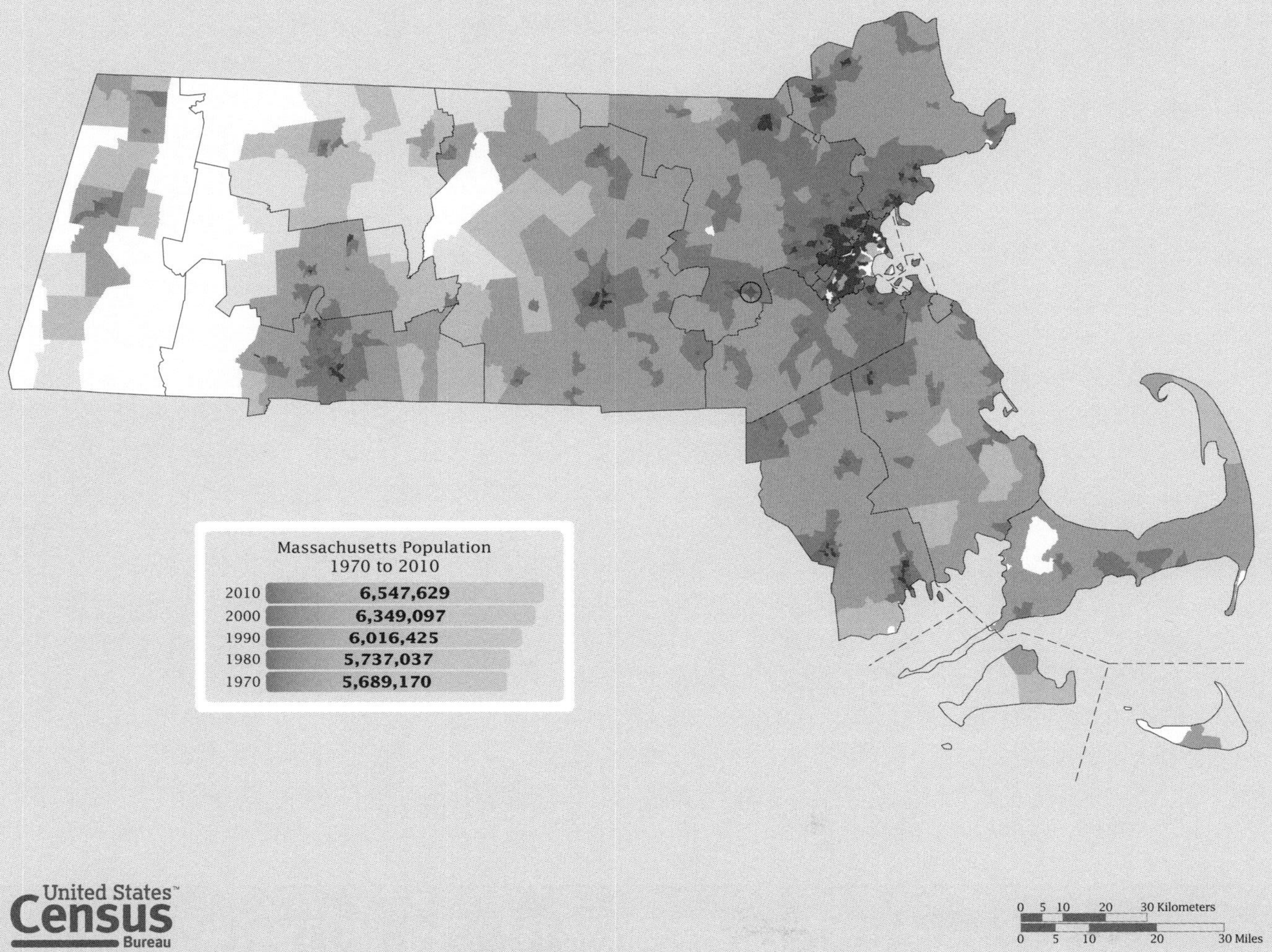

### State Race* Breakdown

White (80.4%)

Black or African American (6.6%)
American Indian and Alaska Native (0.3%)
Asian (5.3%)
Native Hawaiian and Other Pacific Islander (<0.1%)
Some other race (4.7%)
Two or more races (2.6%)

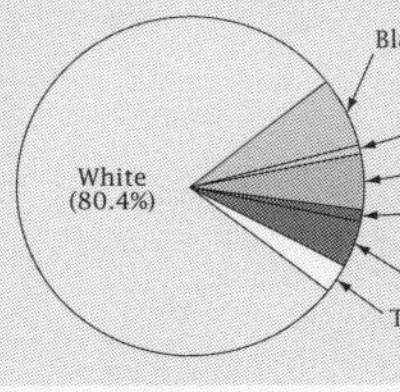

*One race

Hispanic or Latino (of any race) makes up **9.6%** of the state population.

### Population by Sex and Age

Total Population: 6,547,629

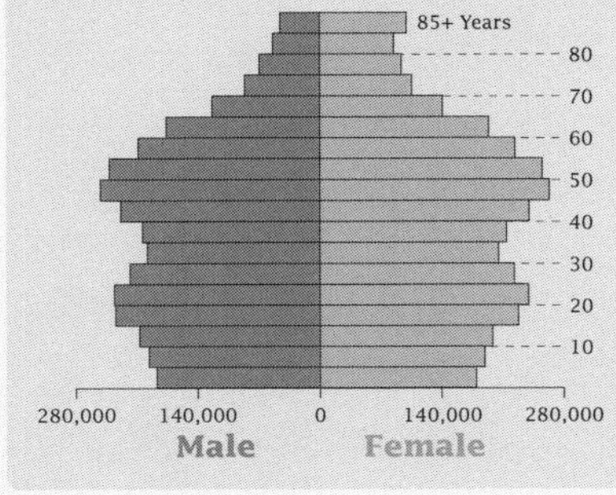

85+ Years
80
70
60
50
40
30
20
10

Male
Female

280,000  140,000  0  140,000  280,000

### Housing Tenure

Total Occupied Housing Units:
2,547,075

62.3% Owner Occupied     37.7% Renter Occupied

Average Household Size of Owner-Occupied Units:
2.66 people

Average Household Size of Renter-Occupied Units:
2.18 people

### People per Square Mile by Census Tract

10,000.0 to 110,107.9
5,000.0 to 9,999.9
1,000.0 to 4,999.9
200.0 to 999.9
88.4 to 199.9
40.0 to 88.3
Less than 40.0

U.S. density is 88.4

County Boundary

Massachusetts Mean Center of Population

Massachusetts Population 1970 to 2010

| Year | Population |
|------|------------|
| 2010 | 6,547,629 |
| 2000 | 6,349,097 |
| 1990 | 6,016,425 |
| 1980 | 5,737,037 |
| 1970 | 5,689,170 |

0  5  10  20  30 Kilometers

0  5  10  20  30 Miles

United States™
Census
Bureau

U.S. Department of Commerce   Economics and Statistics Administration   U.S. CENSUS BUREAU

293

# 2010 Census: Michigan Profile

## Population Density by Census Tract

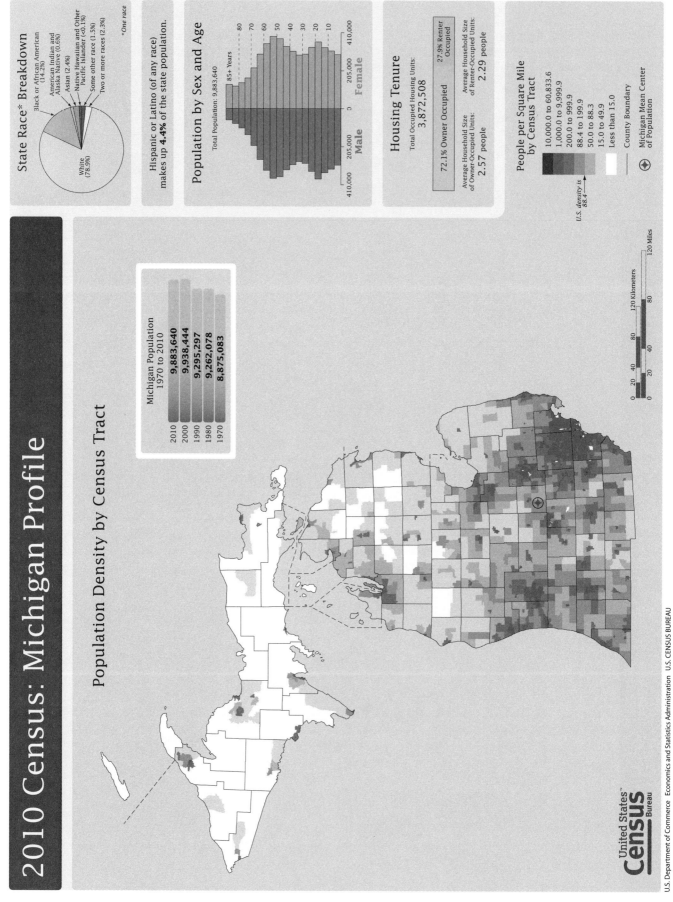

### State Race* Breakdown

White (78.9%)
Black or African American (14.2%)
American Indian and Alaska Native (0.6%)
Asian (2.4%)
Native Hawaiian and Other Pacific Islander (<0.1%)
Some other race (1.5%)
Two or more races (2.3%)

*One race

Hispanic or Latino (of any race) makes up **4.4%** of the state population.

### Population by Sex and Age

Total Population: 9,883,640

85+ Years
80
70
60
50
40
30
20
10

Male          Female

410,000   205,000   0   205,000   410,000

### Housing Tenure

Total Occupied Housing Units:
3,872,508

72.1% Owner Occupied          27.9% Renter Occupied

Average Household Size of Owner-Occupied Units:
2.57 people

Average Household Size of Renter-Occupied Units:
2.29 people

### People per Square Mile by Census Tract

U.S. density is 88.4

10,000.0 to 60,833.6
1,000.0 to 9,999.9
200.0 to 999.9
88.4 to 199.9
50.0 to 88.3
15.0 to 49.9
Less than 15.0

County Boundary

Michigan Mean Center of Population

### Michigan Population 1970 to 2010

| Year | Population |
|------|-----------|
| 2010 | 9,883,640 |
| 2000 | 9,938,444 |
| 1990 | 9,295,297 |
| 1980 | 9,262,078 |
| 1970 | 8,875,083 |

0  20  40  80  120 Kilometers
0  20  40  80  120 Miles

**United States Census Bureau**

U.S. Department of Commerce   Economics and Statistics Administration   U.S. CENSUS BUREAU

# 2010 Census: Minnesota Profile

## State Race* Breakdown

Black or African American (5.2%)
American Indian and Alaska Native (1.1%)
Asian (4.0%)
Native Hawaiian and Other Pacific Islander (<0.1%)
Some other race (1.9%)
Two or more races (2.4%)

White (85.3%)

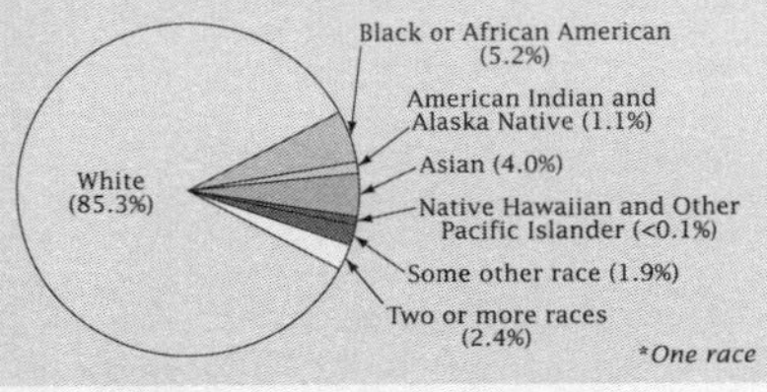

*One race

Hispanic or Latino (of any race) makes up **4.7%** of the state population.

## Population by Sex and Age

Total Population: 5,303,925

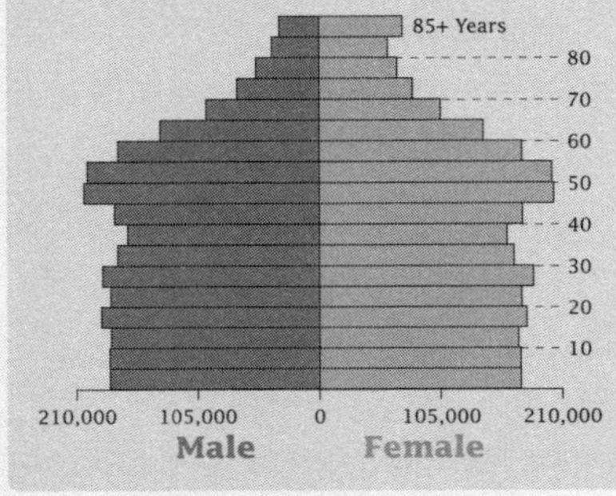

85+ Years
80
70
60
50
40
30
20
10

Male
Female

210,000  105,000  0  105,000  210,000

## Housing Tenure

Total Occupied Housing Units: 2,087,227

73.0% Owner Occupied          27.0% Renter Occupied

Average Household Size of Owner-Occupied Units: 2.59 people

Average Household Size of Renter-Occupied Units: 2.16 people

## Population Density by Census Tract

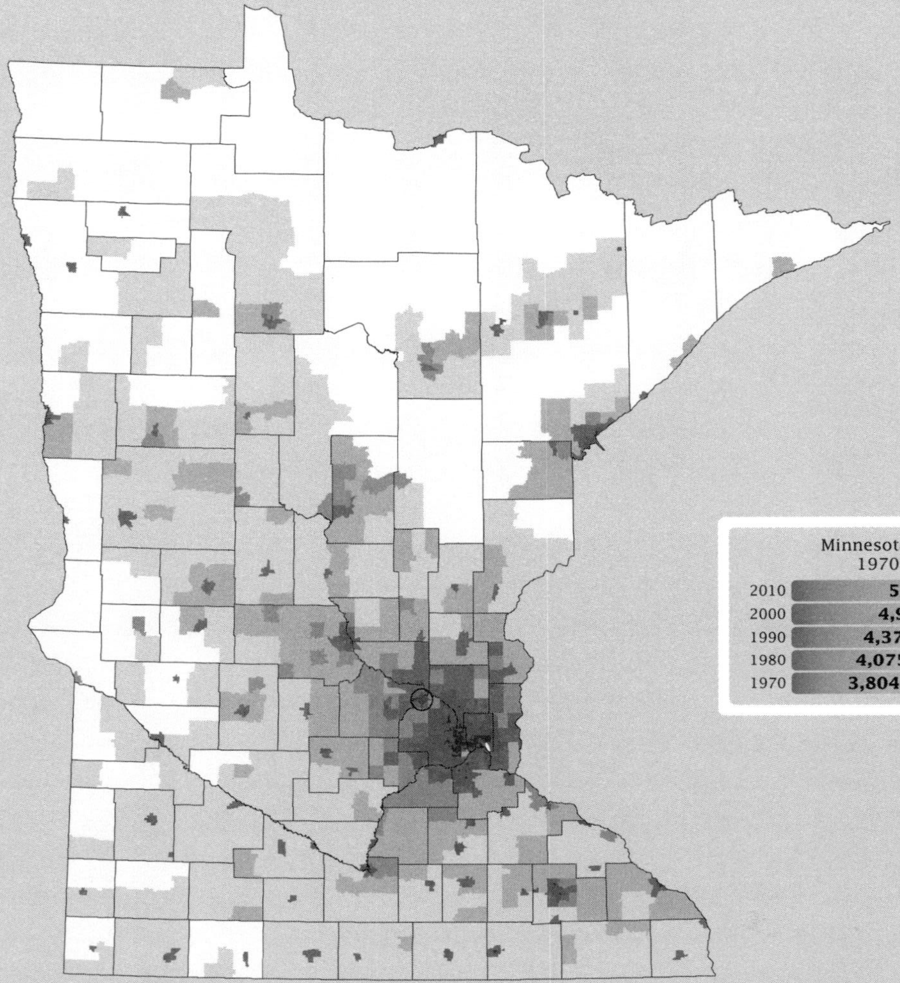

Minnesota Population 1970 to 2010

| Year | Population |
|------|------------|
| 2010 | 5,303,925 |
| 2000 | 4,919,479 |
| 1990 | 4,375,099 |
| 1980 | 4,075,970 |
| 1970 | 3,804,971 |

### People per Square Mile by Census Tract

- 5,000.0 to 25,732.8
- 1,000.0 to 4,999.9
- 200.0 to 999.9
- 88.4 to 199.9
- 30.0 to 88.3
- 10.0 to 29.9
- Less than 10.0

U.S. density is 88.4

County Boundary

Minnesota Mean Center of Population

0  20  40  60  80 Kilometers
0  20  40  60  80 Miles

United States™ Census Bureau

U.S. Department of Commerce   Economics and Statistics Administration   U.S. CENSUS BUREAU

# 2010 Census: Mississippi Profile

## Population Density by Census Tract

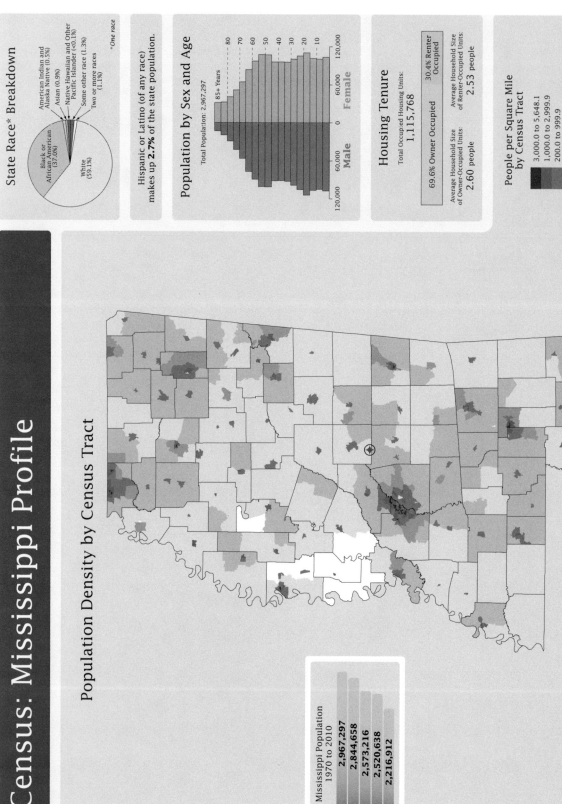

### State Race* Breakdown

White (59.1%)

Black or African American (37.0%)

American Indian and Alaska Native (0.5%)

Asian (0.9%)

Native Hawaiian and Other Pacific Islander (<0.1%)

Some other race (1.3%)

Two or more races (1.1%)

*One race

Hispanic or Latino (of any race) makes up **2.7%** of the state population.

### Population by Sex and Age

Total Population: 2,967,297

85+ Years
80
70
60
50
40
30
20
10

120,000   60,000   0   60,000   120,000

Male                    Female

### Housing Tenure

Total Occupied Housing Units: 1,115,768

69.6% Owner Occupied

30.4% Renter Occupied

Average Household Size of Owner-Occupied Units: 2.60 people

Average Household Size of Renter-Occupied Units: 2.53 people

### People per Square Mile by Census Tract

3,000.0 to 5,648.1
1,000.0 to 2,999.9
200.0 to 999.9
88.4 to 199.9
30.0 to 83.3
10.0 to 29.9
Less than 10.0

U.S. density is 88.4

County Boundary

Mississippi Mean Center of Population

### Mississippi Population 1970 to 2010

2010 — 2,967,297
2000 — 2,844,658
1990 — 2,573,216
1980 — 2,520,638
1970 — 2,216,912

0   20   40   60 Kilometers
0   20   40   60 Miles

United States Census Bureau

U.S. Department of Commerce   Economics and Statistics Administration   U.S. CENSUS BUREAU

# 2010 Census: Missouri Profile

## Population Density by Census Tract

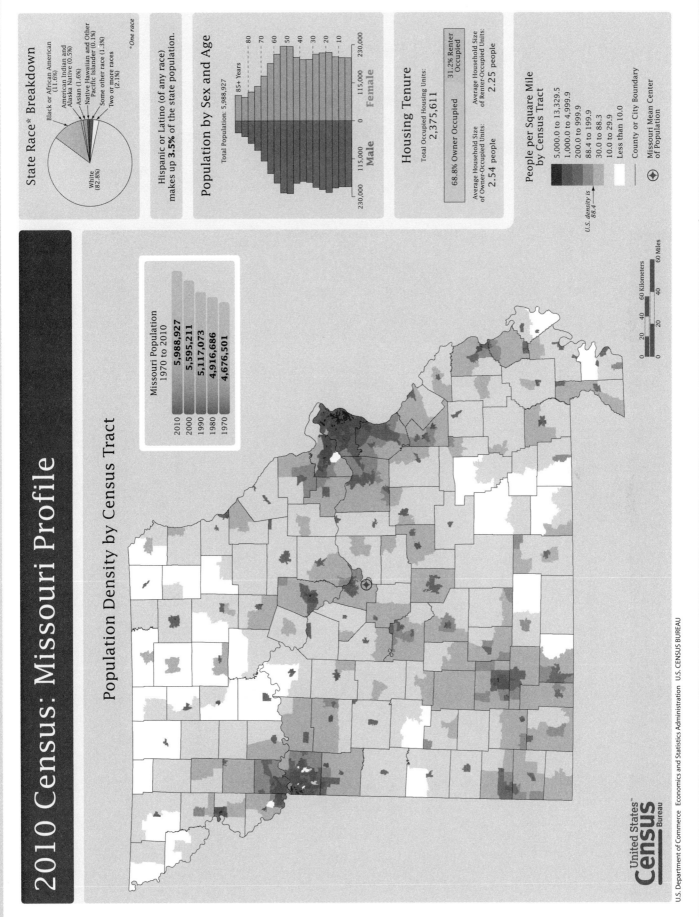

### State Race* Breakdown

White (82.8%)
Black or African American (11.6%)
American Indian and Alaska Native (0.5%)
Asian (1.6%)
Native Hawaiian and Other Pacific Islander (0.1%)
Some other race (1.3%)
Two or more races (2.1%)

*One race

Hispanic or Latino (of any race) makes up **3.5%** of the state population.

### Population by Sex and Age

Total Population: 5,988,927

85+ Years
80
70
60
50
40
30
20
10

230,000    115,000    0    115,000    230,000

**Male**        **Female**

### Housing Tenure

Total Occupied Housing Units:
2,375,611

68.8% Owner Occupied
31.2% Renter Occupied

Average Household Size of Owner-Occupied Units:
2.54 people

Average Household Size of Renter-Occupied Units:
2.25 people

### People per Square Mile by Census Tract

5,000.0 to 13,329.5
1,000.0 to 4,999.9
200.0 to 999.9
88.4 to 199.9
30.0 to 88.3
10.0 to 29.9
Less than 10.0

U.S. density is 88.4

County or City Boundary
Missouri Mean Center of Population

### Missouri Population 1970 to 2010

2010    5,988,927
2000    5,595,211
1990    5,117,073
1980    4,916,686
1970    4,676,501

0    20    40    60 Kilometers
0    20    40    60 Miles

United States Census Bureau

U.S. Department of Commerce   Economics and Statistics Administration   U.S. CENSUS BUREAU

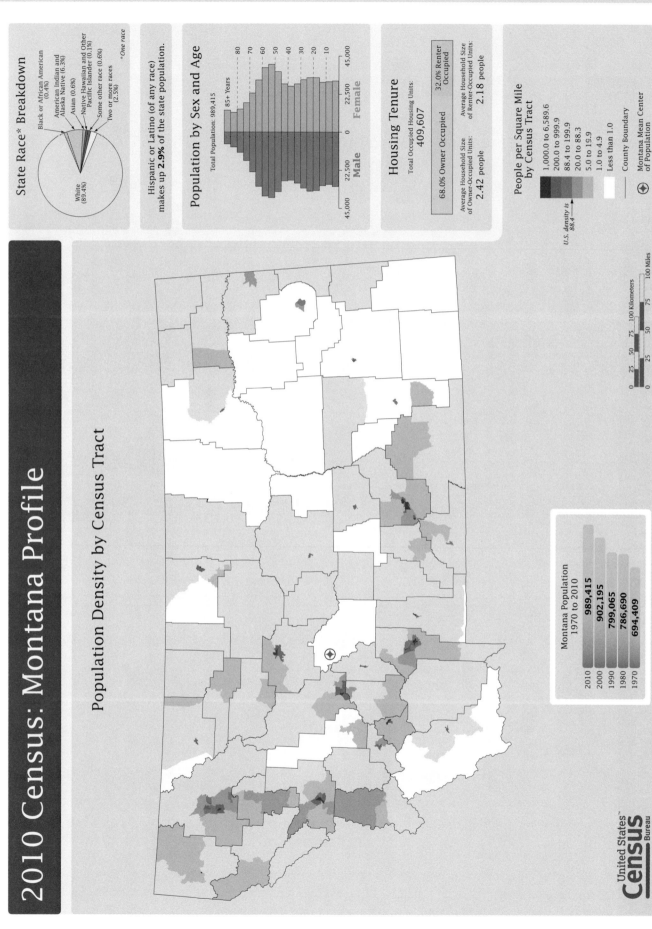

# 2010 Census: Montana Profile

## Population Density by Census Tract

### State Race* Breakdown

Black or African American (0.4%)
American Indian and Alaska Native (6.3%)
Asian (0.6%)
Native Hawaiian and Other Pacific Islander (0.1%)
Some other race (0.6%)
Two or more races (2.5%)
White (89.4%)
*One race

Hispanic or Latino (of any race) makes up **2.9%** of the state population.

### Population by Sex and Age

Total Population: 989,415

85+ Years
80
70
60
50
40
30
20
10

Female
Male

45,000   22,500   0   22,500   45,000

### Housing Tenure

Total Occupied Housing Units: 409,607

68.0% Owner Occupied
32.0% Renter Occupied

Average Household Size of Owner-Occupied Units: 2.42 people
Average Household Size of Renter-Occupied Units: 2.18 people

### People per Square Mile by Census Tract

1,000.0 to 6,589.6
200.0 to 999.9
88.4 to 199.9
20.0 to 88.3
5.0 to 19.9
1.0 to 4.9
Less than 1.0
County Boundary
Montana Mean Center of Population

U.S. density is 88.4

0   25   50   75   100 Kilometers
0   25   50   75   100 Miles

### Montana Population 1970 to 2010

2010    989,415
2000    902,195
1990    799,065
1980    786,690
1970    694,409

United States Census Bureau

U.S. Department of Commerce   Economics and Statistics Administration   U.S. CENSUS BUREAU

# 2010 Census: Nebraska Profile

## Population Density by Census Tract

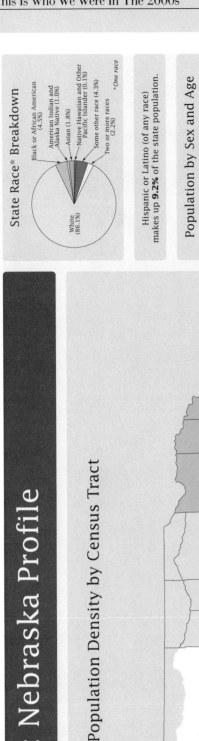

### State Race* Breakdown

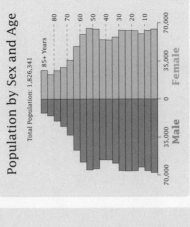

White (86.1%)
Black or African American (4.5%)
American Indian and Alaska Native (1.0%)
Asian (1.8%)
Native Hawaiian and Other Pacific Islander (0.1%)
Some other race (4.3%)
Two or more races (2.2%)

*One race

Hispanic or Latino (of any race) makes up **9.2%** of the state population.

### Population by Sex and Age

Total Population: 1,826,341

85+ Years
80
70
60
50
40
30
20
10

70,000   35,000   0   35,000   70,000

Female          Male

### Housing Tenure

Total Occupied Housing Units:
**721,130**

67.2% Owner Occupied          32.8% Renter Occupied

Average Household Size of Owner-Occupied Units:
**2.58 people**

Average Household Size of Renter-Occupied Units:
**2.21 people**

### People per Square Mile by Census Tract

1,000.0 to 15,573.8
200.0 to 999.9
88.4 to 199.9
20.0 to 88.3
5.0 to 19.9
1.0 to 4.9
Less than 1.0

U.S. density is 88.4

County Boundary
Nebraska Mean Center of Population

### Nebraska Population 1970 to 2010

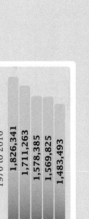

| Year | Population |
|------|------------|
| 2010 | 1,826,341 |
| 2000 | 1,711,263 |
| 1990 | 1,578,385 |
| 1980 | 1,569,825 |
| 1970 | 1,483,493 |

0   20   40   60   80 Miles
0   20   40   60   80 Kilometers

United States Census Bureau

U.S. Department of Commerce  Economics and Statistics Administration  U.S. CENSUS BUREAU

# 2010 Census: Nevada Profile

## Population Density by Census Tract

### State Race* Breakdown

- White (66.2%)
- Black or African American (8.1%)
- American Indian and Alaska Native (1.2%)
- Asian (7.2%)
- Native Hawaiian and Other Pacific Islander (0.6%)
- Some other race (12.0%)
- Two or more races (4.7%)

*One race

Hispanic or Latino (of any race) makes up **26.5%** of the state population.

### Population by Sex and Age

Total Population: 2,700,551

Male | Female

85+ Years
80
70
60
50
40
30
20
10

105,000   52,500   0   52,500   105,000

### Housing Tenure

Total Occupied Housing Units: 1,006,250

58.8% Owner Occupied | 41.2% Renter Occupied

Average Household Size of Owner-Occupied Units: 2.66 people

Average Household Size of Renter-Occupied Units: 2.63 people

### People per Square Mile by Census Tract

U.S. density is 88.4

- 7,000.0 to 24,882.3
- 500.0 to 6,999.9
- 84.4 to 499.9
- 30.0 to 84.3
- 5.0 to 29.9
- 1.0 to 4.9
- Less than 1.0

— County or City Boundary

⊕ Nevada Mean Center of Population

0   30   60   90 Kilometers
0   30   60   90 Miles

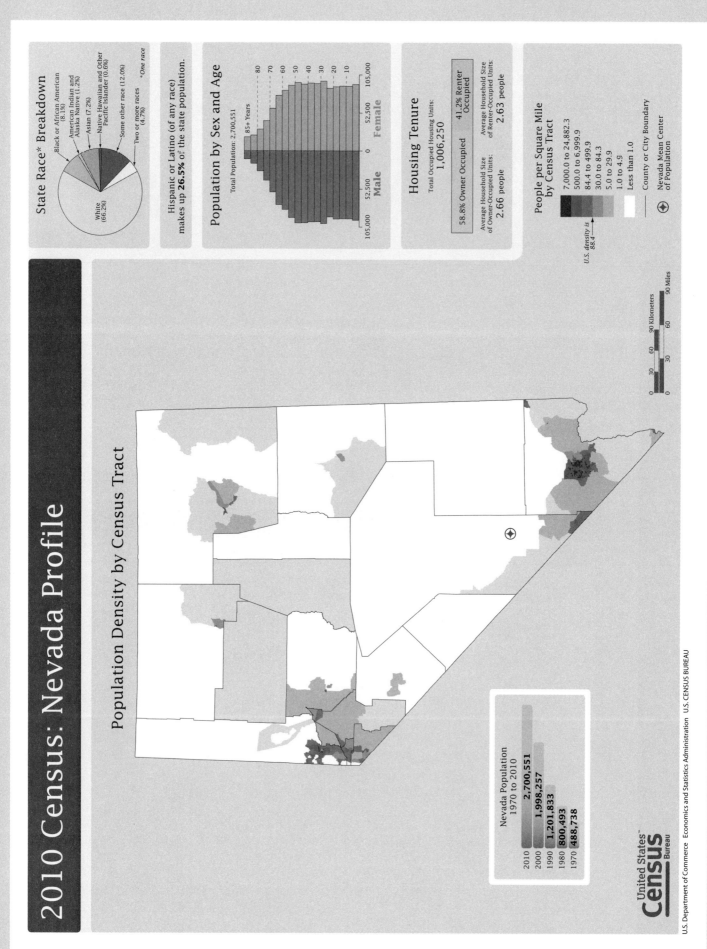

### Nevada Population 1970 to 2010

| Year | Population |
|------|-----------|
| 2010 | 2,700,551 |
| 2000 | 1,998,257 |
| 1990 | 1,201,833 |
| 1980 | 800,493 |
| 1970 | 488,738 |

United States™ Census Bureau

U.S. Department of Commerce   Economics and Statistics Administration   U.S. CENSUS BUREAU

# 2010 Census: New Hampshire Profile

## Population Density by Census Tract

### State Race* Breakdown

Black or African American (1.1%)
American Indian and Alaska Native (0.2%)
Asian (2.2%)
Native Hawaiian and Other Pacific Islander (<0.1%)
Some other race (0.9%)
Two or more races (1.6%)

*One race

White (93.9%)

Hispanic or Latino (of any race) makes up **2.8%** of the state population.

### Population by Sex and Age

Total Population: 1,316,470

85+ Years
80
70
60
50
40
30
20
10

60,000   30,000   0   30,000   60,000
Male                    Female

### Housing Tenure

Total Occupied Housing Units:
518,973

71.0% Owner Occupied          29.0% Renter Occupied

Average Household Size of Owner-Occupied Units:
2.59 people

Average Household Size of Renter-Occupied Units:
2.14 people

### People per Square Mile by Census Tract

5,000.0 to 20,134.9
1,000.0 to 4,999.9
200.0 to 999.9
88.4 to 199.9
50.0 to 88.3
15.0 to 49.9
Less than 15.0

U.S. density is 88.4

County Boundary
New Hampshire Mean Center of Population

0   10   20   30   40 Kilometers
0   10   20   30   40 Miles

### New Hampshire Population 1970 to 2010

| Year | Population |
| --- | --- |
| 2010 | 1,316,470 |
| 2000 | 1,235,786 |
| 1990 | 1,109,252 |
| 1980 | 920,610 |
| 1970 | 737,681 |

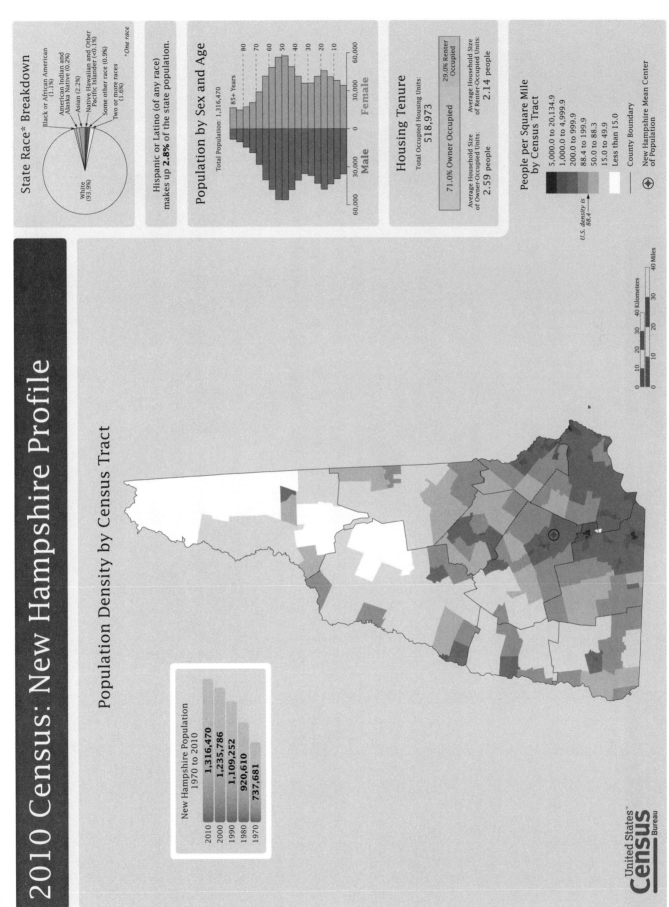

United States Census Bureau

U.S. Department of Commerce   Economics and Statistics Administration   U.S. CENSUS BUREAU

# 2010 Census: New Jersey Profile

## Population Density by Census Tract

### State Race* Breakdown

- Black or African American (13.7%)
- American Indian and Alaska Native (0.3%)
- Asian (8.3%)
- Native Hawaiian and Other Pacific Islander (<0.1%)
- Some other race (6.4%)
- Two or more races (2.7%)
- White (68.6%)

*One race

Hispanic or Latino (of any race) makes up **17.7%** of the state population.

### Population by Sex and Age

Total Population: 8,791,894

85+ Years
80
70
60
50
40
30
20
10

370,000    185,000    0    185,000    370,000

Female          Male

### Housing Tenure

Total Occupied Housing Units: 3,214,360

65.4% Owner Occupied     34.6% Renter Occupied

Average Household Size of Owner-Occupied Units: 2.79 people

Average Household Size of Renter-Occupied Units: 2.47 people

### People per Square Mile by Census Tract

- 10,000.0 to 119,569.9
- 5,000.0 to 9,999.9
- 1,000.0 to 4,999.9
- 200.0 to 999.9
- 88.4 to 199.9
- 40.0 to 88.3
- Less than 40.0

U.S. density is 88.4

— County Boundary

⊕ New Jersey Mean Center of Population

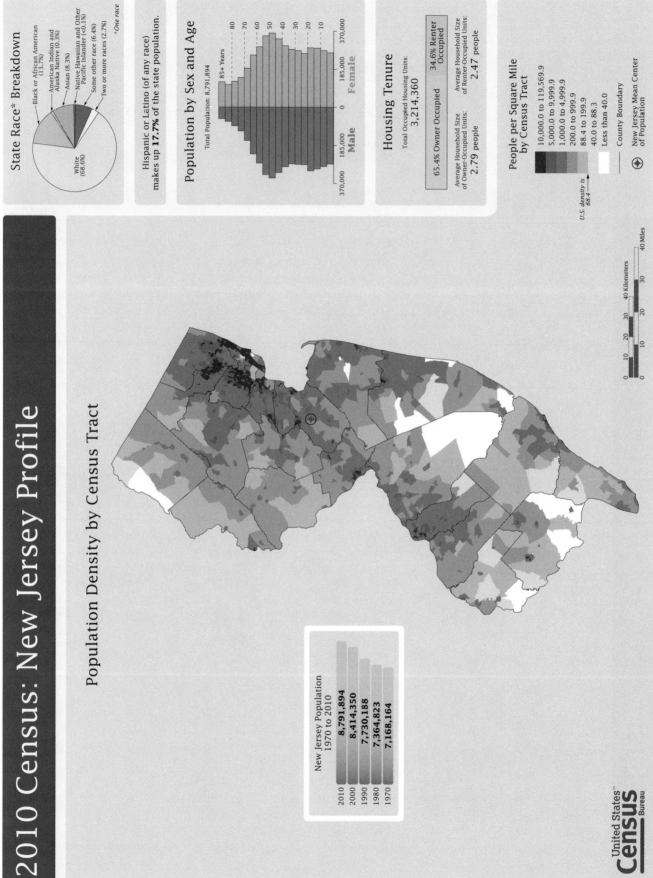

40 Kilometers
0    10    20    30

40 Miles
0    10    20    30    40

New Jersey Population 1970 to 2010

| Year | Population |
|------|-----------|
| 2010 | 8,791,894 |
| 2000 | 8,414,350 |
| 1990 | 7,730,188 |
| 1980 | 7,364,823 |
| 1970 | 7,168,164 |

United States™
**census**
Bureau

U.S. Department of Commerce  Economics and Statistics Administration  U.S. CENSUS BUREAU

# 2010 Census: New Mexico Profile

## State Race* Breakdown

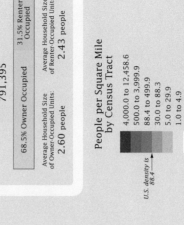

Black or African American (2.1%)
American Indian and Alaska Native (9.4%)
Asian (1.4%)
Native Hawaiian and Other Pacific Islander (0.1%)
Some other race (15.0%)
Two or more races (3.7%)
*One race
White (68.4%)

Hispanic or Latino (of any race) makes up **46.3%** of the state population.

## Population by Sex and Age

Total Population: 2,059,179

85+ Years
80
70
60
50
40
30
20
10

80,000    40,000    0    40,000    80,000
Male                          Female

## Housing Tenure

Total Occupied Housing Units: 791,395

68.5% Owner Occupied | 31.5% Renter Occupied

Average Household Size of Owner-Occupied Units: 2.60 people

Average Household Size of Renter-Occupied Units: 2.43 people

## People per Square Mile by Census Tract

4,000.0 to 12,458.6
500.0 to 3,999.9
88.4 to 499.9
30.0 to 88.3
5.0 to 29.9
1.0 to 4.9
Less than 1.0

U.S. density is 88.4

— County Boundary
⊕ New Mexico Mean Center of Population

## Population Density by Census Tract

New Mexico Population 1970 to 2010

| Year | Population |
|---|---|
| 2010 | 2,059,179 |
| 2000 | 1,819,046 |
| 1990 | 1,515,069 |
| 1980 | 1,302,894 |
| 1970 | 1,016,000 |

0    25    50    75    100 Kilometers
0    25    50    75    100 Miles

United States™ Census Bureau

U.S. Department of Commerce   Economics and Statistics Administration   U.S. CENSUS BUREAU

# 2010 Census: New York Profile

## Population Density by Census Tract

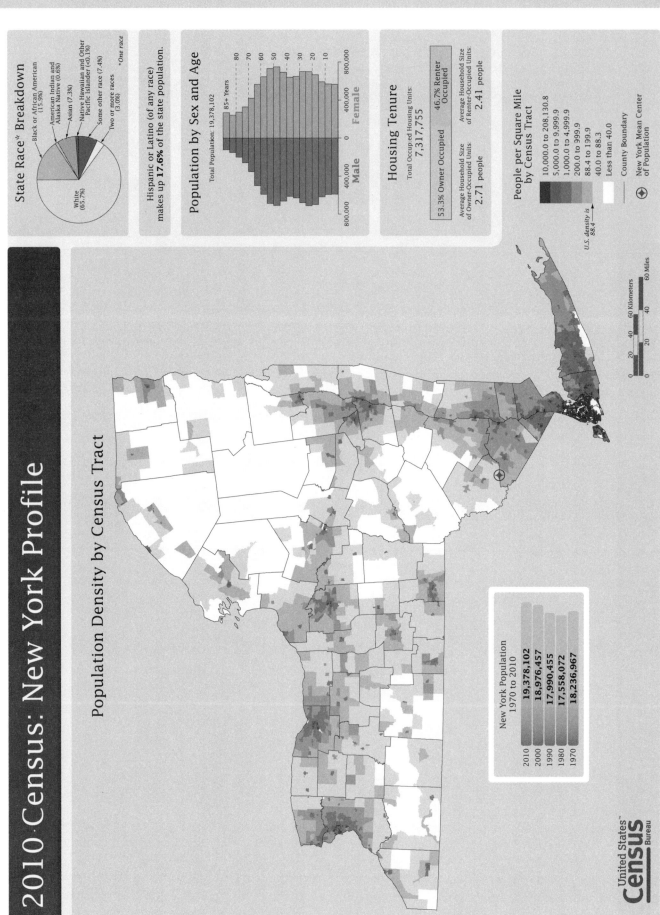

### State Race* Breakdown

Black or African American (15.9%)
American Indian and Alaska Native (0.6%)
Asian (7.3%)
Native Hawaiian and Other Pacific Islander (<0.1%)
Some other race (7.4%)
Two or more races (3.0%)

*One race

White (65.7%)

Hispanic or Latino (of any race) makes up **17.6%** of the state population.

### Population by Sex and Age

Total Population: 19,378,102

85+ Years
80
70
60
50
40
30
20
10

800,000   400,000   0   400,000   800,000
Male        Female

### Housing Tenure

Total Occupied Housing Units:
7,317,755

53.3% Owner Occupied
46.7% Renter Occupied

Average Household Size of Owner-Occupied Units:
2.71 people

Average Household Size of Renter-Occupied Units:
2.41 people

### People per Square Mile by Census Tract

10,000.0 to 208,130.8
5,000.0 to 9,999.9
1,000.0 to 4,999.9
200.0 to 999.9
88.4 to 199.9
40.0 to 88.3
Less than 40.0

U.S. density is 88.4

County Boundary

New York Mean Center of Population

New York Population 1970 to 2010

| Year | Population |
|------|-----------|
| 2010 | 19,378,102 |
| 2000 | 18,976,457 |
| 1990 | 17,990,455 |
| 1980 | 17,558,072 |
| 1970 | 18,236,967 |

0   20   40   60 Miles
0   20   40   60 Kilometers

United States Census Bureau

U.S. Department of Commerce   Economics and Statistics Administration   U.S. CENSUS BUREAU

# 2010 Census: North Carolina Profile

## Population Density by Census Tract

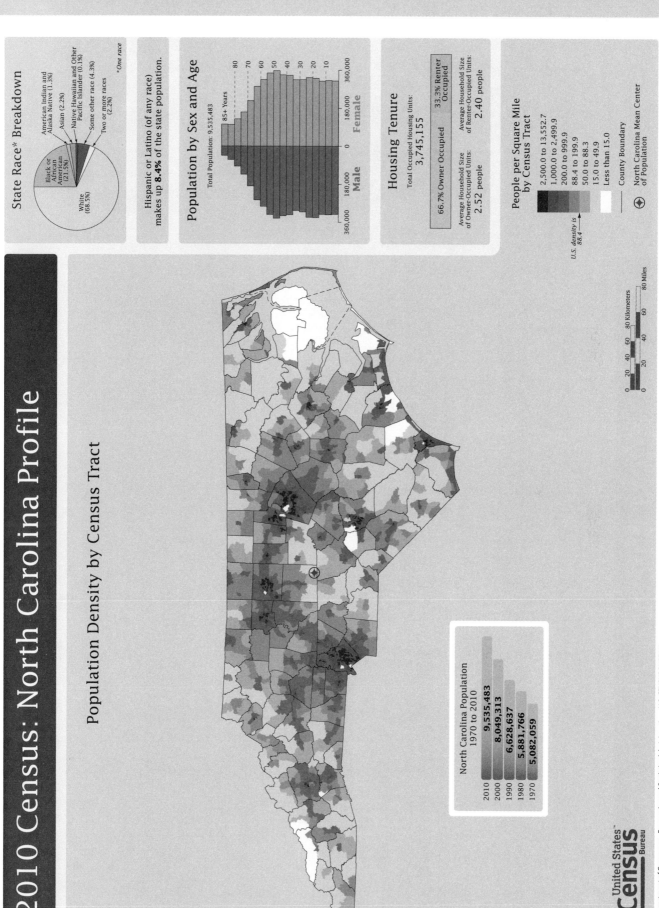

### State Race* Breakdown

- White (68.5%)
- Black or African American (21.5%)
- American Indian and Alaska Native (1.3%)
- Asian (2.2%)
- Native Hawaiian and Other Pacific Islander (0.1%)
- Some other race (4.3%)
- Two or more races (2.2%)

*One race

Hispanic or Latino (of any race) makes up **8.4%** of the state population.

### Population by Sex and Age

Total Population: 9,535,483

85+ Years
80
70
60
50
40
30
20
10

Male        Female

360,000   180,000   0   180,000   360,000

### Housing Tenure

Total Occupied Housing Units:
**3,745,155**

| 66.7% Owner Occupied | 33.3% Renter Occupied |

Average Household Size of Owner-Occupied Units: **2.52 people**

Average Household Size of Renter-Occupied Units: **2.40 people**

### People per Square Mile by Census Tract

- 2,500.0 to 13,552.7
- 1,000.0 to 2,499.9
- 200.0 to 999.9
- 88.4 to 199.9
- 50.0 to 88.3
- 15.0 to 49.9
- Less than 15.0

*U.S. density is 88.4*

- County Boundary
- ⊕ North Carolina Mean Center of Population

0   20   40   60   80 Kilometers
0   20   40   60   80 Miles

### North Carolina Population 1970 to 2010

| Year | Population |
|---|---|
| 2010 | 9,535,483 |
| 2000 | 8,049,313 |
| 1990 | 6,628,637 |
| 1980 | 5,881,766 |
| 1970 | 5,082,059 |

United States™
**Census**
Bureau

U.S. Department of Commerce   Economics and Statistics Administration   U.S. CENSUS BUREAU

# 2010 Census: North Dakota Profile

## Population Density by Census Tract

### State Race* Breakdown

Black or African American (1.2%)
American Indian and Alaska Native (5.4%)
Asian (1.0%)
Native Hawaiian and Other Pacific Islander (<0.1%)
Some other race (0.5%)
Two or more races (1.8%)

*One race

White (90.0%)

### Hispanic or Latino (of any race) makes up 2.0% of the state population.

### Population by Sex and Age

Total Population: 672,591

85+ Years
80
70
60
50
40
30
20
10

Female
Male

35,000    17,500    0    17,500    35,000

### Housing Tenure

Total Occupied Housing Units: 281,192

65.4% Owner Occupied    34.6% Renter Occupied

Average Household Size of Owner-Occupied Units: 2.48 people
Average Household Size of Renter-Occupied Units: 1.96 people

### People per Square Mile by Census Tract

1,000.0 to 8,699.5
200.0 to 999.9
88.4 to 199.9
20.0 to 88.3
5.0 to 19.9
1.0 to 4.9
Less than 1.0

U.S. density is 88.4

County Boundary
North Dakota Mean Center of Population

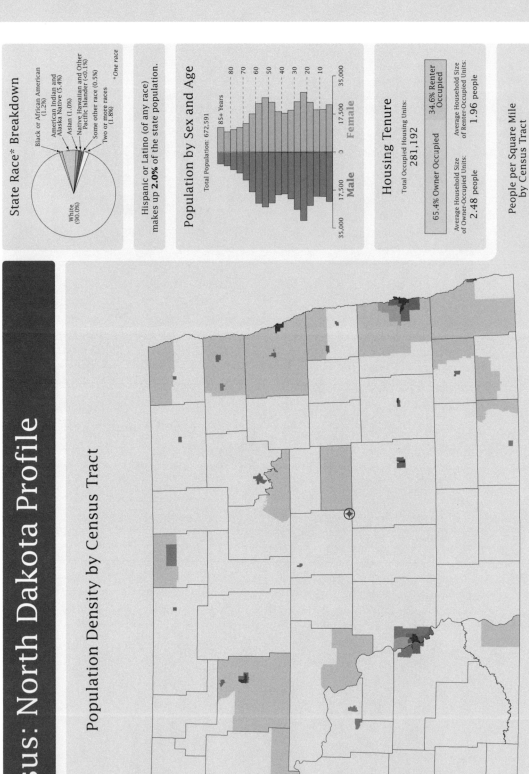

0    20    40    60 Miles
0    20    40    60 Kilometers

North Dakota Population 1970 to 2010

| 2010 | 672,591 |
|------|---------|
| 2000 | 642,200 |
| 1990 | 638,800 |
| 1980 | 652,717 |
| 1970 | 617,761 |

United States™ Census Bureau

U.S. Department of Commerce  Economics and Statistics Administration  U.S. CENSUS BUREAU

# 2010 Census: Ohio Profile

## Population Density by Census Tract

### State Race* Breakdown

- Black or African American (12.2%)
- American Indian and Alaska Native (0.2%)
- Asian (1.7%)
- Native Hawaiian and Other Pacific Islander (<0.1%)
- Some other race (1.1%)
- Two or more races (2.1%)
- White (82.7%)

*One race

Hispanic or Latino (of any race) makes up **3.1%** of the state population.

### Population by Sex and Age

Total Population: 11,536,504

85+ Years
80
70
60
50
40
30
20
10

Male
Female

470,000  235,000  0  235,000  470,000

### Housing Tenure

Total Occupied Housing Units:
**4,603,435**

67.6% Owner Occupied

32.4% Renter Occupied

Average Household Size of Owner-Occupied Units:
**2.54 people**

Average Household Size of Renter-Occupied Units:
**2.24 people**

### People per Square Mile by Census Tract

- 7,500.0 to 29,072.0
- 1,000.0 to 7,499.9
- 200.0 to 999.9
- 88.4 to 199.9
- 50.0 to 88.3
- 25.0 to 49.9
- Less than 25.0

U.S. density is 88.4

— County Boundary

⊕ Ohio Mean Center of Population

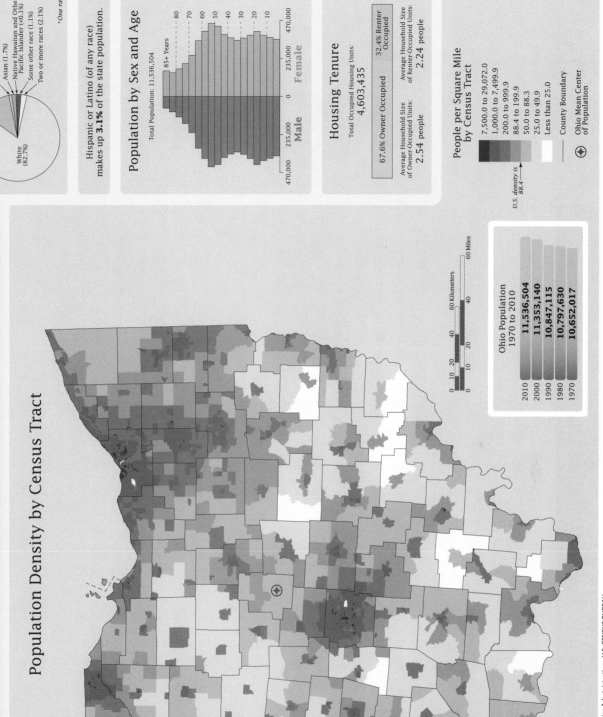

Ohio Population 1970 to 2010

| 2010 | 11,536,504 |
| 2000 | 11,353,140 |
| 1990 | 10,847,115 |
| 1980 | 10,797,630 |
| 1970 | 10,652,017 |

0  10  20  40  60 Kilometers

0  10  20  40  60 Miles

**United States™**
**Census**
Bureau

# 2010 Census: Oklahoma Profile

## Population Density by Census Tract

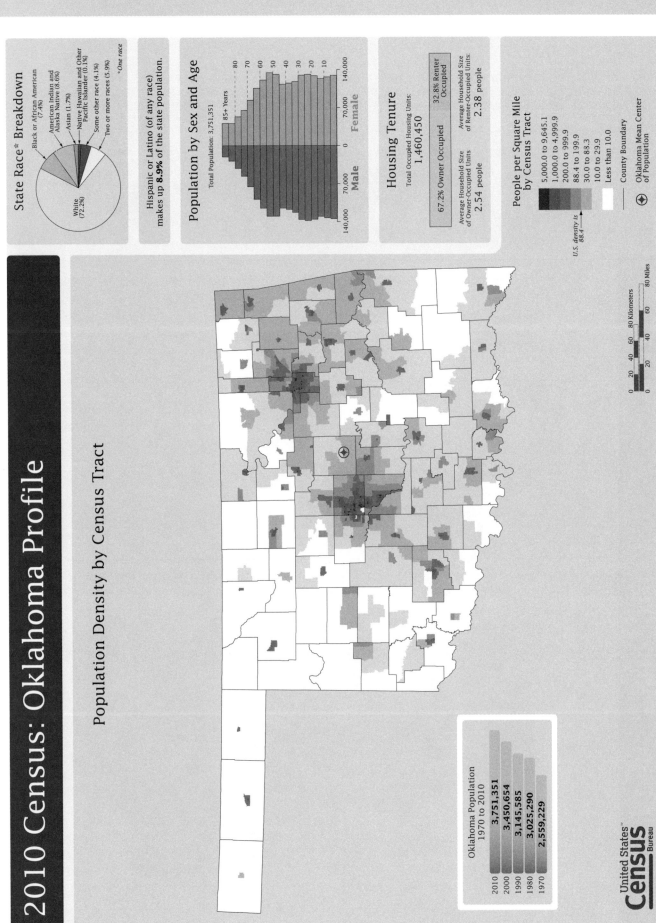

### State Race* Breakdown

White (72.2%)
Black or African American (7.4%)
American Indian and Alaska Native (8.6%)
Asian (1.7%)
Native Hawaiian and Other Pacific Islander (0.1%)
Some other race (4.1%)
Two or more races (5.9%)

*One race

### Hispanic or Latino (of any race) makes up **8.9%** of the state population.

### Population by Sex and Age

Total Population: 3,751,351

85+ Years
80
70
60
50
40
30
20
10

140,000  70,000  0  70,000  140,000

Male          Female

### Housing Tenure

Total Occupied Housing Units:
1,460,450

67.2% Owner Occupied      32.8% Renter Occupied

Average Household Size of Owner-Occupied Units:
2.54 people

Average Household Size of Renter-Occupied Units:
2.38 people

### People per Square Mile by Census Tract

5,000.0 to 9,645.1
1,000.0 to 4,999.9
200.0 to 999.9
88.4 to 199.9
30.0 to 83.3
10.0 to 29.9
Less than 10.0

U.S. density is 88.4

County Boundary
Oklahoma Mean Center of Population

0  20  40  60  80 Kilometers
0  20  40  60  80 Miles

### Oklahoma Population 1970 to 2010

2010   3,751,351
2000   3,450,654
1990   3,145,585
1980   3,025,290
1970   2,559,229

United States Census Bureau

U.S. Department of Commerce   Economics and Statistics Administration   U.S. CENSUS BUREAU

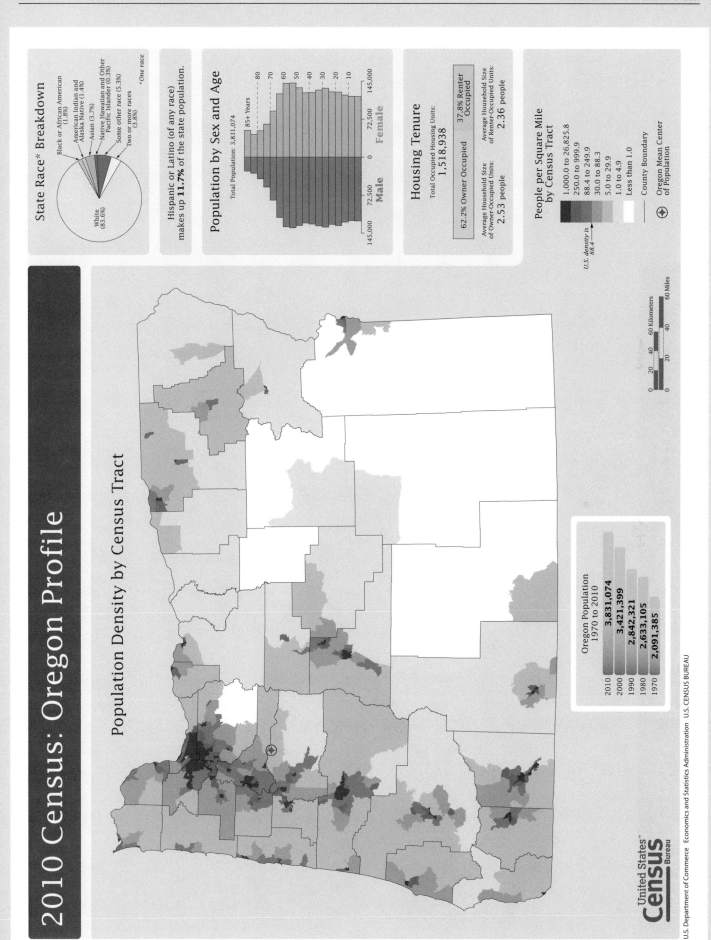

# 2010 Census: Oregon Profile

## Population Density by Census Tract

### State Race* Breakdown

Black or African American (1.8%)
American Indian and Alaska Native (1.4%)
Asian (3.7%)
Native Hawaiian and Other Pacific Islander (0.3%)
Some other race (5.3%)
Two or more races (3.8%)

*One race

White (83.6%)

Hispanic or Latino (of any race) makes up **11.7%** of the state population.

### Population by Sex and Age

Total Population: 3,831,074

85+ Years
80
70
60
50
40
30
20
10

145,000        72,500        0        72,500        145,000
Male                          Female

### Housing Tenure

Total Occupied Housing Units: 1,518,938

62.2% Owner Occupied        37.8% Renter Occupied

Average Household Size of Owner-Occupied Units: 2.53 people

Average Household Size of Renter-Occupied Units: 2.36 people

### People per Square Mile by Census Tract

1,000.0 to 26,825.8
250.0 to 999.9
88.4 to 249.9
30.0 to 88.3
5.0 to 29.9
1.0 to 4.9
Less than 1.0

County Boundary
Oregon Mean Center of Population

U.S. density is 88.4

0    20    40    60 Kilometers
0    20    40    60 Miles

### Oregon Population 1970 to 2010

2010    3,831,074
2000    3,421,399
1990    2,842,321
1980    2,633,105
1970    2,091,385

United States Census Bureau

U.S. Department of Commerce   Economics and Statistics Administration   U.S. CENSUS BUREAU

# 2010 Census: Pennsylvania Profile

## Population Density by Census Tract

### State Race* Breakdown

Black or African American (10.8%)
American Indian and Alaska Native (0.2%)
Asian (2.7%)
Native Hawaiian and Other Pacific Islander (<0.1%)
Some other race (2.4%)
Two or more races (1.9%)

White (81.9%)

*One race

Hispanic or Latino (of any race) makes up **5.7%** of the state population.

### Population by Sex and Age

Total Population: 12,702,379

85+ Years
80
70
60
50
40
30
20
10

510,000  255,000  0  255,000  510,000

Female

Male

### Housing Tenure

Total Occupied Housing Units: 5,018,904

69.6% Owner Occupied   30.4% Renter Occupied

Average Household Size of Owner-Occupied Units: 2.57 people

Average Household Size of Renter-Occupied Units: 2.16 people

### People per Square Mile by Census Tract

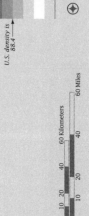

10,000.0 to 64,263.1
1,000.0 to 9,999.9
200.0 to 999.9
88.4 to 199.9
50.0 to 83.3
15.0 to 49.9
Less than 15.0

County Boundary

⊕ Pennsylvania Mean Center of Population

U.S. density is 88.4

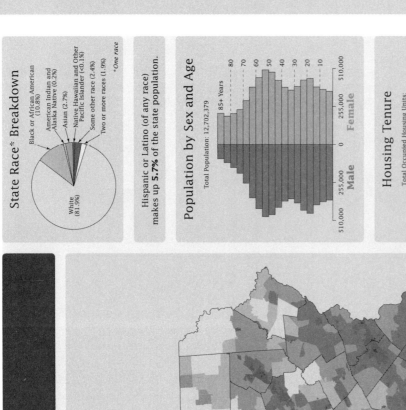

0  10  20  40  60 Kilometers
0  10  20  40  60 Miles

### Pennsylvania Population 1970 to 2010

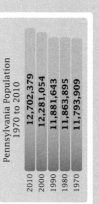

| 2010 | 12,702,379 |
| 2000 | 12,281,054 |
| 1990 | 11,881,643 |
| 1980 | 11,863,895 |
| 1970 | 11,793,909 |

United States™
Census
Bureau

U.S. Department of Commerce  Economics and Statistics Administration  U.S. CENSUS BUREAU

# 2010 Census: Puerto Rico Profile

## Population Density by Census Tract

### State Race* Breakdown

Black or African American (12.4%)
American Indian and Alaska Native (0.5%)
Asian (0.2%)
Native Hawaiian and Other Pacific Islander (<0.1%)
Some other race (7.8%)
Two or more races (3.3%)
*One race

White (75.8%)

Hispanic or Latino (of any race) makes up **99.0%** of the state population.

### Population by Sex and Age

Total Population: 3,725,789

85+ Years
80
70
60
50
40
30
20
10

160,000    80,000    0    80,000    160,000
Male                          Female

### Housing Tenure

Total Occupied Housing Units:
1,376,531

| 71.6% Owner Occupied | 28.4% Renter Occupied |

Average Household Size of Owner-Occupied Units:
2.70 people

Average Household Size of Renter-Occupied Units:
2.63 people

### People per Square Mile by Census Tract

10,000.0 to 47,457.6
5,000.0 to 9,999.9
1,000.0 to 4,999.9
500.0 to 999.9
250.0 to 499.9
88.4 to 249.9
Less than 88.4

U.S. density is 88.4

Municipio Boundary

⊕ Puerto Rico Mean Center of Population

### Puerto Rico Population 1970 to 2010

| Year | Population |
|------|------------|
| 2010 | 3,725,789 |
| 2000 | 3,808,610 |
| 1990 | 3,522,037 |
| 1980 | 3,196,520 |
| 1970 | 2,712,033 |

0  5  10  20  30 Kilometers
0  5  10  20  30 Miles

United States Census Bureau

U.S. Department of Commerce  Economics and Statistics Administration  U.S. CENSUS BUREAU

311

# 2010 Census: Rhode Island Profile

## State Race* Breakdown

- Black or African American (5.7%)
- American Indian and Alaska Native (0.6%)
- Asian (2.9%)
- Native Hawaiian and Other Pacific Islander (0.1%)
- Some other race (6.0%)
- Two or more races (3.3%)
- White (81.4%)

*One race

Hispanic or Latino (of any race) makes up **12.4%** of the state population.

## Population by Sex and Age

Total Population: 1,052,567

85+ Years
80
70
60
50
40
30
20
10

Female

Male

50,000   22,500   0   22,500   50,000

## Housing Tenure

Total Occupied Housing Units: 413,600

| 60.7% Owner Occupied | 39.3% Renter Occupied |

Average Household Size of Owner-Occupied Units: 2.59 people

Average Household Size of Renter-Occupied Units: 2.21 people

## People per Square Mile by Census Tract

- 10,000.0 to 21,760.9
- 5,000.0 to 9,999.9
- 1,000.0 to 4,999.9
- 500.0 to 999.9
- 200.0 to 499.9
- 100.0 to 199.9
- Less than 100.0

U.S. density is 88.4

— County Boundary

⊕ Rhode Island Mean Center of Population

## Population Density by Census Tract

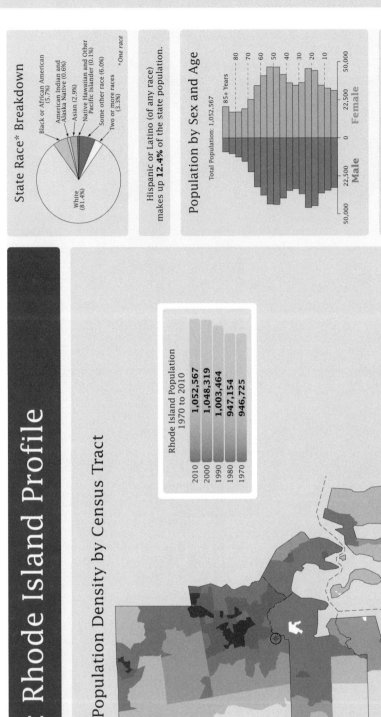

Rhode Island Population 1970 to 2010

| 2010 | 1,052,567 |
| 2000 | 1,048,319 |
| 1990 | 1,003,464 |
| 1980 | 947,154 |
| 1970 | 946,725 |

0   5   10   15 Miles

0   5   10   15 Kilometers

United States Census Bureau

U.S. Department of Commerce  Economics and Statistics Administration  U.S. CENSUS BUREAU

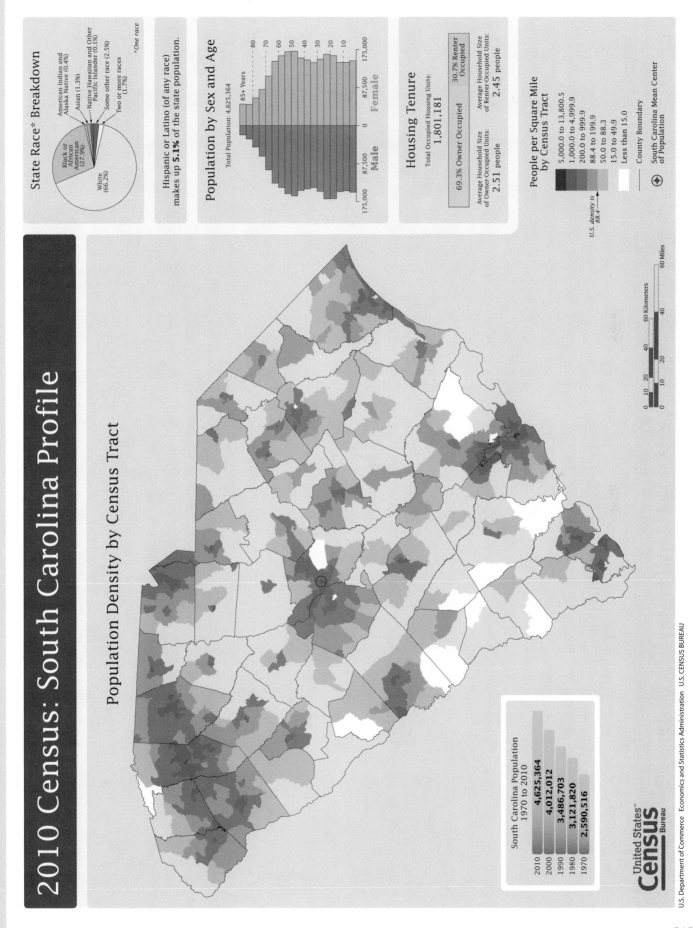

# 2010 Census: South Carolina Profile

## Population Density by Census Tract

### State Race* Breakdown

American Indian and
Alaska Native (0.4%)
Asian (1.3%)
Native Hawaiian and Other
Pacific Islander (0.1%)
Some other race (2.5%)
Two or more races
(1.7%)

*One race

Black or
African
American
(27.9%)

White
(66.2%)

Hispanic or Latino (of any race)
makes up **5.1%** of the state population.

### Population by Sex and Age

Total Population: 4,625,364

85+ Years
80
70
60
50
40
30
20
10

175,000   87,500   0   87,500   175,000

Male                              Female

### Housing Tenure

Total Occupied Housing Units:
1,801,181

69.3% Owner Occupied        30.7% Renter
Occupied

Average Household Size       Average Household Size
of Owner-Occupied Units:     of Renter-Occupied Units:
2.51 people                  2.45 people

### People per Square Mile
by Census Tract

5,000.0 to 13,800.5
1,000.0 to 4,999.9
200.0 to 999.9
88.4 to 199.9
50.0 to 88.3
15.0 to 49.9
Less than 15.0

County Boundary

South Carolina Mean Center
of Population

U.S. density is
88.4

0   10   20        60 Kilometers
0      20   40   60 Miles
10        40

South Carolina Population
1970 to 2010

2010   4,625,364
2000   4,012,012
1990   3,486,703
1980   3,121,820
1970   2,590,516

United States™
**Census**
Bureau

U.S. Department of Commerce  Economics and Statistics Administration  U.S. CENSUS BUREAU

313

# 2010 Census: South Dakota Profile

## Population Density by Census Tract

### State Race* Breakdown

Black or African American (1.3%)
American Indian and Alaska Native (8.8%)
Asian (0.9%)
Native Hawaiian and Other Pacific Islander (<0.1%)
Some other race (0.9%)
Two or more races (2.1%)

*One race

White (85.9%)

### Hispanic or Latino (of any race) makes up **2.7%** of the state population.

### Population by Sex and Age

Total Population: 814,180

85+ Years
80
70
60
50
40
30
20
10

35,000    17,500    0    17,500    35,000

Male                    Female

### Housing Tenure

Total Occupied Housing Units: 322,282

68.1% Owner Occupied          31.9% Renter Occupied

Average Household Size of Owner-Occupied Units: 2.53 people

Average Household Size of Renter-Occupied Units: 2.18 people

### People per Square Mile by Census Tract

1,000.0 to 6,919.7
200.0 to 999.9
88.4 to 199.9
20.0 to 88.3
5.0 to 19.9
1.0 to 4.9
Less than 1.0

U.S. density is 88.4

County Boundary

South Dakota Mean Center of Population

0    20    40    60 Kilometers
0    20    40    60 Miles

South Dakota Population 1970 to 2010

2010    814,180
2000    754,844
1990    696,004
1980    690,768
1970    665,507

United States Census Bureau

# 2010 Census: Tennessee Profile

## Population Density by Census Tract

### State Race* Breakdown

White (77.6%)
Black or African American (16.7%)
American Indian and Alaska Native (0.3%)
Asian (1.4%)
Native Hawaiian and Other Pacific Islander (0.1%)
Some other race (2.2%)
Two or more races (1.7%)

*One race

Hispanic or Latino (of any race) makes up **4.6%** of the state population.

### Population by Sex and Age

Total Population: 6,346,105

85+ Years
80
70
60
50
40
30
20
10

240,000   120,000   0   120,000   240,000

Male            Female

### Housing Tenure

Total Occupied Housing Units:
2,493,552

68.2% Owner Occupied          31.8% Renter Occupied

Average Household Size of Owner-Occupied Units:
2.53 people

Average Household Size of Renter-Occupied Units:
2.38 people

### People per Square Mile by Census Tract

5,000.0 to 11,344.8
1,000.0 to 4,999.9
200.0 to 999.9
88.4 to 199.9
50.0 to 88.3
15.0 to 49.9
Less than 15.0

U.S. density is 88.4

County Boundary
Tennessee Mean Center of Population

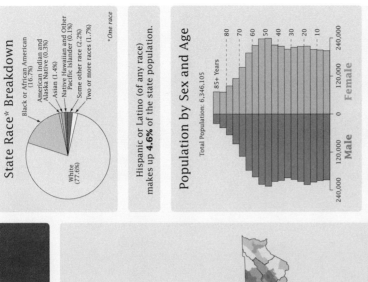

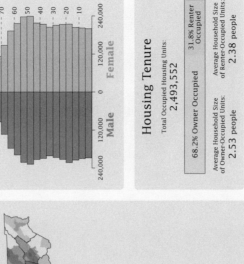

Tennessee Population 1970 to 2010

| Year | Population |
|------|------------|
| 2010 | 6,346,105 |
| 2000 | 5,689,283 |
| 1990 | 4,877,185 |
| 1980 | 4,591,120 |
| 1970 | 3,923,687 |

0   20   40   60   80 Kilometers
0   20   40   60   80 Miles

United States Census Bureau

U.S. Department of Commerce   Economics and Statistics Administration   U.S. CENSUS BUREAU

315

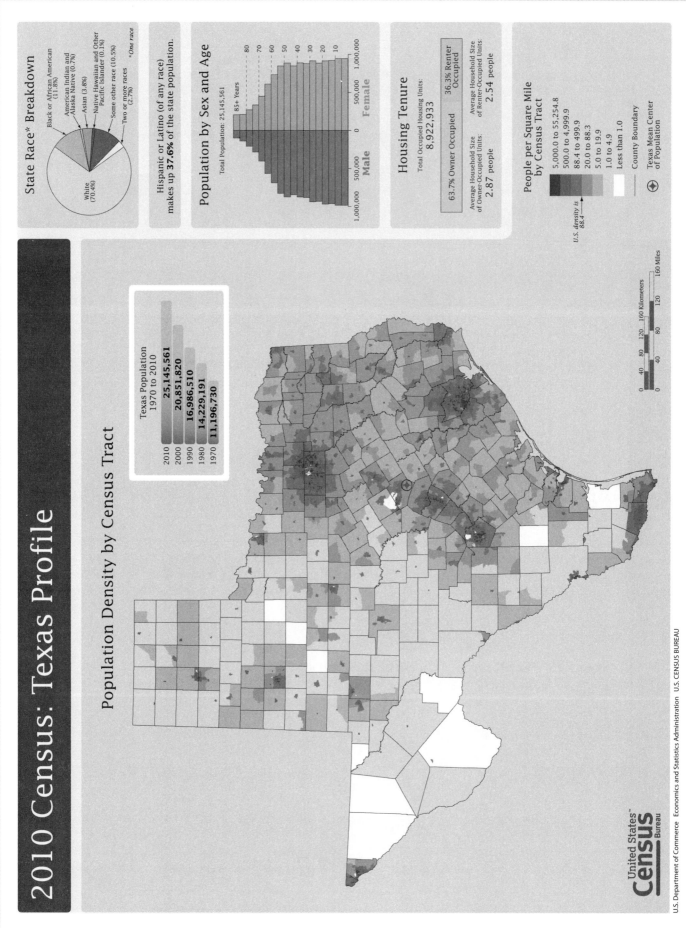

# 2010 Census: Texas Profile

## Population Density by Census Tract

### State Race* Breakdown

- Black or African American (11.8%)
- American Indian and Alaska Native (0.7%)
- Asian (3.8%)
- Native Hawaiian and Other Pacific Islander (0.1%)
- Some other race (10.5%)
- Two or more races (2.7%)
- White (70.4%)

*One race

Hispanic or Latino (of any race) makes up **37.6%** of the state population.

### Population by Sex and Age

Total Population: 25,145,561

Male    Female

85+ Years
80
70
60
50
40
30
20
10

1,000,000   500,000   0   500,000   1,000,000

### Housing Tenure

Total Occupied Housing Units: 8,922,933

63.7% Owner Occupied    36.3% Renter Occupied

Average Household Size of Owner-Occupied Units: 2.87 people

Average Household Size of Renter-Occupied Units: 2.54 people

### People per Square Mile by Census Tract

- 5,000.0 to 55,254.8
- 500.0 to 4,999.9
- 88.4 to 499.9
- 20.0 to 88.3
- 5.0 to 19.9
- 1.0 to 4.9
- Less than 1.0

*U.S. density is 88.4*

County Boundary

Texas Mean Center of Population

### Texas Population 1970 to 2010

- 2010: 25,145,561
- 2000: 20,851,820
- 1990: 16,986,510
- 1980: 14,229,191
- 1970: 11,196,730

0   40   80   120   160 Miles

0   40   80   120   160 Kilometers

United States™ **Census** Bureau

U.S. Department of Commerce   Economics and Statistics Administration   U.S. CENSUS BUREAU

# 2010 Census: Utah Profile

## State Race* Breakdown

- White (86.1%)
- Black or African American (1.1%)
- American Indian and Alaska Native (1.2%)
- Asian (2.0%)
- Native Hawaiian and Other Pacific Islander (0.9%)
- Some other race (6.0%)
- Two or more races (2.7%)

*One race

Hispanic or Latino (of any race) makes up **13.0%** of the state population.

## Population by Sex and Age

Total Population: 2,763,885

Male — Female

85+ Years
80
70
60
50
40
30
20
10

140,000 · 70,000 · 0 · 70,000 · 140,000

## Housing Tenure

Total Occupied Housing Units: 877,692

70.4% Owner Occupied

29.6% Renter Occupied

Average Household Size of Owner-Occupied Units: 3.21 people

Average Household Size of Renter-Occupied Units: 2.82 people

## People per Square Mile by Census Tract

- 5,000.0 to 29,402.3
- 500.0 to 4,999.9
- 88.4 to 499.9
- 30.0 to 88.3
- 5.0 to 29.9
- 1.0 to 4.9
- Less than 1.0

U.S. density is 88.4

— County Boundary

⊕ Utah Mean Center of Population

## Population Density by Census Tract

### Utah Population 1970 to 2010

- 2010: 2,763,885
- 2000: 2,233,169
- 1990: 1,722,850
- 1980: 1,461,037
- 1970: 1,059,273

0 · 20 · 40 · 60 · 80 Kilometers

0 · 20 · 40 · 60 · 80 Miles

United States™ Census Bureau

U.S. Department of Commerce  Economics and Statistics Administration  U.S. CENSUS BUREAU

# 2010 Census: Vermont Profile

## State Race* Breakdown

White (95.3%)

Black or African American (1.0%)
American Indian and Alaska Native (0.4%)
Asian (1.3%)
Native Hawaiian and Other Pacific Islander (<0.1%)
Some other race (0.3%)
Two or more races (1.7%)

*One race

Hispanic or Latino (of any race) makes up **1.5%** of the state population.

## Population by Sex and Age

Total Population: 625,741

85+ Years
80
70
60
50
40
30
20
10

30,000    15,000    0    15,000    30,000

Male                          Female

## Housing Tenure

Total Occupied Housing Units: 256,442

70.7% Owner Occupied          29.3% Renter Occupied

Average Household Size of Owner-Occupied Units: 2.45 people

Average Household Size of Renter-Occupied Units: 2.08 people

## People per Square Mile by Census Tract

5,000.0 to 20,105.9
1,000.0 to 4,999.9
200.0 to 999.9
88.4 to 199.9
30.0 to 88.3
1.0 to 29.9
Less than 1.0

U.S. density is 88.4

County Boundary
⊕ Vermont Mean Center of Population

## Population Density by Census Tract

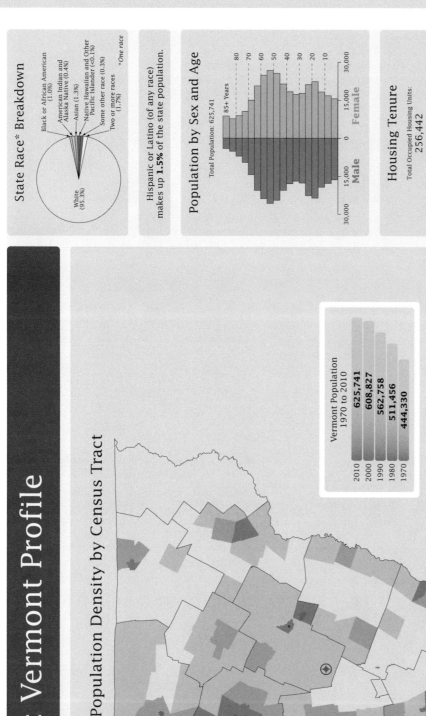

### Vermont Population 1970 to 2010

| Year | Population |
| --- | --- |
| 2010 | 625,741 |
| 2000 | 608,827 |
| 1990 | 562,758 |
| 1980 | 511,456 |
| 1970 | 444,330 |

0    10    20    30 Miles

0    10    20    30 Kilometers

United States Census Bureau

U.S. Department of Commerce  Economics and Statistics Administration  U.S. CENSUS BUREAU

# 2010 Census: Virginia Profile

## Population Density by Census Tract

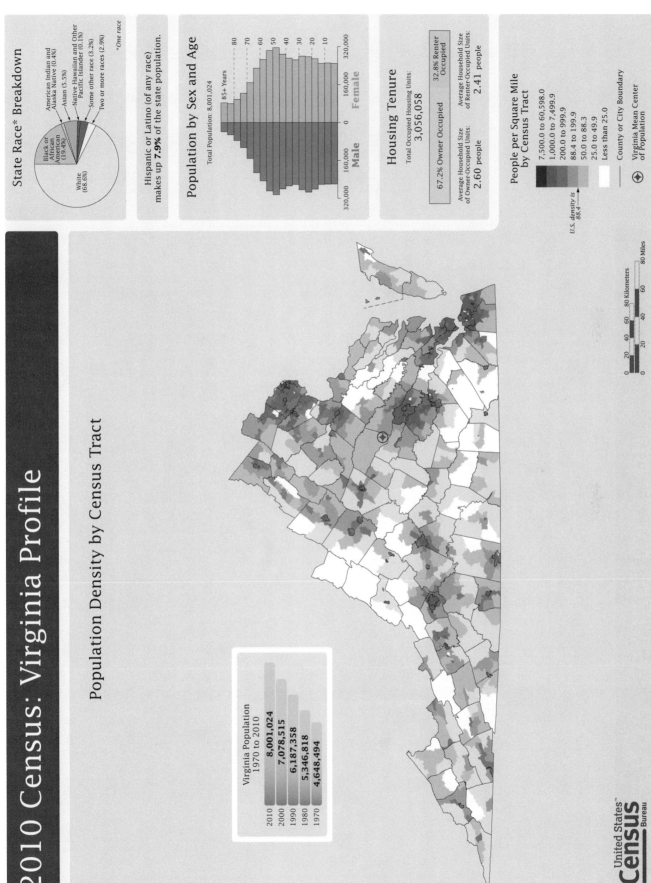

### State Race* Breakdown

Black or African American (19.4%)

American Indian and Alaska Native (0.4%)

Asian (5.5%)

Native Hawaiian and Other Pacific Islander (0.1%)

Some other race (3.2%)

Two or more races (2.9%)

White (68.6%)

*One race

Hispanic or Latino (of any race) makes up **7.9%** of the state population.

### Population by Sex and Age

Total Population: 8,001,024

85+ Years
80
70
60
50
40
30
20
10

320,000   160,000   0   160,000   320,000

Female

Male

### Housing Tenure

Total Occupied Housing Units: 3,056,058

67.2% Owner Occupied

32.8% Renter Occupied

Average Household Size of Owner-Occupied Units: **2.60** people

Average Household Size of Renter-Occupied Units: **2.41** people

### People per Square Mile by Census Tract

7,500.0 to 60,598.0
1,000.0 to 7,499.9
200.0 to 999.9
88.4 to 199.9
50.0 to 88.3
25.0 to 49.9
Less than 25.0

U.S. density is 88.4

County or City Boundary

Virginia Mean Center of Population

0   20   40   60   80 Kilometers

0   20   40   60   80 Miles

### Virginia Population 1970 to 2010

2010  **8,001,024**
2000  **7,078,515**
1990  **6,187,358**
1980  **5,346,818**
1970  **4,648,494**

United States **Census** Bureau

U.S. Department of Commerce   Economics and Statistics Administration   U.S. CENSUS BUREAU

# 2010 Census: Washington Profile

## Population Density by Census Tract

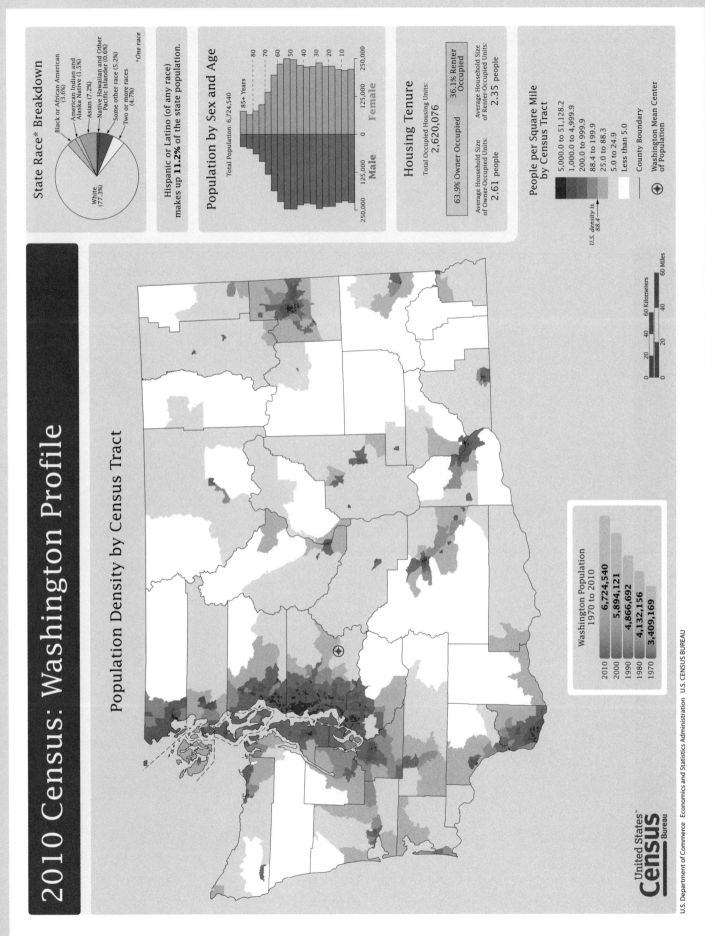

### State Race* Breakdown

Black or African American (3.6%)
American Indian and Alaska Native (1.5%)
Asian (7.2%)
Native Hawaiian and Other Pacific Islander (0.6%)
Some other race (5.2%)
Two or more races (4.7%)
White (77.3%)

*One race

Hispanic or Latino (of any race) makes up **11.2%** of the state population.

### Population by Sex and Age

Total Population: 6,724,540

85+ Years
80
70
60
50
40
30
20
10

250,000   125,000   0   125,000   250,000
**Female**          **Male**

### Housing Tenure

Total Occupied Housing Units: 2,620,076

63.9% Owner Occupied

36.1% Renter Occupied

Average Household Size of Owner-Occupied Units: 2.61 people

Average Household Size of Renter-Occupied Units: 2.35 people

### People per Square Mile by Census Tract

5,000.0 to 51,128.2
1,000.0 to 4,999.9
200.0 to 999.9
88.4 to 199.9
25.0 to 88.3
5.0 to 24.9
Less than 5.0

*U.S. density is 88.4*

County Boundary

Washington Mean Center of Population

0   20   40   60 Kilometers
0   20   40   60 Miles

Washington Population 1970 to 2010

| Year | Population |
|---|---|
| 2010 | 6,724,540 |
| 2000 | 5,894,121 |
| 1990 | 4,866,692 |
| 1980 | 4,132,156 |
| 1970 | 3,409,169 |

United States Census Bureau

U.S. Department of Commerce   Economics and Statistics Administration   U.S. CENSUS BUREAU

# 2010 Census: West Virginia Profile

## Population Density by Census Tract

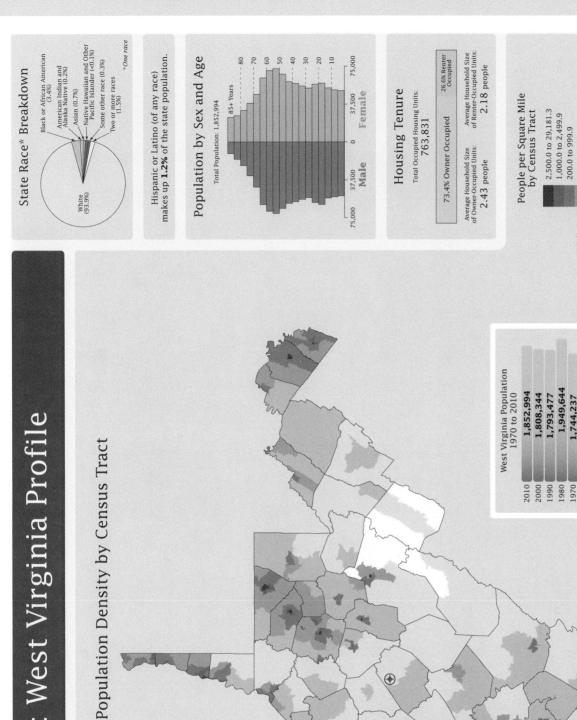

### State Race* Breakdown

White (93.9%)
Black or African American (3.4%)
American Indian and Alaska Native (0.2%)
Asian (0.7%)
Native Hawaiian and Other Pacific Islander (<0.1%)
Some other race (0.3%)
Two or more races (1.5%)

*One race

Hispanic or Latino (of any race) makes up **1.2%** of the state population.

### Population by Sex and Age

Total Population: 1,852,994

85+ Years
80
70
60
50
40
30
20
10

75,000   37,500   0   37,500   75,000

Male            Female

### Housing Tenure

Total Occupied Housing Units: 763,831

73.4% Owner Occupied          26.6% Renter Occupied

Average Household Size of Owner-Occupied Units: 2.43 people

Average Household Size of Renter-Occupied Units: 2.18 people

### People per Square Mile by Census Tract

2,500.0 to 29,181.3
1,000.0 to 2,499.9
200.0 to 999.9
88.4 to 199.9
30.0 to 88.3
10.0 to 29.9
Less than 10.0

U.S. density is 88.4

County Boundary

⊕ West Virginia Mean Center of Population

West Virginia Population 1970 to 2010

2010  1,852,994
2000  1,808,344
1990  1,793,477
1980  1,949,644
1970  1,744,237

0  10  20  30  40 Kilometers
0  10  20  30  40 Miles

United States™ Census Bureau

U.S. Department of Commerce  Economics and Statistics Administration  U.S. CENSUS BUREAU

# 2010 Census: Wisconsin Profile

## Population Density by Census Tract

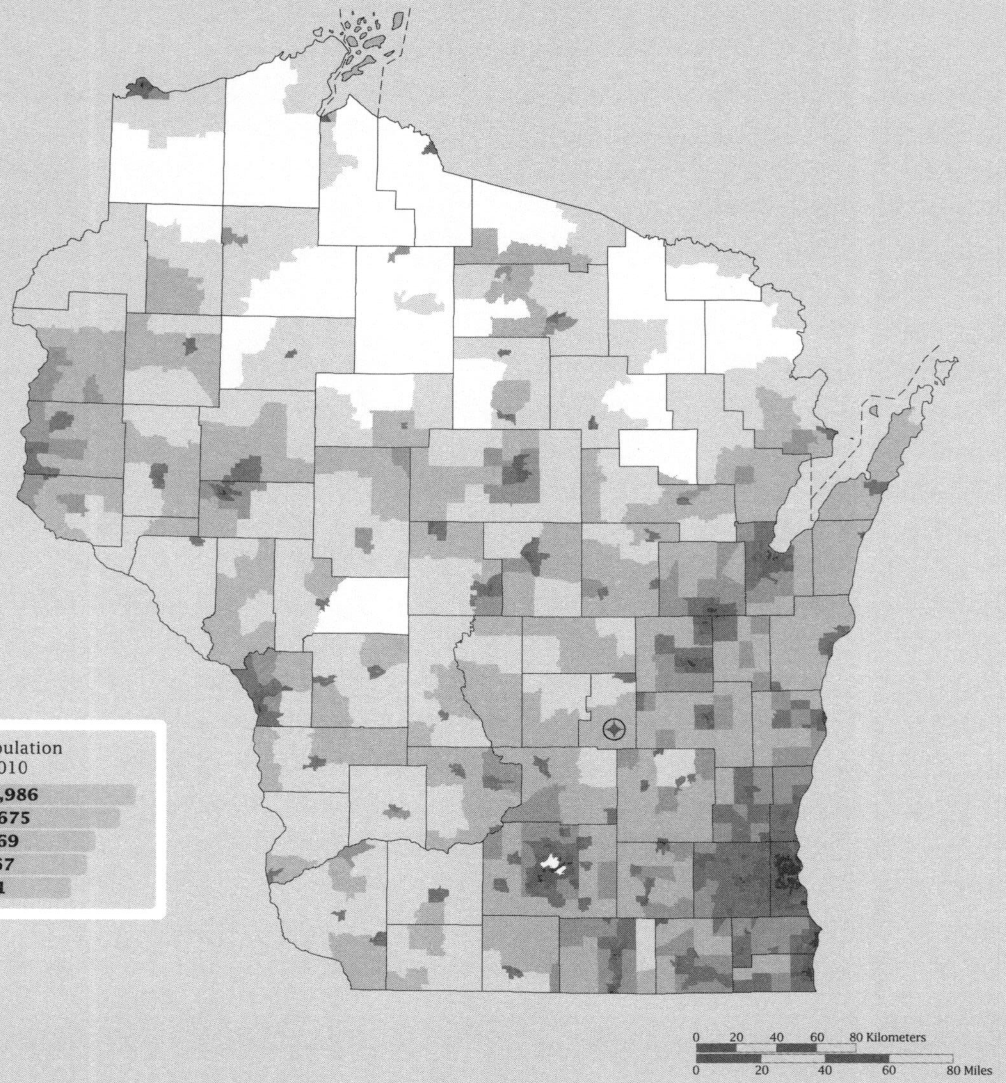

### State Race* Breakdown

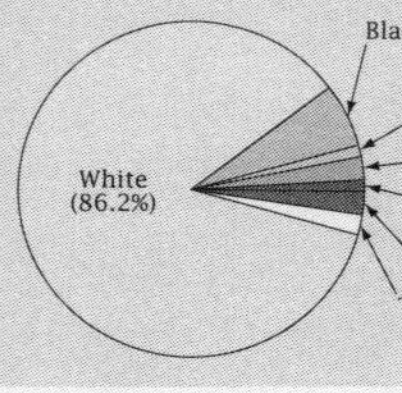

Black or African American (6.3%)
American Indian and Alaska Native (1.0%)
Asian (2.3%)
Native Hawaiian and Other Pacific Islander (<0.1%)
Some other race (2.4%)
Two or more races (1.8%)

*One race

White (86.2%)

### Hispanic or Latino (of any race) makes up 5.9% of the state population.

### Population by Sex and Age

Total Population: 5,686,986

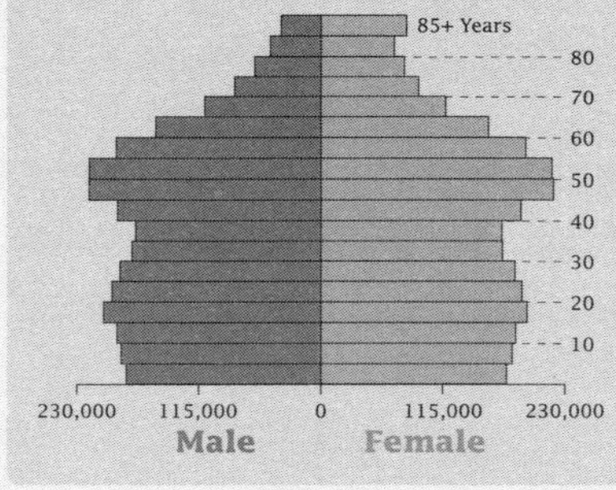

85+ Years
80
70
60
50
40
30
20
10

230,000    115,000    0    115,000    230,000

Male              Female

### Housing Tenure

Total Occupied Housing Units: 2,279,768

68.1% Owner Occupied          31.9% Renter Occupied

Average Household Size of Owner-Occupied Units: 2.56 people

Average Household Size of Renter-Occupied Units: 2.16 people

### People per Square Mile by Census Tract

5,000.0 to 50,310.2
1,000.0 to 4,999.9
200.0 to 999.9
88.4 to 199.9
30.0 to 88.3
10.0 to 29.9
Less than 10.0

U.S. density is 88.4

County Boundary

Wisconsin Mean Center of Population

0    20    40    60    80 Kilometers

0    20    40    60    80 Miles

### Wisconsin Population 1970 to 2010

2010    5,686,986
2000    5,363,675
1990    4,891,769
1980    4,705,767
1970    4,417,731

United States™
Census
Bureau

U.S. Department of Commerce   Economics and Statistics Administration   U.S. CENSUS BUREAU

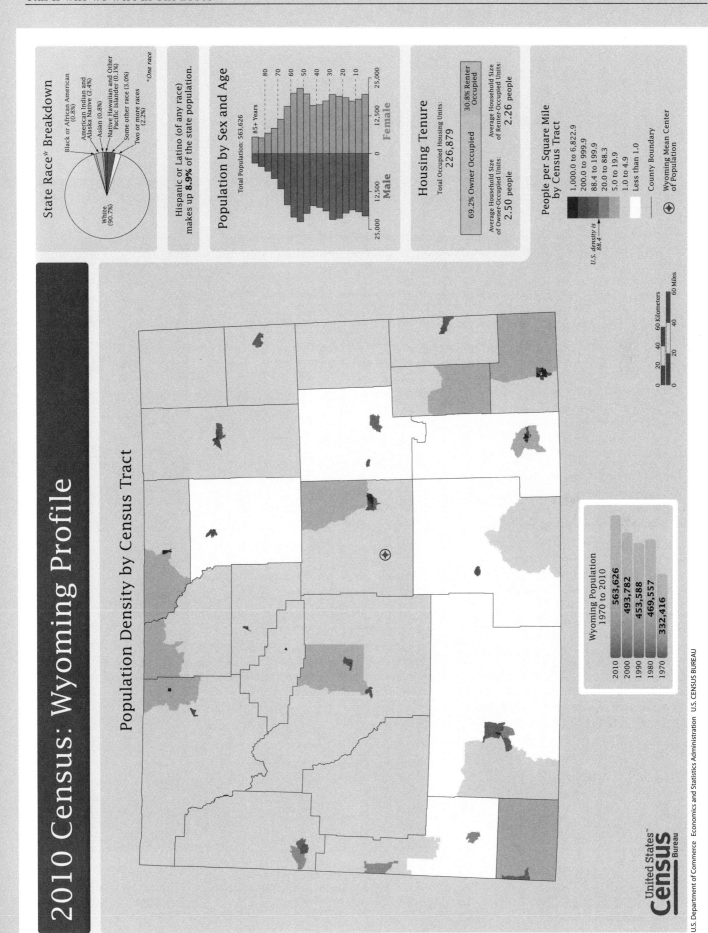

# 2010 Census: Wyoming Profile

## Population Density by Census Tract

### State Race* Breakdown

- Black or African American (0.8%)
- American Indian and Alaska Native (2.4%)
- Asian (0.8%)
- Native Hawaiian and Other Pacific Islander (0.1%)
- Some other race (3.0%)
- Two or more races (2.2%)

White (90.7%)

*One race

Hispanic or Latino (of any race) makes up **8.9%** of the state population.

### Population by Sex and Age

Total Population: 563,626

85+ Years
80
70
60
50
40
30
20
10

Male | Female

25,000 — 12,500 — 0 — 12,500 — 25,000

### Housing Tenure

Total Occupied Housing Units:
226,879

69.2% Owner Occupied | 30.8% Renter Occupied

Average Household Size of Owner-Occupied Units:
2.50 people

Average Household Size of Renter-Occupied Units:
2.26 people

### People per Square Mile by Census Tract

- 1,000.0 to 6,822.9
- 200.0 to 999.9
- 88.4 to 199.9
- 20.0 to 88.3
- 5.0 to 19.9
- 1.0 to 4.9
- Less than 1.0

U.S. density is 88.4

— County Boundary

⊕ Wyoming Mean Center of Population

### Wyoming Population 1970 to 2010

| Year | Population |
|------|-----------|
| 2010 | 563,626 |
| 2000 | 493,782 |
| 1990 | 453,588 |
| 1980 | 469,557 |
| 1970 | 332,416 |

0  20  40  60 Miles
0  20  40  60 Kilometers

United States Census Bureau

U.S. Department of Commerce  Economics and Statistics Administration  U.S. CENSUS BUREAU

323

Table 5.

# American Indian Reservation and Alaska Native Village Statistical Area Population: 2010

(For information on confidentiality protection, nonsampling error, and definitions, see *www.census.gov/prod/cen2010/doc/pl94-171.pdf*)

| Area | Total population | American Indian and Alaska Native | | | Not American Indian and Alaska Native alone or in combination |
|---|---|---|---|---|---|
| | | Alone or in combination | Alone | In combination | |
| Total American Indian areas[1]......................... | 4,576,127 | 1,069,411 | 901,280 | 168,131 | 3,506,716 |
| Total Alaska Native village statistical areas............... | 242,613 | 78,141 | 65,855 | 12,286 | 164,472 |
| Outside American Indian/Alaska Native areas ............ | 303,926,798 | 4,073,027 | 1,965,113 | 2,107,914 | 299,853,771 |

[1] Includes federal reservations and/or off-reservation trust lands, Oklahoma tribal statistical areas, tribal designated statistical areas, state reservations, and state designated American Indian statistical areas.

Note: In this table, the American Indian and Alaska Native alone-or-in-combination population and the not American Indian and Alaska Native alone-or-in-combination population add to the total population for each area.

Source: U.S. Census Bureau, *2010 Census Redistricting Data (Public Law 94-171) Summary File,* Table P1.

---

areas (see Figure 6). In comparison, the proportion of the American Indian and Alaska Native alone population living outside of American Indian and Alaska Native areas was somewhat lower (67 percent), while the vast majority of the American Indian and Alaska Native in combination population (92 percent) lived outside American Indian and Alaska Native areas.

These proportions were similar to Census 2000, when 75 percent of the American Indian and Alaska Native alone-or-in-combination population lived outside American Indian and Alaska Native areas, as did 64 percent of the American Indian and Alaska Native alone population and 92 percent of the American Indian and Alaska Native in combination population.[20]

**A greater proportion of the American Indian and Alaska Native alone population lived inside American Indian areas than did the American Indian and Alaska Native in combination population.**

According to the 2010 Census, 20 percent of the American Indian and Alaska Native alone-or-in-combination population lived inside an American Indian area

[20] Information on the Census 2000 American Indian and Alaska Native population living in American Indian and Alaska Native areas can be found in PCT1 tables in *Census 2000 Summary File 2.*

(i.e., federal reservation and/or off-reservation trust land, Oklahoma tribal statistical area, state reservation, or federal- or state-designated American Indian statistical area).[21] The proportion of the American Indian and Alaska Native alone population that lived inside American Indian areas was 31 percent, while a smaller proportion of the American Indian and Alaska Native in combination population (7 percent) lived inside American Indian areas in 2010. Patterns were similar for the proportion of the American Indian and Alaska Native population that lived inside American Indian areas in 2000.

**The American Indian and Alaska Native alone population was more likely than the American Indian and Alaska Native in combination population to live inside Alaska Native village statistical areas.**

Individuals living inside Alaska Native village statistical areas made up 1 percent of the total American Indian and Alaska Native alone-or-in-combination population in 2010.

[21] For information on American Indian and Alaska Native areas, see the *2010 Census Redistricting Data (Public Law 94-171) Summary File—Technical Documentation* at <www.census.gov/prod/cen2010/doc /pl94-171.pdf> and the wall map, *American Indians and Alaska Natives in the United States* at <www.census.gov/geo/www/maps /aian2010_wall_map/aian_wall_map.html>.

The proportion of the American Indian and Alaska Native alone population living inside Alaska Native village statistical areas (2 percent) in 2010 was higher compared with the American Indian and Alaska Native alone-or-in-combination population. The proportion of the American Indian and Alaska Native in combination population living inside Alaska Native village statistical areas was 1 percent. Patterns were similar for the proportion of the American Indian and Alaska Native population living inside Alaska Native village statistical areas in 2000.

**Most people living in American Indian areas and in Alaska Native village statistical areas did not identify as American Indian and Alaska Native.**

Of the total U.S. population (308.7 million), about 4.6 million individuals lived in American Indian areas and about 243,000 individuals lived in Alaska Native village statistical areas (see Table 5). This means that 98 percent of the U.S. population (303.9 million people) lived outside of American Indian and Alaska Native areas.

Of all people that lived in American Indian areas, 1.1 million identified as American Indian and Alaska Native alone or in combination with another race, compared with

Table 6.
## American Indian Reservations and Alaska Native Village Statistical Areas With Largest American Indian and Alaska Native Populations: 2010
(For information on confidentiality protection, nonsampling error, and definitions, see *www.census.gov/prod/cen2010/doc/pl94-171.pdf*)

| Area | | American Indian and Alaska Native | | | Not American Indian and Alaska Native alone or in combination |
|---|---|---|---|---|---|
| | Total population | Alone or in combination | Alone | In combination | |
| **American Indian Reservation** | | | | | |
| Navajo Nation Reservation and Off-Reservation Trust Land, AZ–NM–UT ... | 173,667 | 169,321 | 166,824 | 2,497 | 4,346 |
| Pine Ridge Reservation, SD–NE.................... | 18,834 | 16,906 | 16,580 | 326 | 1,928 |
| Fort Apache Reservation, AZ ...................... | 13,409 | 13,014 | 12,870 | 144 | 395 |
| Gila River Indian Reservation, AZ................. | 11,712 | 11,251 | 10,845 | 406 | 461 |
| Osage Reservation, OK............................ | 47,472 | 9,920 | 6,858 | 3,062 | 37,552 |
| San Carlos Reservation, AZ....................... | 10,068 | 9,901 | 9,835 | 66 | 167 |
| Rosebud Indian Reservation and Off-Reservation Trust Land, SD......... | 10,869 | 9,809 | 9,617 | 192 | 1,060 |
| Tohono O'odham Nation Reservation and Off-Reservation Trust Land, AZ ... | 10,201 | 9,278 | 9,139 | 139 | 923 |
| Blackfeet Indian Reservation and Off-Reservation Trust Land, MT ........ | 10,405 | 9,149 | 8,944 | 205 | 1,256 |
| Flathead Reservation, MT......................... | 28,359 | 9,138 | 7,042 | 2,096 | 19,221 |
| **Alaska Native Village Statistical Area** | | | | | |
| Knik Alaska Native village statistical area ......... | 65,768 | 6,582 | 3,529 | 3,053 | 59,186 |
| Bethel Alaska Native village statistical area ....... | 6,080 | 4,334 | 3,953 | 381 | 1,746 |
| Kenaitze Alaska Native village statistical area...... | 32,902 | 3,417 | 2,001 | 1,416 | 29,485 |
| Barrow Alaska Native village statistical area....... | 4,212 | 2,889 | 2,577 | 312 | 1,323 |
| Ketchikan Alaska Native village statistical area..... | 12,742 | 2,605 | 1,692 | 913 | 10,137 |
| Kotzebue Alaska Native village statistical area ..... | 3,201 | 2,585 | 2,355 | 230 | 616 |
| Nome Alaska Native village statistical area......... | 3,681 | 2,396 | 1,994 | 402 | 1,285 |
| Chickaloon Alaska Native village statistical area.... | 23,087 | 2,373 | 1,369 | 1,004 | 20,714 |
| Dillingham Alaska Native village statistical area .... | 2,378 | 1,583 | 1,333 | 250 | 795 |
| Sitka Alaska Native village statistical area ......... | 4,480 | 1,240 | 855 | 385 | 3,240 |

Note: In this table, the American Indian and Alaska Native alone-or-in-combination population and the not American Indian and Alaska Native alone-or-in-combination population add to the total population of the reservation or village statistical area. The rankings of the American Indian reservations and Alaska Native village statistical areas are based on the American Indian and Alaska Native alone-or-in-combination population.

Source: U.S. Census Bureau, *2010 Census Redistricting Data (Public Law 94-171) Summary File,* Table P1.

the 3.5 million that did not identify as American Indian and Alaska Native. Therefore, out of the total 4.6 million people in American Indian areas, 77 percent did not identify as American Indian and Alaska Native.

Of all people that lived in Alaska Native village statistical areas, 78,000 individuals identified as American Indian and Alaska Native alone or in combination with another race compared with 164,000 that did not identify as American Indian and Alaska Native. Therefore, out of the total 243,000 people that lived in Alaska Native village statistical areas, 68 percent did not identify as American Indian and Alaska Native.

**The Navajo Nation had the largest American Indian and Alaska Native population of all the American Indian reservations.**

Table 6 provides information on the American Indian and Alaska Native population living on American Indian reservations. The rankings of the American Indian reservations are based on the American Indian and Alaska Native alone-or-in-combination population. The Navajo Nation was the American Indian reservation with the largest total population (174,000), and the largest American Indian and Alaska Native alone-or-in-combination population (169,000) (see Table 6). The second-largest American Indian reservation with regard to total

population size was the Osage reservation. A large majority (38,000 out of 47,000) of residents living on the Osage reservation, however, did not identify as American Indian and Alaska Native alone or in combination with another race. The second-largest American Indian reservation with regard to American Indian and Alaska Native population size was the Pine Ridge reservation, with 17,000 residents identifying as American Indian and Alaska Native alone or in combination with another race.

Figure 7 shows the 20 American Indian reservations with the largest American Indian and Alaska Native alone population. The Navajo Nation was the American Indian

Figure 7.
## Top 20 Reservations and Alaska Native Village Statistical Areas With the Largest American Indian and Alaska Native (AIAN) Alone Population: 2010

(For information on confidentiality protection, nonsampling error, and definitions, see
*www.census.gov/prod/cen2010/doc/pl94-171.pdf*)

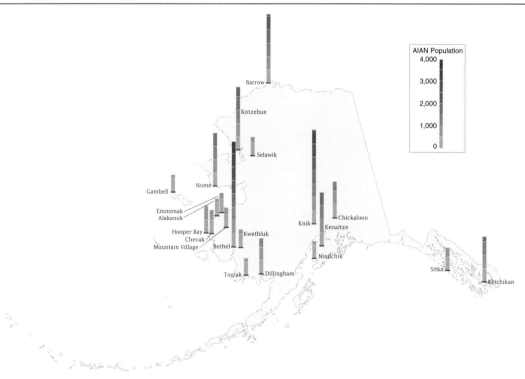

Source: U.S. Census Bureau, *2010 Census Redistricting Data (Public Law 94-171) Summary File*, Table P1.

reservation that had the largest American Indian and Alaska Native alone population (167,000) (see Figure 7), just as it had for the American Indian and Alaska Native alone-or-in-combination population (see Table 6). The second-largest American Indian reservation with regard to the American Indian and Alaska Native alone population size was again the Pine Ridge reservation (17,000).

**Knik had the largest American Indian and Alaska Native alone-or-in-combination population of all Alaska Native village statistical areas.**

Table 6 also provides data for the American Indian and Alaska Native population living in Alaska Native village statistical areas. The rankings of the Alaska Native village statistical areas are based on the American Indian and Alaska Native alone-or-in-combination population. Knik had the largest total population and the largest American Indian and Alaska Native alone-or-in-combination population of all Alaska Native village statistical areas (see Table 6). However, a small proportion of individuals (7,000 out of 66,000) living in Knik identified as American Indian and Alaska Native alone or in combination with another race. Bethel had the second largest American Indian and Alaska Native alone-or-in-combination population (4,000).

The 20 Alaska Native village statistical areas with the largest American Indian and Alaska Native alone population are presented in Figure 7. Bethel and Knik also had the two largest American Indian and Alaska Native alone populations of all Alaska Native village statistical areas (see Figure 7 and Table 6). Both of these villages had about 4,000 people who identified as American Indian and Alaska Native alone.

## PATTERNS AMONG AMERICAN INDIAN AND ALASKA NATIVE TRIBAL GROUPINGS

Table 7 presents data for a number of American Indian and Alaska Native tribal groupings. Data for people who reported only one American Indian and Alaska Native tribal grouping, such as Aleut, are presented in the first data column. Next, data for people who identified with two or more American Indian and Alaska Native tribal groupings, such as Aleut and Inupiat, and no other race group are presented in the second data column. The third data column presents data for people who reported one American Indian and Alaska Native tribal grouping and one or more other races, such as Aleut **and** Black. The fourth data column presents data for people who reported two or more American Indian and Alaska Native tribal groupings and one or more other race groups, such as Aleut, Inupiat, **and** Black.

All of these columns are summed and presented in the last column, American Indian and Alaska Native tribal grouping *alone or in any combination*. Thus, the last column presents the maximum number of people in the selected American Indian and Alaska Native tribal grouping.

## CHANGES TO THE TRIBAL GROUPINGS SINCE CENSUS 2000

Some of the results in this report reflect changes to the composition of selected American Indian and Alaska Native tribal groupings since Census 2000. These changes in tribal groupings were based on specific requests and suggestions from tribal leaders, American Indian advisors, and data users. These suggestions and other research resulted in revisions to the component American Indian tribes that defined a particular tribal grouping. For example, "Hopi" is now a separate tribal grouping, where it was classified under the "Pueblo" tribal grouping in Census 2000. The broad "Latin American Indian" grouping has been replaced by the individual tribal groupings of "Central American Indian," "Mexican American Indian," "South American Indian," and "Spanish American Indian."

For Alaska Natives, there were six tribal groupings in the 2010 Census (see Table 7). Individual "Eskimo" tribal groupings, with the exception of "Yup'ik," shown in Census 2000 are now classified under one tribal grouping ("Inupiat"). "Yup'ik" was included within the 2000 "Eskimo" tribal grouping but became a separate tribal grouping in 2010. "Tlingit-Haida" now includes some Alaska Native tribes that were under "Other specified Alaska Native tribes" in Census 2000.

Comparisons for many tribal groupings across the decade are generally not appropriate due to the multiple changes in the American Indian and Alaska Native tribal groupings between Census 2000 and the 2010 Census. Therefore, discussion of the population change for tribal groupings is not included in this report.

Table 7.

# American Indian and Alaska Native Population by Selected Tribal Groupings: 2010

(For information on confidentiality protection, nonsampling error, and definitions, see *www.census.gov/prod/cen2010/doc/sf1.pdf*)

| Tribal grouping | American Indian and Alaska Native alone | | American Indian and Alaska Native in combination with one or more other races | | American Indian and Alaska Native tribal grouping alone or in any combination[1] |
|---|---|---|---|---|---|
| | One tribal grouping reported | Two or more tribal groupings reported[1] | One tribal grouping reported | Two or more tribal groupings reported[1] | |
| Total ............................... | 2,879,638 | 52,610 | 2,209,267 | 79,064 | 5,220,579 |
| American Indian tribes, specified................... | 1,935,363 | 96,770 | 1,211,938 | 153,180 | 3,397,251 |
| Apache ........................................ | 63,193 | 6,501 | 33,303 | 8,813 | 111,810 |
| Arapaho........................................ | 8,014 | 388 | 2,084 | 375 | 10,861 |
| Blackfeet ...................................... | 27,279 | 4,519 | 54,109 | 19,397 | 105,304 |
| Canadian and French American Indian............... | 6,433 | 618 | 6,981 | 790 | 14,822 |
| Central American Indian ......................... | 15,882 | 572 | 10,865 | 525 | 27,844 |
| Cherokee....................................... | 284,247 | 16,216 | 468,082 | 50,560 | 819,105 |
| Cheyenne ...................................... | 11,375 | 1,118 | 5,311 | 1,247 | 19,051 |
| Chickasaw...................................... | 27,973 | 2,233 | 19,220 | 2,852 | 52,278 |
| Chippewa....................................... | 112,757 | 2,645 | 52,091 | 3,249 | 170,742 |
| Choctaw........................................ | 103,910 | 6,398 | 72,101 | 13,355 | 195,764 |
| Colville........................................ | 8,114 | 200 | 2,148 | 87 | 10,549 |
| Comanche...................................... | 12,284 | 1,187 | 8,131 | 1,728 | 23,330 |
| Cree........................................... | 2,211 | 739 | 4,023 | 1,010 | 7,983 |
| Creek.......................................... | 48,352 | 4,596 | 30,618 | 4,766 | 88,332 |
| Crow .......................................... | 10,332 | 528 | 3,309 | 1,034 | 15,203 |
| Delaware ...................................... | 7,843 | 372 | 9,439 | 610 | 18,264 |
| Hopi........................................... | 12,580 | 2,054 | 3,013 | 680 | 18,327 |
| Houma......................................... | 8,169 | 71 | 2,438 | 90 | 10,768 |
| Iroquois........................................ | 40,570 | 1,891 | 34,490 | 4,051 | 81,002 |
| Kiowa.......................................... | 9,437 | 918 | 2,947 | 485 | 13,787 |
| Lumbee ........................................ | 62,306 | 651 | 10,039 | 695 | 73,691 |
| Menominee ..................................... | 8,374 | 253 | 2,330 | 176 | 11,133 |
| Mexican American Indian ........................ | 121,221 | 2,329 | 49,670 | 2,274 | 175,494 |
| Navajo......................................... | 286,731 | 8,285 | 32,918 | 4,195 | 332,129 |
| Osage ......................................... | 8,938 | 1,125 | 7,090 | 1,423 | 18,576 |
| Ottawa......................................... | 7,272 | 776 | 4,274 | 711 | 13,033 |
| Paiute ......................................... | 9,340 | 865 | 3,135 | 427 | 13,767 |
| Pima .......................................... | 22,040 | 1,165 | 3,116 | 334 | 26,655 |
| Potawatomi .................................... | 20,412 | 462 | 12,249 | 648 | 33,771 |
| Pueblo......................................... | 49,695 | 2,331 | 9,568 | 946 | 62,540 |
| Puget Sound Salish.............................. | 14,320 | 215 | 5,540 | 185 | 20,260 |
| Seminole....................................... | 14,080 | 2,368 | 12,447 | 3,076 | 31,971 |
| Shoshone ...................................... | 7,852 | 610 | 3,969 | 571 | 13,002 |
| Sioux.......................................... | 112,176 | 4,301 | 46,964 | 6,669 | 170,110 |
| South American Indian ........................... | 20,901 | 479 | 25,015 | 838 | 47,233 |
| Spanish American Indian.......................... | 13,460 | 298 | 6,012 | 181 | 19,951 |
| Tohono O'Odham ............................... | 19,522 | 725 | 3,033 | 198 | 23,478 |
| Ute............................................ | 7,435 | 785 | 2,802 | 469 | 11,491 |
| Yakama ........................................ | 8,786 | 310 | 2,207 | 224 | 11,527 |
| Yaqui.......................................... | 21,679 | 1,516 | 8,183 | 1,217 | 32,595 |
| Yuman ......................................... | 7,727 | 551 | 1,642 | 169 | 10,089 |
| All other American Indian tribes ................... | 270,141 | 12,606 | 135,032 | 11,850 | 429,629 |
| American Indian tribes, not specified[2]............... | 131,943 | 117 | 102,188 | 72 | 234,320 |
| Alaska Native tribes, specified..................... | 98,892 | 4,194 | 32,992 | 2,772 | 138,850 |
| Alaskan Athabascan ............................ | 15,623 | 804 | 5,531 | 526 | 22,484 |
| Aleut .......................................... | 11,920 | 723 | 6,108 | 531 | 19,282 |
| Inupiat ......................................... | 24,859 | 877 | 7,051 | 573 | 33,360 |
| Tlingit-Haida ................................... | 15,256 | 859 | 9,331 | 634 | 26,080 |
| Tsimshian ...................................... | 2,307 | 240 | 1,010 | 198 | 3,755 |
| Yup'ik.......................................... | 28,927 | 691 | 3,961 | 310 | 33,889 |
| Alaska Native tribes, not specified[3] ................ | 19,731 | 173 | 9,896 | 133 | 29,933 |
| American Indian or Alaska Native tribes, not specified[4] .. | 693,709 | – | 852,253 | 1 | 1,545,963 |

– Represents zero.

[1] The numbers by American Indian and Alaska Native tribal grouping do not add to the total American Indian and Alaska Native population. This is because the American Indian and Alaska Native tribal groupings are tallies of the number of American Indian and Alaska Native *responses* rather than the number of American Indian or Alaska Native *respondents*. Respondents reporting several American Indian or Alaska Native groups are counted several times. For example, a respondent reporting "Cherokee and Navajo" would be included in the Cherokee as well as the Navajo numbers.

[2] Includes respondents who wrote in an American Indian tribe not specified in the American Indian and Alaska Native Tribal Detailed Classification List for the 2010 Census or wrote in the generic term "American Indian."

[3] Includes respondents who wrote in an Alaska Native tribe not specified in the American Indian and Alaska Native Tribal Detailed Classification List for the 2010 Census or wrote in the generic term "Alaska Native."

[4] Includes respondents who checked the "American Indian or Alaska Native" response category on the census questionnaire.

Source: U.S. Census Bureau, 2010 Census special tabulation.

Figure 8.
**Percentage Distribution of the Largest American Indian Tribal Groupings by Response Type: 2010**
(For information on confidentiality protection, nonsampling error, and definitions, see www.census.gov/prod/cen2010/doc/sf1.pdf)

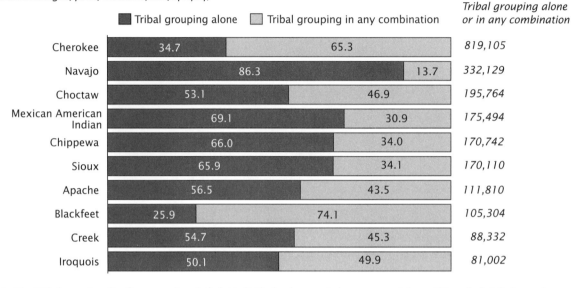

■ Tribal grouping alone  ☐ Tribal grouping in any combination

*Tribal grouping alone or in any combination*

| | Tribal grouping alone | Tribal grouping in any combination | Tribal grouping alone or in any combination |
|---|---|---|---|
| Cherokee | 34.7 | 65.3 | 819,105 |
| Navajo | 86.3 | 13.7 | 332,129 |
| Choctaw | 53.1 | 46.9 | 195,764 |
| Mexican American Indian | 69.1 | 30.9 | 175,494 |
| Chippewa | 66.0 | 34.0 | 170,742 |
| Sioux | 65.9 | 34.1 | 170,110 |
| Apache | 56.5 | 43.5 | 111,810 |
| Blackfeet | 25.9 | 74.1 | 105,304 |
| Creek | 54.7 | 45.3 | 88,332 |
| Iroquois | 50.1 | 49.9 | 81,002 |

Note: The "Tribal grouping alone" response type includes individuals who reported one or more tribes within a single tribal grouping. The "Tribal grouping in any combination" response type includes individuals who reported one or more other races and/or tribal groupings.

Source: U.S. Census Bureau, *2010 Census Summary File 1.*

**The Cherokee tribal grouping had the largest American Indian population in 2010.**

In the 2010 Census, the American Indian and Alaska Native alone-or-in-any-combination tribal groupings with 100,000 or more responses were Cherokee, Navajo, Choctaw, Mexican American Indian, Chippewa, Sioux, Apache, and Blackfeet (see Table 7). The Cherokee tribal grouping had the largest alone-or-in-any-combination population, with 819,000.

The Cherokee tribal grouping had the highest number of individuals who identified with one tribal grouping in combination with multiple races (468,000). Choctaw had the second-highest number of individuals (72,000) who identified with one tribal grouping together with multiple races. With over 50,000 respondents, Cherokee also had the highest number of individuals who identified with multiple

tribal groupings, and who also identified with multiple races.

The Navajo tribal grouping had the highest number of individuals (287,000) who identified with one tribal grouping and no other race. The Cherokee tribal grouping had the second-highest number of individuals (284,000) who identified with one tribal grouping and no other race.

The Cherokee tribal grouping had the highest number of individuals (16,000) who reported multiple tribal groupings but did not report an additional race. The Navajo tribal grouping had the second-highest number of individuals (8,000) who reported multiple tribal groupings but did not report an additional race.

**Of the largest American Indian tribal groupings, Blackfeet had the highest proportion of respondents who reported more than one tribal grouping and/or race.**

Among the largest American Indian tribal groupings, the proportion of respondents who reported at least one other race or tribal grouping varied (see Figure 8 and Table 7). The Blackfeet tribal grouping had the highest proportion of respondents who reported more than one tribal grouping or race. Almost three-fourths (74 percent) of all individuals in the Blackfeet tribal grouping reported an additional race and/or tribal grouping.

The tribal groupings with the next two highest percentages with more than one tribal grouping or race were Cherokee (65 percent) and Iroquois (50 percent). Navajo had the lowest proportion (14 percent) of respondents who identified with another tribal grouping and/or race.

Figure 9.
**Percentage Distribution of Alaska Native Tribal Groupings by Response Type: 2010**
(For information on confidentiality protection, nonsampling error, and definitions, see
*www.census.gov/prod/cen2010/doc/sf1.pdf*)

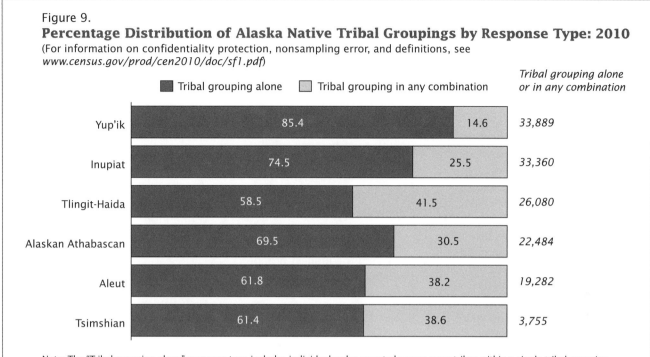

*Tribal grouping alone or in any combination*

| | Tribal grouping alone | Tribal grouping in any combination | Tribal grouping alone or in any combination |
|---|---|---|---|
| Yup'ik | 85.4 | 14.6 | 33,889 |
| Inupiat | 74.5 | 25.5 | 33,360 |
| Tlingit-Haida | 58.5 | 41.5 | 26,080 |
| Alaskan Athabascan | 69.5 | 30.5 | 22,484 |
| Aleut | 61.8 | 38.2 | 19,282 |
| Tsimshian | 61.4 | 38.6 | 3,755 |

Note: The "Tribal grouping alone" response type includes individuals who reported one or more tribes within a single tribal grouping. The "Tribal grouping in any combination" response type includes individuals who reported one or more other races and/or tribal groupings.
Source: U.S. Census Bureau, *2010 Census Summary File 1.*

## PATTERNS AMONG ALASKA NATIVE TRIBAL GROUPINGS

**The Yup'ik tribal grouping and the Inupiat tribal grouping had the largest Alaska Native alone and Alaska Native alone-or-in-any combination populations.**

Table 7 presents data for the six Alaska Native tribal groupings. The Yup'ik tribal grouping contained the greatest number of people (29,000) who identified with one tribal grouping and did not report another race. The Inupiat tribal grouping had the highest number of individuals (900) who identified with multiple tribal groupings, but did not identify with one or more additional races.[22]

[22] The term "Inupiat" is used in the 2010 Census to classify responses (other than Yup'ik) that were classified in previous censuses as "Eskimo."

The two largest Alaska Native alone-or-in-any-combination tribal grouping populations were Yup'ik (34,000) and Inupiat (33,000). The third-largest tribal grouping was Tlingit-Haida, followed by the Alaskan Athabascan tribal grouping and the Aleut tribal grouping. Tsimshians (4,000) had the smallest alone-or-in-any-combination tribal grouping population size.

The Tlingit-Haida tribal grouping had the most individuals (9,000) who identified with multiple races but did not report any additional tribal groupings. The Tlingit-Haida tribal grouping also had the highest number of people (600) who identified with multiple tribal groupings as well as with one or more additional races.

**The Yup'ik tribal grouping had the largest Alaska Native population.**

The majority of Alaska Natives reported only one tribal grouping (see Table 7 and Figure 9). The Yup'ik tribal grouping had the highest proportion of people reporting one tribal grouping alone and no other race (85 percent), followed by the Inupiat tribal grouping (75 percent). On the other hand, the Tlingit-Haida population had the highest proportion (42 percent) of people who identified with more than one tribal grouping and/or another race.

## SUMMARY

This report provides a portrait of the American Indian and Alaska Native population and contributes to our understanding of the nation's changing ethnic and racial diversity.

While both the American Indian and Alaska Native alone and the American Indian and Alaska Native alone-or-in-combination populations grew from 2000 to 2010 (by 18 percent and 27 percent, respectively), the American Indian and Alaska Native in combination population experienced greater growth, increasing by 39 percent. Within this population, the American Indian and Alaska Native **and** White **and** Black population more than doubled in size.

Other notable trends were that the American Indian and Alaska Native population continued to be concentrated in the West and South and increased in these regions between 2000 and 2010. Additionally, concentrations of American Indians tended to be proximate to American Indian and Alaska Native areas.

Other interesting points noted in the report were that a majority of the American Indian and Alaska Native alone-or-in-combination population (78 percent) lived outside of American Indian and Alaska Native areas. This compares with 67 percent of the American Indian and Alaska Native alone population and with 92 percent of the American Indian and Alaska Native in combination population that lived outside of American Indian and Alaska Native areas in 2010.

Of all people that lived in American Indian areas, 3.5 million out of 4.6 million (77 percent) did not identify as American Indian and Alaska Native. Of the people that lived in Alaska Native village statistical areas, 164,000 out of 243,000 (68 percent) did not identify as American Indian and Alaska Native.

In terms of American Indian tribal groupings, the Cherokee tribal grouping and the Navajo tribal grouping had the two largest American Indian alone-or-in-any combination populations in 2010. Of the largest American Indian tribal groupings, the Blackfeet tribal grouping had the highest proportion of respondents who reported more than one tribal grouping and/or race.

In terms of Alaska Native tribal groupings, the Yup'ik tribal grouping and the Inupiat tribal grouping had the two largest Alaska Native alone and Alaska Native alone-or-in-any combination populations. Among the Alaska Native tribal groupings, Tlingit-Haida had the largest proportion of respondents who reported more than one tribal grouping and/or race.

Throughout the decade, the Census Bureau will release additional information on the American Indian and Alaska Native population, including characteristics such as age, sex, and family type, which will provide greater insights to the demographic characteristics of this population at various geographic levels.

## ABOUT THE 2010 CENSUS

### Why was the 2010 Census conducted?

The U.S. Constitution mandates that a census be taken in the United States every 10 years. This is required in order to determine the number of seats each state is to receive in the U.S. House of Representatives.

### Why did the 2010 Census ask the question on race?

The Census Bureau collects data on race to fulfill a variety of legislative and program requirements. Data on race are used in the legislative redistricting process carried out by the states and in monitoring local jurisdictions' compliance with the Voting Rights Act. More broadly, data on race are critical for research that underlies many policy decisions at all levels of government.

### How do data from the question on race benefit me, my family, and my community?

All levels of government need information on race to implement and evaluate programs or enforce laws, such as the Civil Rights Act, Voting Rights Act, Fair Housing Act, Equal Employment Opportunity Act, and the 2010 Census Redistricting Data Program.

Both public and private organizations use race information to find areas where groups may need special services and to plan and implement education, housing, health, and other programs that address these needs. For example, a school system might use this information to design cultural activities that reflect the diversity in their community, or a business could use it to select the mix of merchandise it will sell in a new store. Census information also helps identify areas where residents might need services of particular importance to certain racial groups, such as screening for hypertension or diabetes.

## FOR MORE INFORMATION

For more information on race in the United States, visit the Census Bureau's Internet site at <www.census.gov/population /race>.

Information on confidentiality protection, nonsampling error, and definitions is available at <www.census.gov/prod/cen2010 /doc/pl94-171.pdf>.

Data on race from the *2010 Census Redistricting Data (Public Law 94-171) Summary File* and the *2010 Census Summary File 1* were released on a state-by-state basis. The 2010 Census redistricting data

are available on the Internet at <http://factfinder2.census.gov /main.html>.

For more information on specific race groups in the United States, go to <www.census.gov> and search for "Minority Links." This Web page includes information about the 2010 Census and provides links to reports based on past censuses and surveys focusing on the social and economic characteristics of the Black or African American, American Indian and Alaska Native, Asian, and Native Hawaiian and Other Pacific Islander populations.

Information on other population and housing topics is presented

in the 2010 Census Briefs series, located on the Census Bureau's Web site at <www.census.gov/prod /cen2010>. This series presents information about race, Hispanic origin, age, sex, household type, and housing tenure.

For more information about the 2010 Census, including data products, call the Customer Services Center at 1-800-923-8282. You can also visit the Census Bureau's Question and Answer Center at <ask.census.gov> to submit your questions online.

# The Asian Population: 2010

*2010 Census Briefs*

Issued March 2012

C2010BR-11

By
Elizabeth M. Hoeffel,
Sonya Rastogi,
Myoung Ouk Kim,
and
Hasan Shahid

## INTRODUCTION

According to the 2010 Census, the Asian population grew faster than any other race group in the United States between 2000 and 2010. This was observed for the population who reported Asian alone (increased 43 percent), as well as for the population who reported Asian alone or in combination with another race (increased 46 percent). The Asian population continued to be concentrated in the West, and the Chinese population was the largest detailed Asian group.

This report provides a portrait of the Asian population in the United States and discusses that population's distribution at the national level and at lower levels of geography.[1]  It is part of a series that analyzes population and housing data collected from the 2010 Census.

The data for this report are based on the *2010 Census Redistricting Data (Public Law 94-171) Summary File*, which was the first 2010 Census data product released with data on race and Hispanic origin, including information on the Asian population, and was provided to each state for use in drawing boundaries for legislative districts.[2]  Data for this report also come from the *2010 Census Summary File 1*, which was one of the first 2010 Census

Figure 1.
**Reproduction of the Question on Race From the 2010 Census**

6. **What is this person's race?** *Mark* X *one or more boxes.*
- White
- Black, African Am., or Negro
- American Indian or Alaska Native — *Print name of enrolled or principal tribe.*

- Asian Indian
- Chinese
- Filipino
- Japanese
- Korean
- Vietnamese
- Native Hawaiian
- Guamanian or Chamorro
- Samoan
- Other Asian — *Print race, for example, Hmong, Laotian, Thai, Pakistani, Cambodian, and so on.*
- Other Pacific Islander — *Print race, for example, Fijian, Tongan, and so on.*

- Some other race — *Print race.*

Source: U.S. Census Bureau, 2010 Census questionnaire.

data products to provide information on selected detailed groups, such as Asian Indians, Koreans, and Filipinos.[3]

## UNDERSTANDING RACE DATA FROM THE 2010 CENSUS

**The 2010 Census used federal standards to collect and present data on race.**

For the 2010 Census, the question on race was asked of individuals living in the United States (see Figure 1). An individual's response to the race question was based upon self-identification. The U.S. Census Bureau collects information on race following the guidance of the U.S. Office of Management and Budget's (OMB)

---

[1] This report discusses data for the 50 states and the District of Columbia, but not Puerto Rico.
[2] Information on the *2010 Census Redistricting Data (Public Law 94-171) Summary File* is available online at <http://2010.census.gov/2010census/data/redistricting-data.php>.

[3] Information on the *2010 Census Summary File 1* is available online at <http://2010.census.gov/news/press-kits/summary-file-1.html>.

U.S. Department of Commerce
Economics and Statistics Administration
U.S. CENSUS BUREAU

1997 *Revisions to the Standards for the Classification of Federal Data on Race and Ethnicity.*[4] These federal standards mandate that race and Hispanic origin (ethnicity) are separate and distinct concepts and that when collecting these data via self-identification, two different questions must be used.[5]

Starting in 1997, OMB required federal agencies to use a minimum of five race categories: White, Black or African American, American Indian or Alaska Native, Asian, and Native Hawaiian or Other Pacific Islander. For respondents unable to identify with any of these five race categories, OMB approved the Census Bureau's inclusion of a sixth category—Some Other Race—on the Census 2000 and 2010 Census questionnaires. The 1997 OMB standards also allowed for respondents to identify with more than one race. The definition of the Asian racial category used in the 2010 Census is presented in the text box on this page.

Data on race have been collected since the first U.S. decennial census in 1790, but no distinction was made for people of Asian descent. In 1860, the first Asian response category ("Chinese") was added to the question on race in California only and in other states beginning in 1870. A second Asian response category ("Japanese") was included for the first time

---

[4] The 1997 *Revisions to the Standards for the Classification of Federal Data on Race and Ethnicity*, issued by OMB, is available at <www.whitehouse.gov /omb/fedreg_1997standards>.

[5] The OMB requires federal agencies to use a minimum of two ethnicities: Hispanic or Latino and Not Hispanic or Latino. Hispanic origin can be viewed as the heritage, nationality group, lineage, or country of birth of the person or the person's parents or ancestors before their arrival in the United States. People who identify their origin as Hispanic, Latino, or Spanish may be of any race. "Hispanic or Latino" refers to a person of Cuban, Mexican, Puerto Rican, South or Central American, or other Spanish culture or origin regardless of race.

---

## DEFINITION OF ASIAN USED IN THE 2010 CENSUS

According to OMB, "Asian" refers to a person having origins in any of the original peoples of the Far East, Southeast Asia, or the Indian subcontinent, including, for example, Cambodia, China, India, Japan, Korea, Malaysia, Pakistan, the Philippine Islands, Thailand, and Vietnam.

The Asian population includes people who indicated their race(s) as "Asian" or reported entries such as "Asian Indian," "Chinese," "Filipino," "Korean," "Japanese," and "Vietnamese" or provided other detailed Asian responses.

---

in the 1870 Census in California only and in other states starting in 1890. Additional Asian response categories were collected intermittently in the question on race over the course of seven censuses, from the 1920 Census to the 1980 Census. The use of six detailed Asian response categories in the decennial census question on race has remained unchanged since the 1980 Census (Asian Indian, Chinese, Filipino, Japanese, Korean, and Vietnamese).

Beginning with the 1910 Census, reports of detailed Asian groups that did not have separate response categories in the race question were tabulated from a general "Other" write-in area. In the 1990 Census, a write-in area was introduced that was solely dedicated to the reporting of detailed Asian groups or detailed Native Hawaiian and Other Pacific Islander groups that did not have a separate response category. A shared write-in area for reports of detailed Asian groups or detailed Native Hawaiian and Other Pacific Islander groups that did not have specific response categories in the race question continued for Census 2000 and the 2010 Census.[6]

[6] For information about comparability of 2010 Census data with race and Hispanic origin to data collected in previous censuses, see the *2010 Census Redistricting Data (Public Law 94-171) Summary File—Technical Documentation* at <www.census.gov/prod /cen2010/doc/pl94-171.pdf>.

In Census 2000, for the first time, individuals were presented with the option to self-identify with more than one race, and this continued with the 2010 Census, as prescribed by OMB. There are 57 possible multiple-race combinations involving the five OMB race categories and Some Other Race.[7]

The 2010 Census question on race included 15 separate response categories and three areas where respondents could write in detailed information about their race (see Figure 1).[8] The response categories and write-in answers can be combined to create the five minimum OMB race categories plus Some Other Race. In addition to White, Black or African American, American Indian and Alaska Native, and Some Other Race, 7 of the

---

[7] The 2010 Census provides information on the population reporting more than one race, as well as detailed race combinations (e.g., Asian *and* White; Asian *and* White *and* Native Hawaiian and Other Pacific Islander). In this report, the multiple-race categories are denoted with the conjunction *and* in bold and italicized print to indicate the separate race groups that constitute the particular combination.

[8] There were two changes to the question on race for the 2010 Census. First, the wording of the race question was changed from "What is this person's race? Mark ☒ one or more races to indicate what this person considers himself/herself to be" in 2000 to "What is this person's race? Mark ☒ one or more boxes" for 2010. Second, in 2010, examples were added to the "Other Asian" response category (Hmong, Laotian, Thai, Pakistani, Cambodian, and so on) and the "Other Pacific Islander" response category (Fijian, Tongan, and so on). In 2000, no examples were given in the race question.

15 response categories are Asian groups, and 4 are Native Hawaiian and Other Pacific Islander groups.[9] The 7 Asian response categories are Asian Indian, Chinese, Filipino, Japanese, Korean, Vietnamese, and Other Asian.

For a complete explanation of the race categories used in the 2010 Census, see the 2010 Census Brief, *Overview of Race and Hispanic Origin: 2010*.[10]

## RACE ALONE, RACE IN COMBINATION, AND RACE ALONE-OR-IN-COMBINATION CONCEPTS

This report presents data for the Asian population and focuses on results for three major conceptual groups.

First, people who responded to the question on race by indicating only one race are referred to as the *race alone* population, or the group who reported *only one* race. For example, respondents who reported a single detailed Asian group, such as "Asian Indian" or "Korean," would be included in the *Asian alone* population. Respondents who reported more than one detailed Asian group, such as "Asian Indian" and "Korean" would also be included in the *Asian alone* population. This is because the detailed groups in the example combination are part of the larger Asian race category. The *Asian alone* population can be viewed as the minimum number of people reporting Asian.

Second, individuals who chose more than one of the six race categories are referred to as the *race in combination* population, or as the group who reported *more than one race*. For example, respondents who reported they were Asian **and** White or reported they were Asian **and** White **and** Native Hawaiian and Other Pacific Islander would be included in the *Asian in combination* population. This population is also referred to as the *multiple-race Asian* population.

Third, the maximum number of people reporting Asian is reflected in the *Asian alone-or-in-combination* population. One way to define the Asian population is to combine those respondents who reported *Asian alone* with those who reported *Asian in combination* with one or more other races. The addition of these two groups creates the *Asian alone-or-in-combination* population. Another way to think of the *Asian alone-or-in-combination* population is the total number of people who reported Asian, whether or not they reported any other race(s).

Throughout the report, the discussion of the Asian population includes results for each of these groups and highlights the diversity within the entire Asian population.[11]

## THE ASIAN POPULATION: A SNAPSHOT

The 2010 Census showed that the U.S. population on April 1, 2010, was 308.7 million. Out of the total U.S. population, 14.7 million

people, or 4.8 percent, were Asian alone (see Table 1). In addition, 2.6 million people, or another 0.9 percent, reported Asian in combination with one or more other races.[12] Together, these two groups totaled 17.3 million people. Thus, 5.6 percent of all people in the United States identified as Asian, either alone or in combination with one or more other races.

**The Asian population increased more than four times faster than the total U.S. population.**

The total U.S. population grew by 9.7 percent, from 281.4 million in 2000 to 308.7 million in 2010 (see Table 1). In comparison, the Asian alone population increased more than four times faster than the total U.S. population, growing by 43 percent from 10.2 million to 14.7 million.[13, 14]

The Asian alone-or-in-combination population experienced slightly more growth than the Asian alone population, growing by 46 percent from 11.9 million in 2000 to 17.3 million in 2010. In fact, the Asian population grew at a faster

---

[9] The race categories included in the census questionnaire generally reflect a social definition of race recognized in this country and are not an attempt to define race biologically, anthropologically, or genetically. In addition, it is recognized that the categories of the race question include race and national origin or sociocultural groups.

[10] Humes, K., N. Jones, and R. Ramirez. 2011. *Overview of Race and Hispanic Origin: 2010*, U.S. Census Bureau, 2010 Census Briefs, C2010BR-02, available at <www.census.gov/prod/cen2010/briefs /c2010br-02.pdf>.

[11] As a matter of policy, the Census Bureau does not advocate the use of the *alone* population over the *alone-or-in-combination* population or vice versa. The use of the *alone* population in sections of this report does not imply that it is a preferred method of presenting or analyzing data. The same is true for sections of this report that focus on the *alone-or-in-combination* population. Data on race from the 2010 Census can be presented and discussed in a variety of ways.

[12] For the purposes of this report, the terms "reported," "identified," and "classified" are used interchangeably to refer to the response provided by respondents as well as responses assigned during the editing and imputation process.

[13] Percentages shown in text generally are rounded to the nearest integer, while those shown in tables and figures are shown with decimals. All rounding is based on unrounded calculations. Thus, due to rounding, some percentages shown in tables and figures ending in "5" may round either up or down. For example, unrounded numbers of 14.49 and 14.51 would both be shown as 14.5 in a table, but would be cited in the text as 14 and 15, respectively.

[14] The observed changes in the race counts between Census 2000 and the 2010 Census could be attributed to a number of factors. Demographic change since 2000, which includes births and deaths in a geographic area and migration in and out of a geographic area, will have an impact on the resulting 2010 Census counts. Additionally, some changes in the race question's wording and format since Census 2000 could have influenced reporting patterns in the 2010 Census.

Table 1.
## Asian Population: 2000 and 2010
(For information on confidentiality protection, nonsampling error, and definitions, see *www.census.gov/prod/cen2010/doc/pl94-171.pdf*)

| Race | 2000 | | 2010 | | Change, 2000 to 2010 | |
|---|---|---|---|---|---|---|
| | Number | Percentage of total population | Number | Percentage of total population | Number | Percent |
| Total population.......................... | 281,421,906 | 100.0 | 308,745,538 | 100.0 | 27,323,632 | 9.7 |
| Asian alone or in combination..................... | 11,898,828 | 4.2 | 17,320,856 | 5.6 | 5,422,028 | 45.6 |
| Asian alone .................................... | 10,242,998 | 3.6 | 14,674,252 | 4.8 | 4,431,254 | 43.3 |
| Asian in combination ........................... | 1,655,830 | 0.6 | 2,646,604 | 0.9 | 990,774 | 59.8 |
| Asian; White................................ | 868,395 | 0.3 | 1,623,234 | 0.5 | 754,839 | 86.9 |
| Asian; Some Other Race ..................... | 249,108 | 0.1 | 234,462 | 0.1 | -14,646 | –5.9 |
| Asian; Black or African American............... | 106,782 | – | 185,595 | 0.1 | 78,813 | 73.8 |
| Asian; Native Hawaiian and Other Pacific Islander. . | 138,802 | – | 165,690 | 0.1 | 26,888 | 19.4 |
| Asian; White; Native Hawaiian and Other Pacific Islander................................ | 89,611 | – | 143,126 | – | 53,515 | 59.7 |
| All other combinations including Asian........... | 203,132 | 0.1 | 294,497 | 0.1 | 91,365 | 45.0 |
| Not Asian alone or in combination.................. | 269,523,078 | 95.8 | 291,424,682 | 94.4 | 21,901,604 | 8.1 |

– Percentage rounds to 0.0.

Note: In Census 2000, an error in data processing resulted in an overstatement of the Two or More Races population by about 1 million people (about 15 percent) nationally, which almost entirely affected race combinations involving Some Other Race. Therefore, data users should assess observed changes in race combinations involving Some Other Race between Census 2000 and the 2010 Census with caution. Changes in specific race combinations not involving Some Other Race, such as Asian *and* White or Asian *and* Black or African American, generally should be more comparable.

Sources: U.S. Census Bureau, *Census 2000 Redistricting Data (Public Law 94-171) Summary File,* Table PL1; and *2010 Census Redistricting Data (Public Law 94-171) Summary File,* Table P1.

rate than all race groups in the country.[15]

## MULTIPLE-RACE REPORTING AMONG THE ASIAN POPULATION

### About 15 percent of the Asian population reported multiple races.

Of the 17.3 million people who reported Asian, 14.7 million or 85 percent, identified as Asian alone (see Table 1). An additional 2.6 million people reported Asian in combination with one or more additional races, representing about 15 percent of the Asian alone-or-in-combination population. Of the five OMB race groups, the Asian

population had the third-largest percentage reporting more than one race.[16]

### Asians who reported multiple races grew at a faster rate than the Asian alone population.

From 2000 to 2010, the Asian multiple-race population grew by about 1 million people. The multiple-race Asian population grew at a faster rate than the Asian alone population, growing by 60 percent in size since 2000 (see Table 1).

### Among Asians, the largest multiple-race combination was Asian *and* White.

Among the 2.6 million people who reported they were Asian and one or more additional races, the majority (1.6 million or 61 percent) identified as Asian *and* White (see Figure 2). The next largest

combinations were Asian *and* Some Other Race (9 percent), Asian *and* Black (7 percent), Asian *and* Native Hawaiian and Other Pacific Islander (6 percent), and Asian *and* White *and* Native Hawaiian and Other Pacific Islander (5 percent).[17] Together, these five combinations accounted for nearly 90 percent of all Asians who reported multiple races.

### The Asian *and* White population contributed to most of the growth among Asians who reported multiple races.

Among people who reported their race as Asian and one or more additional races, those who reported Asian *and* White grew by 87 percent, nearly doubling in size from 868,000 in 2000 to 1.6 million in 2010 (see Table 1). The Asian *and* White population represented the greatest increase in the multiple-race Asian population. The Asian *and* White population's share of all

---

[15] Information on national-level 2010 Census redistricting data (Public Law 94-171) for race groups is available online at <http://2010.census.gov/news/press-kits /redistricting.html>.

[16] Humes, K., N. Jones, and R. Ramirez. 2011. *Overview of Race and Hispanic Origin: 2010*, U.S. Census Bureau, 2010 Census Briefs, C2010BR-02, available at <www.census.gov/prod/cen2010/briefs /c2010br-02.pdf>.

[17] The terms "Black" and "Black or African American" are used interchangeably in this report.

Figure 2.
## Percentage Distribution of the Asian in Combination Population: 2000 and 2010

(For information on confidentiality protection, nonsampling error, and definitions, see *www.census.gov/prod/cen2010/doc/pl94-171.pdf*)

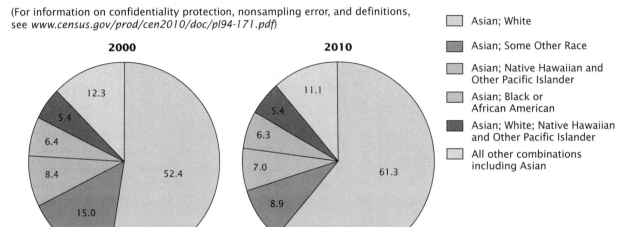

**2000**

12.3
5.4
6.4
8.4
15.0
52.4

**2010**

11.1
5.4
6.3
7.0
8.9
61.3

Legend:
- Asian; White
- Asian; Some Other Race
- Asian; Native Hawaiian and Other Pacific Islander
- Asian; Black or African American
- Asian; White; Native Hawaiian and Other Pacific Islander
- All other combinations including Asian

Note: In Census 2000, an error in data processing resulted in an overstatement of the Two or More Races population by about 1 million people (about 15 percent) nationally, which almost entirely affected race combinations involving Some Other Race. Therefore, data users should assess observed changes in the Two or More Races population and race combinations involving Some Other Race between Census 2000 and the 2010 Census with caution. Changes in specific race combinations not involving Some Other Race, such as Asian *and* White or Asian *and* Black or African American, generally should be more comparable. Percentages may not add to 100.0 due to rounding.

Sources: U.S. Census Bureau, *Census 2000 Redistricting Data (Public Law 94-171) Summary File*, Table PL1; and *2010 Census Redistricting Data (Public Law 94-171) Summary File*, Table P1.

multiple-race Asians also increased substantially, from 52 percent to 61 percent (see Figure 2).

The Asian *and* Native Hawaiian and Other Pacific Islander population's share of the multiple-race Asian population decreased from 8 percent in 2000 to 6 percent in 2010. The Asian *and* Black population's share of the Asian multiple-race population increased from 6 percent to 7 percent. The proportion of the Asian *and* White *and* Native Hawaiian and Other Pacific Islander population remained at 5 percent.

The Asian *and* Some Other Race population decreased from 2000 to 2010. This decrease was likely due to a data processing error in the Two or More Races population, which largely affected the combinations that included Some Other Race, overstating the Asian *and* Some Other Race population in 2000.[18]

---

[18] In Census 2000, an error in data processing resulted in an overstatement of the Two or More Races population by about 1 million people (about 15 percent) nationally, which almost entirely affected race combinations involving Some Other Race. Therefore, data users should assess observed changes in race combinations involving Some Other Race between Census 2000 and the 2010 Census with caution. Changes in specific race combinations not involving Some Other Race, such as Asian *and* White, generally are more comparable.

## THE GEOGRAPHIC DISTRIBUTION OF THE ASIAN POPULATION

**The Asian population was heavily concentrated in the West.**

In the 2010 Census, of all respondents who reported Asian alone or in combination, 46 percent lived in the West (see Figure 3). An additional 22 percent lived in the South, 20 percent in the Northeast, and 12 percent in the Midwest. This pattern was similar for the Asian alone population.

Figure 3.

**Percentage Distribution of the Asian Population by Region: 2000 and 2010**

(For information on confidentiality protection, nonsampling error, and definitions, see *www.census.gov/prod/cen2010/doc/pl94-171.pdf*)

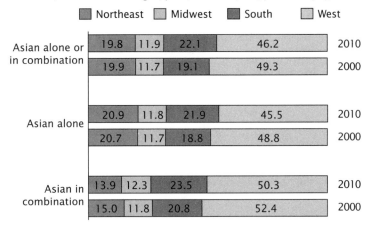

Northeast    Midwest    South    West

| | | | | |
|---|---|---|---|---|
| Asian alone or in combination | 19.8 | 11.9 | 22.1 | 46.2 | 2010 |
| | 19.9 | 11.7 | 19.1 | 49.3 | 2000 |
| Asian alone | 20.9 | 11.8 | 21.9 | 45.5 | 2010 |
| | 20.7 | 11.7 | 18.8 | 48.8 | 2000 |
| Asian in combination | 13.9 | 12.3 | 23.5 | 50.3 | 2010 |
| | 15.0 | 11.8 | 20.8 | 52.4 | 2000 |

Note: Percentages may not add to 100.0 due to rounding.

Sources: U.S. Census Bureau, *Census 2000 Redistricting Data (Public Law 94-171) Summary File*, Table PL1; and *2010 Census Redistricting Data (Public Law 94-171) Summary File*, Table P1.

**Among all regions, Asians constituted the greatest proportion of the region's total population in the West.**

Among all regions, Asians constituted the greatest proportion of the region's total population in the West, at 11 percent (see Table 2).[19] In other regions, the Asian alone-or-in-combination population was a smaller proportion—6 percent of the Northeast and 3 percent of both the South and Midwest. This pattern was similar for the Asian alone population.

[19] The Northeast census region includes Connecticut, Maine, Massachusetts, New Hampshire, New Jersey, New York, Pennsylvania, Rhode Island, and Vermont. The Midwest census region includes Illinois, Indiana, Iowa, Kansas, Michigan, Minnesota, Missouri, Nebraska, North Dakota, Ohio, South Dakota, and Wisconsin. The South census region includes Alabama, Arkansas, Delaware, the District of Columbia, Florida, Georgia, Kentucky, Louisiana, Maryland, Mississippi, North Carolina, Oklahoma, South Carolina, Tennessee, Texas, Virginia, and West Virginia. The West census region includes Alaska, Arizona, California, Colorado, Hawaii, Idaho, Montana, Nevada, New Mexico, Oregon, Utah, Washington, and Wyoming.

**The proportion of Asians declined in the West and increased in the South.**

The proportion of all respondents who reported Asian alone or in combination stayed about the same for the Northeast and Midwest, while the proportions for the South and West changed by 3 percentage points each from 2000 to 2010 (see Figure 3). The proportion of the Asian alone-or-in-combination population living in the South increased from 19 percent to 22 percent, while the proportion living in the West declined from 49 percent to 46 percent. These changes were similar for the Asian alone population.

**When comparing the Asian alone population with the Asian in combination population, the largest differences were found in the proportions living in the West and the Northeast.**

In 2010, 50 percent of the Asian in combination population lived in the West compared with 46 percent of the Asian alone population (see Figure 3). A larger share of the Asian alone population lived in the Northeast (21 percent) compared with the Asian in combination population (14 percent). In the South and Midwest, the differences between the Asian in combination and Asian alone populations were smaller.

**The proportions of the Asian in combination population decreased in the West and Northeast and increased in the South.**

The proportions of multiple-race Asians decreased in the West and Northeast and increased in the South (see Figure 3). In 2000, 52 percent of the Asian in combination population lived in the West, decreasing to 50 percent in 2010. The Asian in combination population increased in the South from 21 percent to 23 percent. The proportion decreased slightly in the Northeast from 15 percent to 14 percent.

**The Asian population grew in every region between 2000 and 2010, experiencing the fastest growth in the South.**

The Asian alone-or-in-combination population grew in every region between 2000 and 2010, growing the fastest in the South (69 percent), followed by the Midwest (48 percent), Northeast (45 percent), and West (36 percent) (see Table 2). These patterns were fairly similar for the Asian alone population.

In comparison, the Asian in combination population grew by 80 percent in the South, followed by the Midwest (66 percent), West (54 percent), and Northeast (48 percent).

Table 2.
## Asian Population for the United States, Regions, and States, and for Puerto Rico: 2000 and 2010

(For information on confidentiality protection, nonsampling error, and definitions, see *www.census.gov/prod/cen2010/doc/pl94-171.pdf*)

| Area | Asian alone or in combination | | | | Asian alone | | | | Asian in combination | | | |
|---|---|---|---|---|---|---|---|---|---|---|---|---|
| | 2000 | 2010 | Percentage of total population, 2010[1] | Percent change | 2000 | 2010 | Percentage of total population, 2010[1] | Percent change | 2000 | 2010 | Percentage of total population, 2010[1] | Percent change |
| United States .. | 11,898,828 | 17,320,856 | 5.6 | 45.6 | 10,242,998 | 14,674,252 | 4.8 | 43.3 | 1,655,830 | 2,646,604 | 0.9 | 59.8 |
| **REGION** | | | | | | | | | | | | |
| Northeast......... | 2,368,297 | 3,428,624 | 6.2 | 44.8 | 2,119,426 | 3,060,773 | 5.5 | 44.4 | 248,871 | 367,851 | 0.7 | 47.8 |
| Midwest.......... | 1,392,938 | 2,053,971 | 3.1 | 47.5 | 1,197,554 | 1,729,059 | 2.6 | 44.4 | 195,384 | 324,912 | 0.5 | 66.3 |
| South............ | 2,267,094 | 3,835,242 | 3.3 | 69.2 | 1,922,407 | 3,213,470 | 2.8 | 67.2 | 344,687 | 621,772 | 0.5 | 80.4 |
| West ............ | 5,870,499 | 8,003,019 | 11.1 | 36.3 | 5,003,611 | 6,670,950 | 9.3 | 33.3 | 866,888 | 1,332,069 | 1.9 | 53.7 |
| **STATE** | | | | | | | | | | | | |
| Alabama ......... | 39,458 | 67,036 | 1.4 | 69.9 | 31,346 | 53,595 | 1.1 | 71.0 | 8,112 | 13,441 | 0.3 | 65.7 |
| Alaska .......... | 32,686 | 50,402 | 7.1 | 54.2 | 25,116 | 38,135 | 5.4 | 51.8 | 7,570 | 12,267 | 1.7 | 62.0 |
| Arizona ......... | 118,672 | 230,907 | 3.6 | 94.6 | 92,236 | 176,695 | 2.8 | 91.6 | 26,436 | 54,212 | 0.8 | 105.1 |
| Arkansas ........ | 25,401 | 44,943 | 1.5 | 76.9 | 20,220 | 36,102 | 1.2 | 78.5 | 5,181 | 8,841 | 0.3 | 70.6 |
| California ........ | 4,155,685 | 5,556,592 | 14.9 | 33.7 | 3,697,513 | 4,861,007 | 13.0 | 31.5 | 458,172 | 695,585 | 1.9 | 51.8 |
| Colorado ........ | 120,779 | 185,589 | 3.7 | 53.7 | 95,213 | 139,028 | 2.8 | 46.0 | 25,566 | 46,561 | 0.9 | 82.1 |
| Connecticut ....... | 95,368 | 157,088 | 4.4 | 64.7 | 82,313 | 135,565 | 3.8 | 64.7 | 13,055 | 21,523 | 0.6 | 64.9 |
| Delaware ........ | 18,944 | 33,701 | 3.8 | 77.9 | 16,259 | 28,549 | 3.2 | 75.6 | 2,685 | 5,152 | 0.6 | 91.9 |
| District of Columbia.. | 17,956 | 26,857 | 4.5 | 49.6 | 15,189 | 21,056 | 3.5 | 38.6 | 2,767 | 5,801 | 1.0 | 109.6 |
| Florida .......... | 333,013 | 573,083 | 3.0 | 72.1 | 266,256 | 454,821 | 2.4 | 70.8 | 66,757 | 118,262 | 0.6 | 77.2 |
| Georgia ......... | 199,812 | 365,497 | 3.8 | 82.9 | 173,170 | 314,467 | 3.2 | 81.6 | 26,642 | 51,030 | 0.5 | 91.5 |
| Hawaii .......... | 703,232 | 780,968 | 57.4 | 11.1 | 503,868 | 525,078 | 38.6 | 4.2 | 199,364 | 255,890 | 18.8 | 28.4 |
| Idaho ........... | 17,390 | 29,698 | 1.9 | 70.8 | 11,889 | 19,069 | 1.2 | 60.4 | 5,501 | 10,629 | 0.7 | 93.2 |
| Illinois.......... | 473,649 | 668,694 | 5.2 | 41.2 | 423,603 | 586,934 | 4.6 | 38.6 | 50,046 | 81,760 | 0.6 | 63.4 |
| Indiana.......... | 72,839 | 126,750 | 2.0 | 74.0 | 59,126 | 102,474 | 1.6 | 73.3 | 13,713 | 24,276 | 0.4 | 77.0 |
| Iowa............ | 43,119 | 64,512 | 2.1 | 49.6 | 36,635 | 53,094 | 1.7 | 44.9 | 6,484 | 11,418 | 0.4 | 76.1 |
| Kansas.......... | 56,049 | 83,930 | 2.9 | 49.7 | 46,806 | 67,762 | 2.4 | 44.8 | 9,243 | 16,168 | 0.6 | 74.9 |
| Kentucky ........ | 37,062 | 62,029 | 1.4 | 67.4 | 29,744 | 48,930 | 1.1 | 64.5 | 7,318 | 13,099 | 0.3 | 79.0 |
| Louisiana ........ | 64,350 | 84,335 | 1.9 | 31.1 | 54,758 | 70,132 | 1.5 | 28.1 | 9,592 | 14,203 | 0.3 | 48.1 |
| Maine........... | 11,827 | 18,333 | 1.4 | 55.0 | 9,111 | 13,571 | 1.0 | 49.0 | 2,716 | 4,762 | 0.4 | 75.3 |
| Maryland ........ | 238,408 | 370,044 | 6.4 | 55.2 | 210,929 | 318,853 | 5.5 | 51.2 | 27,479 | 51,191 | 0.9 | 86.3 |
| Massachusetts..... | 264,814 | 394,211 | 6.0 | 48.9 | 238,124 | 349,768 | 5.3 | 46.9 | 26,690 | 44,443 | 0.7 | 66.5 |
| Michigan ........ | 208,329 | 289,607 | 2.9 | 39.0 | 176,510 | 238,199 | 2.4 | 34.9 | 31,819 | 51,408 | 0.5 | 61.6 |
| Minnesota ....... | 162,414 | 247,132 | 4.7 | 52.2 | 141,968 | 214,234 | 4.0 | 50.9 | 20,446 | 32,898 | 0.6 | 60.9 |
| Mississippi....... | 23,281 | 32,560 | 1.1 | 39.9 | 18,626 | 25,742 | 0.9 | 38.2 | 4,655 | 6,818 | 0.2 | 46.5 |
| Missouri......... | 76,210 | 123,571 | 2.1 | 62.1 | 61,595 | 98,083 | 1.6 | 59.2 | 14,615 | 25,488 | 0.4 | 74.4 |
| Montana......... | 7,101 | 10,482 | 1.1 | 47.6 | 4,691 | 6,253 | 0.6 | 33.3 | 2,410 | 4,229 | 0.4 | 75.5 |
| Nebraska........ | 26,809 | 40,561 | 2.2 | 51.3 | 21,931 | 32,293 | 1.8 | 47.2 | 4,878 | 8,268 | 0.5 | 69.5 |
| Nevada ......... | 112,456 | 242,916 | 9.0 | 116.0 | 90,266 | 195,436 | 7.2 | 116.5 | 22,190 | 47,480 | 1.8 | 114.0 |
| New Hampshire.... | 19,219 | 34,522 | 2.6 | 79.6 | 15,931 | 28,407 | 2.2 | 78.3 | 3,288 | 6,115 | 0.5 | 86.0 |
| New Jersey ....... | 524,356 | 795,163 | 9.0 | 51.6 | 480,276 | 725,726 | 8.3 | 51.1 | 44,080 | 69,437 | 0.8 | 57.5 |
| New Mexico....... | 26,619 | 40,456 | 2.0 | 52.0 | 19,255 | 28,208 | 1.4 | 46.5 | 7,364 | 12,248 | 0.6 | 66.3 |
| New York ........ | 1,169,200 | 1,579,494 | 8.2 | 35.1 | 1,044,976 | 1,420,244 | 7.3 | 35.9 | 124,224 | 159,250 | 0.8 | 28.2 |
| North Carolina..... | 136,212 | 252,585 | 2.6 | 85.4 | 113,689 | 208,962 | 2.2 | 83.8 | 22,523 | 43,623 | 0.5 | 93.7 |
| North Dakota...... | 4,967 | 9,193 | 1.4 | 85.1 | 3,606 | 6,909 | 1.0 | 91.6 | 1,361 | 2,284 | 0.3 | 67.8 |
| Ohio............ | 159,776 | 238,292 | 2.1 | 49.1 | 132,633 | 192,233 | 1.7 | 44.9 | 27,143 | 46,059 | 0.4 | 69.7 |
| Oklahoma ........ | 58,723 | 84,170 | 2.2 | 43.3 | 46,767 | 65,076 | 1.7 | 39.1 | 11,956 | 19,094 | 0.5 | 59.7 |
| Oregon.......... | 127,339 | 186,281 | 4.9 | 46.3 | 101,350 | 141,263 | 3.7 | 39.4 | 25,989 | 45,018 | 1.2 | 73.2 |
| Pennsylvania ...... | 248,601 | 402,587 | 3.2 | 61.9 | 219,813 | 349,088 | 2.7 | 58.8 | 28,788 | 53,499 | 0.4 | 85.8 |
| Rhode Island ..... | 28,290 | 36,763 | 3.5 | 30.0 | 23,665 | 30,457 | 2.9 | 28.7 | 4,625 | 6,306 | 0.6 | 36.3 |
| South Carolina..... | 44,931 | 75,674 | 1.6 | 68.4 | 36,014 | 59,051 | 1.3 | 64.0 | 8,917 | 16,623 | 0.4 | 86.4 |
| South Dakota ..... | 6,009 | 10,216 | 1.3 | 70.0 | 4,378 | 7,610 | 0.9 | 73.8 | 1,631 | 2,606 | 0.3 | 59.8 |
| Tennessee........ | 68,918 | 113,398 | 1.8 | 64.5 | 56,662 | 91,242 | 1.4 | 61.0 | 12,256 | 22,156 | 0.3 | 80.8 |
| Texas............ | 644,193 | 1,110,666 | 4.4 | 72.4 | 562,319 | 964,596 | 3.8 | 71.5 | 81,874 | 146,070 | 0.6 | 78.4 |
| Utah............ | 48,692 | 77,748 | 2.8 | 59.7 | 37,108 | 55,285 | 2.0 | 49.0 | 11,584 | 22,463 | 0.8 | 93.9 |
| Vermont......... | 6,622 | 10,463 | 1.7 | 58.0 | 5,217 | 7,947 | 1.3 | 52.3 | 1,405 | 2,516 | 0.4 | 79.1 |
| Virginia.......... | 304,559 | 522,199 | 6.5 | 71.5 | 261,025 | 439,890 | 5.5 | 68.5 | 43,534 | 82,309 | 1.0 | 89.1 |
| Washington ....... | 395,741 | 604,251 | 9.0 | 52.7 | 322,335 | 481,067 | 7.2 | 49.2 | 73,406 | 123,184 | 1.8 | 67.8 |
| West Virginia ...... | 11,873 | 16,465 | 0.9 | 38.7 | 9,434 | 12,406 | 0.7 | 31.5 | 2,439 | 4,059 | 0.2 | 66.4 |
| Wisconsin ........ | 102,768 | 151,513 | 2.7 | 47.4 | 88,763 | 129,234 | 2.3 | 45.6 | 14,005 | 22,279 | 0.4 | 59.1 |
| Wyoming ........ | 4,107 | 6,729 | 1.2 | 63.8 | 2,771 | 4,426 | 0.8 | 59.7 | 1,336 | 2,303 | 0.4 | 72.4 |
| Puerto Rico ...... | 17,279 | 10,464 | 0.3 | -39.4 | 7,960 | 6,831 | 0.2 | -14.2 | 9,319 | 3,633 | 0.1 | -61.0 |

[1] The percentage of the total population is calculated by using the total population of all races. The totals for each geography can be found in Table 11, page 18 of the 2010 Census Brief, *Overview of Race and Hispanic Origin: 2010*, available at <www.census.gov/prod/cen2010/briefs/c2010br-02.pdf>.

Sources: U.S. Census Bureau, *Census 2000 Redistricting Data (Public Law 94-171) Summary File*, Table PL1; and *2010 Census Redistricting Data (Public Law 94-171) Summary File*, Table P1.

**Nearly three-fourths of all Asians lived in ten states.**

The ten states with the largest Asian alone-or-in-combination populations in 2010 were California (5.6 million), New York (1.6 million), Texas (1.1 million), New Jersey (0.8 million), Hawaii (0.8 million), Illinois (0.7 million), Washington (0.6 million), Florida (0.6 million), Virginia (0.5 million), and Pennsylvania (0.4 million) (see Table 2). Together, these ten states represented nearly three-fourths of the entire Asian population in the United States.

Among these states, the Asian alone-or-in-combination population experienced substantial growth in six states between 2000 and 2010, growing by 72 percent in Texas and Florida, 71 percent in Virginia, 62 percent in Pennsylvania, 53 percent in Washington, and 52 percent in New Jersey. Out of the ten states, the Asian alone-or-in-combination population grew the least in Hawaii (11 percent).

Out of the ten states above, the first nine also had the largest Asian alone populations. The state with the tenth-largest Asian alone population was Massachusetts (0.3 million). In a similar fashion to the Asian alone-or-in-combination population, the Asian alone population experienced considerable growth in Texas, Florida, Virginia, Pennsylvania, Washington, and New Jersey and relatively slower growth in Hawaii.

**The Asian population represented over 50 percent of the total population in Hawaii and over 8 percent of the total population in five other states.**

The states with the highest proportions of the Asian alone-or-in-combination population

were located in the West and the Northeast. The Asian alone-or-in-combination population represented 57 percent of the total population in Hawaii (see Table 2). California had the next highest proportion at 15 percent, followed by New Jersey (9 percent), Nevada (9 percent), Washington (9 percent), and New York (8 percent). These same six states had the highest proportions of the Asian alone population.

The Asian alone-or-in-combination population represented less than 2 percent of the total population in 15 states. Out of these 15 states, 8 were in the South—West Virginia, Mississippi, Alabama, Kentucky, Arkansas, South Carolina, Tennessee, and Louisiana. Three states were in the West—Montana, Wyoming, and Idaho. Two states were in the Midwest—South Dakota and North Dakota—and two states were in the Northeast—Maine and Vermont.

The Asian alone population represented less than 2 percent of the total population in the same states as the Asian alone-or-in-combination population, plus seven additional states—New Mexico, Indiana, Missouri, Ohio, Oklahoma, Iowa, and Nebraska.

**California and Texas had the largest numeric growth of Asians.**

The Asian alone-or-in-combination population grew by 5.4 million people over the decade. California had the largest numeric growth of people reporting Asian alone-or-in-combination (1.4 million), increasing from 4.2 million in 2000 to 5.6 million in 2010. Texas had the next largest numeric growth (466,000), increasing from 644,000 in 2000 to 1.1 million in 2010. This was followed by New York, which

grew by 410,000, increasing from 1.2 million to 1.6 million. The Asian alone population showed a similar pattern of numeric growth.

**The Asian population grew in every state between 2000 and 2010.**

The Asian alone-or-in-combination population grew by at least 30 percent in all states except for Hawaii (11 percent increase) (see Table 2). The top five states that experienced the most growth were Nevada (116 percent), Arizona (95 percent), North Carolina (85 percent), North Dakota (85 percent), and Georgia (83 percent). These same five states also experienced the most growth in the Asian alone population.

Reflecting percentages similar to the Asian alone-or-in-combination population and the Asian alone population, Nevada (114 percent), Arizona (105 percent), and North Carolina (94 percent) were among the top five states that experienced the most growth in the Asian in combination population. In contrast to the Asian alone-or-in-combination population and the Asian alone population, Utah (94 percent) was among the top five states that experienced the most growth in the Asian in combination population. The Asian in combination population also grew considerably in the District of Columbia (110 percent).[20]

**Multiple-race Asians were more likely to live in California and Hawaii.**

More than half of all Asians lived in five states. Of all respondents who reported as Asian alone or in combination, about 32 percent lived in California, 9 percent in New York, 6 percent in Texas, 5 percent in

---

[20] For this report, the District of Columbia is treated as a state equivalent.

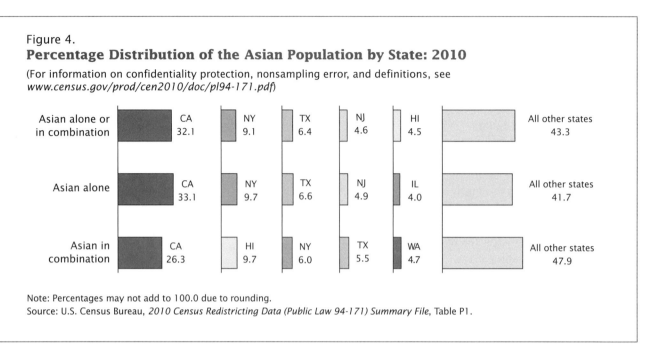

Figure 4.
**Percentage Distribution of the Asian Population by State: 2010**

(For information on confidentiality protection, nonsampling error, and definitions, see *www.census.gov/prod/cen2010/doc/pl94-171.pdf*)

Note: Percentages may not add to 100.0 due to rounding.
Source: U.S. Census Bureau, *2010 Census Redistricting Data (Public Law 94-171) Summary File*, Table P1.

New Jersey, and 5 percent in Hawaii (see Figure 4).

This pattern was similar for the Asian alone population for California (33 percent), New York (10 percent), Texas (7 percent), and New Jersey (5 percent). However, the state with the next highest proportion of the Asian alone population was Illinois (4 percent).

The pattern was slightly different for respondents who identified as Asian in combination and one or more additional races. Among multiple-race Asians, 26 percent lived in California, 10 percent in Hawaii, 6 percent each lived in New York and Texas, and 5 percent in Washington.

**The Asian population was concentrated in counties in the West, especially counties in Hawaii and California.**

Counties with the highest concentration of the Asian alone-or-in-combination population were located in the West and are shown in dark blue on the map (see Figure 5). Honolulu county, HI, had the highest percentage of the Asian

alone-or-in-combination population (62 percent), followed by three additional counties in Hawaii: Kauai (51 percent), Maui (47 percent), and Hawaii (45 percent).

Two county equivalents in Alaska had concentrations of the Asian alone-or-in-combination population of 25 percent or more—Aleutians East Borough and Aleutians West Census Area. Four counties in California had concentrations of 25 percent or more, all of which were located near San Francisco, CA, and San Jose, CA.

These patterns were similar for the Asian alone population, although the proportions of the Asian alone population were smaller relative to the Asian alone-or-in-combination populations in the four Hawaiian counties mentioned above. The Asian alone population represented 44 percent of the population in Honolulu county, 31 percent in Kauai county, 29 percent in Maui county, and 22 percent in Hawaii county.

The Asian alone-or-in-combination population also had concentrations of 10.0 percent to 24.9

percent in other counties near metropolitan statistical areas in the West, such as Los Angeles, CA; Las Vegas, NV; Portland, OR; and Seattle, WA. In the South, the Asian alone-or-in-combination population had concentrations of 10.0 percent to 24.9 percent in counties near Dallas, TX; Houston, TX; Washington, DC; and Atlanta, GA.

In the Midwest, one county (DuPage) near Chicago, IL, and one county (Ramsey) near Minneapolis, MN, had concentrations of the Asian-alone-or-in-combination population between 10.0 percent and 24.9 percent of the total population. This was also true in the Northeast for counties near Boston, MA, and New York, NY.

Counties with concentrations of 5.0 percent to 9.9 percent of the Asian alone-or-in-combination population were near all of the metropolitan statistical areas mentioned above. While there were some differences in the magnitude of the concentrations for some of the metro areas discussed above, the overall pattern was similar for the Asian alone population.

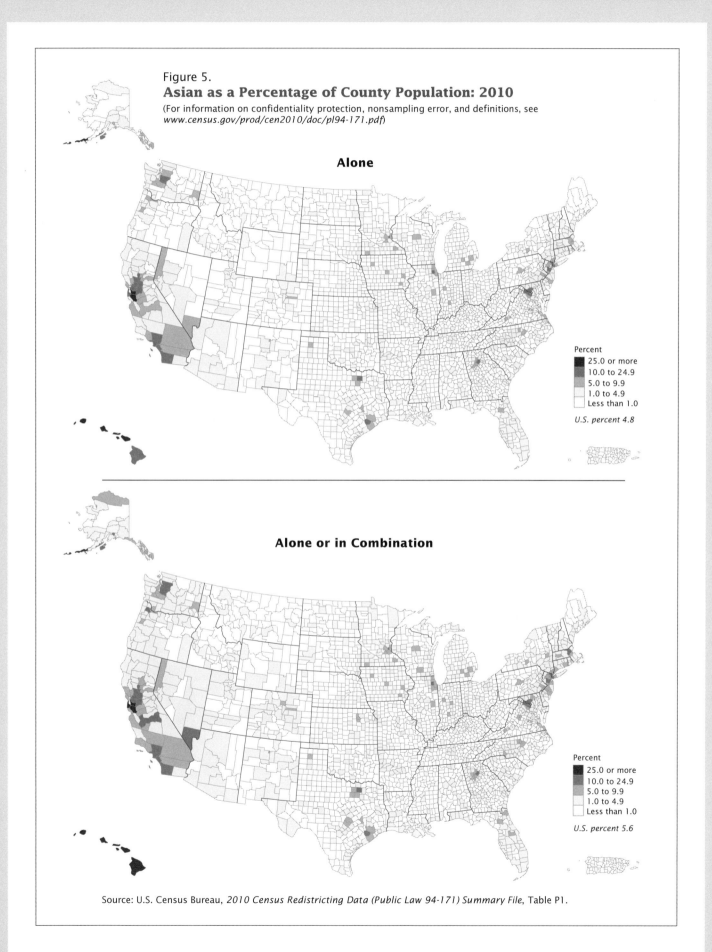

Figure 5.
**Asian as a Percentage of County Population: 2010**
(For information on confidentiality protection, nonsampling error, and definitions, see *www.census.gov/prod/cen2010/doc/pl94-171.pdf*)

**Alone**

Percent
- 25.0 or more
- 10.0 to 24.9
- 5.0 to 9.9
- 1.0 to 4.9
- Less than 1.0

*U.S. percent 4.8*

**Alone or in Combination**

Percent
- 25.0 or more
- 10.0 to 24.9
- 5.0 to 9.9
- 1.0 to 4.9
- Less than 1.0

*U.S. percent 5.6*

Source: U.S. Census Bureau, *2010 Census Redistricting Data (Public Law 94-171) Summary File*, Table P1.

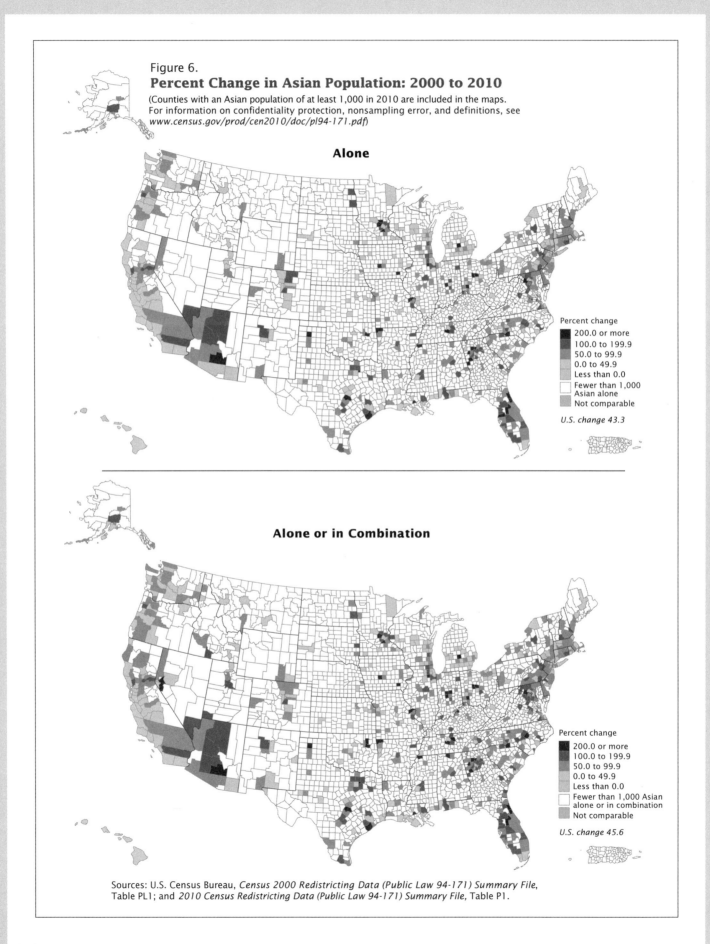

Figure 6.
**Percent Change in Asian Population: 2000 to 2010**

(Counties with an Asian population of at least 1,000 in 2010 are included in the maps.
For information on confidentiality protection, nonsampling error, and definitions, see
*www.census.gov/prod/cen2010/doc/pl94-171.pdf*)

**Alone**

Percent change
200.0 or more
100.0 to 199.9
50.0 to 99.9
0.0 to 49.9
Less than 0.0
Fewer than 1,000
Asian alone
Not comparable

*U.S. change 43.3*

**Alone or in Combination**

Percent change
200.0 or more
100.0 to 199.9
50.0 to 99.9
0.0 to 49.9
Less than 0.0
Fewer than 1,000 Asian
alone or in combination
Not comparable

*U.S. change 45.6*

Sources: U.S. Census Bureau, *Census 2000 Redistricting Data (Public Law 94-171) Summary File,*
Table PL1; and *2010 Census Redistricting Data (Public Law 94-171) Summary File,* Table P1.

Table 3.

## Ten Places With the Largest Number of Asians: 2010

(For information on confidentiality protection, nonsampling error, and definitions, see *www.census.gov/prod/cen2010/doc/pl94-171.pdf*)

| Place | Total population | Asian | | | | | |
|---|---|---|---|---|---|---|---|
| | | Alone or in combination | | Alone | | In combination | |
| | | Rank | Number | Rank | Number | Rank | Number |
| New York, NY................ | 8,175,133 | 1 | 1,134,919 | 1 | 1,038,388 | 1 | 96,531 |
| Los Angeles, CA .............. | 3,792,621 | 2 | 483,585 | 2 | 426,959 | 2 | 56,626 |
| San Jose, CA................. | 945,942 | 3 | 326,627 | 3 | 303,138 | 5 | 23,489 |
| San Francisco, CA............. | 805,235 | 4 | 288,529 | 4 | 267,915 | 6 | 20,614 |
| San Diego, CA................ | 1,307,402 | 5 | 241,293 | 5 | 207,944 | 4 | 33,349 |
| Urban Honolulu CDP, HI[1]........ | 337,256 | 6 | 230,071 | 6 | 184,950 | 3 | 45,121 |
| Chicago, IL ................. | 2,695,598 | 7 | 166,770 | 7 | 147,164 | 7 | 19,606 |
| Houston, TX................. | 2,099,451 | 8 | 139,960 | 8 | 126,378 | 9 | 13,582 |
| Fremont, CA ................ | 214,089 | 9 | 116,755 | 9 | 108,332 | 22 | 8,423 |
| Philadelphia, PA.............. | 1,526,006 | 10 | 106,720 | 10 | 96,405 | 14 | 10,315 |
| | | | | | | | |
| Seattle, WA ................. | 608,660 | 11 | 100,727 | 12 | 84,215 | 8 | 16,512 |
| Sacramento, CA ............. | 466,488 | 12 | 98,705 | 11 | 85,503 | 10 | 13,202 |

[1] Urban Honolulu CDP, HI, is a census designated place (CDP). CDPs are the statistical counterparts of incorporated places and are delineated to provide data for settled concentrations of population that are identifiable by name but are not legally incorporated under the laws of the state in which they are located.

Source: U.S. Census Bureau, *2010 Census Redistricting Data (Public Law 94-171) Summary File,* Table P1.

Many counties in western states, counties in states along the northeastern seaboard, and counties around several metro areas had Asian alone-or-in-combination populations of at least 1 percent of the total population. This population made up less than 1 percent in the majority of counties across the United States (66 percent of all counties). This was more pronounced for the Asian alone population, which accounted for less than 1 percent of the total population in 75 percent of all counties.

**Counties that experienced the fastest growth in the Asian population were primarily located in the South and the Midwest.**

Of the 733 counties that had an Asian alone-or-in-combination population of 1,000 or more, 38 counties experienced 200.0 percent growth or more, 116 counties experienced 100.0 percent to 199.9 percent growth, 299 counties experienced 50.0 percent to 99.9 percent growth,

275 counties experienced up to a 50 percent increase, and in 4 counties the Asian alone-or-in-combination population declined (see Figure 6).[21]

Throughout the South and Midwest, there were several counties where the Asian alone-or-in-combination population grew 200 percent or more. For example, this was seen in counties in Texas, Florida, and Georgia in the South and counties in states in the Midwest such as Minnesota, Ohio, Iowa, and Indiana. Two counties in the West, in Arizona and Nevada, experienced growth over 200 percent. There were no counties in the Northeast that experienced 200 percent growth or more in the Asian alone-or-in-combination population. This pattern was similar for the Asian alone population.

The Asian alone-or-in-combination population grew by 100.0 percent to 199.9 percent in a number of counties in western and northeastern states. For example, the Asian

[21] Of the 733 counties, one county (Broomfield, Colorado) existed in 2010 but not in 2000.

alone-or-in-combination population grew between 100.0 percent and 199.9 percent in counties in Oregon, California, Nevada, and Arizona. Counties in states along the eastern seaboard experienced considerable growth. In the South, counties in Florida also stand out as having experienced substantial growth in the Asian alone-or-in-combination population. There were also pockets of substantial growth in other southern states, such as counties around Atlanta, GA, and counties near Houston, TX, and Dallas, TX. There were also pockets of growth in counties in midwestern states, such as near Minneapolis, MN, and Chicago, IL. These patterns were similar for the Asian alone population.

**The places with the largest Asian populations were New York, NY, and Los Angeles, CA.**

The 2010 Census showed that New York, NY, had the largest Asian alone-or-in-combination population, with 1.1 million, followed by Los Angeles, CA (484,000), and San Jose, CA (327,000) (see Table 3). Three

Table 4.
## Ten Places With the Highest Percentage of Asians: 2010
(For information on confidentiality protection, nonsampling error, and definitions, see *www.census.gov/prod/cen2010/doc/pl94-171.pdf*)

| Place[1] | Total population | Asian | | | | | |
|---|---|---|---|---|---|---|---|
| | | Alone or in combination | | Alone | | In combination | |
| | | Rank | Percentage of total population | Rank | Percentage of total population | Rank | Percentage of total population |
| Urban Honolulu CDP, HI[2]........ | 337,256 | 1 | 68.2 | 2 | 54.8 | 1 | 13.4 |
| Daly City, CA................. | 101,123 | 2 | 58.4 | 1 | 55.6 | 21 | 2.8 |
| Fremont, CA ................. | 214,089 | 3 | 54.5 | 3 | 50.6 | 5 | 3.9 |
| Sunnyvale, CA................ | 140,081 | 4 | 43.7 | 4 | 40.9 | 19 | 2.8 |
| Irvine, CA.................... | 212,375 | 5 | 43.3 | 5 | 39.2 | 4 | 4.1 |
| Santa Clara, CA.............. | 116,468 | 6 | 40.8 | 6 | 37.7 | 11 | 3.2 |
| Garden Grove, CA............. | 170,883 | 7 | 38.6 | 7 | 37.1 | 75 | 1.4 |
| Torrance, CA................. | 145,438 | 8 | 38.2 | 8 | 34.5 | 6 | 3.6 |
| San Francisco, CA............ | 805,235 | 9 | 35.8 | 9 | 33.3 | 25 | 2.6 |
| San Jose, CA................. | 945,942 | 10 | 34.5 | 10 | 32.0 | 27 | 2.5 |
| | | | | | | | |
| Elk Grove, CA ................ | 153,015 | 11 | 30.6 | 12 | 26.3 | 2 | 4.3 |
| Fairfield, CA.................. | 105,321 | 26 | 19.0 | 32 | 14.9 | 3 | 4.1 |
| Berkeley, CA ................. | 112,580 | 21 | 22.8 | 22 | 19.3 | 7 | 3.6 |
| Vallejo, CA................... | 115,942 | 13 | 28.3 | 15 | 24.9 | 8 | 3.3 |
| Enterprise CDP, NV[2] ........... | 108,481 | 20 | 24.5 | 20 | 21.2 | 9 | 3.3 |
| Hayward, CA................. | 144,186 | 17 | 25.2 | 18 | 22.0 | 10 | 3.2 |

[1] Places of 100,000 or more total population. The 2010 Census showed 282 places in the United States with 100,000 or more population. They included 273 incorporated places (including 5 city-county consolidations) and 9 census designated places (CDPs) that were not legally incorporated.

[2] Urban Honolulu CDP, HI, and Enterprise CDP, NV are census designated places. CDPs are the statistical counterparts of incorporated places, and are delineated to provide data for settled concentrations of population that are identifiable by name but are not legally incorporated under the laws of the state in which they are located.

Source: U.S. Census Bureau, *2010 Census Redistricting Data (Public Law 94-171) Summary File*, Table P1.

other places—San Francisco, CA; San Diego, CA; and Urban Honolulu CDP, HI—had Asian alone-or-in-combination populations of over 200,000 people.[22]

Six of the ten places with the largest Asian alone-or-in-combination populations—Los Angeles, CA; San Jose, CA; San Francisco, CA; San Diego, CA; Urban Honolulu CDP, HI; and Fremont, CA were located in the West, and of these six, five were located in California. This ranking was identical for the Asian alone population.

New York, NY (97,000), and Los Angeles, CA (57,000), also had the largest Asian in combination populations, followed by Urban Honolulu CDP, HI (45,000), and San Diego, CA (33,000). Of the ten

[22] Census designated places (CDPs) are the statistical counterparts of incorporated places and are delineated to provide data for settled concentrations of population that are identifiable by name but are not legally incorporated under the laws of the state in which they are located.

places that had the largest Asian alone-or-in-combination and Asian alone populations, eight also had the largest Asian in combination populations. The two places out of the top ten that had the largest Asian in combination populations but were not within the top ten ranking for the Asian alone and Asian alone-or-in-combination populations were Seattle, WA, and Sacramento, CA.

**The place with the greatest proportion of the Asian population was Urban Honolulu CDP, HI.**

Among the places with populations of 100,000 or more, the places with the greatest proportion of the Asian alone-or-in-combination population were Urban Honolulu CDP, HI (68 percent), followed by Daly City, CA (58 percent); Fremont, CA (55 percent); Sunnyvale, CA (44 percent); and Irvine, CA (43 percent) (see Table 4). Of the

top ten places shown, three were majority Asian—Urban Honolulu CDP, HI; Daly City, CA; and Fremont, CA. All of these ten places were in the West, and nine of them were located in California.

These rankings were similar for the Asian alone population, except that Daly City, CA (56 percent) had the greatest Asian alone proportion, followed by Urban Honolulu CDP, HI (55 percent). Also, the proportions for the Asian alone and Asian alone-or-in-combination populations across the ten places shown were similar, with the exception of Urban Honolulu CDP, HI, where the Asian alone-or-in-combination population constituted 68 percent of the total population. This figure was much lower for the Asian alone population (55 percent).

Urban Honolulu CDP, HI, also had the greatest Asian in combination proportion. Similar to the Asian alone and Asian

Table 5.
## Asian Population by Number of Detailed Groups: 2010
(For information on confidentiality protection, nonsampling error, and definitions, see *www.census.gov/prod/cen2010/doc/sf1.pdf*)

| Detailed group | Asian alone | | Asian in combination with one or more other races | | Detailed Asian group alone or in any combination[1] |
|---|---|---|---|---|---|
| | One detailed Asian group reported | Two or more detailed Asian groups reported[1] | One detailed Asian group reported | Two or more detailed Asian groups reported[1] | |
| Total . . . . . . . . . . . . . . . | [2]14,327,580 | 346,672 | 2,429,530 | 217,074 | 17,320,856 |
| Asian Indian. . . . . . . . . . . . . . . | 2,843,391 | 75,416 | 240,547 | 23,709 | 3,183,063 |
| Bangladeshi. . . . . . . . . . . . . . . | 128,792 | 13,288 | 4,364 | 856 | 147,300 |
| Bhutanese . . . . . . . . . . . . . . . | 15,290 | 3,524 | 442 | 183 | 19,439 |
| Burmese . . . . . . . . . . . . . . . | 91,085 | 4,451 | 4,077 | 587 | 100,200 |
| Cambodian . . . . . . . . . . . . . . . | 231,616 | 23,881 | 18,229 | 2,941 | 276,667 |
| Chinese[3] . . . . . . . . . . . . . . . | 3,347,229 | 188,153 | 334,144 | 140,588 | 4,010,114 |
| Chinese, except Taiwanese[4] . . . | 3,137,061 | 185,289 | 317,344 | 140,038 | 3,779,732 |
| Taiwanese[4] . . . . . . . . . . . . . . | 196,691 | 2,501 | 15,781 | 468 | 215,441 |
| Filipino . . . . . . . . . . . . . . . | 2,555,923 | 94,050 | 645,970 | 120,897 | 3,416,840 |
| Hmong. . . . . . . . . . . . . . . | 247,595 | 4,728 | 7,392 | 358 | 260,073 |
| Indonesian. . . . . . . . . . . . . . . | 63,383 | 6,713 | 22,425 | 2,749 | 95,270 |
| Iwo Jiman . . . . . . . . . . . . . . . | 1 | 1 | 7 | 3 | 12 |
| Japanese. . . . . . . . . . . . . . . | 763,325 | 78,499 | 368,094 | 94,368 | 1,304,286 |
| Korean . . . . . . . . . . . . . . . | 1,423,784 | 39,690 | 216,288 | 27,060 | 1,706,822 |
| Laotian. . . . . . . . . . . . . . . | 191,200 | 18,446 | 19,733 | 2,751 | 232,130 |
| Malaysian . . . . . . . . . . . . . . . | 16,138 | 5,730 | 3,214 | 1,097 | 26,179 |
| Maldivian . . . . . . . . . . . . . . . | 98 | 4 | 25 | – | 127 |
| Mongolian . . . . . . . . . . . . . . . | 14,366 | 772 | 2,779 | 427 | 18,344 |
| Nepalese . . . . . . . . . . . . . . . | 51,907 | 5,302 | 1,941 | 340 | 59,490 |
| Okinawan. . . . . . . . . . . . . . . | 2,753 | 2,928 | 3,093 | 2,552 | 11,326 |
| Pakistani . . . . . . . . . . . . . . . | 363,699 | 19,295 | 24,184 | 1,985 | 409,163 |
| Singaporean . . . . . . . . . . . . . . . | 3,418 | 1,151 | 645 | 133 | 5,347 |
| Sri Lankan . . . . . . . . . . . . . . . | 38,596 | 2,860 | 3,607 | 318 | 45,381 |
| Thai . . . . . . . . . . . . . . . | 166,620 | 16,252 | 48,620 | 6,091 | 237,583 |
| Vietnamese . . . . . . . . . . . . . . . | 1,548,449 | 84,268 | 93,058 | 11,658 | 1,737,433 |
| Other Asian, not specified[5] . . . . . | 218,922 | 19,410 | 366,652 | 18,777 | 623,761 |

– Represents zero.

Note: This table shows more detailed Asian groups and response types than tables in *2010 Census Summary File 1*. As a result, some numbers do not match those shown in *2010 Census Summary File 1*.

[1] The numbers by detailed Asian group do not add to the total Asian population. This is because the detailed Asian groups are tallies of the number of Asian *responses* rather than the number of Asian *respondents*. Respondents reporting several Asian groups are counted several times. For example, a respondent reporting "Korean" and "Filipino" would be included in the Korean as well as the Filipino numbers.

[2] The total of 14,327,580 respondents categorized as reporting only one detailed Asian group in this table is higher than the total of 14,314,103 shown in Table PCT5 (U.S. Census Bureau, *2010 Census Summary File 1*). This is because the number shown here *includes* respondents who reported "Chinese" and "Taiwanese" together as a single detailed group, "Chinese", whereas PCT5 *excludes* respondents who reported "Chinese" and "Taiwanese " together.

[3] *Includes* respondents who reported "Chinese" and "Taiwanese" together.

[4] *Excludes* respondents who reported "Chinese" and "Taiwanese" together.

[5] Includes respondents who checked the "Other Asian" response category on the census questionnaire or wrote in a generic term such as "Asian" or "Asiatic."

Source: U.S. Census Bureau, 2010 Census special tabulation.

alone-or-in-combination popula-tions, all the places with the highest Asian in combination proportions were located in the West. Of the ten places that had the highest Asian in combination proportions, four places also were among the top ten Asian alone and Asian alone-or-in-combination proportions.

Six places that had the highest percentage of the Asian in combi-nation population were not within the top ten ranking for the Asian alone population or the Asian alone-or-in-combination popula-tion. These places were Elk Grove, CA; Fairfield, CA; Berkeley, CA; Vallejo, CA; Enterprise CDP, NV; and Hayward, CA.

## PATTERNS AMONG THE DETAILED ASIAN GROUPS

Table 5 presents data for a number of detailed groups. Data for people who reported only one detailed Asian group, such as Filipino, are presented in the first data column.

Next, data for people who identified with two or more detailed Asian groups, such as Filipino and Korean, and no other race group are pre-sented in the second data column. The third data column presents data for people who reported only one detailed Asian group and one or more other races, such as Filipino *and* White. The fourth data col-umn presents data for people who reported two or more detailed Asian groups and one or more other race

Table 6.
## Asian Population by Detailed Group: 2000 and 2010
(For information on confidentiality protection, nonsampling error, and definitions, see *www.census.gov/prod/cen2010/sf1.pdf*)

| Detailed group | Asian alone[1] | | | Asian in combination with one or more other races [1] | | | Detailed Asian group alone or in any combination[1] | | |
|---|---|---|---|---|---|---|---|---|---|
| | 2000 | 2010 | Percent change | 2000 | 2010 | Percent change | 2000 | 2010 | Percent change |
| Total .............. | 10,242,998 | 14,674,252 | 43.3 | 1,655,830 | 2,646,604 | 59.8 | 11,898,828 | 17,320,856 | 45.6 |
| Asian Indian................ | 1,718,778 | 2,918,807 | 69.8 | 180,821 | 264,256 | 46.1 | 1,899,599 | 3,183,063 | 67.6 |
| Bangladeshi................ | 46,905 | 142,080 | 202.9 | 10,507 | 5,220 | −50.3 | 57,412 | 147,300 | 156.6 |
| Bhutanese ................ | 192 | 18,814 | 9,699.0 | 20 | 625 | 3,025.0 | 212 | 19,439 | 9,069.3 |
| Burmese ................. | 14,620 | 95,536 | 553.5 | 2,100 | 4,664 | 122.1 | 16,720 | 100,200 | 499.3 |
| Cambodian ................ | 183,769 | 255,497 | 39.0 | 22,283 | 21,170 | −5.0 | 206,052 | 276,667 | 34.3 |
| Chinese[2] .................. | 2,564,190 | 3,535,382 | 37.9 | 301,042 | 474,732 | 57.7 | 2,865,232 | 4,010,114 | 40.0 |
| Chinese, except Taiwanese[3] .. | 2,432,046 | 3,322,350 | 36.6 | 288,391 | 457,382 | 58.6 | 2,720,437 | 3,779,732 | 38.9 |
| Taiwanese[3]............... | 118,827 | 199,192 | 67.6 | 11,564 | 16,249 | 40.5 | 130,391 | 215,441 | 65.2 |
| Filipino.................. | 1,908,125 | 2,649,973 | 38.9 | 456,690 | 766,867 | 67.9 | 2,364,815 | 3,416,840 | 44.5 |
| Hmong................... | 174,712 | 252,323 | 44.4 | 11,598 | 7,750 | −33.2 | 186,310 | 260,073 | 39.6 |
| Indonesian................ | 44,186 | 70,096 | 58.6 | 18,887 | 25,174 | 33.3 | 63,073 | 95,270 | 51.0 |
| Iwo Jiman ................ | 18 | 2 | −88.9 | 60 | 10 | −83.3 | 78 | 12 | −84.6 |
| Japanese................. | 852,237 | 841,824 | −1.2 | 296,695 | 462,462 | 55.9 | 1,148,932 | 1,304,286 | 13.5 |
| Korean................... | 1,099,422 | 1,463,474 | 33.1 | 129,005 | 243,348 | 88.6 | 1,228,427 | 1,706,822 | 38.9 |
| Laotian.................. | 179,103 | 209,646 | 17.1 | 19,100 | 22,484 | 17.7 | 198,203 | 232,130 | 17.1 |
| Malaysian ................ | 15,029 | 21,868 | 45.5 | 3,537 | 4,311 | 21.9 | 18,566 | 26,179 | 41.0 |
| Maldivian ................ | 29 | 102 | 251.7 | 22 | 25 | 13.6 | 51 | 127 | 149.0 |
| Mongolian ................ | 3,699 | 15,138 | 309.2 | 2,169 | 3,206 | 47.8 | 5,868 | 18,344 | 212.6 |
| Nepalese................. | 8,209 | 57,209 | 596.9 | 1,190 | 2,281 | 91.7 | 9,399 | 59,490 | 532.9 |
| Okinawan................. | 6,138 | 5,681 | −7.4 | 4,461 | 5,645 | 26.5 | 10,599 | 11,326 | 6.9 |
| Pakistani ................ | 164,628 | 382,994 | 132.6 | 39,681 | 26,169 | −34.1 | 204,309 | 409,163 | 100.3 |
| Singaporean .............. | 2,017 | 4,569 | 126.5 | 377 | 778 | 106.4 | 2,394 | 5,347 | 123.4 |
| Sri Lankan................ | 21,364 | 41,456 | 94.0 | 3,223 | 3,925 | 21.8 | 24,587 | 45,381 | 84.6 |
| Thai .................... | 120,918 | 182,872 | 51.2 | 29,365 | 54,711 | 86.3 | 150,283 | 237,583 | 58.1 |
| Vietnamese ............... | 1,169,672 | 1,632,717 | 39.6 | 54,064 | 104,716 | 93.7 | 1,223,736 | 1,737,433 | 42.0 |
| Other Asian, not specified[4] .... | 162,913 | 238,332 | 46.3 | 213,810 | 385,429 | 80.3 | 376,723 | 623,761 | 65.6 |

Note: This table shows more detailed Asian groups and response types than tables in *2010 Census Summary File 1* and *Census 2000 Summary File 1*. As a result, some numbers do not match those shown in the *2010 Census Summary File 1* and *Census 2000 Summary File 1*.

[1] The numbers by detailed Asian group do not add to the total Asian population. This is because the detailed Asian groups are tallies of the number of Asian *responses* rather than the number of Asian *respondents*. Respondents reporting several Asian groups are counted several times. For example, a respondent reporting "Korean" and "Filipino" would be included in the Korean as well as the Filipino numbers.

[2] *Includes* respondents who reported "Chinese" and "Taiwanese" together.

[3] *Excludes* respondents who reported "Chinese" and "Taiwanese" together.

[4] Includes respondents who checked the "Other Asian" response category on the census questionnaire or wrote in a generic term such as "Asian" or "Asiatic."

Source: U.S. Census Bureau, 2010 Census special tabulation.

groups, such as Filipino, Korean, *and* White.

All of these columns are summed and presented in the last data column, detailed Asian group *alone or in any combination*. Thus, the last column presents the maximum number of people who identified as the detailed Asian group.

**The Chinese population was the largest detailed Asian group.**

In the 2010 Census, the detailed Asian groups with one million or more responses for the Asian alone-or-in-any-combination

population were Chinese, Filipino, Asian Indian, Vietnamese, Korean, and Japanese (see Table 5).

The Chinese alone-or-in-any-combination population, the largest detailed Asian group, was 4.0 million. There were 3.3 million people who reported Chinese alone with no additional detailed Asian group or race category.

**Filipino and Asian Indian were the second- and third-largest detailed Asian groups.**

Filipino and Asian Indian were the next largest detailed Asian groups for the Asian

alone-or-in-any-combination population. Filipino was the second-largest detailed Asian group of the Asian alone-or-in-any-combination population (3.4 million), followed by Asian Indian (3.2 million). However, for the Asian alone population where only one detailed Asian group was reported, Asian Indian was the second-largest group (2.8 million), followed by Filipino (2.6 million).

**The Bhutanese population experienced the fastest growth from 2000 to 2010.**

The Bhutanese population experienced the fastest growth from

2000 to 2010, growing from about 200 in 2000 to about 19,000 in 2010 (see Table 6). While the Bhutanese population experienced high percentage growth, its proportion of the Asian alone-or-in-any-combination population remained small.

Of all the detailed Asian alone-or-in-any combination groups that had a population of one million or more, the Asian Indian population grew the fastest, by 68 percent, followed by the Filipino (44 percent), Vietnamese (42 percent), Korean (39 percent), and Chinese (40 percent) populations. The Japanese population experienced the slowest growth among the detailed Asian groups with alone-or-in-any-combination populations of one million or more, growing by 14 percent.

**Asian Indians, Chinese, and Filipinos represented 60 percent of the Asian alone population.**

An analysis of respondents who identified with only one detailed Asian group shows the Chinese population accounted for 23 percent, the Asian Indian population accounted for 19 percent, and the Filipino population accounted for 17 percent of all respondents who identified as Asian alone (see Figure 7). Combined, these three groups accounted for 60 percent of the Asian alone population. Vietnamese (11 percent), Korean (10 percent), Japanese (5 percent), other single detailed Asian groups (13 percent), and two or more detailed Asian groups (2 percent) accounted for smaller proportions of the Asian alone population.

The largest proportion of Asian in combination with another race(s) was for respondents who identified as Filipino (24 percent), followed by all other single detailed Asian

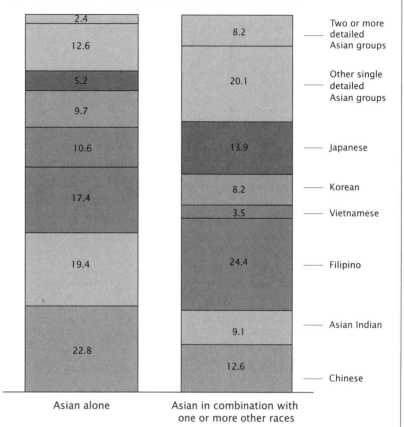

Figure 7.

**Percentage Distribution of the Asian Population by Detailed Group: 2010**

(For information on confidentiality protection, nonsampling error, and definitions, see *www.census.gov/prod/cen2010/doc/sf1.pdf*)

Note: All categories shown, except the "Two or more detailed Asian groups" category, represent respondents who identified with only one detailed Asian group. Percentages may not add to 100.0 due to rounding.

Source: U.S. Census Bureau, 2010 Census special tabulation.

groups (20 percent). The next highest proportions were Japanese (14 percent), Chinese (13 percent), Asian Indian (9 percent), Korean (8 percent), two or more detailed Asian groups (8 percent), and Vietnamese (4 percent).

**Japanese had the highest proportion reporting multiple detailed Asian groups and/or another race(s) relative to the largest detailed Asian groups.**

Among the detailed Asian groups with alone-or-in-any-combination populations of one million or

more, the Japanese population had the highest proportion reporting multiple detailed Asian groups and no other race (6 percent), one group (Japanese) and another race(s) (28 percent), and multiple detailed Asian groups and another races(s) (7 percent) (see Figure 8). Combining these groups, 41 percent of the Japanese population identified with multiple detailed Asian groups and/or another race(s). After Japanese, Filipinos had the highest proportion of respondents reporting

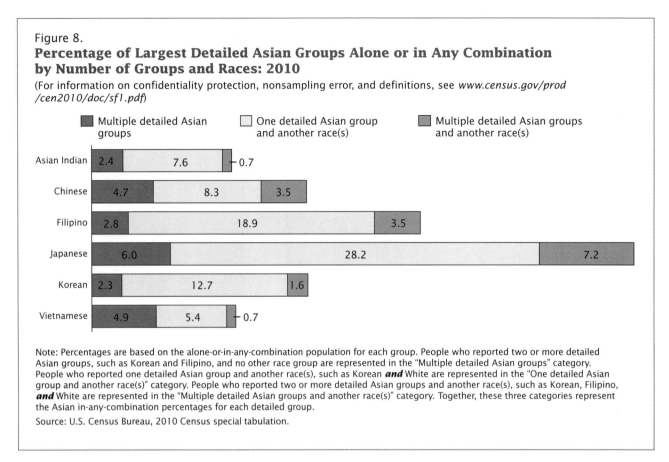

Figure 8.
**Percentage of Largest Detailed Asian Groups Alone or in Any Combination by Number of Groups and Races: 2010**
(For information on confidentiality protection, nonsampling error, and definitions, see *www.census.gov/prod/cen2010/doc/sf1.pdf*)

- Multiple detailed Asian groups
- One detailed Asian group and another race(s)
- Multiple detailed Asian groups and another race(s)

| Group | Multiple detailed Asian groups | One detailed Asian group and another race(s) | Multiple detailed Asian groups and another race(s) |
|---|---|---|---|
| Asian Indian | 2.4 | 7.6 | 0.7 |
| Chinese | 4.7 | 8.3 | 3.5 |
| Filipino | 2.8 | 18.9 | 3.5 |
| Japanese | 6.0 | 28.2 | 7.2 |
| Korean | 2.3 | 12.7 | 1.6 |
| Vietnamese | 4.9 | 5.4 | 0.7 |

Note: Percentages are based on the alone-or-in-any-combination population for each group. People who reported two or more detailed Asian groups, such as Korean and Filipino, and no other race group are represented in the "Multiple detailed Asian groups" category. People who reported one detailed Asian group and another race(s), such as Korean **and** White are represented in the "One detailed Asian group and another race(s)" category. People who reported two or more detailed Asian groups and another race(s), such as Korean, Filipino, **and** White are represented in the "Multiple detailed Asian groups and another race(s)" category. Together, these three categories represent the Asian in-any-combination percentages for each detailed group.
Source: U.S. Census Bureau, 2010 Census special tabulation.

one group (Filipino) and another race(s) (19 percent). Also, 3 percent identified with multiple detailed Asian groups and no other race, and 4 percent reported multiple detailed Asian groups and another race(s). Therefore, 25 percent of those who identified as Filipino identified with multiple detailed Asian groups and/or another race(s).

Among the detailed Asian groups with alone-or-in-any-combination populations of one million or more, Asian Indians and Vietnamese had the lowest proportion who reported multiple detailed Asian groups and/or another race(s) (11 percent each). The Asian Indian population had 2 percent report multiple detailed Asian groups and no other race, 8 percent report one group (Asian Indian) and another

race(s), and almost 1 percent report multiple detailed Asian groups and another race(s). The Vietnamese population had 5 percent report multiple detailed Asian groups and no other race, 5 percent report one group (Vietnamese) and another race(s), and almost 1 percent report multiple detailed Asian groups and another race(s).

Chinese and Koreans both had a slightly higher proportion who reported multiple detailed Asian groups and/or another race (17 percent each). The Chinese population had 5 percent report multiple detailed Asian groups and no other race, 8 percent report one group (Chinese) and another race(s), and 4 percent report multiple detailed Asian groups and another race(s). The Korean population had 2 percent report multiple

detailed Asian groups and no other race, 13 percent report one group (Korean) and another race(s), and 2 percent report multiple detailed Asian groups and another race(s).

## THE GEOGRAPHIC DISTRIBUTION OF DETAILED ASIAN GROUPS

**The Japanese population had the highest proportion living in the West among the largest detailed Asian groups.**

Among detailed Asian groups with alone-or-in-any-combination populations that numbered one million or more, Japanese (71 percent) and Filipinos (66 percent) had the two largest proportions that lived in the West (see Figure 9). Large proportions of Chinese (49 percent), Vietnamese (49 percent), and Koreans (44 percent) lived in the

West as well. A much lower proportion of Asian Indians (25 percent) lived in the West compared to the other groups shown.

Larger proportions of Vietnamese (32 percent), Asian Indians (29 percent), and Koreans (24 percent) lived in the South compared to other groups shown. A greater proportion of Asian Indians (30 percent), Chinese (26 percent), and Koreans (21 percent) lived in the Northeast compared to other groups shown. For all detailed Asian groups shown, the Midwest had the lowest proportion of each group.

**California was the top state for each of the six largest detailed Asian groups.**

Of the detailed Asian groups that numbered one million or more within the Asian alone-or-in-any-combination population, the highest proportion of each group lived in California. The Filipino population (43 percent) had the highest proportion that lived in California, followed by Vietnamese (37 percent), Chinese (36 percent), Japanese (33 percent), and Korean

(30 percent) (see Figure 10). Asian Indians (19 percent) had the lowest proportion living in California relative to all groups shown.

For Chinese (15 percent), Asian Indians (12 percent), and Koreans (9 percent), the state with the second-largest proportion of these populations was New York. The state with the second-largest proportions of Japanese (24 percent) and Filipinos (10 percent) was Hawaii. The second-largest proportion of the Vietnamese population (13 percent) lived in Texas.

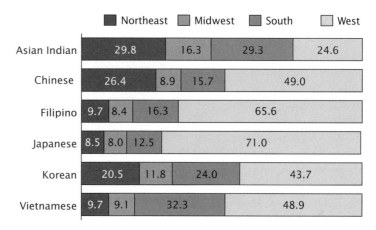

Figure 9.
**Percentage Distribution of Largest Detailed Asian Groups by Region: 2010**
(For information on confidentiality protection, nonsampling error, and definitions, see www.census.gov/prod/cen2010/doc/sf1.pdf)

Note: Percentages are based on the alone-or-in-any-combination population for each group.
Source: U.S. Census Bureau, 2010 Census special tabulation.

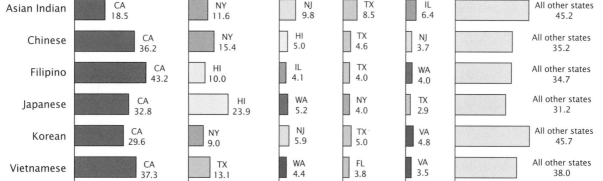

Figure 10.
**Percentage Distribution of Largest Detailed Asian Groups by State: 2010**
(For information on confidentiality protection, nonsampling error, and definitions, see www.census.gov/prod/cen2010/doc/sf1.pdf)

Note: Percentages are based on the alone-or-in-any-combination population for each group. Percentages may not add to 100.0 due to rounding.
Source: U.S. Census Bureau, 2010 Census special tabulation.

**The Asian Indian population was the largest detailed Asian group in nearly half of all states.**

Figure 11 presents a state-level map illustrating the diversity of the largest detailed Asian alone-or-in-any-combination population groups across the country. The different colors denote which detailed Asian group was the largest in each state, and the graduated circles illustrate the relative size of that group.

The Asian Indian population was the largest detailed Asian group in 23 states, more than any other detailed Asian group. Of these states, 13 were in the South (Alabama, Arkansas, Delaware, Florida, Georgia, Kentucky, Maryland, North Carolina, South Carolina, Tennessee, Texas, Virginia, and West Virginia); 6 were in the Midwest (Illinois, Indiana, Iowa, Michigan, Missouri, and Ohio); and 4 were in the Northeast (Connecticut, Pennsylvania, New Hampshire, and New Jersey).

For every state in the West, either the Filipino population or the Chinese population was the largest detailed Asian group. Filipino was the largest detailed Asian group in Alaska, Arizona, California, Hawaii, Idaho, Montana, Nevada, New Mexico, Washington, and Wyoming, while Chinese was the largest in Colorado, Oregon, and Utah. Outside of the West, Filipino was the largest detailed Asian group in South Dakota, while Chinese was the largest in the District of Columbia and North Dakota, as well as several states in the Northeast (Maine, Massachusetts, New York, Rhode Island, and Vermont).

The Vietnamese population was the largest detailed Asian group in five states—Louisiana, Mississippi, and Oklahoma in the South; and Kansas and Nebraska in the Midwest.

The Hmong population was the largest detailed Asian group in two states (Minnesota and Wisconsin).

**The 20 metro areas with the largest Asian population contained many diverse detailed Asian groups.**

Next, the top five detailed Asian groups in the 20 metro areas with the largest Asian alone-or-in-combination population in 2010 are discussed.

In 6 of the 20 metro areas with the largest Asian alone-or-in-combination population, Chinese had the largest alone-or-in-any-combination population of all detailed Asian groups (see Figure 12). Of these metro areas, the New York-Northern New Jersey-Long Island NY-NJ-PA metro area had the largest Chinese population (695,000), followed by Los Angeles-Long Beach-Santa Ana, CA (544,000), San Francisco-Oakland-Fremont, CA (477,000), San Jose-Sunnyvale-Santa Clara, CA (173,000), Boston-Cambridge-Quincy, MA-NH (123,000), and Seattle-Tacoma-Bellevue, WA (101,000). Of these 6 metro areas, 2 were in the Northeast, and 4 were in the West.

The Asian Indian population also had the largest alone-or-in-any-combination population in 6 of the 20 metro areas with the largest Asian alone-or-in-combination population. Of these areas, the metro area with the largest Asian Indian population was Chicago-Joliet-Naperville, IL-IN-WI (186,000), followed by Washington-Arlington-Alexandria, DC-VA-MD-WV (142,000), Dallas-Fort Worth-Arlington, TX (108,000), Philadelphia-Camden-Wilmington, PA-NJ-DE-MD (98,000), Atlanta-Sandy Springs-Marietta, GA (86,000), and Detroit-Warren-Livonia, MI (60,000). Of these 6 metro areas, none was located in the West.

The Filipino population had the highest alone-or-in-any-combination population in 5 of the 20 metro areas with the largest Asian alone-or-in-combination population. Of these 5 areas, San Diego-Carlsbad-San Marcos, CA had the largest Filipino population (182,000), followed by Riverside-San Bernardino-Ontario, CA (118,000), Las Vegas-Paradise, NV (108,000), Sacramento–Arden-Arcade–Roseville, CA (74,000), and Phoenix-Mesa-Glendale, AZ (40,000).

Among the 20 metro areas with the largest Asian alone-or-in-combination populations, Japanese, Hmong, and Vietnamese had the highest alone-or-in-any-combination population in 1 metro area each. The Japanese population (241,000) was the largest detailed Asian group in Honolulu, HI. The Hmong population (64,000) was the largest detailed Asian group in Minneapolis-St. Paul-Bloomington, MN-WI. The Vietnamese population was the largest detailed Asian group in Houston-Sugar Land-Baytown, TX (110,000).

**The Chinese population was represented among the top five detailed Asian groups for each metro area shown.**

The Chinese population was among the top five largest detailed Asian populations for every metro area shown (see Figure 12). The Asian Indian and Filipino populations were within the top five largest detailed Asian alone-or-in-any-combination populations for 18 out of the 20 metro areas with the largest Asian alone-or-in-combination populations. Asian Indians were not represented within the top five detailed Asian groups in Los Angeles-Long Beach-Santa Ana, CA, and Honolulu, HI.

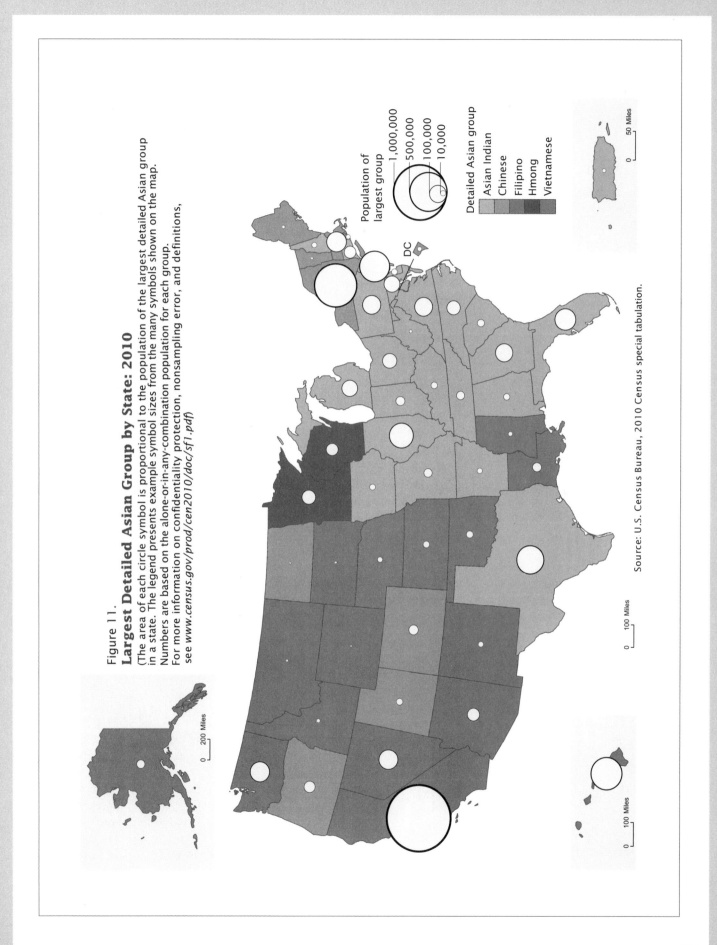

Figure 11.
**Largest Detailed Asian Group by State: 2010**
(The area of each circle symbol is proportional to the population of the largest detailed Asian group
in a state. The legend presents example symbol sizes from the many symbols shown on the map.
Numbers are based on the alone-or-in-any-combination population for each group.
For more information on confidentiality protection, nonsampling error, and definitions,
see *www.census.gov/prod/cen2010/doc/sf1.pdf*)

Population of
largest group

1,000,000
500,000
100,000
10,000

Detailed Asian group

Asian Indian
Chinese
Filipino
Hmong
Vietnamese

DC

Source: U.S. Census Bureau, 2010 Census special tabulation.

0   50 Miles

0   100 Miles

0   200 Miles

0   100 Miles

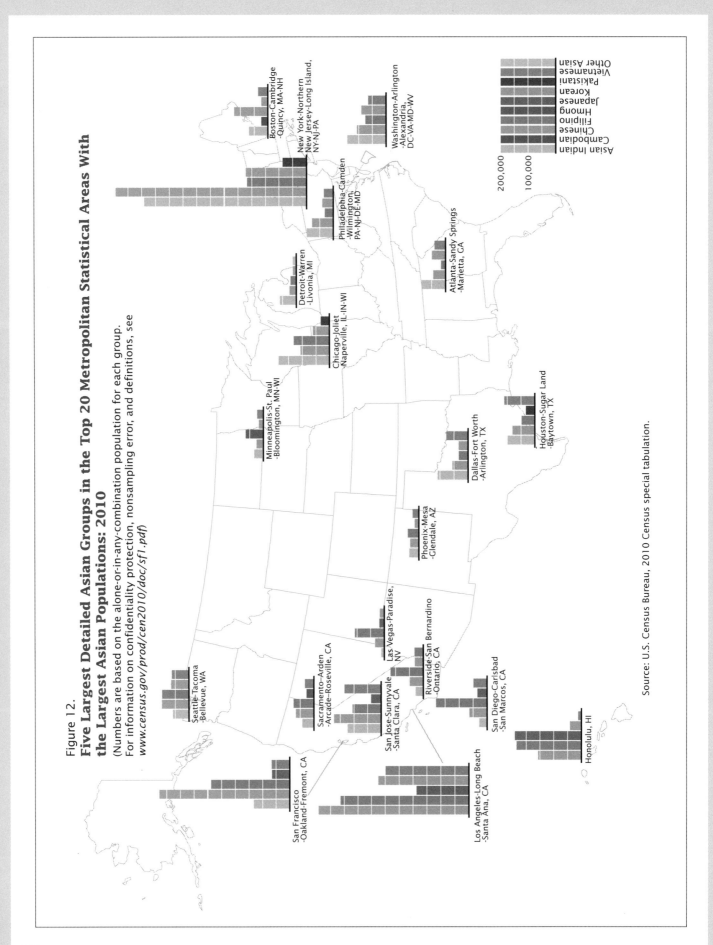

Figure 12.

**Five Largest Detailed Asian Groups in the Top 20 Metropolitan Statistical Areas With the Largest Asian Populations: 2010**

(Numbers are based on the alone-or-in-any-combination population for each group. For information on confidentiality protection, nonsampling error, and definitions, see www.census.gov/prod/cen2010/doc/sf1.pdf)

Source: U.S. Census Bureau, 2010 Census special tabulation.

Filipinos were not represented in the top five detailed Asian groups in Boston-Cambridge-Quincy, MA-NH and Minneapolis-St. Paul-Bloomington, MN-WI. The Korean and Vietnamese populations were represented among the top five detailed Asian groups in 15 and 16 out of the 20 metro areas with the largest Asian alone-or-in-combination population, respectively.

The Japanese population was represented in the top five detailed Asian groups in 6 out of the 20 metro areas, all of which were located in the West. Pakistanis were represented in 3 of the 20 metro areas with the largest Asian alone-or-in-combination population, New York-Northern New Jersey-Long Island NY-NJ-PA (86,000), Houston-Sugar Land-Baytown, TX, and Chicago-Joliet-Naperville, IL-IN-WI (32,000 each). Hmong were represented in 2 metro areas, Minneapolis-St. Paul-Bloomington, MN-WI (64,000) and Sacramento–Arden-Arcade–Roseville, CA (27,000). Cambodians were represented in 1 metro area, Boston-Cambridge-Quincy, MA-NH (25,000).

## SUMMARY

This report provides a detailed portrait of the Asian population in the United States and contributes to our understanding of the nation's changing racial and ethnic diversity.

The Asian alone population and the Asian alone-or-in-combination population both grew substantially from 2000 to 2010, increasing in size by 43 percent and 46 percent, respectively. These populations grew more than any other race group in 2010. The multiple-race Asian population also experienced considerable growth, increasing by 60 percent. Leading this growth was the Asian **and**

White population, which grew by 87 percent.

Additional notable trends were presented in this report. The Asian population continued to be concentrated in the West. However, the proportion of all Asians living in the West decreased from 2000 to 2010, while the proportion living in the South increased.

The report also highlighted results for detailed Asian groups, indicating that the Chinese population was the largest detailed Asian group. For the Asian alone-or-in-any-combination population, Filipinos and Asian Indians were the second- and third-largest detailed Asian groups.

The report also discussed geographic patterns for detailed Asian groups. Of the detailed Asian groups with one million or more alone-or-in-any-combination populations, Japanese, Filipino, Chinese, Vietnamese, and Korean populations were concentrated in the West. However, this pattern was not observed for Asian Indians. In addition, for these same six groups, the largest proportion of each group lived in California.

Another interesting finding is that among the detailed Asian groups with alone-or-in-any-combination populations of one million or more, the Japanese population had the highest proportion that identified with multiple detailed Asian groups and/or another race(s) (41 percent). After Japanese, Filipinos had the next-highest proportion of respondents who identified with multiple detailed Asian groups and/or another race(s) (25 percent).

Throughout the decade, the Census Bureau will release additional information on the Asian population, including characteristics such as age, sex, and family type, which will provide greater insights

into the demographic characteristics of this population at various geographic levels.

## ABOUT THE 2010 CENSUS

### Why was the 2010 Census conducted?

The U.S. Constitution mandates that a census be taken in the United States every 10 years. This is required in order to determine the number of seats each state is to receive in the U.S. House of Representatives.

### Why did the 2010 Census ask the question on race?

The Census Bureau collects data on race to fulfill a variety of legislative and program requirements. Data on race are used in the legislative redistricting process carried out by the states and in monitoring local jurisdictions' compliance with the Voting Rights Act. More broadly, data on race are critical for research that underlies many policy decisions at all levels of government.

### How do data from the question on race benefit me, my family, and my community?

All levels of government need information on race to implement and evaluate programs, or enforce laws, such as the Civil Rights Act, Voting Rights Act, Fair Housing Act, Equal Employment Opportunity Act, and the 2010 Census Redistricting Data Program.

Both public and private organizations use race information to find areas where groups may need special services and to plan and implement education, housing, health, and other programs that address these needs. For example, a school system might use this information to design cultural activities that reflect the diversity in their community, or a business could use it to select the mix of merchandise it will sell in a new store. Census information also helps identify areas where residents might need services of particular importance to certain racial groups, such as screening for hypertension or diabetes.

## FOR MORE INFORMATION

For more information on race in the United States, visit the Census Bureau's Internet site at <www.census.gov/population /race>.

Information on confidentiality protection, nonsampling error, and definitions is available at <www.census.gov/prod/cen2010 /doc/pl94-171.pdf>.

Data on race from the *2010 Census Redistricting Data (Public Law 94-171) Summary File* and the *2010 Census Summary File 1* were released on a state-by-state basis. The 2010 Census redistricting data are available on the Internet at <http://factfinder2.census.gov /main.html>.

For more information on specific race groups in the United States, go to <www.census.gov> and search for "Minority Links." This Web page includes information about the 2010 Census and provides links to reports based on past censuses and surveys focusing on the social and economic characteristics of the Black or African American, American Indian and Alaska Native, Asian, and Native Hawaiian and Other Pacific Islander populations.

Information on other population and housing topics is presented in the 2010 Census Briefs series, located on the Census Bureau's Web site at <www.census.gov/prod/cen2010>. This series presents information about race, Hispanic origin, age, sex, household type, and housing tenure.

For more information about the 2010 Census, including data products, call the Customer Services Center at 1-800-923-8282. You can also visit the Census Bureau's Question and Answer Center at <ask.census.gov> to submit your questions online.

# The Black Population: 2010

*2010 Census Briefs*

Issued September 2011

C2010BR-06

By
Sonya Rastogi,
Tallese D. Johnson,
Elizabeth M. Hoeffel,
and
Malcolm P. Drewery, Jr.

## INTRODUCTION

This report provides a portrait of the Black population in the United States and discusses its distribution at the national level and at lower levels of geography.[1,2] It is part of a series that analyzes population and housing data collected from the 2010 Census. The data for this report are based on the *2010 Census Redistricting Data (Public Law 94-171) Summary File*, which was the first 2010 Census data product released with data on race and Hispanic origin and was provided to each state for use in drawing boundaries for legislative districts.[3]

## UNDERSTANDING RACE DATA FROM THE 2010 CENSUS

**The 2010 Census used established federal standards to collect and present data on race.**

For the 2010 Census, the question on race was asked of individuals living in the United States (see Figure 1). An individual's response to the race question was based upon self-identification. The U.S. Census Bureau collects information on race following the guidance of the U.S. Office of Management and Budget's

Figure 1.

**Reproduction of the Question on Race From the 2010 Census**

**6. What is this person's race?** *Mark* X *one or more boxes.*

- ☐ White
- ☐ Black, African Am., or Negro
- ☐ American Indian or Alaska Native — *Print name of enrolled or principal tribe.* ⟿

[                    ]

- ☐ Asian Indian
- ☐ Chinese
- ☐ Filipino
- ☐ Other Asian — *Print race, for example, Hmong, Laotian, Thai, Pakistani, Cambodian, and so on.* ⟿

- ☐ Japanese
- ☐ Korean
- ☐ Vietnamese

- ☐ Native Hawaiian
- ☐ Guamanian or Chamorro
- ☐ Samoan
- ☐ Other Pacific Islander — *Print race, for example, Fijian, Tongan, and so on.* ⟿

[                    ]

- ☐ Some other race — *Print race.* ⟿

[                    ]

Source: U.S. Census Bureau, 2010 Census questionnaire.

(OMB) 1997 *Revisions to the Standards for the Classification of Federal Data on Race and Ethnicity.*[4] These federal standards mandate that race and Hispanic origin (ethnicity) are separate and distinct concepts and that when collecting these data via self-identification, two different questions must be used.[5]

---

[1] The terms "Black" and "Black or African American" are used interchangeably in this report.

[2] This report discusses data for the 50 states and the District of Columbia, but not Puerto Rico.

[3] Information on the *2010 Census Redistricting Data (Public Law 94-171) Summary File* is available online at <http://2010.census.gov/2010census/data/redistricting-data.php>.

---

[4] The 1997 *Revisions to the Standards for the Classification of Federal Data on Race and Ethnicity*, issued by OMB, is available at <www.whitehouse.gov/omb/fedreg/1997standards.html>.

[5] The OMB requires federal agencies to use a minimum of two ethnicities: Hispanic or Latino and Not Hispanic or Latino. Hispanic origin can be viewed as the heritage, nationality group, lineage, or country of birth of the person or the person's parents or ancestors before their arrival in the United States. People who identify their origin as Hispanic, Latino, or Spanish may be of any race. "Hispanic or Latino" refers to a person of Cuban, Mexican, Puerto Rican, South or Central American, or other Spanish culture or origin regardless of race.

U.S. Department of Commerce
Economics and Statistics Administration
U.S. CENSUS BUREAU

Starting in 1997, OMB required federal agencies to use a minimum of five race categories: White, Black or African American, American Indian or Alaska Native, Asian, and Native Hawaiian or Other Pacific Islander. For respondents unable to identify with any of these five race categories, OMB approved the Census Bureau's inclusion of a sixth category—Some Other Race—on the Census 2000 and 2010 Census questionnaires. The 1997 OMB standards also allowed for respondents to identify with more than one race. The definition of the Black or African American racial category used in the 2010 Census is presented in the text box on this page.

Data on race have been collected since the first U.S. decennial census in 1790.[6] For the first time in Census 2000, individuals were presented with the option to self-identify with more than one race and this continued with the 2010 Census, as prescribed by OMB. There are 57 possible multiple race combinations involving the five OMB race categories and Some Other Race.[7]

The 2010 Census question on race included 15 separate response categories and three areas where respondents could write in detailed information about their race (see

---

## DEFINITION OF BLACK OR AFRICAN AMERICAN USED IN THE 2010 CENSUS

According to OMB, "Black or African American" refers to a person having origins in any of the Black racial groups of Africa.

The Black racial category includes people who marked the "Black, African Am., or Negro" checkbox. It also includes respondents who reported entries such as African American; Sub-Saharan African entries, such as Kenyan and Nigerian; and Afro-Caribbean entries, such as Haitian and Jamaican.*

*Sub-Saharan African entries are classified as Black or African American with the exception of Sudanese and Cape Verdean because of their complex, historical heritage. North African entries are classified as White, as OMB defines White as a person having origins in any of the original peoples of Europe, the Middle East, or North Africa.

---

Figure 1).[8] The response categories and write-in answers can be combined to create the five minimum OMB race categories plus Some Other Race. In addition to White, Black or African American, American Indian and Alaska Native, and Some Other Race, 7 of the 15 response categories are Asian groups and 4 are Native Hawaiian and Other Pacific Islander groups.[9]

For a complete explanation of the race categories used in the 2010 Census, see the 2010 Census Brief, *Overview of Race and Hispanic Origin: 2010.*[10]

---

[8] There were two changes to the question on race for the 2010 Census. First, the wording of the race question was changed from "What is this person's race? Mark ☒ one or more races to indicate what this person considers himself/herself to be" in 2000 to "What is this person's race? Mark ☒ one or more boxes" for 2010. Second, in 2010, examples were added to the "Other Asian" response category (Hmong, Laotian, Thai, Pakistani, Cambodian, and so on) and the "Other Pacific Islander" response category (Fijian, Tongan, and so on). In 2000, no examples were given in the race question.

[9] The race categories included in the census questionnaire generally reflect a social definition of race recognized in this country and are not an attempt to define race biologically, anthropologically, or genetically. In addition, it is recognized that the categories of the race question include race and national origin or sociocultural groups.

[10] Humes, K., N. Jones, and R. Ramirez. 2011. *Overview of Race and Hispanic Origin: 2010*, U.S. Census Bureau, 2010 Census Briefs, C2010BR-02, available at <www.census.gov/prod/cen2010/briefs/c2010br-02.pdf>.

---

## RACE ALONE, RACE IN COMBINATION, AND RACE ALONE-OR-IN-COMBINATION CONCEPTS

This report presents data for the Black population and focuses on results for three major conceptual groups.

People who responded to the question on race by indicating only one race are referred to as the *race alone* population, or the group who reported *only one* race. For example, respondents who marked only the "Black, African Am., or Negro" category on the census questionnaire would be included in the *Black alone* population. This population can be viewed as the minimum number of people reporting Black.

Individuals who chose more than one of the six race categories are referred to as the *race in combination* population, or as the group who reported *more than one race*. For example, respondents who reported they were Black or African American **and** White or Black or African American **and** Asian **and** American Indian and Alaska Native would be included in the *Black in combination* population. This population is also referred to as the *multiple-race Black* population.

---

[6] For information about comparability of 2010 Census data on race and Hispanic origin to data collected in previous censuses, see the *2010 Census Redistricting Data (Public Law 94-171) Summary File—Technical Documentation* at <www.census.gov/prod/cen2010/doc/pl94-171.pdf>.

[7] The 2010 Census provides data on the total population reporting more than one race, as well as detailed race combinations (e.g., Black or African American **and** White; Black or African American **and** Asian **and** American Indian and Alaska Native). In this report, the multiple-race categories are denoted with the conjunction **and** in bold and italicized print to indicate the separate race groups that comprise the particular combination.

Table 1.

## Black or African American Population: 2000 and 2010

(For information on confidentiality protection, nonsampling error, and definitions, see *www.census.gov/prod/cen2010/doc/pl94-171.pdf*)

| Race | 2000 | | 2010 | | Change, 2000 to 2010 | |
|---|---|---|---|---|---|---|
| | Number | Percent of total population | Number | Percent of total population | Number | Percent |
| Total population . . . . . . . . . . . . . . . . . . . . . . . . . . . . . . | 281,421,906 | 100.0 | 308,745,538 | 100.0 | 27,323,632 | 9.7 |
| Black or African American alone or in combination . . . . . . . . . . . . | 36,419,434 | 12.9 | 42,020,743 | 13.6 | 5,601,309 | 15.4 |
| Black or African American alone . . . . . . . . . . . . . . . . . . . . . . . . | 34,658,190 | 12.3 | 38,929,319 | 12.6 | 4,271,129 | 12.3 |
| Black or African American in combination . . . . . . . . . . . . . . . . . . | 1,761,244 | 0.6 | 3,091,424 | 1.0 | 1,330,180 | 75.5 |
| Black or African American; White. . . . . . . . . . . . . . . . . . . . . | 784,764 | 0.3 | 1,834,212 | 0.6 | 1,049,448 | 133.7 |
| Black or African American; Some Other Race. . . . . . . . . . . . . . | 417,249 | 0.1 | 314,571 | 0.1 | −102,678 | −24.6 |
| Black or African American; American Indian and Alaska Native . . | 182,494 | 0.1 | 269,421 | 0.1 | 86,927 | 47.6 |
| Black or African American; White; American Indian and Alaska Native. . . . . . . . . . . . . . . . . . . . . . . . . . . . . . . . . | 112,207 | – | 230,848 | 0.1 | 118,641 | 105.7 |
| Black or African American; Asian. . . . . . . . . . . . . . . . . . . . . | 106,782 | – | 185,595 | 0.1 | 78,813 | 73.8 |
| All other combinations including Black or African American . . . . . | 157,748 | 0.1 | 256,777 | 0.1 | 99,029 | 62.8 |
| Not Black or African American alone or in combination . . . . . . . . . | 245,002,472 | 87.1 | 266,724,795 | 86.4 | 21,722,323 | 8.9 |

– Percentage rounds to 0.0.

Note: In Census 2000, an error in data processing resulted in an overstatement of the Two or More Races population by about 1 million people (about 15 percent) nationally, which almost entirely affected race combinations involving Some Other Race. Therefore, data users should assess observed changes in the Two or More Races population and race combinations involving Some Other Race between Census 2000 and the 2010 Census with caution. Changes in specific race combinations not involving Some Other Race, such as Black or African American **and** White or Black or African American **and** Asian, generally should be more comparable.

Sources: U.S. Census Bureau, *Census 2000 Redistricting Data (Public Law 94-171) Summary File*, Table PL1; and *2010 Census Redistricting Data (Public Law 94-171) Summary File*, Table P1.

The maximum number of people reporting Black is reflected in the *Black alone-or-in-combination* population. One way to define the Black population is to combine those respondents who reported Black alone with those who reported Black in combination with one or more other races. This creates the *Black alone-or-in-combination* population. Another way to think of the *Black alone-or-in-combination* population is the total number of people who reported Black, whether or not they reported any other races.

Throughout the report, the discussion of the Black population compares results for each of these groups and highlights the diversity within the entire Black population.[11]

[11] As a matter of policy, the Census Bureau does not advocate the use of the *alone* population over the *alone-or-in-combination* population or vice versa. The use of the *alone* population in sections of this report does not imply that it is a preferred method of presenting or analyzing data. The same is true for sections of this report that focus on the *alone-or-in-combination* population. Data on race from the 2010 Census can be presented and discussed in a variety of ways.

## THE BLACK POPULATION: A SNAPSHOT

The 2010 Census showed that the United States population on April 1, 2010, was 308.7 million. Out of the total population, 38.9 million people, or 13 percent, identified as Black alone (see Table 1).[12, 13] In addition, 3.1 million people, or 1 percent, reported Black in combination with one or more other races.

Together, these two groups totaled 42.0 million people. Thus, 14 percent of all people in the United States identified as Black, either

[12] Percentages shown in text generally are rounded to the nearest integer, while those shown in tables and figures are shown with decimals. All rounding is based on unrounded calculations. Thus, due to rounding, some percentages shown in tables and figures ending in "5" may round either up or down. For example, unrounded numbers of 14.49 and 14.51 would both be shown as 14.5 in a table, but would be cited in the text as 14 and 15, respectively.

[13] For the purposes of this report, the terms "reported," "identified," and "classified" are used interchangeably to refer to the response provided by respondents as well as responses assigned during the editing and imputation process.

alone, or in combination with one or more other races.

**The Black population increased at a faster rate than the total population.**

The total U.S. population grew by 9.7 percent, from 281.4 million in 2000 to 308.7 million in 2010 (see Table 1). In comparison, the Black alone population grew by 12 percent from 34.7 million to 38.9 million.[14]

The Black alone-or-in-combination population experienced more growth than the total population and the Black alone population, growing by 15 percent. However, both groups grew at a slower rate

[14] The observed changes in the race counts between Census 2000 and the 2010 Census could be attributed to a number of factors. Demographic change since 2000, which includes births and deaths in a geographic area and migration in and out of a geographic area, will have an impact on the resulting 2010 Census counts. Additionally, some changes in the race question's wording and format since Census 2000 could have influenced reporting patterns in the 2010 Census.

Table 2.

## Most Frequent Combinations of Black or African American Population With One or More Other Races by Hispanic or Latino Origin: 2000 and 2010

(For information on confidentiality protection, nonsampling error, and definitions, see *www.census.gov/prod/cen2010/doc/pl94-171.pdf*)

| Black or African American in combination | 2000 | | 2010 | | Change, 2000 to 2010 | |
|---|---|---|---|---|---|---|
| | Number | Percent | Number | Percent | Number | Percent |
| **Total number reporting Black or African American and one or more other races** | **1,761,244** | **100.0** | **3,091,424** | **100.0** | **1,330,180** | **75.5** |
| Black or African American; White | 784,764 | 44.6 | 1,834,212 | 59.3 | 1,049,448 | 133.7 |
| Black or African American; Some Other Race | 417,249 | 23.7 | 314,571 | 10.2 | −102,678 | −24.6 |
| Black or African American; American Indian and Alaska Native | 182,494 | 10.4 | 269,421 | 8.7 | 86,927 | 47.6 |
| Black or African American; White; American Indian and Alaska Native | 112,207 | 6.4 | 230,848 | 7.5 | 118,641 | 105.7 |
| Black or African American; Asian | 106,782 | 6.1 | 185,595 | 6.0 | 78,813 | 73.8 |
| Black or African American; White; Some Other Race | 43,172 | 2.5 | 46,641 | 1.5 | 3,469 | 8.0 |
| All other combinations including Black or African American | 114,576 | 6.5 | 210,136 | 6.8 | 95,560 | 83.4 |
| | | | | | | |
| **Hispanic or Latino** | | | | | | |
| Black or African American in combination | 325,330 | 100.0 | 653,747 | 100.0 | 328,417 | 100.9 |
| Black or African American; White | 87,687 | 27.0 | 245,850 | 37.6 | 158,163 | 180.4 |
| Black or African American; Some Other Race | 161,283 | 49.6 | 227,648 | 34.8 | 66,365 | 41.1 |
| Black or African American; American Indian and Alaska Native | 14,472 | 4.4 | 31,571 | 4.8 | 17,099 | 118.2 |
| Black or African American; White; American Indian and Alaska Native | 18,046 | 5.5 | 50,000 | 7.6 | 31,954 | 177.1 |
| Black or African American; Asian | 7,269 | 2.2 | 15,451 | 2.4 | 8,182 | 112.6 |
| Black or African American; White; Some Other Race | 15,481 | 4.8 | 33,554 | 5.1 | 18,073 | 116.7 |
| All other combinations including Black or African American | 21,092 | 6.5 | 49,673 | 7.6 | 28,581 | 135.5 |
| | | | | | | |
| **Not Hispanic or Latino** | | | | | | |
| Black or African American in combination | 1,435,914 | 100.0 | 2,437,677 | 100.0 | 1,001,763 | 69.8 |
| Black or African American; White | 697,077 | 48.5 | 1,588,362 | 65.2 | 891,285 | 127.9 |
| Black or African American; Some Other Race | 255,966 | 17.8 | 86,923 | 3.6 | −169,043 | −66.0 |
| Black or African American; American Indian and Alaska Native | 168,022 | 11.7 | 237,850 | 9.8 | 69,828 | 41.6 |
| Black or African American; White; American Indian and Alaska Native | 94,161 | 6.6 | 180,848 | 7.4 | 86,687 | 92.1 |
| Black or African American; Asian | 99,513 | 6.9 | 170,144 | 7.0 | 70,631 | 71.0 |
| Black or African American; White; Some Other Race | 27,691 | 1.9 | 13,087 | 0.5 | −14,604 | −52.7 |
| All other combinations including Black or African American | 93,484 | 6.5 | 160,463 | 6.6 | 66,979 | 71.6 |

Note: In Census 2000, an error in data processing resulted in an overstatement of the Two or More Races population by about 1 million people (about 15 percent) nationally, which almost entirely affected race combinations involving Some Other Race. Therefore, data users should assess observed changes in the Two or More Races population and race combinations involving Some Other Race between Census 2000 and the 2010 Census with caution. Changes in specific race combinations not involving Some Other Race, such as Black or African American *and* White or Black or African American *and* Asian, generally should be more comparable.

Sources: U.S. Census Bureau, *Census 2000 Redistricting Data (Public Law 94-171) Summary File,* Tables PL1 and PL2; and *2010 Census Redistricting Data (Public Law 94-171) Summary File,* Tables P1 and P2.

than most other major race and ethnic groups in the country.[15]

[15] Humes, K., N. Jones, and R. Ramirez. 2011. *Overview of Race and Hispanic Origin: 2010*, U.S. Census Bureau, 2010 Census Briefs, C2010BR-02, available at <www.census.gov/prod/cen2010/briefs/c2010br-02.pdf>.

## MULTIPLE-RACE REPORTING AMONG THE BLACK POPULATION

**Blacks who reported more than one race grew at a much faster rate than the Black alone population.**

In the 2010 Census, 3.1 million people reported Black in combination with one or more additional races (see Table 2). The multiple-race Black population grew at a considerably faster rate than the Black alone population, growing by more than three-fourths in size since 2000.

**The largest multiple-race combination was Black *and* White.**

Among people who reported they were Black and one or more additional races, the majority identified as Black *and* White (59 percent) (see Table 2). This was followed by Black and Some Other Race (10 percent), Black *and* American Indian and Alaska Native (9 percent), and Black *and* White *and* American Indian and Alaska Native (7 percent). Together, these four combinations comprised over 85 percent of all Blacks who reported multiple races.

**The Black *and* White population contributed to most of the growth among Blacks who reported multiple races.**

Among people who reported their race as Black and one or more additional races, those who reported Black *and* White more than doubled in size from about 785,000 in 2000 to 1.8 million in 2010. This combination constituted the greatest increase in the multiple-race Black population. The Black *and* White population's share of all multiple-race Blacks also increased substantially, from 45 percent in 2000 to 59 percent in 2010, about a 15 percentage-point difference.

The Black *and* Some Other Race population decreased between 2000 to 2010. This decrease was likely due to a data processing error in the Two or More Races population, which largely affected the combinations that included Some Other Race, overstating the

Black *and* Some Other Race population in 2000.[16]

The Black *and* American Indian and Alaska Native population grew by nearly one-half its size, increasing from 182,000 in 2000 to 269,000 in 2010. However, the Black *and* American Indian and Alaska Native population decreased as a proportion of the Black in combination population, from 10 percent to 9 percent.

The Black *and* White *and* American Indian and Alaska Native population increased both numerically and as a proportion of the Black in combination population. This population more than doubled in size from 112,000 in 2000 to 231,000 in 2010.

The Black *and* Asian population increased numerically from 107,000 in 2000 to 186,000 in 2010, an increase of 74 percent or nearly three-fourths in size. However, the Black *and* Asian population as a proportion of Blacks who reported multiple races remained at about 6 percent.

## PATTERNS AMONG THE NON-HISPANIC BLACK POPULATION AND THE HISPANIC BLACK POPULATION

According to the 1997 OMB standards, Hispanics may be of any race. The 2010 Census results reflect this, demonstrating that

---

[16] In Census 2000, an error in data processing resulted in an overstatement of the Two or More Races population by about 1 million people (about 15 percent) nationally, which almost entirely affected race combinations involving Some Other Race. Therefore, data users should assess observed changes in the Two or More Races population and race combinations involving Some Other Race between Census 2000 and the 2010 Census with caution. Changes in specific race combinations not involving Some Other Race, such as Black or African American *and* White or Black or African American *and* Asian, generally should be more comparable.

Hispanics report a diversity of races (White, Black, American Indian or Alaska Native, etc.), or may also report that they are "Some Other Race" (self-identifying their race as "Latino," "Mexican," "Puerto Rican," "Salvadoran," or other national origins or ethnicities), or identify with various combinations of races. For more details on the race reporting patterns of Hispanics, see the 2010 Census Brief, *The Hispanic Population: 2010.*[17]

This section presents data for the Black population, highlighting patterns for Blacks who reported a Hispanic origin and Blacks who did not report a Hispanic origin.

**About 97 percent of the Black alone population reported that they were non-Hispanic.**

In 2010, the overwhelming majority of the Black alone population was non-Hispanic—about 97 percent of the Black alone population reported as non-Hispanic and 3 percent as Hispanic (see Table 3). Similarly, 95 percent of the Black alone-or-in-combination population reported as non-Hispanic and about 5 percent reported as Hispanic. However, a much lower proportion (79 percent) of people who reported Black in combination with one or more additional races were non-Hispanic.

**Both non-Hispanic Blacks and Hispanic Blacks contributed to the growth of the multiple-race Black population.**

Nationwide, the total multiple-race population grew from 6.8 million in 2000 to 9.0 million in 2010 (see Tables 3 and 4). Both non-Hispanic

---

[17] Ennis, S., M. Rios-Vargas, and N. Albert. 2011. *The Hispanic Population: 2010*, U.S. Census Bureau, 2010 Census Briefs, C2010BR-04, available at <www.census.gov/prod/cen2010/briefs/c2010br-04.pdf>.

Table 3.
## Black or African American Population by Hispanic or Latino Origin: 2010
(For information on confidentiality protection, nonsampling error, and definitions, see *www.census.gov/prod/cen2010/doc/pl94-171.pdf*)

| Race and Hispanic or Latino origin | Alone or in combination | | | Alone | | | In combination | | |
|---|---|---|---|---|---|---|---|---|---|
| | Number | Percent of total population | Percent of Black or African American population | Number | Percent of total population | Percent of Black or African American population | Number | Percent of total population | Percent of Black or African American population |
| Total population ... | 308,745,538 | 100.0 | (X) | 299,736,465 | 100.0 | (X) | 9,009,073 | 100.0 | (X) |
| Black or African American ... | 42,020,743 | 13.6 | 100.0 | 38,929,319 | 13.0 | 100.0 | 3,091,424 | 34.3 | 100.0 |
| Hispanic or Latino ........ | 1,897,218 | 0.6 | 4.5 | 1,243,471 | 0.4 | 3.2 | 653,747 | 7.3 | 21.1 |
| Not Hispanic or Latino ..... | 40,123,525 | 13.0 | 95.5 | 37,685,848 | 12.6 | 96.8 | 2,437,677 | 27.1 | 78.9 |

(X) Not applicable.

Source: U.S. Census Bureau, *2010 Census Redistricting Data (Public Law 94-171) Summary File,* Tables P1 and P2.

Blacks and Hispanic Blacks contributed to this growth. In 2000, non-Hispanic Blacks accounted for 21 percent of all people who reported multiple races, compared with 27 percent in 2010. Hispanic Blacks accounted for 5 percent of all people who reported multiple races in 2000 and increased to 7 percent in 2010.

Over the last 10 years there has been a large increase in the

non-Hispanic Black in combination population who reported Black *and* White (see Table 2). In the 2010 Census, 65 percent of non-Hispanic Blacks who reported multiple races were Black *and* White, compared with 49 percent in 2000. Black *and* American Indian and Alaska Native accounted for 10 percent, and Black *and* White *and* American Indian and Alaska Native, and Black *and* Asian accounted for 7 percent each.

In 2010, among Hispanics who identified as Black and one or more additional races, 38 percent reported Black *and* White, compared with 27 percent in 2000. Black *and* Some Other Race accounted for 35 percent, Black *and* White *and* American Indian and Alaska Native accounted for 8 percent, and Black *and* White *and* Some Other Race accounted for 5 percent.

Table 4.
## Black or African American Population by Hispanic or Latino Origin: 2000
(For information on confidentiality protection, nonsampling error, and definitions, see *www.census.gov/prod/cen2000/doc/pl94-171.pdf*)

| Race and Hispanic or Latino origin | Alone or in combination | | | Alone | | | In combination | | |
|---|---|---|---|---|---|---|---|---|---|
| | Number | Percent of total population | Percent of Black or African American population | Number | Percent of total population | Percent of Black or African American population | Number | Percent of total population | Percent of Black or African American population |
| Total population .. | 281,421,906 | 100.0 | (X) | 274,595,678 | 100.0 | (X) | 6,826,228 | 100.0 | (X) |
| Black or African American .. | 36,419,434 | 12.9 | 100.0 | 34,658,190 | 12.6 | 100.0 | 1,761,244 | 25.8 | 100.0 |
| Hispanic or Latino ....... | 1,035,683 | 0.4 | 2.8 | 710,353 | 0.3 | 2.0 | 325,330 | 4.8 | 18.5 |
| Not Hispanic or Latino .... | 35,383,751 | 12.6 | 97.2 | 33,947,837 | 12.4 | 98.0 | 1,435,914 | 21.0 | 81.5 |

(X) Not applicable.

Source: U.S. Census Bureau, *2000 Census Redistricting Data (Public Law 94-171) Summary File,* Tables PL1 and PL2.

## THE GEOGRAPHIC DISTRIBUTION OF THE BLACK POPULATION

**The South was the region where Blacks comprised the greatest proportion of the total population.**

The South was the region where the Black alone-or-in-combination population comprised the greatest proportion of the total population, at 20 percent (see Table 5).[18] In other regions, the Black alone-or-in-combination population was much smaller in proportion—13 percent in the Northeast, 11 percent in the Midwest, and 6 percent in the West. These results were similar for the Black alone population.

**The majority of Blacks in the United States lived in the South.**

According to the 2010 Census, of all respondents who reported Black alone-or-in-combination, 55 percent lived in the South, 18 percent in the Midwest, 17 percent in the Northeast, and 10 percent in the West (see Figure 2). This pattern was similar for the Black alone population.

Compared to 2000, the proportions of the Black alone-or-in-combination population for the West stayed about the same, while the proportions increased

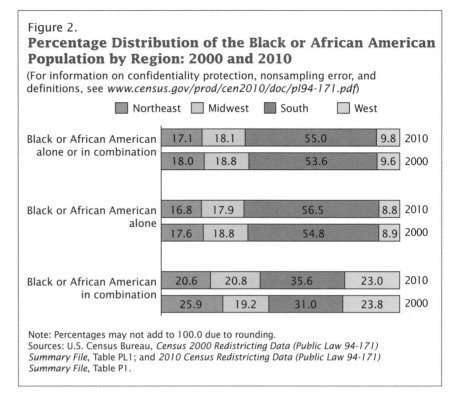

Figure 2.

**Percentage Distribution of the Black or African American Population by Region: 2000 and 2010**

(For information on confidentiality protection, nonsampling error, and definitions, see *www.census.gov/prod/cen2010/doc/pl94-171.pdf*)

■ Northeast  ☐ Midwest  ■ South  ☐ West

| | Northeast | Midwest | South | West | |
|---|---|---|---|---|---|
| Black or African American alone or in combination | 17.1 | 18.1 | 55.0 | 9.8 | 2010 |
| | 18.0 | 18.8 | 53.6 | 9.6 | 2000 |
| Black or African American alone | 16.8 | 17.9 | 56.5 | 8.8 | 2010 |
| | 17.6 | 18.8 | 54.8 | 8.9 | 2000 |
| Black or African American in combination | 20.6 | 20.8 | 35.6 | 23.0 | 2010 |
| | 25.9 | 19.2 | 31.0 | 23.8 | 2000 |

Note: Percentages may not add to 100.0 due to rounding.
Sources: U.S. Census Bureau, *Census 2000 Redistricting Data (Public Law 94-171) Summary File*, Table PL1; and *2010 Census Redistricting Data (Public Law 94-171) Summary File*, Table P1.

[18] The Northeast census region includes Connecticut, Maine, Massachusetts, New Hampshire, New Jersey, New York, Pennsylvania, Rhode Island, and Vermont. The Midwest census region includes Illinois, Indiana, Iowa, Kansas, Michigan, Minnesota, Missouri, Nebraska, North Dakota, Ohio, South Dakota, and Wisconsin. The South census region includes Alabama, Arkansas, Delaware, the District of Columbia, Florida, Georgia, Kentucky, Louisiana, Maryland, Mississippi, North Carolina, Oklahoma, South Carolina, Tennessee, Texas, Virginia, and West Virginia. The West census region includes Alaska, Arizona, California, Colorado, Hawaii, Idaho, Montana, Nevada, New Mexico, Oregon, Utah, Washington, and Wyoming.

in the South and decreased in the Northeast and the Midwest. The proportion of the Black alone population also increased in the South, from 55 percent in 2000 to 57 percent in 2010, whereas the Northeast and the Midwest experienced decreases in their share of the Black alone population.

**The multiple-race Black population was more geographically dispersed than the Black alone population.**

The Black in combination population had a different regional pattern compared to the Black alone population (see Figure 2). A considerably higher proportion of the multiple-race Black population lived in the West (23 percent), relative to the Black alone population (9 percent). While a large proportion of the multiple-race Black population lived in the South (36 percent), this was much lower than the Black alone population (57 percent).

**The Black population grew in every region between 2000 and 2010 with the Black in combination population contributing to this growth, particularly in the South.**

The Black alone-or-in-combination population grew in every region between 2000 and 2010, led by 18 percent growth in both the South and the West (see Table 5). The Black alone population also increased in every region, but at a slower rate than the Black alone-or-in-combination population. The Black alone population grew the most in the South, increasing by 16 percent.

The Black in combination population contributed to population growth in every region, particularly the South. In the South, the Black in combination population doubled from 547,000 to 1.1 million, growing 101 percent over the decade. The Midwest also experienced

Table 5.

# Black or African American Population for the United States, Regions, and States, and for Puerto Rico: 2000 and 2010

(For information on confidentiality protection, nonsampling error, and definitions, see *www.census.gov/prod/cen2010/doc/pl94-171.pdf*)

| Area | Black or African American alone or in combination | | | | Black or African American alone | | | | Black or African American in combination | | | |
|---|---|---|---|---|---|---|---|---|---|---|---|---|
| | 2000 | 2010 | Percent of total popula-tion, 2010[1] | Percent change, 2000 to 2010 | 2000 | 2010 | Percent of total popula-tion, 2010[1] | Percent change, 2000 to 2010 | 2000 | 2010 | Percent of total popula-tion, 2010[1] | Percent change, 2000 to 2010 |
| United States .. | 36,419,434 | 42,020,743 | 13.6 | 15.4 | 34,658,190 | 38,929,319 | 12.6 | 12.3 | 1,761,244 | 3,091,424 | 1.0 | 75.5 |
| **REGION** | | | | | | | | | | | | |
| Northeast ........ | 6,556,909 | 7,187,488 | 13.0 | 9.6 | 6,099,881 | 6,550,217 | 11.8 | 7.4 | 457,028 | 637,271 | 1.2 | 39.4 |
| Midwest ......... | 6,838,669 | 7,594,486 | 11.3 | 11.1 | 6,499,733 | 6,950,869 | 10.4 | 6.9 | 338,936 | 643,617 | 1.0 | 89.9 |
| South ........... | 19,528,231 | 23,105,082 | 20.2 | 18.3 | 18,981,692 | 22,005,433 | 19.2 | 15.9 | 546,539 | 1,099,649 | 1.0 | 101.2 |
| West ............ | 3,495,625 | 4,133,687 | 5.7 | 18.3 | 3,076,884 | 3,422,800 | 4.8 | 11.2 | 418,741 | 710,887 | 1.0 | 69.8 |
| **STATE** | | | | | | | | | | | | |
| Alabama ......... | 1,168,998 | 1,281,118 | 26.8 | 9.6 | 1,155,930 | 1,251,311 | 26.2 | 8.3 | 13,068 | 29,807 | 0.6 | 128.1 |
| Alaska .......... | 27,147 | 33,150 | 4.7 | 22.1 | 21,787 | 23,263 | 3.3 | 6.8 | 5,360 | 9,887 | 1.4 | 84.5 |
| Arizona ......... | 185,599 | 318,665 | 5.0 | 71.7 | 158,873 | 259,008 | 4.1 | 63.0 | 26,726 | 59,657 | 0.9 | 123.2 |
| Arkansas ........ | 427,152 | 468,710 | 16.1 | 9.7 | 418,950 | 449,895 | 15.4 | 7.4 | 8,202 | 18,815 | 0.6 | 129.4 |
| California ........ | 2,513,041 | 2,683,914 | 7.2 | 6.8 | 2,263,882 | 2,299,072 | 6.2 | 1.6 | 249,159 | 384,842 | 1.0 | 54.5 |
| Colorado ........ | 190,717 | 249,812 | 5.0 | 31.0 | 165,063 | 201,737 | 4.0 | 22.2 | 25,654 | 48,075 | 1.0 | 87.4 |
| Connecticut ...... | 339,078 | 405,600 | 11.3 | 19.6 | 309,843 | 362,296 | 10.1 | 16.9 | 29,235 | 43,304 | 1.2 | 48.1 |
| Delaware ........ | 157,152 | 205,923 | 22.9 | 31.0 | 150,666 | 191,814 | 21.4 | 27.3 | 6,486 | 14,109 | 1.6 | 117.5 |
| District of Columbia .. | 350,455 | 314,352 | 52.2 | −10.3 | 343,312 | 305,125 | 50.7 | −11.1 | 7,143 | 9,227 | 1.5 | 29.2 |
| Florida ........... | 2,471,730 | 3,200,663 | 17.0 | 29.5 | 2,335,505 | 2,999,862 | 16.0 | 28.4 | 136,225 | 200,801 | 1.1 | 47.4 |
| Georgia ......... | 2,393,425 | 3,054,098 | 31.5 | 27.6 | 2,349,542 | 2,950,435 | 30.5 | 25.6 | 43,883 | 103,663 | 1.1 | 136.2 |
| Hawaii .......... | 33,343 | 38,820 | 2.9 | 16.4 | 22,003 | 21,424 | 1.6 | −2.6 | 11,340 | 17,396 | 1.3 | 53.4 |
| Idaho ........... | 8,127 | 15,940 | 1.0 | 96.1 | 5,456 | 9,810 | 0.6 | 79.8 | 2,671 | 6,130 | 0.4 | 129.5 |
| Illinois .......... | 1,937,671 | 1,974,113 | 15.4 | 1.9 | 1,876,875 | 1,866,414 | 14.5 | −0.6 | 60,796 | 107,699 | 0.8 | 77.1 |
| Indiana ......... | 538,015 | 654,415 | 10.1 | 21.6 | 510,034 | 591,397 | 9.1 | 16.0 | 27,981 | 63,018 | 1.0 | 125.2 |
| Iowa ............ | 72,512 | 113,225 | 3.7 | 56.1 | 61,853 | 89,148 | 2.9 | 44.1 | 10,659 | 24,077 | 0.8 | 125.9 |
| Kansas .......... | 170,610 | 202,149 | 7.1 | 18.5 | 154,198 | 167,864 | 5.9 | 8.9 | 16,412 | 34,285 | 1.2 | 108.9 |
| Kentucky ........ | 311,878 | 376,213 | 8.7 | 20.6 | 295,994 | 337,520 | 7.8 | 14.0 | 15,884 | 38,693 | 0.9 | 143.6 |
| Louisiana ........ | 1,468,317 | 1,486,885 | 32.8 | 1.3 | 1,451,944 | 1,452,396 | 32.0 | − | 16,373 | 34,489 | 0.8 | 110.6 |
| Maine .......... | 9,553 | 21,764 | 1.6 | 127.8 | 6,760 | 15,707 | 1.2 | 132.4 | 2,793 | 6,057 | 0.5 | 116.9 |
| Maryland ........ | 1,525,036 | 1,783,899 | 30.9 | 17.0 | 1,477,411 | 1,700,298 | 29.4 | 15.1 | 47,625 | 83,601 | 1.4 | 75.5 |
| Massachusetts...... | 398,479 | 508,413 | 7.8 | 27.6 | 343,454 | 434,398 | 6.6 | 26.5 | 55,025 | 74,015 | 1.1 | 34.5 |
| Michigan ......... | 1,474,613 | 1,505,514 | 15.2 | 2.1 | 1,412,742 | 1,400,362 | 14.2 | −0.9 | 61,871 | 105,152 | 1.1 | 70.0 |
| Minnesota ........ | 202,972 | 327,548 | 6.2 | 61.4 | 171,731 | 274,412 | 5.2 | 59.8 | 31,241 | 53,136 | 1.0 | 70.1 |
| Mississippi ........ | 1,041,708 | 1,115,801 | 37.6 | 7.1 | 1,033,809 | 1,098,385 | 37.0 | 6.2 | 7,899 | 17,416 | 0.6 | 120.5 |
| Missouri ......... | 655,377 | 747,474 | 12.5 | 14.1 | 629,391 | 693,391 | 11.6 | 10.2 | 25,986 | 54,083 | 0.9 | 108.1 |
| Montana ......... | 4,441 | 7,917 | 0.8 | 78.3 | 2,692 | 4,027 | 0.4 | 49.6 | 1,749 | 3,890 | 0.4 | 122.4 |
| Nebraska......... | 75,833 | 98,959 | 5.4 | 30.5 | 68,541 | 82,885 | 4.5 | 20.9 | 7,292 | 16,074 | 0.9 | 120.4 |
| Nevada .......... | 150,508 | 254,452 | 9.4 | 69.1 | 135,477 | 218,626 | 8.1 | 61.4 | 15,031 | 35,826 | 1.3 | 138.3 |
| New Hampshire .... | 12,218 | 21,736 | 1.7 | 77.9 | 9,035 | 15,035 | 1.1 | 66.4 | 3,183 | 6,701 | 0.5 | 110.5 |
| New Jersey ....... | 1,211,750 | 1,300,363 | 14.8 | 7.3 | 1,141,821 | 1,204,826 | 13.7 | 5.5 | 69,929 | 95,537 | 1.1 | 36.6 |
| New Mexico ...... | 42,412 | 57,040 | 2.8 | 34.5 | 34,343 | 42,550 | 2.1 | 23.9 | 8,069 | 14,490 | 0.7 | 79.6 |
| New York ........ | 3,234,165 | 3,334,550 | 17.2 | 3.1 | 3,014,385 | 3,073,800 | 15.9 | 2.0 | 219,780 | 260,750 | 1.3 | 18.6 |
| North Carolina .... | 1,776,283 | 2,151,456 | 22.6 | 21.1 | 1,737,545 | 2,048,628 | 21.5 | 17.9 | 38,738 | 102,828 | 1.1 | 165.4 |
| North Dakota ..... | 5,372 | 11,086 | 1.6 | 106.4 | 3,916 | 7,960 | 1.2 | 103.3 | 1,456 | 3,126 | 0.5 | 114.7 |
| Ohio............. | 1,372,501 | 1,541,771 | 13.4 | 12.3 | 1,301,307 | 1,407,681 | 12.2 | 8.2 | 71,194 | 134,090 | 1.2 | 88.3 |
| Oklahoma ........ | 284,766 | 327,621 | 8.7 | 15.0 | 260,968 | 277,644 | 7.4 | 6.4 | 23,798 | 49,977 | 1.3 | 110.0 |
| Oregon .......... | 72,647 | 98,479 | 2.6 | 35.6 | 55,662 | 69,206 | 1.8 | 24.3 | 16,985 | 29,273 | 0.8 | 72.3 |
| Pennsylvania ...... | 1,289,123 | 1,507,965 | 11.9 | 17.0 | 1,224,612 | 1,377,689 | 10.8 | 12.5 | 64,511 | 130,276 | 1.0 | 101.9 |
| Rhode Island ...... | 58,051 | 77,754 | 7.4 | 33.9 | 46,908 | 60,189 | 5.7 | 28.3 | 11,143 | 17,565 | 1.7 | 57.6 |
| South Carolina ..... | 1,200,901 | 1,332,188 | 28.8 | 10.9 | 1,185,216 | 1,290,684 | 27.9 | 8.9 | 15,685 | 41,504 | 0.9 | 164.6 |
| South Dakota ..... | 6,687 | 14,705 | 1.8 | 119.9 | 4,685 | 10,207 | 1.3 | 117.9 | 2,002 | 4,498 | 0.6 | 124.7 |
| Tennessee ........ | 953,349 | 1,107,178 | 17.4 | 16.1 | 932,809 | 1,057,315 | 16.7 | 13.3 | 20,540 | 49,863 | 0.8 | 142.8 |
| Texas ........... | 2,493,057 | 3,168,469 | 12.6 | 27.1 | 2,404,566 | 2,979,598 | 11.8 | 23.9 | 88,491 | 188,871 | 0.8 | 113.4 |
| Utah ............ | 24,382 | 43,209 | 1.6 | 77.2 | 17,657 | 29,287 | 1.1 | 65.9 | 6,725 | 13,922 | 0.5 | 107.0 |
| Vermont ......... | 4,492 | 9,343 | 1.5 | 108.0 | 3,063 | 6,277 | 1.0 | 104.9 | 1,429 | 3,066 | 0.5 | 114.6 |
| Virginia.......... | 1,441,207 | 1,653,563 | 20.7 | 14.7 | 1,390,293 | 1,551,399 | 19.4 | 11.6 | 50,914 | 102,164 | 1.3 | 100.7 |
| Washington ....... | 238,398 | 325,004 | 4.8 | 36.3 | 190,267 | 240,042 | 3.6 | 26.2 | 48,131 | 84,962 | 1.3 | 76.5 |
| West Virginia ...... | 62,817 | 76,945 | 4.2 | 22.5 | 57,232 | 63,124 | 3.4 | 10.3 | 5,585 | 13,821 | 0.7 | 147.5 |
| Wisconsin ........ | 326,506 | 403,527 | 7.1 | 23.6 | 304,460 | 359,148 | 6.3 | 18.0 | 22,046 | 44,379 | 0.8 | 101.3 |
| Wyoming.......... | 4,863 | 7,285 | 1.3 | 49.8 | 3,722 | 4,748 | 0.8 | 27.6 | 1,141 | 2,537 | 0.5 | 122.3 |
| Puerto Rico ....... | 416,296 | 550,259 | 14.8 | 32.2 | 302,933 | 461,498 | 12.4 | 52.3 | 113,363 | 88,761 | 2.4 | −21.7 |

− Percentage rounds to 0.0.

[1] The percent of the total population is calculated by using the total population of all races. The totals for each geography can be found in Table 11, page 18 of the 2010 Census Brief, *Overview of Race and Hispanic Origin: 2010* available at <www.census.gov/prod/cen2010/briefs/c2010br-02.pdf>.

Sources: U.S. Census Bureau, *Census 2000 Redistricting Data (Public Law 94-171) Summary File*, Table PL1; and *2010 Census Redistricting Data (Public Law 94-171) Summary File*, Table P1.

considerable growth in the Black in combination population, increasing 90 percent, followed by increases of 70 percent in the West and 39 percent in the Northeast.

This growth contributed to shifting patterns of the Black in combination population by region. The proportion of the Black in combination population residing in the South increased from 31 percent to 36 percent, and decreased in the Northeast (from 26 percent to 21 percent) (see Figure 2).

**The Black population represented over 50 percent of the total population in the District of Columbia and over 25 percent of the total population in six states, all located in the South.**

The Black alone-or-in-combination population represented 38 percent of the total population in Mississippi (see Table 5). This was followed by Louisiana (33 percent), Georgia (32 percent), Maryland (31 percent), South Carolina (29 percent), and Alabama (27 percent). These same six states had the highest proportion of the Black alone population and the proportions were similar to the Black alone-or-in-combination population. The Black alone-or-in-combination population represented 52 percent of the total population in the District of Columbia.[19]

The Black alone-or-in-combination population represented less than 3 percent of the total population in 12 states, all located outside of the South. More than half of the states in the West had a Black alone-or-in-combination population of less than 3 percent—Hawaii, New Mexico, and Oregon (about 3 percent each); Utah (about 2 percent); and Wyoming, Idaho, and Montana (about 1 percent each).

---

[19] For this report, the District of Columbia is treated as a state equivalent.

The Black alone-or-in-combination population represented less than 3 percent of the total population in two states in the Midwest—South Dakota and North Dakota (about 2 percent each), and three states in the Northeast—New Hampshire, Maine, (about 2 percent each) and Vermont (1 percent). These same 12 states also had less than 3 percent of the Black alone population and the percentages tended to be slightly lower than the Black alone-or-in-combination population. One additional state (Iowa) had a Black alone population of less than 3 percent, and thus 13 states had Black alone populations of less than 3 percent.

**Nearly 60 percent of all people who reported Black lived in ten states.**

The ten states with the largest Black alone-or-in-combination populations in 2010 were New York (3.3 million), Florida (3.2 million), Texas (3.2 million), Georgia (3.1 million), California (2.7 million), North Carolina (2.2 million), Illinois (2.0 million), Maryland (1.8 million), Virginia (1.7 million), and Ohio (1.5 million) (see Table 5). Among these states, four experienced substantial growth between 2000 and 2010. The Black alone-or-in-combination population grew by 29 percent in Florida, 28 percent in Georgia, 27 percent in Texas, and 21 percent in North Carolina.

Out of the ten states above, nine of them also had the largest Black alone populations. The state with the tenth largest Black alone population was Louisiana (1.5 million). In a similar fashion to the Black alone-or-in-combination population, the Black alone population also experienced considerable growth in Florida, Georgia, Texas, and North Carolina.

**The Black population grew in every state between 2000 and 2010, but declined in the District of Columbia.**

Among all states, the states with small Black alone-or-in-combination populations (2 percent or less) in 2010 tended to experience the largest percentage growth. Maine experienced the largest percentage growth in the Black alone-or-in-combination population, increasing by 128 percent between 2000 and 2010. This was followed by South Dakota (120 percent), Vermont (108 percent), North Dakota (106 percent), and Idaho (96 percent).

At the other end of the spectrum, the Black population in the District of Columbia decreased by 10 percent between 2000 and 2010. As discussed earlier, the District of Columbia still had the highest proportion reporting Black among states, with 52 percent in 2010. The same patterns were observed for the Black alone population by state.

The Black in combination population showed even more substantial growth, as it more than doubled in more than half of all states. The states that experienced the most growth were in the South: North Carolina and South Carolina both grew by 165 percent, followed by West Virginia (147 percent), Kentucky (144 percent), and Tennessee (143 percent).

**Of the population who identified as Black, people who reported multiple races were more likely to live in California.**

Of all respondents who reported as Black alone-or-in-combination, about 8 percent lived in each of these states—New York, Florida, and Texas. Another 7 percent lived in Georgia and 6 percent lived in

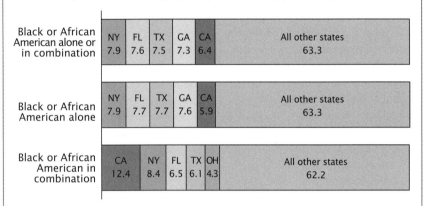

Figure 3.
**Percentage Distribution of the Black or African American Population by State: 2010**
(For information on confidentiality protection, nonsampling error, and definitions, see *www.census.gov/prod/cen2010/doc/pl94-171.pdf*)

| | NY | FL | TX | GA | CA | All other states |
|---|---|---|---|---|---|---|
| Black or African American alone or in combination | 7.9 | 7.6 | 7.5 | 7.3 | 6.4 | 63.3 |

| | NY | FL | TX | GA | CA | All other states |
|---|---|---|---|---|---|---|
| Black or African American alone | 7.9 | 7.7 | 7.7 | 7.6 | 5.9 | 63.3 |

| | CA | NY | FL | TX | OH | All other states |
|---|---|---|---|---|---|---|
| Black or African American in combination | 12.4 | 8.4 | 6.5 | 6.1 | 4.3 | 62.2 |

Note: Percentages may not add to 100.0 due to rounding.
Source: U.S. Census Bureau, *2010 Census Redistricting Data (Public Law 94-171) Summary File*, Table P1.

California (see Figure 3). The pattern for the Black alone population was similar, where 8 percent of the Black alone population lived in New York, Florida, Texas, and Georgia and 6 percent lived in California.

The pattern was slightly different for respondents who identified as Black in combination with one or more additional races. Among multiple-race Blacks, 12 percent lived in California, 8 percent in New York, 6 percent lived in both Florida and Texas, and 4 percent in Ohio.

**The Black population was highly concentrated in counties in the South.**

The Black alone-or-in-combination population was highly concentrated in 2010: 62 percent (1,941 counties) of all counties in the United States had less than 5 percent of the population identified as Black alone-or-in-combination, but in 106 counties, the Black alone-or-in-combination population comprised 50 percent or more of the total county population. All of these counties were located in the South except for the city of St. Louis, MO, which

is considered a county equivalent (see Figure 4). These patterns were similar for the Black alone population.

Concentrations of Blacks outside of the South tended to be in counties located within metropolitan statistical areas. There were 317 counties where the Black alone-or-in-combination population was 25.0 to 49.9 percent of the county population, and only 17 of these counties were not in the South. Of these 17 counties, 15 were in metro areas. This pattern was similar for the Black alone population.

Although the Black alone-or-in-combination population and the Black alone population were not as concentrated in counties in midwestern states, in some metro areas, such as around Chicago, IL, and Detroit, MI, the proportion Black was much higher than the national average of 13 percent. Also, in some metro areas in the West, such as around San Francisco, CA, and Sacramento, CA, the proportion Black was above the national average.

**The Black population in the South experienced mixed growth—some counties experienced an increase, while others experienced a decline.**

Among the 1,558 counties with a Black alone-or-in-combination population of over 1,000 people, over one-third (536 counties) had an increase of 25 percent or more from 2000 to 2010 (see Figure 5). On the other hand, 100 counties had a decrease of over 10 percent. The Black alone-or-in-combination population in counties located in northeastern states such as Maine and Pennsylvania grew significantly, as well as counties in the South, specifically Florida, which had a number of counties that grew by 25 percent or more.

Large growth in the Black alone-or-in-combination population also occurred in the West and sections of the Midwest. Counties in Arizona, Nevada, California, Oregon, and Washington grew substantially between 2000 and 2010. The Midwest had pockets of high growth in states such as Minnesota, Wisconsin, and Illinois.

The Black alone-or-in-combination population in the South experienced the largest percentage declines between 2000 and 2010. Counties located in southern states such as Texas, Arkansas, Louisiana, Mississippi, Alabama, and Georgia experienced greater declines in the Black alone-or-in-combination population compared to the rest of the nation. The Black alone population had similar results.

**The Black in combination population had large concentrations in northeastern states and counties near metro areas in the West, Midwest, and South.**

In 2010, large proportions of the Black in combination population were located in counties

Figure 4.
## Black or African American Population as a Percent of County Population: 2010
(For information on confidentiality protection, nonsampling error, and definitions, see www.census.gov/prod/cen2010/doc/pl94-171.pdf)

**Black or African American Alone**

Percent
- 50.0 or more
- 25.0 to 49.9
- 10.0 to 24.9
- 5.0 to 9.9
- Less then 5.0

*U.S. percent 12.6*

**Black or African American Alone or in Combination**

Percent
- 50.0 or more
- 25.0 to 49.9
- 10.0 to 24.9
- 5.0 to 9.9
- Less then 5.0

*U.S. percent 13.6*

Source: U.S. Census Bureau, *2010 Census Redistricting Data (Public Law 94-171) Summary File*, Table P1.

Figure 5.
## Percent Change in Black or African American Population: 2000 to 2010

(Counties with a Black or African American population of at least 1,000 are included in the maps. For information on confidentiality protection, nonsampling error, and definitions, see *www.census.gov/prod/cen2010/doc/pl94-171.pdf*)

### Black or African American Alone

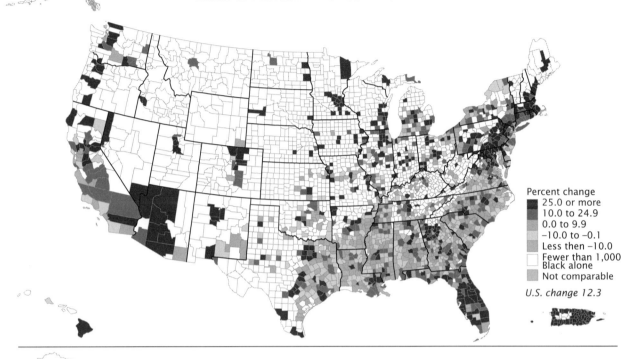

Percent change
- 25.0 or more
- 10.0 to 24.9
- 0.0 to 9.9
- −10.0 to −0.1
- Less then −10.0
- Fewer than 1,000 Black alone
- Not comparable

*U.S. change 12.3*

### Black or African American Alone or in Combination

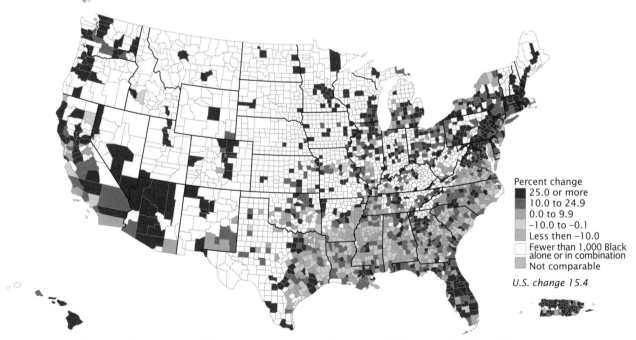

Percent change
- 25.0 or more
- 10.0 to 24.9
- 0.0 to 9.9
- −10.0 to −0.1
- Less then −10.0
- Fewer than 1,000 Black alone or in combination
- Not comparable

*U.S. change 15.4*

Sources: U.S. Census Bureau, *Census 2000 Redistricting Data (Public Law 94-171) Summary File*, Table PL1; and *2010 Census Redistricting Data (Public Law 94-171) Summary File*, Table P1.

Figure 6.
# Black in Combination Population Distribution by County: 2010

(Counties with a Black or African American in combination population of at least 1,000 are included in the map. For information on confidentiality protection, nonsampling error, and definitions, see *www.census.gov/prod/cen2010/doc/pl94-171.pdf*)

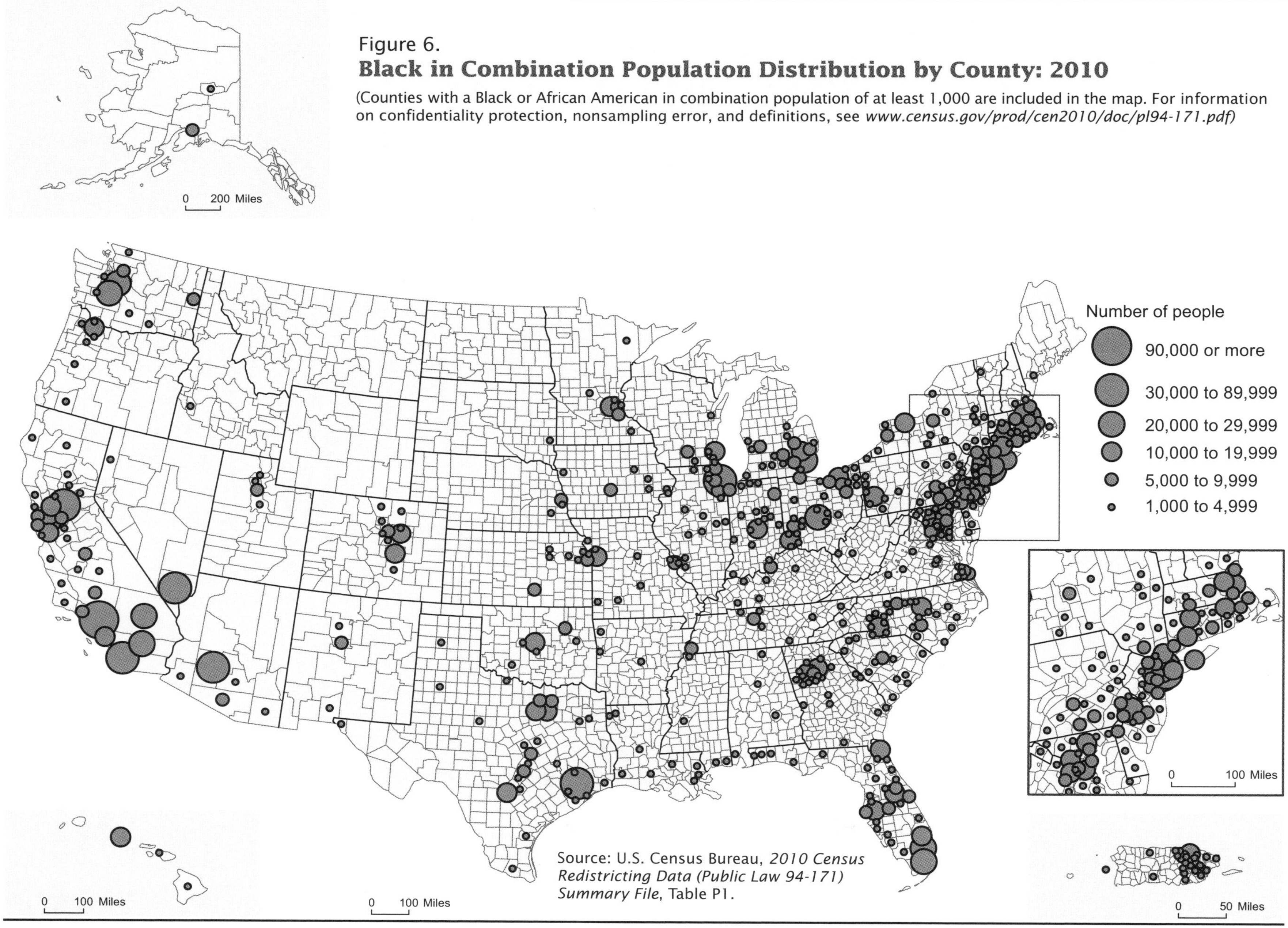

Number of people

90,000 or more

30,000 to 89,999

20,000 to 29,999

10,000 to 19,999

5,000 to 9,999

1,000 to 4,999

Source: U.S. Census Bureau, *2010 Census Redistricting Data (Public Law 94-171) Summary File*, Table P1.

100 Miles

50 Miles

200 Miles

100 Miles

100 Miles

Table 6.
## Ten Places With the Largest Number of Blacks or African Americans: 2010

(For information on confidentiality protection, nonsampling error, and definitions, see *www.census.gov/prod/cen2010/doc/pl94-171.pdf*)

| Place[1] | Total population | Black or African American alone or in combination | | Black or African American alone | | Black or African American in combination | |
|---|---|---|---|---|---|---|---|
| | | Rank | Number | Rank | Number | Rank | Number |
| New York, NY............ | 8,175,133 | 1 | 2,228,145 | 1 | 2,088,510 | 1 | 139,635 |
| Chicago, IL ............. | 2,695,598 | 2 | 913,009 | 2 | 887,608 | 3 | 25,401 |
| Philadelphia, PA.......... | 1,526,006 | 3 | 686,870 | 3 | 661,839 | 4 | 25,031 |
| Detroit, MI .............. | 713,777 | 4 | 601,988 | 4 | 590,226 | 13 | 11,762 |
| Houston, TX............. | 2,099,451 | 5 | 514,217 | 5 | 498,466 | 8 | 15,751 |
| Memphis, TN ............ | 646,889 | 6 | 414,928 | 6 | 409,687 | 58 | 5,241 |
| Baltimore, MD ........... | 620,961 | 7 | 403,998 | 7 | 395,781 | 29 | 8,217 |
| Los Angeles, CA ......... | 3,792,621 | 8 | 402,448 | 8 | 365,118 | 2 | 37,330 |
| Washington, DC.......... | 601,723 | 9 | 314,352 | 9 | 305,125 | 22 | 9,227 |
| Dallas, TX .............. | 1,197,816 | 10 | 308,087 | 10 | 298,993 | 23 | 9,094 |
| | | | | | | | |
| Columbus, OH........... | 787,033 | 15 | 237,077 | 16 | 220,241 | 5 | 16,836 |
| San Diego, CA........... | 1,307,402 | 40 | 104,374 | 43 | 87,949 | 6 | 16,425 |
| Phoenix, AZ............. | 1,445,632 | 37 | 109,544 | 40 | 93,608 | 7 | 15,936 |
| Indianapolis, IN .......... | 829,718 | 14 | 240,789 | 15 | 226,671 | 9 | 14,118 |
| Boston, MA .............. | 617,594 | 21 | 163,629 | 23 | 150,437 | 10 | 13,192 |

[1] Places of 100,000 or more total population. The 2010 Census showed 282 places in the United States with 100,000 or more population. They included 273 incorporated places (including 5 city-county consolidations) and 9 census designated places (CDPs) that were not legally incorporated.

Source: U.S. Census Bureau, *2010 Census Redistricting Data (Public Law 94-171) Summary File*, Table P1.

in northeastern states such as Pennsylvania, New Jersey, New York, and Massachusetts (see Figure 6). The Black in combination population was also concentrated in counties in midwestern states such as Ohio, Michigan, and Indiana, as well as in counties in southern states such as Georgia, North Carolina, and Florida.

Counties near metro areas in the Midwest such as Chicago, IL; Detroit, MI; and Minneapolis, MN, also had large concentrations of the Black in combination population. There were also large concentrations of the Black in combination population in the West in counties near metro areas such as Los Angeles, CA; San Francisco, CA; and Seattle, WA.

### The places with the largest Black population were New York and Chicago.

Among the places with populations of 100,000 or more, the 2010 Census showed that New York, NY, had the largest Black

alone-or-in-combination population with 2.2 million, followed by Chicago, IL (913,000) (see Table 6). Three other places had Black alone-or-in-combination populations of over 500,000 people (Philadelphia, PA; Detroit, MI; and Houston, TX).

Five of the ten places with the largest Black alone-or-in-combination populations—Houston, TX; Memphis, TN; Baltimore, MD; Washington, DC; and Dallas, TX— were in the South. These rankings were identical for the Black alone population.

### The places with the largest Black in combination populations were New York and Los Angeles.

Among the places with populations of 100,000 or more, New York, NY, had the largest Black in combination population (140,000), followed by Los Angeles, CA (37,000) (see Table 6). Two other places, Chicago, IL, and Philadelphia, PA, had populations over 25,000.

In contrast to the patterns observed for the Black alone-or-in-combination population, only one out of the ten places with the largest Black in combination population was in the South and there was more representation of places in the Midwest and the West.

### The place with the greatest proportion Black was Detroit.

Among the places with populations of 100,000 or more, the places with the greatest proportion Black alone-or-in-combination were Detroit, MI (84 percent); followed by Jackson, MS (80 percent); Miami Gardens, FL (78 percent); and Birmingham, AL (74 percent) (see Table 7). Of the top ten places shown, all were majority Black.

Of these places, eight were in the South, and two were in the Midwest, specifically Michigan. These patterns were the same for the Black alone population and the proportions were similar to the Black alone-or-in-combination population.

Table 7.

## Ten Places With the Highest Percentage of Blacks or African Americans: 2010

(For information on confidentiality protection, nonsampling error, and definitions, see *www.census.gov/prod/cen2010/doc/pl94-171.pdf*)

| Place[1] | Total population | Black or African American alone or in combination | | Black or African American alone | | Black or African American in combination | |
|---|---|---|---|---|---|---|---|
| | | Rank | Percent of total population | Rank | Percent of total population | Rank | Percent of total population |
| Detroit, MI .................. | 713,777 | 1 | 84.3 | 1 | 82.7 | 83 | 1.6 |
| Jackson, MS ............... | 173,514 | 2 | 80.1 | 2 | 79.4 | 242 | 0.7 |
| Miami Gardens, FL ........... | 107,167 | 3 | 77.9 | 3 | 76.3 | 91 | 1.6 |
| Birmingham, AL............. | 212,237 | 4 | 74.0 | 4 | 73.4 | 257 | 0.6 |
| Baltimore, MD .............. | 620,961 | 5 | 65.1 | 5 | 63.7 | 134 | 1.3 |
| Memphis, TN ............... | 646,889 | 6 | 64.1 | 6 | 63.3 | 225 | 0.8 |
| New Orleans, LA ............. | 343,829 | 7 | 61.2 | 7 | 60.2 | 184 | 1.0 |
| Flint, MI .................... | 102,434 | 8 | 59.5 | 9 | 56.6 | 9 | 2.9 |
| Montgomery, AL ............. | 205,764 | 9 | 57.4 | 8 | 56.6 | 231 | 0.8 |
| Savannah, GA............... | 136,286 | 10 | 56.7 | 10 | 55.4 | 139 | 1.3 |
| | | | | | | | |
| Lansing, MI ................. | 114,297 | 69 | 27.8 | 78 | 23.7 | 1 | 4.1 |
| Tacoma, WA................. | 198,397 | 132 | 15.0 | 145 | 11.2 | 2 | 3.8 |
| Killeen, TX.................. | 127,921 | 40 | 37.9 | 46 | 34.1 | 3 | 3.8 |
| Syracuse, NY................ | 145,170 | 51 | 33.1 | 57 | 29.5 | 4 | 3.6 |
| Providence, RI .............. | 178,042 | 109 | 19.4 | 114 | 16.0 | 5 | 3.3 |
| Fairfield, CA................. | 105,321 | 111 | 19.0 | 118 | 15.7 | 6 | 3.3 |
| Rochester, NY .............. | 210,565 | 29 | 44.9 | 33 | 41.7 | 7 | 3.2 |
| Fayetteville, NC ............. | 200,564 | 31 | 44.8 | 32 | 41.9 | 8 | 2.9 |
| Vallejo, CA.................. | 115,942 | 81 | 24.9 | 83 | 22.1 | 10 | 2.9 |

[1] Places of 100,000 or more total population. The 2010 Census showed 282 places in the United States with 100,000 or more population. They included 273 incorporated places (including 5 city-county consolidations) and 9 census designated places (CDPs) that were not legally incorporated.

Source: U.S. Census Bureau, *2010 Census Redistricting Data (Public Law 94-171) Summary File*, Table P1.

**The place with the highest proportion of people who identified as multiple-race Black was Lansing, MI.**

Among the places with populations of 100,000 or more, the places with the highest proportion of people who identified as Black and one or more other races were Lansing, MI; Tacoma, WA; Killeen, TX; and Syracuse, NY (about 4 percent each) (see Table 7). Of these ten places, three were in the Northeast, three were in the West, two in the Midwest, and two in the South.

**Among the 20 largest metropolitan statistical areas, New York-Northern New Jersey-Long Island, NY-NJ-PA, had the highest proportion of the non-Hispanic Black alone population living inside the largest principal city.**

The remaining sections discuss geographic patterns for the non-Hispanic Black alone population

and make comparisons to other race and ethnic groups.

Figure 7 shows the proportion of selected race and Hispanic origin groups who lived inside the largest principal city of the 20 largest metro areas in the country versus those who lived outside of that largest principal city.[20] The red bars represent the non-Hispanic Black alone population, the blue bars represent the non-Hispanic White alone population, the green bars represent the Hispanic population, and the orange bars represent other race groups.[21] For example, the red bar denotes the proportion of the

[20] For the remainder of this section, when metro areas are discussed, the report will refer to the largest 20 metropolitan statistical areas.

[21] For this report, the "other" race group refers to the non-Hispanic Asian alone, non-Hispanic American Indian and Alaska Native alone, non-Hispanic Native Hawaiian and Other Pacific Islander alone, and non-Hispanic Some Other Race alone populations, as well as non-Hispanics who reported multiple races.

non-Hispanic Black alone population that lived inside the largest principal city of Boston (46 percent), out of the total non-Hispanic Black alone population in the entire Boston-Cambridge-Quincy, MA-NH metro area.

The top 5 metro areas that had the highest proportion of the non-Hispanic Black alone population living inside their respective largest principal cities were New York-Northern New Jersey-Long Island, NY-NJ-PA (61 percent); Detroit-Warren-Livonia, MI (60 percent); San Diego-Carlsbad-San Marcos, CA (56 percent); Chicago-Joliet-Naperville, IL-IN-WI (54 percent); and Philadelphia-Camden-Wilmington, PA-NJ-DE-MD (53 percent).

The 5 metro areas with the lowest proportion of the non-Hispanic Black alone population living inside their respective largest principal cities were Miami-Fort

Figure 7.
**Proportion of Race and Ethnic Groups Living Inside the Largest Principal City of the 20 Largest Metropolitan Statistical Areas: 2010**

(For information on confidentiality protection, nonsampling error, and definitions, see *www.census.gov/prod/cen2010/doc/pl94-171.pdf*)

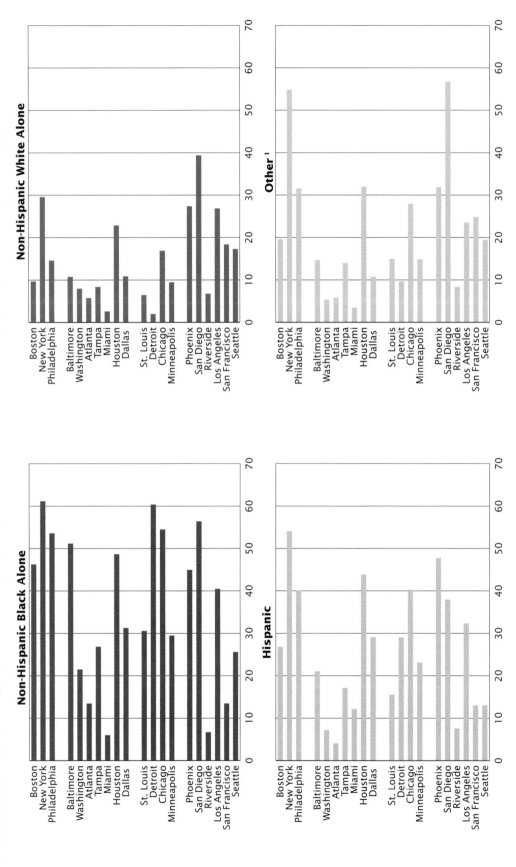

[1] For this figure, the "other" race category refers to the non-Hispanic Asian alone, non-Hispanic American Indian and Alaska Native alone, non-Hispanic Native Hawaiian and Other Pacific Islander alone, and non-Hispanic Some Other Race alone populations, as well as non-Hispanics who reported multiple races.

Note: Principal cities within regions are organized based on proximity to each other. Boston, New York, and Philadelphia are located in the Northeast census region. Baltimore, Washington, Atlanta, Tampa, Miami, Houston, and Dallas are located in the South census region. St. Louis, Detroit, Chicago, and Minneapolis are located in the Midwest census region. Phoenix, San Diego, Riverside, Los Angeles, San Francisco, and Seattle are located in the West census region.

Source: U.S. Census Bureau, 2010 Census special tabulation.

Lauderdale-Pompano Beach, FL (6 percent); Riverside-San Bernardino-Ontario, CA (7 percent); Atlanta-Sandy Springs-Marietta, GA (13 percent); San Francisco-Oakland-Fremont, CA (13 percent); and Washington-Arlington-Alexandria, DC-VA-MD-WV (21 percent).

**The proportion of the non-Hispanic Black alone population living inside the largest principal city surpassed 40 percent in all of the northeastern metro areas shown.**

Across the northeastern metro areas shown, at least 40 percent of the non-Hispanic Black alone population lived inside their respective largest principal city—New York (61 percent), Philadelphia (53 percent), and Boston (46 percent) (see Figure 7).[22]

In the South, 2 out of the 7 metro areas shown had at least 40 percent of the non-Hispanic Black alone population living inside their respective largest principal city—Baltimore (51 percent) and Houston (49 percent). In the Midwest, this was the case for 2 out of the 4 metro areas shown—Chicago (54 percent) and Detroit (60 percent). In the West, half of the metro areas shown had at least 40 percent of the non-Hispanic Black alone population living inside their largest respective principal city—San Diego (56 percent), Phoenix (45 percent), and Los Angeles (40 percent).

---

[22] The Philadelphia-Camden-Wilmington, PA-NJ-DE-MD metro area contains counties that are also part of the South region as defined by the U.S. Census Bureau.

**The non-Hispanic Black alone population was more likely to live inside the largest principal cities compared with non-Hispanic White alone, Hispanic, and other race populations.**

A higher proportion of the non-Hispanic Black alone population lived inside the largest principal cities in 15 out of the 20 largest metro areas, relative to the non-Hispanic White alone, Hispanic, and other race populations (see Figure 7). This was most pronounced in the metro areas of Detroit-Warren-Livonia, MI, and Baltimore-Towson, MD, where the proportion of the non-Hispanic Black alone population living in the largest principal city surpassed the second largest group, Hispanics, by 30 percentage points.

Metro areas that had a lower proportion of the non-Hispanic Black alone population living inside their largest principal city, relative to the Hispanic and other race group populations, were primarily located in the West—the metro areas of Phoenix-Mesa-Glendale, AZ; Riverside-San Bernardino-Ontario, CA; San Diego-Carlsbad-San Marcos, CA; and San Francisco-Oakland-Fremont, CA. However, the metro area with the lowest proportion was Miami-Fort Lauderdale-Pompano Beach, FL, located in the South.

In the metro areas of Miami-Fort Lauderdale-Pompano Beach, FL, and Phoenix-Mesa-Glendale, AZ, a higher proportion of the Hispanic population lived inside the largest principal cities of Miami and Phoenix, relative to the non-Hispanic Black alone population. In the metro area of Riverside-San Bernardino-Ontario, CA, the non-Hispanic Black alone population had the lowest proportion living

inside the city of Riverside, relative to the other groups shown.

In the metro area of San Diego-Carlsbad-San Marcos, CA, the other race category had a slightly higher proportion living in the city of San Diego relative to the non-Hispanic Black alone population. In the metro area of San Francisco-Oakland-Fremont, CA, both the other race category and the non-Hispanic White alone population had a higher proportion living in the city of San Francisco relative to the non-Hispanic Black alone population.

**The proportion of the non-Hispanic Black alone population living inside the largest principal cities within the 20 largest metro areas decreased over the last decade.**

Figure 8 shows the percentage-point difference of a race or Hispanic origin group living inside the largest principal city in a metro area, from 2000 to 2010.[23] The red bars represent the non-Hispanic Black alone population, the blue bars represent the non-Hispanic White alone population, the green bars represent the Hispanic population, and the orange bars represent other race groups. For example, in the Boston-Cambridge-Quincy, MA-NH metro area, 57 percent of the non-Hispanic Black alone population lived in the largest principal city, Boston, in 2000. This figure decreased to 46 percent in 2010, representing a decline of 11 percentage points, which is denoted by the red bar.

Across the 20 largest metro areas in the United States, the non-Hispanic Black alone population declined in the largest principal

---

[23] Data for the metro areas are based on the 2010 Census boundaries.

Figure 8.

## Percentage-Point Difference of Race and Ethnic Groups Living Inside the Largest Principal City of the 20 Largest Metropolitan Statistical Areas: 2000 to 2010

(For information on confidentiality protection, nonsampling error, and definitions, see *www.census.gov/prod/cen2010/doc/pl94-171.pdf*)

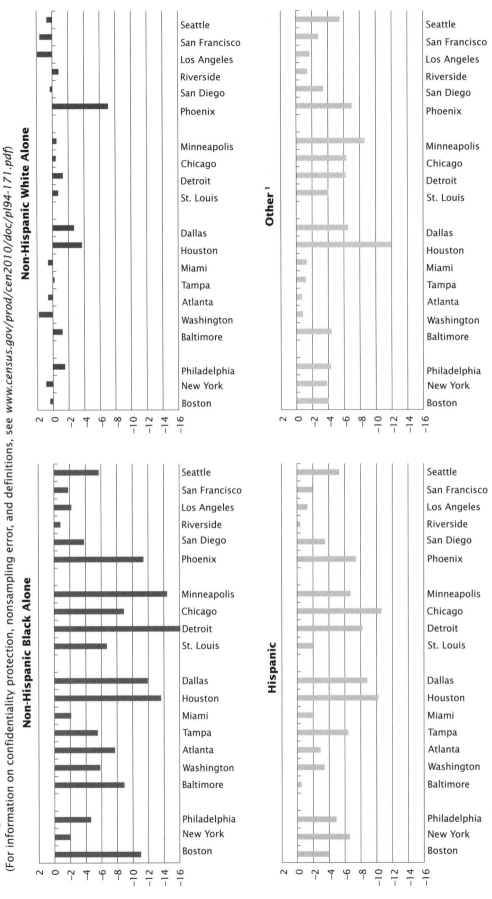

[1] For this figure, the "other" race category refers to the non-Hispanic Asian alone, non-Hispanic Native Hawaiian and Other Pacific Islander alone, and non-Hispanic Some Other Race alone populations, as well as non-Hispanics who reported multiple races.

Note: Principal cities within regions are organized based on proximity to each other. Boston, New York, and Philadelphia are located in the Northeast census region. Baltimore, Washington, Atlanta, Tampa, Miami, Houston, and Dallas are located in the South census region. St. Louis, Detroit, Chicago, and Minneapolis are located in the Midwest census region. Phoenix, San Diego, Riverside, Los Angeles, San Francisco, and Seattle are located in the West census region.

Source: U.S. Census Bureau, 2010 Census special tabulation.

cities and increased outside of these cities from 2000 to 2010. This largely follows the trend of the total population in these metro areas, where the proportion of the total population living inside the largest principal city within a metro area declined in 19 out of the 20 largest metro areas and increased as a proportion outside the largest principal cities from 2000 to 2010. The metro area of Boston-Cambridge-Quincy, MA-NH, was the only metro area that experienced an increase in the proportion of the total population living inside the city of Boston.

The proportion of the non-Hispanic Black alone population in the largest principal cities decreased by at least 10 percentage points in six metro areas from 2000 to 2010, Detroit-Warren-Livonia, MI (16 percentage points); Minneapolis-St. Paul-Bloomington, MN-WI (14 percentage points); Houston-Sugar Land-Baytown, TX (14 percentage points); Dallas-Fort Worth-Arlington, TX (12 percentage points); Phoenix-Mesa-Glendale, AZ (11 percentage points); and Boston-Cambridge-Quincy, MA-NH (11 percentage points).

**Among the 20 largest metro areas, the proportion of the non-Hispanic Black alone population living inside the largest principal cities declined by at least 7 percentage points across all midwestern metro areas.**

The proportion of the non-Hispanic Black alone population living inside the largest principal cities across midwestern metro areas declined by at least 7 percentage points from 2000 to 2010. The largest change was in the Detroit-Warren-Livonia, MI metro area, where the proportion of the non-Hispanic Black alone population living inside the city of Detroit versus outside

the city decreased by 16 percentage points. This was followed by Minneapolis-St. Paul-Bloomington, MN-WI (14 percentage points); Chicago-Joliet-Naperville, IL-IN-WI (9 percentage points); and St. Louis, MO-IL (7 percentage points).

In the Northeast, the proportion of the non-Hispanic Black alone population living inside the largest principal city declined by at least 7 percentage points in 1 out of the 3 metro areas, Boston-Cambridge-Quincy, MA-NH (11 percentage points). In the South, 4 of the 7 metro areas experienced a decline of at least 7 percentage points—Houston-Sugar Land-Baytown, TX (14 percentage points); Dallas-Fort Worth-Arlington, TX (12 percentage points); Baltimore-Towson, MD (9 percentage points); and Atlanta-Sandy Springs-Marietta, GA (8 percentage points).

**The non-Hispanic Black alone population experienced the greatest decline in the proportion living inside the largest principal city for 14 of the 20 largest metro areas.**

The proportion of the non-Hispanic Black alone population living inside the largest principal city declined more than the proportion of other race and ethnic groups that also experienced decreases in the largest principal cities in 14 out of the 20 metro areas. In the metro areas of New York-Northern New Jersey-Long Island, NY-NJ-PA; Philadelphia-Camden-Wilmington, PA-NJ-DE-MD; Tampa-St. Petersburg-Clearwater, FL; and Chicago-Joliet-Naperville, IL-IN-WI; the Hispanic population experienced the greatest declines compared to all groups shown. In the metro areas of Riverside-San Bernardino-Ontario, CA, and San Francisco-Oakland-Fremont, CA, the other race category experienced the greatest declines relative to all groups shown.

Although not as sweeping as the decline in the proportion of the non-Hispanic Black alone population living inside the largest principal cities of most major metro areas, the proportion of the Hispanic population and other race group populations living inside the largest principal city also declined in all of the 20 largest metro areas (see Figure 8). On the other hand, in about half of the largest metro areas, the proportion of the non-Hispanic White alone population living inside the largest principal city increased.

## SUMMARY

This report provided a portrait of the Black population in the United States and contributes to our understanding of the nation's changing racial and ethnic diversity.

While both the Black alone population and the Black alone-or-in-combination population grew from 2000 to 2010 (by 12 percent and 15 percent, respectively), the Black in combination population experienced the most growth, increasing by 76 percent. Within this population, the Black *and* White population more than doubled.

Additional notable trends were presented in this report. The Black population continued to be concentrated in the South and the proportion increased from 2000 to 2010. Additionally, the Black population that lived outside of the South tended to be more concentrated in metro areas.

Other interesting geographic patterns include, for the largest 20 metro areas, the non-Hispanic Black alone population was more likely to live in a largest principal city relative to the non-Hispanic White alone, Hispanic, and other race group populations in 2010. The non-Hispanic Black alone population also experienced the greatest declines in the proportion living in a largest principal city from 2000 to 2010.

Throughout the decade, the Census Bureau will release additional information on the Black population, including characteristics such as age, sex, and family type, which will provide greater insights into the demographic characteristics of this population at various geographic levels.

## ABOUT THE 2010 CENSUS

### Why was the 2010 Census conducted?

The U.S. Constitution mandates that a census be taken in the United States every 10 years. This is required in order to determine the number of seats each state is to receive in the U.S. House of Representatives.

### Why did the 2010 Census ask the question on race?

The Census Bureau collects data on race to fulfill a variety of legislative and program requirements. Data on race are used in the legislative redistricting process carried out by the states and in monitoring local jurisdictions' compliance with the Voting Rights Act. More broadly, data on race are critical for research that underlies many policy decisions at all levels of government.

### How do data from the question on race benefit me, my family, and my community?

All levels of government need information on race to implement and evaluate programs, or enforce laws, such as the Civil Rights Act, Voting Rights Act, Fair Housing Act, Equal Employment Opportunity Act, and the 2010 Census Redistricting Data Program.

Both public and private organizations use race information to find areas where groups may need special services and to plan and implement education, housing, health, and other programs that address these needs. For example, a school system might use this information to design cultural activities that reflect the diversity in their community, or a business could use it to select the mix of merchandise it will sell in a new store. Census information also helps identify areas where residents might need services of particular importance to certain racial groups, such as screening for hypertension or diabetes.

### FOR MORE INFORMATION

For more information on race in the United States, visit the Census Bureau's Internet site at <www.census.gov/population /www/socdemo/race/race.html>.

Information on confidentiality protection, nonsampling error, and definitions is available at <www.census.gov/prod/cen2010 /doc/pl94-171.pdf>.

Data on race from the *2010 Census Redistricting Data (Public Law 94-171) Summary File* were released on a state-by-state basis. The 2010 Census redistricting data are available on the Internet at <http://factfinder2 .census.gov/main.html> and on DVD.

For more information on specific race groups in the United States, go to <www.census.gov> and search for "Minority Links." This Web page includes information about the 2010 Census and provides links to reports based on past censuses and surveys focusing on the social and economic characteristics of the Black or African American, American Indian and Alaska Native, Asian, and Native Hawaiian and Other Pacific Islander populations.

Information on other population and housing topics is presented in the 2010 Census Briefs series, located on the Census Bureau's Web site at <www.census.gov/prod /cen2010>. This series presents information about race, Hispanic origin, age, sex, household type, housing tenure, and people who reside in group quarters.

For more information about the 2010 Census, including data products, call the Customer Services Center at 1-800-923-8282. You can also visit the Census Bureau's Question and Answer Center at <ask.census.gov> to submit your questions online.

# Congressional Apportionment

## 2010 Census Briefs

Issued November 2011

C2010BR-08

By
Kristin D. Burnett

The Constitutional basis for conducting the decennial census of population is to reapportion the U.S. House of Representatives. Apportionment is the process of dividing the 435 memberships, or seats, in the U.S. House of Representatives among the 50 states. With the exception of the 1920 Census, an apportionment has been made by the Congress on the basis of each decennial census from 1790 to 2010.

The apportionment population for 2010 consists of the resident population of the 50 states plus overseas federal employees (military and civilian) and their dependents living with them, who were included in their home states. The population of the District of Columbia is excluded from the apportionment population because it does not have any voting seats in the U.S. House of Representatives. The 2010 Census apportionment population was 309,183,463, as shown in Table 1.[1]

This report examines trends in congressional apportionment and discusses the apportionment population—what it is, who is included, and what method is used to calculate it. The report is part of a series that analyzes population and housing data collected by the 2010 Census.

**The average size of a congressional district will rise.**

The number of representatives or seats in the U.S. House of Representatives has remained constant at 435 since 1911, except for a temporary increase to 437 at the time of admission of Alaska and Hawaii as states in 1959 (see Table 1). However, the apportionment based on the 1960 Census, which took effect for the election in 1962, reverted to 435 seats.

The average size of a congressional district based on the 2010 Census apportionment population will be 710,767, more than triple the average district size of 210,328 based on the 1910 Census apportionment, and 63,815 more than the average size based on Census 2000 (646,952). Based on the 2010 Census apportionment, the state with the largest average district size will be Montana (994,416), and the state with the smallest average district size will be Rhode Island (527,624).

---

[1] The 2010 Census resident population of the United States, including the District of Columbia, was 308,745,538.

U.S. Department of Commerce
Economics and Statistics Administration
U.S. CENSUS BUREAU

Table 1.

# Apportionment Population Based on the 2010 Census and Apportionment of the U.S. House of Representatives: 1910 to 2010

(For information on confidentiality protection, nonsampling error, and definitions, see *www.census.gov/prod/cen2010/pl94-171.pdf*)

| State | 2010 apportionment population[1] | | | Number of representatives | | | | | | | | | | |
|---|---|---|---|---|---|---|---|---|---|---|---|---|---|---|
| | Total | Resident population | U.S. population overseas | 2010 | 2000 | 1990 | 1980 | 1970 | 1960 | 1950 | 1940 | 1930 | 1920[2] | 1910 |
| Total .......... | 309,183,463 | 308,143,815 | 1,039,648 | 435 | 435 | 435 | 435 | 435 | 435 | [3]437 | 435 | 435 | 435 | [4]435 |
| Alabama .............. | 4,802,982 | 4,779,736 | 23,246 | 7 | 7 | 7 | 7 | 7 | 8 | 9 | 9 | 9 | 10 | 10 |
| Alaska ................ | 721,523 | 710,231 | 11,292 | 1 | 1 | 1 | 1 | 1 | 1 | 1 | (X) | (X) | (X) | (X) |
| Arizona ............... | 6,412,700 | 6,392,017 | 20,683 | 9 | 8 | 6 | 5 | 4 | 3 | 2 | 2 | 1 | 1 | 1 |
| Arkansas ............. | 2,926,229 | 2,915,918 | 10,311 | 4 | 4 | 4 | 4 | 4 | 4 | 6 | 7 | 7 | 7 | 7 |
| California .............. | 37,341,989 | 37,253,956 | 88,033 | 53 | 53 | 52 | 45 | 43 | 38 | 30 | 23 | 20 | 11 | 11 |
| Colorado ............. | 5,044,930 | 5,029,196 | 15,734 | 7 | 7 | 6 | 6 | 5 | 4 | 4 | 4 | 4 | 4 | 4 |
| Connecticut ........... | 3,581,628 | 3,574,097 | 7,531 | 5 | 5 | 6 | 6 | 6 | 6 | 6 | 6 | 6 | 5 | 5 |
| Delaware ............. | 900,877 | 897,934 | 2,943 | 1 | 1 | 1 | 1 | 1 | 1 | 1 | 1 | 1 | 1 | 1 |
| Florida ................ | 18,900,773 | 18,801,310 | 99,463 | 27 | 25 | 23 | 19 | 15 | 12 | 8 | 6 | 5 | 4 | 4 |
| Georgia ............... | 9,727,566 | 9,687,653 | 39,913 | 14 | 13 | 11 | 10 | 10 | 10 | 10 | 10 | 10 | 12 | 12 |
| Hawaii ................ | 1,366,862 | 1,360,301 | 6,561 | 2 | 2 | 2 | 2 | 2 | 2 | 1 | (X) | (X) | (X) | (X) |
| Idaho ................. | 1,573,499 | 1,567,582 | 5,917 | 2 | 2 | 2 | 2 | 2 | 2 | 2 | 2 | 2 | 2 | 2 |
| Illinois................ | 12,864,380 | 12,830,632 | 33,748 | 18 | 19 | 20 | 22 | 24 | 24 | 25 | 26 | 27 | 27 | 27 |
| Indiana................ | 6,501,582 | 6,483,802 | 17,780 | 9 | 9 | 10 | 10 | 11 | 11 | 11 | 11 | 12 | 13 | 13 |
| Iowa.................. | 3,053,787 | 3,046,355 | 7,432 | 4 | 5 | 5 | 6 | 6 | 7 | 8 | 8 | 9 | 11 | 11 |
| Kansas................ | 2,863,813 | 2,853,118 | 10,695 | 4 | 4 | 4 | 5 | 5 | 5 | 6 | 6 | 7 | 8 | 8 |
| Kentucky .............. | 4,350,606 | 4,339,367 | 11,239 | 6 | 6 | 6 | 7 | 7 | 7 | 8 | 9 | 9 | 11 | 11 |
| Louisiana.............. | 4,553,962 | 4,533,372 | 20,590 | 6 | 7 | 7 | 8 | 8 | 8 | 8 | 8 | 8 | 8 | 8 |
| Maine................. | 1,333,074 | 1,328,361 | 4,713 | 2 | 2 | 2 | 2 | 2 | 2 | 3 | 3 | 3 | 4 | 4 |
| Maryland .............. | 5,789,929 | 5,773,552 | 16,377 | 8 | 8 | 8 | 8 | 8 | 8 | 7 | 6 | 6 | 6 | 6 |
| Massachusetts........... | 6,559,644 | 6,547,629 | 12,015 | 9 | 10 | 10 | 11 | 12 | 12 | 14 | 14 | 15 | 16 | 16 |
| Michigan .............. | 9,911,626 | 9,883,640 | 27,986 | 14 | 15 | 16 | 18 | 19 | 19 | 18 | 17 | 17 | 13 | 13 |
| Minnesota ............. | 5,314,879 | 5,303,925 | 10,954 | 8 | 8 | 8 | 8 | 8 | 8 | 9 | 9 | 9 | 10 | 10 |
| Mississippi.............. | 2,978,240 | 2,967,297 | 10,943 | 4 | 4 | 5 | 5 | 5 | 5 | 6 | 7 | 7 | 8 | 8 |
| Missouri................ | 6,011,478 | 5,988,927 | 22,551 | 8 | 9 | 9 | 9 | 10 | 10 | 11 | 13 | 13 | 16 | 16 |
| Montana................ | 994,416 | 989,415 | 5,001 | 1 | 1 | 1 | 2 | 2 | 2 | 2 | 2 | 2 | 2 | 2 |
| Nebraska.............. | 1,831,825 | 1,826,341 | 5,484 | 3 | 3 | 3 | 3 | 3 | 3 | 4 | 4 | 5 | 6 | 6 |
| Nevada ............... | 2,709,432 | 2,700,551 | 8,881 | 4 | 3 | 2 | 2 | 1 | 1 | 1 | 1 | 1 | 1 | 1 |
| New Hampshire........... | 1,321,445 | 1,316,470 | 4,975 | 2 | 2 | 2 | 2 | 2 | 2 | 2 | 2 | 2 | 2 | 2 |
| New Jersey ............ | 8,807,501 | 8,791,894 | 15,607 | 12 | 13 | 13 | 14 | 15 | 15 | 14 | 14 | 14 | 12 | 12 |
| New Mexico............ | 2,067,273 | 2,059,179 | 8,094 | 3 | 3 | 3 | 3 | 2 | 2 | 2 | 2 | 1 | 1 | 1 |
| New York .............. | 19,421,055 | 19,378,102 | 42,953 | 27 | 29 | 31 | 34 | 39 | 41 | 43 | 45 | 45 | 43 | 43 |
| North Carolina.......... | 9,565,781 | 9,535,483 | 30,298 | 13 | 13 | 12 | 11 | 11 | 11 | 12 | 12 | 11 | 10 | 10 |
| North Dakota............ | 675,905 | 672,591 | 3,314 | 1 | 1 | 1 | 1 | 1 | 2 | 2 | 2 | 2 | 3 | 3 |
| Ohio.................. | 11,568,495 | 11,536,504 | 31,991 | 16 | 18 | 19 | 21 | 23 | 24 | 23 | 23 | 24 | 22 | 22 |
| Oklahoma ............. | 3,764,882 | 3,751,351 | 13,531 | 5 | 5 | 6 | 6 | 6 | 6 | 6 | 8 | 9 | 8 | 8 |
| Oregon................ | 3,848,606 | 3,831,074 | 17,532 | 5 | 5 | 5 | 5 | 4 | 4 | 4 | 4 | 3 | 3 | 3 |
| Pennsylvania........... | 12,734,905 | 12,702,379 | 32,526 | 18 | 19 | 21 | 23 | 25 | 27 | 30 | 33 | 34 | 36 | 36 |
| Rhode Island........... | 1,055,247 | 1,052,567 | 2,680 | 2 | 2 | 2 | 2 | 2 | 2 | 2 | 2 | 2 | 3 | 3 |
| South Carolina........... | 4,645,975 | 4,625,364 | 20,611 | 7 | 6 | 6 | 6 | 6 | 6 | 6 | 6 | 6 | 7 | 7 |
| South Dakota............ | 819,761 | 814,180 | 5,581 | 1 | 1 | 1 | 1 | 2 | 2 | 2 | 2 | 2 | 3 | 3 |
| Tennessee.............. | 6,375,431 | 6,346,105 | 29,326 | 9 | 9 | 9 | 9 | 8 | 9 | 9 | 10 | 9 | 10 | 10 |
| Texas................. | 25,268,418 | 25,145,561 | 122,857 | 36 | 32 | 30 | 27 | 24 | 23 | 22 | 21 | 21 | 18 | 18 |
| Utah.................. | 2,770,765 | 2,763,885 | 6,880 | 4 | 3 | 3 | 3 | 2 | 2 | 2 | 2 | 2 | 2 | 2 |
| Vermont............... | 630,337 | 625,741 | 4,596 | 1 | 1 | 1 | 1 | 1 | 1 | 1 | 1 | 1 | 2 | 2 |
| Virginia................ | 8,037,736 | 8,001,024 | 36,712 | 11 | 11 | 11 | 10 | 10 | 10 | 10 | 9 | 9 | 10 | 10 |
| Washington ............ | 6,753,369 | 6,724,540 | 28,829 | 10 | 9 | 9 | 8 | 7 | 7 | 7 | 6 | 6 | 5 | 5 |
| West Virginia ........... | 1,859,815 | 1,852,994 | 6,821 | 3 | 3 | 3 | 4 | 4 | 5 | 6 | 6 | 6 | 6 | 6 |
| Wisconsin .............. | 5,698,230 | 5,686,986 | 11,244 | 8 | 8 | 9 | 9 | 9 | 10 | 10 | 10 | 10 | 11 | 11 |
| Wyoming .............. | 568,300 | 563,626 | 4,674 | 1 | 1 | 1 | 1 | 1 | 1 | 1 | 1 | 1 | 1 | 1 |

(X) Not applicable.

[1] Includes the resident population for the 50 states, as ascertained by the 2010 Census under Title 13, U.S. Code, and counts of overseas U.S. military and federal civilian employees (and their dependents living with them) allocated to their home state, as reported by the employing federal agencies. The apportionment population does not include the resident or the overseas population of the District of Columbia.

[2] No reapportionment was made based on the 1920 Census.

[3] The 1950 apportionment originally resulted in the previously fixed House size of 435 representatives; but in 1959, Alaska and Hawaii were both newly admitted to the United States, and each was granted one representative—temporarily increasing the size of the House to 437. Then the 1960 apportionment reverted back to the fixed size of 435.

[4] The apportionment act following the 1910 Census was passed on August 8, 1911. This congressional act (U.S. Statutes at Large, Pub.L. 62-5, 37 Stat. 13) fixed the size of the House at 433 representatives, with a provision for the addition of one seat each for Arizona and New Mexico when they would become states the following year. The resulting House size, 435 members, has been unchanged since, except for a temporary increase to 437 at the time of admission of Alaska and Hawaii as states (see footnote 3).

Sources: U.S. Census Bureau, 2010 Census at <www.census.gov/population/apportionment/data>; and *2000 Census of Population and Housing, Population and Housing Unit Counts, United States Summary: 2000* (PHC-3-1, Part 1), Table 3.

Figure 1.
**Apportionment of the U.S. House of Representatives Based on the 2010 Census**

(For information on confidentiality protection, nonsampling error, and definitions, see *www.census.gov/prod /cen2010/doc/sf1.pdf*)

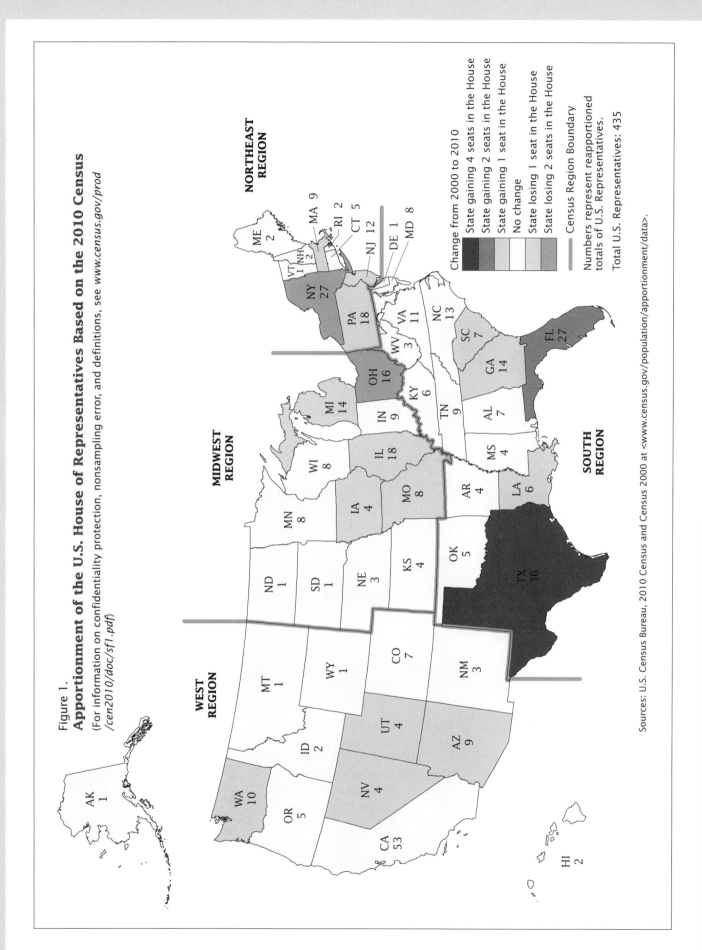

**NORTHEAST REGION**

**MIDWEST REGION**

**WEST REGION**

**SOUTH REGION**

ME 2
VT 1
NH 2
MA 9
RI 2
CT 5
NY 27
NJ 12
PA 18
DE 1
MD 8
VA 11
WV 3
NC 13
SC 7
GA 14
FL 27
OH 16
KY 6
TN 9
AL 7
MI 14
IN 9
IL 18
WI 8
MS 4
AR 4
LA 6
MN 8
IA 4
MO 8
OK 5
TX 36
ND 1
SD 1
NE 3
KS 4
NM 3
CO 7
WY 1
MT 1
UT 4
AZ 9
ID 2
NV 4
WA 10
OR 5
CA 53
AK 1
HI 2

**Change from 2000 to 2010**

State gaining 4 seats in the House
State gaining 2 seats in the House
State gaining 1 seat in the House
No change
State losing 1 seat in the House
State losing 2 seats in the House

Census Region Boundary

Numbers represent reapportioned totals of U.S. Representatives.

Total U.S. Representatives: 435

Sources: U.S. Census Bureau, 2010 Census and Census 2000 at <www.census.gov/population/apportionment/data>.

**Twelve seats in the U.S. House of Representatives will shift from one state to another.**

As a result of the apportionment based on the 2010 Census, 12 seats in the U.S. House of Representatives will shift among 18 states. Eight states will have more representatives in the 113th Congress, which convenes in January 2013, and ten states will have fewer representatives (see Figure 1 and Table 2).

Among the eight states gaining seats, Texas will gain four seats and Florida will gain two seats. The other six states (Arizona, Georgia, Nevada, South Carolina, Utah, and Washington) will each gain one seat.

Of the ten states losing seats, two states, New York and Ohio, will each lose two seats. The other eight states (Illinois, Iowa, Louisiana, Massachusetts, Michigan, Missouri, New Jersey, and Pennsylvania) will each lose one seat.

**The Census 2000 apportionment also shifted 12 seats.**

The seat changes that will occur based on the 2010 Census show many parallels to the seat changes that occurred after Census 2000. For example, the 2000-based reapportionment also led to a shift of 12 seats among 18 states (see Table 2).

Five of the eight states that will gain seats following the 2010 Census also gained seats following Census 2000: Arizona, Florida, Georgia, Nevada, and Texas. Similarly, five of the ten states that will lose seats following the 2010 Census also lost seats following Census 2000: Illinois, Michigan, New York, Ohio, and Pennsylvania.

Table 2.

## Change in the Number of U.S. Representatives by State: 2000 and 2010

(For information on confidentiality protection, nonsampling error, and definitions, see *www.census.gov/prod/cen2010/pl94-171.pdf*)

| State | Gain | State | Loss |
|---|---|---|---|
| **BASED ON 2010 CENSUS** | | **BASED ON 2010 CENSUS** | |
| Total gain in 8 states . . . . . . . . . . . . . | 12 | Total loss in 10 states . . . . . . . . . . | 12 |
| Texas . . . . . . . . . . . . . . . . . . . . . . . | 4 | New York . . . . . . . . . . . . . . . . . . . . . | 2 |
| Florida . . . . . . . . . . . . . . . . . . . . . . | 2 | Ohio . . . . . . . . . . . . . . . . . . . . . . . . . | 2 |
| Arizona . . . . . . . . . . . . . . . . . . . . . | 1 | Illinois . . . . . . . . . . . . . . . . . . . . . . . | 1 |
| Georgia . . . . . . . . . . . . . . . . . . . . . | 1 | Iowa . . . . . . . . . . . . . . . . . . . . . . . . . | 1 |
| Nevada . . . . . . . . . . . . . . . . . . . . . | 1 | Louisiana . . . . . . . . . . . . . . . . . . . . . | 1 |
| South Carolina . . . . . . . . . . . . . . . . | 1 | Massachusetts . . . . . . . . . . . . . . . . . | 1 |
| Utah . . . . . . . . . . . . . . . . . . . . . . . . | 1 | Michigan . . . . . . . . . . . . . . . . . . . . . | 1 |
| Washington . . . . . . . . . . . . . . . . . . . | 1 | Missouri . . . . . . . . . . . . . . . . . . . . . . | 1 |
| | | New Jersey . . . . . . . . . . . . . . . . . . . | 1 |
| | | Pennsylvania . . . . . . . . . . . . . . . . . . | 1 |
| **BASED ON CENSUS 2000** | | **BASED ON CENSUS 2000** | |
| Total gain in 8 states . . . . . . . . . . . . . | 12 | Total loss in 10 states . . . . . . . . . . | 12 |
| Arizona . . . . . . . . . . . . . . . . . . . . . | 2 | New York . . . . . . . . . . . . . . . . . . . . . | 2 |
| Florida . . . . . . . . . . . . . . . . . . . . . . | 2 | Pennsylvania . . . . . . . . . . . . . . . . . . | 2 |
| Georgia . . . . . . . . . . . . . . . . . . . . . | 2 | Connecticut . . . . . . . . . . . . . . . . . . . | 1 |
| Texas . . . . . . . . . . . . . . . . . . . . . . . | 2 | Illinois . . . . . . . . . . . . . . . . . . . . . . . | 1 |
| California . . . . . . . . . . . . . . . . . . . . | 1 | Indiana . . . . . . . . . . . . . . . . . . . . . . | 1 |
| Colorado . . . . . . . . . . . . . . . . . . . . | 1 | Michigan . . . . . . . . . . . . . . . . . . . . . | 1 |
| Nevada . . . . . . . . . . . . . . . . . . . . . | 1 | Mississippi . . . . . . . . . . . . . . . . . . . | 1 |
| North Carolina . . . . . . . . . . . . . . . . | 1 | Ohio . . . . . . . . . . . . . . . . . . . . . . . . . | 1 |
| | | Oklahoma . . . . . . . . . . . . . . . . . . . . | 1 |
| | | Wisconsin . . . . . . . . . . . . . . . . . . . . | 1 |

Sources: U.S. Census Bureau, 2010 Census and Census 2000 at <www.census.gov/population/apportionment/data>.

**Shifts in congressional representation reflect regional trends in population.**

The regional patterns of change in congressional representation between 2000 and 2010 reflect the nation's continuing shift in population from the Northeast and Midwest to the South and West.

Based on the 2010 Census apportionment, the net increase of seven seats in the South reflected a gain of eight seats across four states and a loss of one seat (see Figure 1 and Table 3). The West gained four seats and lost none. The Northeast lost five seats and gained none. The Midwest lost six seats and gained none.

Similar regional shifts occurred after Census 2000. At that time, the net increase of five seats in the South reflected a gain of seven seats in four states and a loss of two seats. The West gained five seats across four states and lost none. The Northeast and Midwest each lost five seats and gained none.

Figure 2 shows the percentage distribution of House seats or memberships by region for each census since 1910. In 1910, the West held the smallest share of House seats out of the four regions (33 seats, or 7.6 percent), but it steadily increased each decade, more than tripling in seats by 2010 (102 seats, or 23.4 percent). After the 1990 apportionment, the West

Table 3.

## Change in the Number of U.S. Representatives by Region: 2000 and 2010

(For information on confidentiality protection, nonsampling error, and definitions, see *www.census.gov/prod/cen2010/pl94-171.pdf*)

| Region | Gain | Loss | Net |
|---|---|---|---|
| **BASED ON 2010 CENSUS** | | | |
| Northeast......................... | – | 5 | –5 |
| Midwest........................... | – | 6 | –6 |
| South............................. | 8 | 1 | 7 |
| West ............................. | 4 | – | 4 |
| **BASED ON CENSUS 2000** | | | |
| Northeast......................... | – | 5 | –5 |
| Midwest........................... | – | 5 | –5 |
| South............................. | 7 | 2 | 5 |
| West ............................. | 5 | – | 5 |

– Represents zero.
Sources: U.S. Census Bureau, 2010 Census and Census 2000 at <www.census.gov/population/apportionment/data>.

(93 seats, or 21.4 percent) surpassed the Northeast (88 seats, or 20.2 percent) in share of seats for the first time; and after the 2010 apportionment, the West (102 seats, or 23.4 percent) will surpass the Midwest (94 seats; 21.6 percent) for the first time.

The South's share of House seats held relatively firm from 1910 to 1970 at about 31 percent (between 133 and 136 seats), and then it increased to 37.0 percent (161 seats) by 2010. After the 2010 apportionment, the South will maintain the largest share of House seats among all four regions, as it has since 1940.

Figure 2.

## Percentage Distribution of Seats in the U.S. House of Representatives by Region: 1910 to 2010

(For information on confidentiality protection, nonsampling error, and definitions, see *www.census.gov/prod/cen2010/pl94-171.pdf*)

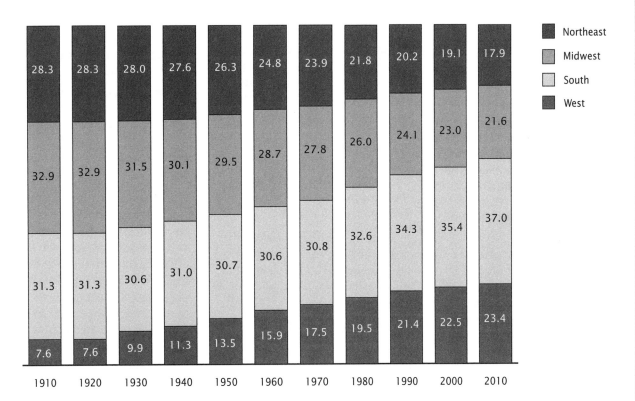

Sources: U.S. Census Bureau, 2010 Census at <www.census.gov/population/apportionment>; and *2000 Census of Population and Housing, Population and Housing Unit Counts, United States Summary* (PHC-3-1, Part 1), Table 3.

Meanwhile, the Midwest, which accounted for the largest regional share of House seats in 1910 through 1930 (between 137 and 143 seats, or between 31.5 and 32.9 percent), showed a steady decline to 21.6 percent (94 seats) by 2010.

After holding relatively stable at about 28 percent (between 120 and 123 seats) from 1910 to 1940, the Northeast's share of House seats gradually decreased to only 17.9 percent (78 seats) by 2010. Therefore, after the 2010 apportionment, the Northeast will hold the smallest share of House seats among all four regions, as it has since 1990.

## CALCULATING APPORTIONMENT

### Congress decides the method to calculate apportionment.

The process of apportionment determines the distribution of congressional seats among the states. Several apportionment methods have been used since the first census in 1790. The apportionment for the 2010 Census was calculated using the method of equal proportions, in accordance with the provisions of Title 2, U.S. Code. The method of equal proportions has been used for apportionment after every census since 1940.

### Step 1: Automatically assign the first 50 seats.

First, each state is assigned one congressional seat, as provided by the Constitution. Then, in the following steps, the method of equal proportions allocates the remaining 385 congressional seats among the 50 states, according to their apportionment populations.

### Step 2: Calculate a list of priority values.

A "priority value" is based on a state's apportionment population and the number of its next potential seat. More specifically, the formula for a priority value (PV) equals the state's apportionment population divided by the geometric mean of its current (n–1) and next (n) potential seat number.

$$PV(n) = \frac{State\ Apportionment\ Population}{\sqrt{n*(n-1)}}$$

Because every state automatically receives its first seat, priority values start with each state's second seat. The maximum number of priority values ever needed for each state would account for the hypothetical situation in which one state is so large that it receives all of the final 385 seats that remain after the first 50 are automatically assigned. This means one could potentially calculate a total list of 19,250 priority values (385 PVs multiplied by 50 states). In general, however, it is more efficient to only calculate enough priority values to account for the largest number of seats any particular state might currently be assigned (or proportionate to each state's actual population). For example, one may choose to calculate approximately 60 priority values for each state because the most populous state in Census 2000 received 53 seats.

In practice, the priority values for a specific state's second and third seats in the 2010 Census are computed as follows. Using Alabama as the example state:

$$PV(2nd\ Seat\ for\ Alabama) = \frac{4,802,982}{\sqrt{2*1}} = 3,396,221$$

$$PV(3rd\ Seat\ for\ Alabama) = \frac{4,802,982}{\sqrt{3*2}} = 1,960,809$$

The rest of the priority values for all of Alabama's potential seats are calculated in a similar fashion. Then the same process is repeated for each of the other states.

### Step 3: Assign the remaining seats in ranked order.

After all of the states' priority values have been calculated, a combined list of priority values from every state is ranked in descending order. The state with the largest priority value in the list is given the 51st seat (because the first 50 seats are automatically assigned); then the state with second largest priority value is given the 52nd seat. This process is continued for each consecutively descending priority value until the last (435th) seat has been filled. The state composition of the reapportioned House of Representatives is then complete.

## ADDITIONAL TOPICS ON CONGRESSIONAL APPORTIONMENT

**When are the apportionment population counts given to the President? To the Congress? To the states?**

*To the President.* Title 13, U.S. Code requires that the apportionment population counts for each state be delivered to the President within 9 months of Census Day, which was April 1, 2010. The 2010 Census counts were delivered to the President on December 21, 2010.

*To the Congress.* According to Title 2, U.S. Code, within 1 week of the opening of the next session of the Congress in the new year, the President must report to the Clerk of the U.S. House of Representatives the apportionment population counts for each state and the number of representatives to which each state is entitled. The President sent the 2010 apportionment results to the House on January 5, 2011.

*To the States.* Also according to Title 2, U.S. Code, within 15 days of receiving the apportionment population counts from the President, the Clerk of the House must inform each state governor of the number of representatives to which each state is entitled. The 2010 apportionment results were transmitted to all the states by January 18, 2011.

**Were children under 18 years old included in the 2010 Census apportionment population counts even though they cannot vote?**

Yes. Being old enough to vote, being registered to vote, or actually voting are not requirements for inclusion in the apportionment counts.

**Did the 2010 Census apportionment population counts include all Americans overseas?**

The overseas portion of the 2010 apportionment counts only included overseas federal employees (military and civilian) and their dependents living with them. Private U.S. citizens living abroad who were not employees of the federal government (or their dependents) were not included in the overseas counts.

**Were undocumented residents in the 50 states included in the 2010 Census apportionment population counts?**

All people (citizens and noncitizens) with a usual residence in one of the 50 states were included in the 2010 Census and thus in the apportionment counts. This has been true since the first census in 1790.

**What is the difference between apportionment and redistricting?**

Population data from the decennial census provide the basis for both apportioning House seats among the states and for redistricting the legislative bodies within each state. Apportionment is the process of determining the number of representatives to which each state is entitled in the U.S. House of Representatives based on the decennial census. Whereas, redistricting is the process of revising the geographic boundaries of areas from which people elect representatives to the U.S. House of Representatives, a state legislature, a county or city council, a school board, and so forth. By law (PL 94-171), redistricting data must be submitted to the states within one year of the census date (so, for this decade, redistricting data had to be submitted to states by no later than April 1, 2011). The Census Bureau released the redistricting population data at the census block level on a state-by-state basis during February and March 2011.

## FOR MORE INFORMATION

For more information on apportionment for both the 2010 and 2000 censuses, visit the U.S. Census Bureau's Internet site at <www.census.gov/population /apportionment>. Data from the 2010 Census are available on the Internet at <http://factfinder2 .census.gov> and on DVD. Information on confidentiality protection, nonsampling error, and definitions is available at <www.census.gov/prod/cen2010 /doc/pl94-171.pdf>.

Information on other population and housing topics is presented in the 2010 Census Briefs series, located on the Census Bureau's Web site at <www.census.gov/prod /cen2010>. This series will present information about race, Hispanic origin, age, sex, household type, housing tenure, and people who reside in group quarters.

For more information about the 2010 Census, including data products, call our Customer Services Center at 301-763-INFO or at 1-800-923-8282. You can also visit our Question and Answer Center at <ask.census.gov> to submit your questions online.

# The Hispanic Population: 2010

*2010 Census Briefs*

Issued May 2011

C2010BR-04

By
Sharon R. Ennis,
Merarys Ríos-Vargas,
and
Nora G. Albert

## INTRODUCTION

This report looks at an important part of our nation's changing ethnic diversity. It is part of a series that analyzes population and housing data collected from the 2010 Census, and it provides a snapshot of the Hispanic or Latino population in the United States. Hispanic population group distributions and growth at the national level and at lower levels of geography are presented.[1]

This report also provides an overview of ethnicity concepts and definitions used in the 2010 Census. The data for this report are based on the *2010 Census Summary File 1*, which is among the first 2010 Census data products to be released and is provided for each state.[2]

### UNDERSTANDING HISPANIC ORIGIN DATA FROM THE 2010 CENSUS

For the 2010 Census, the question on Hispanic origin was asked of individuals living in the United States (see Figure 1). An individual's response to the Hispanic origin question was based

**Figure 1.**

### Reproduction of the Question on Hispanic Origin From the 2010 Census

→ NOTE: Please answer BOTH Question 5 about Hispanic origin and Question 6 about race. For this census, Hispanic origins are not races.

5. Is this person of Hispanic, Latino, or Spanish origin?

☐ **No,** not of Hispanic, Latino, or Spanish origin

☐ Yes, Mexican, Mexican Am., Chicano

☐ Yes, Puerto Rican

☐ Yes, Cuban

☐ Yes, another Hispanic, Latino, or Spanish origin — *Print origin, for example, Argentinean, Colombian, Dominican, Nicaraguan, Salvadoran, Spaniard, and so on.* ↘

Source: U.S. Census Bureau, 2010 Census questionnaire.

upon self-identification. The U.S. Census Bureau collects Hispanic origin information following the guidance of the U.S. Office of Management and Budget's (OMB) 1997 *Revisions to the Standards for the Classification of Federal Data on Race and Ethnicity.*[3] These federal standards mandate that race and ethnicity (Hispanic origin) are separate and distinct concepts and that when collecting these data via self-identification, two different questions must be used.

The OMB definition of Hispanic or Latino origin used in the 2010 Census is presented in the text box "Definition of Hispanic or Latino Origin Used in the 2010 Census." OMB requires federal agencies to use a minimum of two ethnicities: Hispanic or Latino and Not Hispanic or Latino. Hispanic origin can be viewed as

---

[1] The terms "Hispanic or Latino" and "Hispanic" are used interchangeably in this report.

[2] The *2010 Census Summary File 1* provides data on detailed Hispanic origin groups (e.g., Mexican or Puerto Rican) and detailed information about race and tribes (e.g., Chinese, Samoan, or Choctaw). This report discusses data for the 50 states and the District of Columbia. Data for Puerto Rico are shown and discussed separately. For a detailed schedule of 2010 Census products and release dates, visit <www.census.gov/population/www/cen2010/glance/index.html>.

[3] The 1997 *Revisions to the Standards for the Classification of Federal Data on Race and Ethnicity,* issued by OMB, is available at <www.whitehouse.gov/omb/fedreg/1997standards.html>.

**United States Census Bureau**

U.S. Department of Commerce
Economics and Statistics Administration
U.S. CENSUS BUREAU

the heritage, nationality group, lineage, or country of birth of the person or the person's parents or ancestors before their arrival in the United States. People who identify their origin as Hispanic, Latino, or Spanish may be any race.

The question on Hispanic origin was first introduced in the 1970 Census, and subsequently a version of the question has been included in every census since.[4] Spanish surname, place of birth, and Spanish mother tongue responses were also used as identifiers of the Hispanic population in the 1970 Census and were the only Hispanic identifiers in prior censuses.[5] Over the last 40 years the question on Hispanic origin has undergone numerous changes and modifications, all with the aim of improving the quality of Hispanic origin data in the United States, Puerto Rico, and the U.S. Island Areas.[6]

The 2010 Census question on Hispanic origin included five separate response categories and one area where respondents could write in a specific Hispanic origin group. The first response category is intended for respondents who do not identify as Hispanic. The remaining response categories ("Mexican, Mexican Am., Chicano;" "Puerto Rican;" "Cuban;" and "Another Hispanic, Latino, or Spanish origin") and write-in answers can be combined to

---

**Definition of Hispanic or Latino Origin Used in the 2010 Census**

"Hispanic or Latino" refers to a person of Cuban, Mexican, Puerto Rican, South or Central American, or other Spanish culture or origin regardless of race.

---

create data for the OMB category of Hispanic.[7]

## HISPANIC POPULATION

Data from the 2010 Census provide insights to our ethnically diverse nation. According to the 2010 Census, 308.7 million people resided in the United States on April 1, 2010, of which 50.5 million (or 16 percent) were of Hispanic or Latino origin (see Table 1). The Hispanic population increased from 35.3 million in 2000 when this group made up 13 percent of the total population.[8] The majority of

---

the growth in the total population came from increases in those who reported their ethnicity as Hispanic or Latino.[9]

**More than half of the growth in the total population of the United States between 2000 and 2010 was due to the increase in the Hispanic population.**

The Hispanic population increased by 15.2 million between 2000 and 2010, accounting for over half of the 27.3 million increase in the total population of the United States. Between 2000 and 2010, the Hispanic population grew by 43 percent, which was four times the growth in the total population at 10 percent.

Population growth between 2000 and 2010 varied by Hispanic group. The Mexican origin population increased by 54 percent and had the largest numeric change (11.2 million), growing from 20.6 million in 2000 to 31.8 million in 2010.[10] Mexicans accounted for about three-quarters of the 15.2 million increase in the Hispanic population from 2000 to 2010. Puerto Ricans grew by 36 percent, increasing from 3.4 million to 4.6 million. The Cuban population increased by 44 percent, growing from 1.2 million in 2000 to 1.8 million in 2010. Hispanics who reported other

---

[4] The Spanish origin question, now the Hispanic origin question, was originally fielded and tested by the Bureau of the Census in the November 1969 Current Population Survey. It was later used in the 1970 Census of Population (5 percent sample). The Hispanic origin question has been asked on a 100 percent basis in every census since 1980.

[5] U.S. Census Bureau, 1979, *Coverage of the Hispanic Population of the United States in the 1970 Census.* Current Population Reports, Special Studies, P-23, No. 82.

[6] The U.S. Island Areas are the U.S. Virgin Islands, American Samoa, Guam, and the Commonwealth of the Northern Mariana Islands.

---

[7] There were three changes to the Hispanic origin question for the 2010 Census. First, the wording of the question changed from "Is this person Spanish/Hispanic/Latino?" in 2000 to "Is this person of Hispanic, Latino, or Spanish origin?" in 2010. Second, in 2000, the question provided an instruction, "Mark ☒ the '**No**' box if **not** Spanish/Hispanic/Latino." The 2010 Census question provided no specific instruction for non-Hispanic respondents. Third, in 2010, the "Yes, another Hispanic, Latino, or Spanish origin" category provided examples of six Hispanic origin groups (Argentinean, Colombian, Dominican, Nicaraguan, Salvadoran, Spaniard, and so on) and instructed respondents to "print origin." In 2000, no Hispanic origin examples were given.

[8] The observed changes in Hispanic origin counts between Census 2000 and the 2010 Census could be attributed to a number of factors. Demographic change since 2000, which includes births and deaths in a geographic area and migration in and out of a geographic area, will have an impact on the resulting 2010 Census counts. Some changes in the Hispanic origin question's wording and format since Census 2000 could have influenced reporting patterns in the 2010 Census. Additionally, changes to the Hispanic origin edit and coding procedures could have impacted the 2010 counts. These factors should especially be considered when observing changes for detailed Hispanic groups.

---

[9] For the purposes of this report, the term "reported" is used to refer to the response provided by respondents as well as responses assigned during the editing and imputation process.

[10] "People of Mexican origin" refers to people who report their origin as Mexican. It can include people born in Mexico, in the United States, or in other countries. This holds true for all the detailed Hispanic origin groups discussed in this report (e.g., people of Cuban origin, Salvadoran origin, etc). The question on Hispanic origin is an ethnicity question and not a place of birth question. All Hispanic origin responses are based on self-identification. Throughout this report, terms such as Mexican origin and Mexicans or Cuban origin and Cubans are used interchangeably, and in all cases refer to the ethnic origin of the person, not exclusively their place of birth or nationality.

Table 1.
## Hispanic or Latino Origin Population by Type: 2000 and 2010
(For information on confidentiality protection, nonsampling error, and definitions, see *www.census.gov/prod/cen2010/doc/sf1.pdf*)

| Origin and type | 2000 | | 2010 | | Change, 2000 to 2010[1] | |
|---|---|---|---|---|---|---|
| | Number | Percent of total | Number | Percent of total | Number | Percent |
| **HISPANIC OR LATINO ORIGIN** | | | | | | |
| Total | 281,421,906 | 100.0 | 308,745,538 | 100.0 | 27,323,632 | 9.7 |
| Hispanic or Latino | 35,305,818 | 12.5 | 50,477,594 | 16.3 | 15,171,776 | 43.0 |
| Not Hispanic or Latino | 246,116,088 | 87.5 | 258,267,944 | 83.7 | 12,151,856 | 4.9 |
| **HISPANIC OR LATINO BY TYPE** | | | | | | |
| Total | 35,305,818 | 100.0 | 50,477,594 | 100.0 | 15,171,776 | 43.0 |
| Mexican | 20,640,711 | 58.5 | 31,798,258 | 63.0 | 11,157,547 | 54.1 |
| Puerto Rican | 3,406,178 | 9.6 | 4,623,716 | 9.2 | 1,217,538 | 35.7 |
| Cuban | 1,241,685 | 3.5 | 1,785,547 | 3.5 | 543,862 | 43.8 |
| Other Hispanic or Latino | 10,017,244 | 28.4 | 12,270,073 | 24.3 | 2,252,829 | 22.5 |
| Dominican (Dominican Republic) | 764,945 | 2.2 | 1,414,703 | 2.8 | 649,758 | 84.9 |
| Central American (excludes Mexican) | 1,686,937 | 4.8 | 3,998,280 | 7.9 | 2,311,343 | 137.0 |
| Costa Rican | 68,588 | 0.2 | 126,418 | 0.3 | 57,830 | 84.3 |
| Guatemalan | 372,487 | 1.1 | 1,044,209 | 2.1 | 671,722 | 180.3 |
| Honduran | 217,569 | 0.6 | 633,401 | 1.3 | 415,832 | 191.1 |
| Nicaraguan | 177,684 | 0.5 | 348,202 | 0.7 | 170,518 | 96.0 |
| Panamanian | 91,723 | 0.3 | 165,456 | 0.3 | 73,733 | 80.4 |
| Salvadoran | 655,165 | 1.9 | 1,648,968 | 3.3 | 993,803 | 151.7 |
| Other Central American[2] | 103,721 | 0.3 | 31,626 | 0.1 | −72,095 | −69.5 |
| South American | 1,353,562 | 3.8 | 2,769,434 | 5.5 | 1,415,872 | 104.6 |
| Argentinean | 100,864 | 0.3 | 224,952 | 0.4 | 124,088 | 123.0 |
| Bolivian | 42,068 | 0.1 | 99,210 | 0.2 | 57,142 | 135.8 |
| Chilean | 68,849 | 0.2 | 126,810 | 0.3 | 57,961 | 84.2 |
| Colombian | 470,684 | 1.3 | 908,734 | 1.8 | 438,050 | 93.1 |
| Ecuadorian | 260,559 | 0.7 | 564,631 | 1.1 | 304,072 | 116.7 |
| Paraguayan | 8,769 | – | 20,023 | – | 11,254 | 128.3 |
| Peruvian | 233,926 | 0.7 | 531,358 | 1.1 | 297,432 | 127.1 |
| Uruguayan | 18,804 | 0.1 | 56,884 | 0.1 | 38,080 | 202.5 |
| Venezuelan | 91,507 | 0.3 | 215,023 | 0.4 | 123,516 | 135.0 |
| Other South American[3] | 57,532 | 0.2 | 21,809 | – | −35,723 | −62.1 |
| Spaniard | 100,135 | 0.3 | 635,253 | 1.3 | 535,118 | 534.4 |
| All other Hispanic or Latino[4] | 6,111,665 | 17.3 | 3,452,403 | 6.8 | −2,659,262 | −43.5 |

– Percentage rounds to 0.0.

[1] The observed changes in Hispanic origin counts between Census 2000 and the 2010 Census could be attributed to a number of factors. Demographic change since 2000, which includes births and deaths in a geographic area and migration in and out of a geographic area, will have an impact on the resulting 2010 Census counts. Some changes in the Hispanic origin question's wording and format since Census 2000 could have influenced reporting patterns in the 2010 Census. Additionally, changes to the Hispanic origin edit and coding procedures could have impacted the 2010 counts. These factors should especially be considered when observing changes for detailed Hispanic groups.

[2] This category includes people who reported Central American Indian groups, "Canal Zone," and "Central American."

[3] This category includes people who reported South American Indian groups and "South American."

[4] This category includes people who reported "Hispanic" or "Latino" and other general terms.

Sources: U.S. Census Bureau, *Census 2000 Summary File 1* and *2010 Census Summary File 1.*

origins increased by 22 percent, from 10.0 million to 12.3 million.

**Other Hispanic origins refer to a variety of identifications.**

Among the 12.3 million Hispanics who were classified as Other Hispanic in 2010, 1.4 million were of Dominican origin, 4.0 million were of Central American origin (other than Mexican), 2.8 million were of South American origin, 635,000 were Spaniard, and 3.5 million reported general terms such as "Hispanic" or "Latino."

Among Central American Hispanics (excluding Mexicans), those of Salvadoran origin were the largest group at 1.6 million, followed by Guatemalans (1.0 million) and Hondurans (633,000). Of the South American Hispanic population, those of Colombian origin were the largest group at 909,000, followed by Ecuadorians at 565,000 and Peruvians at 531,000.

Although people of Mexican, Puerto Rican, and Cuban origin were the largest detailed Hispanic groups, they grew at slower rates than the other detailed groups. Over the decade, the Spaniard population showed the largest percent increase. The Spaniard population in 2010 was more than six times larger than reported in 2000, increasing from 100,000 to 635,000. Other Hispanic groups with origins from Central and South America (Uruguayan, Honduran, Guatemalan, Salvadoran, Bolivian, Venezuelan, Paraguayan, Peruvian, Argentinean, and Ecuadorian) also showed large percent increases, increasing to more than twice their population sizes from 2000 to 2010.

All detailed Hispanic groups showed large percentage increases between 2000 and 2010. On the other hand, the "Other Central American," "Other South American," and "All other Hispanic or Latino" groups—which include general terms such as Central American, South American, and Latino—experienced large percentage decreases during this period.[11,12]

_____

[11] "Other Central American" includes people who reported Central American Indian groups, "Canal Zone," and "Central American." "Other South American" includes people who reported South American Indian groups and "South American." "Other Hispanic or Latino" includes people who reported "Hispanic" or "Latino" and other general terms.

[12] Empirical evidence of question-design effects on the question of Hispanic origin is well documented in several Census Bureau studies. Results for the Census 2000 Alternative Questionnaire Experiment for example, showed changes in wording and omission of specific Hispanic origin examples contributed to a significant number of people reporting general Hispanic terms such as "Hispanic" and "Latino" instead of reporting a specific Hispanic origin group such as Colombian or Dominican. For more information, see *Questionnaire Effects on Reporting of Race and Hispanic Origin: Results of a Replication of the 1990 Mail Short Form in Census 2000* at <www.census.gov/pred /www/rpts/AQE%20R&HO%20Final%20Report .pdf> and *Results of the 2003 National Census Test of Race and Hispanic Questions* at <www.census.gov/srd/papers/pdf /rsm2007-34.pdf>.

The "Other Central American" group declined from about 104,000 in 2000 to 32,000 in 2010, decreasing 70 percent. The "Other South American" group decreased from about 58,000 to 22,000 (down 62 percent). The "All other Hispanic or Latino" group decreased by 44 percent, from 6.1 million in 2000 to 3.5 million in 2010.

### About three-quarters of Hispanics reported as Mexican, Puerto Rican, or Cuban origin.

In 2010, people of Mexican origin comprised the largest Hispanic group, representing 63 percent of the total Hispanic population in the United States (up from 58 percent in 2000) as shown in Figure 2. The second largest group was Puerto Rican, which comprised 9 percent of the Hispanic population in 2010 (down from 10 percent in 2000). The Cuban population represented approximately 4 percent of the total Hispanic population in both the 2000 and 2010 censuses. These three groups accounted for about three-quarters of the Hispanic population in the United States.

Central American Hispanics, including Mexicans, represented 71 percent of the total Hispanic population residing in the United States. There were 1.6 million people of Salvadoran origin (3 percent of the total Hispanic population) in 2010, rising from 655,000 in 2000. The Salvadoran population grew significantly between 2000 and 2010, increasing by 152 percent. Between 2000 and 2010, Guatemalans increased considerably, growing by 180 percent. Guatemalans represented 2 percent of the total Hispanic population in 2010. This population rose from 372,000 in 2000 to over 1 million in 2010.

South American Hispanics grew by 105 percent, increasing from

1.4 million in 2000 to 2.8 million in 2010. The South American Hispanic population represented 5 percent of the total Hispanic population in 2010.

Dominicans accounted for 3 percent of the total Hispanic population in the United States. This population grew by 85 percent, increasing from 765,000 in 2000 to 1.4 million in 2010. The remaining Hispanic origin groups represented about 8 percent of the total Hispanic population in the United States (see Figure 2).

## GEOGRAPHIC DISTRIBUTION

### More than three-quarters of the Hispanic population lived in the West or South.[13]

In 2010, 41 percent of Hispanics lived in the West and 36 percent lived in the South. The Northeast and Midwest accounted for 14 percent and 9 percent, respectively, of the Hispanic population.

Hispanics accounted for 29 percent of the population in the West, the only region in which Hispanics exceeded the national level of 16 percent (see Table 2). Hispanics accounted for 16 percent of the population of the South, 13 percent of the Northeast, and 7 percent of the Midwest's population.

The Hispanic population grew in every region between 2000 and 2010, and most significantly in the South and Midwest. The South

_____

[13] The Northeast census region includes Connecticut, Maine, Massachusetts, New Hampshire, New Jersey, New York, Pennsylvania, Rhode Island, and Vermont. The Midwest census region includes Illinois, Indiana, Iowa, Kansas, Michigan, Minnesota, Missouri, Nebraska, North Dakota, Ohio, South Dakota, and Wisconsin. The South census region includes Alabama, Arkansas, Delaware, the District of Columbia, Florida, Georgia, Kentucky, Louisiana, Maryland, Mississippi, North Carolina, Oklahoma, South Carolina, Tennessee, Texas, Virginia, and West Virginia. The West census region includes Alaska, Arizona, California, Colorado, Hawaii, Idaho, Montana, Nevada, New Mexico, Oregon, Utah, Washington, and Wyoming.

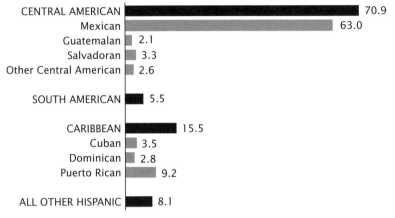

Figure 2.
**Percent Distribution of the Hispanic Population
by Type of Origin: 2010**

(For more information on confidentiality protection, nonsampling error, and
definitions, see *www.census.gov/prod/cen2010/doc/sf1.pdf*)

CENTRAL AMERICAN — 70.9
Mexican — 63.0
Guatemalan — 2.1
Salvadoran — 3.3
Other Central American — 2.6

SOUTH AMERICAN — 5.5

CARIBBEAN — 15.5
Cuban — 3.5
Dominican — 2.8
Puerto Rican — 9.2

ALL OTHER HISPANIC — 8.1

Notes:

1) The "Other Central American" group includes people who reported "Costa Rican,"
"Honduran," "Nicaraguan," "Panamanian," Central American Indian groups, "Canal
Zone," and "Central American."

2) The "South American" group includes people who reported "Argentinean," "Bolivian,"
"Chilean," "Colombian," "Ecuadorian," "Paraguayan," "Peruvian," "Uruguayan,"
"Venezuelan," South American Indian groups, and "South American."

3) The "All Other Hispanic" group includes people who reported "Spaniard," as well as
"Hispanic" or "Latino" and other general terms.

Source: U.S. Census Bureau, *2010 Census Summary File 1.*

experienced a growth of 57 percent in its Hispanic population, which was four times the growth of the total population in the South (14 percent). Significant growth also occurred in the Midwest, with the Hispanic population increasing by 49 percent. This was more than twelve times the growth of the total population in the Midwest (4 percent).

While the Hispanic population grew at a slower rate in the West and Northeast, significant growth still occurred between 2000 and 2010. The Hispanic population grew by 34 percent in the West, which was more than twice the growth of the total population in the West (14 percent). The Northeast's Hispanic population grew by 33 percent—ten times the growth in the total population of the Northeast (3 percent).

Among Hispanic groups with a population of one million or more in 2010, three of the largest Central American groups were concentrated in the West. About two-fifths of people with origins from Guatemala and El Salvador (38 percent and 40 percent, respectively) and half with Mexican origin (52 percent) resided in the West (see Table 3). Unlike Guatemalans, Mexicans, and Salvadorans, all Other Central Americans were more likely to reside in the South.[14] More than half of all Other Central Americans (53 percent) lived in

[14] The "Other Central American" group shown in Table 3 is different than the group with the same name shown in Table 1. The "Other Central American" group in Table 1 includes people who reported Central American Indian groups, "Canal Zone," and "Central American." The "Other Central American" group in Table 3 includes people who reported "Costa Rican," "Honduran," "Nicaraguan," "Panamanian," Central American Indian groups, "Canal Zone," and "Central American."

the South, while 21.9 percent lived in the West. Mexicans were less likely to reside in the Northeast (3 percent) than Guatemalans, Salvadorans, and Other Central Americans.

South American Hispanics were less likely to reside in the West and more likely to reside in the Northeast than the Central American Hispanic groups. About two-fifths of South American Hispanics (42 percent) lived in the South, 37 percent in the Northeast, 15 percent in the West, and 6 percent in the Midwest.

The largest Caribbean Hispanic groups were concentrated in different regions of the United States. Compared to Central and South American Hispanics, the Cuban, Dominican, and Puerto Rican origin populations were less likely to reside in the West. Cubans were much more likely to live in the South and Dominicans and Puerto Ricans were more likely to live in the Northeast. More than three-quarters of the Cuban population (77 percent) resided in the South, more than three-quarters of Dominicans (78 percent) resided in the Northeast, and more than half of the Puerto Rican population (53 percent) lived in the Northeast.

**Over half of the Hispanic population in the United States resided in just three states: California, Texas, and Florida.**

In 2010, 37.6 million, or 75 percent, of Hispanics lived in the eight states with Hispanic populations of one million or more (California, Texas, Florida, New York, Illinois, Arizona, New Jersey, and Colorado). Hispanics in California accounted for 14.0 million (28 percent) of the total Hispanic population, while the Hispanic population in Texas accounted for 9.5 million (19 percent) as shown in Figure 3.

Table 2.
## Hispanic or Latino Population for the United States, Regions, and States, and for Puerto Rico: 2000 and 2010
(For information on confidentiality protection, nonsampling error, and definitions, see *www.census.gov/prod/cen2010/doc/sf1.pdf*)

| Area | 2000 | | | 2010 | | | Population change, 2000 to 2010 | | | |
| --- | --- | --- | --- | --- | --- | --- | --- | --- | --- | --- |
| | | Hispanic or Latino | | | Hispanic or Latino | | Total | | Hispanic or Latino | |
| | Total | Number | Percent of total population | Total | Number | Percent of total population | Number | Per-cent | Number | Per-cent |
| United States... | 281,421,906 | 35,305,818 | 12.5 | 308,745,538 | 50,477,594 | 16.3 | 27,323,632 | 9.7 | 15,171,776 | 43.0 |
| **REGION** | | | | | | | | | | |
| Northeast............ | 53,594,378 | 5,254,087 | 9.8 | 55,317,240 | 6,991,969 | 12.6 | 1,722,862 | 3.2 | 1,737,882 | 33.1 |
| Midwest............. | 64,392,776 | 3,124,532 | 4.9 | 66,927,001 | 4,661,678 | 7.0 | 2,534,225 | 3.9 | 1,537,146 | 49.2 |
| South.............. | 100,236,820 | 11,586,696 | 11.6 | 114,555,744 | 18,227,508 | 15.9 | 14,318,924 | 14.3 | 6,640,812 | 57.3 |
| West .............. | 63,197,932 | 15,340,503 | 24.3 | 71,945,553 | 20,596,439 | 28.6 | 8,747,621 | 13.8 | 5,255,936 | 34.3 |
| **STATE** | | | | | | | | | | |
| Alabama ........... | 4,447,100 | 75,830 | 1.7 | 4,779,736 | 185,602 | 3.9 | 332,636 | 7.5 | 109,772 | 144.8 |
| Alaska ............ | 626,932 | 25,852 | 4.1 | 710,231 | 39,249 | 5.5 | 83,299 | 13.3 | 13,397 | 51.8 |
| Arizona ........... | 5,130,632 | 1,295,617 | 25.3 | 6,392,017 | 1,895,149 | 29.6 | 1,261,385 | 24.6 | 599,532 | 46.3 |
| Arkansas .......... | 2,673,400 | 86,866 | 3.2 | 2,915,918 | 186,050 | 6.4 | 242,518 | 9.1 | 99,184 | 114.2 |
| California .......... | 33,871,648 | 10,966,556 | 32.4 | 37,253,956 | 14,013,719 | 37.6 | 3,382,308 | 10.0 | 3,047,163 | 27.8 |
| Colorado .......... | 4,301,261 | 735,601 | 17.1 | 5,029,196 | 1,038,687 | 20.7 | 727,935 | 16.9 | 303,086 | 41.2 |
| Connecticut ........ | 3,405,565 | 320,323 | 9.4 | 3,574,097 | 479,087 | 13.4 | 168,532 | 4.9 | 158,764 | 49.6 |
| Delaware .......... | 783,600 | 37,277 | 4.8 | 897,934 | 73,221 | 8.2 | 114,334 | 14.6 | 35,944 | 96.4 |
| District of Columbia.... | 572,059 | 44,953 | 7.9 | 601,723 | 54,749 | 9.1 | 29,664 | 5.2 | 9,796 | 21.8 |
| Florida ............ | 15,982,378 | 2,682,715 | 16.8 | 18,801,310 | 4,223,806 | 22.5 | 2,818,932 | 17.6 | 1,541,091 | 57.4 |
| Georgia ........... | 8,186,453 | 435,227 | 5.3 | 9,687,653 | 853,689 | 8.8 | 1,501,200 | 18.3 | 418,462 | 96.1 |
| Hawaii ............ | 1,211,537 | 87,699 | 7.2 | 1,360,301 | 120,842 | 8.9 | 148,764 | 12.3 | 33,143 | 37.8 |
| Idaho ............. | 1,293,953 | 101,690 | 7.9 | 1,567,582 | 175,901 | 11.2 | 273,629 | 21.1 | 74,211 | 73.0 |
| Illinois............ | 12,419,293 | 1,530,262 | 12.3 | 12,830,632 | 2,027,578 | 15.8 | 411,339 | 3.3 | 497,316 | 32.5 |
| Indiana............ | 6,080,485 | 214,536 | 3.5 | 6,483,802 | 389,707 | 6.0 | 403,317 | 6.6 | 175,171 | 81.7 |
| Iowa.............. | 2,926,324 | 82,473 | 2.8 | 3,046,355 | 151,544 | 5.0 | 120,031 | 4.1 | 69,071 | 83.7 |
| Kansas............ | 2,688,418 | 188,252 | 7.0 | 2,853,118 | 300,042 | 10.5 | 164,700 | 6.1 | 111,790 | 59.4 |
| Kentucky .......... | 4,041,769 | 59,939 | 1.5 | 4,339,367 | 132,836 | 3.1 | 297,598 | 7.4 | 72,897 | 121.6 |
| Louisiana.......... | 4,468,976 | 107,738 | 2.4 | 4,533,372 | 192,560 | 4.2 | 64,396 | 1.4 | 84,822 | 78.7 |
| Maine............. | 1,274,923 | 9,360 | 0.7 | 1,328,361 | 16,935 | 1.3 | 53,438 | 4.2 | 7,575 | 80.9 |
| Maryland .......... | 5,296,486 | 227,916 | 4.3 | 5,773,552 | 470,632 | 8.2 | 477,066 | 9.0 | 242,716 | 106.5 |
| Massachusetts....... | 6,349,097 | 428,729 | 6.8 | 6,547,629 | 627,654 | 9.6 | 198,532 | 3.1 | 198,925 | 46.4 |
| Michigan .......... | 9,938,444 | 323,877 | 3.3 | 9,883,640 | 436,358 | 4.4 | −54,804 | −0.6 | 112,481 | 34.7 |
| Minnesota ......... | 4,919,479 | 143,382 | 2.9 | 5,303,925 | 250,258 | 4.7 | 384,446 | 7.8 | 106,876 | 74.5 |
| Mississippi......... | 2,844,658 | 39,569 | 1.4 | 2,967,297 | 81,481 | 2.7 | 122,639 | 4.3 | 41,912 | 105.9 |
| Missouri........... | 5,595,211 | 118,592 | 2.1 | 5,988,927 | 212,470 | 3.5 | 393,716 | 7.0 | 93,878 | 79.2 |
| Montana........... | 902,195 | 18,081 | 2.0 | 989,415 | 28,565 | 2.9 | 87,220 | 9.7 | 10,484 | 58.0 |
| Nebraska.......... | 1,711,263 | 94,425 | 5.5 | 1,826,341 | 167,405 | 9.2 | 115,078 | 6.7 | 72,980 | 77.3 |
| Nevada ........... | 1,998,257 | 393,970 | 19.7 | 2,700,551 | 716,501 | 26.5 | 702,294 | 35.1 | 322,531 | 81.9 |
| New Hampshire....... | 1,235,786 | 20,489 | 1.7 | 1,316,470 | 36,704 | 2.8 | 80,684 | 6.5 | 16,215 | 79.1 |
| New Jersey ......... | 8,414,350 | 1,117,191 | 13.3 | 8,791,894 | 1,555,144 | 17.7 | 377,544 | 4.5 | 437,953 | 39.2 |
| New Mexico......... | 1,819,046 | 765,386 | 42.1 | 2,059,179 | 953,403 | 46.3 | 240,133 | 13.2 | 188,017 | 24.6 |
| New York .......... | 18,976,457 | 2,867,583 | 15.1 | 19,378,102 | 3,416,922 | 17.6 | 401,645 | 2.1 | 549,339 | 19.2 |
| North Carolina....... | 8,049,313 | 378,963 | 4.7 | 9,535,483 | 800,120 | 8.4 | 1,486,170 | 18.5 | 421,157 | 111.1 |
| North Dakota........ | 642,200 | 7,786 | 1.2 | 672,591 | 13,467 | 2.0 | 30,391 | 4.7 | 5,681 | 73.0 |
| Ohio.............. | 11,353,140 | 217,123 | 1.9 | 11,536,504 | 354,674 | 3.1 | 183,364 | 1.6 | 137,551 | 63.4 |
| Oklahoma .......... | 3,450,654 | 179,304 | 5.2 | 3,751,351 | 332,007 | 8.9 | 300,697 | 8.7 | 152,703 | 85.2 |
| Oregon............ | 3,421,399 | 275,314 | 8.0 | 3,831,074 | 450,062 | 11.7 | 409,675 | 12.0 | 174,748 | 63.5 |
| Pennsylvania ....... | 12,281,054 | 394,088 | 3.2 | 12,702,379 | 719,660 | 5.7 | 421,325 | 3.4 | 325,572 | 82.6 |
| Rhode Island........ | 1,048,319 | 90,820 | 8.7 | 1,052,567 | 130,655 | 12.4 | 4,248 | 0.4 | 39,835 | 43.9 |
| South Carolina....... | 4,012,012 | 95,076 | 2.4 | 4,625,364 | 235,682 | 5.1 | 613,352 | 15.3 | 140,606 | 147.9 |
| South Dakota........ | 754,844 | 10,903 | 1.4 | 814,180 | 22,119 | 2.7 | 59,336 | 7.9 | 11,216 | 102.9 |
| Tennessee.......... | 5,689,283 | 123,838 | 2.2 | 6,346,105 | 290,059 | 4.6 | 656,822 | 11.5 | 166,221 | 134.2 |
| Texas............. | 20,851,820 | 6,669,666 | 32.0 | 25,145,561 | 9,460,921 | 37.6 | 4,293,741 | 20.6 | 2,791,255 | 41.8 |
| Utah.............. | 2,233,169 | 201,559 | 9.0 | 2,763,885 | 358,340 | 13.0 | 530,716 | 23.8 | 156,781 | 77.8 |
| Vermont............ | 608,827 | 5,504 | 0.9 | 625,741 | 9,208 | 1.5 | 16,914 | 2.8 | 3,704 | 67.3 |
| Virginia............ | 7,078,515 | 329,540 | 4.7 | 8,001,024 | 631,825 | 7.9 | 922,509 | 13.0 | 302,285 | 91.7 |
| Washington ......... | 5,894,121 | 441,509 | 7.5 | 6,724,540 | 755,790 | 11.2 | 830,419 | 14.1 | 314,281 | 71.2 |
| West Virginia ........ | 1,808,344 | 12,279 | 0.7 | 1,852,994 | 22,268 | 1.2 | 44,650 | 2.5 | 9,989 | 81.4 |
| Wisconsin .......... | 5,363,675 | 192,921 | 3.6 | 5,686,986 | 336,056 | 5.9 | 323,311 | 6.0 | 143,135 | 74.2 |
| Wyoming ........... | 493,782 | 31,669 | 6.4 | 563,626 | 50,231 | 8.9 | 69,844 | 14.1 | 18,562 | 58.6 |
| Puerto Rico ........ | 3,808,610 | 3,762,746 | 98.8 | 3,725,789 | 3,688,455 | 99.0 | −82,821 | −2.2 | −74,291 | −2.0 |

Sources: U.S. Census Bureau, *Census 2000 Summary File 1* and *2010 Census Summary File 1*.

415

Table 3.
## Detailed Hispanic or Latino Origin Groups With a Population Size of One Million or More for the United States and Regions: 2010

(For information on confidentiality protection, nonsampling error, and definitions, see *www.census.gov/prod/cen2010/doc/sf1.pdf*)

| Origin | United States | | Northeast | | Midwest | | South | | West | |
|---|---|---|---|---|---|---|---|---|---|---|
| | Number | Percent | Number | Percent | Number | Percent | Number | Percent | Number | Percent |
| **Total Hispanic** . . . . . . | **50,477,594** | **100.0** | **6,991,969** | **13.9** | **4,661,678** | **9.2** | **18,227,508** | **36.1** | **20,596,439** | **40.8** |
| Central American. . . . . . . . . | 35,796,538 | 100.0 | 1,644,749 | 4.6 | 3,700,814 | 10.3 | 12,642,799 | 35.3 | 17,808,176 | 49.7 |
| Mexican . . . . . . . . . . . . . . | 31,798,258 | 100.0 | 918,188 | 2.9 | 3,470,726 | 10.9 | 10,945,244 | 34.4 | 16,464,100 | 51.8 |
| Guatemalan . . . . . . . . . . . | 1,044,209 | 100.0 | 203,931 | 19.5 | 95,588 | 9.2 | 348,287 | 33.4 | 396,403 | 38.0 |
| Salvadoran. . . . . . . . . . . . | 1,648,968 | 100.0 | 270,509 | 16.4 | 61,894 | 3.8 | 655,184 | 39.7 | 661,381 | 40.1 |
| Other Central American[1] . . | 1,305,103 | 100.0 | 252,121 | 19.3 | 72,606 | 5.6 | 694,084 | 53.2 | 286,292 | 21.9 |
| South American[2] . . . . . . . . . | 2,769,434 | 100.0 | 1,033,473 | 37.3 | 158,768 | 5.7 | 1,150,536 | 41.5 | 426,657 | 15.4 |
| Caribbean . . . . . . . . . . . . . | 7,823,966 | 100.0 | 3,745,150 | 47.9 | 523,524 | 6.7 | 3,008,377 | 38.5 | 546,915 | 7.0 |
| Cuban . . . . . . . . . . . . . . . | 1,785,547 | 100.0 | 197,173 | 11.0 | 62,990 | 3.5 | 1,376,453 | 77.1 | 148,931 | 8.3 |
| Dominican . . . . . . . . . . . . | 1,414,703 | 100.0 | 1,104,802 | 78.1 | 25,799 | 1.8 | 258,383 | 18.3 | 25,719 | 1.8 |
| Puerto Rican . . . . . . . . . . | 4,623,716 | 100.0 | 2,443,175 | 52.8 | 434,735 | 9.4 | 1,373,541 | 29.7 | 372,265 | 8.1 |
| All other Hispanic[3] . . . . . . . . | 4,087,656 | 100.0 | 568,597 | 13.9 | 278,572 | 6.8 | 1,425,796 | 34.9 | 1,814,691 | 44.4 |

[1] This category includes people who reported "Costa Rican," "Honduran," "Nicaraguan," "Panamanian," Central American Indian groups, "Canal Zone," and "Central American."

[2] This category includes people who reported "Argentinean," "Bolivian," "Chilean," "Colombian," "Ecuadorian," "Paraguayan," "Peruvian," "Uruguayan," "Venezuelan," South American Indian groups, and "South American."

[3] This category includes people who reported "Spaniard," as well as "Hispanic" or "Latino" and other general terms.

Source: U.S. Census Bureau, 2010 Census special tabulation.

Hispanics in Florida accounted for 4.2 million (8 percent) of the U.S. Hispanic population.

The Hispanic population experienced growth between 2000 and 2010 in all 50 states and the District of Columbia. The Hispanic population in eight states in the South (Alabama, Arkansas, Kentucky, Maryland, Mississippi, North Carolina, South Carolina, and Tennessee) and South Dakota more than doubled in size between 2000 and 2010. However, even with this large growth, the percent Hispanic in 2010 for each of these states remained less than 9 percent, far below the national level of 16 percent. The Hispanic population in South Carolina grew the fastest, increasing from 95,000 in 2000 to 236,000 in 2010 (a 148 percent increase). Alabama showed the second fastest rate of growth at 145 percent, increasing from 76,000 to 186,000.

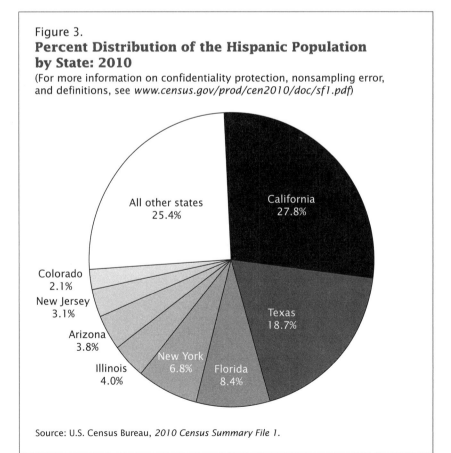

Figure 3.
## Percent Distribution of the Hispanic Population by State: 2010

(For more information on confidentiality protection, nonsampling error, and definitions, see *www.census.gov/prod/cen2010/doc/sf1.pdf*)

California 27.8%
Texas 18.7%
Florida 8.4%
New York 6.8%
Illinois 4.0%
Arizona 3.8%
New Jersey 3.1%
Colorado 2.1%
All other states 25.4%

Source: U.S. Census Bureau, *2010 Census Summary File 1.*

Table 4.

## Top Five States for Detailed Hispanic or Latino Origin Groups With a Population Size of One Million or More in the United States: 2010

(For information on confidentiality protection, nonsampling error, and definitions, see *www.census.gov/prod/cen2010/doc/sf1.pdf*)

| Origin | Total | Rank | | | | |
|---|---|---|---|---|---|---|
| | | First | Second | Third | Fourth | Fifth |
| **MEXICAN** | | | | | | |
| Area................ | United States | California | Texas | Arizona | Illinois | Colorado |
| Population .......... | 31,798,258 | 11,423,146 | 7,951,193 | 1,657,668 | 1,602,403 | 757,181 |
| **PUERTO RICAN** | | | | | | |
| Area................ | United States | New York | Florida | New Jersey | Pennsylvania | Massachusetts |
| Population .......... | 4,623,716 | 1,070,558 | 847,550 | 434,092 | 366,082 | 266,125 |
| **CUBAN** | | | | | | |
| Area................ | United States | Florida | California | New Jersey | New York | Texas |
| Population .......... | 1,785,547 | 1,213,438 | 88,607 | 83,362 | 70,803 | 46,541 |
| **DOMINICAN** | | | | | | |
| Area................ | United States | New York | New Jersey | Florida | Massachusetts | Pennsylvania |
| Population .......... | 1,414,703 | 674,787 | 197,922 | 172,451 | 103,292 | 62,348 |
| **GUATEMALAN** | | | | | | |
| Area................ | United States | California | Florida | New York | Texas | New Jersey |
| Population .......... | 1,044,209 | 332,737 | 83,882 | 73,806 | 66,244 | 48,869 |
| **SALVADORAN** | | | | | | |
| Area................ | United States | California | Texas | New York | Virginia | Maryland |
| Population .......... | 1,648,968 | 573,956 | 222,599 | 152,130 | 123,800 | 123,789 |
| **OTHER HISPANIC**[1] | | | | | | |
| Area................ | United States | California | Florida | Texas | New York | New Jersey |
| Population .......... | 8,162,193 | 1,393,873 | 1,221,623 | 1,030,415 | 917,550 | 516,652 |

[1] This category includes all remaining Hispanic groups with population size less than 1 million.

Source: U.S. Census Bureau, *2010 Census Summary File 1.*

Hispanics in New Mexico were 46 percent of the total state population, the highest proportion for any state. Hispanics were 16 percent (the national level) or more of the state population in eight other states (Arizona, California, Colorado, Florida, Nevada, New Jersey, New York, and Texas). Hispanics accounted for less than 16 percent of the population in 41 states and the District of Columbia.

The top five states for detailed Hispanic origin groups with a national population size of one million or more in 2010 are shown in Table 4. More than one-half (61 percent) of the Mexican origin population in the United States resided in California (11.4 million) and Texas (8.0 million) alone. About two-fifths (41 percent) of the Puerto Rican population lived in two states,

New York (1.1 million) and Florida (848,000). More than two-thirds (68 percent) of all Cubans lived in one state: Florida (1.2 million). Dominicans were highly concentrated in the state of New York with nearly half of them residing there in 2010 (675,000 or 48 percent). About one-third (32 percent) of people of Guatemalan origin resided in California (333,000) and nearly half (48 percent) of the Salvadoran population was concentrated in California (574,000) and Texas (223,000). The remaining other Hispanic origin groups with less than one million in population size were concentrated in California (1.4 million or 17 percent), Florida (1.2 million or 15 percent), Texas (1.0 million or 13 percent), New York (918,000 or 11 percent), and New Jersey (517,000 or 6 percent).

**Salvadorans were the largest Hispanic group in the nation's capital.**

The Mexican origin population represented the largest Hispanic group in 40 states, with more than half of these states in the South and West regions of the country, two in the Northeast region, and in all 12 states in the Midwest region (see Figure 4). Meanwhile Puerto Ricans were the largest group in six of the nine states in the Northeast region and in one Western state, Hawaii (44,000). Dominicans were the largest group in one Northeastern state, Rhode Island (35,000). In the South region, Cubans were the largest Hispanic origin group in Florida (1.2 million) and Salvadorans were the largest group in Maryland (124,000) and the District of Columbia (17,000).

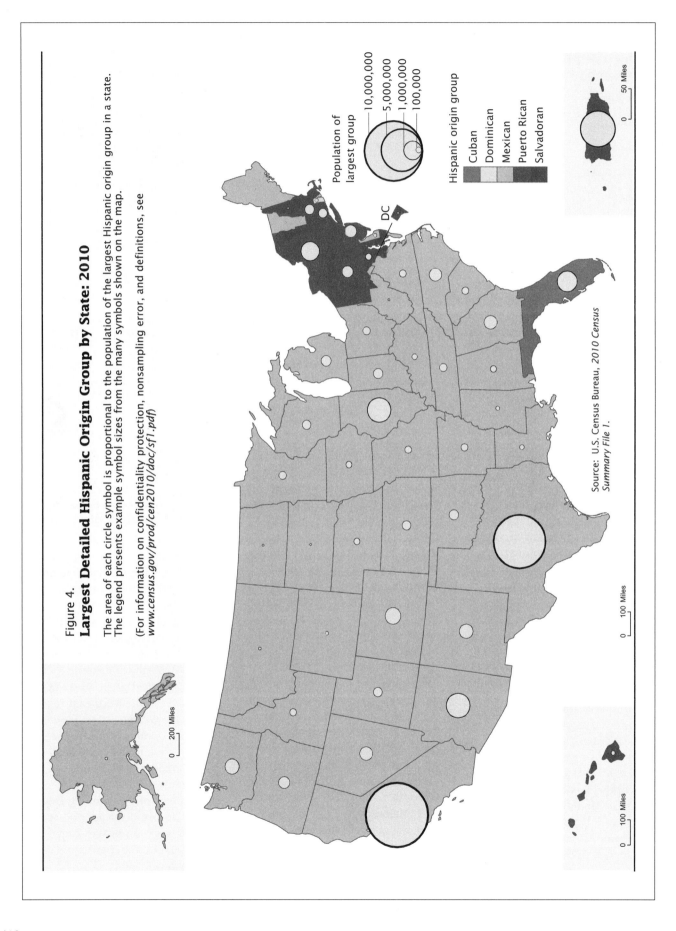

Figure 4.
**Largest Detailed Hispanic Origin Group by State: 2010**

The area of each circle symbol is proportional to the population of the largest Hispanic origin group in a state. The legend presents example symbol sizes from the many symbols shown on the map.

(For information on confidentiality protection, nonsampling error, and definitions, see www.census.gov/prod/cen2010/doc/sf1.pdf)

Population of largest group

10,000,000
5,000,000
1,000,000
100,000

Hispanic origin group

Cuban
Dominican
Mexican
Puerto Rican
Salvadoran

Source: U.S. Census Bureau, *2010 Census Summary File 1.*

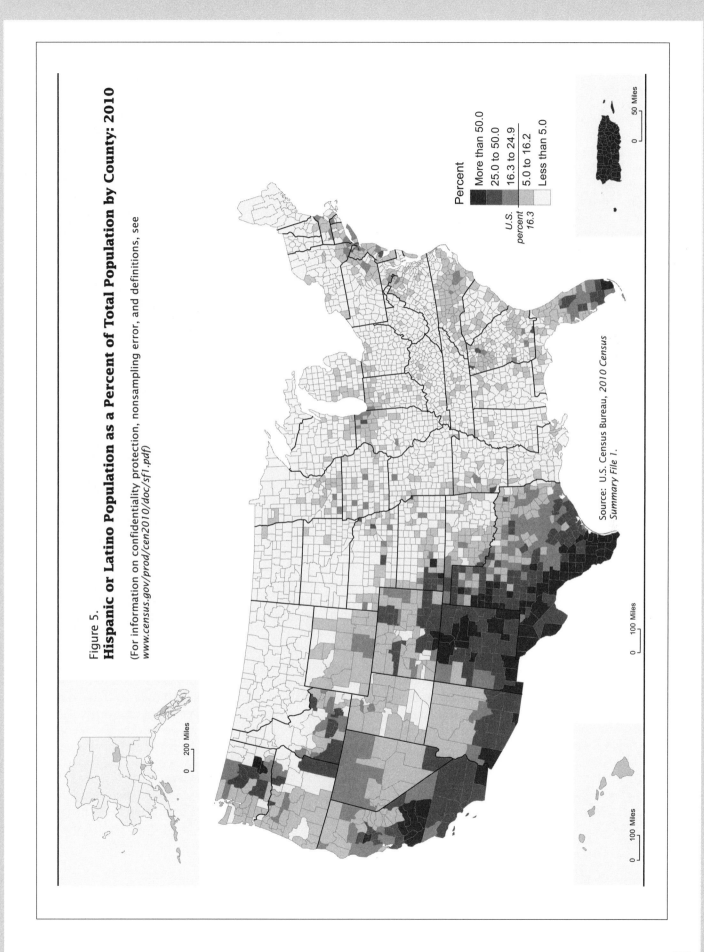

Figure 5.
**Hispanic or Latino Population as a Percent of Total Population by County: 2010**

(For information on confidentiality protection, nonsampling error, and definitions, see
www.census.gov/prod/cen2010/doc/sf1.pdf)

Percent

More than 50.0
25.0 to 50.0
16.3 to 24.9
5.0 to 16.2
Less than 5.0

U.S.
percent
16.3

Source: U.S. Census Bureau, 2010 Census
Summary File 1.

**The Commonwealth of Puerto Rico was 99 percent Hispanic.**

Although the vast majority of the total population in Puerto Rico was of Hispanic origin (99 percent), the total population declined since Census 2000, from 3.8 million to 3.7 million in 2010. Puerto Ricans made up 96 percent of all Hispanics on the island and accounted for 83 percent of the total population loss. On the other hand, the Dominican population, the second largest Hispanic group on the island, increased by 21 percent or 12,000 since Census 2000.[15] Dominicans made up 2 percent of all Hispanics on the island.

**Counties with the highest proportions of Hispanics were along the southwestern border of the United States.**

Hispanics were concentrated in bands of counties along the states bordering Mexico (Texas, New Mexico, Arizona, and California). They were also concentrated outside these four states. In particular, Hispanic concentrations occurred in counties within central Washington, in counties within the states of Kansas, Idaho, Oklahoma, Nebraska, and Colorado, in counties around Chicago, and along the East Coast from New York to Virginia, in counties within central and southern Florida, and the District of Columbia (see Figure 5).

Hispanics were the majority of the population in 82 out of 3,143 counties, accounting for 16 percent of the total Hispanic population.[16] In the South, Hispanics were the majority in 51 counties in Texas and one (Miami-Dade) in Florida. In the West, Hispanics were the majority in 12 counties in New

[15] For more information, see the *2010 Census Summary File 1.*

[16] The counties where Hispanics were the majority of the total population are represented by the More than 50.0 percent class in Figure 5.

Table 5.

## Ten Places With the Highest Number and Percentage of Hispanics or Latinos: 2010

(For information on confidentiality protection, nonsampling error, and definitions, see *www.census.gov/prod/cen2010/doc/sf1.pdf*)

| Place | Total population | Hispanic or Latino population | |
|---|---|---|---|
| | | Rank | Number |
| **NUMBER** | | | |
| New York, NY | 8,175,133 | 1 | 2,336,076 |
| Los Angeles, CA | 3,792,621 | 2 | 1,838,822 |
| Houston, TX | 2,099,451 | 3 | 919,668 |
| San Antonio, TX | 1,327,407 | 4 | 838,952 |
| Chicago, IL | 2,695,598 | 5 | 778,862 |
| Phoenix, AZ | 1,445,632 | 6 | 589,877 |
| El Paso, TX | 649,121 | 7 | 523,721 |
| Dallas, TX | 1,197,816 | 8 | 507,309 |
| San Diego, CA | 1,307,402 | 9 | 376,020 |
| San Jose, CA | 945,942 | 10 | 313,636 |

| Place[1] | Total population | Rank | Percent of total population |
|---|---|---|---|
| **PERCENT** | | | |
| East Los Angeles, CA[2] | 126,496 | 1 | 97.1 |
| Laredo, TX | 236,091 | 2 | 95.6 |
| Hialeah, FL | 224,669 | 3 | 94.7 |
| Brownsville, TX | 175,023 | 4 | 93.2 |
| McAllen, TX | 129,877 | 5 | 84.6 |
| El Paso, TX | 649,121 | 6 | 80.7 |
| Santa Ana, CA | 324,528 | 7 | 78.2 |
| Salinas, CA | 150,441 | 8 | 75.0 |
| Oxnard, CA | 197,899 | 9 | 73.5 |
| Downey, CA | 111,772 | 10 | 70.7 |

[1] Places of 100,000 or more total population. The 2010 Census showed 282 places in the United States with 100,000 or more population. They included 273 incorporated places (including 5 consolidated cities) and 9 census designated places that were not legally incorporated.

[2] East Los Angeles, CA, is a census designated place and is not legally incorporated.

Source: U.S. Census Bureau, *2010 Census Summary File 1.*

Mexico, nine counties in California and two counties in each of the following states: Arizona (Santa Cruz and Yuma), Colorado (Conejos and Costilla), and Washington (Adams and Franklin). In the Midwest, Hispanics were the majority in two counties in Kansas (Ford and Seward), and in the Northeast, Hispanics were the majority in one county (Bronx) in New York.

In 2010, the proportion of Hispanics within a county exceeded the national level (16 percent) most often in the counties of the South and West, especially in counties along the border with Mexico. Hispanics exceeded the national level of 16 percent of the total

population in 429 counties, 14 percent of all counties. Hispanics represented one-quarter to less than half of the county population in 177 counties. The percent Hispanic exceeded the national level of 16 percent but was less than 25.0 percent of the population in 170 counties. More than 86 percent of all counties (2,714 counties) were below the national level. The percent Hispanic ranged from 5.0 percent to just under the national level in 721 counties and were less than 5.0 percent of the county's population in the majority of the U.S. counties (1,993 of the nation's 3,143 counties).

Table 1.
## Population 65 Years and Older by Age and Sex: 2000 and 2010
(For information on confidentiality protection, nonsampling error, and definitions, see *www.census.gov/prod/cen2010/doc/sf1.pdf*)

| Sex and age | 2000 | | | 2010 | | | Change, 2000 to 2010 | |
|---|---|---|---|---|---|---|---|---|
| | Number | Percentage of 65 years and over population | Percentage of U.S. total population | Number | Percentage of 65 years and over population | Percentage of U.S. total population | Number | Percentage |
| **Both sexes, all ages** .... | **281,421,906** | (X) | 100.0 | **308,745,538** | (X) | 100.0 | **27,323,632** | 9.7 |
| 65 years and over ....... | 34,991,753 | 100.0 | 12.4 | 40,267,984 | 100.0 | 13.0 | 5,276,231 | 15.1 |
| 65 to 74 years ......... | 18,390,986 | 52.6 | 6.5 | 21,713,429 | 53.9 | 7.0 | 3,322,443 | 18.1 |
| 65 to 69 years ....... | 9,533,545 | 27.2 | 3.4 | 12,435,263 | 30.9 | 4.0 | 2,901,718 | 30.4 |
| 70 to 74 years ....... | 8,857,441 | 25.3 | 3.1 | 9,278,166 | 23.0 | 3.0 | 420,725 | 4.7 |
| 75 to 84 years ......... | 12,361,180 | 35.3 | 4.4 | 13,061,122 | 32.4 | 4.2 | 699,942 | 5.7 |
| 75 to 79 years ....... | 7,415,813 | 21.2 | 2.6 | 7,317,795 | 18.2 | 2.4 | −98,018 | −1.3 |
| 80 to 84 years ....... | 4,945,367 | 14.1 | 1.8 | 5,743,327 | 14.3 | 1.9 | 797,960 | 16.1 |
| 85 to 94 years ......... | 3,902,349 | 11.2 | 1.4 | 5,068,825 | 12.6 | 1.6 | 1,166,476 | 29.9 |
| 85 to 89 years ....... | 2,789,818 | 8.0 | 1.0 | 3,620,459 | 9.0 | 1.2 | 830,641 | 29.8 |
| 90 to 94 years ....... | 1,112,531 | 3.2 | 0.4 | 1,448,366 | 3.6 | 0.5 | 335,835 | 30.2 |
| 95 years and over ...... | 337,238 | 1.0 | 0.1 | 424,608 | 1.1 | 0.1 | 87,370 | 25.9 |
| 95 to 99 years ....... | 286,784 | 0.8 | 0.1 | 371,244 | 0.9 | 0.1 | 84,460 | 29.5 |
| 100 years and over .... | 50,454 | 0.1 | − | 53,364 | 0.1 | − | 2,910 | 5.8 |
| Median age, 65 years and over............. | 74.5 | (X) | (X) | 74.1 | (X) | (X) | −0.4 | (X) |
| **Male, all ages** ......... | **138,053,563** | (X) | 49.1 | **151,781,326** | (X) | 49.2 | **13,727,763** | 9.9 |
| 65 years and over ....... | 14,409,625 | 41.2 | 5.1 | 17,362,960 | 43.1 | 5.6 | 2,953,335 | 20.5 |
| 65 to 74 years ......... | 8,303,274 | 23.7 | 3.0 | 10,096,519 | 25.1 | 3.3 | 1,793,245 | 21.6 |
| 65 to 69 years ....... | 4,400,362 | 12.6 | 1.6 | 5,852,547 | 14.5 | 1.9 | 1,452,185 | 33.0 |
| 70 to 74 years ....... | 3,902,912 | 11.2 | 1.4 | 4,243,972 | 10.5 | 1.4 | 341,060 | 8.7 |
| 75 to 84 years ......... | 4,879,353 | 13.9 | 1.7 | 5,476,762 | 13.6 | 1.8 | 597,409 | 12.2 |
| 75 to 79 years ....... | 3,044,456 | 8.7 | 1.1 | 3,182,388 | 7.9 | 1.0 | 137,932 | 4.5 |
| 80 to 84 years ....... | 1,834,897 | 5.2 | 0.7 | 2,294,374 | 5.7 | 0.7 | 459,477 | 25.0 |
| 85 to 94 years ......... | 1,158,826 | 3.3 | 0.4 | 1,698,254 | 4.2 | 0.6 | 539,428 | 46.5 |
| 85 to 89 years ....... | 876,501 | 2.5 | 0.3 | 1,273,867 | 3.2 | 0.4 | 397,366 | 45.3 |
| 90 to 94 years ....... | 282,325 | 0.8 | 0.1 | 424,387 | 1.1 | 0.1 | 142,062 | 50.3 |
| 95 years and over ...... | 68,172 | 0.2 | − | 91,425 | 0.2 | − | 23,253 | 34.1 |
| 95 to 99 years ....... | 58,115 | 0.2 | − | 82,263 | 0.2 | − | 24,148 | 41.6 |
| 100 years and over .... | 10,057 | − | − | 9,162 | − | − | −895 | −8.9 |
| Median age, 65 years and over............. | 73.5 | (X) | (X) | 73.2 | (X) | (X) | −0.3 | (X) |
| **Female, all ages**........ | **143,368,343** | (X) | 50.9 | **156,964,212** | (X) | 50.8 | **13,595,869** | 9.5 |
| 65 years and over ....... | 20,582,128 | 58.8 | 7.3 | 22,905,024 | 56.9 | 7.4 | 2,322,896 | 11.3 |
| 65 to 74 years ......... | 10,087,712 | 28.8 | 3.6 | 11,616,910 | 28.8 | 3.8 | 1,529,198 | 15.2 |
| 65 to 69 years ....... | 5,133,183 | 14.7 | 1.8 | 6,582,716 | 16.3 | 2.1 | 1,449,533 | 28.2 |
| 70 to 74 years ....... | 4,954,529 | 14.2 | 1.8 | 5,034,194 | 12.5 | 1.6 | 79,665 | 1.6 |
| 75 to 84 years ......... | 7,481,827 | 21.4 | 2.7 | 7,584,360 | 18.8 | 2.5 | 102,533 | 1.4 |
| 75 to 79 years ....... | 4,371,357 | 12.5 | 1.6 | 4,135,407 | 10.3 | 1.3 | −235,950 | −5.4 |
| 80 to 84 years ....... | 3,110,470 | 8.9 | 1.1 | 3,448,953 | 8.6 | 1.1 | 338,483 | 10.9 |
| 85 to 94 years ......... | 2,743,523 | 7.8 | 1.0 | 3,370,571 | 8.4 | 1.1 | 627,048 | 22.9 |
| 85 to 89 years ....... | 1,913,317 | 5.5 | 0.7 | 2,346,592 | 5.8 | 0.8 | 433,275 | 22.6 |
| 90 to 94 years ....... | 830,206 | 2.4 | 0.3 | 1,023,979 | 2.5 | 0.3 | 193,773 | 23.3 |
| 95 years and over ...... | 269,066 | 0.8 | 0.1 | 333,183 | 0.8 | 0.1 | 64,117 | 23.8 |
| 95 to 99 years ....... | 228,669 | 0.7 | 0.1 | 288,981 | 0.7 | 0.1 | 60,312 | 26.4 |
| 100 years and over .... | 40,397 | 0.1 | − | 44,202 | 0.1 | − | 3,805 | 9.4 |
| Median age, 65 years and over............. | 75.2 | (X) | (X) | 74.8 | (X) | (X) | −0.4 | (X) |

(X) Not applicable

− Percentage rounds to 0.0

Sources: U.S. Census Bureau, *Census 2000 Summary File 1* and *2010 Census Summary File 1*.

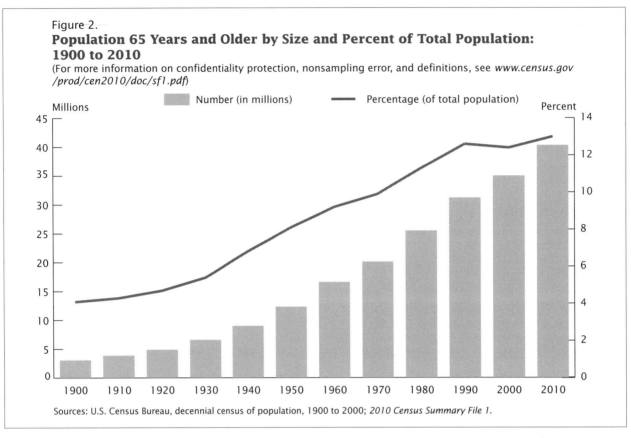

Figure 2.

**Population 65 Years and Older by Size and Percent of Total Population: 1900 to 2010**

(For more information on confidentiality protection, nonsampling error, and definitions, see *www.census.gov/prod/cen2010/doc/sf1.pdf*)

Sources: U.S. Census Bureau, decennial census of population, 1900 to 2000; *2010 Census Summary File 1.*

derived from a two-part age question in which both age and date of birth were asked of all people. Similar to Census 2000, the age question in the 2010 Census asked for age in complete years as well as month, day, and year of birth. In 2010, however, an instruction was added to the age question that guided respondents to report babies less than one year old as age 0.

### THE 65 YEARS AND OLDER POPULATION: A SNAPSHOT

Data from the 2010 Census provide detailed age statistics on the total population as well as the population 65 years and over.[5] According

[5] For additional 2010 Census age and sex information, see U.S. Census Bureau, 2011, *Age and Sex Composition: 2010*, by Lindsay M. Howden and Julie A. Meyer, 2010 Census Briefs, C2010BR-03, available at <www.census.gov/prod/cen2010/briefs/c2010br-03.pdf>.

to the 2010 Census, there were 40.3 million people who were 65 years and over on April 1, 2010 (Table 1). This is an increase of 5.3 million over Census 2000, when this population numbered 35.0 million. The percentage of the population 65 years and over also increased from 2000 to 2010. In 2010, the older population represented 13.0 percent of the total population, an increase from 12.4 percent found in 2000.

When compared with the number of older people in the past, the population 65 years and over has notably increased over time. In 1900, there were 3.1 million people aged 65 and over in the United States (Figure 2). As the population 65 years and over steadily increased throughout the twentieth century, the older population reached its

highest level at 40.3 million in 2010—up from 31.2 million in 1990 and 35.0 million in 2000.

The older population's share of the total population has also been trending upward. The population 65 years and over made up just 4.1 percent of the total population in 1900, and since then steadily increased except for the period between 1990 and 2000. The population aged 65 and over grew slower than that of younger ages during the 1990 to 2000 decade and resulted in a smaller share of the older population in 2000 than 1990. In 1990, the older population represented 12.6 percent of the total population compared with 12.4 percent in 2000. However, in 2010, the population 65 years and over was larger than in any other decennial census at 13.0 percent.

**The 65 years and over population grew at a faster rate than the total population.**

Between 2000 and 2010, the total population increased by 9.7 percent, from 281.4 million to 308.7 million. Growth over the decade was even faster for the population 65 years and over, which grew 15.1 percent. This is the opposite of what happened between 1990 and 2000 when the growth of the older population was slower than the growth of the total population. From 1990 to 2000, the total population grew by 13.2 percent and the population 65 years and over grew by only 12.0 percent.

**Population size and growth varied among the older age groups.**

Table 1 presents data on the distribution of the population for selected older age groups. In 2010, the number of people aged 65 to 74 was 21.7 million and represented 53.9 percent of the population 65 years and over. The number of people 75 to 84 years old totaled 13.1 million and made up 32.4 percent of the population 65 years and over. The population 85 to 94 years old contained 5.1 million people and made up 12.6 percent of the population 65 years and over. Finally, the population 95 years and over was roughly 425,000 persons and represented 1.1 percent of the older population.

An examination of the growth of ten-year age groups among the older population shows that the 85 to 94 year old group experienced the fastest growth between 2000 and 2010. This group grew by 29.9 percent, increasing from 3.9 million to 5.1 million. Within this age group, 85 to 89 year olds increased by 29.8 percent and 90 to 94 year olds increased by 30.2 percent. The

population 95 years and over experienced a similar rate of growth (25.9 percent), and increased from 337,000 to 425,000 between 2000 and 2010.

As shown in Table 1, the population 65 to 74 years experienced relatively slower growth (18.1 percent) than the other older ten-year age groups. However, within the 65 to 74 year old age group, 65 to 69 year olds experienced faster growth than any other five-year age group within the older population. The 65 to 69 year old age group grew by 30.4 percent and increased from 9.5 million to 12.4 million. This age group represents the leading edge of the Baby Boom and is expected to grow more rapidly over the next decade as the first Baby Boomers start turning 65 in 2011.[6]

The ten-year age group with the slowest growth between 2000 and 2010 was the group 75 to 84 years (5.7 percent), which increased from 12.4 million to 13.1 million. Growth in this age group was mainly due to those aged 80 to 84, which grew by 16.1 percent. During the decade, a decrease was noted in the number of people aged 75 to 79 from 7.4 million to 7.3 million, resulting in a decline of 1.3 percent.[7]

---

[6] The Baby Boom includes people born from mid-1946 to 1964. The Baby Boom is distinguished by a dramatic increase in birth rates following World War II, and is one of the largest generations in U.S. history. For more information, see: Hogan, Perez, and Bell, 2008, *Who (Really) Are the First Baby Boomers?* In Joint Statistical Meetings Proceedings, Social Statistics Section, Alexandria, VA: American Statistical Association, pp. 1009–1016.

[7] The changes in the 75 to 79 year old age group mainly reflect the relatively low number of births during the late 1920s and early 1930s. The relatively low number of births during that period has resulted in fewer numbers of people entering these older ages during the previous decade. Between 1990 and 2000, decreases were noted in the 65 to 69 year old age group, and this population has aged forward to now show decreases in the 75 to 79 year old population.

Evidence of varied growth in the older ages can also be seen in the median age of the population 65 years and over, which decreased from 74.5 in 2000 to 74.1 in 2010. Median age indicates the age at which half of the population is above and half of the population is below a certain age. While the rapid rate of growth has been occurring in the oldest ages, growth in the 65 to 69 year old age group has contributed to lowering the median age of the population 65 years and over.

**Males experienced more rapid growth than females in the older ages.**

Males show more rapid growth in the older population than females over the decade. While females continue to outnumber males in the older ages, males continued to close the gap over the decade by increasing at a faster rate than females. The largest growth rate for a ten-year age group was for males 85 to 94 years old (46.5 percent). Females in this age group also increased but to a smaller degree (22.9 percent). When five-year age groups are compared, males 90 to 94 years old had the largest growth rate (50.3 percent) while females in this age group grew by 23.3 percent.

The age group that experienced the largest growth for females was 65 to 69 year olds (28.2 percent). When ten-year age groups are compared, the age group that experienced the largest growth rate for females was for those 95 years and over (23.8 percent). The only five-year age group in which females experienced larger growth than males was the age group 100 years and older. This age group grew by 9.4 percent for females and declined by 8.9 percent for males.

Figure 3.
## Population by Age and Sex: 2000 and 2010

(For more information on confidentiality protection, nonsampling error, and definitions, see *www.census.gov/prod/cen2010/doc/sf1.pdf*)

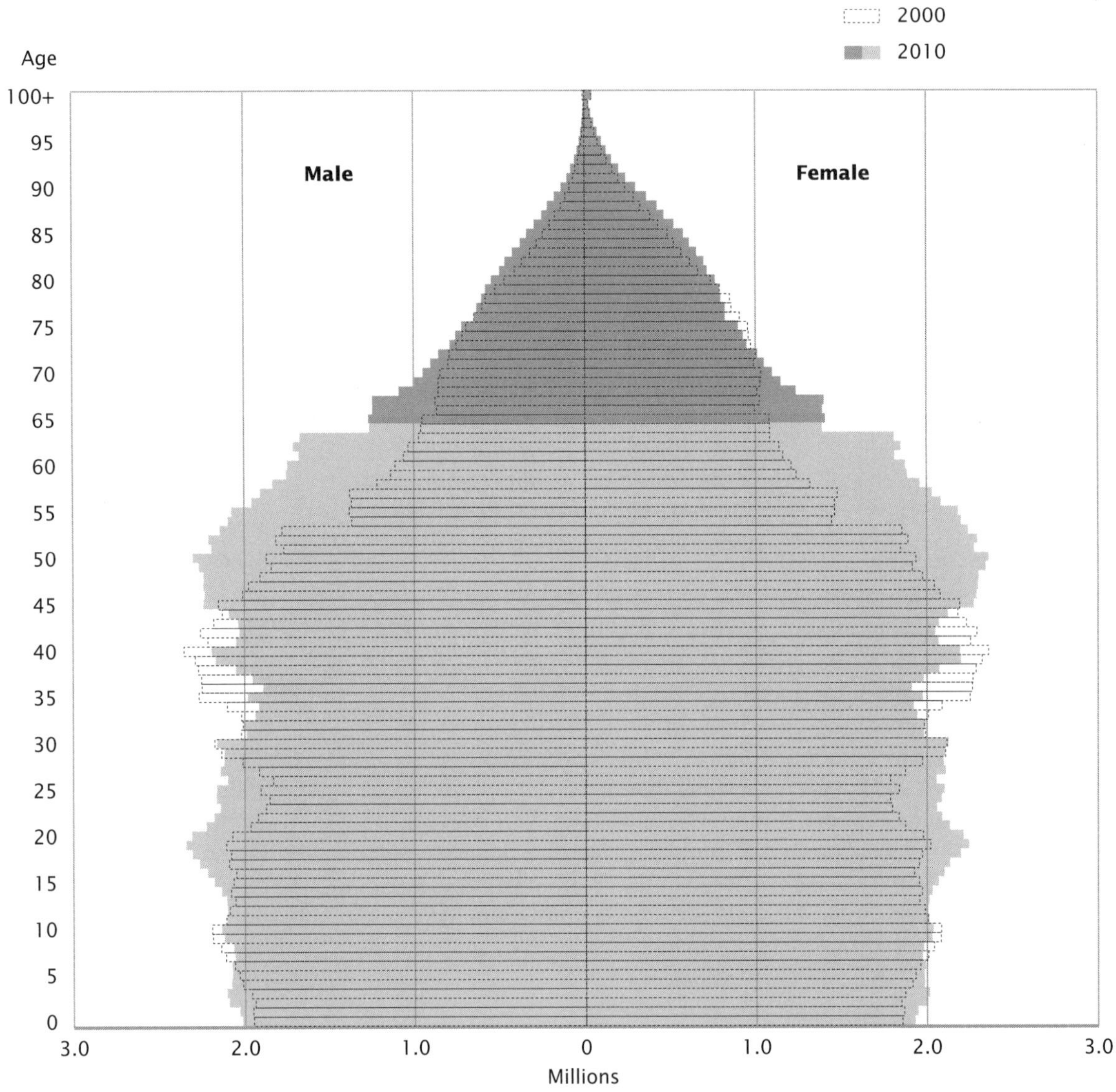

Note: The lighter shade of blue represents ages 0 to 64 in the 2010 Census. The darker shade of blue represents ages 65 years and over in the 2010 Census.

Sources: U.S. Census Bureau, *Census 2000 Summary File 1* and *2010 Census Summary File 1*.

In addition to examining the number, percent, and growth rate of certain age groups, the age-sex pyramid is another key tool for assessing a population's age and sex composition (Figure 3). The age-sex pyramid shows the numeric distribution of males (on the left) and females (on the right) by single years of age. Both the 2000 and 2010 pyramids are shown together so that population shifts in the shape of the pyramid can be more easily assessed. The older population is also shaded darker for easier identification. As the pyramid shows, there was notable growth in the older ages between 2000 and 2010 for both males and females. The population pyramid also gives some context to how the population distribution will likely shift in the near future. The Baby Boom population in 2010

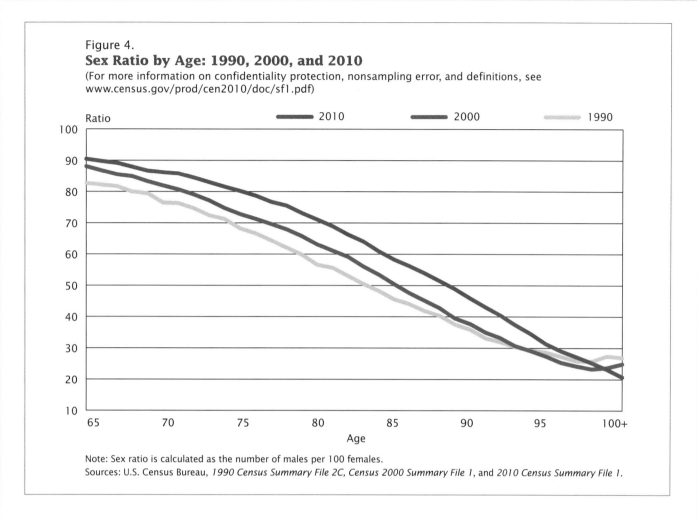

Figure 4.
**Sex Ratio by Age: 1990, 2000, and 2010**
(For more information on confidentiality protection, nonsampling error, and definitions, see www.census.gov/prod/cen2010/doc/sf1.pdf)

Note: Sex ratio is calculated as the number of males per 100 females.
Sources: U.S. Census Bureau, *1990 Census Summary File 2C, Census 2000 Summary File 1*, and *2010 Census Summary File 1*.

appears as a bulge in the middle of the pyramid (at ages 46 to 64). This bulge will begin aging into the 65 and older ages in coming years, and indicates that future growth of the older population is both highly probable and unprecedented in the United States.

**Females continue to outnumber males at older ages, but the gap is narrowing.**

The lines at the topmost part of the age-sex pyramid display the differences that exist between the number of males and the number of females at the older ages. In both 2000 and 2010, women outnumbered men in the older population at every single year of age (i.e., 65 to 100 years and over).

This is apparent by the longer lines at the top of the pyramid for females when compared with males. While this gender-gap has been narrowing, females continue to outpace males with longer life expectancy and lower mortality rates at older ages.[8] The disparity between males and females at the older ages is also apparent in the sex ratio at older ages.

The sex ratio is a common measure used to indicate the balance of males and females in a population. It is derived by taking the number of males divided by the number of females and multiplying by 100. Simply stated, the sex ratio is the

[8] Kochanek, Kenneth, et al., 2011, *Deaths: Preliminary Data for 2009,* National Center for Health Statistics, National Vital Statistics Reports, Vol. 59, No. 4.

number of males per 100 females. For example, a sex ratio of exactly 100 would indicate equal numbers of males and females. A sex ratio higher than 100 shows more males in a population, and a sex ratio under 100 shows more females. Typically, the sex ratio at birth is about 105 males to every 100 females. Then, as males experience higher rates of mortality than females at almost every age, the sex ratio declines as age increases. This results in more women than men in the older populations.

As the results in Figure 4 illustrate, there have been more females than males in the older population across the last three censuses. This is evidenced by the lines on the graph

Figure 5.
**Percent Distribution of the Oldest-Old Population by Age and Sex: 1990, 2000, and 2010**
(For more information on confidentiality protection, nonsampling error, and definitions, see *www.census.gov/prod/cen2010/doc/sf1.pdf*)

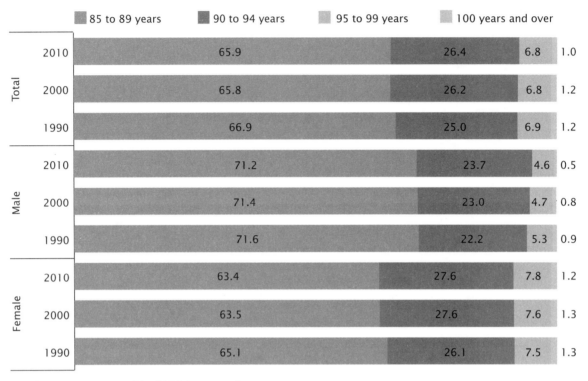

| | | 85 to 89 years | 90 to 94 years | 95 to 99 years | 100 years and over |
|---|---|---|---|---|---|
| **Total** | 2010 | 65.9 | 26.4 | 6.8 | 1.0 |
| | 2000 | 65.8 | 26.2 | 6.8 | 1.2 |
| | 1990 | 66.9 | 25.0 | 6.9 | 1.2 |
| **Male** | 2010 | 71.2 | 23.7 | 4.6 | 0.5 |
| | 2000 | 71.4 | 23.0 | 4.7 | 0.8 |
| | 1990 | 71.6 | 22.2 | 5.3 | 0.9 |
| **Female** | 2010 | 63.4 | 27.6 | 7.8 | 1.2 |
| | 2000 | 63.5 | 27.6 | 7.6 | 1.3 |
| | 1990 | 65.1 | 26.1 | 7.5 | 1.3 |

Note: Percentages may not add to 100.0 due to rounding.
Sources: U.S. Census Bureau, *1990 Census Summary File 2C, Census 2000 Summary File 1*, and *2010 Census Summary File 1*.

being below the 100 mark for all data points. The graph also reveals a noteworthy increase in the sex ratio over time as male and female mortality differentials continue to narrow and more males enter and age into the older population. For single years of age above age 65, the sex ratios were higher in 2010 than in 2000 and 1990.[9] This means that there are increasing numbers of males per females in the older ages.

In 2010, there were 90.5 males per 100 females in the 65 year old population, an increase from 2000 and 1990 when the sex ratios were 88.1 and 82.7, respectively (Figure 4). Increases are also apparent in the older ages where the sex ratio for the population at age 75 was 80.2 in 2010, up from 72.8 in 2000 and 68.2 in 1990. The population 85 years old also experienced increases in the sex ratio over the past three censuses. The population at the age of 85 had 58.3 males per 100 females in 2010, 50.5 males per 100 females in 2000, and 45.6 males per 100 females in 1990.

**Of the oldest-old, 90 to 94 year olds had the greatest increase in percentage.**

In addition to examining the sex ratio, the percent distribution of the population aged 85 and over (the oldest-old) by sex can provide additional findings about differences that exist in the oldest ages of the population (Figure 5).[10] Among the oldest-old, the age group 85 to 89 years made up the greatest share of the distribution in 1990, 2000, and 2010. The largest percentage point increase for the oldest-old population over the previous two decades was concentrated in the 90 to 94 year old age group, which increased from 25.0 percent

[9] The sex ratio at age 99 and above is lower in 2010 than it was in 2000 or 1990. This could be due to a variety of factors associated with the centenarian population, including data quality. For additional information on the centenarian population, see U.S. Census Bureau, 1999, *Centenarians in the United States: 1990* by Constance Krach and Victoria Velkoff, Current Population Reports, Series P23-199RV, available at <www.census.gov/prod/99pubs/p23-199.pdf>.

[10] In this report, the term "oldest-old" population refers to the population 85 years and over.

in 1990 to 26.2 percent in 2000, and 26.4 percent in 2010. The age group 95 to 99 years, while showing numeric increase and positive percent change, maintained the same share of the oldest-old age distribution in 2010 as it did in 2000. Similarly, the population 100 years and over increased in number from 1990 to 2000 to 2010. However, due to larger growth in the other "oldest-old" ages, the share of the oldest-old population that was 100 years and over in the 2010 Census has decreased since Census 2000.

For both males and females 85 years and over, the majority of the oldest-old population was concentrated in the 85 to 89 year old age group. However, differences emerge between the sexes when the distribution of the male population 85 years and over is compared with the distribution of the female population 85 years and over. For males, a greater portion of the population 85 years and over was concentrated in the 85 to 89 year old age group than the female population. In 2010, 71.2 percent of the oldest-old male population was in the 85 to 89 year old age group, compared with 63.4 percent of the oldest-old female population in the 85 to 89 year old age group. These differences in percentages between males and females were due to larger shares of the female population living longer and experiencing lower mortality in the older ages than males.

**The proportion of males 90 to 94 years old increased more than females within the oldest-old distribution between 2000 and 2010.**

Even though females still outnumber males in the oldest-old ages, the gap between males and females in the oldest ages is narrowing. Males 90 to 94 years have been

increasing so that in 2010, 23.7 percent of males who were 85 years and over were in the 90 to 94 year old age group. This is up from 23.0 percent in 2000 and 22.2 percent in 1990. Females, while still increasing in number for this age group, did not have as large a gain between 2000 and 2010. Females 85 years and over that were ages 90 to 94 maintained a share of 27.6 percent in both 2010 and 2000. This is an increase from 26.1 percent in 1990.

## GEOGRAPHIC DISTRIBUTION

In addition to providing national level population statistics, the census also provides data for lower levels of geography. The following section contains information on the older population by regions, states, inside or outside metropolitan/micropolitan areas, counties, and places with a total population of at least 100,000.

## REGION AND STATE

**The South had the largest number of people in the older ages, while the Northeast had the largest percentage of people in the older ages.**

Comparisons across the four census regions in 2010 show that the South contained the greatest number of people 65 years and over and 85 years and over (Table 2).[11] The Midwest contained the second largest number of people 65 years and over and 85 years and over

---

[11] The Northeast region includes Connecticut, Maine, Massachusetts, New Hampshire, New Jersey, New York, Pennsylvania, Rhode Island, and Vermont. The Midwest includes Illinois, Indiana, Iowa, Kansas, Michigan, Minnesota, Missouri, Nebraska, North Dakota, Ohio, South Dakota, and Wisconsin. The South includes Alabama, Arkansas, Delaware, the District of Columbia, Florida, Georgia, Kentucky, Louisiana, Maryland, Mississippi, North Carolina, Oklahoma, South Carolina, Tennessee, Texas, Virginia, and West Virginia. The West includes Alaska, Arizona, California, Colorado, Hawaii, Idaho, Montana, Nevada, New Mexico, Oregon, Utah, Washington, and Wyoming.

while the West contained the third largest number of people 65 years and over and the smallest number of people 85 years and over. The Northeast, on the other hand, contained the smallest number of people 65 years and over and the third largest number of people 85 years and over.

In addition to comparing the older population by number in each region, a comparison of the older population by percentage yields a different ranking. The Northeast had the largest percentage of people 65 years and over (14.1 percent), followed by the Midwest (13.5 percent), the South (13.0 percent), and the West (11.9 percent). The Northeast also contained the largest percentage of people 85 years and over (2.2 percent), followed by the Midwest (2.0 percent), and the West and South (each with 1.6 percent).

**The West had the fastest growth in the population 65 years and over and the population 85 years and over.**

When compared with Census 2000, all regions show positive growth in both the 65 years and over and 85 years and over population. The region with the most rapid growth in the population 65 years and over was the West (23.5 percent), increasing from 6.9 million in 2000 to 8.5 million in 2010. The region with the fastest growth in the population 85 years and over was also the West (42.8 percent), increasing from 806,000 in 2000 to 1.2 million in 2010. To note, the South had the fastest total population growth between 2000 and 2010 followed by the West (14.3 percent and 13.8 percent, respectively).

Table 2.

## Population 65 Years and Older and Population 85 Years and Older for the United States, Regions, and States, and for Puerto Rico: 2000 and 2010

(For information on confidentiality protection, nonsampling error, and definitions, see *www.census.gov/prod/cen2010/doc/sf1.pdf*)

| Area | 2000 Total population | 2000 65 years and over Number | Per-cent | 2000 85 years and over Number | Per-cent | 2010 Total population | 2010 65 years and over Number | Per-cent | 2010 85 years and over Number | Per-cent | Percent change, 2000 to 2010 Total population | 65 years and over | 85 years and over |
|---|---|---|---|---|---|---|---|---|---|---|---|---|---|
| United States... | 281,421,906 | 34,991,753 | 12.4 | 4,239,587 | 1.5 | 308,745,538 | 40,267,984 | 13.0 | 5,493,433 | 1.8 | 9.7 | 15.1 | 29.6 |
| **REGION** | | | | | | | | | | | | | |
| Northeast | 53,594,378 | 7,372,282 | 13.8 | 938,459 | 1.8 | 55,317,240 | 7,804,833 | 14.1 | 1,199,702 | 2.2 | 3.2 | 5.9 | 27.8 |
| Midwest | 64,392,776 | 8,259,075 | 12.8 | 1,064,295 | 1.7 | 66,927,001 | 9,022,334 | 13.5 | 1,320,640 | 2.0 | 3.9 | 9.2 | 24.1 |
| South | 100,236,820 | 12,438,267 | 12.4 | 1,430,546 | 1.4 | 114,555,744 | 14,893,985 | 13.0 | 1,821,982 | 1.6 | 14.3 | 19.7 | 27.4 |
| West | 63,197,932 | 6,922,129 | 11.0 | 806,287 | 1.3 | 71,945,553 | 8,546,832 | 11.9 | 1,151,109 | 1.6 | 13.8 | 23.5 | 42.8 |
| **STATE** | | | | | | | | | | | | | |
| Alabama | 4,447,100 | 579,798 | 13.0 | 67,301 | 1.5 | 4,779,736 | 657,792 | 13.8 | 75,684 | 1.6 | 7.5 | 13.5 | 12.5 |
| Alaska | 626,932 | 35,699 | 5.7 | 2,634 | 0.4 | 710,231 | 54,938 | 7.7 | 4,711 | 0.7 | 13.3 | 53.9 | 78.9 |
| Arizona | 5,130,632 | 667,839 | 13.0 | 68,525 | 1.3 | 6,392,017 | 881,831 | 13.8 | 103,400 | 1.6 | 24.6 | 32.0 | 50.9 |
| Arkansas | 2,673,400 | 374,019 | 14.0 | 46,492 | 1.7 | 2,915,918 | 419,981 | 14.4 | 51,402 | 1.8 | 9.1 | 12.3 | 10.6 |
| California | 33,871,648 | 3,595,658 | 10.6 | 425,657 | 1.3 | 37,253,956 | 4,246,514 | 11.4 | 600,968 | 1.6 | 10.0 | 18.1 | 41.2 |
| Colorado | 4,301,261 | 416,073 | 9.7 | 48,216 | 1.1 | 5,029,196 | 549,625 | 10.9 | 69,613 | 1.4 | 16.9 | 32.1 | 44.4 |
| Connecticut | 3,405,565 | 470,183 | 13.8 | 64,273 | 1.9 | 3,574,097 | 506,559 | 14.2 | 84,898 | 2.4 | 4.9 | 7.7 | 32.1 |
| Delaware | 783,600 | 101,726 | 13.0 | 10,549 | 1.3 | 897,934 | 129,277 | 14.4 | 15,744 | 1.8 | 14.6 | 27.1 | 49.2 |
| District of Columbia | 572,059 | 69,898 | 12.2 | 8,975 | 1.6 | 601,723 | 68,809 | 11.4 | 10,315 | 1.7 | 5.2 | −1.6 | 14.9 |
| Florida | 15,982,378 | 2,807,597 | 17.6 | 331,287 | 2.1 | 18,801,310 | 3,259,602 | 17.3 | 434,125 | 2.3 | 17.6 | 16.1 | 31.0 |
| Georgia | 8,186,453 | 785,275 | 9.6 | 87,857 | 1.1 | 9,687,653 | 1,032,035 | 10.7 | 113,823 | 1.2 | 18.3 | 31.4 | 29.6 |
| Hawaii | 1,211,537 | 160,601 | 13.3 | 17,564 | 1.4 | 1,360,301 | 195,138 | 14.3 | 30,238 | 2.2 | 12.3 | 21.5 | 72.2 |
| Idaho | 1,293,953 | 145,916 | 11.3 | 18,057 | 1.4 | 1,567,582 | 194,668 | 12.4 | 25,242 | 1.6 | 21.1 | 33.4 | 39.8 |
| Illinois | 12,419,293 | 1,500,025 | 12.1 | 192,031 | 1.5 | 12,830,632 | 1,609,213 | 12.5 | 234,912 | 1.8 | 3.3 | 7.3 | 22.3 |
| Indiana | 6,080,485 | 752,831 | 12.4 | 91,558 | 1.5 | 6,483,802 | 841,108 | 13.0 | 115,272 | 1.8 | 6.6 | 11.7 | 25.9 |
| Iowa | 2,926,324 | 436,213 | 14.9 | 65,118 | 2.2 | 3,046,355 | 452,888 | 14.9 | 74,658 | 2.5 | 4.1 | 3.8 | 14.7 |
| Kansas | 2,688,418 | 356,229 | 13.3 | 51,770 | 1.9 | 2,853,118 | 376,116 | 13.2 | 59,318 | 2.1 | 6.1 | 5.6 | 14.6 |
| Kentucky | 4,041,769 | 504,793 | 12.5 | 58,261 | 1.4 | 4,339,367 | 578,227 | 13.3 | 69,208 | 1.6 | 7.4 | 14.5 | 18.8 |
| Louisiana | 4,468,976 | 516,929 | 11.6 | 58,676 | 1.3 | 4,533,372 | 557,857 | 12.3 | 65,686 | 1.4 | 1.4 | 7.9 | 11.9 |
| Maine | 1,274,923 | 183,402 | 14.4 | 23,316 | 1.8 | 1,328,361 | 211,080 | 15.9 | 29,136 | 2.2 | 4.2 | 15.1 | 25.0 |
| Maryland | 5,296,486 | 599,307 | 11.3 | 66,902 | 1.3 | 5,773,552 | 707,642 | 12.3 | 98,126 | 1.7 | 9.0 | 18.1 | 46.7 |
| Massachusetts | 6,349,097 | 860,162 | 13.5 | 116,692 | 1.8 | 6,547,629 | 902,724 | 13.8 | 145,199 | 2.2 | 3.1 | 4.9 | 24.4 |
| Michigan | 9,938,444 | 1,219,018 | 12.3 | 142,460 | 1.4 | 9,883,640 | 1,361,530 | 13.8 | 191,881 | 1.9 | −0.6 | 11.7 | 34.7 |
| Minnesota | 4,919,479 | 594,266 | 12.1 | 85,601 | 1.7 | 5,303,925 | 683,121 | 12.9 | 106,664 | 2.0 | 7.8 | 15.0 | 24.6 |
| Mississippi | 2,844,658 | 343,523 | 12.1 | 42,891 | 1.5 | 2,967,297 | 380,407 | 12.8 | 44,359 | 1.5 | 4.3 | 10.7 | 3.4 |
| Missouri | 5,595,211 | 755,379 | 13.5 | 98,571 | 1.8 | 5,988,927 | 838,294 | 14.0 | 113,779 | 1.9 | 7.0 | 11.0 | 15.4 |
| Montana | 902,195 | 120,949 | 13.4 | 15,337 | 1.7 | 989,415 | 146,742 | 14.8 | 20,021 | 2.0 | 9.7 | 21.3 | 30.5 |
| Nebraska | 1,711,263 | 232,195 | 13.6 | 33,953 | 2.0 | 1,826,341 | 246,677 | 13.5 | 39,308 | 2.2 | 6.7 | 6.2 | 15.8 |
| Nevada | 1,998,257 | 218,929 | 11.0 | 16,989 | 0.9 | 2,700,551 | 324,359 | 12.0 | 30,187 | 1.1 | 35.1 | 48.2 | 77.7 |
| New Hampshire | 1,235,786 | 147,970 | 12.0 | 18,231 | 1.5 | 1,316,470 | 178,268 | 13.5 | 24,761 | 1.9 | 6.5 | 20.5 | 35.8 |
| New Jersey | 8,414,350 | 1,113,136 | 13.2 | 135,999 | 1.6 | 8,791,894 | 1,185,993 | 13.5 | 179,611 | 2.0 | 4.5 | 6.5 | 32.1 |
| New Mexico | 1,819,046 | 212,225 | 11.7 | 23,306 | 1.3 | 2,059,179 | 272,255 | 13.2 | 31,993 | 1.6 | 13.2 | 28.3 | 37.3 |
| New York | 18,976,457 | 2,448,352 | 12.9 | 311,488 | 1.6 | 19,378,102 | 2,617,943 | 13.5 | 390,874 | 2.0 | 2.1 | 6.9 | 25.5 |
| North Carolina | 8,049,313 | 969,048 | 12.0 | 105,461 | 1.3 | 9,535,483 | 1,234,079 | 12.9 | 147,461 | 1.5 | 18.5 | 27.3 | 39.8 |
| North Dakota | 642,200 | 94,478 | 14.7 | 14,726 | 2.3 | 672,591 | 97,477 | 14.5 | 16,688 | 2.5 | 4.7 | 3.2 | 13.3 |
| Ohio | 11,353,140 | 1,507,757 | 13.3 | 176,796 | 1.6 | 11,536,504 | 1,622,015 | 14.1 | 230,429 | 2.0 | 1.6 | 7.6 | 30.3 |
| Oklahoma | 3,450,654 | 455,950 | 13.2 | 57,175 | 1.7 | 3,751,351 | 506,714 | 13.5 | 61,912 | 1.7 | 8.7 | 11.1 | 8.3 |
| Oregon | 3,421,399 | 438,177 | 12.8 | 57,431 | 1.7 | 3,831,074 | 533,533 | 13.9 | 77,872 | 2.0 | 12.0 | 21.8 | 35.6 |
| Pennsylvania | 12,281,054 | 1,919,165 | 15.6 | 237,567 | 1.9 | 12,702,379 | 1,959,307 | 15.4 | 305,676 | 2.4 | 3.4 | 2.1 | 28.7 |
| Rhode Island | 1,048,319 | 152,402 | 14.5 | 20,897 | 2.0 | 1,052,567 | 151,881 | 14.4 | 26,750 | 2.5 | 0.4 | −0.3 | 28.0 |
| South Carolina | 4,012,012 | 485,333 | 12.1 | 50,269 | 1.3 | 4,625,364 | 631,874 | 13.7 | 70,717 | 1.5 | 15.3 | 30.2 | 40.7 |
| South Dakota | 754,844 | 108,131 | 14.3 | 16,086 | 2.1 | 814,180 | 116,581 | 14.3 | 19,226 | 2.4 | 7.9 | 7.8 | 19.5 |
| Tennessee | 5,689,283 | 703,311 | 12.4 | 81,465 | 1.4 | 6,346,105 | 853,462 | 13.4 | 99,917 | 1.6 | 11.5 | 21.3 | 22.7 |
| Texas | 20,851,820 | 2,072,532 | 9.9 | 237,940 | 1.1 | 25,145,561 | 2,601,886 | 10.3 | 305,179 | 1.2 | 20.6 | 25.5 | 28.3 |
| Utah | 2,233,169 | 190,222 | 8.5 | 21,751 | 1.0 | 2,763,885 | 249,462 | 9.0 | 30,991 | 1.1 | 23.8 | 31.1 | 42.5 |
| Vermont | 608,827 | 77,510 | 12.7 | 9,996 | 1.6 | 625,741 | 91,078 | 14.6 | 12,797 | 2.0 | 2.8 | 17.5 | 28.0 |
| Virginia | 7,078,515 | 792,333 | 11.2 | 87,266 | 1.2 | 8,001,024 | 976,937 | 12.2 | 122,403 | 1.5 | 13.0 | 23.3 | 40.3 |
| Washington | 5,894,121 | 662,148 | 11.2 | 84,085 | 1.4 | 6,724,540 | 827,677 | 12.3 | 117,271 | 1.7 | 14.1 | 25.0 | 39.5 |
| West Virginia | 1,808,344 | 276,895 | 15.3 | 31,779 | 1.8 | 1,852,994 | 297,404 | 16.0 | 35,921 | 1.9 | 2.5 | 7.4 | 13.0 |
| Wisconsin | 5,363,675 | 702,553 | 13.1 | 95,625 | 1.8 | 5,686,986 | 777,314 | 13.7 | 118,505 | 2.1 | 6.0 | 10.6 | 23.9 |
| Wyoming | 493,782 | 57,693 | 11.7 | 6,735 | 1.4 | 563,626 | 70,090 | 12.4 | 8,602 | 1.5 | 14.1 | 21.5 | 27.7 |
| Puerto Rico | 3,808,610 | 425,137 | 11.2 | 47,706 | 1.3 | 3,725,789 | 541,998 | 14.5 | 62,596 | 1.7 | −2.2 | 27.5 | 31.2 |

Sources: U.S. Census Bureau, *Census 2000 Summary File 1* and *2010 Census Summary File 1*.

Table 3.
## Residence in Metropolitan or Micropolitan Statistical Areas by Age and by Region: 2010
(For information on confidentiality protection, nonsampling error, and definitions, see *www.census.gov/prod/cen2010/doc/sf1.pdf*)

| Area of residence and age | Total population | | Northeast | | Midwest | | South | | West | |
|---|---|---|---|---|---|---|---|---|---|---|
| | Number | Per-cent | Number | Per-cent | Number | Per-cent | Number | Per-cent | Number | Per-cent |
| **Total population** | | | | | | | | | | |
| All ages[1] . . . . . . . . . . . . . . . . . . . . . | 308,745,538 | 100.0 | 55,317,240 | 17.9 | 66,927,001 | 21.7 | 114,555,744 | 37.1 | 71,945,553 | 23.3 |
| 65 years and over . . . . . . . . . . . | 40,267,984 | 13.0 | 7,804,833 | 2.5 | 9,022,334 | 2.9 | 14,893,985 | 4.8 | 8,546,832 | 2.8 |
| 85 years and over . . . . . . . . . . | 5,493,433 | 1.8 | 1,199,702 | 0.4 | 1,320,640 | 0.4 | 1,821,982 | 0.6 | 1,151,109 | 0.4 |
| **Inside metropolitan or micropolitan statistical area** | | | | | | | | | | |
| All ages[1] . . . . . . . . . . . . . . . . . . . | 289,261,315 | 100.0 | 53,868,425 | 18.6 | 60,443,283 | 20.9 | 105,279,729 | 36.4 | 69,669,878 | 24.1 |
| 65 years and over . . . . . . . . . . . | 36,917,778 | 12.8 | 7,554,783 | 2.6 | 7,831,177 | 2.7 | 13,358,307 | 4.6 | 8,173,511 | 2.8 |
| 85 years and over . . . . . . . . . . | 5,065,675 | 1.8 | 1,167,488 | 0.4 | 1,142,622 | 0.4 | 1,646,940 | 0.6 | 1,108,625 | 0.4 |
| **Outside metropolitan or micropolitan statistical area** | | | | | | | | | | |
| All ages[1] . . . . . . . . . . . . . . . . . . . | 19,484,223 | 100.0 | 1,448,815 | 7.4 | 6,483,718 | 33.3 | 9,276,015 | 47.6 | 2,275,675 | 11.7 |
| 65 years and over . . . . . . . . . . | 3,350,206 | 17.2 | 250,050 | 1.3 | 1,191,157 | 6.1 | 1,535,678 | 7.9 | 373,321 | 1.9 |
| 85 years and over . . . . . . . . . . | 427,758 | 2.2 | 32,214 | 0.2 | 178,018 | 0.9 | 175,042 | 0.9 | 42,484 | 0.2 |

[1] Percentage shown for all ages is the regional distribution. Percentages shown for age groups 65 years and over and 85 years and over for the total population, inside metropolitan/micropolitan, and outside metropolitan/micropolitan are based on the total U.S. population in each area.

Note: Metropolitan and micropolitan statistical areas defined by the Office of Management and Budget as of December 2009 <www.whitehouse.gov/sites/default/files/omb/assets/bulletins/b10-02.pdf>.

Source: U.S. Census Bureau, *2010 Census Summary File 1*.

**Rhode Island was the only state to exhibit numeric decline in the population 65 years and over.**

Among the 50 states, Rhode Island was the only one to exhibit a decrease in the number of people 65 years and over, declining from 152,402 in 2000 to 151,881 in 2010 (–0.3 percent). The decrease in the older population in Rhode Island was largely driven by decreases in the 70 to 74 and 75 to 79 year old age groups.[12]

Compared with other states, Florida had the greatest share of the population that was 65 years and over in both 2000 and 2010 (17.6 percent and 17.3 percent, respectively). In 2010, it was followed by

[12] The decreases noted in the 70 to 74 and 75 to 79 year old age groups in Rhode Island between 2000 and 2010 could be due to several factors. Changes could reflect the relatively low number of births during the late 1920s and early 1930s. The lower fertility rates for that time period resulted in a smaller generation of people who are now aging into the 70 to 74 and 75 to 79 year old age groups. Out-migration of older adults from the state may also be contributing to decreases noted in selected older population age groups.

West Virginia (16.0 percent), Maine (15.9 percent), Pennsylvania (15.4 percent), and Iowa (14.9 percent).

The state with the lowest share of the population 65 years and over was Alaska in both 2000 and 2010 (5.7 percent and 7.7 percent, respectively). Alaska is also notable as the state with the largest growth rate for the population 65 years and over. The state's older population grew from 35,699 in 2000 to 54,938 in 2010, resulting in a percent change of 53.9 percent.

The District of Columbia's older population declined from 69,898 in 2000 to 68,809 in 2010, resulting in a decrease of 1.6 percent. The percentage of the population that was 65 years and over also decreased from 12.2 percent in 2000 to 11.4 percent in 2010.

**The population 85 years and over increased in all states.**

Between 2000 and 2010, all states experienced increases in the number of people that were 85 years and over. However, the magnitude of growth varied among the states for the oldest-old population.

Alaska had the largest percent change between 2000 and 2010 for the population 85 years and over, which grew 78.9 percent by increasing from 2,634 in 2000 to 4,711 in 2010. Mississippi had the slowest growth (3.4 percent) and increased from 42,891 in 2000 to 44,359 in 2010. Alaska was also the state with the lowest number and percentage of the population 85 years and over when compared with other states.

The state containing the largest percentage of the population 85 years and over in 2010 was Rhode Island. In 2010, people 85 years and over made up 2.5 percent of the total state population compared with 2.0 percent in 2000. This increase in the share of total state population in the oldest-old ages moved Rhode Island from being ranked fifth in 2000 to first in 2010 among states ranked by percentage of the population in the age group 85 years and over. North Dakota, which had been ranked first in 2000, was ranked second in 2010.

Only two states, Mississippi and Oklahoma, maintained the same share of the total state population that was 85 years and over in 2010 as in 2000 (1.5 percent and 1.7 percent, respectively). However, as noted earlier, the size of the oldest-old population still grew between 2000 and 2010 in these states.

## METROPOLITAN AND MICROPOLITAN STATISTICAL AREAS

**The older population was more likely to live inside a metropolitan or micropolitan statistical area than outside a metropolitan or micropolitan statistical area.**

In 2010, 36.9 million people aged 65 and over lived inside a metropolitan or micropolitan statistical area and 3.4 million lived outside of a metropolitan or micropolitan area (Table 3).[13] However, the older population, which made up 13.0 percent of the total population in 2010, accounted for a dispropor-tionally larger share of the population that lived outside metro or

[13] There were 942 metropolitan or micropolitan statistical areas defined by the U.S. Office of Management and Budget (OMB) as of December 2009. Metropolitan and micropolitan statistical areas—metro and micro areas—are geographic entities defined by the OMB for use by federal statistical agencies in collecting, tabulating, and publishing federal statistics. Metro and micro areas are collectively known as core based statistical areas (CBSAs). A metro area contains a core urban area population of 50,000 or more. A micro area contains a core urban area population of at least 10,000 (but less than 50,000). Each metro or micro area consists of one or more counties and includes the counties containing the core urban area, as well as any adjacent counties that have a high degree of social and economic integration (as measured by commuting to work) with the urban core. A metro or micro area's geographic delineation, or list of geographic components at a particular point in time, is referred to as its definition. This report uses metro and micro area definitions published by OMB as of December 2009. For additional information see <www.census.gov/geo/www/2010census/GTC_10.pdf>.

micro areas. Of the 19.5 million people that lived outside metro or micro areas, 17.2 percent were aged 65 and older. Of the 289.3 million people that lived inside metro or micro areas, 12.8 percent were 65 years and over.

The population 85 years and over follows a similar pattern as the population 65 years and over. They were most likely to live inside a metropolitan or micropolitan area. In 2010, 427,758 people aged 85 and over lived outside of a metro or micro statistical area while 5.1 million people aged 85 and over lived inside these areas. Although a larger number of people 85 years and over lived inside metro or micro areas, people in these ages made up a greater share of the population that lived outside a metro or micro area. The oldest-old population made up 2.2 percent of the population that lived out-side a metro or micro area and 1.8 percent of the population that lived inside a metro or micro area.

**The older population was more likely to live inside a metropolitan or micropolitan statistical area in the South when compared with other regions.**

The metropolitan or micropolitan statistical area distribution of the older population further varies by region. Of the total population that lived inside a metro or micro area, 36.4 percent were located in the South, 24.1 percent in the West, 20.9 percent in the Midwest, and 18.6 percent in the Northeast.

The population 65 years and over that lived inside metro or micro areas was 4.6 percent in the South, 2.8 percent in the West, 2.7 percent in the Midwest, and 2.6 percent in the Northeast.

In contrast to the regional patterns for the total population and older population that lived inside a met-ropolitan or micropolitan statistical area, the population 85 years and over maintained the same share of the population across three of the four census regions. In the Northeast, the Midwest, and the West, the population 85 years and over made up 0.4 percent of the total population that lived inside a metro or micro area. In the South, the population 85 years and over made up 0.6 percent.

When the population living outside a metropolitan or micropolitan statistical area is examined, differ-ent findings emerge. Of the total population living outside a metro or micro area, 47.6 percent were located in the South, 33.3 percent in the Midwest, 11.7 percent in the West, and 7.4 percent in the Northeast.

Of the U.S. population that lived outside metro or micro areas, 7.9 percent were 65 years and over and in the South, 6.1 percent in the Midwest, 1.9 percent in the West, and 1.3 percent in the Northeast. Of the U.S. population that lived outside metro or micro areas, 0.9 percent were 85 years and over and in the Midwest, 0.9 percent in the South, 0.2 percent in the West, and 0.2 percent in the Northeast.

## COUNTIES AND PLACES

**Three of the top five counties with the greatest percentage of the population in the 65 years and over age group are found in Florida.**

When the older population is viewed at the county-level, pat-terns of distribution of people 65 years and over generally follow the state and regional trends noted earlier.[14]  Higher shares of the older population can be seen in counties across the Midwest, particularly the Great Plains and Northern Rocky Mountain area as well as the Northeastern Appalachia areas and clustered in states such as Florida and Arizona (Figure 6). The relatively high percentages of the population 65 years and over in much of the Great Plains and Appalachia areas is largely due to continued out-migration of the younger population and population aging of the older residents, known as "aging in place." Clusters of counties with high percentages of the population 65 years and over in states such as Florida and Arizona reflect a growing in-migration of retirees as these states also have notable growth in the size of the older population between 2000 and 2010.

In 2010, three of the top five counties with the highest percentages of the population in the age group 65 years and over were in Florida. The county with the highest share of the population 65 years and over was Sumter County, Florida (43.4 percent), followed by Charlotte County, Florida (34.1 percent), McIntosh County, North Dakota (34.0 percent), La Paz County, Arizona (32.6 percent), and Highlands County, Florida (32.2 percent).

---

[14] The primary legal divisions of most states are termed "counties." In Louisiana, these divisions are known as parishes. In Alaska, which has no counties, the statistically equivalent entities are census areas, city and boroughs (as in Juneau City and Borough), a municipality (Anchorage), and organized boroughs. Census areas are delineated cooperatively for data presentation purposes by the state of Alaska and the U.S. Census Bureau. In four states (Maryland, Missouri, Nevada, and Virginia), there are one or more incorporated places that are independent of any county organization and thus constitute primary divisions of their states; these incorporated places are known as "independent cities" and are treated as equivalent to counties for data presentation purposes. The District of Columbia has no primary divisions, and the entire area is considered equivalent to a county and a state for data presentation purposes.

In Sumter County, Florida, Charlotte County, Florida, La Paz County, Arizona, and Highlands County, Florida the population 65 years and over increased between 2000 and 2010. The high percentage of residents in these counties that were 65 years and over thus largely reflects the fact that these areas were popular retiree destinations. Conversely, in McIntosh County, North Dakota, the older population decreased between 2000 and 2010. Although still maintaining a large share of the older population, the population decline in this county likely indicates that a degree of out-migration is occurring for younger ages and the remaining older adults are "aging in place."

Similar to patterns noted with the population 65 years and over, the percentage of the population in the oldest-old ages also clusters in the Great Plains area as well as areas in Southern Florida (Figure 6). Reflective of the "aging in place" of the older population in the Midwest, the county with the highest percentage of the population 85 years and over was Hooker County, Nebraska (8.3 percent), followed by McIntosh County, North Dakota (7.5 percent), Divide County, North Dakota (6.5 percent), Traverse County, Minnesota (6.2 percent) and Jerauld County, South Dakota (6.1 percent).

**Among counties that contained a population of at least 100 people in the 65 and over age group in 2010, the number of people 65 years and over more than doubled in 20 counties in the United States between 2000 and 2010.**

Growth in the number of people 65 years and over was primarily in the Sierra Nevada and Rocky Mountain areas of the nation (Figure 7). Counties in Texas, Georgia, Alaska,

and Virginia also experienced notable growth in the older population. Of these twenty counties that experienced at least a doubling of their population 65 years and over when the 65 and over population contained at least 100 people in 2010, four were located in Colorado, five in Georgia, five in Texas, three in Alaska, two in Virginia, and one in Florida. The five counties with the greatest percent change between 2000 and 2010 are as follows: Summit County, Colorado, (180.3 percent), Douglas County, Colorado (177.8 percent), Sumter County, Florida (177.3 percent), Denali Borough, Alaska (136.2 percent), and Eagle County, Colorado (135.2 percent).

As shown in Figure 7, many counties in the Great Plains experienced population decline in the older ages as the number of people 65 years and over decreased over the decade. Contributing to this decline in the Great Plains area was cohort aging, older age mortality, and out-migration.[15]

Patterns of growth for the oldest-old population also follow patterns noted with the population 65 years and over (Figure 7). Counties in the Sierra Nevada and Rocky Mountain areas experienced the most pronounced growth while counties in the Great Plains to Central Texas areas and counties extending into areas of Louisiana, southern Arkansas, Mississippi, and Alabama display the most pronounced population decline in ages 85 years and over.

---

[15] A cohort is a group of people born during a specified period of time. For example, the relatively low number of births during the 1930s resulted in a small generation of people who aged into the 70 to 74 and 75 to 79 year old age groups by 2010.

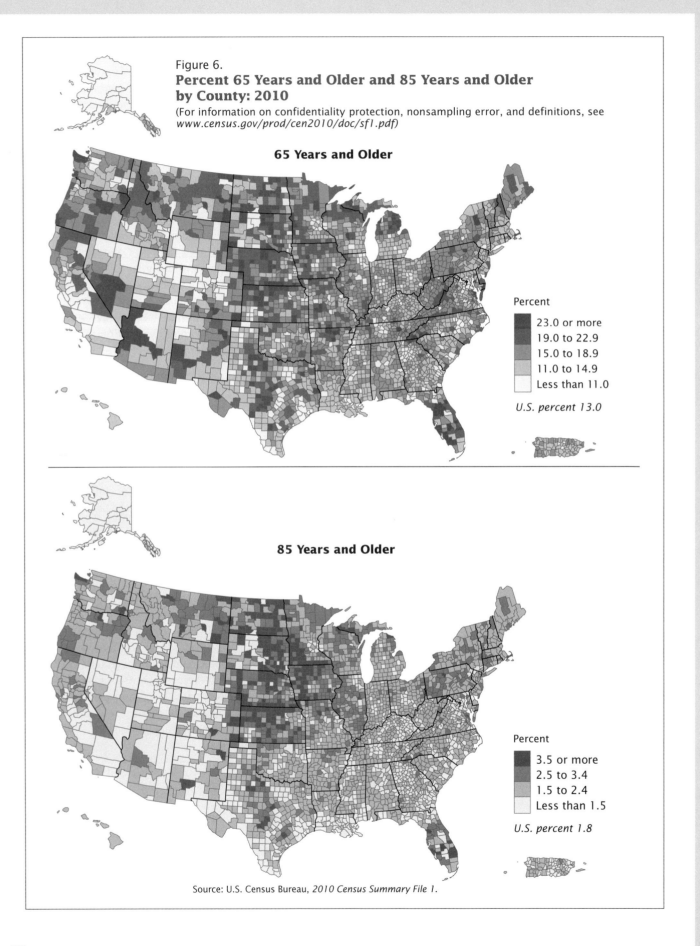

Figure 6.
**Percent 65 Years and Older and 85 Years and Older by County: 2010**
(For information on confidentiality protection, nonsampling error, and definitions, see *www.census.gov/prod/cen2010/doc/sf1.pdf*)

**65 Years and Older**

Percent
23.0 or more
19.0 to 22.9
15.0 to 18.9
11.0 to 14.9
Less than 11.0

*U.S. percent 13.0*

**85 Years and Older**

Percent
3.5 or more
2.5 to 3.4
1.5 to 2.4
Less than 1.5

*U.S. percent 1.8*

Source: U.S. Census Bureau, *2010 Census Summary File 1.*

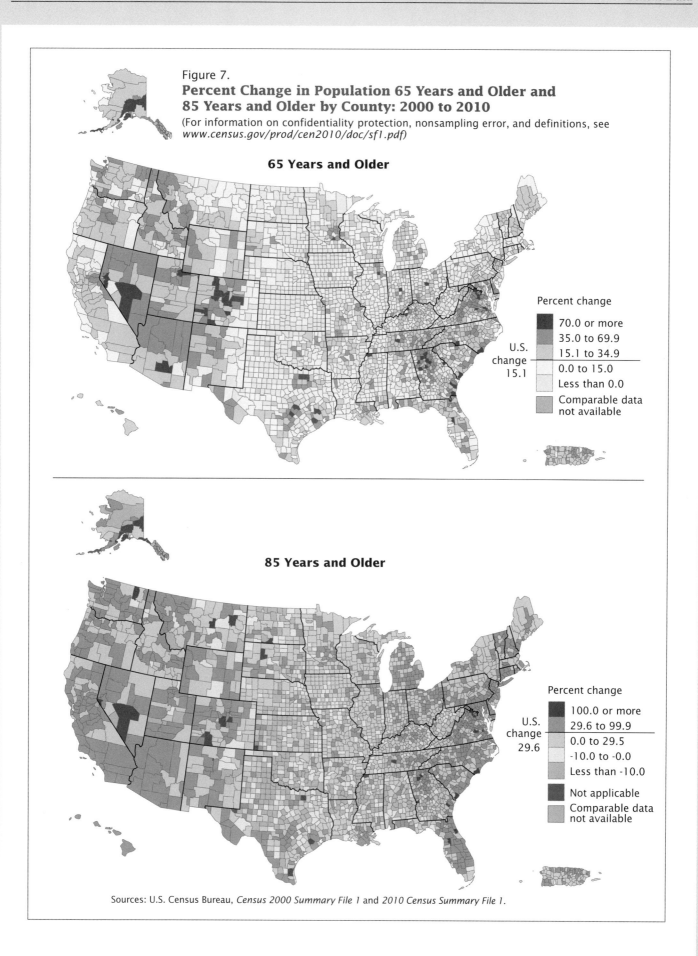

Figure 7.

**Percent Change in Population 65 Years and Older and 85 Years and Older by County: 2000 to 2010**

(For information on confidentiality protection, nonsampling error, and definitions, see *www.census.gov/prod/cen2010/doc/sf1.pdf*)

**65 Years and Older**

Percent change

70.0 or more
35.0 to 69.9
15.1 to 34.9
0.0 to 15.0
Less than 0.0
Comparable data not available

U.S. change 15.1

**85 Years and Older**

Percent change

100.0 or more
29.6 to 99.9
0.0 to 29.5
-10.0 to -0.0
Less than -10.0

Not applicable

Comparable data not available

U.S. change 29.6

Sources: U.S. Census Bureau, *Census 2000 Summary File 1* and *2010 Census Summary File 1*.

**All counties in Rhode Island and Maine contained higher percentages of the 65 years and older population than the nation.**

Following similar regional level analyses earlier in the report, the Northeast and the Midwest contained large percentages of counties where the percentage of the population 65 years and over exceeded that of the nation. However, while the Northeast region of the United States showed the largest overall percentage of the population 65 years and over, there were higher percentages of counties in the Midwest that had shares of the population in the older age group (Table 4). Specifically, 83.4 percent of the counties in the Northeast and 85.7 percent of the counties in the Midwest exceeded the U.S. percentage of the population 65 years and over.[16]

There were also two states, both located in the Northeast, where the percentage of the population that was 65 years and over exceeded the U.S. percent in all counties. In both Maine and Rhode Island, 100 percent of the counties within the states had shares of the population in the older ages that were greater than the national percentage of 13.0 percent.

In addition to containing the greatest percentage of counties that had shares of the population 65 years and over that were higher than the nation, the Northeast and the Midwest also contained the greatest share of counties with

[16] In 2010, the percentage of the population in the age group 65 years and over was 13.0 percent for the nation. Of the 3,143 total counties in the United States, 2,378 counties (75.7 percent) exceeded the national percentage.

Table 4.
## Counties Exceeding the U.S. Percent 65 Years and Older and 85 Years and Older by Region and State: 2010
(For information on confidentiality protection, nonsampling error, and definitions, see www.census.gov/prod/cen2010/doc/sf1.pdf)

| Area | Total counties | Counties exceeding U.S. percent 65 years and over[1] | | Counties exceeding U.S. percent 85 years and over[2] | |
|---|---|---|---|---|---|
| | | Number | Percent | Number | Percent |
| United States ..... | 3,143 | 2,378 | 75.7 | 1,871 | 59.5 |
| Northeast ........... | 217 | 181 | 83.4 | 183 | 84.3 |
| Connecticut ........... | 8 | 6 | 75.0 | 7 | 87.5 |
| Maine............... | 16 | 16 | 100.0 | 16 | 100.0 |
| Massachusetts......... | 14 | 10 | 71.4 | 12 | 85.7 |
| New Hampshire........ | 10 | 7 | 70.0 | 7 | 70.0 |
| New Jersey ........... | 21 | 9 | 42.9 | 16 | 76.2 |
| New York ............. | 62 | 53 | 85.5 | 50 | 80.6 |
| Pennsylvania .......... | 67 | 63 | 94.0 | 61 | 91.0 |
| Rhode Island .......... | 5 | 5 | 100.0 | 5 | 100.0 |
| Vermont.............. | 14 | 12 | 85.7 | 9 | 64.3 |
| Midwest ............ | 1,055 | 904 | 85.7 | 854 | 80.9 |
| Illinois............... | 102 | 87 | 85.3 | 88 | 86.3 |
| Indiana.............. | 92 | 75 | 81.5 | 55 | 59.8 |
| Iowa................ | 99 | 93 | 93.9 | 95 | 96.0 |
| Kansas.............. | 105 | 89 | 84.8 | 92 | 87.6 |
| Michigan ............ | 83 | 72 | 86.7 | 60 | 72.3 |
| Minnesota ........... | 87 | 67 | 77.0 | 75 | 86.2 |
| Missouri............. | 115 | 100 | 87.0 | 86 | 74.8 |
| Nebraska............ | 93 | 87 | 93.5 | 82 | 88.2 |
| North Dakota.......... | 53 | 47 | 88.7 | 48 | 90.6 |
| Ohio................ | 88 | 73 | 83.0 | 58 | 65.9 |
| South Dakota......... | 66 | 54 | 81.8 | 51 | 77.3 |
| Wisconsin ........... | 72 | 60 | 83.3 | 64 | 88.9 |
| South .............. | 1,423 | 1,026 | 72.1 | 618 | 43.4 |
| Alabama ............ | 67 | 55 | 82.1 | 29 | 43.3 |
| Arkansas............ | 75 | 64 | 85.3 | 47 | 62.7 |
| Delaware ............ | 3 | 2 | 66.7 | 1 | 33.3 |
| District of Columbia ..... | 1 | – | – | – | – |
| Florida ............. | 67 | 51 | 76.1 | 31 | 46.3 |
| Georgia ............. | 159 | 91 | 57.2 | 39 | 24.5 |
| Kentucky ............ | 120 | 87 | 72.5 | 38 | 31.7 |
| Louisiana............ | 64 | 30 | 46.9 | 12 | 18.8 |
| Maryland ............ | 24 | 12 | 50.0 | 11 | 45.8 |
| Mississippi........... | 82 | 48 | 58.5 | 30 | 36.6 |
| North Carolina......... | 100 | 78 | 78.0 | 51 | 51.0 |
| Oklahoma ........... | 77 | 65 | 84.4 | 46 | 59.7 |
| South Carolina........ | 46 | 36 | 78.3 | 10 | 21.7 |
| Tennessee........... | 95 | 82 | 86.3 | 38 | 40.0 |
| Texas............... | 254 | 175 | 68.9 | 128 | 50.4 |
| Virginia.............. | 134 | 98 | 73.1 | 70 | 52.2 |
| West Virginia ......... | 55 | 52 | 94.5 | 37 | 67.3 |
| West ............... | 448 | 267 | 59.6 | 216 | 48.2 |
| Alaska ............. | 29 | 3 | 10.3 | – | – |
| Arizona ............. | 15 | 10 | 66.7 | 5 | 33.3 |
| California ............ | 58 | 28 | 48.3 | 27 | 46.6 |
| Colorado ............ | 64 | 34 | 53.1 | 28 | 43.8 |
| Hawaii .............. | 5 | 4 | 80.0 | 3 | 60.0 |
| Idaho............... | 44 | 28 | 63.6 | 21 | 47.7 |
| Montana............. | 56 | 49 | 87.5 | 43 | 76.8 |
| Nevada ............. | 17 | 10 | 58.8 | 3 | 17.6 |
| New Mexico.......... | 33 | 23 | 69.7 | 14 | 42.4 |
| Oregon.............. | 36 | 29 | 80.6 | 30 | 83.3 |
| Utah................ | 29 | 11 | 37.9 | 7 | 24.1 |
| Washington .......... | 39 | 26 | 66.7 | 25 | 64.1 |
| Wyoming ............ | 23 | 12 | 52.2 | 10 | 43.5 |

– Represents zero or rounds to 0.0

[1] U.S. percent 65 years and older was 13.0 percent.

[2] U.S. percent 85 years and older was 1.8 percent.

Source: U.S. Census Bureau, *2010 Census Summary File 1.*

percentages of the population 85 years and over that exceeded the national percentage.[17] In the Northeast, 84.3 percent of counties exceeded the U.S. percentage 85 years and over. In the Midwest, 80.9 percent of counties exceeded the U.S. percentage 85 years and over.

While more than half of the counties in the West and the South did exceed the national proportion of the population 65 years and over, the share of counties in the West and the South that exceeded the national percentage for both the 65 years and older and 85 years and older population was lower than the share of counties in the Northeast and the Midwest. Higher rates of in-migration and fertility patterns in the West and the South for many counties contribute to the lower share of counties having proportions of the population 65 years and over that exceeded the national figure.

**Among places with a population of 100,000 or more, four of the ten places with the highest percentage of the population 65 years and over were located in Florida.**

Table 5 lists the ten places (among places with a population of 100,000 or more) with the highest and lowest percentage of the population 65 years and over in 2010.[18] Of the ten places with the highest percentage of the population 65 years and over, five places were located in the South (four of which were in Florida), three in the West, and two in the Midwest. All

Table 5.
**Ten Places With the Highest and Lowest Percentage of Their Population 65 Years and Older: 2010**
(For information on confidentiality protection, nonsampling error, and definitions, see *www.census.gov/prod/cen2010/doc/sf1.pdf*)

| Place[1] | Total population | Population 65 years and over | |
|---|---|---|---|
| | | Number | Percent |
| **Highest percent 65 years and over** | | | |
| Scottsdale city, AZ | 217,385 | 43,471 | 20.0 |
| Clearwater city, FL | 107,685 | 21,330 | 19.8 |
| Hialeah city, FL | 224,669 | 42,864 | 19.1 |
| Surprise city, AZ | 117,517 | 22,327 | 19.0 |
| Urban Honolulu CDP, HI | 337,256 | 60,162 | 17.8 |
| Metairie CDP, LA | 138,481 | 23,716 | 17.1 |
| Cape Coral city, FL | 154,305 | 26,180 | 17.0 |
| Warren city, MI | 134,056 | 21,644 | 16.1 |
| Independence city, MO | 116,830 | 18,769 | 16.1 |
| Miami city, FL | 399,457 | 63,987 | 16.0 |
| | | | |
| **Lowest percent 65 years and over** | | | |
| West Jordan city, UT | 103,712 | 4,817 | 4.6 |
| Killeen city, TX | 127,921 | 6,618 | 5.2 |
| Frisco city, TX | 116,989 | 6,298 | 5.4 |
| Fontana city, CA | 196,069 | 11,084 | 5.7 |
| Provo city, UT | 112,488 | 6,570 | 5.8 |
| Gilbert town, AZ | 208,453 | 12,628 | 6.1 |
| Enterprise CDP, NV | 108,481 | 6,734 | 6.2 |
| Moreno Valley city, CA | 193,365 | 12,134 | 6.3 |
| Aurora city, IL | 197,899 | 12,789 | 6.5 |
| Thornton city, CO | 118,772 | 7,726 | 6.5 |

[1] Places of 100,000 or more total population. The 2010 Census showed 282 places in the United States with 100,000 or more population. They included 273 incorporated places (including 5 consolidated cities) and 9 census designated places (CDPs) that were not legally incorporated.

Source: U.S. Census Bureau, *2010 Census Summary File 1.*

ten places had percentages of the population in the age group 65 years and over that were higher than the national percentage of 13.0 percent.

Scottsdale city, Arizona contained the highest percentage of people 65 years and over among places with 100,000 or more people in 2010 (20.0 percent). Reflective of the growth in the older population between 2000 and 2010, the share of the population in the 65 and over age group increased from 2000, when the city was ranked ninth among places with the highest proportion of their population 65 years and over.

Of the ten places with the lowest percentage of the population 65 years and over, seven places were located in the West, two in

the South, and one in the Midwest. Utah, Texas, and California each contained two places where the percentage of the population in the 65 years and over age group ranked in the bottom ten.

West Jordan city, Utah, contained the lowest percentage of people 65 years and over among places with 100,000 or more people in 2010 (4.6 percent), followed by Killeen city, Texas (5.2 percent) and Frisco city, Texas (5.4 percent). In these places, as well as other places listed as having the lowest percentage of people 65 years and older, higher concentrations of people in the younger ages resulted in a smaller relative share of older adults in 2010. Many of the places listed in the lower panel of Table 5 were suburbs of large metropolitan

[17] In 2010, the percentage of the population in the age group 85 years and over was 1.8 percent. Of the 3,143 total counties in the United States, 1,871 counties (59.5 percent) exceeded the national percentage.

[18] The 2010 Census showed 282 places in the United States with 100,000 or more population. They included 273 incorporated places (including 5 city/county consolidations) and 9 census designated places (CDPs) that were not legally incorporated.

Table 6.
## Ten Places With the Highest and Lowest Percentage of Their Population 85 Years and Older: 2010
(For information on confidentiality protection, nonsampling error, and definitions, see *www.census.gov/prod/cen2010/doc/sf1.pdf*)

| Place[1] | Total population | Population 85 years and over | |
| --- | --- | --- | --- |
| | | Number | Percent |
| **Highest percent 85 years and over** | | | |
| Urban Honolulu CDP, HI . . . . . | 337,256 | 11,781 | 3.5 |
| Clearwater city, FL. . . . . . . . . . | 107,685 | 3,725 | 3.5 |
| Santa Rosa city, CA. . . . . . . . | 167,815 | 4,654 | 2.8 |
| Warren city, MI. . . . . . . . . . . . | 134,056 | 3,636 | 2.7 |
| Scottsdale city, AZ. . . . . . . . . . | 217,385 | 5,821 | 2.7 |
| Metairie CDP, LA . . . . . . . . . . . | 138,481 | 3,665 | 2.6 |
| Pueblo city, CO . . . . . . . . . . . . | 106,595 | 2,818 | 2.6 |
| Billings city, MT . . . . . . . . . . . | 104,170 | 2,749 | 2.6 |
| Springfield city, MO . . . . . . . . | 159,498 | 4,209 | 2.6 |
| Rockford city, IL. . . . . . . . . . . . | 152,871 | 3,970 | 2.6 |
| **Lowest percent 85 years and over** | | | |
| West Jordan city, UT . . . . . . . . | 103,712 | 390 | 0.4 |
| Enterprise CDP, NV. . . . . . . . . | 108,481 | 423 | 0.4 |
| Frisco city, TX . . . . . . . . . . . . | 116,989 | 470 | 0.4 |
| Killeen city, TX. . . . . . . . . . . . | 127,921 | 524 | 0.4 |
| Gilbert town, AZ. . . . . . . . . . . . | 208,453 | 999 | 0.5 |
| North Las Vegas city, NV . . . . . | 216,961 | 1,068 | 0.5 |
| Fontana city, CA . . . . . . . . . . | 196,069 | 1,020 | 0.5 |
| West Valley City city, UT . . . . . | 129,480 | 689 | 0.5 |
| Moreno Valley city, CA. . . . . . . | 193,365 | 1,083 | 0.6 |
| Miramar city, FL. . . . . . . . . . . . | 122,041 | 725 | 0.6 |

[1] Places of 100,000 or more total population. The 2010 Census showed 282 places in the United States with 100,000 or more population. They included 273 incorporated places (including 5 consolidated cities) and 9 census designated places (CDPs) that were not legally incorporated.

Source: U.S. Census Bureau, *2010 Census Summary File 1.*

areas where residents aged 18 to 64 (working ages) and under 18 years made up greater shares of the total population. To note, Killeen city, Texas was associated with the Fort Hood military base, which contributed to the lower percentage of people 65 years and over. Provo city, Utah is home to a large university that contributes to the lower share of older adults.

**Among places with a population of 100,000 or more, the places with the highest and lowest proportion of their population in the 85 and over age group were located in the West.**

Of the ten places with a population of 100,000 or more with the highest percentage of their population 85 years and over, five

were located in the West, three in the Midwest, and two in the South (Table 6). Four of the places appearing among the top ten in Table 6 for having a high percentage of their population in the 85 years and over age group are also listed among the top ten places for percentage of the population in the 65 years and over age group. This includes Urban Honolulu CDP, Hawaii; Clearwater city, Florida; Warren city, Michigan; and Metairie CDP, Louisiana.

The place with the highest percentage of its population in the 85 and over age group was Urban Honolulu CDP, located in Hawaii (3.5 percent), followed by Clearwater city, Florida (3.5 percent) and Santa Rosa city, California

(2.8 percent).[19] Interestingly, Florida, which contained more places among the top ten places with the highest proportion of their population in the 65 years and over age group than other states, contains only one place on the list of the top ten places for the highest percentage of their population in the 85 years and over age group.

While the West contained the most places among the top ten places with the highest proportion of their population 85 years and over, the West also had seven cities listed among the top ten places with the lowest percentage of their population 85 years and over (Table 6). Specifically, Utah, Nevada, Arizona, and California were states in the West that contained places with low percentages of their population 85 years and over. The place with the lowest percentage of its population in the 85 and over age group, West Jordan city, Utah (0.4 percent), was also the place with the lowest percentage of its population in the 65 years and over age group.

The South had three places appearing on the list of the ten places with the lowest proportion of their population in the oldest-old age group. Two of the southern places were located in Texas while one was located in Florida.

_____

[19] Urban Honolulu CDP, Hawaii, has a higher percentage of its population in the 85 years and over age group than Clearwater city, Florida, when the percent is rounded to two decimal places. However, for data presentation purposes, only one decimal place appears in the table.

## ADDITIONAL FINDINGS ON THE OLDER POPULATION

### At what age were there almost twice as many women as men?[20]

In the 2010 Census, there were approximately twice as many women as men at age 89 (361,309 compared with 176,689, respectively). This point occurred about 4 years older than it did in 2000, and 6 years older than it did in 1990. This increase is further evidence of the narrowing gap in mortality between men and women occurring at the older ages.

### How many people 65 years and over lived in skilled-nursing facilities in 2010?

Approximately 1.3 million people 65 years and over were in skilled-nursing facilities in 2010 (Table 7).[21] This represents 3.1 percent of the total population 65 years and over.

Of the population 65 years and over in skilled-nursing facilities in 2010, there were about 2.5 times the number of women 65 years and over than men 65 years and over (891,873 and 360,762, respectively). Males were most likely to be concentrated in the 75 to 84 year old age group in skilled-nursing facilities (137,850) followed by the 85 to 94 year old age group (120,089) and then the 65 to 74 year old group (88,814). Women, on the other hand, were more concentrated in the 85 to 94 year old age group (409,600), followed by the 75 to 84 year old group

[20] This finding originally appeared in the U.S. Census Bureau brief on age and sex, issued May 2011. See U.S. Census Bureau, 2011, *Age and Sex Composition: 2010*, by Lindsay M. Howden and Julie A. Meyer, 2010 Census Briefs, C2010BR-03, available at <www.census.gov/prod/cen2010/briefs /c2010br-03.pdf>.

[21] Skilled-nursing facilities are considered group quarters. The 2010 Census definition for group quarters can be found at <www.census.gov/prod/cen2010/doc/sf1 .pdf>.

Table 7.

## Population 65 Years and Older in Skilled-Nursing Facilities by Selected Age Groups and Sex: 2010

(For information on confidentiality protection, nonsampling error, and definitions, see *www.census.gov/prod/cen2010/doc/sf1.pdf*)

| Sex and age | Total population | In skilled-nursing facilities | |
|---|---|---|---|
| | | Number | Percent |
| Both sexes, all ages . . . . . . . . . . . | 308,745,538 | 1,502,264 | 0.5 |
| Total 65 years and over . . . . . . . | 40,267,984 | 1,252,635 | 3.1 |
| 65 to 74 years . . . . . . . . . . . . . . . . | 21,713,429 | 197,310 | 0.9 |
| 75 to 84 years . . . . . . . . . . . . . . . . | 13,061,122 | 420,790 | 3.2 |
| 85 to 94 years . . . . . . . . . . . . . . . . | 5,068,825 | 529,689 | 10.4 |
| 95 years and over . . . . . . . . . . . . . | 424,608 | 104,846 | 24.7 |
| 95 to 99 years . . . . . . . . . . . . . | 371,244 | 87,621 | 23.6 |
| 100 years and over . . . . . . . . . . | 53,364 | 17,225 | 32.3 |
| Male, all ages . . . . . . . . . . . . . . . | 151,781,326 | 500,185 | 0.3 |
| Total 65 years and over . . . . . . . | 17,362,960 | 360,762 | 2.1 |
| 65 to 74 years . . . . . . . . . . . . . . . . | 10,096,519 | 88,814 | 0.9 |
| 75 to 84 years . . . . . . . . . . . . . . . . | 5,476,762 | 137,850 | 2.5 |
| 85 to 94 years . . . . . . . . . . . . . . . . | 1,698,254 | 120,089 | 7.1 |
| 95 years and over . . . . . . . . . . . . . | 91,425 | 14,009 | 15.3 |
| 95 to 99 years . . . . . . . . . . . . . | 82,263 | 12,345 | 15.0 |
| 100 years and over . . . . . . . . . . | 9,162 | 1,664 | 18.2 |
| Female, all ages . . . . . . . . . . . . . . | 156,964,212 | 1,002,079 | 0.6 |
| Total 65 years and over . . . . . . . | 22,905,024 | 891,873 | 3.9 |
| 65 to 74 years . . . . . . . . . . . . . . . . | 11,616,910 | 108,496 | 0.9 |
| 75 to 84 years . . . . . . . . . . . . . . . . | 7,584,360 | 282,940 | 3.7 |
| 85 to 94 years . . . . . . . . . . . . . . . . | 3,370,571 | 409,600 | 12.2 |
| 95 years and over . . . . . . . . . . . . . | 333,183 | 90,837 | 27.3 |
| 95 to 99 years . . . . . . . . . . . . . | 288,981 | 75,276 | 26.0 |
| 100 years and over . . . . . . . . . . | 44,202 | 15,561 | 35.2 |

Source: U.S. Census Bureau, *2010 Census Summary File 1*.

(282,940) and the 65 to 74 year old age group (108,496).

As age increases, the share of the older population in a skilled-nursing facility also increases. In 2010, 0.9 percent of the total population 65 to 74 years old resided in a nursing home compared with 24.7 percent of the population 95 and over, and 32.3 percent of the population 100 and above. Females were more likely to be in a nursing home as they aged compared with males. In 2010, 3.9 percent of females 65 years and over were in skilled-nursing facilities compared with 2.1 percent of males 65 years and over. For both males and females, 0.9 percent of people 65 to 74 years old were in a nursing home. However, only 15.3 percent of males 95 years and over were in a nursing home compared with 27.3 percent of females 95 years and over.

### How many centenarians were there in the 2010 Census?[22]

In the 2010 Census, there were 53,364 centenarians, defined as people 100 years and over. This is a 5.8 percent increase from 2000 when there were 50,454 people who were at least 100 years old. Of the total population in 2010, 1 out of every 5,786 people was a centenarian.

Females outnumbered males in the centenarian population. In 2010, there were 9,162 males and 44,202 females who were 100 years and over. Females made up 82.8 percent

[22] The centenarian population can potentially be affected by data quality issues, such as age misreporting by respondents. For more information about data quality at the extreme older ages, please see U.S. Census Bureau, 1999, *Centenarians in the United States: 1990* by Constance Krach and Victoria Velkoff, Current Population Reports, Series P23-199RV, available at <www.census.gov /prod/99pubs/p23-199.pdf>.

of the total centenarian population while males made up 17.2 percent. Of the total U.S. female population, 1 out of every 3,551 females was a centenarian. Of the total U.S. male population, 1 out of every 16,566 males was a centenarian.

## ABOUT THE 2010 CENSUS

### Why was the 2010 Census conducted?

The U.S. Constitution mandates that a census be taken in the United States every 10 years. This is required in order to determine the number of seats each state is to receive in the U.S. House of Representatives. Age data are used to determine the voting age population (age 18 and older) for use in the legislative redistricting process.

### Why did the 2010 Census ask the question on age?

The Census Bureau collects data on age to support a variety of legislative and program requirements. These data are also used to aid in the allocation of funds from federal programs, in particular to programs targeting the older population. This includes planning for hospitals, roads, and housing assistance. For example, the Department of Veterans Affairs uses census data to plan for nursing homes, hospitals, cemeteries, domiciliary services, and veterans benefits; the Department of Health and Human Services uses age data as part of the formula used to allocate funds for services to seniors with low incomes under the Older Americans Act; and the Equal Employment

Opportunity Commission uses age data to enforce equal employment opportunities. These data are also used to forecast the number of people eligible for Social Security and Medicare benefits.

### How are data on age beneficial?

Federal, state and local governments need information on age to implement, evaluate, and aid programs that plan and develop services for older adults. This includes, but is not limited to, the Equal Employment Opportunity Act, the Older Americans Act, the Nutrition Education Program, the Rehabilitation Act, the Long Term Care Ombudsman Services for Older Americans Program, and the Supportive Housing for the Elderly Program.

Other important uses for census data on age are in the planning and funding of services for the older population, such as health service centers, retirement homes, assisted living or skilled-nursing facilities, transportation availability, Social Security, and Medicare benefits. Census data can also be used by the private sector to determine business locations and advertising for goods and services targeting older adults, investment planning, employment opportunities, and specialized consumer needs. Researchers can use age data to project future population trends, assess mortality patterns, evaluate shifts in the geographic distribution of the older population, and plan ways to better serve the needs of a given community.

## FOR MORE INFORMATION

For more information on age in the United States, visit the U.S. Census Bureau's Internet site at <www.census.gov/population /www/socdemo/age/>.

Data on age and sex from the 2010 Census Summary File 1 provide information at the state level and below and are available on the Internet at <factfinder2 .census.gov/main.html> and on DVD. Information on confidentiality protection, nonsampling error, and definitions is available on the Census Bureau's Internet site at <www.census.gov/prod/cen2010 /doc/sf1.pdf>.

Information on other population and housing topics is presented in the 2010 Census Briefs series, located on the U.S. Census Bureau's Web site at <www.census.gov /prod/cen2010/>. This series presents information about race, Hispanic origin, age, sex, household type, housing tenure, and people who reside in group quarters.

For more information about the 2010 Census, including data products, call the Customer Services Center at 1-800-923-8282. You can also visit the Census Bureau's Question and Answer Center at <ask.census.gov> to submit your questions online.

# Overview of Race and Hispanic Origin: 2010

## 2010 Census Briefs

Issued March 2011

C2010BR-02

By
Karen R. Humes,
Nicholas A. Jones, and
Roberto R. Ramirez

## INTRODUCTION

This report looks at our nation's changing racial and ethnic diversity. It is part of a series that analyzes population and housing data collected from the 2010 Census, and it provides a snapshot of race and Hispanic origin in the United States. Racial and ethnic population group distributions and growth at the national level and at lower levels of geography are presented.

This report also provides an overview of race and ethnicity concepts and definitions used in the 2010 Census. The data for this report are based on the *2010 Census Redistricting Data (Public Law 94-171) Summary File*, which is among the first 2010 Census data products to be released and is provided to each state for use in drawing boundaries for legislative districts.[1]

---

[1] The *2010 Census Redistricting Data (Public Law 94-171) Summary File* provides data on Hispanic origin and race, including information on the population reporting more than one race as well as detailed race combinations (e.g., White *and* Asian; White *and* Black or African American *and* American Indian and Alaska Native). In this report, the multiple-race combination categories are denoted with the conjunction *and* in bold and italicized print to indicate the specific race groups that comprise the particular combination. This report discusses data for the 50 states and the District of Columbia but not Puerto Rico.

The *2010 Census Redistricting Data (Public Law 94-171) Summary File* does not contain data for detailed Hispanic origin groups (e.g., Mexican or Puerto Rican) or detailed information about race or tribes (e.g., Chinese, Samoan, or Choctaw). Therefore, these specific groups are not discussed in this report. Data on detailed Hispanic origin groups and detailed information about race and tribes will be released on a state-by-state basis as part of the *2010 Census Demographic Profile* and the *2010 Census Summary File 1*. Additional reports on the Hispanic or Latino population and selected race population groups will be released as part of the 2010 Census Briefs series. For a detailed schedule of 2010 Census products and release dates, visit <www.census.gov /population/www/cen2010/glance/index.html>.

### Figure 1.

## Reproduction of the Questions on Hispanic Origin and Race From the 2010 Census

→ NOTE: Please answer BOTH Question 5 about Hispanic origin and Question 6 about race. For this census, Hispanic origins are not races.

5. Is this person of Hispanic, Latino, or Spanish origin?

☐ **No,** not of Hispanic, Latino, or Spanish origin
☐ Yes, Mexican, Mexican Am., Chicano
☐ Yes, Puerto Rican
☐ Yes, Cuban
☐ Yes, another Hispanic, Latino, or Spanish origin — *Print origin, for example, Argentinean, Colombian, Dominican, Nicaraguan, Salvadoran, Spaniard, and so on.* ⤵

6. What is this person's race? *Mark* ☒ *one or more boxes.*

☐ White
☐ Black, African Am., or Negro
☐ American Indian or Alaska Native — *Print name of enrolled or principal tribe.* ⤵

☐ Asian Indian ☐ Japanese ☐ Native Hawaiian
☐ Chinese ☐ Korean ☐ Guamanian or Chamorro
☐ Filipino ☐ Vietnamese ☐ Samoan
☐ Other Asian — *Print race, for example, Hmong, Laotian, Thai, Pakistani, Cambodian, and so on.* ⤵ ☐ Other Pacific Islander — *Print race, for example, Fijian, Tongan, and so on.* ⤵

☐ Some other race — *Print race.* ⤵

Source: U.S. Census Bureau, 2010 Census questionnaire.

## UNDERSTANDING RACE AND HISPANIC ORIGIN DATA FROM THE 2010 CENSUS

**The 2010 Census used established federal standards to collect and present data on race and Hispanic origin.**

For the 2010 Census, the questions on race and Hispanic origin were asked of individuals living in the United States (see Figure 1). An individual's responses to the race question and to the Hispanic origin question were based upon

**United States™**

U.S. Department of Commerce

self-identification. The U.S. Census Bureau collects race and Hispanic origin information following the guidance of the U.S. Office of Management and Budget's (OMB) 1997 *Revisions to the Standards for the Classification of Federal Data on Race and Ethnicity*.[2] These federal standards mandate that race and Hispanic origin (ethnicity) are separate and distinct concepts and that when collecting these data via self-identification, two different questions must be used.

## Hispanic Origin

The OMB definition of Hispanic or Latino origin used in the 2010 Census is presented in the text box "Definition of Hispanic or Latino Origin Used in the 2010 Census." OMB requires federal agencies to use a minimum of two ethnicities: Hispanic or Latino and Not Hispanic or Latino. Hispanic origin can be viewed as the heritage, nationality group, lineage, or country of birth of the person or the person's parents or ancestors before their arrival in the United States. People who identify their origin as Hispanic, Latino, or Spanish may be any race.[3]

### Definition of Hispanic or Latino Origin Used in the 2010 Census

"Hispanic or Latino" refers to a person of Cuban, Mexican, Puerto Rican, South or Central American, or other Spanish culture or origin regardless of race.

[2] The 1997 *Revisions to the Standards for the Classification of Federal Data on Race and Ethnicity*, issued by OMB, is available at <www.whitehouse.gov/omb /fedreg/1997standards.html>.
[3] The terms "Hispanic or Latino" and "Hispanic" are used interchangeably in this report.

The 2010 Census question on Hispanic origin included five separate response categories and one area where respondents could write-in a specific Hispanic origin group. The first response category is intended for respondents who do not identify as Hispanic. The remaining response categories ("Mexican, Mexican Am., or Chicano"; "Puerto Rican"; "Cuban"; and "Another Hispanic, Latino, or Spanish origin") and write-in answers can be combined to create the OMB category of Hispanic.[4]

## Race

The OMB definitions of the race categories used in the 2010 Census, plus the Census Bureau's definition of Some Other Race, are presented in the text box "Definition of Race Categories Used in the 2010 Census." Starting in 1997, OMB required federal agencies to use a minimum of five race categories: White, Black or African American, American Indian or Alaska Native, Asian, and Native Hawaiian or Other Pacific Islander. For respondents unable to identify with any of these five race categories, OMB approved the Census Bureau's inclusion of a sixth category—Some Other Race—on the Census 2000 and 2010 Census questionnaires.

[4] There were three changes to the Hispanic origin question for the 2010 Census. First, the wording of the question changed from "Is this person Spanish/Hispanic/ Latino?" in 2000 to "Is this person of Hispanic, Latino, or Spanish origin?" in 2010. Second, in 2000, the question provided an instruction, "Mark ☒ the '**No**' box if **not** Spanish/ Hispanic/Latino." The 2010 Census question provided no specific instruction for non-Hispanic respondents. Third, in 2010, the "Yes, another Hispanic, Latino, or Spanish origin" category provided examples of six Hispanic origin groups (Argentinean, Colombian, Dominican, Nicaraguan, Salvadoran, Spaniard, and so on) and instructed respondents to "print origin." In 2000, no Hispanic origin examples were given.

Data on race have been collected since the first U.S. decennial census in 1790.[5] For the first time in Census 2000, individuals were presented with the option to self-identify with more than one race and this continued with the 2010 Census, as prescribed by OMB. There are 57 possible multiple race combinations involving the five OMB race categories and Some Other Race.

The 2010 Census question on race included 15 separate response categories and three areas where respondents could write-in detailed information about their race.[6] The response categories and write-in answers can be combined to create the five minimum OMB race categories plus Some Other Race. In addition to White, Black or African American, American Indian and Alaska Native, and Some Other Race, 7 of the 15 response categories are Asian groups and 4 are Native Hawaiian and Other Pacific Islander groups.[7]

[5] For information about comparability of 2010 Census data on race and Hispanic origin to data collected in previous censuses, see the *2010 Census Redistricting Data (Public Law 94-171) Summary File—Technical Documentation* at <www.census.gov/prod /cen2010/doc/pl94-171.pdf>.
[6] There were two changes to the question on race for the 2010 Census. First, the wording of the race question was changed from "What is this person's race? Mark ☒ one or more races to indicate what this person considers himself/herself to be" in 2000 to "What is this person's race? Mark ☒ one or more boxes" for 2010. Second, in 2010, examples were added to the "Other Asian" response category (Hmong, Laotian, Thai, Pakistani, Cambodian, and so on) and the "Other Pacific Islander" response category (Fijian, Tongan, and so on). In 2000, no examples were given in the race question.
[7] The race categories included in the census questionnaire generally reflect a social definition of race recognized in this country and are not an attempt to define race biologically, anthropologically, or genetically. In addition, it is recognized that the categories of the race question include race and national origin or sociocultural groups.

### Definition of Race Categories Used in the 2010 Census

"White" refers to a person having origins in any of the original peoples of Europe, the Middle East, or North Africa. It includes people who indicated their race(s) as "White" or reported entries such as Irish, German, Italian, Lebanese, Arab, Moroccan, or Caucasian.

"Black or African American" refers to a person having origins in any of the Black racial groups of Africa. It includes people who indicated their race(s) as "Black, African Am., or Negro" or reported entries such as African American, Kenyan, Nigerian, or Haitian.

"American Indian or Alaska Native" refers to a person having origins in any of the original peoples of North and South America (including Central America) and who maintains tribal affiliation or community attachment. This category includes people who indicated their race(s) as "American Indian or Alaska Native" or reported their enrolled or principal tribe, such as Navajo, Blackfeet, Inupiat, Yup'ik, or Central American Indian groups or South American Indian groups.

"Asian" refers to a person having origins in any of the original peoples of the Far East, Southeast Asia, or the Indian subcontinent, including, for example, Cambodia, China, India, Japan, Korea, Malaysia, Pakistan, the Philippine Islands, Thailand, and Vietnam. It includes people who indicated their race(s) as "Asian" or reported entries such as "Asian Indian," "Chinese," "Filipino," "Korean," "Japanese," "Vietnamese," and "Other Asian" or provided other detailed Asian responses.

"Native Hawaiian or Other Pacific Islander" refers to a person having origins in any of the original peoples of Hawaii, Guam, Samoa, or other Pacific Islands. It includes people who indicated their race(s) as "Pacific Islander" or reported entries such as "Native Hawaiian," "Guamanian or Chamorro," "Samoan," and "Other Pacific Islander" or provided other detailed Pacific Islander responses.

"Some Other Race" includes all other responses not included in the White, Black or African American, American Indian or Alaska Native, Asian, and Native Hawaiian or Other Pacific Islander race categories described above. Respondents reporting entries such as multiracial, mixed, interracial, or a Hispanic or Latino group (for example, Mexican, Puerto Rican, Cuban, or Spanish) in response to the race question are included in this category.

something other than White alone and those who reported their ethnicity as Hispanic or Latino.[8]

**More than half of the growth in the total population of the United States between 2000 and 2010 was due to the increase in the Hispanic population.**

In 2010, there were 50.5 million Hispanics in the United States, composing 16 percent of the total population (see Table 1). Between 2000 and 2010, the Hispanic population grew by 43 percent—rising from 35.3 million in 2000, when this group made up 13 percent of the total population.[9] The Hispanic population increased by 15.2 million between 2000 and 2010, accounting for over half of the 27.3 million increase in the total population of the United States.

The non-Hispanic population grew relatively slower over the decade, about 5 percent. Within the non-Hispanic population, the number of people who reported their race as White alone grew even slower between 2000 and 2010 (1 percent). While the non-Hispanic White alone population increased numerically from 194.6 million to 196.8 million over the 10-year period, its proportion of the total population declined from 69 percent to 64 percent.

---

[8] For the purposes of this report, the term "reported" is used to refer to the response provided by respondents as well as responses assigned during the editing and imputation process.

[9] The observed changes in race and Hispanic origin counts between Census 2000 and the 2010 Census could be attributed to a number of factors. Demographic change since 2000, which includes births and deaths in a geographic area and migration in and out of a geographic area, will have an impact on the resulting 2010 Census counts. Additionally, some changes in the race and Hispanic origin questions' wording and format since Census 2000 could have influenced reporting patterns in the 2010 Census.

## RACE AND HISPANIC ORIGIN IN THE 2010 CENSUS

Data from the 2010 Census provide insights to our racially and ethnically diverse nation. According to the 2010 Census, 308.7 million people resided in the United States on April 1, 2010—an increase of 27.3 million people, or 9.7 percent, between 2000 and 2010. The vast majority of the growth in the total population came from increases in those who reported their race(s) as

Table 1.
## Population by Hispanic or Latino Origin and by Race for the United States: 2000 and 2010
(For information on confidentiality protection, nonsampling error, and definitions, see *www.census.gov/prod/cen2010/doc/pl94-171.pdf*)

| Hispanic or Latino origin and race | 2000 | | 2010 | | Change, 2000 to 2010 | |
|---|---|---|---|---|---|---|
| | Number | Percentage of total population | Number | Percentage of total population | Number | Percent |
| **HISPANIC OR LATINO ORIGIN AND RACE** | | | | | | |
| Total population ................. | **281,421,906** | 100.0 | **308,745,538** | 100.0 | **27,323,632** | **9.7** |
| Hispanic or Latino ....................... | 35,305,818 | 12.5 | 50,477,594 | 16.3 | 15,171,776 | 43.0 |
| Not Hispanic or Latino.................... | 246,116,088 | 87.5 | 258,267,944 | 83.7 | 12,151,856 | 4.9 |
| White alone ......................... | 194,552,774 | 69.1 | 196,817,552 | 63.7 | 2,264,778 | 1.2 |
| **RACE** | | | | | | |
| Total population ................. | **281,421,906** | 100.0 | **308,745,538** | 100.0 | **27,323,632** | **9.7** |
| One Race ........................... | 274,595,678 | 97.6 | 299,736,465 | 97.1 | 25,140,787 | 9.2 |
| White ............................ | 211,460,626 | 75.1 | 223,553,265 | 72.4 | 12,092,639 | 5.7 |
| Black or African American ............... | 34,658,190 | 12.3 | 38,929,319 | 12.6 | 4,271,129 | 12.3 |
| American Indian and Alaska Native......... | 2,475,956 | 0.9 | 2,932,248 | 0.9 | 456,292 | 18.4 |
| Asian ............................ | 10,242,998 | 3.6 | 14,674,252 | 4.8 | 4,431,254 | 43.3 |
| Native Hawaiian and Other Pacific Islander.... | 398,835 | 0.1 | 540,013 | 0.2 | 141,178 | 35.4 |
| Some Other Race ..................... | 15,359,073 | 5.5 | 19,107,368 | 6.2 | 3,748,295 | 24.4 |
| Two or More Races[1] ..................... | 6,826,228 | 2.4 | 9,009,073 | 2.9 | 2,182,845 | 32.0 |

[1] In Census 2000, an error in data processing resulted in an overstatement of the Two or More Races population by about 1 million people (about 15 percent) nationally, which almost entirely affected race combinations involving Some Other Race. Therefore, data users should assess observed changes in the Two or More Races population and race combinations involving Some Other Race between Census 2000 and the 2010 Census with caution. Changes in specific race combinations not involving Some Other Race, such as White *and* Black or African American or White *and* Asian, generally should be more comparable.

Sources: U.S. Census Bureau, *Census 2000 Redistricting Data (Public Law 94-171) Summary File*, Tables PL1 and PL2; and *2010 Census Redistricting Data (Public Law 94-171) Summary File*, Tables P1 and P2.

**The overwhelming majority of the total population of the United States reported only one race in 2010.**

In the 2010 Census, 97 percent of all respondents (299.7 million) reported only one race (see Table 1).[10] The largest group reported

[10] Individuals who responded to the question on race by indicating only one race are referred to as the *race-alone* population or the group that reported only one race category. Six categories make up this population: White alone, Black or African American alone, American Indian and Alaska Native alone, Asian alone, Native Hawaiian and Other Pacific Islander alone, and Some Other Race alone. Individuals who chose more than 1 of the 6 race categories are referred to as the Two or More Races population. All respondents who indicated more than one race can be collapsed into the Two or More Races category which, combined with the six race-alone categories, yields seven mutually exclusive and exhaustive categories. Thus, the six race-alone categories and the Two or More Races category sum to the total population.

White alone (223.6 million), accounting for 72 percent of all people living in the United States.[11] The Black or African-American alone population was 38.9 million and represented 13 percent of the total population.[12] There were 2.9 million respondents who indicated American Indian and Alaska Native alone (0.9 percent). Approximately 14.7 million (about 5 percent of all respondents) identified their race

[11] As a matter of policy, the Census Bureau does not advocate the use of the *alone* population over the *alone-or-in-combination* population or vice versa. The use of the *alone* population in sections of this report does not imply that it is a preferred method of presenting or analyzing data. The same is true for sections of this report that focus on the *alone-or-in-combination* population. Data on race from the 2010 Census can be presented and discussed in a variety of ways.

[12] The terms "Black or African American" and "Black" are used interchangeably in this report.

as Asian alone. The smallest major race group was Native Hawaiian and Other Pacific Islander alone (0.5 million) and represented 0.2 percent of the total population. The remainder of respondents who reported only one race—19.1 million (6 percent of all respondents)—were classified as Some Other Race alone. People who reported more than one race numbered 9.0 million in the 2010 Census and made up about 3 percent of the total population.

**The Asian population grew faster than any other major race group between 2000 and 2010.**

In the United States, all major race groups increased in population size between 2000 and 2010, but they grew at different rates. Over the decade, the Asian alone population experienced the fastest rate of growth and the White alone population experienced the slowest rate of growth, with the other major race groups' growth spanning the range in between. Of the 27.3 million people added to the total population of the United States between 2000 and 2010, the White alone population made up just under half of the growth—increasing 12.1 million. Within the White alone population, the vast majority of the growth was propelled by the Hispanic population.

The Asian alone population increased by 43 percent between 2000 and 2010, more than any other major race group. The Asian alone population had the second-largest numeric change (4.4 million), growing from 10.2 million in 2000 to 14.7 million in 2010. The Asian alone population gained the most in share of the total population, moving up from about 4 percent in 2000 to about 5 percent in 2010.

The Native Hawaiian and Other Pacific Islander alone population, the smallest major race group, also grew substantially between 2000 and 2010, increasing by more than one-third. This population numbered 398,835 in 2000, rising to 540,013 in 2010 with its proportion of the total population changing from 0.1 percent to 0.2 percent, respectively.

Between 2000 and 2010, the population classified as Some Other Race alone increased considerably,

growing by about one-quarter. This population climbed from 15.4 million in 2000 to 19.1 million in 2010 and was approximately 6 percent of the total population in both decennial censuses. Most of this growth was due to increases in the Hispanic population.

An 18 percent growth in the American Indian and Alaska Native alone population occurred between 2000 and 2010. This population, also relatively small numerically, maintained its proportion of the total population between decennial censuses (0.9 percent) while growing from 2.5 million to 2.9 million.

While the Black alone population had the third-largest numeric increase in population size over the decade (4.3 million), behind the White alone and Asian alone populations, it grew slower than most other major race groups. In fact, the Black alone population exhibited the smallest percentage growth outside of the White alone population, increasing 12 percent between 2000 and 2010. This population rose from 34.7 million in 2000 to 38.9 million in 2010, making up 12 percent and 13 percent of the total population, respectively.

The only major race group to experience a decrease in its proportion of the total population was the White alone population. While this group increased the most numerically between decennial censuses (211.5 million to 223.6 million), its share of the total population fell from 75 percent in 2000 to 72 percent in 2010.

The Two or More Races population was one of the fastest-growing groups over the decade. This population increased approximately one-third between 2000 and 2010.[13]

## The Hispanic population predominantly identified as either White or Some Other Race.

People of Hispanic origin may be any race. For the 2010 Census, a new instruction was added immediately preceding the questions on Hispanic origin and race, which was not used in Census 2000. The instruction stated that "For this census, Hispanic origins are not races" because in the federal statistical system, Hispanic origin is considered to be a separate concept from race. However, this did not preclude individuals from self-identifying their race as "Latino," "Mexican," "Puerto Rican," "Salvadoran," or other national origins or ethnicities; in fact, many did so. If the response provided to the race question could not be classified in one or more of the five OMB race groups, it was generally classified in the category Some Other Race. Therefore, responses to the question on race that reflect a Hispanic origin were classified in the Some Other Race category.

[13] In Census 2000, an error in data processing resulted in an overstatement of the Two or More Races population by about 1 million people (about 15 percent) nationally, which almost entirely affected race combinations involving Some Other Race. Therefore, data users should assess observed changes in the Two or More Races population and race combinations involving Some Other Race between Census 2000 and the 2010 Census with caution. Changes in specific multiple-race combinations not involving Some Other Race, such as White **and** Black or White **and** Asian, generally, should be more comparable.

The 2010 Census racial distributions of the Hispanic population and of the non-Hispanic population differ and are shown in Table 2. Over half of the Hispanic population identified as White and no other race, while about one-third provided responses that were classified as Some Other Race alone when responding to the question on race. Much smaller proportions of Hispanics identified as other race groups alone: Black alone (3 percent), American Indian and Alaska Native alone (1 percent), Asian alone (0.4 percent), and Native Hawaiian and Other Pacific Islander alone (0.1 percent).

The racial distribution of the non-Hispanic population, on the other hand, was mostly White alone (76 percent), Black alone (15 percent), and Asian alone (6 percent). Less than 1 percent of non-Hispanics provided responses to the race question that were classified as Some Other Race alone (0.2 percent).

In 2010, 6 percent of Hispanics reported multiple races. Among non-Hispanics, 2 percent reported more than one race.

**Native Hawaiians and Other Pacific Islanders and American Indians and Alaska Natives were more likely than other groups to report multiple races.**

In the 2010 Census, the population reporting their race as White, either alone or with at least one other race, was the largest of all the alone-or-in-combination categories (231.0 million) and represented about three-fourths of the total

Table 2.
**Population by Hispanic or Latino Origin and Race for the United States: 2010**

(For information on confidentiality protection, nonsampling error, and definitions, see www.census.gov/prod/cen2010/doc/pl94-171.pdf)

| Hispanic or Latino origin and race | Number | Percent |
|---|---|---|
| **HISPANIC OR LATINO** | | |
| Total | 50,477,594 | 100.0 |
| **Race** | | |
| One Race | 47,435,002 | 94.0 |
| White | 26,735,713 | 53.0 |
| Black or African American | 1,243,471 | 2.5 |
| American Indian and Alaska Native | 685,150 | 1.4 |
| Asian | 209,128 | 0.4 |
| Native Hawaiian and Other Pacific Islander | 58,437 | 0.1 |
| Some Other Race | 18,503,103 | 36.7 |
| Two or More Races | 3,042,592 | 6.0 |
| **NOT HISPANIC OR LATINO** | | |
| Total | 258,267,944 | 100.0 |
| **Race** | | |
| One Race | 252,301,463 | 97.7 |
| White | 196,817,552 | 76.2 |
| Black or African American | 37,685,848 | 14.6 |
| American Indian and Alaska Native | 2,247,098 | 0.9 |
| Asian | 14,465,124 | 5.6 |
| Native Hawaiian and Other Pacific Islander | 481,576 | 0.2 |
| Some Other Race | 604,265 | 0.2 |
| Two or More Races | 5,966,481 | 2.3 |

Source: U.S. Census Bureau, *2010 Census Redistricting Data (Public Law 94-171) Summary File*, Tables P1 and P2.

population (see Table 3).[14] People who reported their race as White in combination with one or more additional races numbered 7.5 million, making up 2 percent of the total population. About 14 percent of the total population reported their race as Black, either alone or with at least one other race, which was the second-largest of the alone-or-in-combination categories (42.0 million).

There were 21.7 million people classified as Some Other Race alone or in combination and 17.3 million people classified as Asian alone or in combination in the 2010 Census, making up 7 percent and 6 percent of the total population, respectively. There were comparable levels and proportions of the total population who indicated race groups in combination with Some Other Race (2.6 million and 0.9 percent) and with Asian (2.6 million and 0.9 percent).

[14] The maximum number of people reporting a particular race is reflected in the race-alone-or-in-combination concept. This represents the number of times responses were part of 1 of the 6 major race categories, either alone or in combination with the other five race categories. There are six race-alone-or-in-combination categories, which are not mutually exclusive: White alone or in combination, Black alone or in combination, American Indian and Alaska Native alone or in combination, Asian alone or in combination, Native Hawaiian and Other Pacific Islander alone or in combination, and Some Other Race alone or in combination. For example, a respondent who indicated Asian **and** White was counted in the Asian alone-or-in-combination category as well as in the White alone-or-in-combination category. Therefore, the sum of all race-alone-or-in-combination categories equals the number of races reported (i.e., responses), which exceeds the total population.

Table 3.
## Race by the Alone-or-In-Combination, Alone, and In-Combination Categories for the United States: 2010

(For information on confidentiality protection, nonsampling error, and definitions, see *www.census.gov/prod/cen2010/doc/pl94-171.pdf*)

| Race | Number | Percentage of total population | Percentage of alone or in combination |
|---|---|---|---|
| Total population ................. | 308,745,538 | 100.0 | (X) |
| **WHITE** | | | |
| Alone or in combination.................... | 231,040,398 | 74.8 | (X) |
| Alone ............................... | 223,553,265 | 72.4 | 96.8 |
| In combination ........................ | 7,487,133 | 2.4 | 3.2 |
| **BLACK OR AFRICAN AMERICAN** | | | |
| Alone or in combination.................... | 42,020,743 | 13.6 | (X) |
| Alone ............................... | 38,929,319 | 12.6 | 92.6 |
| In combination ........................ | 3,091,424 | 1.0 | 7.4 |
| **AMERICAN INDIAN AND ALASKA NATIVE** | | | |
| Alone or in combination.................... | 5,220,579 | 1.7 | (X) |
| Alone ............................... | 2,932,248 | 0.9 | 56.2 |
| In combination ........................ | 2,288,331 | 0.7 | 43.8 |
| **ASIAN** | | | |
| Alone or in combination.................... | 17,320,856 | 5.6 | (X) |
| Alone ............................... | 14,674,252 | 4.8 | 84.7 |
| In combination ........................ | 2,646,604 | 0.9 | 15.3 |
| **NATIVE HAWAIIAN AND OTHER PACIFIC ISLANDER** | | | |
| Alone or in combination.................... | 1,225,195 | 0.4 | (X) |
| Alone ............................... | 540,013 | 0.2 | 44.1 |
| In combination ........................ | 685,182 | 0.2 | 55.9 |
| **SOME OTHER RACE** | | | |
| Alone or in combination.................... | 21,748,084 | 7.0 | (X) |
| Alone ............................... | 19,107,368 | 6.2 | 87.9 |
| In combination ........................ | 2,640,716 | 0.9 | 12.1 |

(X) Not applicable.

Note: The total population is equal to the number of respondents. In the 2010 Census, there were 308,745,538 respondents. The total of all race categories alone or in combination with one or more other races is equal to the number of responses; therefore, it adds to more than the total population.

Source: U.S. Census Bureau, *2010 Census Redistricting Data (Public Law 94-171) Summary File*, Table P1.

The two smallest alone-or-in-combination categories were American Indian and Alaska Native (5.2 million) and Native Hawaiian and Other Pacific Islander (1.2 million), making up 2 percent and 0.4 percent of the total population, respectively. These two categories were unique in that large proportions of these populations indicated more than one race, compared with other major race groups (see Figure 2). There were more reports of Native Hawaiian and Other Pacific Islander in combination with one or more additional races than there were of Native Hawaiian and Other Pacific Islander alone (0.7 million and 0.5 million, respectively). Almost as many people indicated American Indian and Alaska Native in combination with one or more additional races as people who indicated American Indian and Alaska Native alone (2.3 million and 2.9 million, respectively). Thus, over half of the Native Hawaiian and Other Pacific Islander population and almost half of the American Indian and Alaska Native population reported more than one race.

**Most people who reported multiple races provided exactly two races in 2010; White *and* Black was the largest multiple-race combination.**

Over the last 10 years, considerable research has been conducted on people of multiple races, and how they self-identify has become a more common part of our discussions and understanding of race and ethnicity. Results from the 2010 Census provide new information on the diversity and changes in the Two or More Races population in the United States.

Among people who reported more than one race in 2010, the vast majority (about 92 percent) reported exactly two races (see Table 4). An additional 8 percent of the Two or More Races population reported three races and less than 1 percent reported four or more races.

In 2010, four groups were, by far, the largest multiple-race combinations in the United States: White *and* Black (1.8 million), White *and* Some Other Race (1.7 million), White *and* Asian (1.6 million), and White *and* American Indian and Alaska Native (1.4 million). Together, these four combinations composed nearly three-fourths of the multiple-race population in the 2010 Census (see Figure 3).

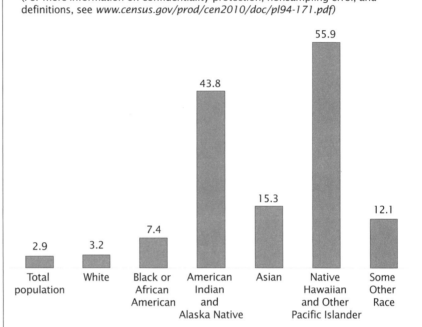

Figure 2.
**Percentage of Major Race Groups Reporting Multiple Races: 2010**

(For more information on confidentiality protection, nonsampling error, and definitions, see *www.census.gov/prod/cen2010/doc/pl94-171.pdf*)

Note:  Specified race group refers to the alone or in-combination population.
Source: U.S. Census Bureau, *2010 Census Redistricting Data (Public Law 94-171) Summary File*, Table P1.

**Different multiple-race reporting patterns occurred for Hispanics and non-Hispanics.**

Tables 5 through 10 present data for the major race groups and their largest multiple-race combinations by Hispanic origin. A general pattern existed in these data tables for people who reported more than one race in the 2010 Census. There were more reports of multiple-race combinations that included White than reports of combinations involving any other group. This basic pattern also existed among non-Hispanics. However, among Hispanics, relatively large proportions reported multiple-race combinations involving Some Other Race, as well as combinations involving White.

Table 4.
## Two or More Races Population by Number of Races and Selected Combinations for the United States: 2010

(For information on confidentiality protection, nonsampling error, and definitions, see *www.census.gov/prod/cen2010/doc/pl94-171.pdf*)

| Race | Number | Percent |
|---|---|---|
| Two or More Races population | 9,009,073 | 100.0 |
| Two races | 8,265,318 | 91.7 |
| White; Black or African American | 1,834,212 | 20.4 |
| White; American Indian and Alaska Native | 1,432,309 | 15.9 |
| White; Asian | 1,623,234 | 18.0 |
| White; Native Hawaiian and Other Pacific Islander | 169,991 | 1.9 |
| White; Some Other Race | 1,740,924 | 19.3 |
| Black or African American; American Indian and Alaska Native | 269,421 | 3.0 |
| Black or African American; Asian | 185,595 | 2.1 |
| Black or African American; Native Hawaiian and Other Pacific Islander | 50,308 | 0.6 |
| Black or African American; Some Other Race | 314,571 | 3.5 |
| American Indian and Alaska Native; Asian | 58,829 | 0.7 |
| American Indian and Alaska Native; Native Hawaiian and Other Pacific Islander | 11,039 | 0.1 |
| American Indian and Alaska Native; Some Other Race | 115,752 | 1.3 |
| Asian; Native Hawaiian and Other Pacific Islander | 165,690 | 1.8 |
| Asian; Some Other Race | 234,462 | 2.6 |
| Native Hawaiian and Other Pacific Islander; Some Other Race | 58,981 | 0.7 |
| Three races | 676,469 | 7.5 |
| White; Black or African American; American Indian and Alaska Native | 230,848 | 2.6 |
| White; Black or African American; Asian | 61,511 | 0.7 |
| White; Black or African American; Native Hawaiian and Other Pacific Islander | 9,245 | 0.1 |
| White; Black or African American; Some Other Race | 46,641 | 0.5 |
| White; American Indian and Alaska Native; Asian | 45,960 | 0.5 |
| White; American Indian and Alaska Native; Native Hawaiian and Other Pacific Islander | 8,656 | 0.1 |
| White; American Indian and Alaska Native; Some Other Race | 30,941 | 0.3 |
| White; Asian; Native Hawaiian and Other Pacific Islander | 143,126 | 1.6 |
| White; Asian; Some Other Race | 35,786 | 0.4 |
| White; Native Hawaiian and Other Pacific Islander; Some Other Race | 9,181 | 0.1 |
| Black or African American; American Indian and Alaska Native; Asian | 9,460 | 0.1 |
| Black or African American; American Indian and Alaska Native; Native Hawaiian and Other Pacific Islander | 2,142 | – |
| Black or African American; American Indian and Alaska Native; Some Other Race | 8,236 | 0.1 |
| Black or African American; Asian; Native Hawaiian and Other Pacific Islander | 7,295 | 0.1 |
| Black or African American; Asian; Some Other Race | 8,122 | 0.1 |
| Black or African American; Native Hawaiian and Other Pacific Islander; Some Other Race | 4,233 | – |
| American Indian and Alaska Native; Asian; Native Hawaiian and Other Pacific Islander | 3,827 | – |
| American Indian and Alaska Native; Asian; Some Other Race | 3,785 | – |
| American Indian and Alaska Native; Native Hawaiian and Other Pacific Islander; Some Other Race | 2,000 | – |
| Asian; Native Hawaiian and Other Pacific Islander; Some Other Race | 5,474 | 0.1 |
| Four races | 57,875 | 0.6 |
| Five races | 8,619 | 0.1 |
| Six races | 792 | – |

– Percentage rounds to 0.0.

Source: U.S. Census Bureau, *2010 Census Redistricting Data (Public Law 94-171) Summary File*, Table P1.

Figure 3.
**Percentage Distribution of People Who Reported Multiple Races: 2010**
(For more information on confidentiality protection, nonsampling error, and definitions, see
*www.census.gov/prod/cen2010/doc/pl94-171.pdf*)

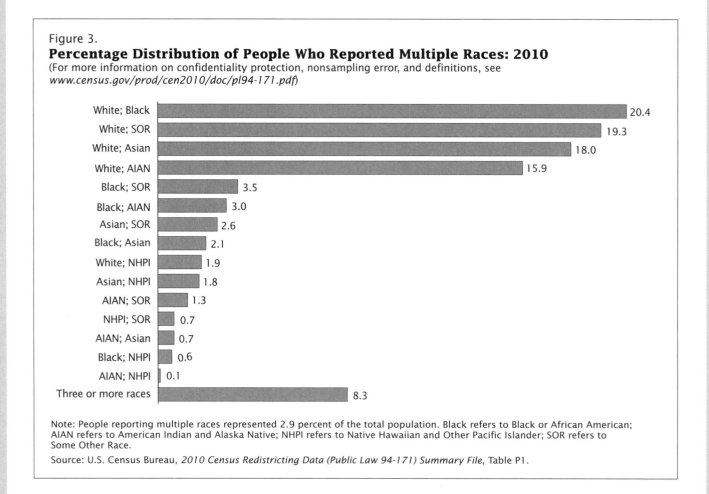

Note: People reporting multiple races represented 2.9 percent of the total population. Black refers to Black or African American; AIAN refers to American Indian and Alaska Native; NHPI refers to Native Hawaiian and Other Pacific Islander; SOR refers to Some Other Race.

Source: U.S. Census Bureau, *2010 Census Redistricting Data (Public Law 94-171) Summary File*, Table P1.

**People who identified as White were the most likely to report only one race.**

In the 2010 Census, 97 percent of people in the White alone-or-in-combination category reported White and no other race (see Table 5). Among the 7.5 million people who reported they were White and one or more additional races, one-fourth reported White *and* Black, and nearly one-fourth reported White *and* Some Other Race. Another one-fifth reported White *and* Asian, and nearly one-fifth reported White *and* American Indian and Alaska Native. This was a fairly even distribution of responses among the four largest combinations.

Table 5.
## The White Population and Largest Multiple-Race Combinations by Hispanic or Latino Origin for the United States: 2010

(For information on confidentiality protection, nonsampling error, and definitions, see *www.census.gov/prod/cen2010/doc/pl94-171.pdf*)

| Race | Number | Percent | Percentage of White in combination |
|---|---|---|---|
| **WHITE ALONE OR IN COMBINATION** | | | |
| **Total** | **231,040,398** | **100.0** | **(X)** |
| White alone | 223,553,265 | 96.8 | (X) |
| White in combination | 7,487,133 | 3.2 | 100.0 |
| White; Black or African American | 1,834,212 | 0.8 | 24.5 |
| White; Some Other Race | 1,740,924 | 0.8 | 23.3 |
| White; Asian | 1,623,234 | 0.7 | 21.7 |
| White; American Indian and Alaska Native | 1,432,309 | 0.6 | 19.1 |
| White; Black or African American; American Indian and Alaska Native | 230,848 | 0.1 | 3.1 |
| All other combinations including White | 625,606 | 0.3 | 8.4 |
| | | | |
| **Hispanic or Latino** | **29,184,290** | **100.0** | **(X)** |
| White alone | 26,735,713 | 91.6 | (X) |
| White in combination | 2,448,577 | 8.4 | 100.0 |
| White; Black or African American | 245,850 | 0.8 | 10.0 |
| White; Some Other Race | 1,601,125 | 5.5 | 65.4 |
| White; Asian | 135,522 | 0.5 | 5.5 |
| White; American Indian and Alaska Native | 226,385 | 0.8 | 9.2 |
| White; Black or African American; American Indian and Alaska Native | 50,000 | 0.2 | 2.0 |
| All other combinations including White | 189,695 | 0.6 | 7.7 |
| | | | |
| **Not Hispanic or Latino** | **201,856,108** | **100.0** | **(X)** |
| White alone | 196,817,552 | 97.5 | (X) |
| White in combination | 5,038,556 | 2.5 | 100.0 |
| White; Black or African American | 1,588,362 | 0.8 | 31.5 |
| White; Some Other Race | 139,799 | 0.1 | 2.8 |
| White; Asian | 1,487,712 | 0.7 | 29.5 |
| White; American Indian and Alaska Native | 1,205,924 | 0.6 | 23.9 |
| White; Black or African American; American Indian and Alaska Native | 180,848 | 0.1 | 3.6 |
| All other combinations including White | 435,911 | 0.2 | 8.7 |

(X) Not applicable.

Note: Largest combinations based on White in-combination population.

Source: U.S. Census Bureau, *2010 Census Redistricting Data (Public Law 94-171) Summary File*, Tables P1 and P2.

Table 5 shows that 29.2 million people of Hispanic origin reported that they were either White alone or White in combination with another race. Of the 2.4 million Hispanics who reported their race as White in combination with one or more additional races, almost two-thirds were classified as White *and* Some Other Race.

The multiple-race reporting pattern was different for non-Hispanic Whites. Of the 5.0 million non-Hispanics who reported that they were White and one or more additional races, about one-third reported White *and* Black, nearly one-third reported White *and* Asian, and about one-fourth reported White *and* American Indian and Alaska Native.

Table 6.
## The Black or African-American Population and Largest Multiple-Race Combinations by Hispanic or Latino Origin for the United States: 2010

(For information on confidentiality protection, nonsampling error, and definitions, see *www.census.gov/prod/cen2010/doc/pl94-171.pdf*)

| Race | Number | Percent | Percentage of Black or African American in combination |
|---|---|---|---|
| **BLACK OR AFRICAN AMERICAN ALONE OR IN COMBINATION** | | | |
| **Total** | **42,020,743** | **100.0** | (X) |
| Black or African American alone | 38,929,319 | 92.6 | (X) |
| Black or African American in combination | 3,091,424 | 7.4 | 100.0 |
| Black or African American; White | 1,834,212 | 4.4 | 59.3 |
| Black or African American; Some Other Race | 314,571 | 0.7 | 10.2 |
| Black or African American; American Indian and Alaska Native | 269,421 | 0.6 | 8.7 |
| Black or African American; White; American Indian and Alaska Native | 230,848 | 0.5 | 7.5 |
| Black or African American; Asian | 185,595 | 0.4 | 6.0 |
| All other combinations including Black or African American | 256,777 | 0.6 | 8.3 |
| **Hispanic or Latino** | **1,897,218** | **100.0** | (X) |
| Black or African American alone | 1,243,471 | 65.5 | (X) |
| Black or African American in combination | 653,747 | 34.5 | 100.0 |
| Black or African American; White | 245,850 | 13.0 | 37.6 |
| Black or African American; Some Other Race | 227,648 | 12.0 | 34.8 |
| Black or African American; American Indian and Alaska Native | 31,571 | 1.7 | 4.8 |
| Black or African American; White; American Indian and Alaska Native | 50,000 | 2.6 | 7.6 |
| Black or African American; Asian | 15,451 | 0.8 | 2.4 |
| All other combinations including Black or African American | 83,227 | 4.4 | 12.7 |
| **Not Hispanic or Latino** | **40,123,525** | **100.0** | (X) |
| Black or African American alone | 37,685,848 | 93.9 | (X) |
| Black or African American in combination | 2,437,677 | 6.1 | 100.0 |
| Black or African American; White | 1,588,362 | 4.0 | 65.2 |
| Black or African American; Some Other Race | 86,923 | 0.2 | 3.6 |
| Black or African American; American Indian and Alaska Native | 237,850 | 0.6 | 9.8 |
| Black or African American; White; American Indian and Alaska Native | 180,848 | 0.5 | 7.4 |
| Black or African American; Asian | 170,144 | 0.4 | 7.0 |
| All other combinations including Black or African American | 173,550 | 0.4 | 7.1 |

(X) Not applicable.

Note: Largest combinations based on Black or African American in-combination population.

Source: U.S. Census Bureau, *2010 Census Redistricting Data (Public Law 94-171) Summary File*, Tables P1 and P2.

**Within the population who identified as Black, Hispanics were more likely to report multiple races than non-Hispanics.**

In the 2010 Census, 93 percent of people in the Black alone-or-in-combination category reported Black and no other race (see Table 6). Among the 3.1 million people who reported that they were Black and one or more additional races,

the majority reported being Black *and* White (59 percent).

The Black alone-or-in-combination population included 1.9 million people of Hispanic origin, 35 percent of whom reported multiple races. This is more than five times greater than the proportion reporting multiple races among non-Hispanics who identified as Black (6 percent). Most Hispanics who

identified as Black in combination with one or more additional races reported one of two combinations: Black *and* White (38 percent) and Black *and* Some Other Race (35 percent). This contrasts with non-Hispanics who identified as Black in combination with one or more additional races, where about two-thirds reported one combination, Black *and* White.

Table 7.
## The American Indian and Alaska Native Population and Largest Multiple-Race Combinations by Hispanic or Latino Origin for the United States: 2010

(For information on confidentiality protection, nonsampling error, and definitions, see *www.census.gov/prod/cen2010/doc/pl94-171.pdf*)

| Race | Number | Percent | Percentage of American Indian and Alaska Native in combination |
|---|---|---|---|
| **AMERICAN INDIAN AND ALASKA NATIVE ALONE OR IN COMBINATION** | | | |
| **Total** . . . . . . . . . . . . . . . . . . . . . . . . . . . . . . . . . . . . . . . . . . . . . . . . | **5,220,579** | **100.0** | **(X)** |
| American Indian and Alaska Native alone. . . . . . . . . . . . . . . . . . . . . . . . . . . . | 2,932,248 | 56.2 | (X) |
| American Indian and Alaska Native in combination . . . . . . . . . . . . . . . . . . . . . | 2,288,331 | 43.8 | 100.0 |
| American Indian and Alaska Native; White . . . . . . . . . . . . . . . . . . . . . . . . . . | 1,432,309 | 27.4 | 62.6 |
| American Indian and Alaska Native; Black or African American . . . . . . . . . . . . . . | 269,421 | 5.2 | 11.8 |
| American Indian and Alaska Native; White; Black or African American. . . . . . . . . . . | 230,848 | 4.4 | 10.1 |
| American Indian and Alaska Native; Some Other Race . . . . . . . . . . . . . . . . . . | 115,752 | 2.2 | 5.1 |
| American Indian and Alaska Native; Asian . . . . . . . . . . . . . . . . . . . . . . . . . . | 58,829 | 1.1 | 2.6 |
| All other combinations including American Indian and Alaska Native . . . . . . . . . . . . . . | 181,172 | 3.5 | 7.9 |
| | | | |
| **Hispanic or Latino** . . . . . . . . . . . . . . . . . . . . . . . . . . . . . . . . . . . . . . . . | **1,190,904** | **100.0** | **(X)** |
| American Indian and Alaska Native alone. . . . . . . . . . . . . . . . . . . . . . . . . . . . | 685,150 | 57.5 | (X) |
| American Indian and Alaska Native in combination . . . . . . . . . . . . . . . . . . . . . | 505,754 | 42.5 | 100.0 |
| American Indian and Alaska Native; White . . . . . . . . . . . . . . . . . . . . . . . . . . | 226,385 | 19.0 | 44.8 |
| American Indian and Alaska Native; Black or African American . . . . . . . . . . . . . . | 31,571 | 2.7 | 6.2 |
| American Indian and Alaska Native; White; Black or African American. . . . . . . . . . . | 50,000 | 4.2 | 9.9 |
| American Indian and Alaska Native; Some Other Race . . . . . . . . . . . . . . . . . . | 106,604 | 9.0 | 21.1 |
| American Indian and Alaska Native; Asian . . . . . . . . . . . . . . . . . . . . . . . . . . | 12,257 | 1.0 | 2.4 |
| All other combinations including American Indian and Alaska Native . . . . . . . . . . . . . . | 78,937 | 6.6 | 15.6 |
| | | | |
| **Not Hispanic or Latino**. . . . . . . . . . . . . . . . . . . . . . . . . . . . . . . . . . . . . . | **4,029,675** | **100.0** | **(X)** |
| American Indian and Alaska Native alone. . . . . . . . . . . . . . . . . . . . . . . . . . . . | 2,247,098 | 55.8 | (X) |
| American Indian and Alaska Native in combination . . . . . . . . . . . . . . . . . . . . . | 1,782,577 | 44.2 | 100.0 |
| American Indian and Alaska Native; White . . . . . . . . . . . . . . . . . . . . . . . . . . | 1,205,924 | 29.9 | 67.7 |
| American Indian and Alaska Native; Black or African American . . . . . . . . . . . . . . | 237,850 | 5.9 | 13.3 |
| American Indian and Alaska Native; White; Black or African American. . . . . . . . . . . | 180,848 | 4.5 | 10.1 |
| American Indian and Alaska Native; Some Other Race . . . . . . . . . . . . . . . . . . | 9,148 | 0.2 | 0.5 |
| American Indian and Alaska Native; Asian . . . . . . . . . . . . . . . . . . . . . . . . . . | 46,572 | 1.2 | 2.6 |
| All other combinations including American Indian and Alaska Native . . . . . . . . . . . . . . | 102,235 | 2.5 | 5.7 |

(X) Not applicable.

Note: Largest combinations based on American Indian and Alaska Native in-combination population.

Source: U.S. Census Bureau, *2010 Census Redistricting Data (Public Law 94-171) Summary File*, Tables P1 and P2.

## Nearly half of all people who identified as American Indian and Alaska Native reported multiple races.

In 2010, 56 percent of people in the American Indian and Alaska Native alone-or-in-combination category reported one race (see Table 7). Of the 2.3 million who reported American Indian and Alaska Native along with one or more additional races, about 63 percent reported one combination: American Indian and Alaska Native *and* White. American Indian and Alaska Native *and* Black (12 percent) as well as American Indian and Alaska Native *and* White *and* Black (10 percent) were also common combinations reported among this population.

Among those who identified as American Indian and Alaska Native, the proportion of Hispanics and non-Hispanics who reported more than one race was about the same—unlike any other race group.

There were 1.2 million people of Hispanic origin who identified as American Indian and Alaska Native, 43 percent of whom reported multiple races. The majority of Hispanics who reported more than one race within the American Indian and Alaska Native population identified as one of two combinations: American Indian and Alaska Native *and* White (45 percent) and American Indian and Alaska Native *and* Some Other Race (21 percent). Similar to Hispanic American Indians and Alaska Natives, 44 percent of non-Hispanics who identified as American Indian and Alaska Native reported more than one race. However, unlike Hispanics, over two-thirds reported one combination: American Indian and Alaska Native *and* White.

**Among people who identified as Asian, 15 percent reported more than one race.**

About 85 percent of the Asian alone-or-in-combination population reported Asian and no other race in the 2010 Census, compared to 15 percent who reported Asian along with one or more additional races (see Table 8). Of the 2.6 million who indicated Asian along with one or more additional races, well over half reported being Asian *and* White (61 percent).

The majority of the 0.6 million people of Hispanic origin who identified as Asian alone or in combination reported more than one race (65 percent). Among Hispanics who identified as Asian along with one or more additional races, the most frequently reported combinations were Asian *and* White (35 percent) and Asian *and* Some Other Race (27 percent). About 14 percent of non-Hispanics who identified as Asian reported multiple races—two-thirds of whom identified as one combination, Asian *and* White.

Table 8.

## The Asian Population and Largest Multiple-Race Combinations by Hispanic or Latino Origin for the United States: 2010

(For information on confidentiality protection, nonsampling error, and definitions, see *www.census.gov/prod/cen2010/doc/pl94-171.pdf*)

| Race | Number | Percent | Percentage of Asian in combination |
|---|---|---|---|
| **ASIAN ALONE OR IN COMBINATION** | | | |
| **Total** | **17,320,856** | **100.0** | **(X)** |
| Asian alone | 14,674,252 | 84.7 | (X) |
| Asian in combination | 2,646,604 | 15.3 | 100.0 |
| Asian; White | 1,623,234 | 9.4 | 61.3 |
| Asian; Some Other Race | 234,462 | 1.4 | 8.9 |
| Asian; Black or African American | 185,595 | 1.1 | 7.0 |
| Asian; Native Hawaiian and Other Pacific Islander | 165,690 | 1.0 | 6.3 |
| Asian; White; Native Hawaiian and Other Pacific Islander | 143,126 | 0.8 | 5.4 |
| All other combinations including Asian | 294,497 | 1.7 | 11.1 |
| **Hispanic or Latino** | **598,146** | **100.0** | **(X)** |
| Asian alone | 209,128 | 35.0 | (X) |
| Asian in combination | 389,018 | 65.0 | 100.0 |
| Asian; White | 135,522 | 22.7 | 34.8 |
| Asian; Some Other Race | 103,591 | 17.3 | 26.6 |
| Asian; Black or African American | 15,451 | 2.6 | 4.0 |
| Asian; Native Hawaiian and Other Pacific Islander | 16,129 | 2.7 | 4.1 |
| Asian; White; Native Hawaiian and Other Pacific Islander | 22,799 | 3.8 | 5.9 |
| All other combinations including Asian | 95,526 | 16.0 | 24.6 |
| **Not Hispanic or Latino** | **16,722,710** | **100.0** | **(X)** |
| Asian alone | 14,465,124 | 86.5 | (X) |
| Asian in combination | 2,257,586 | 13.5 | 100.0 |
| Asian; White | 1,487,712 | 8.9 | 65.9 |
| Asian; Some Other Race | 130,871 | 0.8 | 5.8 |
| Asian; Black or African American | 170,144 | 1.0 | 7.5 |
| Asian; Native Hawaiian and Other Pacific Islander | 149,561 | 0.9 | 6.6 |
| Asian; White; Native Hawaiian and Other Pacific Islander | 120,327 | 0.7 | 5.3 |
| All other combinations including Asian | 198,971 | 1.2 | 8.8 |

(X) Not applicable.

Note: Largest combinations based on Asian in-combination population.

Source: U.S. Census Bureau, *2010 Census Redistricting Data (Public Law 94-171) Summary File*, Tables P1 and P2.

Table 9.

## The Native Hawaiian and Other Pacific Islander Population and Largest Multiple-Race Combinations by Hispanic or Latino Origin for the United States: 2010

(For information on confidentiality protection, nonsampling error, and definitions, see *www.census.gov/prod/cen2010/doc/pl94-171.pdf*)

| Race | Number | Percent | Percentage of Native Hawaiian and Other Pacific Islander in combination |
|---|---|---|---|
| **NATIVE HAWAIIAN AND OTHER PACIFIC ISLANDER ALONE OR IN COMBINATION** | | | |
| **Total** | **1,225,195** | **100.0** | **(X)** |
| Native Hawaiian and Other Pacific Islander alone | 540,013 | 44.1 | (X) |
| Native Hawaiian and Other Pacific Islander in combination | 685,182 | 55.9 | 100.0 |
| Native Hawaiian and Other Pacific Islander; White | 169,991 | 13.9 | 24.8 |
| Native Hawaiian and Other Pacific Islander; Asian | 165,690 | 13.5 | 24.2 |
| Native Hawaiian and Other Pacific Islander; White; Asian | 143,126 | 11.7 | 20.9 |
| Native Hawaiian and Other Pacific Islander; Some Other Race | 58,981 | 4.8 | 8.6 |
| Native Hawaiian and Other Pacific Islander; Black or African American | 50,308 | 4.1 | 7.3 |
| All other combinations including Native Hawaiian and Other Pacific Islander | 97,086 | 7.9 | 14.2 |
| **Hispanic or Latino** | **210,307** | **100.0** | **(X)** |
| Native Hawaiian and Other Pacific Islander alone | 58,437 | 27.8 | (X) |
| Native Hawaiian and Other Pacific Islander in combination | 151,870 | 72.2 | 100.0 |
| Native Hawaiian and Other Pacific Islander; White | 22,187 | 10.5 | 14.6 |
| Native Hawaiian and Other Pacific Islander; Asian | 16,129 | 7.7 | 10.6 |
| Native Hawaiian and Other Pacific Islander; White; Asian | 22,799 | 10.8 | 15.0 |
| Native Hawaiian and Other Pacific Islander; Some Other Race | 46,909 | 22.3 | 30.9 |
| Native Hawaiian and Other Pacific Islander; Black or African American | 4,913 | 2.3 | 3.2 |
| All other combinations including Native Hawaiian and Other Pacific Islander | 38,933 | 18.5 | 25.6 |
| **Not Hispanic or Latino** | **1,014,888** | **100.0** | **(X)** |
| Native Hawaiian and Other Pacific Islander alone | 481,576 | 47.5 | (X) |
| Native Hawaiian and Other Pacific Islander in combination | 533,312 | 52.5 | 100.0 |
| Native Hawaiian and Other Pacific Islander; White | 147,804 | 14.6 | 27.7 |
| Native Hawaiian and Other Pacific Islander; Asian | 149,561 | 14.7 | 28.0 |
| Native Hawaiian and Other Pacific Islander; White; Asian | 120,327 | 11.9 | 22.6 |
| Native Hawaiian and Other Pacific Islander; Some Other Race | 12,072 | 1.2 | 2.3 |
| Native Hawaiian and Other Pacific Islander; Black or African American | 45,395 | 4.5 | 8.5 |
| All other combinations including Native Hawaiian and Other Pacific Islander | 58,153 | 5.7 | 10.9 |

(X) Not applicable.

Note: Largest combinations based on Native Hawaiian and Other Pacific Islander in-combination population.

Source: U.S. Census Bureau, *2010 Census Redistricting Data (Public Law 94-171) Summary File*, Tables P1 and P2.

**More than half of all people who identified as Native Hawaiian and Other Pacific Islander reported multiple races.**

About 44 percent of people in the Native Hawaiian and Other Pacific Islander alone-or-in-combination category reported this race and no other (see Table 9). Of the 0.7 million who indicated Native Hawaiian and Other Pacific Islander along with one or more additional races, 25 percent reported Native Hawaiian and Other Pacific Islander *and* White, 24 percent reported Native Hawaiian and Other Pacific Islander *and* Asian, and 21 percent reported Native Hawaiian and Other Pacific Islander *and* White *and* Asian—representing a fairly even distribution of responses among the largest combinations.

Within the population who identified as Native Hawaiian and Other Pacific Islander, high proportions of both Hispanics (72 percent) and non-Hispanics (53 percent) reported multiple races (0.2 million and 1.0 million, respectively). For Hispanics, the largest combination was Native Hawaiian and Other Pacific Islander **and** Some Other Race (31 percent). Among non-Hispanics, similar proportions (about 28 percent each) reported the following: Native Hawaiian and Other Pacific Islander **and** Asian and Native Hawaiian and Other Pacific Islander **and** White.

**Hispanics made up 97 percent of all those classified as only Some Other Race.**

Table 10 shows the Some Other Race alone-or-in-combination population (21.7 million) by Hispanic origin in the United States in 2010. Respondents who were classified as Some Other Race alone represented the vast majority of the total (88 percent).

Among the 2.6 million people who reported multiple races that included Some Other Race, the most common combinations were Some Other Race **and** White (66 percent), followed by Some Other Race **and** Black (12 percent), Some Other Race **and** Asian (9 percent), Some Other Race **and** American Indian and Alaska Native (4 percent), and Some Other Race **and** Native Hawaiian and Other Pacific Islander (2 percent). All other combinations including Some Other Race represented 7 percent of the Some Other Race alone-or-in-combination population.

Table 10.

**The Some Other Race Population and Largest Multiple-Race Combinations by Hispanic or Latino Origin for the United States: 2010**

(For information on confidentiality protection, nonsampling error, and definitions, see *www.census.gov/prod/cen2010/doc/pl94-171.pdf*)

| Race | Number | Percent | Percentage of Some Other Race in combination |
|---|---|---|---|
| **SOME OTHER RACE ALONE OR IN COMBINATION** | | | |
| Total | **21,748,084** | **100.0** | (X) |
| Some Other Race alone | 19,107,368 | 87.9 | (X) |
| Some Other Race in combination | 2,640,716 | 12.1 | 100.0 |
| Some Other Race; White | 1,740,924 | 8.0 | 65.9 |
| Some Other Race; Black or African American | 314,571 | 1.4 | 11.9 |
| Some Other Race; Asian | 234,462 | 1.1 | 8.9 |
| Some Other Race; American Indian and Alaska Native | 115,752 | 0.5 | 4.4 |
| Some Other Race; Native Hawaiian and Other Pacific Islander | 58,981 | 0.3 | 2.2 |
| All other combinations including Some Other Race | 176,026 | 0.8 | 6.7 |
| **Hispanic or Latino** | **20,714,218** | **100.0** | (X) |
| Some Other Race alone | 18,503,103 | 89.3 | (X) |
| Some Other Race in combination | 2,211,115 | 10.7 | 100.0 |
| Some Other Race; White | 1,601,125 | 7.7 | 72.4 |
| Some Other Race; Black or African American | 227,648 | 1.1 | 10.3 |
| Some Other Race; Asian | 103,591 | 0.5 | 4.7 |
| Some Other Race; American Indian and Alaska Native | 106,604 | 0.5 | 4.8 |
| Some Other Race; Native Hawaiian and Other Pacific Islander | 46,909 | 0.2 | 2.1 |
| All other combinations including Some Other Race | 125,238 | 0.6 | 5.7 |
| **Not Hispanic or Latino** | **1,033,866** | **100.0** | (X) |
| Some Other Race alone | 604,265 | 58.4 | (X) |
| Some Other Race in combination | 429,601 | 41.6 | 100.0 |
| Some Other Race; White | 139,799 | 13.5 | 32.5 |
| Some Other Race; Black or African American | 86,923 | 8.4 | 20.2 |
| Some Other Race; Asian | 130,871 | 12.7 | 30.5 |
| Some Other Race; American Indian and Alaska Native | 9,148 | 0.9 | 2.1 |
| Some Other Race; Native Hawaiian and Other Pacific Islander | 12,072 | 1.2 | 2.8 |
| All other combinations including Some Other Race | 50,788 | 4.9 | 11.8 |

(X) Not applicable.

Note: Largest combinations based on Some Other Race in-combination population.

Source: U.S. Census Bureau, *2010 Census Redistricting Data (Public Law 94-171) Summary File*, Tables P1 and P2.

In the 2010 Census, approximately 20.7 million people of Hispanic origin were classified as Some Other Race either alone or in combination, compared with only 1 million people of non-Hispanic origin. Nearly all of those who were classified as Some Other Race alone were of Hispanic origin (18.5 million out of 19.1 million, or 97 percent).

The majority of Hispanics classified as Some Other Race reported only one race (89 percent). However, notable reporting differences were observed for non-Hispanics. Among non-Hispanics who were classified as Some Other Race, about

42 percent reported more than one race (nearly four times higher than their Hispanic counterparts).

In 2010, among Hispanics classified as Some Other Race in combination with one or more additional races, the most common multiple-race group by far was Some Other Race *and* White (72 percent), followed by Some Other Race *and* Black (10 percent). Among non-Hispanics who were classified as Some Other Race and one or more additional races, the most common multiple-race combinations were more evenly distributed—Some Other Race *and* White (33 percent) and Some Other Race *and* Asian (31 percent).

## GEOGRAPHIC DISTRIBUTION OF THE MINORITY POPULATION

### Nearly half of the West region's population was minority.

In the 2010 Census, just over one-third of the U.S. population reported their race and ethnicity as something other than non-Hispanic White alone. This group, referred to as the "minority" population for this report, increased from 86.9 million

to 111.9 million between 2000 and 2010 (see Table 11). This represented a growth of 29 percent over the decade. The non-Hispanic White alone population also grew over the decade, from 194.6 million to 196.8 million; however, growth was relatively slow for this population (1 percent).

In the four census regions, the proportion of the total population that was minority (proportion minority) ranged from about one-fifth to just under one-half of the total population in 2010.[15] The minority population numbered 33.9 million (47 percent) in the West, 45.8 million (40 percent) in the South, and 17.3 million (31 percent) in the Northeast. In the Midwest, the minority population was 14.8 million and made up 22 percent of the total population.

The minority population grew in every region between 2000 and 2010, but most significantly in the South and West. The South experienced growth of 34 percent in its minority population. Similar growth occurred in the West, with the minority population increasing by 29 percent. The non-Hispanic White alone population also grew in the

---

[15] The Northeast census region includes Connecticut, Maine, Massachusetts, New Hampshire, New Jersey, New York, Pennsylvania, Rhode Island, and Vermont. The Midwest census region includes Illinois, Indiana, Iowa, Kansas, Michigan, Minnesota, Missouri, Nebraska, North Dakota, Ohio, South Dakota, and Wisconsin. The South census region includes Alabama, Arkansas, Delaware, the District of Columbia, Florida, Georgia, Kentucky, Louisiana, Maryland, Mississippi, North Carolina, Oklahoma, South Carolina, Tennessee, Texas, Virginia, and West Virginia. The West census region includes Alaska, Arizona, California, Colorado, Hawaii, Idaho, Montana, Nevada, New Mexico, Oregon, Utah, Washington, and Wyoming.

South and West between the two decennial censuses, but at a slower rate (4 percent and 3 percent, respectively).

The minority population in the Northeast and Midwest experienced considerable growth between 2000 and 2010. The minority population grew by 21 percent in the Northeast, and the Midwest minority population grew 24 percent. In contrast, the non-Hispanic White alone population in both of these regions declined since 2000 (–3 percent in the Northeast and –1 percent in the Midwest).

### California had the largest minority population in 2010.

In 2010, the states with the largest minority populations frequently also had the largest non-Hispanic White alone populations. California led the nation with the largest minority population (22.3 million). Texas (13.7 million), New York (8.1 million), Florida (7.9 million), and Illinois (4.7 million) round out the top five states with the largest minority populations. Most of these states also had the largest non-Hispanic White alone populations—California with 15.0 million, Texas with 11.4 million, New York with 11.3 million, and Florida with 10.9 million. The state with the fifth-largest non-Hispanic White alone population in 2010 was Pennsylvania (10.1 million).

Table 11.
## Non-Hispanic White Alone Population and the Minority Population for the United States, Regions, States, and for Puerto Rico: 2000 and 2010

(For information on confidentiality protection, nonsampling error, and definitions, see www.census.gov/prod/cen2010/doc/pl94-171.pdf)

| Area | 2000 | | | | 2010 | | | | Percentage change, 2000 to 2010 | |
|---|---|---|---|---|---|---|---|---|---|---|
| | Total | Non-Hispanic White alone | Minority[1] | Percentage minority[1] | Total | Non-Hispanic White alone | Minority[1] | Percentage minority[1] | Non-Hispanic White alone | Minority[1] |
| **United States.....** | 281,421,906 | 194,552,774 | 86,869,132 | 30.9 | 308,745,538 | 196,817,552 | 111,927,986 | 36.3 | 1.2 | 28.8 |
| **REGION** | | | | | | | | | | |
| Northeast............... | 53,594,378 | 39,327,262 | 14,267,116 | 26.6 | 55,317,240 | 38,008,094 | 17,309,146 | 31.3 | −3.4 | 21.3 |
| Midwest ............... | 64,392,776 | 52,386,131 | 12,006,645 | 18.6 | 66,927,001 | 52,096,633 | 14,830,368 | 22.2 | −0.6 | 23.5 |
| South ................ | 100,236,820 | 65,927,794 | 34,309,026 | 34.2 | 114,555,744 | 68,706,462 | 45,849,282 | 40.0 | 4.2 | 33.6 |
| West ................. | 63,197,932 | 36,911,587 | 26,286,345 | 41.6 | 71,945,553 | 38,006,363 | 33,939,190 | 47.2 | 3.0 | 29.1 |
| **STATE** | | | | | | | | | | |
| Alabama ............. | 4,447,100 | 3,125,819 | 1,321,281 | 29.7 | 4,779,736 | 3,204,402 | 1,575,334 | 33.0 | 2.5 | 19.2 |
| Alaska ............... | 626,932 | 423,788 | 203,144 | 32.4 | 710,231 | 455,320 | 254,911 | 35.9 | 7.4 | 25.5 |
| Arizona .............. | 5,130,632 | 3,274,258 | 1,856,374 | 36.2 | 6,392,017 | 3,695,647 | 2,696,370 | 42.2 | 12.9 | 45.2 |
| Arkansas............. | 2,673,400 | 2,100,135 | 573,265 | 21.4 | 2,915,918 | 2,173,469 | 742,449 | 25.5 | 3.5 | 29.5 |
| California ............ | 33,871,648 | 15,816,790 | 18,054,858 | 53.3 | 37,253,956 | 14,956,253 | 22,297,703 | 59.9 | −5.4 | 23.5 |
| Colorado ............ | 4,301,261 | 3,202,880 | 1,098,381 | 25.5 | 5,029,196 | 3,520,793 | 1,508,403 | 30.0 | 9.9 | 37.3 |
| Connecticut .......... | 3,405,565 | 2,638,845 | 766,720 | 22.5 | 3,574,097 | 2,546,262 | 1,027,835 | 28.8 | −3.5 | 34.1 |
| Delaware ............ | 783,600 | 567,973 | 215,627 | 27.5 | 897,934 | 586,752 | 311,182 | 34.7 | 3.3 | 44.3 |
| District of Columbia ....... | 572,059 | 159,178 | 412,881 | 72.2 | 601,723 | 209,464 | 392,259 | 65.2 | 31.6 | −5.0 |
| Florida.............. | 15,982,378 | 10,458,509 | 5,523,869 | 34.6 | 18,801,310 | 10,884,722 | 7,916,588 | 42.1 | 4.1 | 43.3 |
| Georgia .............. | 8,186,453 | 5,128,661 | 3,057,792 | 37.4 | 9,687,653 | 5,413,920 | 4,273,733 | 44.1 | 5.6 | 39.8 |
| Hawaii ............... | 1,211,537 | 277,091 | 934,446 | 77.1 | 1,360,301 | 309,343 | 1,050,958 | 77.3 | 11.6 | 12.5 |
| Idaho ................ | 1,293,953 | 1,139,291 | 154,662 | 12.0 | 1,567,582 | 1,316,243 | 251,339 | 16.0 | 15.5 | 62.5 |
| Illinois .............. | 12,419,293 | 8,424,140 | 3,995,153 | 32.2 | 12,830,632 | 8,167,753 | 4,662,879 | 36.3 | −3.0 | 16.7 |
| Indiana .............. | 6,080,485 | 5,219,373 | 861,112 | 14.2 | 6,483,802 | 5,286,453 | 1,197,349 | 18.5 | 1.3 | 39.0 |
| Iowa ................ | 2,926,324 | 2,710,344 | 215,980 | 7.4 | 3,046,355 | 2,701,123 | 345,232 | 11.3 | −0.3 | 59.8 |
| Kansas .............. | 2,688,418 | 2,233,997 | 454,421 | 16.9 | 2,853,118 | 2,230,539 | 622,579 | 21.8 | −0.2 | 37.0 |
| Kentucky............. | 4,041,769 | 3,608,013 | 433,756 | 10.7 | 4,339,367 | 3,745,655 | 593,712 | 13.7 | 3.8 | 36.9 |
| Louisiana............. | 4,468,976 | 2,794,391 | 1,674,585 | 37.5 | 4,533,372 | 2,734,884 | 1,798,488 | 39.7 | −2.1 | 7.4 |
| Maine ............... | 1,274,923 | 1,230,297 | 44,626 | 3.5 | 1,328,361 | 1,254,297 | 74,064 | 5.6 | 2.0 | 66.0 |
| Maryland ............. | 5,296,486 | 3,286,547 | 2,009,939 | 37.9 | 5,773,552 | 3,157,958 | 2,615,594 | 45.3 | −3.9 | 30.1 |
| Massachusetts........... | 6,349,097 | 5,198,359 | 1,150,738 | 18.1 | 6,547,629 | 4,984,800 | 1,562,829 | 23.9 | −4.1 | 35.8 |
| Michigan ............. | 9,938,444 | 7,806,691 | 2,131,753 | 21.4 | 9,883,640 | 7,569,939 | 2,313,701 | 23.4 | −3.0 | 8.5 |
| Minnesota ............ | 4,919,479 | 4,337,143 | 582,336 | 11.8 | 5,303,925 | 4,405,142 | 898,783 | 16.9 | 1.6 | 54.3 |
| Mississippi ........... | 2,844,658 | 1,727,908 | 1,116,750 | 39.3 | 2,967,297 | 1,722,287 | 1,245,010 | 42.0 | −0.3 | 11.5 |
| Missouri ............. | 5,595,211 | 4,686,474 | 908,737 | 16.2 | 5,988,927 | 4,850,748 | 1,138,179 | 19.0 | 3.5 | 25.2 |
| Montana ............. | 902,195 | 807,823 | 94,372 | 10.5 | 989,415 | 868,628 | 120,787 | 12.2 | 7.5 | 28.0 |
| Nebraska............. | 1,711,263 | 1,494,494 | 216,769 | 12.7 | 1,826,341 | 1,499,753 | 326,588 | 17.9 | 0.4 | 50.7 |
| Nevada .............. | 1,998,257 | 1,303,001 | 695,256 | 34.8 | 2,700,551 | 1,462,081 | 1,238,470 | 45.9 | 12.2 | 78.1 |
| New Hampshire .......... | 1,235,786 | 1,175,252 | 60,534 | 4.9 | 1,316,470 | 1,215,050 | 101,420 | 7.7 | 3.4 | 67.5 |
| New Jersey ........... | 8,414,350 | 5,557,209 | 2,857,141 | 34.0 | 8,791,894 | 5,214,878 | 3,577,016 | 40.7 | −6.2 | 25.2 |
| New Mexico ........... | 1,819,046 | 813,495 | 1,005,551 | 55.3 | 2,059,179 | 833,810 | 1,225,369 | 59.5 | 2.5 | 21.9 |
| New York ............. | 18,976,457 | 11,760,981 | 7,215,476 | 38.0 | 19,378,102 | 11,304,247 | 8,073,855 | 41.7 | −3.9 | 11.9 |
| North Carolina .......... | 8,049,313 | 5,647,155 | 2,402,158 | 29.8 | 9,535,483 | 6,223,995 | 3,311,488 | 34.7 | 10.2 | 37.9 |
| North Dakota .......... | 642,200 | 589,149 | 53,051 | 8.3 | 672,591 | 598,007 | 74,584 | 11.1 | 1.5 | 40.6 |
| Ohio................ | 11,353,140 | 9,538,111 | 1,815,029 | 16.0 | 11,536,504 | 9,359,263 | 2,177,241 | 18.9 | −1.9 | 20.0 |
| Oklahoma ............ | 3,450,654 | 2,556,368 | 894,286 | 25.9 | 3,751,351 | 2,575,381 | 1,175,970 | 31.3 | 0.7 | 31.5 |
| Oregon .............. | 3,421,399 | 2,857,616 | 563,783 | 16.5 | 3,831,074 | 3,005,848 | 825,226 | 21.5 | 5.2 | 46.4 |
| Pennsylvania........... | 12,281,054 | 10,322,455 | 1,958,599 | 15.9 | 12,702,379 | 10,094,652 | 2,607,727 | 20.5 | −2.2 | 33.1 |
| Rhode Island........... | 1,048,319 | 858,433 | 189,886 | 18.1 | 1,052,567 | 803,685 | 248,882 | 23.6 | −6.4 | 31.1 |
| South Carolina .......... | 4,012,012 | 2,652,291 | 1,359,721 | 33.9 | 4,625,364 | 2,962,740 | 1,662,624 | 35.9 | 11.7 | 22.3 |
| South Dakota .......... | 754,844 | 664,585 | 90,259 | 12.0 | 814,180 | 689,502 | 124,678 | 15.3 | 3.7 | 38.1 |
| Tennessee ........... | 5,689,283 | 4,505,930 | 1,183,353 | 20.8 | 6,346,105 | 4,800,782 | 1,545,323 | 24.4 | 6.5 | 30.6 |
| Texas ............... | 20,851,820 | 10,933,313 | 9,918,507 | 47.6 | 25,145,561 | 11,397,345 | 13,748,216 | 54.7 | 4.2 | 38.6 |
| Utah ................ | 2,233,169 | 1,904,265 | 328,904 | 14.7 | 2,763,885 | 2,221,719 | 542,166 | 19.6 | 16.7 | 64.8 |
| Vermont ............. | 608,827 | 585,431 | 23,396 | 3.8 | 625,741 | 590,223 | 35,518 | 5.7 | 0.8 | 51.8 |
| Virginia.............. | 7,078,515 | 4,965,637 | 2,112,878 | 29.8 | 8,001,024 | 5,186,450 | 2,814,574 | 35.2 | 4.4 | 33.2 |
| Washington ........... | 5,894,121 | 4,652,490 | 1,241,631 | 21.1 | 6,724,540 | 4,876,804 | 1,847,736 | 27.5 | 4.8 | 48.8 |
| West Virginia .......... | 1,808,344 | 1,709,966 | 98,378 | 5.4 | 1,852,994 | 1,726,256 | 126,738 | 6.8 | 1.0 | 28.8 |
| Wisconsin ............ | 5,363,675 | 4,681,630 | 682,045 | 12.7 | 5,686,986 | 4,738,411 | 948,575 | 16.7 | 1.2 | 39.1 |
| Wyoming ............. | 493,782 | 438,799 | 54,983 | 11.1 | 563,626 | 483,874 | 79,752 | 14.1 | 10.3 | 45.0 |
| **Puerto Rico .............** | 3,808,610 | 33,966 | 3,774,644 | 99.1 | 3,725,789 | 26,946 | 3,698,843 | 99.3 | −20.7 | −2.0 |

[1] For this report, "minority" refers to people who reported their ethnicity and race as something other than non-Hispanic White alone in the decennial census.

Sources: U.S. Census Bureau, *Census 2000 Redistricting Data (Public Law 94-171) Summary File*, Tables PL1 and PL2; and *2010 Census Redistricting Data (Public Law 94-171) Summary File*, Tables P1 and P2.

**Texas joined California, the District of Columbia, Hawaii, and New Mexico in having a "majority-minority" population.**

In California, the District of Columbia, Hawaii, New Mexico, and Texas, the population was majority-minority (i.e., over 50 percent of the population was minority) in 2010 (see Table 11). Hawaii had the highest proportion minority (77 percent), followed by California and New Mexico, each with 60 percent. California, New Mexico, and Hawaii had a majority-minority population in 2000 as well, and this population grew 24 percent, 22 percent, and 13 percent, respectively, between 2000 and 2010. About 55 percent of Texas' population was minority in 2010, up from 48 percent in 2000. Over the decade, the minority population in Texas grew by 39 percent. The District of Columbia's population was also majority-minority (65 percent) but was down from 72 percent in 2000.

In 2010, the vast majority of the population identified as non-Hispanic White alone in four states. In the New England area, Maine, New Hampshire, and Vermont all had populations that were predominantly non-Hispanic White alone (94 percent, 92 percent, and 94 percent, respectively). The minority population grew by at least 50 percent in each of these states between 2000 and 2010—by 66 percent in Maine, by 68 percent in New Hampshire, and by 52 percent in Vermont, which outpaced growth of the non-Hispanic White alone population (2 percent, 3 percent, and 1 percent, respectively). West Virginia also had a predominantly non-Hispanic White alone population in 2010 (93 percent). While West Virginia's non-Hispanic White alone population increased by 1 percent over the decade, the

state's minority population grew 29 percent.

**Nevada's minority population grew the fastest between 2000 and 2010.**

There were a number of other states where significant proportions of the population were minority. The minority population in Arizona, Florida, Georgia, Maryland, and Nevada approached 50 percent in 2010. Among these states, Nevada had the highest proportion minority (46 percent), followed by Maryland (45 percent), Georgia (44 percent), and Arizona and Florida (each about 42 percent).

The minority population grew in all 50 states between 2000 and 2010. Among all states, Nevada's minority population increased the most (78 percent). Each of the five states that had a proportion minority approaching 50 percent also experienced at least 30 percent growth in this population. The minority population grew by 40 percent in Georgia and by 30 percent in Maryland across the decade. Arizona's and Florida's minority population increased even more (45 percent and 43 percent, respectively). In the District of Columbia, the minority population declined by 5 percent.

The non-Hispanic White alone population also experienced growth between 2000 and 2010 in 35 states and the District of Columbia. Eight states and the District of Columbia had non-Hispanic White alone populations that increased at least 10 percent between the decennial censuses. The District of Columbia had the largest percentage increase in the non-Hispanic White alone population (32 percent), followed by Utah (17 percent), Idaho (16 percent), and Arizona (13 percent). Hawaii, Nevada, and South Carolina all

had about 12 percent growth in the non-Hispanic White alone population. The non-Hispanic White alone population grew by about 10 percent in North Carolina and Wyoming.

The non-Hispanic White alone population declined in 15 states between 2000 and 2010. Eleven of the states with declines in the non-Hispanic White alone population were in the Northeast and Midwest. In particular, 6 of the 9 states in the Northeast had declines in the non-Hispanic White alone population—Connecticut (–4 percent), Massachusetts (–4 percent), New Jersey (–6 percent), New York (–4 percent), Pennsylvania (–2 percent), and Rhode Island (–6 percent). The five states in the Midwest with declines in the non-Hispanic White alone population were Illinois (–3 percent), Iowa (–0.3 percent), Kansas (–0.2 percent), Michigan (–3 percent), and Ohio (–2 percent). Fewer states in the South saw declines in the non-Hispanic White alone population (Louisiana, –2 percent; Maryland, –4 percent; and Mississippi, –0.3 percent). California was the only state in the West with a non-Hispanic White alone population that declined (–5 percent).

**In about one-tenth of all counties, the minority population composed 50 percent or more of the total population.**

Out of 3,143 counties, there were 348 where at least half of the population was minority in 2010 (see Figure 4). The minority population was concentrated in counties along the East coast from Massachusetts to Florida and in counties within the Gulf Coast states of Alabama, Mississippi, and Louisiana. A band of counties where a high proportion of the population was minority stretched

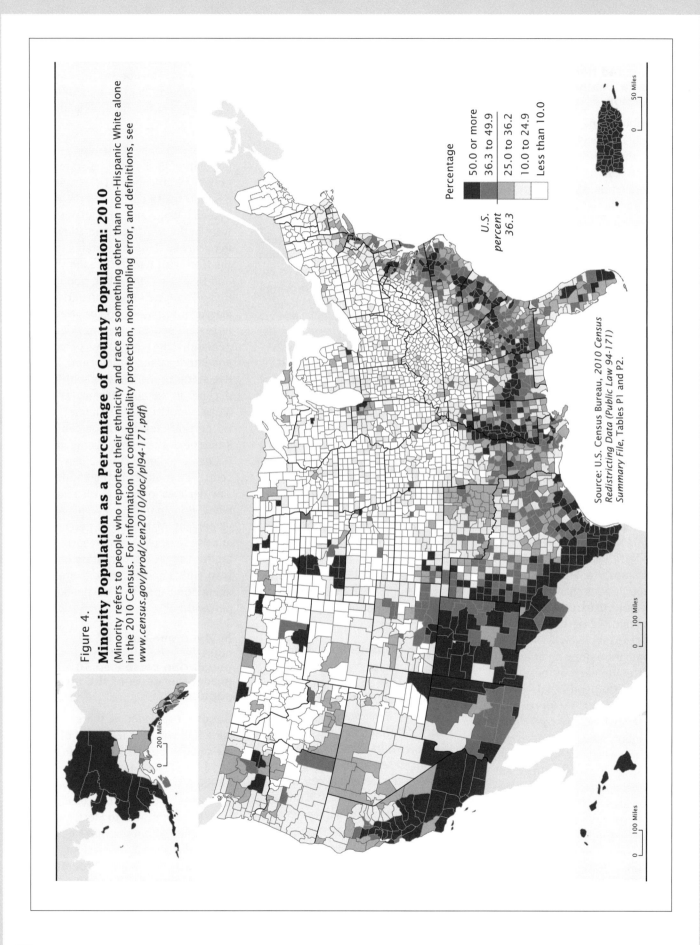

Figure 4.

**Minority Population as a Percentage of County Population: 2010**

(Minority refers to people who reported their ethnicity and race as something other than non-Hispanic White alone in the 2010 Census. For information on confidentiality protection, nonsampling error, and definitions, see www.census.gov/prod/cen2010/doc/pl94-171.pdf)

Percentage

50.0 or more
36.3 to 49.9
25.0 to 36.2
10.0 to 24.9
Less than 10.0

U.S. percent
36.3

Source: U.S. Census Bureau, 2010 Census Redistricting Data (Public Law 94-171) Summary File, Tables P1 and P2.

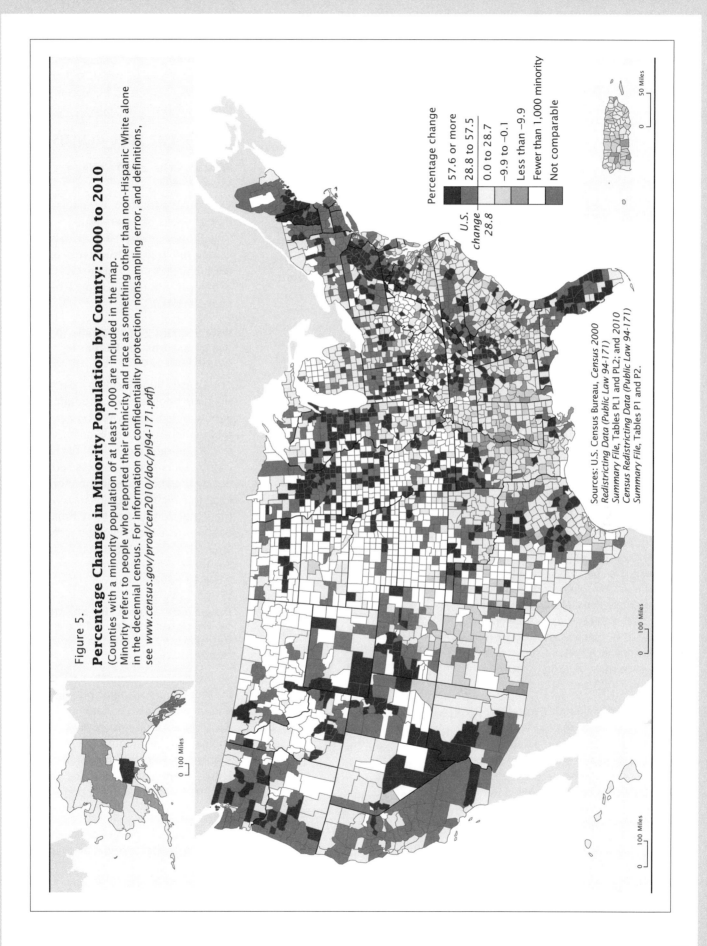

Figure 5.

**Percentage Change in Minority Population by County: 2000 to 2010**

(Counties with a minority population of at least 1,000 are included in the map. Minority refers to people who reported their ethnicity and race as something other than non-Hispanic White alone in the decennial census. For information on confidentiality protection, nonsampling error, and definitions, see *www.census.gov/prod/cen2010/doc/pl94-171.pdf*)

Percentage change

- 57.6 or more
- 28.8 to 57.5
- 0.0 to 28.7
- –9.9 to –0.1
- Less than –9.9
- Fewer than 1,000 minority
- Not comparable

U.S. change 28.8

Sources: U.S. Census Bureau, *Census 2000 Redistricting Data (Public Law 94-171) Summary File*, Tables PL1 and PL2; and 2010 *Census Redistricting Data (Public Law 94-171) Summary File*, Tables P1 and P2.

across the southwest through the states lining the U.S.-Mexico border (Texas, New Mexico, Arizona, and California). Additionally, counties in states along the Pacific coast, and in Hawaii and Alaska, also had high proportions of the population that were minority.

In 2010, there were 1,205 counties where less than 10 percent of the population was minority. The majority of these counties were located in Appalachia, in the upper Northeast, and in the central and upper Midwest.

### Growth in the minority population occurred in many counties across the nation.

The map in Figure 5 illustrates the percentage change in the minority population between 2000 and 2010 for counties with a minority population of at least 1,000 in 2010. Minority population growth was concentrated in counties in the Pacific Northwest, Pacific Southwest, western Arizona, southern Nevada, and areas of the interior West. Counties in the mid-Atlantic corridor, Florida, and in clusters throughout the southeastern states also had significant growth in their minority population. Additionally, multiple groupings of counties in Texas, northern Illinois, southern Wisconsin, and southern Minnesota experienced substantial growth in their minority population between 2000 and 2010.

There were 53 counties with a minority population of at least 1,000 that experienced a decline of at least 10 percent in their minority population between 2000 and 2010. Many of these counties were located along the Mississippi River in Arkansas, Louisiana, and

Mississippi, as well as in central and western Alabama.

## SUMMARY

This report presented data from the 2010 Census that illustrated the nation's changing racial and ethnic diversity. The examination of racial and ethnic group distributions nationally shows that while the non-Hispanic White alone population is still numerically and proportionally the largest major race and ethnic group in the United States, it is also growing at the slowest rate. During the past 10 years, it has been the Hispanic population and the Asian population that have grown considerably, in part due to relatively higher levels of immigration.

Additional notable trends were presented in this report. The Black population, the second-largest major race group, did experience growth over the decade; however, it grew at a slower rate than all other major race groups except for White. Racial classification issues continue to persist among those who identify as Hispanic, resulting in a substantial proportion of that population being categorized as Some Other Race. People reporting more than one race was another fast-growing population and made up large proportions of the American Indian and Alaska Native population and Native Hawaiian and Other Pacific Islander population. Geographically, there are a number of areas, particularly in the South and West, that have large proportions minority, which also grew considerably between 2000 and 2010. Overall, the U.S. population has become more racially and ethnically diverse over time. Throughout the decade, the Census

Bureau will release additional information on race and Hispanic origin population groups, which will provide more insights to the nation's racial and ethnic diversity.

## ABOUT THE 2010 CENSUS

### Why was the 2010 Census conducted?

The U.S. Constitution mandates that a census be taken in the United States every 10 years. This is required in order to determine the number of seats each state is to receive in the U.S. House of Representatives.

### Why did the 2010 Census ask the questions on Hispanic origin and race?

The Census Bureau collects data on Hispanic origin and race to fulfill a variety of legislative and program requirements. Data on Hispanic origin and race are used in the legislative redistricting process carried out by the states and in monitoring local jurisdictions' compliance with the Voting Rights Act. More broadly, data on Hispanic origin and race are critical for research that underlies many policy decisions at all levels of government.

### How do data from the question on Hispanic origin and race benefit me, my family, and my community?

All levels of government need information on Hispanic origin and race to implement and evaluate programs, or enforce laws, such as the Civil Rights Act, Voting Rights Act, Fair Housing Act, Equal Employment Opportunity Act, and the 2010 Census Redistricting Data Program.

Both public and private organizations use Hispanic origin and race information to find areas where groups may need special services and to plan and implement education, housing, health, and other programs that address these needs. For example, a school system might use this information to design cultural activities that reflect the diversity in their community, or a business could use it to select the mix of merchandise it will sell in a new store. Census information also helps identify areas where residents might need services of particular importance to certain racial or ethnic groups, such as screening for hypertension or diabetes.

## FOR MORE INFORMATION

For more information on race and Hispanic origin in the United States, visit the Census Bureau's Internet site at <www.census.gov /population/www/socdemo /hispanic/hispanic.html> and <www.census.gov/population /www/socdemo/race/race.html>.

Information on confidentiality protection, nonsampling error, and definitions is available at <www.census.gov/prod/cen2010 /doc/pl94-171.pdf>.

Data on race and Hispanic origin from the *2010 Census Redistricting Data (Public Law 94-171) Summary File* were released on a state-by-state basis. The 2010 Census redistricting data are available on the Internet at <http://factfinder2 .census.gov/main.html> and on DVD.

For more information on specific race and ethnic groups in the United States, go to <www.census .gov/> and click on "Minority Links." This Web page includes information about the 2010 Census and provides links to reports based on past censuses and surveys focusing on the social and economic characteristics of the Hispanic or Latino, Black or African American, American Indian and

Alaska Native, Asian, and Native Hawaiian and Other Pacific Islander populations.

Information on other population and housing topics is presented in the 2010 Census Briefs series, located on the Census Bureau's Web site at <www.census.gov/prod /cen2010/>. This series presents information about race, Hispanic origin, age, sex, household type, housing tenure, and people who reside in group quarters.

For more information about the 2010 Census, including data products, call the Customer Services Center at 1-800-923-8282. You can also visit the Census Bureau's Question and Answer Center at <ask.census.gov> to submit your questions online.

# Population Distribution and Change: 2000 to 2010

*2010 Census Briefs*

Issued March 2011

C2010BR-01

By
Paul Mackun
and
Steven Wilson

(With Thomas Fischetti
and Justyna Goworowska)

## INTRODUCTION

The 2010 Census reported 308.7 million people in the United States, a 9.7 percent increase from the Census 2000 population of 281.4 million. This report discusses population change between 2000 and 2010 for several geographic levels, including regions, states, metropolitan and micropolitan statistical areas, counties, and places.

## NATIONAL AND REGIONAL CHANGE

The increase of 9.7 percent over the last decade was lower than the 13.2 percent increase for the 1990s and comparable to the growth during the 1980s of 9.8 percent (Figure 1). Since 1900, only the 1930s experienced a lower growth rate (7.3 percent) than this past decade.[1]

From 2000 to 2010, regional growth was much faster for the South and West (14.3 and 13.8 percent, respectively) than for the Midwest (3.9 percent) and Northeast (3.2 percent)

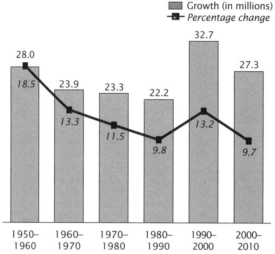

Figure 1.
**U.S. Population Change: 1950–1960 to 2000–2010**
(For more information on confidentiality protection, nonsampling error, and definitions, see *www.census.gov/prod/cen2010/doc/pl94-171.pdf*)

Growth (in millions)
Percentage change

Note: Change for 1950–1960 includes the populations of Alaska and Hawaii in the U.S. total, although they were not U.S. states at the time of the 1950 census.

Source: U.S. Census Bureau, 2010 Census; Census 2000; Frank Hobbs and Nicole Stoops, *Demographic Trends in the 20th Century*, Census 2000 Special Reports, CENSR-4, U.S. Census Bureau, Washington, DC, 2002; and Richard L. Forstall, *Population of States and Counties of the United States: 1790 to 1990*, U.S. Census Bureau, Washington, DC, 1996.

[1] References to historical data in the report are based on the Census 2000 PHC-T series <www.census.gov/population/www/cen2000/briefs/tablist.html>; Frank Hobbs and Nicole Stoops, *Demographic Trends in the 20th Century*, Census 2000 Special Reports, CENSR-4, U.S. Census Bureau, Washington, DC, 2002; and Richard L. Forstall, *Population of States and Counties of the United States: 1790 to 1990*, U.S. Census Bureau, Washington, DC, 1996. National historical data calculations before 1960 include Alaska and Hawaii.

(Table 1, Figure 2). The South grew by 14.3 million over the decade to 114.6 million people, while the West increased by 8.7 million to reach 71.9 million people—surpassing the population of the Midwest. The Midwest gained 2.5 million, increasing that region's population to 66.9 million, and the Northeast's gain of 1.7 million brought that region's

U.S. Department of Commerce
Economics and Statistics Administration
U.S. CENSUS BUREAU

Table 1.
## Population Change for the United States, Regions, States, and Puerto Rico: 2000 to 2010

(For information on confidentiality protection, nonsampling error, and definitions, see www.census.gov/prod/cen2010/doc/pl94-171.pdf)

| Area | Population 2000 | Population 2010 | Change Number | Change Percent |
|---|---|---|---|---|
| United States......... | 281,421,906 | 308,745,538 | 27,323,632 | 9.7 |
| **REGION** | | | | |
| Northeast................... | 53,594,378 | 55,317,240 | 1,722,862 | 3.2 |
| Midwest.................... | 64,392,776 | 66,927,001 | 2,534,225 | 3.9 |
| South...................... | 100,236,820 | 114,555,744 | 14,318,924 | 14.3 |
| West ..................... | 63,197,932 | 71,945,553 | 8,747,621 | 13.8 |
| **STATE** | | | | |
| Alabama .................. | 4,447,100 | 4,779,736 | 332,636 | 7.5 |
| Alaska .................... | 626,932 | 710,231 | 83,299 | 13.3 |
| Arizona ................... | 5,130,632 | 6,392,017 | 1,261,385 | 24.6 |
| Arkansas ................. | 2,673,400 | 2,915,918 | 242,518 | 9.1 |
| California ................. | 33,871,648 | 37,253,956 | 3,382,308 | 10.0 |
| Colorado ................. | 4,301,261 | 5,029,196 | 727,935 | 16.9 |
| Connecticut .............. | 3,405,565 | 3,574,097 | 168,532 | 4.9 |
| Delaware ................. | 783,600 | 897,934 | 114,334 | 14.6 |
| District of Columbia .......... | 572,059 | 601,723 | 29,664 | 5.2 |
| Florida ................... | 15,982,378 | 18,801,310 | 2,818,932 | 17.6 |
| Georgia .................. | 8,186,453 | 9,687,653 | 1,501,200 | 18.3 |
| Hawaii ................... | 1,211,537 | 1,360,301 | 148,764 | 12.3 |
| Idaho .................... | 1,293,953 | 1,567,582 | 273,629 | 21.1 |
| Illinois.................... | 12,419,293 | 12,830,632 | 411,339 | 3.3 |
| Indiana................... | 6,080,485 | 6,483,802 | 403,317 | 6.6 |
| Iowa..................... | 2,926,324 | 3,046,355 | 120,031 | 4.1 |
| Kansas................... | 2,688,418 | 2,853,118 | 164,700 | 6.1 |
| Kentucky ................. | 4,041,769 | 4,339,367 | 297,598 | 7.4 |
| Louisiana................. | 4,468,976 | 4,533,372 | 64,396 | 1.4 |
| Maine.................... | 1,274,923 | 1,328,361 | 53,438 | 4.2 |
| Maryland ................. | 5,296,486 | 5,773,552 | 477,066 | 9.0 |
| Massachusetts............. | 6,349,097 | 6,547,629 | 198,532 | 3.1 |
| Michigan ................. | 9,938,444 | 9,883,640 | −54,804 | −0.6 |
| Minnesota ................ | 4,919,479 | 5,303,925 | 384,446 | 7.8 |
| Mississippi................ | 2,844,658 | 2,967,297 | 122,639 | 4.3 |
| Missouri.................. | 5,595,211 | 5,988,927 | 393,716 | 7.0 |
| Montana.................. | 902,195 | 989,415 | 87,220 | 9.7 |
| Nebraska................. | 1,711,263 | 1,826,341 | 115,078 | 6.7 |
| Nevada .................. | 1,998,257 | 2,700,551 | 702,294 | 35.1 |
| New Hampshire............. | 1,235,786 | 1,316,470 | 80,684 | 6.5 |
| New Jersey ............... | 8,414,350 | 8,791,894 | 377,544 | 4.5 |
| New Mexico............... | 1,819,046 | 2,059,179 | 240,133 | 13.2 |
| New York................. | 18,976,457 | 19,378,102 | 401,645 | 2.1 |
| North Carolina............. | 8,049,313 | 9,535,483 | 1,486,170 | 18.5 |
| North Dakota.............. | 642,200 | 672,591 | 30,391 | 4.7 |
| Ohio..................... | 11,353,140 | 11,536,504 | 183,364 | 1.6 |
| Oklahoma ................ | 3,450,654 | 3,751,351 | 300,697 | 8.7 |
| Oregon................... | 3,421,399 | 3,831,074 | 409,675 | 12.0 |
| Pennsylvania.............. | 12,281,054 | 12,702,379 | 421,325 | 3.4 |
| Rhode Island.............. | 1,048,319 | 1,052,567 | 4,248 | 0.4 |
| South Carolina............. | 4,012,012 | 4,625,364 | 613,352 | 15.3 |
| South Dakota.............. | 754,844 | 814,180 | 59,336 | 7.9 |
| Tennessee................ | 5,689,283 | 6,346,105 | 656,822 | 11.5 |
| Texas.................... | 20,851,820 | 25,145,561 | 4,293,741 | 20.6 |
| Utah..................... | 2,233,169 | 2,763,885 | 530,716 | 23.8 |
| Vermont.................. | 608,827 | 625,741 | 16,914 | 2.8 |
| Virginia................... | 7,078,515 | 8,001,024 | 922,509 | 13.0 |
| Washington ............... | 5,894,121 | 6,724,540 | 830,419 | 14.1 |
| West Virginia ............. | 1,808,344 | 1,852,994 | 44,650 | 2.5 |
| Wisconsin ................ | 5,363,675 | 5,686,986 | 323,311 | 6.0 |
| Wyoming ................. | 493,782 | 563,626 | 69,844 | 14.1 |
| **Puerto Rico** ............. | 3,808,610 | 3,725,789 | −82,821 | −2.2 |

Source: U.S. Census Bureau, 2010 Census and Census 2000.

population to 55.3 million. Overall, the South and West accounted for 84.4 percent of the U.S. population increase from 2000 to 2010, an increase from their 77.0 percent share of the total change from 1990 to 2000.

## STATE-LEVEL CHANGE

Nevada was the fastest-growing state between 2000 and 2010, growing by 35.1 percent (Table 1). It was followed by Arizona (24.6 percent), Utah (23.8 percent), Idaho (21.1 percent), and Texas (20.6 percent). Rhode Island, Louisiana, and Ohio were the slowest-increasing states, all of which grew by less than 2.0 percent. Unlike the 1990s in which every state grew, one state (Michigan) declined over this decade, losing 0.6 percent of its population.[2] (Puerto Rico's population declined by 2.2 percent to 3.7 million people.)

Between 2000 and 2010, Texas experienced the highest numeric increase, up by 4.3 million people. California, which had the largest population increase in the previous decade, increased by 3.4 million over the same period; followed by Florida (2.8 million), Georgia (1.5 million), North Carolina (1.5 million), and Arizona (1.3 million). These six states, which were the only states to gain over a million people during the decade, accounted for over half (54.0 percent) of the overall increase for the United States.

The concentration of high percentage changes among the western and southern states maintains a pattern from recent decades (Figure 3). Nevada is the only state that has maintained a growth rate of 25.0 percent or greater for the last three decades; it has been the fastest-growing state for five

---

[2] The District of Columbia's population declined between 1990 and 2000.

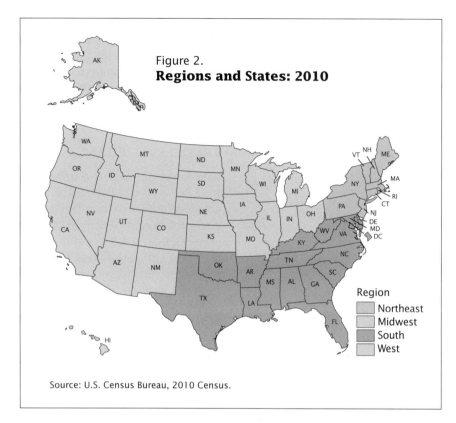

Figure 2.
**Regions and States: 2010**

Region
Northeast
Midwest
South
West

Source: U.S. Census Bureau, 2010 Census.

2010, the fifth straight decade it has grown at a rate faster than any other state in the Northeast. Whereas New York and New Jersey had the largest numeric gains in the region in the 1990s, Pennsylvania gained the most population in the region between 2000 and 2010, increasing by 421,000 people.

South Dakota, growing by 7.9 percent between 2000 and 2010, was the fastest-growing state in the Midwest during this period—replacing Minnesota, which had been the fastest-growing state over the previous three decades. Illinois and Indiana had the largest numeric increases in that region over the decade, increasing by 411,000 and 403,000, respectively.

## MOST POPULOUS STATES

The ten most populous states contained 54.0 percent of the U.S. population in 2010 (similar to the percentage in 2000) with one-fourth (26.5 percent) of the U.S. population in the three largest states: California (the most populous state since the 1970 Census), Texas, and New York. These three states had April 1, 2010, populations of

straight decades. Six states, including five in the West, grew by 25.0 percent or more between 1990 and 2000. Wyoming, after having lost population between 1980 and 1990, has grown over the past two decades, surpassing the national level between 2000 and

2010. Between 2000 and 2010, the District of Columbia experienced its first decennial population increase since the 1940s, increasing by 5.2 percent to surpass 600,000 people.

New Hampshire increased by 6.5 percent between 2000 and

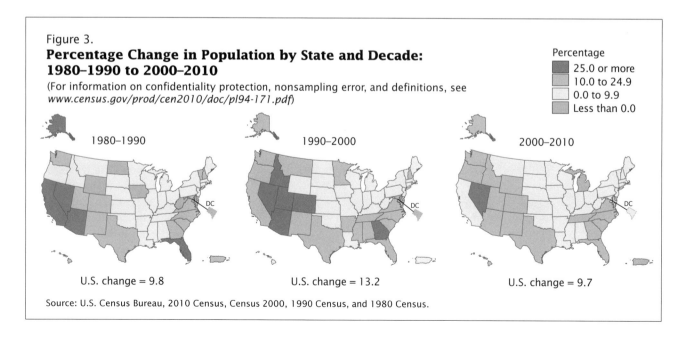

Figure 3.
**Percentage Change in Population by State and Decade: 1980–1990 to 2000–2010**
(For information on confidentiality protection, nonsampling error, and definitions, see *www.census.gov/prod/cen2010/doc/pl94-171.pdf*)

Percentage
25.0 or more
10.0 to 24.9
0.0 to 9.9
Less than 0.0

1980–1990

1990–2000

2000–2010

U.S. change = 9.8

U.S. change = 13.2

U.S. change = 9.7

Source: U.S. Census Bureau, 2010 Census, Census 2000, 1990 Census, and 1980 Census.

37.3 million, 25.1 million, and 19.4 million, respectively. The next seven most populous states—Florida, Illinois, Pennsylvania, Ohio, Michigan, Georgia, and North Carolina—contained an additional 27.5 percent of the population. Nine of the ten largest states in 2000 were also among the ten largest in 2010. North Carolina, which was the eleventh largest state in 2000, moved into the top ten for 2010 (tenth largest)—replacing New Jersey, which fell from ninth largest in 2000 to eleventh in 2010.

The ten most populous and the ten least populous states are distributed among the four regions. The South contained the greatest number (four) of the ten largest states, with three others in the Midwest, two in the Northeast, and one in the West. Furthermore, the Northeast contained four of the ten least populous states (Maine, New Hampshire, Rhode Island, and Vermont), with three others in the West (Alaska, Montana, and Wyoming), two in the Midwest (North Dakota and South Dakota), and one in the South (Delaware).

## METROPOLITAN AND MICROPOLITAN STATISTICAL AREAS

Over four-fifths (83.7 percent) of the U.S. population in 2010 lived in the nation's 366 metro areas, and another one-tenth (10.0 percent)

**Metropolitan and micropolitan statistical areas**—metro and micro areas—are geographic entities defined by the U.S. Office of Management and Budget for use by federal statistical agencies in collecting, tabulating, and publishing federal statistics. Metro and micro areas are collectively known as core based statistical areas (CBSAs). A metro area contains a core urban area population of 50,000 or more. A micro area contains a core urban area population of at least 10,000 (but less than 50,000). Each metro or micro area consists of one or more counties and includes the counties containing the core urban area, as well as any adjacent counties that have a high degree of social and economic integration (as measured by commuting to work) with the urban core.

of the population resided in the nation's 576 micro areas (Table 2). Metro areas grew almost twice as fast as micro areas, 10.8 percent compared to 5.9 percent. Population growth of at least twice the national rate occurred in many metro and micro areas, such as some areas in parts of California, Nevada, Arizona, Texas, Florida, and the Carolinas. No metro area in the West region declined (Figure 4).

All ten of the most populous metro areas in 2010 grew over the decade, with Houston, Atlanta, and Dallas-Fort Worth (26.1 percent, 24.0 percent, and 23.4 percent, respectively) the fastest-growing among them (Table 3). The Atlanta metro area accounted for over one-half (54.4 percent) of Georgia's 2010 population and over two-thirds (68.0 percent) of the state's population growth during the last decade. In addition, the Houston

and Dallas-Fort Worth metro areas together accounted for almost one-half (49.0 percent) of Texas' population and over one-half (56.9 percent) of its population growth.

Two other top-ten metro areas experienced double-digit growth: Washington, DC (16.4 percent) and Miami (11.1 percent). The New York metro area, with a population of 18.9 million (6.1 percent of the U.S. population), and Los Angeles, with a population of 12.8 million (4.2 percent of the U.S. population), were the two most populous metro areas in the nation. Combined, approximately 1 of every 10 people in the United States lived in either the New York or Los Angeles metro areas in 2010.

Among all 366 metro areas, Palm Coast, FL, was the fastest-growing between 2000 and 2010 (up 92.0 percent), followed by St. George, UT, (up 52.9 percent), and by three

Table 2.
## Population by Core Based Statistical Area (CBSA) Status: 2000 and 2010

(For information on confidentiality protection, nonsampling error, and definitions, see *www.census.gov/prod/cen2010/doc/pl94-171.pdf*)

| Area | Population | | Share of U.S. population | | Change | |
|---|---|---|---|---|---|---|
| | 2000 | 2010 | 2000 | 2010 | Number | Percent |
| United States...................... | 281,421,906 | 308,745,538 | 100.0 | 100.0 | 27,323,632 | 9.7 |
| Inside CBSA ............................. | 262,290,227 | 289,261,315 | 93.2 | 93.7 | 26,971,088 | 10.3 |
| Metropolitan............................ | 233,069,827 | 258,317,763 | 82.8 | 83.7 | 25,247,936 | 10.8 |
| Micropolitan............................ | 29,220,400 | 30,943,552 | 10.4 | 10.0 | 1,723,152 | 5.9 |
| Outside CBSA............................. | 19,131,679 | 19,484,223 | 6.8 | 6.3 | 352,544 | 1.8 |

Note: Metropolitan and micropolitan statistical areas defined by the Office of Management and Budget as of December 2009.

Source: U.S. Census Bureau, 2010 Census and Census 2000.

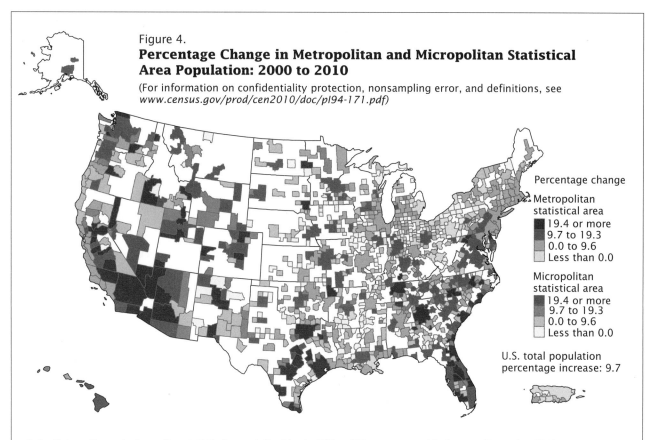

Figure 4.
**Percentage Change in Metropolitan and Micropolitan Statistical Area Population: 2000 to 2010**

(For information on confidentiality protection, nonsampling error, and definitions, see www.census.gov/prod/cen2010/doc/pl94-171.pdf)

Percentage change

Metropolitan statistical area
- 19.4 or more
- 9.7 to 19.3
- 0.0 to 9.6
- Less than 0.0

Micropolitan statistical area
- 19.4 or more
- 9.7 to 19.3
- 0.0 to 9.6
- Less than 0.0

U.S. total population percentage increase: 9.7

Note: Metropolitan and micropolitan statistical areas defined by the Office of Management and Budget as of December 2009. Broomfield County, CO, was formed from parts of Adams, Boulder, Jefferson, and Weld Counties, CO, on November 15, 2001, and was coextensive with Broomfield city. For purposes of presenting data for metropolitan and micropolitan statistical areas, Broomfield is treated as if it were a county at the time of Census 2000.

Source: U.S. Census Bureau, 2010 Census and Census 2000.

other areas with population growth rates over 40.0 percent: Las Vegas, Raleigh, and Cape Coral (Table 3).

The ten fastest-growing metro areas included both large and small metro areas, ranging from three areas with 2010 populations of more than 1.0 million (Las Vegas, Austin, and Raleigh) to one below 100,000 (Palm Coast, FL). The Las Vegas metro area accounted for almost three-quarters (72.3 percent) of Nevada's 2010 population and over four-fifths (81.9 percent) of the state's growth.

Many of the fast-growing micro areas were located near fast-growing metro areas. Likewise, many of the micro areas that were slow-growing or declining were located near slow-growing or declining metro areas.

## COUNTIES

Almost two-thirds of the nation's 3,143 counties gained population between 2000 and 2010. Most counties along the Pacific, Atlantic, and Gulf Coasts grew between 2000 and 2010, as did most counties adjacent to the southern U.S. border (Figure 5). Furthermore, many counties in the South— such as those in parts of Florida, northern Georgia, North Carolina, Virginia, and the eastern half of Texas—experienced growth at or above 10 percent. In the West, all counties in Utah experienced population growth in the last decade, with some of those gains being

25 percent or more. Most New England counties grew, but most of these increased at rates below 10 percent.[3]

The counties that lost population were mostly regionally clustered and mirrored decades of population loss for those areas; for example, many Appalachian counties in eastern Kentucky and West Virginia; many Great Plains counties in the Dakotas, Kansas, Nebraska, and Texas; and a group of counties in and around the Mississippi Delta saw population declines. In addition, many counties along the Great Lakes and on the northern U.S.

---
[3] New England consists of Maine, New Hampshire, Vermont, Massachusetts, Rhode Island, and Connecticut.

Table 3.
## Population Change for the Ten Most Populous and Ten Fastest-Growing Metropolitan Statistical Areas: 2000 to 2010

(For information on confidentiality protection, nonsampling error, and definitions, see *www.census.gov/prod/cen2010/doc/pl94-171.pdf*)

| Metropolitan statistical area | Population | | Change | |
|---|---|---|---|---|
| | 2000 | 2010 | Number | Percent |
| **MOST POPULOUS** | | | | |
| New York-Northern New Jersey-Long Island, NY-NJ-PA . . . . . . . . . . . . . . . . . | 18,323,002 | 18,897,109 | 574,107 | 3.1 |
| Los Angeles-Long Beach-Santa Ana, CA . . . . . . . . . . . . . . . . . . . . . . . . . . . | 12,365,627 | 12,828,837 | 463,210 | 3.7 |
| Chicago-Joliet-Naperville, IL-IN-WI . . . . . . . . . . . . . . . . . . . . . . . . . . . . . . . | 9,098,316 | 9,461,105 | 362,789 | 4.0 |
| Dallas-Fort Worth-Arlington, TX. . . . . . . . . . . . . . . . . . . . . . . . . . . . . . . . . . | 5,161,544 | 6,371,773 | 1,210,229 | 23.4 |
| Philadelphia-Camden-Wilmington, PA-NJ-DE-MD . . . . . . . . . . . . . . . . . . . . | 5,687,147 | 5,965,343 | 278,196 | 4.9 |
| Houston-Sugar Land-Baytown, TX . . . . . . . . . . . . . . . . . . . . . . . . . . . . . . . | 4,715,407 | 5,946,800 | 1,231,393 | 26.1 |
| Washington-Arlington-Alexandria, DC-VA-MD-WV . . . . . . . . . . . . . . . . . . . . | 4,796,183 | 5,582,170 | 785,987 | 16.4 |
| Miami-Fort Lauderdale-Pompano Beach, FL. . . . . . . . . . . . . . . . . . . . . . . . | 5,007,564 | 5,564,635 | 557,071 | 11.1 |
| Atlanta-Sandy Springs-Marietta, GA . . . . . . . . . . . . . . . . . . . . . . . . . . . . . | 4,247,981 | 5,268,860 | 1,020,879 | 24.0 |
| Boston-Cambridge-Quincy, MA-NH. . . . . . . . . . . . . . . . . . . . . . . . . . . . . . | 4,391,344 | 4,552,402 | 161,058 | 3.7 |
| **FASTEST-GROWING** | | | | |
| Palm Coast, FL . . . . . . . . . . . . . . . . . . . . . . . . . . . . . . . . . . . . . . . . . . . . | 49,832 | 95,696 | 45,864 | 92.0 |
| St. George, UT. . . . . . . . . . . . . . . . . . . . . . . . . . . . . . . . . . . . . . . . . . . . | 90,354 | 138,115 | 47,761 | 52.9 |
| Las Vegas-Paradise, NV . . . . . . . . . . . . . . . . . . . . . . . . . . . . . . . . . . . . . | 1,375,765 | 1,951,269 | 575,504 | 41.8 |
| Raleigh-Cary, NC. . . . . . . . . . . . . . . . . . . . . . . . . . . . . . . . . . . . . . . . . . | 797,071 | 1,130,490 | 333,419 | 41.8 |
| Cape Coral-Fort Myers, FL . . . . . . . . . . . . . . . . . . . . . . . . . . . . . . . . . . . | 440,888 | 618,754 | 177,866 | 40.3 |
| Provo-Orem, UT . . . . . . . . . . . . . . . . . . . . . . . . . . . . . . . . . . . . . . . . . . | 376,774 | 526,810 | 150,036 | 39.8 |
| Greeley, CO. . . . . . . . . . . . . . . . . . . . . . . . . . . . . . . . . . . . . . . . . . . . . . | 180,926 | 252,825 | 71,899 | 39.7 |
| Austin-Round Rock-San Marcos, TX. . . . . . . . . . . . . . . . . . . . . . . . . . . . . | 1,249,763 | 1,716,289 | 466,526 | 37.3 |
| Myrtle Beach-North Myrtle Beach-Conway, SC . . . . . . . . . . . . . . . . . . . . . | 196,629 | 269,291 | 72,662 | 37.0 |
| Bend, OR. . . . . . . . . . . . . . . . . . . . . . . . . . . . . . . . . . . . . . . . . . . . . . . | 115,367 | 157,733 | 42,366 | 36.7 |

Note: The full names of the metropolitan statistical areas are shown in this table; abbreviated versions of the names are shown in the text.
Source: U.S. Census Bureau, 2010 Census and Census 2000.

border either lost population or grew below 10 percent.

Some counties in midwestern metro areas grew rapidly (50 percent or more), even though the surrounding counties grew more slowly or declined. Examples include (metro area in parentheses): Delaware County, OH, (Columbus); Hamilton County, IN, (Indianapolis); Kendall County, IL, (Chicago), and Dallas County, IA, (Des Moines).

Some counties with the largest numeric gains in population contained large cities, such as Phoenix and Houston. Some of the largest numeric losses also occurred in counties containing or coextensive with large cities, such as Detroit, Chicago, Cleveland, Pittsburgh, Buffalo, Baltimore, St. Louis, and New Orleans. Not surprisingly, many of the counties with large numeric change were also the ones with large populations (Figure 6), such as some counties in parts of

California, Arizona, Texas, Florida, and in the corridor from Boston to Washington, DC. In contrast to the many large counties found in California, for example, the most populous counties in states such as Montana, Wyoming, and the Dakotas were much smaller. In fact, none of these four states contained a county with a 2010 Census population of 200,000 or more. Montana and South Dakota each possessed only two counties with populations of 100,000 or more; North Dakota only contained one; and Wyoming did not have any county of that population size.

Los Angeles County, CA, with a population of 9.8 million, remained the most populous county in the United States since 1960, followed by Cook County, IL, (containing Chicago), and Harris County, TX, (containing Houston) (Table 4). Nine of the ten largest counties grew, led

by Maricopa County, AZ, (containing Phoenix) and Harris County, TX, with rates of 24.2 and 20.3 percent, respectively. Cook County, IL, was the exception, declining by 3.4 percent.

In 2010, Maricopa County contained 59.7 percent of Arizona's population and accounted for 59.1 percent of the state's growth between 2000 and 2010. Large counties in other states also accounted for large portions of their state's population and growth. For example, the two Texas counties (Harris and Dallas) that were among the ten largest nationally accounted for over one-quarter (25.7 percent) of the population of the nation's second-largest state and 19.6 percent of its growth.

As with the largest counties and those with the largest numeric gains, many of the fastest-growing counties with a Census 2000 population of 10,000 or more were

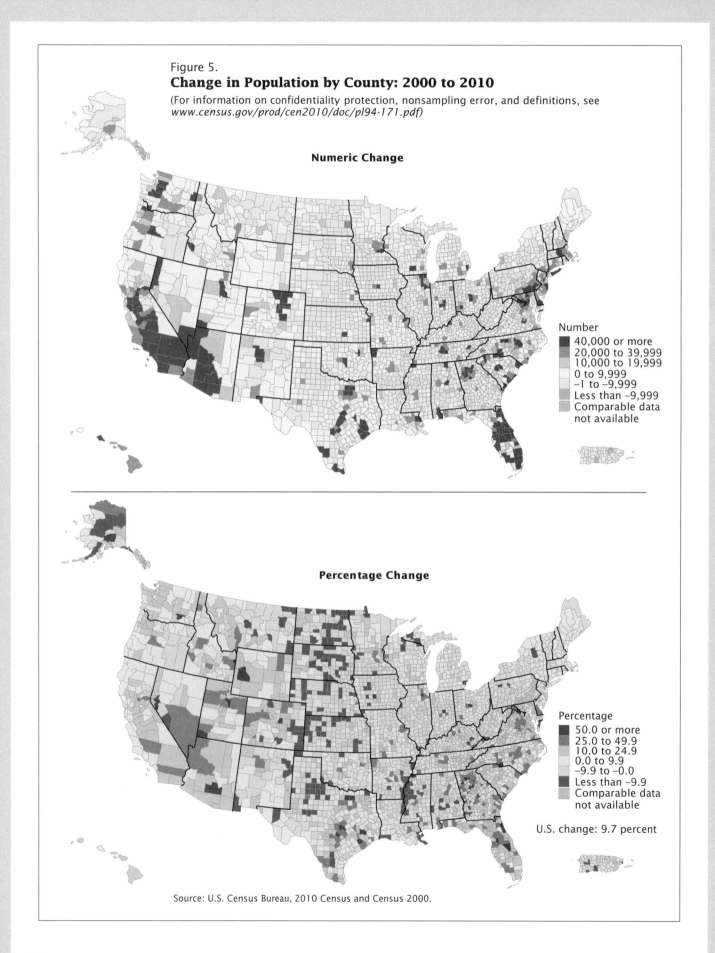

Figure 5.

**Change in Population by County: 2000 to 2010**

(For information on confidentiality protection, nonsampling error, and definitions, see *www.census.gov/prod/cen2010/doc/pl94-171.pdf*)

**Numeric Change**

Number

40,000 or more
20,000 to 39,999
10,000 to 19,999
0 to 9,999
−1 to −9,999
Less than −9,999
Comparable data
not available

**Percentage Change**

Percentage

50.0 or more
25.0 to 49.9
10.0 to 24.9
0.0 to 9.9
−9.9 to −0.0
Less than −9.9
Comparable data
not available

U.S. change: 9.7 percent

Source: U.S. Census Bureau, 2010 Census and Census 2000.

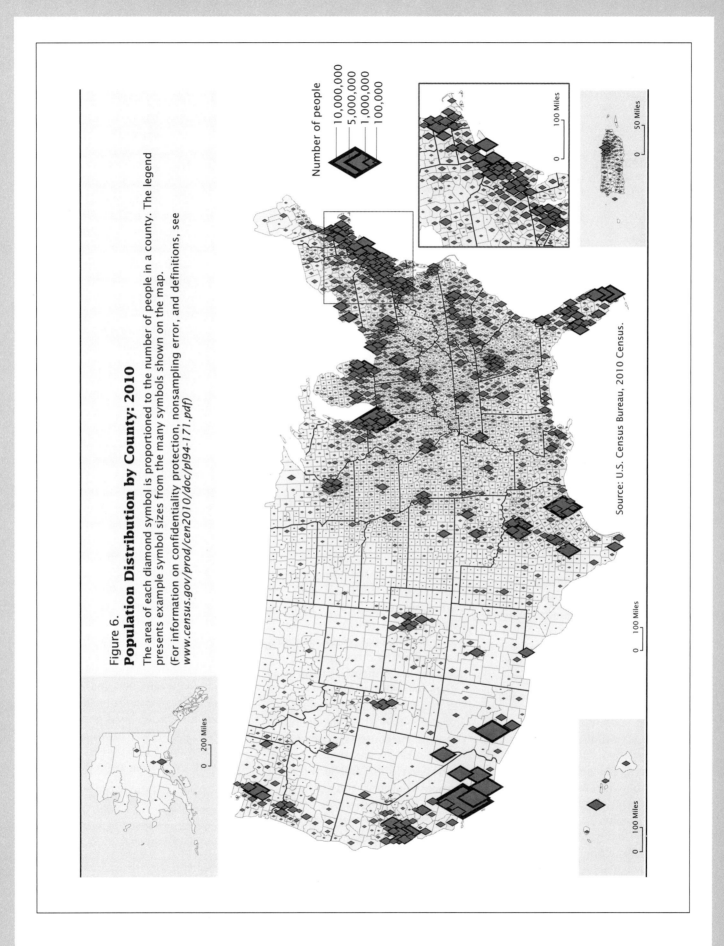

Figure 6.
**Population Distribution by County: 2010**

The area of each diamond symbol is proportioned to the number of people in a county. The legend presents example symbol sizes from the many symbols shown on the map.

(For information on confidentiality protection, nonsampling error, and definitions, see *www.census.gov/prod/cen2010/doc/pl94-171.pdf*)

Number of people

10,000,000
5,000,000
1,000,000
100,000

Source: U.S. Census Bureau, 2010 Census.

0    100 Miles

0    50 Miles

0    100 Miles

0    200 Miles

0    100 Miles

Table 4.

**Population Change for the Ten Most Populous and Ten Fastest-Growing Counties: 2000 to 2010**

(For information on confidentiality protection, nonsampling error, and definitions, see www.census.gov/prod/cen2010/doc/pl94-171.pdf)

| County | Population | | Change | |
|---|---|---|---|---|
| | 2000 | 2010 | Number | Percent |
| **MOST POPULOUS** | | | | |
| Los Angeles, CA . . . . . . . . . . . . . . | 9,519,338 | 9,818,605 | 299,267 | 3.1 |
| Cook, IL. . . . . . . . . . . . . . . . . . . . . | 5,376,741 | 5,194,675 | −182,066 | −3.4 |
| Harris, TX. . . . . . . . . . . . . . . . . . . . | 3,400,578 | 4,092,459 | 691,881 | 20.3 |
| Maricopa, AZ. . . . . . . . . . . . . . . . . | 3,072,149 | 3,817,117 | 744,968 | 24.2 |
| San Diego, CA. . . . . . . . . . . . . . . . | 2,813,833 | 3,095,313 | 281,480 | 10.0 |
| Orange, CA . . . . . . . . . . . . . . . . . . | 2,846,289 | 3,010,232 | 163,943 | 5.8 |
| Kings, NY. . . . . . . . . . . . . . . . . . . . | 2,465,326 | 2,504,700 | 39,374 | 1.6 |
| Miami-Dade, FL. . . . . . . . . . . . . . . | 2,253,362 | 2,496,435 | 243,073 | 10.8 |
| Dallas, TX . . . . . . . . . . . . . . . . . . . | 2,218,899 | 2,368,139 | 149,240 | 6.7 |
| Queens, NY. . . . . . . . . . . . . . . . . . | 2,229,379 | 2,230,722 | 1,343 | 0.1 |
| | | | | |
| **FASTEST-GROWING[1]** | | | | |
| Kendall, IL . . . . . . . . . . . . . . . . . . . | 54,544 | 114,736 | 60,192 | 110.4 |
| Pinal, AZ . . . . . . . . . . . . . . . . . . . . | 179,727 | 375,770 | 196,043 | 109.1 |
| Flagler, FL . . . . . . . . . . . . . . . . . . . | 49,832 | 95,696 | 45,864 | 92.0 |
| Lincoln, SD . . . . . . . . . . . . . . . . . . | 24,131 | 44,828 | 20,697 | 85.8 |
| Loudoun, VA . . . . . . . . . . . . . . . . . | 169,599 | 312,311 | 142,712 | 84.1 |
| Rockwall, TX . . . . . . . . . . . . . . . . . | 43,080 | 78,337 | 35,257 | 81.8 |
| Forsyth, GA. . . . . . . . . . . . . . . . . . | 98,407 | 175,511 | 77,104 | 78.4 |
| Sumter, FL. . . . . . . . . . . . . . . . . . . | 53,345 | 93,420 | 40,075 | 75.1 |
| Paulding, GA . . . . . . . . . . . . . . . . . | 81,678 | 142,324 | 60,646 | 74.3 |
| Henry, GA . . . . . . . . . . . . . . . . . . . | 119,341 | 203,922 | 84,581 | 70.9 |

[1] Among counties with Census 2000 populations of 10,000 or more.

Source: U.S. Census Bureau, 2010 Census and Census 2000.

in metro areas. Two counties with Census 2000 populations of 10,000 or greater more than doubled their populations between 2000 and 2010 (metro area in parentheses): Kendall County, IL, (Chicago) and Pinal County, AZ, (Phoenix) (Table 4). In comparison, three counties with 1990 populations of 10,000 or greater more than doubled their populations between 1990 and 2000: Douglas County, CO, (Denver); Forsyth County, GA; and Henry County, GA (Atlanta).

Another six counties in this size range experienced growth rates between 75 percent and 100 percent between 2000 and 2010: Flagler County, FL, (Palm Coast); Lincoln County, SD, (Sioux Falls); Loudoun County, VA, (Washington, DC); Rockwall County, TX, (Dallas-Fort Worth); Forsyth County, GA, (Atlanta); and Sumter County, FL,

(located in a micro area to the west of Orlando).

Population density for counties continued to vary widely across the country in 2010 (Figure 7). Counties in the Northeast and South were generally more densely populated than many of the counties in the Midwest and West, which contained numerous counties with densities lower than 10 people per square mile. The highest densities included some of the counties along the Atlantic, Pacific, and Gulf coasts, some counties adjacent to the Great Lakes, and some counties in western North Carolina, western South Carolina, and northern Georgia, among others. An almost unbroken chain of coastal counties with population densities of 300 people per square mile or more runs from New Hampshire through northern Virginia.

**PLACES**

In this section, we examine population change from 2000 to 2010 for incorporated places that had populations of 10,000 or more in Census 2000. Nine of the ten most populous cities gained population this past decade (Table 5). Led by New York (8.2 million), Los Angeles (3.8 million), and Chicago (2.7 million), the six most populous cities kept their same rank as in 2000; fourth-ranked Houston surpassed the 2 million mark during the decade. San Antonio—which had the largest numeric increase and the largest percentage increase among the top ten—moved ahead of San Diego and Dallas into seventh place, while San Jose replaced Detroit as the tenth most populous city. Chicago, which had grown between 1990 and 2000, was the only top-ten city in 2010 to experience decline over the decade (−6.9 percent), while Philadelphia's gain between 2000 and 2010 was its first decennial gain since the 1940–1950 period. The seven cities that were not only in the top ten in both 2000 and 2010, but also grew between 1990–2000 and 2000–2010 (New York, Los Angeles, Houston, Phoenix, San Antonio, San Diego, and Dallas) experienced smaller numeric and percentage increases between 2000 and 2010 than they did between 1990 and 2000.[4] Furthermore, the cumulative gain between 2000 and 2010 for the ten largest cities (including the loss for Chicago) was approximately 670,000, which was less than the roughly 686,000 gain for New York alone from 1990 to 2000.

Of incorporated places with Census 2000 populations of 10,000 or greater, nine of the ten fastest-growing ones between 2000 and

[4] Philadelphia was in the top ten between 1990 and 2000 but declined over that decade.

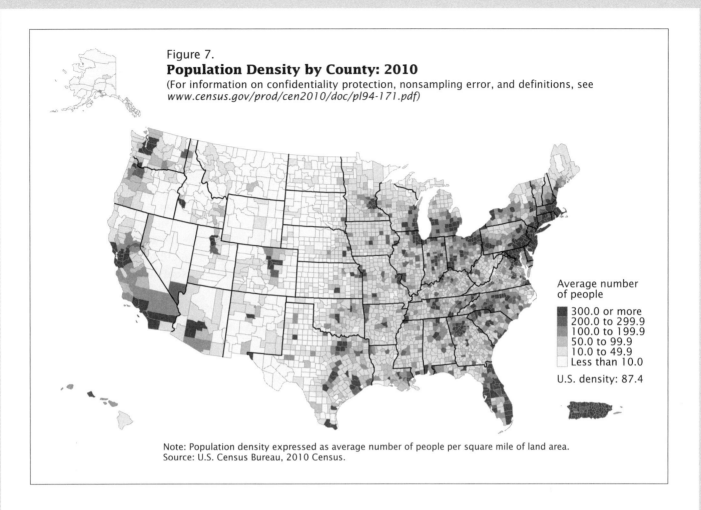

Figure 7.
**Population Density by County: 2010**
(For information on confidentiality protection, nonsampling error, and definitions, see *www.census.gov/prod/cen2010/doc/pl94-171.pdf*)

Average number of people

300.0 or more
200.0 to 299.9
100.0 to 199.9
50.0 to 99.9
10.0 to 49.9
Less than 10.0

U.S. density: 87.4

Note: Population density expressed as average number of people per square mile of land area.
Source: U.S. Census Bureau, 2010 Census.

2010 were located in either western or southern states—one was located in the Midwest (Plainfield, IL)—and all ten were located in metro areas with 2010 Census populations of 1 million or more (metro area in parentheses): Lincoln, CA, (Sacramento); Surprise, AZ, and Goodyear, AZ, (Phoenix); Frisco, TX, and Wylie, TX, (Dallas-Fort Worth); Beaumont, CA, (Riverside-San Bernardino); Plainfield, IL, (Chicago); Louisville/Jefferson County, KY (Louisville/Jefferson County); Pflugerville, TX, (Austin); and Indian Trail, NC, (Charlotte). Six of the places more than tripled their populations between 2000 and 2010: Lincoln (282.1 percent); Surprise (281.0 percent); Frisco (247.0 percent); Goodyear (245.2 percent); Beaumont (223.9 percent);

and Plainfield (203.6 percent). The next four places grew between 170 and 190 percent.

## METHODOLOGY AND SOURCES OF DATA

This report used decennial census data primarily for the years 1990, 2000, and 2010. The population universe is the resident population of the United States (50 states and the District of Columbia) and Puerto Rico. All derived values were computed using unrounded data. For readability, most whole numbers in the text are expressed in millions or rounded to the nearest hundred or thousand, and percentages are rounded to tenths. In the tables, whole numbers are unrounded and percentages are rounded to the nearest tenth. In the maps, data are

categorized based on unrounded percentages. In Figure 5 and the tables, numeric and percentage change for counties are only calculated for the universe of counties that existed in both Census 2000 and the 2010 Census.

## FOR MORE INFORMATION

Data for state and local areas from the *2010 Census Redistricting Data (Public Law 94-171) Summary File* are available on the Internet at <http://factfinder2.census .gov/main.html> and on DVD. For more information on confidentiality protection, nonsampling error, and definitions, see <www.census .gov/prod/cen2010/doc/pl94 -171.pdf>. For more information on metropolitan and micropolitan statistical areas, including concepts,

Table 5.

## Population Change for the Ten Most Populous and Ten Fastest-Growing Incorporated Places: 2000 to 2010

(For information on confidentiality protection, nonsampling error, and definitions, see *www.census.gov/prod/cen2010/doc/pl94-171.pdf*)

| Place | Population | | Change | |
|---|---|---|---|---|
| | 2000 | 2010 | Number | Percent |
| **MOST POPULOUS** | | | | |
| New York city, NY............ | 8,008,278 | 8,175,133 | 166,855 | 2.1 |
| Los Angeles city, CA ........ | 3,694,820 | 3,792,621 | 97,801 | 2.6 |
| Chicago city, IL ............ | 2,896,016 | 2,695,598 | −200,418 | −6.9 |
| Houston city, TX............ | 1,953,631 | 2,099,451 | 145,820 | 7.5 |
| Philadelphia city, PA......... | 1,517,550 | 1,526,006 | 8,456 | 0.6 |
| Phoenix city, AZ............ | 1,321,045 | 1,445,632 | 124,587 | 9.4 |
| San Antonio city, TX ........ | 1,144,646 | 1,327,407 | 182,761 | 16.0 |
| San Diego city, CA.......... | 1,223,400 | 1,307,402 | 84,002 | 6.9 |
| Dallas city, TX ............. | 1,188,580 | 1,197,816 | 9,236 | 0.8 |
| San Jose city, CA........... | 894,943 | 945,942 | 50,999 | 5.7 |
| | | | | |
| **FASTEST-GROWING**[1] | | | | |
| Lincoln city, CA ............ | 11,205 | 42,819 | 31,614 | 282.1 |
| Surprise city, AZ ........... | 30,848 | 117,517 | 86,669 | 281.0 |
| Frisco city, TX ............. | 33,714 | 116,989 | 83,275 | 247.0 |
| Goodyear city, AZ .......... | 18,911 | 65,275 | 46,364 | 245.2 |
| Beaumont city, CA.......... | 11,384 | 36,877 | 25,493 | 223.9 |
| Plainfield village, IL ......... | 13,038 | 39,581 | 26,543 | 203.6 |
| Louisville/Jefferson County metro government, KY[2] ..... | 256,231 | 741,096 | 484,865 | 189.2 |
| Pflugerville city, TX ......... | 16,335 | 46,936 | 30,601 | 187.3 |
| Indian Trail town, NC ........ | 11,905 | 33,518 | 21,613 | 181.5 |
| Wylie city, TX.............. | 15,132 | 41,427 | 26,295 | 173.8 |

[1] Among incorporated places with Census 2000 populations of 10,000 or more.

[2] Louisville city and Jefferson County, Kentucky, formed a consolidated government after Census 2000. The 2000 population for the incorporated place of Louisville city is before consolidation.

Source: U.S. Census Bureau, 2010 Census and Census 2000.

definitions, reports, and maps, go to <www.census.gov /population/www/metroareas /metroarea.html>. For more information on historical census data, go to <www.census.gov/population /www/censusdata/hiscendata .html>.

Information on other population and housing topics is presented in the 2010 Census Briefs series, located on the U.S. Census Bureau's Web site at <www.census.gov /prod/cen2010/>. This series also presents information about race, Hispanic origin, age, sex, household type, housing tenure, and people who reside in group quarters.

If you have questions or need additional information, please call the Customer Services Center at 1-800-923-8282. You can also visit the Census Bureau's Question and Answer Center at <ask.census.gov> to submit your questions online.

# The White Population: 2010

*2010 Census Briefs*

Issued September 2011

C2010BR-05

By
Lindsay Hixson,
Bradford B. Hepler,
and
Myoung Ouk Kim

## INTRODUCTION

This report provides a portrait of the White population in the United States and discusses its distribution at the national level and at lower levels of geography.[1] It is part of a series that analyzes population and housing data collected from the 2010 Census. The data for this report are based on the *2010 Census Redistricting Data (Public Law 94-171) Summary File*, which was the first 2010 Census data product released with data on race and Hispanic origin and was provided to each state for use in drawing boundaries for legislative districts.[2]

## UNDERSTANDING RACE DATA FROM THE 2010 CENSUS

**The 2010 Census used established federal standards to collect and present data on race.**

For the 2010 Census, the question on race was asked of individuals living in the United States (see Figure 1). An individual's response to the race question was based upon self-identification. The U.S. Census Bureau collects information on race following the guidance of the U.S. Office of Management and Budget's (OMB) 1997 *Revisions to the Standards for the Classification of Federal Data on*

Figure 1.

**Reproduction of the Question on Race From the 2010 Census**

6. **What is this person's race?** *Mark* ☒ *one or more boxes.*
☐ White
☐ Black, African Am., or Negro
☐ American Indian or Alaska Native — *Print name of enrolled or principal tribe.* ↘

☐ Asian Indian ☐ Japanese ☐ Native Hawaiian
☐ Chinese ☐ Korean ☐ Guamanian or Chamorro
☐ Filipino ☐ Vietnamese ☐ Samoan
☐ Other Asian — *Print race, for example, Hmong, Laotian, Thai, Pakistani, Cambodian, and so on.* ↘  ☐ Other Pacific Islander — *Print race, for example, Fijian, Tongan, and so on.* ↘

☐ Some other race — *Print race.* ↘

Source: U.S. Census Bureau, 2010 Census questionnaire.

*Race and Ethnicity.*[3] These federal standards mandate that race and Hispanic origin (ethnicity) are separate and distinct concepts and that when collecting these data via self-identification, two different questions must be used.[4]

Starting in 1997, OMB required federal agencies to use a minimum of five race categories: White, Black or African

[1] This report discusses data for the 50 states and the District of Columbia, but not Puerto Rico.
[2] Information on the *2010 Census Redistricting Data (Public Law 94-171) Summary File* is available online at <http://2010.census.gov/2010census/data/redistricting-data.php>.

[3] The 1997 *Revisions to the Standards for the Classification of Federal Data on Race and Ethnicity*, issued by OMB is available at <www.whitehouse.gov/omb/fedreg/1997standards.html>.
[4] The OMB requires federal agencies to use a minimum of two ethnicities: Hispanic or Latino and Not Hispanic or Latino. Hispanic origin can be viewed as the heritage, nationality group, lineage, or country of birth of the person or the person's parents or ancestors before their arrival in the United States. People who identify their origin as Hispanic, Latino, or Spanish may be of any race. "Hispanic or Latino" refers to a person of Cuban, Mexican, Puerto Rican, South or Central American, or other Spanish culture or origin regardless of race.

U.S. Department of Commerce
Economics and Statistics Administration
U.S. CENSUS BUREAU

American, American Indian or Alaska Native, Asian, and Native Hawaiian or Other Pacific Islander.[5] For respondents unable to identify with any of these five race categories, OMB approved the Census Bureau's inclusion of a sixth category—Some Other Race—on the 2000 and 2010 Census questionnaires. The 1997 OMB standards also allowed for respondents to identify with more than one race. The definition of the White racial category used in the 2010 Census is presented in the text box on this page.

Data on race have been collected since the first U.S. decennial census in 1790, and the White population has been enumerated in every census.[6] For the first time in Census 2000, individuals were presented with the option to self-identify with more than one race and this continued with the 2010 Census, as prescribed by OMB. There are 57 possible multiple race combinations involving the five OMB race categories and Some Other Race.[7]

The 2010 Census question on race included 15 separate response categories and three areas where respondents could write in detailed information about their race (see

---

**DEFINITION OF WHITE USED IN THE 2010 CENSUS**

According to OMB, "White" refers to a person having origins in any of the original peoples of Europe, the Middle East, or North Africa.

The White racial category includes people who marked the "White" checkbox. It also includes respondents who reported entries such as Caucasian or White; European entries, such as Irish, German, and Polish; Middle Eastern entries, such as Arab, Lebanese, and Palestinian; and North African entries, such as Algerian, Moroccan, and Egyptian.

---

Figure 1).[8] The response categories and write-in answers can be combined to create the five minimum OMB race categories plus Some Other Race. In addition to White, Black or African American, American Indian and Alaska Native, and Some Other Race, 7 of the 15 response categories are Asian groups and 4 are Native Hawaiian and Other Pacific Islander groups.[9]

For a complete explanation of the race categories used in the 2010 Census, see the 2010 Census Brief, *Overview of Race and Hispanic Origin: 2010*.[10]

---

## RACE ALONE, RACE IN COMBINATION, AND RACE ALONE-OR-IN-COMBINATION CONCEPTS

This report presents data for the White population and focuses on results for three major conceptual groups.

People who responded to the question on race by indicating only one race are referred to as the *race alone* population, or the group who reported *only one* race. For example, respondents who marked only the "White" category on the census questionnaire would be included in the *White alone* population. This population can be viewed as the minimum number of people reporting White.

Individuals who chose more than one of the six race categories are referred to as the *race in combination* population, or as the group who reported *more than one race*. For example, respondents who reported they were White **and** Black or White **and** Asian **and** American Indian and Alaska Native would be included in the *White in combination* population. This population is also referred to as the *multiple-race White* population.

---

[5] The terms "Black or African American" and "Black" are used interchangeably in this report.

[6] For information about comparability of 2010 Census data on race and Hispanic origin to data collected in previous censuses, see the *2010 Census Redistricting Data (Public Law 94-171) Summary File—Technical Documentation* at <www.census.gov/prod /cen2010/doc/pl94-171.pdf>.

[7] The 2010 Census provides data on the total population reporting more than one race, as well as detailed race combinations, (e.g., Asian **and** White; White **and** Black or African American **and** American Indian and Alaska Native). In this report, the multiple-race categories are denoted with the conjunction **and** in bold and italicized print to indicate the separate race groups that comprise the particular combination.

[8] There were two changes to the question on race for the 2010 Census. First, the wording of the race question was changed from "What is this person's race? Mark ☒ one or more races to indicate what this person considers himself/herself to be" in 2000 to "What is this person's race? Mark ☒ one or more boxes" for 2010. Second, in 2010, examples were added to the "Other Asian" response category (Hmong, Laotian, Thai, Pakistani, Cambodian, and so on) and the "Other Pacific Islander" response category (Fijian, Tongan, and so on). In 2000, no examples were given in the race question.

[9] The race categories included in the census questionnaire generally reflect a social definition of race recognized in this country and are not an attempt to define race biologically, anthropologically, or genetically. In addition, it is recognized that the categories of the race question include racial and national origin or sociocultural groups.

[10] Humes, K., N. Jones, and R. Ramirez. 2011. *Overview of Race and Hispanic Origin: 2010*, U.S. Census Bureau, 2010 Census Briefs, C2010BR-02, available at <www.census.gov/prod/cen2010/briefs /c2010br-02.pdf>.

Table 1.
# White Population: 2000 and 2010
(For information on confidentiality protection, nonsampling error, and definitions, see *www.census.gov/prod/cen2010/doc/pl94-171.pdf*)

| Race and Hispanic or Latino origin | 2000 | | 2010 | | Change, 2000 to 2010 | |
|---|---|---|---|---|---|---|
| | Number | Percentage of total population | Number | Percentage of total population | Number | Percent |
| Total population .................. | 281,421,906 | 100.0 | 308,745,538 | 100.0 | 27,323,632 | 9.7 |
| White alone or in combination............... | 216,930,975 | 77.1 | 231,040,398 | 74.8 | 14,109,423 | 6.5 |
| White alone ........................... | 211,460,626 | 75.1 | 223,553,265 | 72.4 | 12,092,639 | 5.7 |
| Hispanic or Latino...................... | 16,907,852 | 6.0 | 26,735,713 | 8.7 | 9,827,861 | 58.1 |
| Not Hispanic or Latino .................. | 194,552,774 | 69.1 | 196,817,552 | 63.7 | 2,264,778 | 1.2 |
| White in combination .................... | 5,470,349 | 1.9 | 7,487,133 | 2.4 | 2,016,784 | 36.9 |
| White; Black or African American........... | 784,764 | 0.3 | 1,834,212 | 0.6 | 1,049,448 | 133.7 |
| White; Some Other Race ................ | 2,206,251 | 0.8 | 1,740,924 | 0.6 | −465,327 | −21.1 |
| White; Asian ......................... | 868,395 | 0.3 | 1,623,234 | 0.5 | 754,839 | 86.9 |
| White; American Indian and Alaska Native.... | 1,082,683 | 0.4 | 1,432,309 | 0.5 | 349,626 | 32.3 |
| White; Black or African American; American Indian and Alaska Native....... | 112,207 | – | 230,848 | 0.1 | 118,641 | 105.7 |
| All other combinations including White....... | 416,049 | 0.1 | 625,606 | 0.2 | 209,557 | 50.4 |
| Not White alone or in combination ............ | 64,490,931 | 22.9 | 77,705,140 | 25.2 | 13,214,209 | 20.5 |

– Percentage rounds to 0.0.

Note: In Census 2000, an error in data processing resulted in an overstatement of the Two or More Races population by about 1 million people (about 15 percent) nationally, which almost entirely affected race combinations involving Some Other Race. Therefore, data users should assess observed changes in the Two or More Races population and race combinations involving Some Other Race between Census 2000 and the 2010 Census with caution. Changes in specific race combinations not involving Some Other Race, such as White *and* Black or African American or White *and* Asian, generally should be more comparable.

Sources: U.S. Census Bureau, *Census 2000 Redistricting Data (Public Law 94-171) Summary File*, Tables PL1 and PL2; and *2010 Census Redistricting Data (Public Law 94-171) Summary File,* Tables P1 and P2.

The maximum number of people who reported White is reflected in the *White alone-or-in-combination* population. One way to define the White population is to combine those respondents who reported White alone with those who reported White in combination with one or more other races. This creates the *White alone-or-in-combination* population. Another way to think about the *White alone-or-in-combination* population is the total number of people who reported White, whether or not they reported any other races.

Throughout the report, the discussion of the White population compares results for each of these groups and highlights the diversity within the entire White population.[11]

## THE WHITE POPULATION: A SNAPSHOT

The 2010 Census showed that the U.S. population on April 1, 2010, was 308.7 million. Out of the total population, 223.6 million people, or 72 percent, identified as White alone (see Table 1).[12, 13] In addition, 7.5 million people, or 2 percent, reported White in combination with one or more other races.

Together, these two groups totaled 231.0 million people. Thus, 75 percent of all people in the United States identified as White, either alone, or in combination with one or more other races.

[11] As a matter of policy, the Census Bureau does not advocate the use of the *alone* population over the *alone-or-in-combination* population or vice versa. The use of the *alone* population in sections of this report does not imply that it is a preferred method of presenting or analyzing data. The same is true for sections of this report that focus on the *alone-or-in-combination* population. Data on race from the 2010 Census can be presented and discussed in a variety of ways.

[12] Percentages shown in text generally are rounded to the nearest integer, while those shown in tables and figures are shown with decimals. All rounding is based on unrounded calculations. Thus, due to rounding, some percentages shown in tables and figures ending in "5" may round either up or down. For example, unrounded numbers of 14.49 and 14.51 would both be shown as 14.5 in a table, but would be cited in the text as 14 and 15, respectively.

[13] For the purposes of this report, the terms "reported," "identified," and "classified" are used interchangeably to refer to the response provided by respondents as well as responses assigned during the editing and imputation process.

Table 2.

## Largest White Multiple-Race Combinations by Hispanic or Latino Origin: 2010

(For information on confidentiality protection, nonsampling error, and definitions, see *www.census.gov/prod/cen2010/doc/pl94-171.pdf*)

| White in combination | Total | | Hispanic or Latino | | Not Hispanic or Latino | |
|---|---|---|---|---|---|---|
| | Number | Percent | Number | Percent | Number | Percent |
| **Total number reporting White and one or more other races** .............. | 7,487,133 | 100.0 | 2,448,577 | 100.0 | 5,038,556 | 100.0 |
| White; Black or African American .............. | 1,834,212 | 24.5 | 245,850 | 10.0 | 1,588,362 | 31.5 |
| White; Some Other Race..................... | 1,740,924 | 23.3 | 1,601,125 | 65.4 | 139,799 | 2.8 |
| White; Asian............................... | 1,623,234 | 21.7 | 135,522 | 5.5 | 1,487,712 | 29.5 |
| White; American Indian and Alaska Native ....... | 1,432,309 | 19.1 | 226,385 | 9.2 | 1,205,924 | 23.9 |
| White; Black or African American; American Indian and Alaska Native.................... | 230,848 | 3.1 | 50,000 | 2.0 | 180,848 | 3.6 |
| All other combinations including White .......... | 625,606 | 8.4 | 189,695 | 7.7 | 435,911 | 8.7 |

Source: U.S. Census Bureau, *2010 Census Redistricting Data (Public Law 94-171) Summary File*, Tables P1 and P2.

## The White population increased at a slower rate than the total population.

The total U.S. population grew by 9.7 percent, from 281.4 million in 2000 to 308.7 million in 2010 (see Table 1). In comparison, the White alone population grew by 6 percent from 211.5 million to 223.6 million.[14] But while the White alone population increased numerically over the 10-year period, its proportion of the total population declined from 75 percent to 72 percent.

The White alone-or-in-combination population experienced slightly more growth than the White alone population, growing by 7 percent. However, both groups grew at a slower rate than the total population, as well as all other major race and ethnic groups in the country.[15]

[14] The observed changes in the race counts between Census 2000 and the 2010 Census could be attributed to a number of factors. Demographic change since 2000, which includes births and deaths in a geographic area and migration in and out of a geographic area, will have an impact on the resulting 2010 Census counts. Additionally, some changes in the race question's wording and format since Census 2000 could have influenced reporting patterns in the 2010 Census.

[15] Humes, K., N. Jones, and R. Ramirez. 2011. *Overview of Race and Hispanic Origin: 2010*, U.S. Census Bureau, 2010 Census Briefs, C2010BR-02, available at <www.census.gov/prod/cen2010/briefs /c2010br-02.pdf>.

## MULTIPLE-RACE REPORTING AMONG THE WHITE POPULATION

### The proportion of Whites who reported more than one race grew by 37 percent.

In the 2010 Census, 7.5 million people reported White in combination with one or more additional races (see Table 1). The multiple-race White population grew at a faster rate than the White alone population, with an increase of more than one-third in size since 2000.

### The largest multiple-race combination was White *and* Black.

Among people who reported they were White and one or more additional races, there was a fairly even distribution of the four largest multiple-race combinations. One-fourth of Whites who reported multiple races identified as White *and* Black, and nearly one-fourth identified as White *and* Some Other Race; over one-fifth reported White *and* Asian, and nearly one-fifth reported White *and* American Indian and Alaska Native. Together, these four combinations comprised 89 percent of all Whites who reported multiple races (see Table 2).

## Two of the race combinations contributed to most of the growth among Whites who reported multiple races.

The majority of the increase of the multiple-race White population was driven by the growth of two race combinations. Of the 2.0 million increase of Whites who reported multiple races, over half of the growth was attributed to White *and* Black, and over one-third was due to White *and* Asian.

The White *and* Black population grew by 134 percent or over 1 million people (see Table 1). The White *and* Asian population increased by 87 percent or more than 750,000 people over the decade.

On the other hand, the White *and* Some Other Race population decreased by almost one-half million over the decade. This decrease was likely due to a data processing error in the Two or More Races population in 2000, which overstated the White *and* Some Other Race population and largely affected the

Table 3.
# White Population by Hispanic or Latino Origin: 2000 and 2010

(For information on confidentiality protection, nonsampling error, and definitions, see *www.census.gov/prod/cen2010/doc/pl94-171.pdf*)

| Race and Hispanic or Latino origin | 2000 | | 2010 | | Change, 2000 to 2010 | |
|---|---|---|---|---|---|---|
| | Number | Percentage of total population | Number | Percentage of total population | Number | Percent |
| Total population ........... | 281,421,906 | 100.0 | 308,745,538 | 100.0 | 27,323,632 | 9.7 |
| White alone or in combination ........ | 216,930,975 | 77.1 | 231,040,398 | 74.8 | 14,109,423 | 6.5 |
| Hispanic or Latino ................ | 18,753,075 | 6.7 | 29,184,290 | 9.4 | 10,431,215 | 55.6 |
| Not Hispanic or Latino ............. | 198,177,900 | 70.4 | 201,856,108 | 65.4 | 3,678,208 | 1.9 |
| White alone ....................... | 211,460,626 | 75.1 | 223,553,265 | 72.4 | 12,092,639 | 5.7 |
| Hispanic or Latino ................ | 16,907,852 | 6.0 | 26,735,713 | 8.7 | 9,827,861 | 58.1 |
| Not Hispanic or Latino ............. | 194,552,774 | 69.1 | 196,817,552 | 63.7 | 2,264,778 | 1.2 |
| White in combination................ | 5,470,349 | 1.9 | 7,487,133 | 2.4 | 2,016,784 | 36.9 |
| Hispanic or Latino ................ | 1,845,223 | 0.7 | 2,448,577 | 0.8 | 603,354 | 32.7 |
| Not Hispanic or Latino ............. | 3,625,126 | 1.3 | 5,038,556 | 1.6 | 1,413,430 | 39.0 |

Sources: U.S. Census Bureau, *Census 2000 Redistricting Data (Public Law 94-171) Summary File*, Tables PL1 and PL2; and *2010 Census Redistricting Data (Public Law 94-171) Summary File,* Tables P1 and P2.

combinations that included Some Other Race.[16]

## PATTERNS AMONG THE NON-HISPANIC WHITE POPULATION AND THE HISPANIC WHITE POPULATION

According to the 1997 OMB standards, Hispanics may be of any race. The 2010 Census results reflect this, demonstrating that Hispanics report a diversity of races (White, Black, American Indian or Alaska Native, etc.), or may also report that they are "Some Other Race" (self-identifying their race as "Latino," "Mexican," "Puerto Rican," "Salvadoran," or other national origins or ethnicities), or identify with various combinations of races. For more details on the race reporting patterns of Hispanics, see the

---

[16] In Census 2000, an error in data processing resulted in an overstatement of the Two or More Races population by about 1 million people (about 15 percent) nationally, which almost entirely affected race combinations involving Some Other Race. Therefore, data users should assess observed changes in the Two or More Races population and race combinations involving Some Other Race between Census 2000 and the 2010 Census with caution. Changes in specific race combinations not involving Some Other Race, such as White *and* Black or White *and* Asian, generally should be more comparable.

2010 Census Brief, *The Hispanic Population: 2010*.[17]

This section presents data for the White population, highlighting patterns for Whites who reported they are of Hispanic origin (*Hispanic Whites*), and Whites who reported they are not of Hispanic origin (*Non-Hispanic Whites*).

### More than 29 million people of Hispanic origin reported that they were White.

In 2010, the number of Whites who reported one race and identified as Hispanic was 26.7 million, or 9 percent of the total population (see Table 3). In comparison, the number of Whites who reported one race and identified as non-Hispanic numbered 196.8 million, or 64 percent of the total population.

Among the 7.5 million people who reported White in combination with an additional race group(s), 2.4 million were Hispanic. Multiple-race White respondents who were of Hispanic origin represented 1 percent of the total population.

---

[17] Ennis, S., M. Rios-Vargas, and N. Albert. 2011. *The Hispanic Population: 2010*, U.S. Census Bureau, 2010 Census Briefs, C2010BR-04, available at <www.census.gov/prod/cen2010/briefs /c2010br-04.pdf>.

### The White population who identified as Hispanic grew by 56 percent.

Whites who identified as being of Hispanic origin increased by 56 percent between 2000 and 2010 (see Table 3). Of the 231.0 million White alone-or-in-combination population in the 2010 Census, 29.2 million or 13 percent reported they were Hispanic. In comparison, 9 percent of the White alone-or-in-combination population identified as Hispanic in 2000. The 4 percentage point increase in the proportion of all Whites who identified as Hispanic represented the largest increase in share of the total White population among all of the groups within the White population.

### The non-Hispanic White population share of the total population decreased.

While the non-Hispanic White alone-or-in-combination population increased numerically from 198.2 million to 201.9 million, it grew by only 2 percent over the decade (see Table 3). This, coupled with the tremendous growth in other groups such as Hispanics and Asians, contributed to the non-Hispanic White alone-or-in combination population's proportion of the total population to decline from 70 percent to 65 percent.

**Three-fourths of the growth in the White population was due to growing numbers of Hispanic Whites.**

The White alone-or-in-combination population increased by 7 percent, from 216.9 million in 2000 to 231.0 million in 2010 (see Table 3). Most of this growth was a result of the increase in the White Hispanic population.

Whites who reported one race and identified as Hispanic accounted for 70 percent of the growth of the White alone-or-in-combination population (see Figure 2). Multiple-race Whites who identified as Hispanic accounted for another 4 percent of the growth of the White alone-or-in-combination population. Thus, Hispanics accounted for about three-fourths of the increase in the White alone-or-in-combination population.

On the other hand, non-Hispanic single-race Whites contributed to only 16 percent of the growth of the White alone-or-in-combination population, and non-Hispanic multiple-race Whites accounted for 10 percent of the growth.

**Hispanic Whites comprised a larger proportion of the multiple-race White population than the White alone population.**

Overall, Hispanic Whites comprised 12 percent of the White alone population, but they represented 33 percent of the multiple-race White population (see Figure 3). In comparison, non-Hispanic Whites were 88 percent of the White alone population, but comprised 67 percent of the multiple-race White population.

Figure 2.

**Percentage Distribution of the Growth of the White Population by Hispanic or Latino Origin: 2000 to 2010**

(For information on confidentiality protection, nonsampling error, and definitions, see *www.census.gov/prod/cen2010/doc/pl94-171.pdf*)

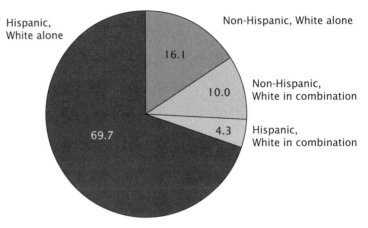

Total growth = 14.1 million

Note: Percentages do not add to 100.0 due to rounding.
Source: U.S. Census Bureau, *2010 Census Redistricting Data (Public Law 94-171) Summary File*, Tables P1 and P2.

Figure 3.

**Percentage Distribution of the White Population by Hispanic or Latino Origin: 2010**

(For information on confidentiality protection, nonsampling error, and definitions, see *www.census.gov/prod/cen2010/doc/pl94-171.pdf*)

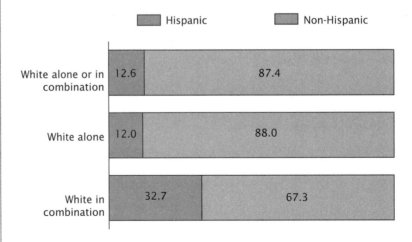

Source: U.S. Census Bureau, *2010 Census Redistricting Data (Public Law 94-171) Summary File*, Tables P1 and P2.

Although Hispanic Whites were more likely to report multiple races than non-Hispanic Whites, growth over the last 10 years was faster among the non-Hispanic multiple-race White population. The non-Hispanic multiple-race White population grew by 39 percent, whereas the Hispanic multiple-race White population grew by 33 percent (see Table 3).

**Hispanic Whites and non-Hispanic Whites reported different multiple-race groups.**

The largest multiple-race combinations reported by non-Hispanic Whites were White *and* Black (1.6 million), White *and* Asian (1.5 million), and White *and* American Indian and Alaska Native (1.2 million). Among non-Hispanic Whites who reported more than one race, the top combinations were White *and* Black (32 percent), White *and* Asian (30 percent), and White *and* American Indian and Alaska Native (24 percent), as shown in Table 2. These three race combination categories accounted for the vast majority of all non-Hispanic Whites who reported multiple races.

White *and* Some Other Race was the largest multiple-race combination reported by Hispanic Whites (1.6 million). Among Hispanic Whites who reported more than one race, the majority indicated they were White *and* Some Other Race (65 percent), followed by White *and* Black (10 percent), White *and* American Indian and Alaska Native (9 percent), and White *and* Asian (6 percent), as shown in Table 2.

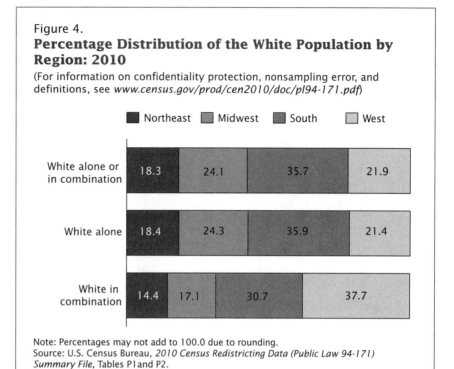

Figure 4.

**Percentage Distribution of the White Population by Region: 2010**

(For information on confidentiality protection, nonsampling error, and definitions, see *www.census.gov/prod/cen2010/doc/pl94-171.pdf*)

Note: Percentages may not add to 100.0 due to rounding.
Source: U.S. Census Bureau, *2010 Census Redistricting Data (Public Law 94-171) Summary File,* Tables P1 and P2.

## THE GEOGRAPHIC DISTRIBUTION OF THE WHITE POPULATION

**The majority of the White alone-or-in-combination population lived in the South and the Midwest.**

According to the 2010 Census, of all respondents who reported White alone-or-in-combination, 36 percent lived in the South, 24 percent lived in the Midwest, 22 percent lived in the West, and 18 percent lived in the Northeast (see Figure 4).[18]

The distribution of the White alone population was almost identical to the White alone-or-in-combination population across the regions, with 36 percent living in the South, 24 percent in the Midwest, 21 percent in the West, and 18 percent in the Northeast.

[18] The Northeast census region includes Connecticut, Maine, Massachusetts, New Hampshire, New Jersey, New York, Pennsylvania, Rhode Island, and Vermont. The Midwest census region includes Illinois, Indiana, Iowa, Kansas, Michigan, Minnesota, Missouri, Nebraska, North Dakota, Ohio, South Dakota, and Wisconsin. The South census region includes Alabama, Arkansas, Delaware, the District of Columbia, Florida, Georgia, Kentucky, Louisiana, Maryland, Mississippi, North Carolina, Oklahoma, South Carolina, Tennessee, Texas, Virginia, and West Virginia. The West census region includes Alaska, Arizona, California, Colorado, Hawaii, Idaho, Montana, Nevada, New Mexico, Oregon, Utah, Washington, and Wyoming.

Table 4.
# White Population for the United States, Regions, and States, and for Puerto Rico: 2000 and 2010

(For information on confidentiality protection, nonsampling error, and definitions, see www.census.gov/prod/cen2010/doc/sf1.pdf)

| Area | White alone or in combination | | | White alone, not Hispanic or Latino | | | White in combination | | |
|---|---|---|---|---|---|---|---|---|---|
| | 2000 | 2010 | Percentage change, 2000 to 2010 | 2000 | 2010 | Percentage change, 2000 to 2010 | 2000 | 2010 | Percentage change, 2000 to 2010 |
| United States.... | 216,930,975 | 231,040,398 | 6.5 | 194,552,774 | 196,817,552 | 1.2 | 5,470,349 | 7,487,133 | 36.9 |
| **REGION** | | | | | | | | | |
| Northeast............. | 42,395,625 | 42,246,801 | −0.4 | 39,327,262 | 38,008,094 | −3.4 | 862,123 | 1,078,463 | 25.1 |
| Midwest.............. | 54,709,407 | 55,704,560 | 1.8 | 52,386,131 | 52,096,633 | −0.6 | 875,756 | 1,281,037 | 46.3 |
| South................ | 74,303,744 | 82,475,187 | 11.0 | 65,927,794 | 68,706,462 | 4.2 | 1,484,345 | 2,302,042 | 55.1 |
| West ................ | 45,522,199 | 50,613,850 | 11.2 | 36,911,587 | 38,006,363 | 3.0 | 2,248,125 | 2,825,591 | 25.7 |
| **STATE** | | | | | | | | | |
| Alabama ............. | 3,199,953 | 3,337,077 | 4.3 | 3,125,819 | 3,204,402 | 2.5 | 37,145 | 61,683 | 66.1 |
| Alaska ............... | 463,999 | 518,949 | 11.8 | 423,788 | 455,320 | 7.4 | 29,465 | 45,373 | 54.0 |
| Arizona ............. | 3,998,154 | 4,852,961 | 21.4 | 3,274,258 | 3,695,647 | 12.9 | 124,543 | 185,840 | 49.2 |
| Arkansas ............ | 2,170,534 | 2,296,665 | 5.8 | 2,100,135 | 2,173,469 | 3.5 | 31,936 | 51,436 | 61.1 |
| California ............ | 21,490,973 | 22,953,374 | 6.8 | 15,816,790 | 14,956,253 | −5.4 | 1,320,914 | 1,499,440 | 13.5 |
| Colorado ............ | 3,665,638 | 4,240,231 | 15.7 | 3,202,880 | 3,520,793 | 9.9 | 105,633 | 151,029 | 43.0 |
| Connecticut ......... | 2,835,974 | 2,846,192 | 0.4 | 2,638,845 | 2,546,262 | −3.5 | 55,619 | 73,782 | 32.7 |
| Delaware ............ | 594,425 | 637,392 | 7.2 | 567,973 | 586,752 | 3.3 | 9,652 | 18,775 | 94.5 |
| District of Columbia..... | 184,309 | 243,650 | 32.2 | 159,178 | 209,464 | 31.6 | 8,208 | 12,179 | 48.4 |
| Florida .............. | 12,734,292 | 14,488,435 | 13.8 | 10,458,509 | 10,884,722 | 4.1 | 269,263 | 379,273 | 40.9 |
| Georgia ............. | 5,412,371 | 5,951,521 | 10.0 | 5,128,661 | 5,413,920 | 5.6 | 85,090 | 164,081 | 92.8 |
| Hawaii .............. | 476,162 | 564,323 | 18.5 | 277,091 | 309,343 | 11.6 | 182,060 | 227,724 | 25.1 |
| Idaho................ | 1,201,113 | 1,432,824 | 19.3 | 1,139,291 | 1,316,243 | 15.5 | 23,809 | 36,337 | 52.6 |
| Illinois.............. | 9,322,831 | 9,423,048 | 1.1 | 8,424,140 | 8,167,753 | −3.0 | 197,360 | 245,171 | 24.2 |
| Indiana.............. | 5,387,174 | 5,583,367 | 3.6 | 5,219,373 | 5,286,453 | 1.3 | 67,152 | 115,461 | 71.9 |
| Iowa................ | 2,777,183 | 2,830,454 | 1.9 | 2,710,344 | 2,701,123 | −0.3 | 28,543 | 48,893 | 71.3 |
| Kansas.............. | 2,363,412 | 2,468,364 | 4.4 | 2,233,997 | 2,230,539 | −0.2 | 49,468 | 77,320 | 56.3 |
| Kentucky ............ | 3,678,740 | 3,878,336 | 5.4 | 3,608,013 | 3,745,655 | 3.8 | 37,851 | 68,799 | 81.8 |
| Louisiana............ | 2,894,983 | 2,895,868 | − | 2,794,391 | 2,734,884 | −2.1 | 38,822 | 59,676 | 53.7 |
| Maine............... | 1,247,776 | 1,284,877 | 3.0 | 1,230,297 | 1,254,297 | 2.0 | 11,762 | 19,906 | 69.2 |
| Maryland ............ | 3,465,697 | 3,488,887 | 0.7 | 3,286,547 | 3,157,958 | −3.9 | 74,389 | 129,603 | 74.2 |
| Massachusetts........ | 5,472,809 | 5,400,458 | −1.3 | 5,198,359 | 4,984,800 | −4.1 | 105,523 | 135,222 | 28.1 |
| Michigan ............ | 8,133,283 | 8,006,969 | −1.6 | 7,806,691 | 7,569,939 | −3.0 | 167,230 | 203,849 | 21.9 |
| Minnesota ........... | 4,466,325 | 4,634,915 | 3.8 | 4,337,143 | 4,405,142 | 1.6 | 66,043 | 110,853 | 67.8 |
| Mississippi........... | 1,761,658 | 1,782,807 | 1.2 | 1,727,908 | 1,722,287 | −0.3 | 15,559 | 28,123 | 80.8 |
| Missouri............. | 4,819,487 | 5,070,826 | 5.2 | 4,686,474 | 4,850,748 | 3.5 | 71,404 | 112,056 | 56.9 |
| Montana............. | 831,978 | 908,645 | 9.2 | 807,823 | 868,628 | 7.5 | 14,749 | 23,684 | 60.6 |
| Nebraska............ | 1,554,164 | 1,607,717 | 3.4 | 1,494,494 | 1,499,753 | 0.4 | 20,903 | 34,879 | 66.9 |
| Nevada ............. | 1,565,866 | 1,890,043 | 20.7 | 1,303,001 | 1,462,081 | 12.2 | 63,980 | 103,355 | 61.5 |
| New Hampshire........ | 1,198,927 | 1,255,950 | 4.8 | 1,175,252 | 1,215,050 | 3.4 | 12,076 | 19,900 | 64.8 |
| New Jersey .......... | 6,261,187 | 6,210,995 | −0.8 | 5,557,209 | 5,214,878 | −6.2 | 156,482 | 181,747 | 16.1 |
| New Mexico.......... | 1,272,116 | 1,473,005 | 15.8 | 813,495 | 833,810 | 2.5 | 57,863 | 65,129 | 12.6 |
| New York ............ | 13,275,834 | 13,155,274 | −0.9 | 11,760,981 | 11,304,247 | −3.9 | 382,145 | 414,300 | 8.4 |
| North Carolina........ | 5,884,608 | 6,697,465 | 13.8 | 5,647,155 | 6,223,995 | 10.2 | 79,952 | 168,515 | 110.8 |
| North Dakota......... | 599,918 | 616,350 | 2.7 | 589,149 | 598,007 | 1.5 | 6,737 | 10,901 | 61.8 |
| Ohio................ | 9,779,512 | 9,751,547 | −0.3 | 9,538,111 | 9,359,263 | −1.9 | 134,059 | 212,110 | 58.2 |
| Oklahoma ........... | 2,770,035 | 2,906,285 | 4.9 | 2,556,368 | 2,575,381 | 0.7 | 141,601 | 199,440 | 40.8 |
| Oregon.............. | 3,055,670 | 3,337,309 | 9.2 | 2,857,616 | 3,005,848 | 5.2 | 94,047 | 132,695 | 41.1 |
| Pennsylvania ......... | 10,596,409 | 10,604,187 | 0.1 | 10,322,455 | 10,094,652 | −2.2 | 112,206 | 197,899 | 76.4 |
| Rhode Island ......... | 910,630 | 882,280 | −3.1 | 858,433 | 803,685 | −6.4 | 19,439 | 25,411 | 30.7 |
| South Carolina........ | 2,727,208 | 3,127,075 | 14.7 | 2,652,291 | 2,962,740 | 11.7 | 31,648 | 67,075 | 111.9 |
| South Dakota......... | 678,604 | 715,167 | 5.4 | 664,585 | 689,502 | 3.7 | 9,200 | 15,775 | 71.5 |
| Tennessee........... | 4,617,553 | 5,019,639 | 8.7 | 4,505,930 | 4,800,782 | 6.5 | 54,243 | 97,691 | 80.1 |
| Texas............... | 15,240,387 | 18,276,506 | 19.9 | 10,933,313 | 11,397,345 | 4.2 | 440,882 | 574,954 | 30.4 |
| Utah................ | 2,034,448 | 2,447,583 | 20.3 | 1,904,265 | 2,221,719 | 16.7 | 41,473 | 68,023 | 64.0 |
| Vermont............. | 596,079 | 606,588 | 1.8 | 585,431 | 590,223 | 0.8 | 6,871 | 10,296 | 49.8 |
| Virginia.............. | 5,233,601 | 5,681,937 | 8.6 | 4,965,637 | 5,186,450 | 4.4 | 113,491 | 195,085 | 71.9 |
| Washington .......... | 5,003,180 | 5,471,864 | 9.4 | 4,652,490 | 4,876,804 | 4.8 | 181,357 | 275,502 | 51.9 |
| West Virginia ......... | 1,733,390 | 1,765,642 | 1.9 | 1,709,966 | 1,726,256 | 1.0 | 14,613 | 25,654 | 75.6 |
| Wisconsin ........... | 4,827,514 | 4,995,836 | 3.5 | 4,681,630 | 4,738,411 | 1.2 | 57,657 | 93,769 | 62.6 |
| Wyoming ............ | 462,902 | 522,739 | 12.9 | 438,799 | 483,874 | 10.3 | 8,232 | 11,460 | 39.2 |
| **Puerto Rico** .......... | 3,199,547 | 2,928,808 | −8.5 | 33,966 | 26,946 | −20.7 | 134,685 | 103,708 | −23.0 |

− Percentage rounds to 0.0.

Sources: U.S. Census Bureau, *Census 2000 Redistricting Data (Public Law 94-171) Summary File*, Tables PL1 and PL2; and *2010 Census Redistricting Data (Public Law 94-171) Summary File*, Tables P1 and P2.

Figure 5.
**Percentage Distribution of the White Alone Population by Hispanic or Latino Origin and State: 2010**
(For information on confidentiality protection, nonsampling error, and definitions, see *www.census.gov/prod/cen2010/doc/pl94-171.pdf*)

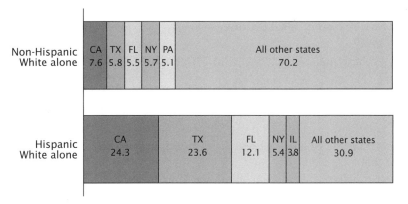

Non-Hispanic White alone: CA 7.6 | TX 5.8 | FL 5.5 | NY 5.7 | PA 5.1 | All other states 70.2

Hispanic White alone: CA 24.3 | TX 23.6 | FL 12.1 | NY 5.4 | IL 3.8 | All other states 30.9

Note: Percentages do not add to 100.0 due to rounding.
Source: U.S. Census Bureau, *2010 Census Redistricting Data (Public Law 94-171) Summary File*, Tables P1 and P2.

However, the distribution of Whites who reported multiple races was very different. Multiple-race Whites were much more likely to live in the West (38 percent) than other regions.

**The White-alone-or-in-combination population grew in the South and West regions but was constant or declined in the Northeast and Midwest regions.**

Between 2000 and 2010, the White alone-or-in-combination population grew by 11 percent in the South and the West. However, the White alone-or-in-combination population grew by only 2 percent in the Midwest, and actually dropped in the Northeast (see Table 4).

The non-Hispanic White alone population grew at an even slower rate. The non-Hispanic White alone population grew by 4 percent in the South and 3 percent in the West, and actually dropped in the Northeast and the Midwest.

**The population of Whites who reported more than one race grew in every region between 2000 and 2010, particularly in the South and the Midwest.**

On the other hand, the White in combination population experienced growth in every region, particularly in the South and the Midwest (see Table 4). In the South, the White in combination population grew by more than half (55 percent), and by nearly half (46 percent) in the Midwest. The Northeast and the West also experienced growth in the White in combination population, increasing by about 25 percent in both regions.

**Almost one-third of all people who reported White lived in just four states.**

In 2010, the four states with the largest White alone-or-in-combination populations were California, Texas, Florida, and New York (see Table 4). Combined, these states represented nearly one-third (30 percent) of the White

alone-or-in-combination population, or 68.9 million of the 231.0 million people. These four states were also the four states with the largest total populations in the United States.

The four states with the largest multiple-race White populations were also California, Texas, New York, and Florida. However, these four states comprised a high proportion (nearly two-fifths) of the multiple-race White population, with multiple-race White populations ranging from 379,000 to 1.5 million (see Table 4). As an example of the differences, one-in-five Whites who reported multiple races resided in California, compared with one-in-ten Whites who reported a single race.

**The Hispanic White alone population was even more heavily concentrated in these same four states.**

Almost half of the Hispanic White alone population lived in California and Texas (24 percent each), followed by Florida (12 percent) and New York (5 percent). Together, these four states comprised nearly two-thirds of the Hispanic White alone population. In contrast, the four states with the largest non-Hispanic White alone populations comprised one-fourth of the non-Hispanic White alone population (see Figure 5).

**The White-alone-or-in-combination population grew the fastest in western states and southern states.**

Among all people who reported their race as White, the fastest growth between 2000 and 2010 was observed in states in the West and states in the South (see Table 4). Nine states in the West experienced a growth of greater than 10 percent in their White alone-or-in-combination population: Arizona (21 percent), Nevada (21 percent), Utah (20 percent), Idaho (19 percent), Hawaii (19 percent), New Mexico (16 percent), Colorado (16 percent), Wyoming (13 percent), and Alaska (12 percent).

In the South, the White alone-or-in-combination population grew by more than 10 percent in four states (Texas, 20 percent; South Carolina, 15 percent; North Carolina, 14 percent; and Florida, 14 percent) and in the District of Columbia (32 percent). The White alone-or-in-combination population did not experience growth greater than 10 percent in any midwestern state, nor in any northeastern state.

### The multiple-race White population increased by at least 8 percent in every state.

While the White alone population generally experienced slow or negative growth in most states, the multiple-race White population increased by at least 8 percent in every state in the country. Of particular note was the tremendous change seen among the top ten states with the greatest increase in the multiple-race White population. Of the top ten states, nine were in the South. South Carolina had the largest percentage increase in the multiple-race White population (112 percent), followed by North Carolina (111 percent), Delaware (95 percent), Georgia (93 percent), Kentucky (82 percent), Mississippi (81 percent), Tennessee (80 percent), West Virginia (76 percent), and Maryland (74 percent).

The increase of multiple-race Whites in the South is noteworthy, considering the relatively small proportions seen in 2000. While the White *and* Black population represented 24 percent of the total Two or More Races population at the

national level, the White *and* Black population represented between 28 percent and 43 percent of the Two or More Races population in the Southern states listed above.

### Few states had fast growth in their non-Hispanic White alone population.

Comparatively, the growth of the non-Hispanic White alone population was slower in the South (4 percent) and the West (3 percent). Only eight states and the District of Columbia had non-Hispanic White alone populations that increased by at least 10 percent between the decennial censuses. The District of Columbia had the largest percent change in the non-Hispanic White alone population (32 percent), followed by Utah (17 percent), Idaho (16 percent), and Arizona (13 percent). Hawaii, Nevada, and South Carolina all had about 12 percent change in their non-Hispanic White alone population, while the non-Hispanic White alone population grew by about 10 percent in North Carolina and in Wyoming (see Table 4).

### The non-Hispanic White alone population declined in 15 states.

Eleven of the states with declines in their non-Hispanic White alone population were in the Northeast and the Midwest. In particular, two-thirds of the states in the Northeast had declines in the non-Hispanic White alone population—Connecticut (–4 percent), Massachusetts (–4 percent), New Jersey (–6 percent), New York (–4 percent), Pennsylvania (–2 percent), and Rhode Island (–6 percent). Nearly half of the states in the Midwest had declines in the non-Hispanic White alone population—Illinois (–3 percent), Iowa (–0.3 percent), Kansas (–0.2 percent), Michigan (–3 percent), and Ohio (–2 percent).

Fewer states in the South saw declines in the non-Hispanic White alone population—Louisiana (–2 percent), Maryland (–4 percent), and Mississippi (–0.3 percent). California was the only state in the West with a non-Hispanic White alone population that declined (–5 percent).

### The White alone-or-in-combination population was concentrated in counties in the Northeast and the Midwest.

The majority of all counties throughout the country had a high percentage of non-Hispanic White alone-or-in-combination respondents in their populations (see Figure 6). Out of all 3,143 counties in the United States, there were 2,146 counties where the non-Hispanic White alone-or-in-combination population was 75 percent or more of the total population.

Several distinct patterns can be seen in the distribution of the non-Hispanic White alone-or-in-combination population across the country. The non-Hispanic White population was generally most prevalent in counties across the northern half of the country throughout the Northeast and the Midwest regions. The most prevalent non-Hispanic White population counties also stretched into parts of the South and comprised much of the West. Another distinctive boundary was across central Alaska, where non-Hispanic Whites were concentrated in the southeastern portion of the state.

### The Hispanic White population was concentrated in counties throughout the Southwest.

The Hispanic White alone-or-in-combination population was concentrated in counties throughout the Southwest in the states lining the U.S.-Mexico border (Texas, New Mexico, Arizona, and California)

Figure 6.

## Non-Hispanic and Hispanic White Alone or in Combination Population as a Percentage of County Population: 2010

(For information on confidentiality protection, nonsampling error, and definitions, see www.census.gov/prod/cen2010/doc/pl94-171.pdf)

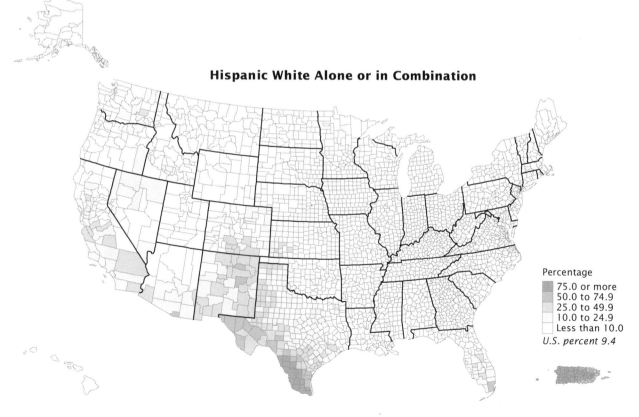

**Non-Hispanic White Alone or in Combination**

Percentage
- 75.0 or more
- 50.0 to 74.9
- 25.0 to 49.9
- 10.0 to 24.9
- Less than 10.0

*U.S. percent 65.4*

**Hispanic White Alone or in Combination**

Percentage
- 75.0 or more
- 50.0 to 74.9
- 25.0 to 49.9
- 10.0 to 24.9
- Less than 10.0

*U.S. percent 9.4*

Source: U.S. Census Bureau, *2010 Census Redistricting Data (Public Law 94-171) Summary File*, Tables P1 and P2.

Figure 7.

## Percentage Change in Non-Hispanic and Hispanic White Alone or in Combination Population by County: 2000 to 2010

(Counties with a White Alone or in Combination population of at least 1,000 are included in the maps. For information on confidentiality protection, nonsampling error, and definitions, see www.census.gov/prod/cen2010/doc/pl94-171.pdf)

### Non-Hispanic White Alone or in Combination

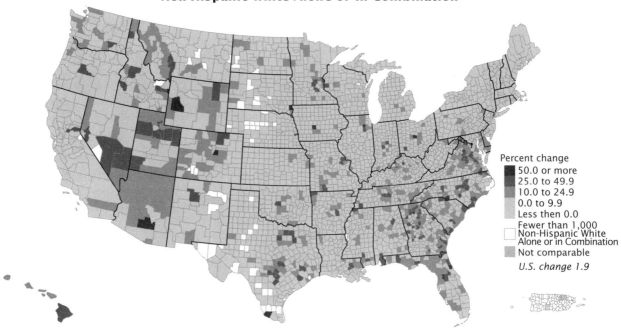

Percent change
50.0 or more
25.0 to 49.9
10.0 to 24.9
0.0 to 9.9
Less then 0.0
Fewer than 1,000 Non-Hispanic White Alone or in Combination
Not comparable

U.S. change 1.9

### Hispanic White Alone or in Combination

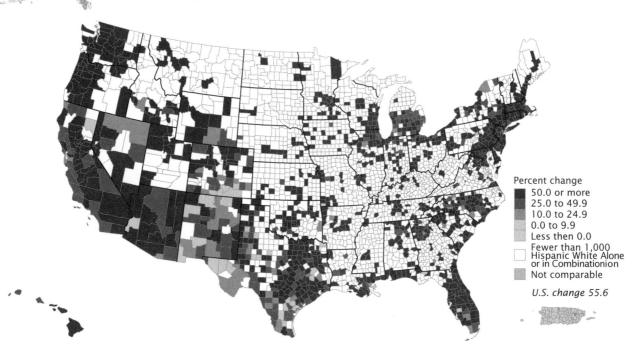

Percent change
50.0 or more
25.0 to 49.9
10.0 to 24.9
0.0 to 9.9
Less then 0.0
Fewer than 1,000 Hispanic White Alone or in Combinationion
Not comparable

U.S. change 55.6

Sources: U.S. Census Bureau, *2000 Census Redistricting Data (Public Law 94-171) Summary File*, Tables PL1 and PL2; and *2010 Census Redistricting Data (Public Law 94-171) Summary File*, Table P1 and P2.

Table 5.
## Ten Places With the Largest Number of Whites: 2010
(For information on confidentiality protection, nonsampling error, and definitions, see *www.census.gov/prod/cen2010/doc/pl94-171.pdf*)

| Place[1] | Total population | White alone or in combination | | White alone | | White in combination | |
|---|---|---|---|---|---|---|---|
| | | Rank | Number | Rank | Number | Rank | Number |
| New York, NY.............. | 8,175,133 | 1 | 3,797,402 | 1 | 3,597,341 | 1 | 200,061 |
| Los Angeles, CA.......... | 3,792,621 | 2 | 2,031,586 | 2 | 1,888,158 | 2 | 143,428 |
| Chicago, IL ............... | 2,695,598 | 3 | 1,270,097 | 3 | 1,212,835 | 3 | 57,262 |
| Houston, TX.............. | 2,099,451 | 4 | 1,116,036 | 4 | 1,060,491 | 4 | 55,545 |
| San Antonio, TX........... | 1,327,407 | 5 | 1,001,202 | 5 | 963,413 | 9 | 37,789 |
| Phoenix, AZ.............. | 1,445,632 | 6 | 995,467 | 6 | 951,958 | 6 | 43,509 |
| San Diego, CA............ | 1,307,402 | 7 | 824,542 | 7 | 769,971 | 5 | 54,571 |
| Philadelphia, PA........... | 1,526,006 | 8 | 655,021 | 8 | 626,221 | 11 | 28,800 |
| Dallas, TX ............... | 1,197,816 | 9 | 633,355 | 9 | 607,415 | 13 | 25,940 |
| Austin, TX ............... | 790,390 | 10 | 562,451 | 10 | 539,760 | 18 | 22,691 |
| | | | | | | | |
| Honolulu, HI.............. | 337,256 | 154 | 99,213 | 255 | 60,409 | 7 | 38,804 |
| San Jose, CA............. | 945,942 | 19 | 442,231 | 20 | 404,437 | 8 | 37,794 |
| San Francisco, CA......... | 805,235 | 21 | 420,823 | 21 | 390,387 | 10 | 30,436 |

[1] Places of 100,000 or more total population. The 2010 Census showed 282 places in the United States with 100,000 or more population. They included 273 incorporated places (including 5 city-county consolidations) and 9 census designated places that were not legally incorporated.

Source: U.S. Census Bureau, *2010 Census Redistricting Data (Public Law 94-171) Summary File,* Table P1.

and also in Nevada and Colorado (see Figure 6). Additionally, multiple groupings of counties in Florida and in the Pacific Northwest also had high proportions of the population that were Hispanic White.

**The growth in the Hispanic White population and the decline in the non-Hispanic White population were seen in different parts of the country.**

The maps in Figure 7 illustrate the percent change in the non-Hispanic White alone-or-in-combination population and the Hispanic White alone-or-in-combination population between 2000 and 2010 by county. About half of all counties with a non-Hispanic White population of at least 1,000 experienced a decline in their non-Hispanic White population between 2000 and 2010. Among all non-Hispanic Whites, the mid-section of the country showed the largest decrease in the non-Hispanic White population, in areas stretching from Montana to the Dakotas southward to western Texas and eastern New Mexico.

There were also observable declines in the non-Hispanic White alone-or-in-combination population stretching eastward to New England and in Arkansas and the Gulf Coast states. There were also declines in the non-Hispanic White population in counties in California and parts of the Pacific Northwest.

The growth of the non-Hispanic White alone-or-in-combination population was concentrated in counties in the mid-Atlantic corridor and clusters throughout the southeastern states and in Florida. Counties in the Pacific Northwest, northern California, Arizona, Nevada, and areas of the interior West also had increases in their non-Hispanic White populations. Additionally, counties in Texas, Missouri, Hawaii, and Alaska experienced growth in their non-Hispanic White populations between 2000 and 2010.

The Hispanic White alone-or-in-combination population growth was concentrated in counties in the Pacific Northwest and Southwest, especially in Arizona and California. Counties in Texas, Florida, the

Northeast corridor, the Great Lakes, Colorado, and Wyoming had significant growth in their Hispanic White populations. Hawaii also experienced growth in the Hispanic White population between 2000 and 2010.

**The places with the largest White populations were New York, NY; Los Angeles, CA; Chicago, IL; Houston, TX; and San Antonio, TX.**

The 2010 Census showed that, of all places in the United States with populations of 100,000 or more, New York, NY, had the largest White alone-or-in-combination population with almost 3.8 million people (see Table 5).[19] Los Angeles, CA; Chicago, IL; Houston, TX; and San Antonio, TX, each had White populations between 1 and 3 million. These places were also the five largest places in the United States, with the exception of San Antonio, TX, which ranked seventh.

[19] The 2010 Census showed 282 places in the United States with 100,000 or more population. They included 273 incorporated places (including 5 city-county consolidations) and 9 census designated places that were not legally incorporated.

503

Table 6.
## Ten Places With the Highest Percentage of Whites: 2010
(For information on confidentiality protection, nonsampling error, and definitions, see *www.census.gov/prod/cen2010/doc/pl94-171.pdf*)

| Place[1] | Total population | White alone or in combination | | White alone | | White in combination | |
|---|---|---|---|---|---|---|---|
| | | Rank | Percentage of total population | Rank | Percentage of total population | Rank | Percentage of total population |
| Hialeah, FL | 224,669 | 1 | 94.0 | 1 | 92.6 | 268 | 1.4 |
| Arvada, CO | 106,433 | 2 | 92.4 | 3 | 89.8 | 194 | 2.5 |
| Billings, MT | 104,170 | 3 | 92.3 | 4 | 89.6 | 167 | 2.7 |
| Fargo, ND | 105,549 | 4 | 92.1 | 2 | 90.2 | 250 | 1.9 |
| Fort Collins, CO | 143,986 | 5 | 91.9 | 6 | 89.0 | 153 | 2.8 |
| Boise City, ID | 205,671 | 6 | 91.7 | 7 | 89.0 | 158 | 2.8 |
| Springfield, MO | 159,498 | 7 | 91.7 | 8 | 88.7 | 140 | 3.0 |
| Scottsdale, AZ | 217,385 | 8 | 91.3 | 5 | 89.3 | 237 | 2.0 |
| Spokane, WA | 208,916 | 9 | 90.8 | 15 | 86.7 | 53 | 4.1 |
| Cedar Rapids, IA | 126,326 | 10 | 90.7 | 10 | 88.0 | 173 | 2.7 |
| | | | | | | | |
| Cape Coral, FL | 154,305 | 11 | 90.2 | 9 | 88.2 | 232 | 2.1 |
| Honolulu, HI | 337,256 | 275 | 29.4 | 281 | 17.9 | 1 | 11.5 |
| Fairfield, CA | 105,321 | 211 | 52.8 | 226 | 46.0 | 2 | 6.8 |
| Anchorage, AK | 291,826 | 102 | 72.8 | 117 | 66.0 | 3 | 6.8 |
| Tacoma, WA | 198,397 | 106 | 71.6 | 127 | 64.9 | 4 | 6.7 |
| Antioch, CA | 102,372 | 195 | 55.0 | 213 | 48.9 | 5 | 6.1 |
| Elk Grove, CA | 153,015 | 217 | 51.9 | 225 | 46.1 | 6 | 5.8 |
| Concord, CA | 122,067 | 116 | 70.1 | 130 | 64.5 | 7 | 5.5 |
| Lansing, MI | 114,297 | 135 | 66.6 | 149 | 61.2 | 8 | 5.4 |
| Berkeley, CA | 112,580 | 146 | 64.8 | 161 | 59.5 | 9 | 5.3 |
| Murrieta, CA | 103,466 | 94 | 75.0 | 100 | 69.7 | 10 | 5.2 |

[1] Places of 100,000 or more total population. The 2010 Census showed 282 places in the United States with 100,000 or more population. They included 273 incorporated places (including 5 city-county consolidations) and 9 census designated places that were not legally incorporated.

Source: U.S. Census Bureau, *2010 Census Redistricting Data (Public Law 94-171) Summary File,* Table P1.

**The places with the largest multiple-race White populations were New York and Los Angeles.**

Of all places with populations of 100,000 or more, New York, NY, had the largest multiple-race White population (200,000) followed by Los Angeles (143,000) (see Table 5). Three other places, Chicago, IL; Houston, TX; and San Diego, CA, had populations over 50,000.

**More than half of the top ten places with the highest percentage of Whites were in the West.**

Six of the ten places with the highest proportions of Whites alone-or-in-combination were in the West, three in the Midwest, and one in the South (see Table 6). The highest proportion of Whites was in Hialeah, FL, with 94 percent. In Hialeah, 95 percent of the population was Hispanic, indicating a large White Hispanic population, which is unique among the other top 10 places with the highest proportion of Whites in 2010.

Among the places with populations of 100,000 or more, the top ten places with the greatest proportion of people who identified as White, alone or in combination, had populations over 90 percent White. Even among these places, the population was less homogeneous than in 2000.

**The place with the greatest proportion of multiple-race Whites was Honolulu, HI.**

Among the places with populations of 100,000 or more, Honolulu, HI, had the highest proportion of people who identified as White and one or more other races (12 percent), followed by Fairfield, CA; Anchorage, AK; and Tacoma, WA (7 percent each) (see Table 6). Of these ten places, nine were in the West (with six in California alone) and one was in the Midwest.

## Figure 8.
## Proportion of the Non-Hispanic White Alone Population Living Inside the Largest Principal City of the 20 Largest Metropolitan Areas: 2000 and 2010

(For information on confidentiality protection, nonsampling error, and definitions, see *www.census.gov/prod/cen2010/doc/pl94-171.pdf*)

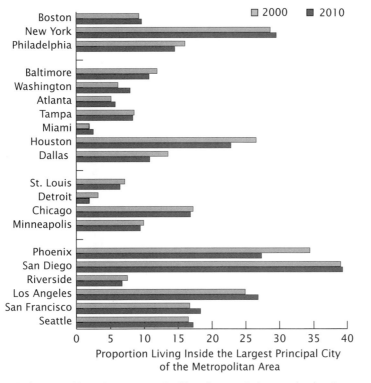

Proportion Living Inside the Largest Principal City of the Metropolitan Area

Note: Principal cities within regions are organized based on proximity to each other. Boston, New York, and Philadelphia are located in the Northeast census region. Baltimore, Washington, Atlanta, Tampa, Miami, Houston, and Dallas are located in the South census region. St. Louis, Detroit, Chicago, and Minneapolis are located in the Midwest census region. Phoenix, San Diego, Riverside, Los Angeles, San Francisco, and Seattle are located in the West census region.

Source: U.S. Census Bureau, 2010 Census special tabulation.

**In the 20 largest metropolitan statistical areas, the proportion of the non-Hispanic White alone population living inside the largest principal cities varied by metro area.**

Figure 8 shows the proportion of the non-Hispanic White alone population who lived inside the largest principal city of the 20 largest metropolitan statistical areas in the country versus those who lived outside of that largest principal

city, in 2000 and in 2010.[20, 21] For example, the dark blue bar denotes the proportion of the non-Hispanic White alone population who lived inside the largest principal city of Boston in 2010 (9.6 percent), out of the total non-Hispanic White alone population in the entire Boston-Cambridge-Quincy, MA-NH metro area.

[20] For the remainder of this section, when metro areas are discussed, the report will refer to the largest 20 metropolitan statistical areas.

[21] Data for the metro areas are based on the 2010 Census boundaries.

In all of the 20 metro areas (except for the San Diego-Carlsbad-San Marcos, CA metro area), less than one-third of the non-Hispanic White alone population lived inside their respective largest principal city in 2010. The metro areas that had the highest proportion of the non-Hispanic White alone population living inside their respective largest principal cities were San Diego-Carlsbad-San Marcos, CA (39 percent); New York-Northern New Jersey-Long Island, NY-NJ-PA (29 percent); Phoenix-Mesa-Glendale, AZ (27 percent); Los Angeles-Long Beach-Santa Ana, CA (27 percent); and Houston-Sugar Land-Baytown, TX (23 percent).

The metro areas with the lowest proportion of the non-Hispanic White alone population living inside their respective largest principal cities were Detroit-Warren-Livonia, MI (2 percent), and Miami-Fort Lauderdale-Pompano Beach, FL (2 percent).

**The proportion of the non-Hispanic White alone population living inside the largest principal city was 15 percent or less in most of the selected metro areas in the Northeast, the Midwest, and the South, but higher in the West.**

In 2 of the 3 northeastern metro areas shown (see Figure 8), 15 percent or less of the non-Hispanic White alone population lived inside their respective largest principal city—Boston (10 percent) and Philadelphia (15 percent).

In 6 of the 7 metro areas that represent the South, less than 15 percent of the non-Hispanic White alone population lived inside their respective largest principal city—Atlanta (6 percent), Baltimore (11 percent), Dallas (11 percent), Miami

Figure 9.

# Percentage-Point Difference of Race and Ethnic Groups Living Inside the Largest Principal City of the 20 Largest Metropolitan Statistical Areas: 2000 to 2010

(For information on confidentiality protection, nonsampling error, and definitions, see *www.census.gov/prod/cen2010/doc/pl94-171.pdf*)

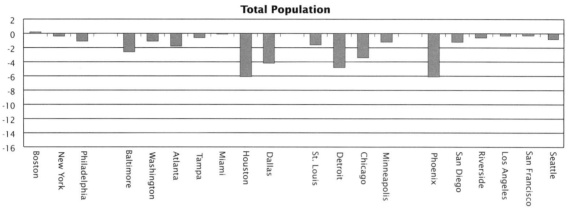

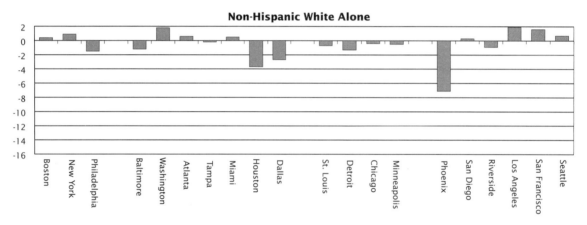

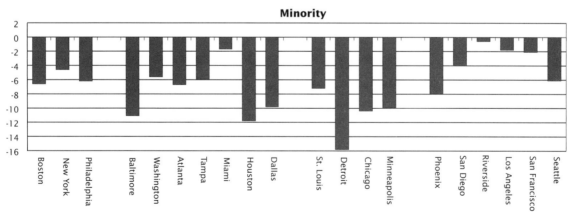

Note: Minority refers to people who reported their race and ethnicity as something other than non-Hispanic White alone.

Principal cities within regions are organized based on proximity to each other. Boston, New York, and Philadelphia are located in the Northeast census region. Baltimore, Washington, Atlanta, Tampa, Miami, Houston, and Dallas are located in the South census region. St. Louis, Detroit, Chicago, and Minneapolis are located in the Midwest census region. Phoenix, San Diego, Riverside, Los Angeles, San Francisco, and Seattle are located in the West census region.

Source: U.S. Census Bureau, 2010 Census special tabulation.

(2 percent), Tampa (8 percent), and Washington (8 percent).

In the Midwest, this was the case for 3 out of the 4 metro areas shown, with lower proportions of the non-Hispanic White alone population living inside their respective largest principal city—Detroit (2 percent), Minneapolis (9 percent), and St. Louis (6 percent).

The selected metro areas in the West generally had higher proportions of their non-Hispanic White alone population living inside the largest principal city. In 5 of the 6 metro areas in the West, more than 15 percent of the non-Hispanic White alone population lived inside their respective largest principal city—Los Angeles (27 percent), Phoenix (27 percent), San Diego (39 percent), San Francisco (18 percent), and Seattle (17 percent).

**The proportion of the non-Hispanic White alone population living inside the largest principal city increased over the past 10 years in about half of the 20 largest metro areas.**

Figure 9 shows the percentage-point difference of a race or Hispanic origin group living inside the largest principal city in the 20 largest metro areas, from 2000 to 2010. For example, in the Boston-Cambridge-Quincy, MA-NH metro area, 9.2 percent of the non-Hispanic White alone population lived in the largest principal city, Boston, in 2000. This figure increased to 9.6 percent in 2010. This represents an increase of 0.4 percentage points.

In about half of the 20 largest metro areas in the United States, the proportion of the non-Hispanic White alone population living inside the largest principal cities increased, while the proportion living outside of these cities

decreased, from 2000 to 2010. This unique pattern differed largely from the total population, where the proportions of people living inside the largest principal cities decreased in 19 of the 20 largest metro areas.

The largest growth in the proportion of the non-Hispanic White alone population living inside the largest principal city of a metro area was seen in Los Angeles (up 1.9 percentage points), Washington (up 1.8 percentage points), and San Francisco (up 1.6 percentage points). The proportion living inside versus outside the largest principal cities of New York, Seattle, Atlanta, Miami, Boston, and San Diego also increased over the decade.

In contrast, the largest principal cities' share of their respective metro area's total population decreased between 2000 and 2010 in all of the major metro areas, with the exception of the Boston-Cambridge-Quincy, MA-NH metro area.

Data for the 20 largest metro areas show that the largest principal cities' share of the non-Hispanic White alone metro area population declined in each of the Midwestern metro areas—Detroit (down 1.3 percentage points), St. Louis (down 0.7 percentage points), Minneapolis (down 0.5 percentage points), and Chicago (down 0.4 percentage points).

In the 2010 Census, just over one-third of the U.S. population reported their race and ethnicity as something other than non-Hispanic White alone. This group is referred to as the "minority" population for this report. The proportion of the minority population living inside the largest principal city declined in all of the 20 largest metros over the decade. Four of these metro areas experienced declines greater than 10 percentage points

in the proportion of the minority population that lived inside the city: Detroit (down 15.8 percentage points), Houston (down 11.8 percentage points), Baltimore (down 11.1 percentage points), and Chicago (down 10.4 percentage points).

## SUMMARY

This report provided a portrait of the White population in the United States and contributes to our understanding of the nation's changing racial and ethnic diversity.

While the White population continued to be the largest race group, representing 75 percent of the total population, it grew at a slower rate than the total population. The majority of the growth in the White population was due to the growth among Hispanic Whites. The increase in the multiple-race reporting of groups that included White, specifically the White **and** Black population and the White **and** Asian population also contributed to the growth of the White population.

Additional notable trends were presented in this report. The White population has become more diverse as evidenced by the growth of the Hispanic White population and the multiple-race White population. The increase of the non-Hispanic White alone population accounted for 16 percent of the growth of the total White population between 2000 and 2010, whereas the Hispanic White alone population accounted for 70 percent, and the multiple-race White population accounted for 14 percent.

Geographically, the White alone-or-in-combination population grew in the South and West regions, but was constant or declined in the Northeast and Midwest regions.

The non-Hispanic White alone population grew at an even slower rate. On the other hand, multiple-race Whites grew in every region between 2000 and 2010, particularly in the South and the Midwest.

Additionally, while the largest principal cities' share of their respective metropolitan statistical area's total population decreased between 2000 and 2010 in 19 of the 20 largest metro areas, the non-Hispanic White alone population living inside versus outside the largest principal cities increased over the decade in Los Angeles, Washington, San Francisco, New York, Seattle, Atlanta, Miami, Boston, and San Diego.

Throughout the decade, the Census Bureau will release additional information on the White population, including characteristics such as age, sex, and family type, which will provide greater insights to the demographic characteristics of this population at various geographic levels.

## ABOUT THE 2010 CENSUS

### Why was the 2010 Census conducted?

The U.S. Constitution mandates that a census be taken in the United States every 10 years. This is required in order to determine the number of seats each state is to receive in the U.S. House of Representatives.

### Why did the 2010 Census ask the question on race?

The Census Bureau collects data on race to fulfill a variety of legislative and program requirements. Data on race are used in the legislative redistricting process carried out by the states and in monitoring local jurisdictions' compliance with the Voting Rights Act. More broadly, data on race are critical for research that underlies many policy decisions at all levels of government.

### How do data from the question on race benefit me, my family, and my community?

All levels of government need information on race to implement and evaluate programs, or enforce laws, such as the Civil Rights Act, Voting Rights Act, Fair Housing Act, Equal Employment Opportunity Act, and the 2010 Census Redistricting Data Program.

Both public and private organizations use race information to find areas where groups may need special services and to plan and implement education, housing, health, and other programs that address these needs. For example, a school system might use this information to design cultural activities that reflect the diversity in their community, or a business could use it to select the mix of merchandise it will sell in a new store. Census information also helps identify areas where residents might need services of particular importance to certain racial groups, such as screening for hypertension or diabetes.

### FOR MORE INFORMATION

For more information on race in the United States, visit the Census Bureau's Internet site at <www.census.gov/population /www/socdemo/race/race.html>.

Information on confidentiality protection, nonsampling error, and definitions is available at <www.census.gov/prod/cen2010 /doc/pl94-171.pdf>.

Data on race from the *2010 Census Redistricting Data (Public Law 94-171) Summary File* were released on a state-by-state basis. The 2010 Census redistricting data are available on the Internet at <http://factfinder2.census.gov /main.html> and on DVD.

For more information on specific race groups in the United States, go to <www.census.gov> and search for "Minority Links." This Web page includes information about the 2010 Census and provides links to reports based on past censuses and surveys focusing on the social and economic characteristics of the Black or African American, American Indian and Alaska Native, Asian, and Native Hawaiian and Other Pacific Islander populations.

Information on other population and housing topics is presented in the 2010 Census Briefs series, located on the Census Bureau's Web site at <www.census.gov/prod /cen2010>. This series presents information about race, Hispanic origin, age, sex, household type, housing tenure, and people who reside in group quarters.

For more information about the 2010 Census, including data products, call the Customer Services Center at 1-800-923-8282. You can also visit the Census Bureau's Question and Answer Center at <ask.census.gov> to submit your questions online.

Adams, Mary and Michael Oleksak. *Intangible Capital: Putting Knowledge to Work in the 21st-Century Organization.* Praeger, 2010.

Banville, Lee. *Covering American Politics in the 21st Century: An Encyclopedia of News Media Titans, Trends, and Controversies.* ABC-CLIO, 2016.

Batchelor, Bob. *The 2000s.* Greenwood, 2008.

Belanger, Craig, ed. *The 2000s in America.* Salem Press, 2013.

Blanchard, Joy, ed. *Controversies on Campus: Debating the Issues Confronting American Universities in the 21st Century.* Praeger, 2018.

Chandler, Kimberley and Molly Sandling. *Exploring America in the 2000s: New Millennium, New U.S.* Prufrock Press, 2014.

Cromwell, David and David Edwards. *Newspeak in the 21st Century.* Pluto Press, 2009.

Crume, Richard, ed. *Environmental Health in the 21st Century: From Air Pollution to Zoonotic Diseases.* Greenwood, 2018.

Damico, Amy M. and Sara E. Quay. *21st-Century TV Dramas: Exploring the New Golden Age.* Praeger, 2016.

Dávila, Alberto and Marie T. Mora. *Hispanic Entrepreneurs in the 2000s: An Economic Profile and Policy Implications.* Stanford Economics and Finance, 2013.

Deitche, Scott M. *Green Collar Jobs: Environmental Careers for the 21st Century.* Praeger, 2010.

Eckert, Amy E. and Laura Sjoberg. *Rethinking the 21st Century: 'New' Problems, 'Old' Solutions.* Zed Books, 2009.

Feinstein, Stephen. *The 2000s.* Enslow Publishing, 2016.

Gigliotti, Jim and John Walters. *Sports in America! 2000-2009.* Chelsea House Publishers, 2010.

Grant, Alan R. *American Politics: 2000 and Beyond (Routledge Revivals).* Routledge, 2017.

Hargrove, Thomas K. and Guido Stempel III, eds. *The 21st-Century Voter Who Votes, How They Vote, and Why They Vote.* ABC-CLIO, 2015.

Hill, Joshua B. and Nancy E. Marion. *Introduction to Cybercrime: Computer Crimes, Laws, and Policing in the 21st Century.* Praeger, 2016.

Lind, Nancy S. and Erik Rankin, eds. *Privacy in the Digital Age: 21st-Century Challenges to the Fourth Amendment.* Praeger, 2015.

O'Neill, Kevin. *Internet Afterlife: Virtual Salvation in the 21st Century.* Praeger, 2016.

Robson, David. *The Decade of the 2000s.* ReferencePoint Press, 2012.

Rycroft, Robert S., ed. *The Economics of Inequality, Poverty, and Discrimination in the 21st Century.* Praeger, 2013.

Tucker, Spencer C., ed. *U.S. Conflicts in the 21st Century: Afghanistan War, Iraq War, and the War on Terror.* ABC-CLIO, 2015.

Wayne, Stephen J. and Clyde Wilcox. *The Election of the Century: The 2000 Election and What it Tells Us About American Politics in the New Millennium.* Routledge, 2002.

Wright, Katheryn. *The New Heroines: Female Embodiment and Technology in 21st-Century Popular Culture.* Praeger, 2016.

## General Reference
America's College Museums
American Environmental Leaders: From Colonial Times to the Present
Encyclopedia of African-American Writing
Encyclopedia of Constitutional Amendments
Encyclopedia of Human Rights and the United States
Encyclopedia of Invasions & Conquests
Encyclopedia of Prisoners of War & Internment
Encyclopedia of Religion & Law in America
Encyclopedia of Rural America
Encyclopedia of the Continental Congress
Encyclopedia of the United States Cabinet, 1789-2010
Encyclopedia of War Journalism
Encyclopedia of Warrior Peoples & Fighting Groups
The Environmental Debate: A Documentary History
The Evolution Wars: A Guide to the Debates
From Suffrage to the Senate: America's Political Women
Gun Debate: An Encyclopedia of Gun Rights & Gun Control in the U.S.
Opinions throughout History: National Security vs. Civil and Privacy Rights
Opinions throughout History: Immigration
Opinions throughout History: Drug Abuse & Drug Epidemics
Political Corruption in America
Privacy Rights in the Digital Era
The Religious Right: A Reference Handbook
Speakers of the House of Representatives, 1789-2009
This is Who We Were: 1880-1900
This is Who We Were: A Companion to the 1940 Census
This is Who We Were: In the 1900s
This is Who We Were: In the 1910s
This is Who We Were: In the 1920s
This is Who We Were: In the 1940s
This is Who We Were: In the 1950s
This is Who We Were: In the 1960s
This is Who We Were: In the 1970s
This is Who We Were: In the 1980s
This is Who We Were: In the 1990s
This is Who We Were: In the 2000s
U.S. Land & Natural Resource Policy
The Value of a Dollar 1600-1865: Colonial Era to the Civil War
The Value of a Dollar: 1860-2014
Working Americans 1770-1869 Vol. IX: Revolutionary War to the Civil War
Working Americans 1880-1999 Vol. I: The Working Class
Working Americans 1880-1999 Vol. II: The Middle Class
Working Americans 1880-1999 Vol. III: The Upper Class
Working Americans 1880-1999 Vol. IV: Their Children
Working Americans 1880-2015 Vol. V: Americans At War
Working Americans 1880-2005 Vol. VI: Women at Work
Working Americans 1880-2006 Vol. VII: Social Movements
Working Americans 1880-2007 Vol. VIII: Immigrants
Working Americans 1880-2009 Vol. X: Sports & Recreation
Working Americans 1880-2010 Vol. XI: Inventors & Entrepreneurs
Working Americans 1880-2011 Vol. XII: Our History through Music
Working Americans 1880-2012 Vol. XIII: Education & Educators
Working Americans 1880-2016 Vol. XIV: Industry Through the Ages
Working Americans 1880-2017 Vol. XV: Politics & Politicians
World Cultural Leaders of the 20th & 21st Centuries

## Education Information
Charter School Movement
Comparative Guide to American Elementary & Secondary Schools
Complete Learning Disabilities Directory
Educators Resource Handbook
Special Education: Policy and Curriculum Development

## Health Information
Comparative Guide to American Hospitals
Complete Directory for Pediatric Disorders
Complete Directory for People with Chronic Illness
Complete Directory for People with Disabilities
Complete Mental Health Directory
Diabetes in America: Analysis of an Epidemic
Guide to Health Care Group Purchasing Organizations
Guide to U.S. HMO's & PPO's
Medical Device Market Place
Older Americans Information Directory

## Business Information
Complete Television, Radio & Cable Industry Directory
Directory of Business Information Resources
Directory of Mail Order Catalogs
Directory of Venture Capital & Private Equity Firms
Environmental Resource Handbook
Financial Literacy Starter Kit
Food & Beverage Market Place
Grey House Homeland Security Directory
Grey House Performing Arts Directory
Grey House Safety & Security Directory
Hudson's Washington News Media Contacts Directory
New York State Directory
Sports Market Place Directory

## Statistics & Demographics
American Tally
America's Top-Rated Cities
America's Top-Rated Smaller Cities
Ancestry & Ethnicity in America
The Asian Databook
Comparative Guide to American Suburbs
The Hispanic Databook
Profiles of America
"Profiles of" Series – State Handbooks
Weather America

## Financial Ratings Series
Financial Literacy Basics
TheStreet Ratings' Guide to Bond & Money Market Mutual Funds
TheStreet Ratings' Guide to Common Stocks
TheStreet Ratings' Guide to Exchange-Traded Funds
TheStreet Ratings' Guide to Stock Mutual Funds
TheStreet Ratings' Ultimate Guided Tour of Stock Investing
Weiss Ratings' Consumer Guides
Weiss Ratings' Financial Literary Basic Guides
Weiss Ratings' Guide to Banks
Weiss Ratings' Guide to Credit Unions
Weiss Ratings' Guide to Health Insurers
Weiss Ratings' Guide to Life & Annuity Insurers
Weiss Ratings' Guide to Property & Casualty Insurers

## Bowker's Books In Print® Titles
American Book Publishing Record® Annual
American Book Publishing Record® Monthly
Books In Print®
Books In Print® Supplement
Books Out Loud™
Bowker's Complete Video Directory™
Children's Books In Print®
El-Hi Textbooks & Serials In Print®
Forthcoming Books®
Law Books & Serials In Print™
Medical & Health Care Books In Print™
Publishers, Distributors & Wholesalers of the US™
Subject Guide to Books In Print®
Subject Guide to Children's Books In Print®

## Canadian General Reference
Associations Canada
Canadian Almanac & Directory
Canadian Environmental Resource Guide
Canadian Parliamentary Guide
Canadian Venture Capital & Private Equity Firms
Canadian Who's Who
Financial Post Directory of Directors
Financial Services Canada
Governments Canada
Health Guide Canada
The History of Canada
Libraries Canada
Major Canadian Cities

# 2018 Title List

Visit **www.SalemPress.com** for Product Information, Table of Contents, and Sample Pages

## Science, Careers & Mathematics

Ancient Creatures
Applied Science
Applied Science: Engineering & Mathematics
Applied Science: Science & Medicine
Applied Science: Technology
Biomes and Ecosystems
Careers in the Arts: Fine, Performing & Visual
Careers in Building Construction
Careers in Business
Careers in Chemistry
Careers in Communications & Media
Careers in Environment & Conservation
Careers in Financial Services
Careers in Green Energy
Careers in Healthcare
Careers in Hospitality & Tourism
Careers in Human Services
Careers in Law, Criminal Justice & Emergency Services
Careers in Manufacturing
Careers in Outdoor Jobs
Careers in Overseas Jobs
Careers in Physics
Careers in Sales, Insurance & Real Estate
Careers in Science & Engineering
Careers in Sports & Fitness
Careers in Social Media
Careers in Sports Medicine & Training
Careers in Technology Services & Repair
Computer Technology Innovators
Contemporary Biographies in Business
Contemporary Biographies in Chemistry
Contemporary Biographies in Communications & Media
Contemporary Biographies in Environment & Conservation
Contemporary Biographies in Healthcare
Contemporary Biographies in Hospitality & Tourism
Contemporary Biographies in Law & Criminal Justice
Contemporary Biographies in Physics
Earth Science
Earth Science: Earth Materials & Resources
Earth Science: Earth's Surface and History
Earth Science: Physics & Chemistry of the Earth
Earth Science: Weather, Water & Atmosphere
Encyclopedia of Energy
Encyclopedia of Environmental Issues
Encyclopedia of Environmental Issues: Atmosphere and Air Pollution
Encyclopedia of Environmental Issues: Ecology and Ecosystems
Encyclopedia of Environmental Issues: Energy and Energy Use
Encyclopedia of Environmental Issues: Policy and Activism
Encyclopedia of Environmental Issues: Preservation/Wilderness Issues
Encyclopedia of Environmental Issues: Water and Water Pollution
Encyclopedia of Global Resources
Encyclopedia of Global Warming
Encyclopedia of Mathematics & Society
Encyclopedia of Mathematics & Society: Engineering, Tech, Medicine
Encyclopedia of Mathematics & Society: Great Mathematicians
Encyclopedia of Mathematics & Society: Math & Social Sciences
Encyclopedia of Mathematics & Society: Math Development/Concepts
Encyclopedia of Mathematics & Society: Math in Culture & Society
Encyclopedia of Mathematics & Society: Space, Science, Environment
Encyclopedia of the Ancient World
Forensic Science
Geography Basics
Internet Innovators
Inventions and Inventors
Magill's Encyclopedia of Science: Animal Life
Magill's Encyclopedia of Science: Plant life
Notable Natural Disasters
Principles of Artificial Intelligence & Robotics
Principles of Astronomy
Principles of Biology
Principles of Biotechnology
Principles of Chemistry
Principles of Climatology
Principles of Physical Science
Principles of Physics
Principles of Programming & Coding
Principles of Research Methods
Principles of Sustainability
Science and Scientists
Solar System
Solar System: Great Astronomers
Solar System: Study of the Universe
Solar System: The Inner Planets
Solar System: The Moon and Other Small Bodies
Solar System: The Outer Planets
Solar System: The Sun and Other Stars
World Geography

## Literature

American Ethnic Writers
Classics of Science Fiction & Fantasy Literature
Critical Approaches: Feminist
Critical Approaches: Multicultural
Critical Approaches: Moral
Critical Approaches: Psychological
Critical Insights: Authors
Critical Insights: Film
Critical Insights: Literary Collection Bundles
Critical Insights: Themes
Critical Insights: Works
Critical Survey of American Literature
Critical Survey of Drama
Critical Survey of Graphic Novels: Heroes & Super Heroes
Critical Survey of Graphic Novels: History, Theme & Technique
Critical Survey of Graphic Novels: Independents/Underground Classics
Critical Survey of Graphic Novels: Manga
Critical Survey of Long Fiction
Critical Survey of Mystery & Detective Fiction
Critical Survey of Mythology and Folklore: Heroes and Heroines
Critical Survey of Mythology and Folklore: Love, Sexuality & Desire
Critical Survey of Mythology and Folklore: World Mythology
Critical Survey of Novels into Film
Critical Survey of Poetry
Critical Survey of Poetry: American Poets
Critical Survey of Poetry: British, Irish & Commonwealth Poets
Critical Survey of Poetry: Cumulative Index
Critical Survey of Poetry: European Poets
Critical Survey of Poetry: Topical Essays
Critical Survey of Poetry: World Poets
Critical Survey of Science Fiction & Fantasy
Critical Survey of Shakespeare's Plays
Critical Survey of Shakespeare's Sonnets
Critical Survey of Short Fiction
Critical Survey of Short Fiction: American Writers
Critical Survey of Short Fiction: British, Irish, Commonwealth Writers
Critical Survey of Short Fiction: Cumulative Index
Critical Survey of Short Fiction: European Writers
Critical Survey of Short Fiction: Topical Essays
Critical Survey of Short Fiction: World Writers
Critical Survey of World Literature
Critical Survey of Young Adult Literature
Cyclopedia of Literary Characters
Cyclopedia of Literary Places
Holocaust Literature
Introduction to Literary Context: American Poetry of the 20th Century
Introduction to Literary Context: American Post-Modernist Novels
Introduction to Literary Context: American Short Fiction
Introduction to Literary Context: English Literature
Introduction to Literary Context: Plays
Introduction to Literary Context: World Literature
Magill's Literary Annual 2018
Masterplots
Masterplots II: African American Literature
Masterplots II: American Fiction Series
Masterplots II: British & Commonwealth Fiction Series
Masterplots II: Christian Literature
Masterplots II: Drama Series
Masterplots II: Juvenile & Young Adult Literature, Supplement
Masterplots II: Nonfiction Series
Masterplots II: Poetry Series
Masterplots II: Short Story Series
Masterplots II: Women's Literature Series
Notable African American Writers
Notable American Novelists
Notable Playwrights
Notable Poets
Recommended Reading: 600 Classics Reviewed
Short Story Writers

**Grey House Publishing | Salem Press | H.W. Wilson** | 4919 Route, 22 PO Box 56, Amenia NY 12501-0056

## History and Social Science

The 2000s in America
50 States
African American History
Agriculture in History
American First Ladies
American Heroes
American Indian Culture
American Indian History
American Indian Tribes
American Presidents
American Villains
America's Historic Sites
Ancient Greece
The Bill of Rights
The Civil Rights Movement
The Cold War
Countries, Peoples & Cultures
Countries, Peoples & Cultures: Central & South America
Countries, Peoples & Cultures: Central, South & Southeast Asia
Countries, Peoples & Cultures: East & South Africa
Countries, Peoples & Cultures: East Asia & the Pacific
Countries, Peoples & Cultures: Eastern Europe
Countries, Peoples & Cultures: Middle East & North Africa
Countries, Peoples & Cultures: North America & the Caribbean
Countries, Peoples & Cultures: West & Central Africa
Countries, Peoples & Cultures: Western Europe
Defining Documents: American Revolution
Defining Documents: American West
Defining Documents: Ancient World
Defining Documents: Asia
Defining Documents: Civil Rights
Defining Documents: Civil War
Defining Documents: Court Cases
Defining Documents: Dissent & Protest
Defining Documents: Emergence of Modern America
Defining Documents: Exploration & Colonial America
Defining Documents: Immigration & Immigrant Communities
Defining Documents: LGBTQ
Defining Documents: Manifest Destiny
Defining Documents: Middle Ages
Defining Documents: Middle East
Defining Documents: Nationalism & Populism
Defining Documents: Native Americans
Defining Documents: Political Campaigns, Candidates & Discourse
Defining Documents: Postwar 1940s
Defining Documents: Reconstruction
Defining Documents: Renaissance & Early Modern Era
Defining Documents: Secrets, Leaks & Scandals
Defining Documents: 1920s
Defining Documents: 1930s
Defining Documents: 1950s
Defining Documents: 1960s
Defining Documents: 1970s
Defining Documents: The 17th Century
Defining Documents: The 18th Century
Defining Documents: The 19th Century
Defining Documents: The 20th Century: 1900-1950
Defining Documents: Vietnam War
Defining Documents: Women
Defining Documents: World War I
Defining Documents: World War II
Education Today
The Eighties in America
Encyclopedia of American Immigration
Encyclopedia of Flight
Encyclopedia of the Ancient World
Fashion Innovators
The Fifties in America
The Forties in America
Great Athletes
Great Athletes: Baseball
Great Athletes: Basketball
Great Athletes: Boxing & Soccer
Great Athletes: Cumulative Index
Great Athletes: Football
Great Athletes: Golf & Tennis
Great Athletes: Olympics

Great Athletes: Racing & Individual Sports
Great Contemporary Athletes
Great Events from History: 17th Century
Great Events from History: 18th Century
Great Events from History: 19th Century
Great Events from History: 20th Century (1901-1940)
Great Events from History: 20th Century (1941-1970)
Great Events from History: 20th Century (1971-2000)
Great Events from History: 21st Century (2000-2016)
Great Events from History: African American History
Great Events from History: Cumulative Indexes
Great Events from History: LGBTG
Great Events from History: Middle Ages
Great Events from History: Secrets, Leaks & Scandals
Great Events from History: Renaissance & Early Modern Era
Great Lives from History: 17th Century
Great Lives from History: 18th Century
Great Lives from History: 19th Century
Great Lives from History: 20th Century
Great Lives from History: 21st Century (2000-2017)
Great Lives from History: American Women
Great Lives from History: Ancient World
Great Lives from History: Asian & Pacific Islander Americans
Great Lives from History: Cumulative Indexes
Great Lives from History: Incredibly Wealthy
Great Lives from History: Inventors & Inventions
Great Lives from History: Jewish Americans
Great Lives from History: Latinos
Great Lives from History: Notorious Lives
Great Lives from History: Renaissance & Early Modern Era
Great Lives from History: Scientists & Science
Historical Encyclopedia of American Business
Issues in U.S. Immigration
Magill's Guide to Military History
Milestone Documents in African American History
Milestone Documents in American History
Milestone Documents in World History
Milestone Documents of American Leaders
Milestone Documents of World Religions
Music Innovators
Musicians & Composers 20th Century
The Nineties in America
The Seventies in America
The Sixties in America
Sociology Today
Survey of American Industry and Careers
The Thirties in America
The Twenties in America
United States at War
U.S. Court Cases
U.S. Government Leaders
U.S. Laws, Acts, and Treaties
U.S. Legal System
U.S. Supreme Court
Weapons and Warfare
World Conflicts: Asia and the Middle East

## Health

Addictions & Substance Abuse
Adolescent Health & Wellness
Cancer
Complementary & Alternative Medicine
Community & Family Health
Genetics & Inherited Conditions
Health Issues
Infectious Diseases & Conditions
Magill's Medical Guide
Nutrition
Nursing
Psychology & Behavioral Health
Psychology Basics

**Grey House Publishing | Salem Press | H.W. Wilson |** 4919 Route, 22 PO Box 56, Amenia NY 12501-0056

# 2018 Title List
Visit www.HWWilsonInPrint.com for Product Information, Table of Contents and Sample Pages

## Current Biography
Current Biography Cumulative Index 1946-2013
Current Biography Monthly Magazine
Current Biography Yearbook: 2003
Current Biography Yearbook: 2004
Current Biography Yearbook: 2005
Current Biography Yearbook: 2006
Current Biography Yearbook: 2007
Current Biography Yearbook: 2008
Current Biography Yearbook: 2009
Current Biography Yearbook: 2010
Current Biography Yearbook: 2011
Current Biography Yearbook: 2012
Current Biography Yearbook: 2013
Current Biography Yearbook: 2014
Current Biography Yearbook: 2015
Current Biography Yearbook: 2016
Current Biography Yearbook: 2017

## Core Collections
Children's Core Collection
Fiction Core Collection
Graphic Novels Core Collection
Middle & Junior High School Core
Public Library Core Collection: Nonfiction
Senior High Core Collection
Young Adult Fiction Core Collection

## The Reference Shelf
Aging in America
Alternative Facts: Post Truth & the Information War
The American Dream
American Military Presence Overseas
The Arab Spring
Artificial Intelligence
The Brain
The Business of Food
Campaign Trends & Election Law
Conspiracy Theories
The Digital Age
Dinosaurs
Embracing New Paradigms in Education
Faith & Science
Families: Traditional and New Structures
The Future of U.S. Economic Relations: Mexico, Cuba, and Venezuela
Global Climate Change
Graphic Novels and Comic Books
Guns in America
Immigration
Immigration in the U.S.
Internet Abuses & Privacy Rights
Internet Safety
LGBTQ in the 21st Century
Marijuana Reform
The News and its Future
The Paranormal
Politics of the Ocean
Prescription Drug Abuse
Racial Tension in a "Postracial" Age
Reality Television
Representative American Speeches: 2008-2009
Representative American Speeches: 2009-2010
Representative American Speeches: 2010-2011
Representative American Speeches: 2011-2012
Representative American Speeches: 2012-2013
Representative American Speeches: 2013-2014
Representative American Speeches: 2014-2015
Representative American Speeches: 2015-2016
Representative American Speeches: 2016-2017
Representative American Speeches: 2017-2018
Rethinking Work
Revisiting Gender
Robotics
Russia
Social Networking
Social Services for the Poor
South China Seas Conflict
Space Exploration & Development
Sports in America

The Supreme Court
The Transformation of American Cities
U.S. Infrastructure
U.S. National Debate Topic: Educational Reform
U.S. National Debate Topic: Surveillance
U.S. National Debate Topic: The Ocean
U.S. National Debate Topic: Transportation Infrastructure
Whistleblowers

## Readers' Guide
Abridged Readers' Guide to Periodical Literature
Readers' Guide to Periodical Literature

## Indexes
Index to Legal Periodicals & Books
Short Story Index
Book Review Digest

## Sears List
Sears List of Subject Headings
Sears: Lista de Encabezamientos de Materia

## Facts About Series
Facts About American Immigration
Facts About China
Facts About the 20th Century
Facts About the Presidents
Facts About the World's Languages

## Nobel Prize Winners
Nobel Prize Winners: 1901-1986
Nobel Prize Winners: 1987-1991
Nobel Prize Winners: 1992-1996
Nobel Prize Winners: 1997-2001

## World Authors
World Authors: 1995-2000
World Authors: 2000-2005

## Famous First Facts
Famous First Facts
Famous First Facts About American Politics
Famous First Facts About Sports
Famous First Facts About the Environment
Famous First Facts: International Edition

## American Book of Days
The American Book of Days
The International Book of Days

## Monographs
American Reformers
The Barnhart Dictionary of Etymology
Celebrate the World
Guide to the Ancient World
Indexing from A to Z
Nobel Prize Winners
The Poetry Break
Radical Change: Books for Youth in a Digital Age
Speeches of American Presidents

## Wilson Chronology
Wilson Chronology of Asia and the Pacific
Wilson Chronology of Human Rights
Wilson Chronology of Ideas
Wilson Chronology of the Arts
Wilson Chronology of the World's Religions
Wilson Chronology of Women's Achievements

**Grey House Publishing** | **Salem Press** | **H.W. Wilson** | 4919 Route, 22 PO Box 56, Amenia NY 12501-0056